CULTURGRAMS:

The Nations around Us

Produced by the
David M. Kennedy Center
for International Studies

Brigham Young University

Volume II

Africa, Asia, and Oceania

About the Culturgram Series...

This book (Volume II) includes *Culturgrams* for Africa, Asia, and Oceania.

A related volume (Volume I) includes *Culturgrams* for the Americas and Europe.

Bound volumes of *Culturgrams* may be ordered from Ferguson Publishing Company, 200 West Madison Street, Suite 300, Chicago, IL 60606; phone (800) 306–9941; fax (800) 306–9942, or Brigham Young University, David M. Kennedy Center for International Studies, PO Box 24538, Provo, UT 84602–4538; phones (800) 528–6279 and (801) 378–6528; fax (801) 378–5882. The internet address is: http://www.byu.edu/culturgrams. The prices for Volume I are $35.00 for education and nonprofit groups, $50.00 retail for profit-making organizations. The prices for Volume II are $40.00 for education and nonprofit groups, $65.00 retail for profit-making organizations.

Because the reproduction of the *Culturgrams* in this volume is strictly prohibited, copies should be ordered directly from Kennedy Center Publications. *Culturgrams* are currently available as a complete set (both bound and loose-leaf), as area and language sets, and individually. To order, contact Kennedy Center Publications at the address above.

R
910
C899
1997
v. 2

Library of Congress Cataloging-in-Publication Data

Culturgrams : the nations around us /
developed by the David M. Kennedy Center for International Studies, Brigham Young University. 2 v. : maps : 28 cm.

ISBN 0-89434-191-X (set)

Contents: v. 1. The Americas and Europe — v. 2. Africa, Asia, and Oceania.

1. Manners and customs. 2. Intercultural communication. I. David M. Kennedy Center for International Studies.

GT150.C85 1993
390—dc20   93-29643

David M. Kennedy Center for International Studies,
Grant P. Skabelund, Managing Editor; Susan M. Sims, Editor; Lisa M. Ralph and Amy L. Andrus, Associate Editors.

ISBN 0-89434-190-1

Library of Congress Card 93-29643 (for set)

Contents

Foreword

For years the best-known introduction of many Americans to many foreign countries has come by way of the four-page *Culturgrams* prepared and distributed by the David M. Kennedy Center for International Studies at Brigham Young University in Provo, Utah. Millions of these simple, straightforward handouts have been distributed to Americans in all levels of our society and by all types of organizations.

Culturgrams are particularly useful because they put so much emphasis on the unique values, customs, and cultural assumptions of the people they describe. One can find the population statistics or the square mileage of the country from many other standard sources, but the "people maps" are much more difficult to locate. I believe this is why *Culturgrams* remain at the top of the list in people's minds, and this is what justifies their continuing success as the most widely distributed publications explaining the customs and traditions of the world's peoples.

With a high concern for accuracy and current validity of the data *Culturgrams* contain, Kennedy Center Publications keeps the reports up-to-date and continues to add more countries to their expanding coverage.

The inclusion of the set in two bound volumes (*Culturgrams: The Nations around Us*, Volumes I and II) places a wealth of information about more than 150 countries in a single repository, so that those who need handy access to such data will be able to keep the book within reach of their desk.

I sincerely hope new editions of *Culturgrams: The Nations around Us* will continue to be forthcoming well into the 21st century.

L. Robert Kohls
Scholar in Residence
Institute for Intercultural Leadership

Introduction

In 1974, President Spencer W. Kimball of the Church of Jesus Christ of Latter-day Saints issued a challenge to Mormons to build more effective bridges of understanding and friendship with people all over the world. Brigham Young University contributed to the effort by inviting people from about 50 countries to share what they thought was essential information about their country and its people. These interviews laid the foundation for *Culturgrams*, which were first published by BYU's Language and Intercultural Research Center and were later transferred to the David M. Kennedy Center for International Studies (1981).

The 1996–97 edition consists of 154 *Culturgrams*. Included in both volumes is a glossary; it contains some of the concepts used throughout *Culturgrams*. Also part of this edition are 11 new *Culturgrams*. Volume I of *The Nations around Us* now includes Albania, Guyana, Saint Kitts and Nevis, and Slovenia. Volume II now contains Burkina Faso, Kyrgyzstan, Mauritania, Namibia, Swaziland, Tajikistan, and United Arab Emirates. In addition, for the first time, Turkey is included in Volume I and Russia in Volume II. Our readers suggested these two countries, which straddle Asia and Europe geographically and culturally, be included in both volumes. We concurred with their feedback by instituting the change.

Each four-page *Culturgram* introduces the reader to the daily customs and lifestyle of a society, as well as its political and economic structure. Each text represents the efforts of individuals from all over the world who have lived and worked in that country. Kennedy Center Publications requests and receives input from scholars within the target culture, U.S. and European academics, volunteers from organizations such as the Peace Corps and International Red Cross, expatriate diplomats and businesspeople, educators, and many others.

This approach allows the Center to take advantage of a wide variety of perspectives and professional backgrounds to bring our readers a unique look at daily life around the globe. It also means that *Culturgrams* contain information based as much on opinion as fact. *Culturgrams* do not focus on statistical data. Other resources present country statistics, but none tells a reader about people on a personal level. Our goal is to present the people of a culture to the reader, thus encouraging understanding and appreciation between people of different nationalities.

Each new *Culturgram* is written by someone who meets certain residence, educational, and professional criteria. The draft is reviewed by a panel of individuals with similar qualifications but usually different backgrounds. This panel is asked to correct errors, comment on accuracy, and generally help us determine whether the expressed opinions and facts form a fair and broad description of the culture. A *Culturgram* cannot describe every aspect of a culture or ethnic group in a particular country, but it does paint a broad picture about life for the majority of people there. All project participants are asked to be as fair and up-to-date as possible. Once a new *Culturgram* has been published (after six to twelve months of work), it is reviewed periodically by qualified reviewers and annually by our professional staff of editors trained in international studies. When necessary, our editors revise the text to keep it current. This helps ensure that each *Culturgram* is a timely source of information about people's lives, society, and culture.

The list of contributors to and supporters of *Culturgrams* is long and irretrievable. We thank the hundreds of individuals who have shared their valuable expertise to make *Culturgrams* a beneficial intercultural learning tool. We also acknowledge the enthusiastic support of the current university leadership. Specific to this volume, we thank Matt Scherer (designer) and John Rees (photographer), whose talents are so beautifully displayed on the cover.

Students, teachers, resource librarians, international student advisors, business travelers, health-care workers, government and military personnel, tourists, missionaries, international development workers, and many others benefit from *Culturgrams*. With your purchase of *Culturgrams*, you join the millions who have come to count on the accurate, up-to-date information that continues to build bridges of understanding between Earth's peoples. Enjoy.

Grant Paul Skabelund
Managing Editor
Kennedy Center Publications

CULTURGRAM '97

Aa Glossary Zz

The following is a list of some common concepts found in Culturgrams. *These are not definitions; they are explanations of how the terms are used in the series, what significance they hold in regard to understanding cultures, and often how they are calculated. For explanations of international organizations (United Nations, European Union, and so forth), please refer to reference sources in a library.*

Cash Crops

A cash crop is an agricultural product that is grown for sale, not for the farmer's consumption. It is often a crop (coffee, cotton, sugarcane, rice and other grains) that requires manufacturing or processing. It may also be a crop (oranges, potatoes, bananas) that can be consumed upon harvest but is cultivated primarily to be sold. Cash crops are most effectively produced on a large scale, but they can be grown on small plots of land. When grown on a large scale, the crops are more likely to be exported than consumed locally, although small growers in developing countries may sell to a local buyer who then sells larger quantities domestically and abroad. The economies of many countries depend heavily on the sale of cash crops.

Diversified Economy

An economy is considered diversified if its stability relies on a variety of industries rather than one or two commodities. For example, oil-rich countries that rely almost solely on the petroleum industry for their income are vulnerable to changes in the price of oil on the world market. When the price drops significantly, the countries are suddenly unable to pay debts or finance social development projects. The same is true for countries that rely on agricultural products such as coffee or on minerals such as copper for their income. Countries whose economies are based not only on agricultural products but also on manufacturing, services, technology, and so forth are better able to withstand global price changes. Thus, the more diversified a country's economic base, the better.

What is a *Culturgram*?

Each four-page *Culturgram* is designed to introduce readers to the daily customs and lifestyles, as well as the political and economic structure, of a nation. *Culturgrams* represent the contributions of individuals worldwide who have experienced living and working in each country. BYU's David M. Kennedy Center for International Studies requests and receives input from scholars within each target culture, U.S. and European academics, volunteers from organizations such as the Peace Corps and International Red Cross, expatriate diplomats and businesspeople, educators, and others.

This approach allows us to draw from a wide variety of perspectives and professional backgrounds in bringing our readers a unique look at culture. It also means that *Culturgrams* contain information based as much on opinion as on fact; however, we consult a wide variety of perspectives before publishing any information. A *Culturgram* cannot describe every ethnic group or cultural aspect of a given country, but it does paint a broad picture about life for the majority of people there.

Culturgrams do not focus on statistical data. A number of other fine resources present national statistics, but none really informs readers about people on a personal level. Our goal is to give readers an accurate view of a culture in order to encourage understanding and appreciation between people of different nationalities.

Each new *Culturgram* is written by someone who meets certain residency, educational, and professional criteria.

Drafts are reviewed by panels of individuals with similar qualifications but differing backgrounds. Panels are asked to correct errors and generally comment on whether the expressed opinions and facts form a broad, fair description of the culture. All project participants are asked to be as fair and up-to-date as possible.

Once a new *Culturgram* has been published (after six to twelve months of work), it is reviewed periodically by qualified reviewers and annually by our professional staff of editors trained in international relations. When necessary, the editors revise and update the text to reflect current events. This helps ensure that each text is a timely source of information about people's lives, their society, and the cultural environment in which they live.

GLOSSARY

Extended Family

As used in *Culturgrams*, this term refers to a family unit that includes parents, their children, and one or more relatives. The relatives most often include grandparents and sometimes cousins, aunts, and uncles. Some extended family units are organized with older parents, their married sons (occasionally daughters) and their families, and all unmarried sons and daughters. Extended families may share a single household or live in a compound that includes living structures for each nuclear unit, in which case families share work and other responsibilities. When a *Culturgram* states the extended family is the basic unit of society, it means households generally are composed of the extended family or the extended family network, both of which are essential to personal and social security.

Foreign Language Phrases

Most *Culturgrams* contain phrases and words in the target culture's official or common language. In general, a *Culturgram* does not provide a pronunciation guide for these phrases due to limited space. Also, including pronunciation and a translation tends to interrupt the flow of the text. A *Culturgram* is not designed to teach foreign languages. Rather, the phrases contained in a *Culturgram* are there to facilitate the description of how people interact with one another. Their translation often provides insights about the culture, but pronunciation is not necessary to gain that insight. In the few cases where pronunciation hints are provided, they are necessary for English-speakers to properly pronounce a word. For instance, the country Lesotho is not pronounced as it would seem. Instead of saying "le-SEW-tho," one should say "le-SUE-too."

Free and Compulsory Education

Most countries provide free education to their citizens, meaning the government operates a public school system open to all children who fall into a certain age group. It does not necessarily mean there are no costs involved in attending school. Students may be required to wear uniforms (which must be purchased), might live far from the nearest school (and parents must pay for transportation), or may need to supply their own paper, pencils, and other basic items. In addition, having a child in school can cost a rural family one laborer on the family farm. This can become such a burden to poorer families that free education is still not accessible to them.

Compulsory education refers to the fact that the law requires children to attend school for a certain number of years. In many countries this rule is seldom enforced. Therefore, it may reflect the government's target for how long children should remain in school to obtain a basic education, rather than how long they are actually required to attend. Compulsory education usually encompasses six to nine years, and optional schooling usually continues for three or more years.

Gross Domestic Product (GDP) Per Capita

This economic statistic refers to the value of all goods and services produced annually in an economy per person. Naturally, not every person produces goods and services, but the total is averaged for the entire population. If the term is expressed as "gross national product" (GNP), it is essentially the same statistic except for the addition of income earned abroad, minus the income earned in the country by noncitizens. This is significant when part of the population works in other countries and sends back money to their families. It is also significant for countries that have substantial investments abroad. For most countries, the two statistics, GDP and GNP, are almost interchangeable.

In the past, GDP was calculated in terms of the U.S. dollar after conversion from the local currency at official exchange rates. This caused accuracy problems because of artificially set exchange rates and because a dollar may not buy the same amount of goods in the United States as it does in another country. Social scientists have recently developed the concept of Purchasing Power Parity (PPP), a measurement that tries to account for the inconsistencies of the past. When GDP is figured in terms of PPP, an *international dollar* not affected by exchange rates is used. Likewise, PPP attempts to express the relative ability of a person to purchase goods with the local currency. Therefore, measured with PPP, $500 will buy essentially the same things in the United States as it will in Brazil or Japan. For many countries, PPP data does not yet exist and only estimates are available for others. Most *Culturgrams* use PPP with GDP, as expressed with the phrase "real gross domestic product." When the word "real" is absent, only the GDP has been calculated. The real GDPs in *Culturgrams* are usually taken from the *Human Development Report 1995* (New York: Oxford University Press for the United Nations Development Program, 1995). In cases where the real GDP is low (less than $1,000, for example), one can assume that people have very little disposable income. But one should also remember that rural families may grow their own food and, therefore, need less disposable income to meet basic needs. In other cases, such a low figure indicates people may indeed be without food, shelter, clothing, or other necessities.

Human Development and
Gender-related Development Indexes

Originating with the United Nations's Development Program, the Human Development Index (HDI) and Gender-related Development Index (GDI) attempt to compensate for the inability of traditional economic indicators to accurately portray the environment in which people live—whether that environment nurtures personal development or hinders it. The project functions under the assumption that human development is "a process of enlarging people's choices" (UNDP 1995, 11). The three essential choices that people must have in order to access others include the ability to "lead a long and healthy life, to acquire knowledge and to have access to the resources needed for a decent standard of living" (UNDP, 11). Accordingly, the basis of the HDI and GDI are statistics related to literacy, infant mortality, life expectancy, and real GDP. If people have access to a useful education, adequate health care, and a decent wage, they are more likely to be involved in community affairs, join the middle class, and contribute skills and time to society. Such societies are more often democratic and respecting of human rights.

Each country is ranked in relation to the others according to its index rating, which falls between 0 and 1. The HDI "shows how far a country has to travel to provide . . . essential choices to all its people. It is not a measure of well-being. Nor is it a measure of happiness. Instead, it is a measure of empowerment" (UNDP, p. 12). The GDI looks at the same data as the HDI but is restricted to women. It is common for women to lag behind men in having access to the same basic resources and choices. Only 130 nations have been ranked for the GDI, whereas 174 have been listed for the HDI. Each *Culturgram* for which HDI and GDI data are available lists the country's index and rank. Some interpretation is also given. For more detailed analysis and additional data, refer to the entire *Human Development Report*, which is revised and updated each year.

Income Distribution

This phrase is generally used in connection with the gap between what the poorest people in a country earn and what the richest earn. If income distribution is highly unequal, a small wealthy class generally controls the economy (and often the government) and owns most property. The much larger poor class is often landless, which is significant since the people are probably farmers who must rent property and receive only a small share of the benefits from their labor. An unequal, but not highly unequal, income distribution often indicates that a middle class is beginning to grow. When the distribution is fairly equal, as is the case in a minority of countries, it is due mostly to a large and prosperous middle class. However, it can also indicate the presence of a broad poor class and absence of a wealthy elite. Generally, having a highly unequal income distribution means the economy is unhealthy, whereas the existence of a strong middle (consumer) class is good for an economy.

Infant Mortality Rate

This statistic is expressed as the number of children per 1,000 live births who die before their first birthday. It is an important indicator of the overall health of a population, since infants who die at this age usually are subject to preventable diseases or birth defects related to the mother's health. Those who die at birth often do so because of a lack of prenatal care and medical attention at birth. People who have access to health care, clean water, nutritious food, and education are more likely to have a low infant mortality rate than people who lack such access. Industrialized countries generally have a low rate (fewer than 10 per 1,000), while developing countries usually have a higher rate (averaging more than 30). The poorest countries may have rates exceeding 100.

Life Expectancy

This measurement refers to how long a person can expect to live from birth if mortality patterns remain unchanged. Someone born today may be expected to live 80 years if living in some European countries but only 58 years if living in parts of Africa. However, since mortality patterns do change throughout a person's lifetime, the statistic is really a better reflection of how long an adult who is currently living can expect to live. So a person who is 50 today can expect to live until 80 in some countries or only a few more years in others. Women live longer than men in most countries, and people in industrialized countries live longer than those in developing countries. People in countries with high pollution have lower rates of life expectancy.

Culturgrams usually express this statistic as a range of years, which most often corresponds to an average for women at the longer-living end and men at the shorter-living end. This statistic, like infant mortality, helps the reader understand the overall health of a population and whether the people have access to nutritious food, clean water, health care, and proper sanitation.

Literacy Rate

Most countries and international organizations define literacy in terms of those older than 15 years of age who can read and write. Sometimes that only means they can read and write their names or perform other basic tasks. In a few cases, literacy is defined as having attended school, even if only for a short time. Most educational experts agree that current definitions fall short of actually measuring whether the population is literate, since being able to write one's name does not mean one can read a newspaper or understand a bus schedule or work instructions.

Literacy may also be defined in terms of an official language not spoken on a daily basis by a majority of the population, which can make the definition even more irrelevant. However, since world organizations cannot agree on how to measure literacy, and since collecting such data is difficult, the current definitions remain in force. Researchers try to add to the statistic by looking at other factors, such as how many years of schooling the average person completes, whether the labor force is skilled or unskilled, and so forth. *Culturgrams* usually list the official literacy rate or an expert estimate and often contain other relevant information.

Nuclear Family

 As used in *Culturgrams*, this term refers to a family unit that includes one or two parents and their children. The nuclear family usually lives in a single-family dwelling. When a *Culturgram* states the nuclear family is the basic social unit, it means the average household is composed of a nuclear family.

Population and Population Growth Rate

The population listed for each country in the *Culturgram* series is an estimate for the year previous to publication (i.e., 1995 population for text published in 1996). The estimate is based on the actual population at the last census multiplied by an annual growth rate. The estimate may seem to conflict with other sources, since other sources often only print the population as of the latest census (whenever it may have been taken) or an estimate made in a base year (i.e., 1990). *Culturgram* estimates are in keeping with figures in

U.S. government publications, but they are sometimes modified by information from the target culture's government. Each population estimate is revised on an annual basis; it is rounded to the nearest 100,000 or 10,000, depending on the size of the population.

The population growth rate is an estimate, rounded to the nearest tenth of a percent, based on the previous year's difference between births and deaths and the net number of migrants leaving or entering the country. The growth rate may change substantially in a single year if there is a large influx of immigrants, a massive emigration, a natural disaster, or an epidemic. Growth rates tend to be low in industrialized countries because families are small, averaging one or two children. Growth rates are generally high in developing countries, especially in areas where subsistence farming is the primary economic activity. These cultures require large families to help farm the land, but they often have a high infant mortality rate; many children are conceived to ensure that enough will survive into adulthood. In small nations, the growth rate may be low due to emigration, as people must go elsewhere to find work.

Staple Food

Staple foods are those foods that supply the majority of the average person's calories and nutrition. A culture's primary staple food is usually starchy, such as cassava (manioc), corn, rice, millet, or wheat. Staple foods also include any meats, fruits, and vegetables eaten in large quantities or on a frequent basis.

Subsistence Farming

Subsistence farming refers to farming as the main source of a family's livelihood. That is, a family will grow its own food, raise its own livestock, build its own home, and often make its own clothing. Members of such a family generally do not earn a wage by working at a job, but they usually are not entirely without a cash income. Family members might sell surplus produce or livestock, or make crafts or other items (blankets, baskets, etc.), in order to buy things they cannot provide for themselves. These usually include items such as sugar, cooking oil, clothing, rice or another staple food, and so forth. Subsistence farmers may also set aside part of their land to grow cash crops in order to earn money. Subsistence farmers generally do not grow an abundance of anything. They often live on small owned or rented plots of land, and they seldom enjoy the luxuries of running water or electricity.

Underemployment

Underemployment refers to the case when workers are not officially unemployed but either are not able to find enough work in their profession or are working in jobs below their skill level. For example, if a country's universities graduate many people in engineering or other professional fields but the economy is not diversified or well developed, those people may find themselves unemployed, working in jobs that do not take advantage of their skills, or only working part-time in their fields. In the latter case, they may return to farming or local retailing. In too many cases, the most educated people simply emigrate to another country to find work, resulting in what is called a "brain drain."

Government unemployment figures generally do not include underemployment; it must be estimated. However, when unemployment is high (more than 10 percent), one usually can assume that underemployment affects at least as many or more workers. This condition reflects an economy that is not growing, and it can lead to social unrest. High underemployment (more than 40 percent) often leads to political turmoil and violence. Employing and paying people according to their skill level helps secure social stability and encourage economic growth.

Western/Western-style

This term usually refers to the dress and eating customs, culture, and traditions of Western Europe, the United States, and Canada. This culture is often referred to as Western because of its common ancient (primarily Greek and Roman) philosophical, legal, political, and social heritage. The term *Western* can also refer to cultures that have a Judeo-Christian value system and religious orientation.

Metric Conversions

Celsius	Fahrenheit	Kilometers	Miles	Meters	Inches/Feet
0°	32°	1	.62	1mm	.039"
4°	39°	10	6.2	50mm	1.95"
8°	46°	50	31	100mm	3.9"
12°	54°	100	62	1m	39.37"
16°	61°	250	155	50m	164'
20°	68°	500	311	100m	328'
24°	75°	750	465	500m	1,640'
28°	82°	1,000	621	1,000m	3,280'
32°	90°	2,000	1,242	1,609m	5,280'
36°	97°	3,000	1,860	5,000m	16,400'
40°	104°	5,000	3,100	10,000m	22,960'

Islamic State of
Afghanistan

Boundary representations not necessarily authoritative.

**A
S
I
A**

BACKGROUND

Land and Climate

Afghanistan is located in central Asia. With an area of 251,773 square miles (652,090 square kilometers), it is a bit smaller than Texas. It is a landlocked country of rugged mountains, the highest of which reaches 24,550 feet. The most important mountain range is the Hindu Kush, which extends about 600 miles from the far northeast to the southwest, effectively bisecting the country. North of the Hindu Kush, the Turkestan Plains run down to the Amu River on the northern border. After broadening into the Hazarajat central plateau, the mountains disappear into western deserts like the Registan. Afghanistan relies on four major river systems (Amu Darya, Kabul, Helmand, Hari Rud) for water.

The climate varies according to elevation and location. For instance, Kabul (at 6,000 feet) has cold winters and nice summers; Jalalabad (1,800 feet) has a subtropical climate; and Kandahar's (3,500 feet) is mild year-round.

History

Located along the famous Silk Road, Afghanistan has been the "Crossroads of Asia" since ancient times and, as such, has always been subject to invasion. Emperors and conquerors (Greeks, Persians, Central Asians, Indians, and others) throughout history have attempted to control or pacify the region's inhabitants, always finding them fiercely independent and formidable military opponents.

Islam was introduced in the seventh century and flourished in the Ghaznavid Empire (977–1186). Great destruction occurred in the 13th century with the Mongol invasions of Genghis Khan. His Turko-Mongol descendant, Tamerlane, established the Timurid Dynasty (1370–1506), famed for its

arts and architecture. The Moghul Dynasty (1526–1707) rose to control eastern Afghanistan and the Indian subcontinent, while the Persian Safavid Dynasty (1501–1732) held western Afghanistan.

Afghanistan's modern roots are in the Durrani Dynasty founded in 1747 by Ahmed Shah Durrani. Members of his Pashtun subtribe basically ruled Afghanistan until 1978. During the 19th century, Afghanistan was caught in the "Great Game" between the Russian Empire in Central Asia and the rival British Empire in India. Although internal unification was achieved under the "Iron Amir," Abdur Rahman Khan (1880–1901), Britain maintained nominal control over foreign policy until Afghanistan's independence in 1919.

Cold War politics after World War II subjected Afghanistan to U.S. and Soviet competition. Five years after the monarchy was overthrown in 1973, a Soviet-backed internal coup prompted popular rebellion. The Communist government received Soviet aid in the form of an invasion in 1979. The resulting Soviet-Afghan War produced widespread destruction throughout Afghanistan, killed 1.5 million people, and drove more than 6 million refugees into Pakistan and Iran. When Soviet troops withdrew in 1989, civil war continued between the Communist government and Muslim *mujahideen* (holy warriors) from several political parties.

In 1992, Kabul fell to an uneasy alliance between opposing forces, but the war did not end. Indeed, it began a new and more brutal one between factions seeking total control of the country. By early 1996, a force that had emerged only in 1994 controlled the southern half of the country. This fundamentalist group, the *Taliban*, then pressed on Kabul, which was already threatened by other groups. The resulting chaos and *Taliban's* strict interpretation of Islamic law dashed the hopes of most Afghans for an end to violence and poverty.

PEOPLE

Population

Afghanistan's population is disputed but estimated to be about 17 million. More than 40 percent is younger than age 14. The country's Human Development Index (0.228) ranks it 170th out of 174 nations. Adjusted for women, the rank falls to last out of 130 countries. About 80 percent of the people live in rural areas. Kabul is the capital and traditionally the largest city, with 1.5 million residents before 1992. Fighting has reduced its numbers to fewer than 500,000. Other major cities are Kandahar, Herat, Mazar-i-Sharif, and Jalalabad.

Afghanistan has many ethnic groups. The largest is the Pashtun tribal society, which comprises 40 to 45 percent of the population and is divided into several major subtribes. Most Pashtuns live in the east and south. Most Tajiks (25 percent) live in the north, Uzbeks (6–9 percent) in the north-center, and Hazara (9–19 percent) in the center. Smaller numbers of Baluchi, Brahui, Kirgiz, Nuristani, Qizilbash, and Turkmen together comprise 10 to 12 percent of the population. Fewer than half of the refugees who left during the 1980s have returned.

Language

Some 32 languages and dialects are spoken in Afghanistan. Dari (a form of Persian) is spoken most widely and has several dialects. Pashto, spoken by Pashtuns, has two major variants and many dialects. Uzbeks speak Uzbeki and Turkmen speak Turkic languages. Smaller ethnic groups speak their own languages or a dialect of a major language. For instance, the Hazara speak a Dari dialect.

Religion

Islam is the religion of virtually all Afghans, but as a unifying force it has not overcome ethnic differences. About 84 percent of people are Sunni Muslims, while 15 percent (primarily Hazara and some Persian speakers) are *Sh'a* (Shiite) Muslims. Small numbers of Sikhs and Hindus live in the cities.

Founded by Muhammad of Arabia in 622, Islam is based on the belief in one God (*Allah*). Islam shares many biblical figures with Judaism and Christianity, but Muslims accept Muhammad as the last and greatest prophet. The *Qur'an* (Koran) is said to contain *Allah's* will as revealed through the angel Gabriel to Muhammad. The war against the Soviets was considered a holy war waged by the *mujahideen*, and through it Islam's political power increased. Culturally, Islam dominates most people's lives from birth to death. Its influence on daily activities is often shared with such local behavior codes as *Pushtunwali* (code of the Pashtuns). Many Muslims pray five times daily and observe the dawn-to-dusk fast for the month of *Ramadan*. In areas controlled by the *Taliban*, Islam's strictest tenets are enforced.

General Attitudes

Afghans typically are friendly and hospitable, but they can also be stern and hard depending on their experience in the war. Although people are aware of themselves as Afghans, primary loyalty is usually to their family, kin group, clan, or tribe, through which they express their identity. Their various codes are often strict and inflexible, stressing honor and one's responsibility to fulfill expected roles. Personal disputes are not easily solved because of the need to protect one's honor. Family honor is also affected by personal behavior, so living the code properly is considered essential. Piety and stoicism are admired traits.

Rural Afghans value wealth as defined by land ownership or a large family. Urban residents are more likely to view wealth in terms of money or possessions, and they value education highly. Nomadic people define wealth by the size of their herds.

People's outlook on life is influenced by a great faith that *Allah* controls everything and that everything happens according to his will. This belief helps them accept a hard life, even if it somewhat dampens personal initiative.

Personal Appearance

Nearly all Afghans wear a *Perahan tunban*, a long, knee-length shirt worn over baggy trousers that are pulled tight with a drawstring. Flat sandals, sneakers, boots, or dress shoes—all common footwear—are removed for prayers. Men may wear a dress coat or vest over the *Perahan tunban*, and women may wear a short jacket, long coat, or shawl. The harsh winters compel most people to cover their heads with a flat wool cap, a turban with *kolah* (turban cap) in a color and design distinctive to the wearer's ethnic background, or the *qarakuli* cap made from the skin of the karakul sheep.

Women rarely appear in public, but if they do, they wear a *chadiri* (head-to-toe covering) over their clothing; others wear a *chador* (shawl/veil). Jewelry made from gold and silver is common and often features lapis lazuli and garnet, locally abundant semiprecious stones. Many people, especially children, wear a *tawiz* (amulet) to protect against evil.

CUSTOMS AND COURTESIES

Greetings

A handshake is common among men, who tend to be expressive in greeting friends and may pat backs during an embrace. Lengthy verbal greetings are often accompanied by placing the right hand over the heart. A man does not shake hands with or otherwise touch a woman in public, although he may greet her verbally in an indirect way. Women friends embrace and kiss three times on alternating cheeks. Women might also shake hands.

Greetings vary by region and ethnic group, but Arabic greetings are universally accepted. *Assalaam alaikum* (Peace be upon you) is replied to with *Waalaikum assalaam* (And peace also upon you). A common Dari greeting is *Khubus ti?* (How are you?), and the Pashto equivalent is *Sanga ye?* Goodbye is *Khoda hafiz.*

When one addresses others in formal situations, using an academic or professional title is essential. *Haji* (pilgrim) is reserved for those who have made a pilgrimage to Makkah, Saudi Arabia. Socioeconomic status can also determine which title to use (such as *Khan*, meaning "sir"). Some people are respectfully referred to only by title (e.g., *Haji Khan*). Usually, however, titles are combined with names. Parents often are called by a child's name, such as *Umm* (mother of) *Muhammad* or *Abu* (father of) *Alam*. Friends use given names and nicknames among themselves.

Gestures

Afghans do not use the hands much while speaking. Men often finger worry beads (*tasbe*) during conversation. Male friends link arms or hold hands while walking, but members of the opposite sex do not touch in public. To beckon a person, one motions downward with the palm of the hand facing down. To request divine assistance at the beginning or end of an activity (trip, meal, project), one holds both hands in front of the chest, palms up as if holding a book. Afghans typically sit with legs crossed, and it is impolite to let the soles of the feet point toward someone else. Using the left hand for passing items is also impolite and considered unclean.

Visiting

Visiting between family, friends, and neighbors provides the mainstay of social life. However, it is common for women to spend their adult lives in *purdah*, which means they are not seen by males who are not close family members. Consequently, visiting is mostly segregated by gender. Homes often have a special room (*hujra*) where the male host receives male guests. Females socialize elsewhere in the compound. Hosts serve guests tea and, depending on the time of day, perhaps something to eat. Guests are expected to have at least three cups of hospitality tea. Any business discussions occur after refreshments. Guests do not bring gifts. The ability of an Afghan to generously receive guests is a sign of social status.

Eating

Rural Afghans commonly eat only breakfast and dinner, but some may have a light lunch. Most have snacks between meals. At meals, Afghans usually sit on the floor around a mat on which food is served in a communal dish. To eat, one uses the fingers of the right hand or a piece of *nan* (unleavened bread). One never uses the left hand to serve oneself, as it is traditionally reserved for cleaning after using the toilet. One eats until satisfied, and leftover food is saved for later or the next day's breakfast. In many areas, belches are considered a sign of a satisfied diner. Families normally eat together, but if a male guest is present, females eat separately. Most Afghans do not eat at restaurants, but some restaurants have booths or a separate dining area for families so women may dine out.

LIFESTYLE

Family

Life centers on the extended family, which provides the basis for most social, economic, and political interaction. The rural family may be quite large, with several generations living together in the same, adjoining, or nearby compounds. The most common dwelling of the settled population is a mud-brick structure of several rooms, surrounded by high mud walls that provide security from enemies, seclusion for women, and a pen for animals. Within the compound, the senior male (father or grandfather) leads the family. Household tasks are divided by gender, age, and experience. Women do all the cooking, washing, and cleaning. They may engage in light farming, but their lives center on the household. The wife of the senior male is the dominant female. Males work in the fields or family business and handle all contacts with the outside world, such as shopping in the market or dealing with local officials. In many cases, men even shop for personal items (clothing) for their wives so that women need not threaten their modesty by leaving home. Only adult males participate in the *jirga* (village council) or other political events, but women are well-informed about local happenings and are influential in shaping men's opinions.

Dating and Marriage

Dating is virtually nonexistent since the sexes are segregated at puberty. Teenage girls enter *purdah* and therefore have no contact with nonfamily males. Marriages normally are arranged, often with senior females playing a prominent role in the decision. Among urban or Westernized families, the prospective bride and groom may be permitted to meet or view each other and approve or reject the union. Marriages between cousins are common and often preferred, as they strengthen family ties. Matchmakers engage in lengthy negotiations over the bride-price (paid by the groom's family to the bride's) and/or dowry (what the bride brings to the marriage).

Marriage and engagement rituals are numerous, varied, and complex. Traditionally the wedding lasts three days, with some festivities at the bride's family home and some at the groom's. Most activities occur with the sexes segregated, but all gather for the contract signing and *Qur'an* recitation. Divorce is simple (e.g., the man need only announce it in public three times) but rare. A man may have up to four wives, but he must provide for each equally; this limits most to one wife. Premarital and extramarital sex are strictly forbidden and may be grounds for severe punishment (including death).

Diet

Afghan cuisine is influenced by the foods of South and Central Asia, China, and Iran. Common meals include many types of *pilau* (rice mixed with meat and/or vegetables), *qorma* (vegetable sauce), *kebab* (skewered meat), *ashak* or *mantu* (pasta dishes), and *nan*. Tomatoes, spinach, potatoes, peas, carrots, cucumbers, and eggplant are popular. Yogurt and other dairy products are dietary staples. Sugarcane, pudding, a variety of fruits (fresh and dried), and nuts are eaten as desserts and snacks. *Chai* (tea), either green or black, is the most popular drink. Most Afghans cannot regularly afford meat, but they enjoy beef, mutton, chicken, and many types of game. An urban diet usually is more varied than a rural one, but shortages are severe at times. Islamic law forbids the consumption of alcohol and pork, and most people comply. Local tobacco, hashish, and opium are smoked widely among men.

Recreation

Afghanistan's unique national sport is *buzkashi*, a precursor to polo, in which teams of horsemen compete to see who can carry the headless carcass of a calf from a circle to a spot a few hundred feet away and return it to the circle. Any player in possession of the calf will suffer all manner of abuse to make him drop it, sometimes even from his own teammates who may want the game prolonged. Only truly superb horsemen are able to master the game. Afghans also enjoy soccer, volleyball, and wrestling. Television and radio play a limited role in people's lives. Most leisure activities occur in the evening and center on the family. Music is popular and is based on singing, drums, stringed instruments similar to lutes, and a clarinet-like instrument called a *surnai*.

Holidays

Secular holidays include Victory of the Muslim Nation (28 April), Remembrance Day (4 May), and Independence Day (18 August). Islamic holidays are more important and are scheduled according to the lunar calendar. They include the first day of *Ramadan*, the three-day feast at the end of *Ramadan* (called *Id al-Fitr*), *Nawrooz* (New Year's Day), *Id al-Adha* (Feast of Sacrifice honoring Abraham for his willingness to sacrifice his son), *Ashura* (a Shiite day to mark the martyrdom of Imam Husayn), and *Roze-Maulud* (the birthday of the prophet Muhammad). During *Ramadan*, families and friends gather in the evening to eat and visit.

Commerce

Banking and government hours are from 8:00 A.M. to 5:00 P.M., March through October, and 9:00 A.M. to 3:30 P.M. the rest of the year. During *Ramadan*, offices close at 2:00 P.M. each day. Large urban *bazaars* (markets) are divided into many small shops that are grouped together by product. Prices may be fixed, but large purchases involve extensive haggling, preceded and accompanied by tea. Small stalls and open-air vendors service rural and other areas.

SOCIETY

Government

Afghanistan is in disarray. The 1993 interim constitution allows for a president (Burhanuddin Rabbani since 1992) and leadership council to govern with a prime minister and cabinet, whose members are drawn from the 205-member Parliament. In reality, Parliament does not function and the president and his military supporters under Ahmad Shah Massoud control only a limited amount of territory around Kabul. Other regions are ruled by opposing warlords or movements. Each is connected to a particular ethnic, family, religious, and/or linguistic group. *Taliban* was the most powerful in 1996, but its members' harsh treatment of people has many wondering about the future for peace and potential for any form of democracy.

Economy

The economy relies on agriculture, pastoralism, and mining, with the bulk of the labor force engaged in these activities. Agricultural products are mostly for domestic consumption. Major exports include natural gas and textiles. Afghan carpets are well-known. Major trading partners include the republics of the former Soviet Union. Economic disruption due to the war has led to an increase in high-profit opium/heroin production, making Afghanistan the second largest producer in the world. The government controls large industries, mining, and transportation, but private enterprises also function.

The civil war limits prospects for development and naturally restricts the amount of vital international aid and investment the country receives. Still, Afghanistan is in a geographic position important for regional trade and might be able to capitalize on that in the future. Afghanistan's real gross domestic product per capita is about $819. Poverty affects more than half of the population and many families are unable to meet basic needs. Economic infrastructure is underdeveloped and in disrepair, and building a viable economy will require substantial efforts. The currency is the *afghani* (AF).

Transportation and Communication

Afghanistan's one major road, the Ring Road, creates a large "U" as it runs south from Herat to Kandahar, northeast to Kabul, and then north through the Salang Tunnel (at 11,100 feet in elevation) to Kunduz, and on to Mazar-i-Sharif. Paved roads run from these major cities to the nearest border towns, such as from Kabul through Jalalabad to the Khyber Pass on the Pakistani border. However, these roads have been substantially damaged in the war and travel is difficult. Off-road travel is dangerous because of land mines. Many rural areas are essentially inaccessible to vehicles, so people walk, ride animals, or use horse-drawn carts. Buses and minibuses provide transportation in cities and over major transit routes. Few people own private cars. There are no railroads, but a national airline offers limited service.

The government runs one television station, but service has been irregular during the fighting, and television sets are not widely available. Radio service is more reliable; most men regularly listen to the British Broadcasting Corporation (BBC) news broadcasts. Phones are limited but functioning, and postal service exists throughout the country.

Education

Although some urban schools operated during the war, disruptions and other factors kept attendance at about 15 percent. Total literacy is estimated at less than 30 percent (12 percent for women). Many scholars and teachers fled or were killed during the war, and the curriculum was changed in the 1980s to reflect Communist ideology. Students also fled, were killed, or were engaged in the war. Many were and still are needed as laborers at home. The Communist curriculum has been replaced, but serious problems remain. Enrollment is actually falling, and in *Taliban* areas girls and women are being denied education altogether.

Health

Medical services are extremely limited and funded almost entirely by international relief organizations. There is only one doctor for every ten thousand people. Hospitals are found only in some cities, and these are not well equipped. Rural areas completely lack modern medical care. Accordingly, the infant mortality rate is 162 per 1,000 and rising; life expectancy is 45 years. Less than 2 percent of the population is older than age 65. Water is not safe and many diseases affect the population.

FOR THE TRAVELER

U.S. citizens need a passport and visa to travel to Afghanistan, but travel is not recommended. For recorded advisories, call the U.S. State Department at (202) 647–5225. Yellow fever immunizations are required for all travelers coming from infected areas. There are few operating hotels. Many archaeological sites have been destroyed or are off-limits. For information, contact the Embassy of Afghanistan, 2341 Wyoming Avenue NW, Washington, DC 20008; phone (202) 234–3770.

 Printed on recycled paper

Democratic and Popular Republic of

Algeria

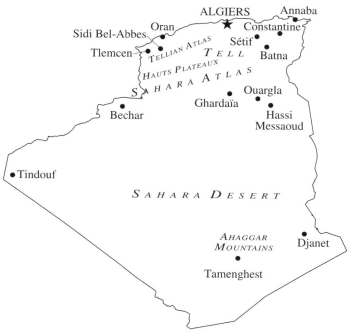

Boundary representations not necessarily authoritative.

BACKGROUND

Land and Climate

Algeria, with an area of 919,590 square miles (2,381,740 square kilometers), is the world's tenth largest country. About 90 percent of the population inhabits the northern coastal region called the Tell. Central and southern Algeria form part of the vast Sahara, where only an occasional oasis is capable of supporting life. The Tell enjoys a mild Mediterranean climate and moderate rainfall, with a rainy season that extends from December to March. A hot, dusty wind called *sirocco* is common during the summer. The Tell is separated from the Sahara by mountains and the *Hauts Plateaux* (highlands).

History

Algeria's earliest inhabitants were not a homogenous people, but they were collectively called Berbers (from the Greek *barbaros*, or *barbarian*) by the Greeks and Romans because of their different customs. The term was adopted by successive invaders and is still used by non-Berbers today. A movement among indigenous Berbers has developed to collectively call themselves *Imazighen* (free men; *Amazigh*, singular). Algeria was conquered by the Phoenicians, whose Carthaginian Empire flourished (c. 800–146 B.C.) until its destruction by the Romans. The coastal region was held by the Romans and then the Vandals until the Umayyad (Arab) invasion in the seventh century A.D. Algiers, Oran, Constantine, and Annaba owe their development to this period. The Umayyads introduced Islam to the Imazighen who, in the eighth century, regained control of the region and established their own Islamic empire. Several indigenous empires followed until the 13th century, when immigrating Bedouins introduced the nomadic lifestyle.

From the early 1500s, the area was part of the Turkish Ottoman Empire. During this time, Barbary Coast pirates consistently attacked European ships and disrupted trade. This piracy was one reason France invaded in 1830. Fighting lasted for several years, but Algeria eventually became a French-controlled territory and, ultimately, a department of the French Republic. Present-day borders were set in 1902.

A smoldering independence movement erupted into open warfare in 1954. After years of bitter fighting, Algeria was granted independence in 1962. Nearly one million French and other European colonists evacuated when the French Army withdrew. During the 1960s and 1970s, Algeria went through a challenging period of adjustment before emerging as a firm socialist republic.

The National Liberation Front (FLN) was the republic's only political party until February 1989, when it set forth a new constitution for a multiparty system. The nation's first free elections (local and regional) were held in 1990, and full national elections were set for late 1991. The Islamic Salvation Front (FIS) gained surprising victories in the 1990 elections and staged strikes in 1991 to protest questionable election laws. Subsequent violence led President Chadli Bendjedid to postpone voting, but elections were eventually held in December 1991. Voter turnout was low among more secular Algerians and the Islamists appeared to be heading for victory.

To prevent the FIS from taking power, the military took control and forced Chadli to resign. The nation's High Security Council canceled election results, banned the FIS, and instituted a High State Council to govern in Chadli's place. This council soon found itself presiding over Algeria's slide into economic and political chaos. In January 1994, the council appointed General Liamine Zeroual as president.

Meanwhile, the FIS developed an armed resistance, and a substantial guerrilla army eventually gained control of some towns and considerable influence in some urban enclaves. More radical militants ordered all foreigners to leave the country in 1993 and began killing anyone deemed a supporter of the military regime. Abuses by government forces, as well as factional fighting on both sides of the conflict, contributed to a chaos that seemed destined for civil war.

Fortunately, the government sponsored limited multiparty presidential elections in 1995, restoring a semblance of peace to the country. President Zeroual was elected by a wide margin in a fair vote. Nevertheless, the FIS was excluded from the process, and many believe full peace is only possible with their participation in parliamentary elections set for 1997. A national peace conference opened in 1996 to discuss ways to broaden political participation, but the government demands the FIS renounce violence and other policies before it can legally participate in any official discussions or elections. A new constitution is expected by the end of 1996. Even if the FIS then joins the political mainstream, the more radical Armed Islamic Groups (GIA), as well as hardline military factions, may not be so willing to reconcile their differences.

THE PEOPLE

Population

Algeria's population of 28.5 million is growing anually at 2.2 percent. Some 75 percent of all residents are younger than age 25. About half live in urban areas. Algiers has two million residents. About 83 percent of Algerians are of Arabic descent or mixed heritage (Amazigh/Arab), while 16 percent are of Amazigh lineage. The Imazighen and Arabs are well integrated, although some Imazighen (especially the Mozabit of the Sahara) do not intermarry with other groups. The Imazighen call themselves by different names (Kabyle, Shawya, Mozabit, Tuareg, etc.). They inhabit primarily the Aures and Djurdjura Mountains or desert regions—due to a historical tendency to seek refuge from invading armies.

Algeria's Human Development Index (0.732) ranks it 85th out of 174 countries. Adjusted for women, the index is only 0.508, reflecting gaps in income and literacy. In times of peace, Algerians have access to some resources necessary for them to pursue personal goals.

Language

Arabic is the official language. French, the primary language of business before 1992, is now far less prominent. Algerian Arabic incorporates many French and Amazigh words into daily speech. Classical Arabic is used for school instruction, government administration, and media reports. The Algerian dialect is used in casual conversation. It can be understood by speakers of other North African Arabic dialects but not by Middle East Arabic speakers. Imazighen speak their own languages (Kabyle, Shawya, etc.) and Arabic.

Religion

Although Islam is the state religion, Algeria is not an Islamic republic. Still, since 99 percent of the people are Sunni Muslim, Islamic philosophy is deeply rooted in their minds, hearts, and behavior. Islamic scripture, the *Qur'an* (Koran), is considered the complete word of God. Muslims revere major Judeo-Christian prophets, but they accept Muhammad as the last and greatest emissary of *Allah* (God). Friday is the day of worship when men go to mosque for a sermon and prayer. Women pray in a different area of the mosque. Islam is practiced every day through dress, dietary codes, five daily prayers, and constant references to *Allah*.

General Attitudes

Algerians are formal and courteous with strangers but warm and expressive among friends. They may be frank and even personal in expressing opinions, although it is impolite to publicly offend another person. Urban Algerians are becoming more individualistic, a character trait at odds with the traditional habit of placing group needs over personal ones. Algerians value family solidarity, intelligence, honesty, loyalty, courage, social status, and simplicity. Manliness is admired, as are traditional feminine qualities. The average Algerian man wants to buy a home, have a family, and own a car. Algerians desire a good education and health, but most of all they want peace.

Many outside observers interpret recent events as a battle between secular society and a dominating religion. However, the situation is more accurately portrayed in terms of a social revolution. Widening socioeconomic gaps between the powerful wealthy class and poor masses, as well as a decline in social mores (rising crime, corruption, materialism, etc.), were the primary complaints of a fringe movement of educated conservatives. When they appealed to the structure, safety, and equality of Islam, religion became a powerful and unifying symbol for disenchanted people. But the conflict is essentially between those who supported the 1992 military takeover and those who opposed it. The former are mostly secularists opposed to democracy. The latter may be secularists who support the separation of religion and politics in a democracy. Or they may be Islamists, presently divided between those who insist on an Islamic, nondemocratic state and those who support a democracy influenced by Islamic principles.

Personal Appearance

Most urban men and about half of all urban women wear Western attire, but some urban dwellers and most rural people wear traditional North African styles. For women, this includes a blouse and skirt covered in public by a long, dark, full dress. Some (not Amazigh women) wear veils in public. Most cover their hair with a scarf in public. Women wear considerable jewelry, an important part of a their dowry and financial security. Although secular urban women may have Western hairstyles, most Algerian women have long, braided hair.

Traditional attire for men may include long, flowing robes or a long shirt, vest, and loose-fitting pants. Head coverings are common. Most men have a mustache, the traditional symbol of manhood. In fact, to curse someone's mustache is one of the worst possible insults. Men who wear beards do so mostly as an expression of religious orientation.

CUSTOMS AND COURTESIES

Greetings

Greetings are genuinely cordial and open. They usually are accompanied by a handshake and frequently an embrace (between members of the same sex). Anything less friendly is considered impolite. Men shake hands with women unless one or both of them avoids contact with the opposite sex on religious grounds. Some people follow the French custom of kissing each other on both cheeks when embracing. Others may hold and kiss the other person's right hand. Although different situations call for different greetings, a few phrases are appropriate in most cases. *Ahlan wa sahlan* (May your way be easy) is an Arabic welcome. *Marhaban bikoum* (Hello to you) is also common.

People address strangers and acquaintances by title and family name. Informally, the title may be combined with one's given name. Elders, always greeted first, are often called "uncle" or "aunt," even if not related. Friends and relatives use given names, whereas people within the same social or religious circles address one another as "brother" or "sister," often combined with the first or last name, depending on the degree of familiarity. Imazighen show respect to their elders, including siblings, by addressing them as "dada" or "nana."

Gestures

Algerians commonly use hand gestures during or instead of conversation. Two clasped hands is a greeting at a distance. Men often slap the palm of a friend's hand to express something like "brilliant," "good joke," or "touché." Pressing a flat right hand to the heart shows appreciation or thanks. To ask for patience, one joins the right hand's fingertips, palm up, and moves it up and down slightly. The index finger may be extended to indicate a warning, but it is impolite to point directly at someone or something. Algerians avoid using the left hand for gestures. One passes items with the right hand or both hands. Facial gestures, such as expressing doubt by tightening the lips and raising the eyebrows, are also common. Algerians take care not to let the bottom of the foot point at others, and they do not place feet on furniture.

Visiting

Visiting is a social occasion in Algeria. Guests are usually offered refreshments and it is impolite to refuse them. Hosts typically serve mint tea or coffee and pastries. Algerians visit parents and siblings weekly whenever possible. Close friends also visit one another frequently and without prior arrangement. Others are expected to make plans in advance. Fridays and holidays are popular times for visiting.

Men and women tend to socialize separately. In traditional homes or on formal occasions, they occupy different rooms. Even in Westernized families, they congregate in separate corners of the living room after eating a meal together.

Visitors, especially invited guests, often take gifts to their hosts. In urban areas, guests might give flowers, but food (pastries, fruit, etc.) is the most common gift throughout Algeria. During nonsocial visits, people spend considerable time on small talk before shifting the conversation to the intended subject.

Eating

Urban families usually eat main meals together, but rural or traditional men and women eat separately. In many urban homes, the father serves the meat, and each person takes portions of other foods from serving dishes. The eldest is served first. Rural families are more likely to eat from a common bowl, females after males. Some foods (meat, desserts) are eaten with the right hand, but most are eaten with utensils. Bread is sometimes used as a scoop. Throughout Algeria, people wash their hands and say *Bismi Allah* (In the name of God) before eating. After the meal, they say *Elhamduli Allah* (Praise be to God) and wash the hands. Meals may be followed by tea.

LIFESTYLE

Family

The Algerian family is an important, private, and male-dominated entity, often including three or more generations (parents, married sons and their families, and unmarried children) in a single home. Families have an average of four or five children. Smaller, nuclear families are found in cities. Although some Algerians live in apartments, most prefer large, concrete homes with four or five rooms. High walls surround the home and its vegetable garden.

Mothers care for the children and household, while fathers are responsible for income and discipline. Children are expected to obey parents as youths and take care of them in their old age. An employed man not only provides for his family but also for the families of any unemployed brothers.

Dating and Marriage

Algerians do not date in the Western tradition. Marriage represents the linking of families, not just individuals. Consequently, matchmaking is often a family affair, and romantic love is seen as something that grows with time after marriage. Women generally marry in their early twenties and men a few years later.

Not all Algerians have traditional weddings, nor are all weddings similar. However, it is common for festivities to last at least three days. Men and women usually have separate parties prior to getting married. At one, henna (a plant dye) is applied to the bride's hands and feet and to the groom's hands to signify the approaching change in life. Each betrothed person saves a portion of the henna and sends it to the other; doing so has nearly the same significance as exchanging rings. Before all of this, it is customary for the families to hold an engagement ceremony at a mosque and in each home. The dowry is later agreed upon and both families prepare for the wedding festivities, including the henna ritual. On the wedding day, the groom's family calls for the bride at her home. After they are served food and drink, they take the bride to the groom's home (traditionally riding on a horse, camel, or mule, but now in a nice car) where he is waiting or will appear later in the evening for the ceremony and wedding night.

Diet

Algerian cuisine is influenced by French cooking and features rich sauces. Couscous, a pasta-like semolina cooked with lamb or chicken and vegetables, is perhaps the most popular dish—particularly for special occasions. *Tajine* is a meat-and-vegetable stew named for the type of pot in which it is cooked. *Chorba* is a soup made with small pieces of meat and vermicelli. Staple grains are wheat, rice, maize, and barley. Local produce includes oranges, grapes, watermelon, tomatoes, potatoes, onions, green beans, and cauliflower. Although pastries like *makrout* (a semolina pastry with date filling) are popular, fruit is nearly always served for dessert. Devout Muslims eat no port and drink no alcohol.

Recreation

Soccer is the most popular sport in Algeria. Only men attend matches at stadiums; school girls might attend boys' school matches. Algerians also play basketball, volleyball, and handball. Women participate in sports and track but far less often than men. Families go to the beach or on picnics. Individuals like to take walks, although rural women are always accompanied by relatives. For winter recreation, women watch television and socialize at home while men play cards or dominoes in cafés. Algerians play the guitar, luth, and flute. A *gaspa* is a unique long flute made from bamboo.

Holidays

National holidays include New Year's Day, Labor Day (1 May), Independence Day (5 July), and Revolution Day (1 November). Muslim holy days are set according to the lunar calendar. *Eid el Fitr*, a two-day feast at the end of *Ramadan*, is a time for visiting, feasting, and worshiping. *Ramadan* is the month in which the *Qur'an* was revealed to Muhammad, so for each day Muslims do not eat, drink, or smoke from sunrise to sunset. After an evening prayer (*tarawih*), they eat and visit with family and friends. *Eid el Adha* is a two-day event held in conjunction with the summer pilgrimage to Makkah, Saudi Arabia. It also commemorates Abraham's willingness to sacrifice his son to prove his faith. Muslims observe the prophet Muhammad's birthday as well.

Commerce

Normal business hours are Saturday through Wednesday, 8:00 A.M. to noon and 2:00 to 6:00 P.M. The Western (Gregorian) calendar is used for business. Urban residents buy staple foods from state-owned supermarkets, while small shops are more common in rural areas. Many people buy perishables every day. In remote areas, meat and vegetables are only available on weekly market days.

SOCIETY

Government

Prior to 1991, Algeria had a president, prime minister, and 281-seat National Assembly, but the canceled elections would have been the first to seat a multiparty assembly. The 1995 elections marked the first step back toward a democratic government. President Zeroual appointed Ahmed Ouyahia as prime minister, although Zeroual retains most executive authority. Algeria is divided in 48 *wilayaat* (prefectures), each of which is headed by an appointed *wali* (prefect).

Economy

Algeria's main exports include crude oil, other petroleum products, and natural gas. With four major natural gas deposits, Algeria holds 3.4 percent of the world's total reserves. Agriculture employs about one-fourth of the labor force, but the country is not self-sufficient in food production. Nomadic herding is the primary economic activity in the sparsely populated desert regions.

Real gross domestic product per capita is $4,870, a figure that reflects the country's petroleum wealth. Most people do not enjoy such a high income, and many have been impacted by high inflation, unemployment, the political strife, and the withdrawal of foreign companies.

The government has introduced austerity measures to control inflation and balance the budget. In 1996, the economy grew (3.2 percent) for the first time in four years. If the political situation improves, foreign investment and imports are expected to resume. The currency is the Algerian *dinar* (DA).

Transportation and Communication

Most highways are paved, but desert roads are less reliable. Some people have cars but more rely on buses, especially in major cities. Travel by train is possible but not popular. Seven international airports link Algeria's major cities with other countries. As with transportation, communications systems are very good in the north but less reliable in the south. Telephones are concentrated in urban areas. The state controls local radio and television, but most urban Algerians have access to international television broadcasts via satellite. Newspapers print only authorized material or risk being suspended. Still, the Algerian press is considered one of the freest in the region.

Education

Algeria's adult literacy rate is 57 percent (44 percent for women, 71 percent for men). Schooling is free and compulsory to age 15. Instruction is mainly in Arabic. Beginning at age six, students attend nine years at a "fundamental" school that stresses basic skills, science, and technology. More than three-fourths of all pupils go on to secondary school. Boys are more likely than girls to complete those three years. The University of Algiers and other universities admit only about 15 percent of all candidates. Other students can obtain training at vocational schools and other technological institutes.

Health

Algerians receive free or low-cost care in hospitals, clinics, and mobile health facilities. Lines are long, so many prefer the expensive care of private facilities. Disease, poverty, and malnutrition are still serious, but the health of Algerians is better than a decade ago. Life expectancy (67–69 years) is rising, and the infant mortality rate (50 per 1,000) is dropping. These improvements are partly the result of improved prenatal education and a massive immunization campaign.

FOR THE TRAVELER

The United States issued a travel warning in 1995, advising U.S. citizens not to travel to Algeria because of the risk of being killed by militants. For updates, call the U.S. Department of State: (202) 647–5225. Algeria requires U.S. travelers to have a valid passport and visa. No immunizations are required, but some may be recommended according to one's length of stay. Water should be boiled, even for brushing teeth, although water in major hotels is generally safe. Peel all fruit and cook vegetables before eating. For more information, contact the Consular Section of the Embassy of Algeria, 2137 Wyoming Avenue NW, Washington, DC 20008.

Commonwealth of
Australia

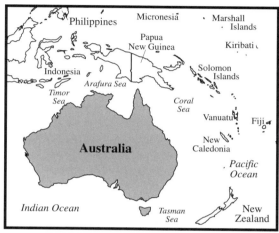

Boundary representations not necessarily authoritative.

BACKGROUND

Land and Climate

Australia is the sixth largest country in the world (2,967,892 square miles or 7,686,850 square kilometers) and is only slightly smaller than the United States. It is the only country that occupies a complete continent. It is also the driest continent in the world. About one-third of the land is desert and another third is composed of poor-quality land. A long chain of mountains, the Great Dividing Range, runs along the Pacific Coast. Fertile farmland lies between the coast and the Great Dividing Range. The western slopes and plains are important wheat-producing areas. Cattle stations reach the edge of the barren interior desert. Australia is known for its marsupials, including koalas, kangaroos, spiny anteaters, and the platypus. Summer is December through February and winter is June through August. The climate ranges from tropical in the north to temperate in the south.

History

The Aborigines were the only inhabitants when the Dutch explored parts of the continent in the 1620s. Most of Australia was left largely undisturbed until 1770, when Captain James Cook took formal possession of the eastern coast for Britain. The British arrived in 1788 and founded penal colonies in what became modern-day Sydney, Hobart, and Brisbane. Many of the early settlers of Australia, therefore, were convicts or soldiers. Free settlements were established in Melbourne, Adelaide, and Perth. With the discovery of gold in 1851, the number of free men immigrating to Australia increased rapidly. In 1868, the practice of transporting convicts to Australia ceased.

In 1901, the six colonies agreed to federate as the Commonwealth of Australia. The country has enjoyed stability and growth throughout the 20th century. Attempts in Western Australia to secede from the Commonwealth in the 1930s failed. Australia established close ties with the United States during World War II. Since that conflict, Australia has been active in global politics.

Robert Hawke became prime minister in 1983 and was reelected in 1990. Due to the recession that began in the 1990s, Hawke's popularity declined and he was removed as head of the Labour Party. Because the leader of the dominant political party is automatically prime minister, Hawke also lost that position to Paul Keating in 1991. Parliamentary elections were held in March 1993, and Keating maintained his position as prime minister. Public dissatisfaction with Keating's policies, unemployment (8 percent), and other issues led to a landslide victory for his opponent, John Howard, in 1996 national elections. As head of a coalition of the Liberal and National Parties, Howard now serves as prime minister.

THE PEOPLE

Population

The population of Australia, about 18.3 million, is growing at about 1.3 percent a year. While the overall population

OCEANIA

density rate is low, approximately 85 percent of the people live in urban areas, mostly in coastal cities. Sydney is the largest city with more than six million people. Nearly 40 percent of all Australians live in Sydney and Melbourne combined. Australia has a young population; about one-third of the population is younger than age 20. Australia's Human Development Index (0.927) ranks it 11th out of 174 nations. Most people have access to opportunities for economic prosperity and personal advancement.

At least 95 percent of the people are Caucasian. Sixty percent of these have an Anglo-Celtic heritage. Because of heavy immigration, Australia is a mosaic of many different nationalities, including Cambodian, Dutch, Estonian, French, German, Greek, Italian, Latvian, Lithuanian, Polish, Polynesian, Vietnamese, Yugoslavian, and other Asian and Latin American peoples. The Asian population has grown from 1 to 4 percent since 1975.

Aborigines (Australia's original inhabitants) make up 1.5 percent of the population. They have a distinct culture, which was once nearly destroyed but is now recognized as an integral and important part of Australia's heritage. Large tracts of land (including one-third of the Northern Territory) have been granted to Aborigines, and efforts are being made to preserve their culture. Aborigines feel a spiritual link to the land. This relationship guides their entire lives as they care for and are cared for by the land. Aboriginal society is complex, but the family is its center. Rituals, ceremonies, and social responsibilities help the Aborigines maintain their link to each other and the land.

Language

English is the national language and is taught in all schools. Immigrant groups often continue to use their native languages at home. The Aborigines once had more than 250 languages, but only about 50 have survived in teachable form. There is now an effort to reverse a trend toward stressing English over Aboriginal languages. Aborigines have their own radio system that broadcasts in their languages, and more families are speaking traditional languages at home. In many Aborigine schools, Aborigine languages are used for instruction at first; English is introduced later.

Australian English uses many words and phrases that are expressions of the country's unique culture, such as *No worries, mate* (No problem, pal), *rubbish* (garbage), *over the road* (across the street), or *rubber* (eraser). The hood of a car is a *bonnet*, while the trunk is a *boot*. Colloquialisms and idioms also add to Australian English. For example, *Spot on* means "Right on." A *bingle* is a "fender bender." Something *dinky-di* is "genuine," as in truly Australian. *Fairdinkum!* more generally means something is true, good, or genuine. And to say someone or something is moving fast, one might use the phrase *like a possum up a gum tree*.

Australians, or *Aussies* as they are often called, also shorten words for everyday conversation. Examples include *uni* (university), *kindi* (kindergarten), and *teli* (television). Because some Australian slang might be offensive to other English speakers, and vice versa, visitors should use standard English.

Religion

Approximately 76 percent of the people are Christians, divided among Anglicans (26 percent), Catholics (26 percent), and other denominations (24 percent). Other religions and nonreligious parts of the population account for the remaining 24 percent. Generally, religion does not play a strong role in daily life.

General Attitudes

Australia is a clean country and people are expected to maintain its standards. In fact, there is a stiff fine for littering. Australians are amiable and easygoing about most things in life; clubs and social groups are popular. Many people frequent local *pubs* (bars) after work and on weekends. Being prompt is important. When conversing, Australians often gesture with their hands to emphasize and clarify. Australians are outgoing and relaxed in public; they are quite comfortable with expressing feelings openly.

Personal Appearance

Australians generally follow European and North American fashion trends. They tend to dress casually. However, this does not mean dress is sloppy. For example, while short pants are common in the summer, tattered clothing is not acceptable. People tend to dress up to go into the city or for social functions. Many people wear hats in the summer as protection from the sun. In winter, warmer clothing (sweaters, etc.) is necessary even in private homes, as most do not have central heating.

CUSTOMS AND COURTESIES

Greetings

Australians greet friends with a casual *G' Day* (Good day) and a warm handshake. Close female friends might hug and kiss lightly on the right cheek. More formal greetings involve a simple *Hello, how are you?* People generally prefer to use first names, even with those they have just met. From a distance, a wave is an acceptable greeting. For casual passerby greetings, Australians may nod their head up and to the right instead of saying *Good day* or *Hello*.

Gestures

Rules of basic etiquette are strongly adhered to in Australia. Winking at women is considered inappropriate. When yawning, one covers the mouth and then excuses oneself. Most hand gestures are the same as in the United States, but a few typical U.S. American gestures may be considered offensive. For example, forming a "V" with the index and middle fingers, palm facing in, is vulgar. (U.S. Americans often use this gesture to express the number two.) Pointing at someone with the index finger is impolite. One preferably points with an open hand in the person's general direction. Sniffing several times when one has a cold is impolite. A person should blow his or her nose in private.

Visiting

Australians often entertain in the home and enjoy inviting others to dinner. When invited by friends, people normally offer to bring something to the meal. The hosts can accept or decline the offer, depending on the event. Hosts greet guests warmly at the door before being inviting them to enter their home. Guests invited for lunch or dinner often bring flowers or a bottle of wine to the hostess. After dinner, the company sometimes "goes out" to a dance club, movie, or sports club.

One popular reason for getting together is the barbecue. It may be informal, where guests bring their own meat and maybe another item, but it is just as common for hosts to provide all the food. Parties and card games are also popular.

Eating

Australians generally eat in the continental style: the fork is held in the left hand and the knife remains in the right. In a private home, guests do not serve themselves from various dishes at the table but receive a plate already served. At a restaurant, a simple, polite hand gesture will attract the waiter's attention. Water is not served with a meal unless asked for. Salads are usually served at the same time as the main course, not before. Persons who want a salad before the meal order it as an entrée. An entrée in Australia is an appetizer rather than a main dish. Placing utensils on the plate together indicates one is finished and wishes to have the dish cleared away. The bill is usually paid at the register after the meal. While tipping is not necessary, it is becoming more common in many restaurants due to the influence of tourists. If the service is good, a small tip is appreciated.

LIFESTYLE

Family

The average family has two or three children, although larger families are not uncommon. Society is family oriented, and Australian family life is similar to family life in the United States. As in other parts of the world, there are increasing numbers of single-parent homes and families in which both father and mother work outside the home. Women comprise about 38 percent of the workforce. They are generally considered equal to men in Australia, with about the same amount of education, fairly equal wages, and important leadership positions in the private and public sectors. Teenagers are rather independent. Communities for senior citizens are funded by church, government, and community groups. Home ownership is valued highly and is part of the *Australian Dream*. Despite usually high interest rates on home loans, about 70 percent of all Australians have their own homes.

Dating and Marriage

Australian dating habits are similar to those in the United States. Dating usually begins by age 15, perhaps beginning with small groups. Going to movies, dancing, and socializing are the most popular activities. The average age for a woman to marry is 23; for men it is 25. Church weddings are still common. A growing number of couples also choose to live together before or instead of marrying. This is referred to as a *de facto marriage*.

Diet

Eating habits are similar to those in the United States. Fruits and vegetables are grown year-round. *Take-away* (take-out) and fast-food businesses are popular. All varieties of fish and meat are common. As in many countries, there is a trend toward eating lighter foods. Salads, seafood, and fresh vegetables are increasing in popularity. The main meal of the day is eaten in the evening; it is usually called *dinner*, but may also be called *tea* if it is a smaller meal. A snack before bedtime is called *supper*.

Recreation

Physical fitness and exercise are important to most Australians. People of all ages enjoy football (played by Australian rules, it is different than U.S. American football), soccer, rugby, cricket, basketball, cycling, *bush walking* (hiking), tennis, lawn bowling, and swimming. Horse racing and golf are also popular. The Melbourne Cup horse race is a nationally televised event. *Netball*, a game similar to basketball and played by girls, is popular all over the country. Girls learn *netball* as early as age five and play it throughout school. Australians consider sportsmanship to be important. Of all outdoor recreational activities, fishing is by far the most popular. It is also important for the economy and creates thousands of jobs.

Holidays

Australia Day (26 January) commemorates the arrival of the first European settlers to Australia. Other holidays are New Year's Day, Good Friday, Easter, Easter Monday, Anzac Day (or Veterans Memorial Day, 25 April), Queen Elizabeth's Birthday (second Monday in June), Christmas, and Boxing Day (26 December). Boxing Day comes from an old British tradition of boxing up unwanted items to give to the poor. It is now simply a day to visit friends and relatives and to "box up" exchange items for return to the store. Labour Day, bank holidays, and holidays for local horse races or cultural festivals vary from state to state. Ethnic festivals and local holidays provide an opportunity to celebrate cultural diversity. These are popular throughout Australia.

Commerce

Most Australians work 38 to 40 hours a week, and some work overtime on weekends or in the evening. Nearly all salaried workers receive four weeks of paid vacation each year. Businesses are generally open Monday through Friday from 8:30 A.M. to 5:30 P.M., and from 9:00 A.M. to noon on Saturday. One evening a week, usually Thursday, shops stay open until 9:00 P.M. In large cities, these shops often remain open late on the weekends as well. Some shops are open on Sunday. Banking hours are generally from 9:30 A.M. to 4:00 P.M. on weekdays.

SOCIETY

Government

Australia is a federal parliamentary state, consisting of six federated states, the Australian Capital Territory around Canberra, and the Northern Territory. Each state enjoys much autonomy, although national law overrides any state laws that conflict with it. The federal Parliament consists of a 76-seat Senate and a 148-seat House of Representatives. All citizens age 18 and older are required to vote in federal and state elections. Those who do not vote may be fined. John Howard is the prime minister. With the Liberal and National Parties now in power, the Labour Party forms the official opposition.

Although Australia is a sovereign nation, it is still a member of Britain's Commonwealth and officially recognizes

Queen Elizabeth II as its monarch. A governor-general (William George Hayden) formally represents the queen. Paul Keating and others support converting Australia into a full republic and withdrawing from the Commonwealth, a move that would require a national referendum and constitutional change. Other political groups strongly oppose such a move, and it is unclear whether the change in government will have any impact on the issue.

Economy

Australia has a strong economy, although its mineral and agricultural exports are sensitive to fluctuations in world market prices. These fluctuations restricted economic growth in the 1980s and were a factor in the 1990–92 recession. Australia exports many minerals, including iron ore, bauxite, diamonds, coal, silver, gold, and copper. Livestock is important in Australia, the world's leading exporter of wool and beef (much of which is exported to the United States). It also ranks high in sheep production. Australia is self-sufficient in food production.

The country's manufacturing industry mainly supplies domestic demand, but a growing number of items are being exported to Asian and Pacific nations. Australia has a large and diversified service sector. Tariff barriers that protect local manufacturing industries are being reduced dramatically to stimulate trade. Inflation is at about 3 percent. The currency is the Australian dollar ($A).

Real gross domestic product per capita is $18,220, which has more than doubled in the last generation. Poverty does exist, and the poorest 40 percent of all households together earn less than 16 percent of the country's income. This indicates there is a fairly wide gap between the wealthy and the poor, but even the poor have the potential to earn a decent income.

Transportation and Communication

The transportation system includes taxis, rental cars, interstate bus lines, railways, and an extensive airline system. The bus system is very good in metropolitan areas. On fixed routes, such as from the airport to a hotel, taxi drivers tell passengers the fare of the trip before they begin. Otherwise, meters are used. Sydney has a ferry system. The Able Tasman overnight ferry service travels from Victoria to Tasmania. Melbourne has an extensive *tram* (streetcar) system. Australia ranks fifth in the world in number of automobiles per capita, with many families owning two cars. Because of their British heritage, Australians drive on the left side of the road.

Nearly all Australian households have a telephone. There are three major communications network companies, as well as one national and several smaller companies. In recent years, the Australian film industry has seen great success at home and in the United States.

Education

Public education is administered by state governments and financed by federal funds. Schooling is compulsory from ages six to fifteen (sixteen in Tasmania). Correspondence instruction, supplemented by two-way radio, reaches children in remote areas. Approximately one-fourth of all Australian children attend private schools. All states have universities, colleges, and institutes. The school year is divided into four terms of about ten weeks each; breaks occur in April, July, and October. Tasmania has three terms with breaks in June and September. The literacy rate is 99 percent. Most Australian adults have completed an average of 11 years of schooling; that is, most finish compulsory education and go on to finish high school as well. A significant portion of the population has completed some higher education.

Health

A national health-care system, called Medicare, is financed by a 1.25 percent income tax. It covers all care provided by public-hospital doctors. There is also a private health-care system. Patients treated in public or private hospitals by private doctors pay for their care. About two-thirds of all hospitals are public. The infant mortality rate is 7 per 1,000; life expectancy averages 75 to 81 years.

FOR THE TRAVELER

A valid passport and visa are required of U.S. citizens traveling to Australia. If one has traveled through nations known to be infected with yellow fever, one must have a certificate of vaccination to enter Australia. Otherwise, no vaccinations are required. A departure tax must be paid at the airport. Dual-voltage small appliances and plug adaptors are necessary to use electrical outlets. For a free copy of *Destination Australia,* call the Aussie Help Line: (800) 333–0199. For other travel information, contact the Australian Tourist Commission, 2049 Century Park East, Los Angeles, CA 90067; phone (310) 229–4870. The Embassy of Australia is located at 1601 Massachusetts Avenue NW, Washington, DC 20036–2273; phone (202) 797–3000. Consulates, which offer the same services as embassies, are located in several major U.S. cities.

Azerbaijan

(Azerbaijani Republic)

Boundary representations not necessarily authoritative.

BACKGROUND

Land and Climate

Azerbaijan, a country slightly larger than the state of Maine, is situated south of Russia. It also borders Georgia, Armenia, and Iran. The province of Nakhichevan, which borders Iran, is cut off from the main part of Azerbaijan by Armenia. Mountains, including the Caucasus and Talysh ranges, and the Karabakh Plateau dominate three sides of the country. Between the mountains are valleys and lowlands with rich flora and fauna. Azerbaijan also has a subtropical zone known for its exotic plants, including pomegranate, pistachio, persimmon, fig, olive, and saffron. The amount of saffron grown on plantations is enough for commercial processing.

The Caspian Sea forms Azerbaijan's eastern border. Enormous oil and natural gas reserves beneath the sea hold greath wealth potential. The Caspian is also rich in biological life; it holds 90 percent of the world's sturgeons. Their habitat is threatened by oil extraction, which began in 1870 and was poorly managed for decades, but efforts are being made to clean up the environment. Two major rivers, the Kura and the Aras, cross the republic, as do a number of smaller rivers, lakes, and springs.

Azerbaijan has a mild climate with more than three hundred days of sunshine each year. Winters are short and cool, and summers are hot and sunny. Fall is pleasant with warm days and cool nights.

History

Azerbaijan originates from the ancient *Atrapatakan*, which was mentioned by the Greek historian Strabo (c. 64 B.C.–

A.D. 23) as the name of a country on Azerbaijan's present territory. Caucasian Albania, another ancient country unrelated to present-day Albania, also inhabited the territory. Both nations were well developed, had trade links with various countries, and had their own languages. Beginning in the seventh century, the area was dominated by Arabs. They introduced Islam, which replaced Zoroastrianism and Christianity as the major religion. They also introduced Arabic. While it did not replace existing languages, its script was used for the Azeri language until 1924.

Because of its geographical location at the juncture of Europe and Asia, the area was dominated by either Turkey or Iran (Persia) for much of its history. It was also ruled by the Mongols and the Russians. According to an 1828 treaty between Russia and Iran, northern Azerbaijan became part of Russia, while the south became part of Iran. The divided Azeris have since experienced different destinies. Present-day Iran has an Azeri population larger than that of Azerbaijan. During the Soviet era, it was difficult for relatives to visit one another across the border, but people are now able to maintain much closer ties.

Azerbaijan declared itself independent in 1918 but was suppressed by Russia's Red Army in 1920 and made part of the Soviet Union. In 1922, it was joined with Georgia and Armenia as the Trancaucasian Soviet Federal Socialist Republic. In 1936, it became a Soviet Socialist Republic, remaining so through the 1980s. A violent conflict with Armenia erupted in the late 1980s regarding the area of Nagorno-Karabakh, which is part of Azerbaijan but is inhabited mostly by

Armenians. It became the subject of fierce fighting as the Armenians sought self-determination rights. A large refugee problem, battles over supply lines, and the Soviet Union's inability to stop the fighting caused great hardship in the country. In 1994, the United Nations Security Council demanded that Armenia withdraw from Azerbaijan, where it had seized up to 20 percent of the territory and displaced one million people. A ceasefire went into effect, but Armenian troops remained; progress seems uncertain.

As Soviet central authority began to weaken, Azerbaijan's Popular Front emerged in opposition to the local Communist Party. But it was Azeri Communist leaders who declared independence in 1991, a few months before the Soviet Union dissolved. Still, Popular Front Chairman Abulfez Elchibey won the first contested elections in 1992 and became the country's president. Major setbacks in the war for Nagorno-Karabakh and economic troubles led Elchibey to call on a former Communist leader, Heydar Aliyev, to help stabilize the government. During a 1993 rebel assault on Baku, Elchibey fled the capital. Aliyev was named interim president, and he named the rebel military commander as prime minister. He soon sponsored elections and carried 97 percent of the vote. Aliyev's government has been more stable. And even though the president faced at least four coup attempts and other difficulties, his New Azerbaijan Party gained a majority in 1995 National Assembly elections.

THE PEOPLE

Population

Azeris descend from the early Caucasian Albanians and migrating Turks. The Seljuks, who came in the 11th century, constituted the largest wave of Turks. Their numbers account for the region's adoption of the Turkish language and culture. The current population is about 7.78 million, of which 83 percent is Azeri. The rest includes Russians, Tatars, Talyshs, Georgians, Ukrainians, Armenians, Lezghians, Kurds, and others. The proportions of these groups is unknown due to the war. For instance, most Armenians have fled the country. Some minority groups, such as the Talyshs, settled in the region long ago, but others were attracted to the rich oil fields of Baku in the late 1800s. More than two million people live in Baku, a cosmopolitan city with many grand buildings and mosques. Azerbaijan's Human Development Index (0.696) ranks it 99th out of 174 countries. This ranking reflects Azerbaijan's past efforts to educate and provide health care to citizens as well as its economic and political instability. The country still has much to do to provide adequate access to a decent standard of living for its people.

Language

Azeri belongs to the Oghuz group of Turkish languages and is similar to modern Turkish. In the 1920s, the Arabic script was changed to a Latin script, which was changed to a Cyrillic script in the 1930s. The Azeri script is now returning to the Latin alphabet. During the Soviet era, Russian and Azeri were official languages, with Russian dominating for government purposes. Today, Azeri dominates for all purposes. Many Azeris can speak Russian, and many of the country's publications are in Russian. Government decrees are published in both Azeri and Russian.

Religion

Traditionally, Azerbaijan is an Islamic nation, but religious worship was outlawed during the Soviet era. This weakened devotion to Islam, as two generations grew up with little knowledge of it. Today, people freely practice their religion, praying at home and attending mosque. Jews and Armenian Christians also practice their respective religions. Still, society is more secular than in neighboring countries.

Most people go to mosque for prayers on Friday, the Muslim day of worship. Men and women pray separately. Most Azeris are Shi'a Muslims (Shiites). They accept the *Qur'an* (Koran) as the word of *Allah* (God) revealed to Muhammad the Prophet. Shiites, in contrast to Sunni Muslims, also revere Fatima, Muhammad's daughter; her husband, Ali; and their sons, Hassan and Hussein. They believe Fatima's descendants, called *Imams* (holy men), disappeared but will reappear in the future to guide Muslims to their destiny.

General Attitudes

The attitude of Azeris as a nation has changed over the years. Conditioned to view themselves as Soviets after World War II, the people still felt separate from Russians. The nation experienced a revival of native literature and history in the 1970s that has provided the basis for Azeri feelings in today's political climate. Desire for national prosperity, love for the motherland, and pride in the native language and culture are strong and being fostered. Unfortunately, an initial optimism about Azerbaijan's future has been dampened by the long war with Armenia. On a daily basis, the war does not touch most people's lives, but it does affect the nation's mood, economic welfare, and ability to develop and progress.

Personal Appearance

Men and women generally wear Western clothing. However, rural women sometimes wear traditional clothing that includes a long, pleated skirt, a long-sleeved blouse, and a *charshab*—a long piece of cloth wrapped loosely around the skirt. Young women cover their heads with light kerchiefs or an *orpack*, a small piece of cloth that wraps around the head and shoulders. Older men usually wear the traditional *papah*, a high, round lambskin hat.

CUSTOMS AND COURTESIES

Greetings

When greeting each other, men shake hands and say *Salem* (Peace). Women also say *Salem*, but they do not shake hands. Female friends or relatives might hug and kiss. Another common greeting is *Sagh ol* (Be well), which is also used at parting. If people are acquainted, they follow the greeting with *Nejasiniz?* (How are you?). One often asks about the health of the other's family.

People of the same age call each other by first names. It is common to use *hanum* (Miss or Mrs.) or *hala* (aunt) after a woman's given name, and *ami* or *dayi* (uncle) after a man's given name. *Bey* (Mr.) is also used after a man's given name at social gatherings or work. Its use was banned in 1920 when Russia invaded, but it is again becoming a preferred way to address men.

Gestures

People remove shoes before entering mosques. When an older person or woman enters a room, those present stand to greet him or her. It is impolite to cross one's legs, smoke, or chew gum in the presence of elders. Speaking loudly to one's colleagues is impolite. One uses the right hand in handshakes and other interactions; using the left hand is rude, unless the right hand is busy. One may point at objects but not people with the index finger. Shaking it while it is vertical is used to reprimand or warn someone. People also use the index finger to attract a listener's attention. The "thumbs-up" gesture means "fine" or "okay." Forming a circle by rounding the finger to touch the thumb tip is obscene.

Visiting

Visiting relatives or friends is popular in Azerbaijan. Hospitality is part of the culture. Friends and family visit without prior notice. Guests are often invited for a meal or for "tea." Tea is a mid-afternoon affair that includes pastries, fruit preserves (not jam), fruit, candy, and tea. At other times, any guest will be offered tea and some sweets. Tea is served in *armudi stakan* (small, pear-shaped glasses). Rural inhabitants customarily invite guests to have tea in the backyard during the spring and summer. People also visit in open-air teahouses. Men like to have tea in a *chaihana* (a light building or tent), especially in the summer along Baku's Caspian shore.

Visitors, particularly those who have adopted Russian customs, often take gifts to their hosts, such as flowers, candy, or pastries. A wrapped present is not opened in the presence of the giver.

Eating

People usually eat three meals a day. For breakfast, tea and bread with butter, cheese, or marmalade is common. Dinner, eaten in the afternoon, includes a meat or vegetable soup, followed by *pilau* (pilaf), a meat dish, potatoes, or macaroni. People commonly eat these same foods for supper, excepting the soup. They eat vegetables and fresh herbs at both dinner and supper.

Azeris hold the fork in the left hand and the knife in the right. In most traditional homes, the cook prepares the plates in the kitchen for each person. In other homes, serving dishes are placed on the table. Guests do not serve themselves; they are served by others. Tea is usually served at the end of each meal.

In cities, women and men eat together at large social gatherings, but they eat separately in rural areas. Eating at restaurants is not common; it is generally reserved for special occasions. The host pays the entire bill and tip.

LIFESTYLE

Family

Azeris value family over the individual, and family needs come first. Men are protective of women in the family. An Azeri would commonly swear by his mother (as opposed to Deity), because she is the most valuable person on earth. Parents feel a lifelong commitment to provide their children with financial support, even after marriage.

Rural Azeris tend to live in extended families. The father is the undisputed head of the family. Married sons and their families live with their parents until financially independent, and all members of the family are loyal to and dependent on the group. This tradition is less evident in cities, where nuclear families are somewhat more common. Rural parents usually build a house for their married sons, and urban parents might buy them apartments.

Unmarried adults generally live with their parents, regardless of age. Adult children are expected to care for their elderly parents. Relatives remain close, visiting each other often and gathering for special occasions. Grandparents help care for grandchildren when necessary.

Dating and Marriage

Dating in the Western sense is not common in Azerbaijan. If urban men and women go out, their relationship is expected to lead to marriage. Premarital sex is strongly discouraged. Urban Azeris choose their spouses, but rural Azeris are expected to follow their parents' wishes regarding a mate.

To become engaged, a man sends a formal proposal to the woman's parents through an older relative. Weddings are celebrated elaborately. A folk music group usually accompanies a groom and his relatives to the bride's house in several cars decorated with flowers and ribbons. The party moves inside the bride's home where the couple's parents and relatives dance. A special wedding melody is played as a signal for the bride to say good-bye to her parents and join the groom. The bride's parents then give the couple their blessings. The actual wedding ceremony usually takes place at night. The bride is accompanied by friends and relatives carrying candles and a decorated mirror.

Diet

Azeris are proud of their cuisine, which they refer to as the "French cuisine of the East." The area's abundance of vegetables, fruits, and fragrant herbs and spices has inspired Azeri cooks to create distinctive national dishes. Cooks often use cilantro, dill, mint, saffron, ginger, garlic, cinnamon, pepper, and other flavors in their dishes. The most popular dish, *pilau,* is made of rice that is steamed for a long time and topped by a variety of foods. These toppings might include chicken, lamb, dried fruit, or milk. *Kebab* is grilled pieces of meat (lamb, chicken, or sturgeon) on a stick. *Piti* is a lamb broth with potatoes and peas cooked in clay pots in the oven. *Dovga* (yogurt, rice, and herbs) is often served after the main meal at celebrations. It is believed to improve digestion. Dinner ends with sherbet or tea, *mürebbe* (preserves), and pastries. The preserves are made from quince, figs, apricots, peaches, cherries, grapes, plums, strawberries, raspberries, walnuts, or mulberries.

Recreation

The most popular sports are wrestling and soccer. Azeri wrestlers compete internationally. Going to movies or theaters is common in the cities, and visiting is a favorite everywhere. For middle- and upper-class families, vacations (three to four weeks) are spent in summer houses that dot the Caspian seashore.

It is common during social gatherings to recite poems of native poets. Azeris enjoy folk music and have many unique musical instruments. In rural areas, members of larger families often perform as folk groups.

Holidays

Azerbaijan has replaced Soviet-era holidays with its own. For example, Day of Commemoration (19 January) honors victims of the 1990 Soviet invasion of Baku. A favorite holiday is *Novrus Bairami*, the New Year celebration that occurs at the beginning of spring. For days before the holiday, women gather in families to bake pastries. Then on New Year's Eve, families come together to eat *pilau* and have tea with pastries. Young people make fires in front of their homes and jump over them; they dance and play games. One can hear national melodies everywhere.

There are two Independence Day celebrations: one on 28 May, marking the 1918 declaration of independence, and one on 18 October, marking freedom in 1991. Azeris also recognize various Muslim holidays, the most important being the feast to end the month of *Ramadan*. During that month, Muslims fast from sunrise to sunset, eating only in the evenings. Forty days later, *Kurban Bairami*, the holiday of sacrifice, commemorates the pilgrimage season and Abraham's willingness to sacrifice his son.

Commerce

Offices are open weekdays from 8:00 or 9:00 A.M. to 5:00 or 6:00 P.M. Stores and shops are also open on Saturday, but they often close an hour each afternoon for dinner. Open-air markets offer fruits, vegetables, meats, herbs, eggs, and other dairy products. Prices at markets are not fixed, so one may bargain with the merchant.

SOCIETY

Government

Azerbaijan is a republic divided into 59 *rayons*. Its constitution allows for a president elected on a five-year term, a prime minister, and a national assembly, known as *Milli Majlis*. All citizens may vote at age 18. Despite the turmoil of its first years, the fledgling government generally seeks to create a democratic, stable country with all of its fundamental freedoms and rights. This effort will be a long process that will depend on the outcome of the war, relations with Russia and other neighbors, economic development, and stable transfers of executive authority. Prominent political parties include the president's New Azerbaijan Party and the Azerbaijan Popular Front (led by Elchibey), but many other parties exist.

Economy

The economy is based on the production of oil and natural gas. With its huge untapped Caspian oil reserves, Azerbaijan has great potential for economic development. Construction, exploration, and production contracts with Western and Russian oil firms will benefit Azerbaijan in the form of new jobs, foreign capital, and high revenues. A new pipeline is being planned to deliver oil from the Caspian to the Mediterranean, one leg through Russia and the other through Georgia. Early oil will travel through existing pipes beginning in 1997.

The chemical industry and production of oil-extraction equipment are important sectors of the economy that likely will be modernized with help from the West. Progress probably will be slow, as Azerbaijan's planned transition to a market economy has not been smooth or substantive.

In agriculture, the most important cash crops are cotton and tobacco. They provide employment in rural areas. Azerbaijan also exports fruits, vegetables, nuts, grapes, and saffron. Trade disruption due to the war, the Soviet Union's collapse, rising unemployment, and the refugee problem has led to decreased agricultural output and exports.

Azerbaijan's currency is the *manat*. Real gross domestic product per capita is $2,550. This figure has been slipping due to negative economic growth, but the country's educated workforce and natural resources show potential for a stronger economy once political issues are settled.

Transportation and Communication

Buses, a subway, trolleys, taxis, and suburban trains provide public transportation in Baku. People travel between cities mainly by train and bus. Most roads are paved, but urban roads are in better condition. In 1992, Azerbaijan's airlines began flying internationally.

A number of daily national newspapers and some regional and local papers are in circulation. Postal service is not effective at present because old postal connections were destroyed and new ones have not yet been fully established. Most urban homes have telephones, but most rural families do not. The entire communications system needs modernization.

Education

Education is provided free through the university level. The government spends more of its budget on education than on anything else except defense. The literacy rate is nearly 96 percent. Due to the lack of facilities, schools must operate in two shifts: morning and afternoon. Classes are held Monday through Saturday. Schools are not divided into levels. Children graduate from the same school they began attending at age six or seven. Eight years of attendance are mandatory and the final three are optional. Those who choose not to complete the full 11 years may attend trade schools to learn a profession. A number of colleges and universities are available; most are located in Baku.

Health

Medical care is provided free, but facilities are not well equipped. Rural areas especially lack clinics and equipment. Drugs and vaccines are in short supply. This has led to an increase of measles and diphtheria. Childhood immunization has become a government priority. The fighting has created a great need for drugs and other medical supplies. Azerbaijan's infant mortality rate is 34 per 1,000; life expectancy is between 67 and 74 years.

FOR THE TRAVELER

U.S. travelers need a valid passport and visa to enter Azerbaijan. Although a visa can be obtained on arrival, one must surrender a passport for at least a day and pay a large fee to get it. Because registration at a hotel is impossible without a passport, obtain a visa in advance. A letter of invitation from someone in Azerbaijan is necessary to obtain a visa. Tourist travel may not be safe due to instability. Credit cards are not accepted; only the local currency and U.S. dollars are accepted. Travelers should drink boiled or bottled water. For travel or other information, contact the Embassy of the Azerbaijani Republic, 927 15th Street NW, Suite 700, Washington, DC 20005.

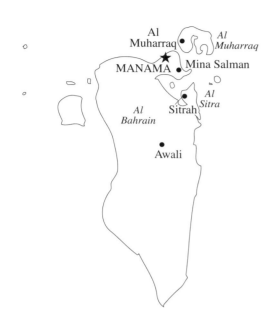

State of
Bahrain

Boundary representations not necessarily authoritative.

A
S
I
A

BACKGROUND

Land and Climate

Bahrain consists of 33 islands, only three of which are inhabited: Al Bahrain, Al Muharraq, and Al Sitra. Manama, the capital, is located on the largest island, Al Bahrain. A causeway links that island to Al Muharraq, where the international airport is located. Many of the country's smaller islands are actually under water during high tides. Bahrain's total land area is 240 square miles (620 square kilometers).

Bahrain is nestled on the western side of the Arabian (Persian) Gulf between Saudi Arabia and Qatar. It is connected to Saudi Arabia by a causeway. Generally flat, the country is dominated by desert terrain. However, it contains a number of natural springs that foster the growth of vegetation and abundant date palm trees. The climate is hot and humid. Summer months often see temperatures above 100°F (38°C). It is cooler between late December and February.

History

Owing to its strategic location in the Gulf and its natural springs, Bahrain has been the object of invaders' and traders' attention for thousands of years. The Romans, Greeks, Portuguese, British, and others ventured to Al Bahrain to conquer the island or trade with its inhabitants. For many years, people in the Gulf region buried their dead on the islands and there are some 175,000 burial mounds still visible. Many mounds have been excavated and some are up to three thousand years old. The Portuguese captured Bahrain in 1521 and ruled until 1602. After the Portuguese were forced from the region, the islands were alternately controlled by different Arab and Persian groups until the Arab Utub tribe expelled the Persians in 1783. At that time, the current ruling Al Khalifa family (part of the Utub tribe) took control of Bahrain. Modern-day Iran (Persia) still maintains a claim to Bahrain and has renewed that claim as recently as 1993.

British influence and military domination in Bahrain began in the early 1800s, when Britain used force to establish a shipping and trading outpost that remained until 1971. At that time, Bahrain became a fully independent state headed by Emir Shaikh Issa bin Salman Al Khalifa. The emir had been the Bahraini monarch since 1961, but he became the sovereign leader at full independence. He continues to hold the throne today.

In 1993, a *shura* council was formed by the emir and the prime minister, who appointed its citizen members. The council was formed in response to demands for greater democracy. Although the *shura* does give some democratic opportunities to the people, many people insist that Parliament (dissolved in 1975) be reinstated. Protests in 1994 ended in violence, while more unrest in 1995 was answered with a crackdown on militant (mostly Shiite) clerics and activists.

THE PEOPLE

Population

Bahrain's population of about 576,000 is growing at 2.6 percent annually. Approximately one-fourth of all residents are expatriates from the Middle East, Asia, Europe, Africa, and North America. The other 75 percent are Arabs. About 65 percent of the total population are Bahraini citizens. Non-Bahraini residents can become naturalized citizens by petitioning the emir, prime minister, or crown prince. Of the Arab population, most (70 percent) are *Shì'a* (Shiite) Muslims. The others, including the royal family, are Sunni Muslims. Bahrain, Iraq, and Iran are the only countries in the Gulf region that have Shiite majorities. Most people live in urban areas.

Bahrain's Human Development Index (0.862) ranks it 44th out of 174 nations. Adjusted for women, the index is only 0.686. These figures indicate that a growing number of Bahrainis have access to resources that allow them to pursue personal goals but that women are less likely to earn an income or make decisions about their lives.

Language

The official language of Bahrain is Arabic. English is also widely used, especially in business and banking circles. Farsi, a Persian dialect, is spoken by many Shiite Muslims, but it is not officially recognized. Many other languages are spoken by various expatriate groups. It is common for people living in Bahrain to be bilingual or multilingual.

Religion

The majority of people living in Bahrain are Muslims. *Islam* literally means "submission to the will of *Allah* (God)." A devout Muslim prays five times daily (prayer times shift by season according to sun position) and obeys the laws of the Muslim holy book, the *Qur'an* (Koran). These laws include avoiding alcohol, pork, and gambling. A Muslim fasts from sunrise to sunset during the month of *Ramadan* and must make a pilgrimage (*Hajj*) to the city of Makkah (Mecca) in Saudi Arabia at least once in a lifetime. Sunni and Shiite Muslims have opposing traditions in Islam, especially in regards to the succession of the prophet Muhammad; they also differ in their approach to certain teachings.

Religion is a central part of Bahraini culture. Work often stops during prayer times. Religion and government are deeply interwoven; it is *Shari'a* (the law of Islam) that establishes social order in connection with the civil law code. Religious freedom is the policy of Bahrain and a number of Christian organizations hold services. Due to social pressure, very few local Arabs would attend these services or convert to Christianity, but it is legal to do so.

General Attitudes

Bahrainis are proud of their country and its image as a nation of warm and friendly inhabitants. Bahrain's citizens are among the best educated in the Gulf. Most view their country as a key trading and banking center. As such, Bahrain is exposed to many foreign cultures and depends upon this interaction for its post-oil economic success. Bahrainis are also proud of their country's relatively low crime rate.

Although the population as a whole is familiar with the material ways of the West, Bahrainis remain dedicated to traditional values. The extended family remains the most important social institution. People fiercely defend their family's name and honor. After a death, relatives are close at hand to help with the grieving process. They also come to the aid of one another in times of need or financial hardship.

Personal Appearance

In villages, dress is traditional. Men wear a long, light robe (*thobe*) that reaches to the ankles. The head is covered by a light cloth headdress (*gutra*) clamped down by a heavy cloth ring (*ocal*). During warmer months, the *thobe* is white. As temperatures get cooler, men wear the *thobe* in various colors. The *gutra* is usually white but may also be white and red checked. The royal family and some of the very wealthy often adorn their attire with gold trim and wear an outer robe (*mishlah*) over the *thobe*. Women wear a full-length black robe (*ubaiya*) year-round. They wear a colorful dress underneath, but it cannot be seen in public. Some women also cover their hair with a scarf (*hijab*), and the most conservative cover their faces with a *burqa*, a veil that covers the bridge of the nose and cheeks. Both genders wear sandals.

Urban attire is generally a combination of traditional and Western dress. For example, a man may wear a sport coat over the *thobe* and choose shoes over sandals. Bahrainis tend to dress neatly; modesty is the norm. Both men and women use perfume.

CUSTOMS AND COURTESIES
Greetings

Personal greetings are important in Bahraini society. The most common way to say "Hello" is *Assalam alikum* (The peace of *Allah* be upon you). The usual reply is *Alikum essalam*, which has virtually the same meaning. The reply to *SabaHel khair* (Good morning) is *SabaHel nur* and to *MasaEl khair* (Good evening) is *MasaEl nur*. People respond to "How are you?" (*Eshloanak* for a man, *Eshloanich* for a woman) with *Zain, al-Humdulillah* (Good, thanks be to *Allah*). "Goodbye" is *Ma'assalameh*.

Handshakes are common and may last the length of the conversation. This or a hand lightly grasping the person's arm shows friendliness. Good friends of the same sex sometimes kiss a number of times on the right and left cheeks. It is socially unacceptable for a man to greet a woman, unless the greeting is part of business protocol. Women, especially those from traditional rural families, look down in the presence of men.

One customarily greets a member of the royal family with the title *Shaikh* (for a man) or *Shaikha* (for a woman). For instance, Mohammed bin Rashid Al Khalifa would be addressed as *Shaikh Mohammed* or *Shaikh Mohammed bin Rashid Al Khalifa*. *Bin* means "son of."

Nicknames, formal and informal, are common. *Abu* means "father of" when it is used before the given name of the oldest son. For example, *Abu Mohammed* is the father of Mohammed. *Ibn* means "son of." So, *Ibn Khuldoon* is the son of Khuldoon. Informal nicknames used among friends are often adapted forms of a person's given name: Aboud for Abdulla, Hamoud for Mohammed, Fatoum for Fatima, Abbasi for Abbas, Salmano for Salman, and so on.

Gestures

Most Bahrainis have become Westernized to the extent that using one's left hand to pass items or using fingers or hands to point is no longer considered rude. People beckon one another with all four fingers and the palm facing up. Waving with the palm down is used to assert authority over someone. Shaking a finger means "no." Bringing the tips of all fingers together facing up can mean "wait," "let me finish," impatience, or exasperation. The more the hand moves vertically, the more intense the message. It is disrespectful to show others the soles of one's feet. Smoking is considered mature and many Bahrainis smoke, but it is rude to do so in the presence of elders. Many Bahrainis also chew gum or cardamom seeds.

Visiting

Bahrainis often invite relatives, friends, and even foreigners into their homes. They visit immediate family almost daily and visit cousins and other relatives usually every week. For more formal visits, guests customarily phone ahead and state the expected time of arrival. Visitors often bring a small gift for the host, such as sweets or flowers. Close friends and relatives might bring gifts such as perfume or clothing. Usually an invitation includes the offering of a large meal. Depending on the host's lifestyle, men and women might eat together at one table. But if the host is more traditional, men do not socialize with unmarried women who are not their daughters or sisters.

In traditional homes, guests stay until the hosts bring out incense (*Bakhour*) and perfume for them. The incense is burned over a hot coal on a special stand (*mabkhara*). The incense and perfume are waved inward towards one's body and hair. After this ritual, a guest is expected to leave. To stay longer is impolite.

Eating

People eat while seated on an Arabic sofa that rests on the floor. Using the hands, everyone eats out of communal dishes. The names of the daily meals are *Iftar* or *Foutour* (breakfast), *Ghada* (lunch), and *Esha* (supper). Devout Muslims do not eat or drink with the left hand, but others will eat with either hand. Guests are fed well during a meal or even given a light snack. Bahraini hosts are pleased when guests enjoy the food and try all the dishes. Guests who are full must act quickly with polite firmness to refuse more food. If they hesitate, more food is served. It is polite in traditional settings to leave a small amount of food on one's plate. Typically a sweet tea is served with meals. Tea is also offered as the social drink for any occasion.

Bahrain has many fine restaurants and fast-food establishments. At better restaurants, servers usually do not receive the standard 10 percent service charge. To personally reward a server, one must add a tip to the service charge. The eldest man in a group customarily pays the restaurant bill and tip, especially on a family outing.

LIFESTYLE

Family

Extended family ties are a strong and dominant part of Bahraini culture. The father is the ultimate authority in the home. Children, especially daughters, do not lightly disobey their father's wishes. Married daughters often return to their parents' home before they give birth and stay for 40 days after the birth to receive care from their mothers and female relatives. The closeness of the family is also evident in the respectful and loving treatment given the elderly. Though traditionally large, families are growing smaller due to greater family planning, more women staying in school longer, and concerns for economic welfare.

Families typically live in free-standing, concrete dwellings. The home usually surrounds an open-air courtyard and has few windows. This protects the family's privacy. In older homes, wind towers provide air circulation and ventilation. Newer homes have air conditioners and electric ceiling fans.

Dating and Marriage

Dating is a controversial subject in Bahrain. Some young people are beginning to date with or without parental permission, but they do so mostly in secret to avoid embarrassing their families. This is because a girl traditionally is looked down upon if she goes out in the company of men other than family members. Society considers these women to be of lesser virtue, so parents worry that they will not be able to marry. Any woman who becomes pregnant out of wedlock faces difficult choices and must often bear the child in secret. Such children may be left to the care of the state, since single motherhood is not socially acceptable.

Some marriages are still arranged, while most marriages that are not arranged in the strict sense still have parental approval; few people marry without family authorization. In the past, women married in their early teens. This is increasingly rare and most marry in their late teens or early twenties.

Marriage celebrations usually last for three days, with separate festivities for men and women. On one night, the bride's hands and feet are decorated with henna, a brown plant dye that stays on the skin for days. The bride is also adorned with gold jewelry, including a *qobqob* (head piece). The bride's family pays for the henna day and the groom's family pays for the other two days.

A man is allowed to have four wives if he provides equally for each wife. However, polygamy is now typically practiced only among the older generations. Few young persons, even in the royal family, consider it a desirable lifestyle.

Diet

Breakfast often consists of fresh *kobouz* (unleavened bread), scrambled eggs mixed with thin noodles and sprinkled with sugar, and cooked beans. Lunch usually consists of some type of spicy rice dish like *beryani* (rice with meat) or *machbous* (rice, meat, tomatoes, and lentils). Other popular dishes include *saloneh* (mixed vegetables) and *harees*, a traditional dish served during the month of *Ramadan*. *Harees* is a blend of wheat and meat cooked until mushy, with lard melted over the top. *Halwa*, a starch pudding mixed with crushed cardamom seeds, saffron, sugar, and fat, is traditionally served before *qahwa* (unsweetened coffee) to conclude the noon meal. The evening meal consists mainly of *bajella* (boiled beans), *kobouz*, an assortment of cheeses, and lots of sweet tea and milk. *Rottab* (dates) are served with every meal. Fish and seafood are also staples of the typical diet. Western influence on the diet is increasingly evident, especially in urban homes. Some Bahrainis now eat packaged breakfast cereals and fast-food.

Recreation

The most popular sport is soccer. Basketball, volleyball, field hockey, and cricket are also enjoyed. There are organized leagues for men, but women's leagues were dissolved in 1979 after the Iranian revolution. Currently, girls and women play sports only in connection with school, but there is talk that leagues may again be established. Bahrainis and expatriates participate in a variety of recreational activities, including sailing, waterskiing, fishing, falconry, horse racing, desert camping, aerobics, softball, ice skating, horseback riding, tennis, and more. Renting videos is also popular.

Holidays

Religious holidays are celebrated according to the lunar *Hijri* calendar, which is shorter than the Western (Gregorian) year by about 11 days. Since dates are set according to the moon's phases, the Gregorian dates for holidays vary from year to year. The most important holidays include *Eid al Fitr*, a three-day feast at the end of the month of *Ramadan*; *Eid al Adha*, which commemorates Abraham's willingness to sacrifice his son and also marks the time for the *Hajj*; and the prophet Muhammad's birthday. The Shiites celebrate *Assura*, a two-day holiday through which they express their beliefs. They parade in the streets, enacting the suffering of the martyr Hussain, the grandson of Muhammad. National Day is celebrated on 16 December. Many Bahrainis also celebrate New Year's on 1 January. The Christmas season is celebrated as the "festive season"; even though the religious significance of the holiday is minimal, it is not uncommon for Bahrainis to have Christmas trees and exchange gifts.

Commerce

Shops are typically open Saturday through Thursday from 8:00 A.M. to 1:00 P.M. They often close from 1:00 to 3:30 P.M. and then reopen until about 8:00 P.M. Business hours are gradually becoming longer. Certain stores now remain open until midnight and some fast-food outlets are open 24 hours. Banking hours are normally from 8:00 A.M. to noon, Saturday through Thursday, and individual branches remain open three afternoons from 3:30 to 5:30 P.M.

When conducting business or shopping in Bahrain, people customarily exchange greetings and converse politely before getting down to details. Many messages important to the transaction are conveyed in the context of this conversation.

SOCIETY

Government

Bahrain is a traditional monarchy. The majority of key government positions are held by members of the Al Khalifa family. The emir is a respected leader, and the royal family is generally well liked. There is, however, growing distrust in the Shiite community. The country employs the traditional Islamic administrative system of the *majlis*, which allows people to directly petition the emir. In practice, the few times available for citizens to meet with the emir reduce the interaction to greetings and other pleasantries rather than serious discussion. But it still gives people the chance to have valuable, direct contact with the monarch. The emir is said to have a remarkable ability to remember people from year to year and take a genuine interest in what they have to say. All inquiries are met with an official reply and have often led to government action. Bahrain has no legislature, but the appointed members of the *shura* council can be nonroyal citizens. There are no political parties or elections.

Economy

As an island nation with limited natural resources, Bahrain must rely on foreign trade to thrive economically. It has one of the world's largest oil refineries. Bahrain is also home to the world's largest aluminum smelter; the nation is trying to find its niche in the competitive world aluminum market. Bahrain pursues an ambition to be a regional banking center, despite heavy competition from Hong Kong and the United Arab Emirates. Progress in the industry was hampered in the 1980s because of the crash of oil prices. Economic growth for 1994 was 2 percent.

Pearl diving was a prominent and honored occupation in the past, but the industry has been in serious decline since the introduction of cultured pearls harvested in other countries. Fishing, another traditional occupation, continues to be important to the domestic economy but is only a small portion of the export economy. The currency is the Bahraini *dinar* (BD).

Real gross domestic product per capita is $14,590. This is a high figure that reflects the country's oil wealth but not necessarily personal prosperity.

Transportation and Communication

Bahrain's transportation network is modern, and most people own cars. Public buses are used mostly by poor expatriates. Bahrainis prefer taxis for public transportation. Most homes have telephones. Cellular phones and mobile pagers have become a status symbol for men. Newspapers from around the world are available. Three local newspapers, which are subject to government control, have a wide readership. International programming is available through radio and television broadcasts.

Education

Bahrain is respected in the Gulf for its strong education system. Compulsory schooling exists for boys and girls through the secondary level. Public schools are single sex through grade 12, but most private schools are coeducational. Bahrain University admits both men and women. The overall literacy rate is 84 percent, but among the youth it approaches 100 percent.

Health

Health care is provided through a system of local clinics and a few major hospitals. Most services are available for free or at low cost to all residents. Private practices and facilities also exist. Bahrain's infant mortality rate is 18 per 1,000; the average life expectancy is 74 years. Nearly all children receive immunizations, and all women have access to prenatal care.

FOR THE TRAVELER

U.S. travelers need a valid passport and a visa to enter Bahrain. A three-to-seven-day transit visa can be obtained at the airport upon arrival, provided the traveler can prove he or she is in transit. Tourists will want to see the Grand Mosque, the Arad Fort, the burial mounds, the National Museum, the main *souq* near Bab Al Bahrain, and archaeological sites. A sea trip by wooden *dhow* is also interesting. Packaged tours are available, but one can also rent a car and set a personal itinerary. Dress conservatively and learn some Arabic. For more information, contact the Bahrain Embassy, 3502 International Drive NW, Washington, DC 20008; phone (202) 342–0741.

People's Republic of
Bangladesh

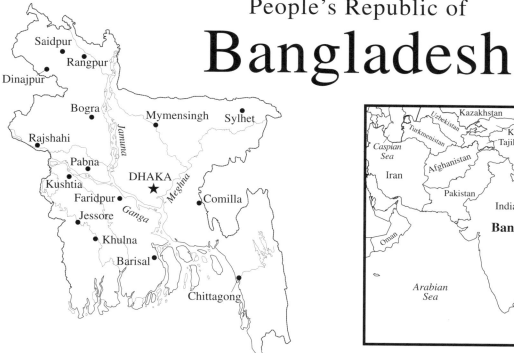

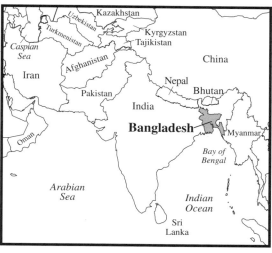

Boundary representations not necessarily authoritative.

BACKGROUND

Land and Climate

With 55,599 square miles (144,000 square kilometers), Bangladesh is about the same size as Wisconsin. It is a fertile delta, except in the southeast and northeast, where it is hilly. Rivers and channels run throughout the country; the three largest rivers are the Ganga, Jamuna, and Meghna. Winter (October–March) is cool and mild; summer (March–June) is hot and humid. The monsoon season (June–October) brings most of Bangladesh's yearly rain; floods, tidal waves, and cyclones are common. In 1991, a cyclone took more than 139,000 lives in the coastal area, destroying entire villages and flooding croplands. A better warning system prevented such a tragedy during storms in 1994.

History

In the 12th century, Muslims began to conquer Hindus in the area now known as Bangladesh. British rule came in the 18th century and the area was part of British India for nearly two hundred years. When British rule ended in 1947, the area became part of the new nation of Pakistan and was called East Pakistan. While linked by religion, the two areas were separated culturally and geographically. East Pakistan did not feel it enjoyed equality with West Pakistan. Calls for autonomy peaked in 1971 and a nine-month civil war began in March. The war eventually involved India because it was flooded by refugees. After the stranded Pakistani Army surrendered to Indian forces, Bangladesh became independent.

Sheikh Mujibur Rahman, leader of the Awami League political party, became the first president and is considered the father of the country. He was assassinated in a 1975 coup.

Following a shaky interim period, Ziaur Rahman governed from 1977 to 1981, when he was assassinated. Hussain Mohammed Ershad took control and governed until 1990, when public protests forced his resignation. A transitional government sponsored free national elections in 1991 and Begum Khaleda Zia, widow of Ziaur Rahman, was elected to lead a new democracy. Challenged by natural disasters, regional problems, and a long-running insurgency in the southeast, Zia faced continual difficulty in stabilizing the country. While some progress was made, political opponents tried to force her from office. All opposition members of Parliament resigned at the end of 1994 and called for a series of strikes in 1995 to force early elections under a neutral caretaker government. Zia refused to step down and sponsored elections in February 1996. These were boycotted by all opposition parties and her subsequent victory became meaningless.

More strikes eventually convinced Zia to step down, and a neutral government held fair, free elections in June 1996. Voter turnout was high, as were hopes for an end to the political stalemate and turmoil. Sheikh Hasina Wazed, daughter of Sheikh Mujibur Rahman and leader of the Awami League, led her party to victory over Zia's Bangladesh Nationalist Party. Wazed soon formed a government as the new prime minister and promised reconciliation and progress.

THE PEOPLE

Population

Bangladesh has more than 128 million people and is growing at about 2.3 percent annually. With a population density of more than 2,300 persons per square mile (890 per square kilometer), Bangladesh is one of the most densely populated countries in the world. Most people live in Bangladesh's thousands of small villages. Only about 16 percent live in cities.

Except for about 250,000 Biharis (Muslims who immigrated from Bihar, India) and some small groups in the southeast, Bangladeshis consider themselves a homogeneous people. They have an Indo-European heritage, with some Arab, Persian, and Turkish influence. The people of West Bengal in India are of the same ethnic group as the Bangladeshis, but they are mostly Hindus. To emphasize this difference, most people refer to themselves as Bangladeshis rather than Bangalis (the technical term for Bangla speakers).

Bangladesh's Human Development Index (0.364) ranks it 146th out of 174 countries. As one of the world's poorest people, most Bangladeshis still lack access to resources that allow for personal advancement or economic prosperity.

Language

Bangla, the official language, is also spoken in India's West Bengal. Spoken Bangla has several distinct dialects, the strongest (most guttural) of which are spoken in the northeastern and southeastern districts of Bangladesh. Most Bangla dialects are soft and somewhat musical. People with a university education usually speak English. They incorporate various colloquialisms derived from Bangla into spoken English. The Biharis speak Urdu, an official language in Pakistan. Small groups along the southeast border speak their own languages.

Religion

Bangladesh has the second largest Muslim population in the world; more than 85 percent of the people are Muslim. Most Bangladeshis are Sunni Muslims. Muslims pray five times daily. The midday *Ju'mma* service on Friday is the most important prayer time. Muslims accept the *Qur'an* (Koran) as scripture, believing it was revealed to Muhammad by *Allah* through the angel Gabriel.

Hindus (13 percent) make up the other major religious group. Christians are few in number, but Christian churches are appreciated for their relief efforts and educational institutions.

Muslims do not drink alcohol or eat pork. Hindus do not eat beef. Muslims fast from sunrise to sundown during the month of *Ramzan* (Ramadan). Each evening the fast is broken with special snacks called *iftar*. It is polite for non-Muslims to avoid daytime public eating, drinking, or smoking during *Ramzan*. Bangladeshis stress cleanliness near holy books and places. They remove the shoes before entering mosques and temples.

General Attitudes

A calm and serious face is considered a sign of maturity. Therefore, while Bangladeshis might not smile in public, they are not being unfriendly. It is not customary to thank someone for a favor. Although the word *dhannabad* (thanks) exists, Bangladeshis avoid using it in everyday life. Instead, one returns the favor. People do use *dhannabad*, however, in formal situations. Bangladeshis value the group more than the individual, so family needs come first. Friendships are expected to be strong and durable. Society is male dominated. Men are protective of women in the family. Women are discouraged from being out alone after sunset. Except in the upper class, women generally have a low status in society, but there is a growing movement to promote women's rights. Women comprise just 7 percent of the labor force.

Social classes play an integral but diminishing role in Bangladesh. For example, class often is still an important factor in the choice of a marriage partner. The way a woman is treated by her husband's family is often determined by her father's wealth; if he is poor, she may be treated poorly.

Bangladeshis are proud of their artistic tradition, which is much older than their young country. They appreciate poetry, music, and literature. Bangali poetry, known for its passion and emotion, reflects the character of the Bangladeshi people. Fatalism—reflected in the arts—plays an important role in people's lives. Many are happy to lead simple, modest lives without various material comforts.

Personal Appearance

Although many men wear Western clothing, especially in urban areas, women generally wear a traditional *saree*—a long piece of printed cloth wrapped around the body in a special way. Jewelry is important to a woman's wardrobe; it also serves as financial security. Women do not wear pants. Adults do not wear shorts. Some men wear white religious clothing called *pajama* (like a Western pajama bottom) and *panjabi* (like a knee-length pajama top). Men in rural villages often wear a *lungi* (a circular piece of cloth, knotted at the waist, that extends to the ankles) with a *genji* (a sleeveless vest).

CUSTOMS AND COURTESIES

Greetings

Muslim Bangladeshis greet each other with *Assalaa-mualaikum* (Peace be upon you) and respond with *Waalaikum assalaam* (And peace be upon you). Each person may raise the right hand to his forehead, palm curved and relaxed, in a salute-like gesture. Men might also shake hands and may embrace during religious festivals. One does not shake hands with, kiss, or embrace a member of the opposite sex in public. A common Hindu greeting is *Adab* (Hello). At parting, a Muslim might say *Khoda hafiz* (May God be with you). *Ashi* (So long) is common for all groups.

In addressing people, Bangladeshis add different suffixes to names to show both respect and closeness. For example, a man adds *-bhabi* (wife of older brother) to the name of his friend's wife, even though they have no family ties. The terms "sister" and "brother" are used as commonly for friends and colleagues as for family members. Age difference is the key factor in determining how to address another person. A person of the same age is usually addressed by name, whereas an older person (regardless of how few years separate the two) may be addressed by name plus a family-related suffix ("older brother," "son of father's brother," "older sister," etc.) or by the suffix alone. So, a young adult might address an older woman by adding *-apa* (older sister) to her name or simply by calling her *apa*.

Gestures

Eye contact during conversation shows sincerity. However, to show respect to an older person or someone of higher social standing, one usually looks down and speaks only when spoken to. In general, it is impolite to cross one's legs or smoke in the presence of an elder, regardless of what the older person does. One does not point the bottom of the shoe or foot at a person because it is thought to lower that person's worth. Bangladeshis are also sensitive about one's foot touching books or other reading materials. Should a person accidently touch a book with a foot, the person apologizes by touching the book with the fingertips of the right hand, then touching the chest, and then the lips.

Pointing with the chin is polite; whistling or winking in public is not. Beckoning with the index finger is very rude. In general, it is impolite to beckon adults, but beckoning is done with the palm turned down and all fingers waving together. The U.S. American sign for "OK" (thumb and index finger touching to form a circle) is obscene. The "thumbs-up" gesture is a sign of rejection in Bangladesh.

Visiting

Bangladeshis visit each other often, usually in the late morning or late afternoon. Hosts offer guests tea (rarely coffee) and sometimes sweets. It is customary to decline the offer a few times but to eventually accept at least some tea. Guests visiting at mealtime are usually invited to eat.

At social occasions, most people avoid being the first or among the last to arrive. When people are invited to an event but cannot go, they still say they will try to attend. Saying "no" may be interpreted as not valuing the host's friendship. The entire extended family is expected to be invited.

Because Bangladeshis are class conscious, they avoid inviting people they think they cannot entertain satisfactorily. Also, people evade certain invitations, such as birthday parties, if they feel they cannot take a proper gift. Dinner guests are not expected to bring gifts, but they usually reciprocate the dinner invitation.

Eating

Bangladeshis generally do not use knives and forks at home, but they use spoons to eat sweets. They eat food with the right hand, which is washed before each meal. Because the left hand is used for sanitation, it is not used to pass objects or to eat. *Shu'ra* (a sauce) is often served with meals. For reasons of cleanliness, people do not let *shu'ra* touch above their knuckles when they eat.

Bangladeshis do not converse much during a meal, especially at home. Food is not passed around the table; rather, plates are taken to a main dish for serving. One places bones and other food wastes on bone plates so they are separate from one's meal. On special occasions, children often eat first. Men and women eat separately at large social gatherings (such as weddings) but not for everyday meals.

At restaurants, the wealthiest person often pays for everyone's meal, particularly among relatives. However, it is becoming more common among students to pay individually. Expensive restaurants have utensils, but others often do not.

LIFESTYLE

Family

Due to economic necessity, extended families often share the same dwelling, but the nuclear family is becoming more popular with the younger generation. Children, especially sons, are expected to care for their elderly parents. Bangladesh has no social security system or nursing homes. Grandparents or older siblings are responsible for child care when the parents are away or working.

Dating and Marriage

Young people have fewer opportunities for social interaction with the opposite sex as they grow older. Dating is unknown. When men and women go out together, as do a small number of university students, the relationship is expected to lead to marriage. Sexual relations outside of marriage are strongly discouraged; self-restraint is considered an indicator of one's potential to build a strong marriage. Women often marry before they are 18, especially in rural areas. Men marry after they finish their education or have some financial security.

Marriage is often arranged through a *ghatak* (matchmaker), who could be a relative or family friend. If a man and woman get to know each other on their own, the man sends a formal proposal to the woman's parents through an older relative. For weddings, both the bride's and groom's houses are decorated with lights. Bamboo gates, decorated with colorful pieces of cloth, are placed at the entrance. The bride wears a *saree* and jewelry; the groom wears a *shirwani* (knee-length coat), a *pagri* (traditional cap), and *nagra* (flat shoes that curl upward in front). A Muslim groom pledges money for the bride's future if the marriage fails; it is recorded in the *ka'been* (marriage registry). Although polygamy and divorce are legal, both carry a negative stigma. While having more than one wife is increasingly rare, divorce is slowly becoming more common.

Diet

Rice is the main staple food. Because Bangladesh has many rivers, fish is cheaper and more available than meat. With a few exceptions (carrots, cucumbers, and tomatoes), vegetables are fried in oil. Bangladeshis prefer spicy food. Popular spices include cumin, ginger, coriander, tumeric, and pepper. Food is often marinated in *shu'ra* (made from chopped onions and spices marinated in warm cooking oil). A good *shu'ra* is considered an index of fine cooking. People usually do not dessert after meals, but they eat sweets on special occasions. Two popular sweets (*rashogolla* and *kalojam*) are variations of dough boiled in syrup.

Recreation

The most popular sports are soccer, field hockey, cricket, table tennis, and badminton. Visiting friends and relatives is another form of recreation; in fact, it is expected because it reinforces the family support network. Televisions and VCRs are becoming popular in cities. Movie theaters are plentiful. Hindu movies (often musicals) from India are favorites, and the youth enjoy movies from the United States. The wealthy attend dance and music performances. There are no discotheques in Bangladesh.

In villages, the most popular youth game, *ha-dudu* or *kabaddi*, is played on a square court. While holding his breath, one team's player enters the other side's area and tries to touch as many of the other players as possible. If he returns to his side while still holding his breath, the other team loses the players he touched and his team gains an equal number of its own players back (from previous rounds). However, if he is trapped by the opposite team and is forced to release his breath, he is out and the opposing team gains one of its members back. The first team to eliminate all players on the other side wins.

Holidays

Political and cultural holidays follow the Western calendar, but religious holidays follow the lunar calendar (so they are on different days each year). A third Bangla calendar determines seasons and the new year (*Pahela Baishak*). Political holidays include *Ekushe February* (21 February, honoring six students killed in a 1952 political protest), Independence Day (26 March, when independence was declared), Labor Day (1 May), and Victory Day (16 December, when independence was actually achieved). The most important religious (Muslim) holidays are *Eid-ul-Fitr* (at the end of *Ramzan*), *Eid-ul-Azha* (commemorating Abraham's willingness to sacrifice his son), and *Shab-i-Barat* (a special night for asking blessings). Some Hindu, Buddhist, and Christian feasts are also celebrated as national holidays.

The *Eid* holidays begin with prayer services and are marked by three days of feasting and visiting. It is common for children to bow and touch the feet of older people in the extended family to show respect. The older people then give the children gifts, usually money. People customarily exchange one-third of the meat sacrificed during *Eid-ul-Azha* as gifts (they donate one-third to the poor and keep one-third). During *Shab-i-Barat*, neighbors exchange sweets.

Commerce

Weekdays are from Saturday to Thursday; offices are closed Friday. Small grocery and retail stores may stay open every day late into the night. Prices in stores are neither marked nor fixed, so bartering is common. Businesspeople interact socially to build trust and a network of acquaintances. Problems are best solved privately by appealing to civility, honor, and goodwill, although legal channels are available.

SOCIETY

Government

Bangladesh is a democracy divided into four regions. The central government is led by a prime minister (Sheikh Hasina Wazed) as head of government. The president, Abdur Rahman Biswas, is a head of state with mostly ceremonial duties. The *Jatiya Sangsad* (National Parliament) has 300 elected seats. The Awami League holds 146 seats. The Bangladesh Nationalist Party is the main opposition group with 116 seats. Various smaller parties are also represented in Parliament. A person can run for and win more than one seat, so there are not always equal numbers of members and seats. An additional 30 seats are reserved for women. All citizens older than age 18 may vote.

Economy

The economy is based on agriculture, which employs 60 percent of the labor force. Jute, a plant whose fiber is used to make carpets, is the main export. In fact, Bangladesh is the world's largest exporter of jute. Other important exports include tea, leather, and shrimp. The country imports many of its consumer goods and food. The relatively young textile industry is expanding rapidly, producing clothing for import to many Western nations, including the United States. Wages sent home from Bangladeshis working abroad is an important source of revenue.

Real gross domestic product per capita is $1,230. Most people either do not earn an income or do not earn enough to meet basic needs. Economic growth in 1994 was nearly 5 percent. Strikes in 1995 and 1996 hampered economic growth, but prospects for future growth are bright if the political situation stabilizes. And while three-fourths of all people live in poverty, new industries are providing employment and other opportunities to a growing number of Bangladeshis. The currency is the *taka* (Tk).

Transportation and Communication

Traffic moves on the left. Roads are not extensive and most are not paved. The main forms of public transportation include buses (often crowded), rickshaws, and *babi-taxis* (three-wheeled motor scooters). For private transport, most people walk or ride bicycles. Because of the many rivers but few bridges, land transportation links are poorly developed. However, rivers are used to transport people and goods throughout the country. Railways are also important.

Telephones are available in urban areas. A person is billed for every call, even local ones. Bangladesh has a national television station and nine radio stations. There are a number of daily newspapers. Mail delivery is slow.

Education

Bangladesh's literacy rate is 36 percent (48 percent for men, 24 percent for women). Boys and girls attend separate schools. Fewer than one-fifth get a secondary education. Universities are coeducational. Approximately 3 percent of the people complete ten years of school, two years of college (comparable to grades 12 and 13), and three or more years at a university.

Health

Bangladesh has a high infant mortality rate (105 per 1,000 births) due partly to malnutrition. Life expectancy for men and women averages 55 years; it is higher in urban areas than in rural areas. Sanitation is poor and water is not potable in most areas. Hospital care is free, but it is inadequate to meet most people's needs. Private clinics provide better care, but only the wealthy can afford them. Services are limited in rural areas.

FOR THE TRAVELER

A passport, visa, and proof of onward passage are required for U.S. visitors to enter Bangladesh. Malaria and cholera are common, as are typhoid and hepatitis. Consult a doctor for recommended vaccinations, or call the U.S. Centers for Disease Control and Prevention International Travel Hotline at (404) 332–4559. Avoid drinking water that has not been boiled; do not eat food from street vendors or poorly maintained restaurants. Wash and peel all fruits and vegetables. Be sure meat is well cooked and served hot. For travel information, contact the Embassy of Bangladesh, 2201 Wisconsin Avenue NW, Suite 300, Washington, DC 20007.

Republic of
Benin

Boundary representations not necessarily authoritative.

BACKGROUND

Land and Climate

Benin is a small western African nation located between Togo and Nigeria. Covering 43,482 square miles (112,620 square kilometers), it is just smaller than Pennsylvania. From its coast on the Atlantic Ocean, Benin runs only 420 miles (680 kilometers) to the northern border. Rolling hills and plains dominate the landscape, but the Atacora Mountains provide variety in the north. Major rivers include the Ouéme, Zou, Pendjari, Mékrou, Alibori, Sota, and Niger. The capital is Porto-Novo.

Benin's north is generally higher in elevation and drier; rain falls between June and September. The hot season is October to April, with January temperatures reaching above 100°F (37°C). Between December and March, the harmattan (dry, hot wind) blows from north to south. The lower-lying south experiences four seasons: a long rainy season between March and July, followed by a short hot season until September; and a short rainy season to November, followed by a long hot season until March. Temperatures are cooler than in the north but are still hot (95°F or 35°C).

Deforestation has destroyed many southern forests, but ceiba, ebony, mahogany, and palm trees are still found. Elephants, lions, giraffes, antelopes, monkeys, boars, crocodiles, wildebeests, and snakes all inhabit Benin. Most snakes are poisonous, and the python is considered sacred.

History

The history of Benin (called Dahomey until 1975) cannot be separated from the history of the powerful Fon kingdom of Danhomê. It was known for its slave trade and production of palm oil and for having an army of women (the Amazons). Other kingdoms were prominent at the same time as Danhomê, such as the Kingdom of Porto-Novo in the south and the northern kingdoms of Borgu, Nikki, Djougou, and Kouande. Danhomê expanded its northern frontier in the early 1800s to acquire more slaves from neighboring tribes. It also fiercely resisted French incursions beginning in 1857. In 1893, the French finally defeated King Gbehanzin, the hero of the resistance, and gradually spread their administrative control throughout the region. By 1904, Dahomey was fully integrated into French West Africa.

Independence came in 1960, but the first 12 years were marked by regional strife, trade union and student strikes, and six military coups. No one could unite the nation until Major Matthieu Kérékou seized power. He eventually (1974) adopted Marxism-Leninism as the official ideology, renamed the country the People's Republic of Benin, and governed with a strong hand until 1989.

When communism disintegrated in Europe, Kérékou sponsored a national conference in which it was decided that Benin would become a multiparty democracy with regularly scheduled elections. Although the transition period was unstable due to strikes and opposition activities, national elections were held on schedule in 1991. Nicéphore Soglo defeated Kérékou to become president of the newly declared Republic of Benin. The peaceful transfer of power was followed by another relatively peaceful election in 1996. Kérékou was elected president.

PEOPLE

Population

The population of 5.5 million grows annually at 3.3 percent. Benin's diversity of ethnic groups is the result of migrations, conquests, and the mixing of groups over time. The Fon is the largest single group with 47.1 percent of the population. Other larger groups include the Adja (12.2 percent), Bariba (9.7), and Yoruba or Aizo (5.1). In the north, a number of smaller groups form 5 percent of the population; these include the Dendi, Betamari, Berba, Kountemba, Ouama, and others. Southern and northern Beninese do not have the best relations, and northerners often are insultingly referred to as *Somba* by southerners. More recent immigrants to Benin include Togolese, Ghanaians, and Nigerians. Two-thirds of all people live in the south, particularly between Abomey and Cotonou, the main commercial city. Cotonou claims 12 percent of the total population, but most people (70 percent) live in rural areas. Benin's Human Development Index (0.332) ranks it 155th out of 174 countries. Adjusted for women, the index (0.314) ranks Benin 114th out of 130 nations. The index reflects Benin's need to better empower people to access opportunities for personal development.

Language

French, the official language, is used in government and education. No indigenous language has been accepted as a national language, so French remains the unifying tongue. Still, many rural people have trouble speaking it. The Adja-Fon language group (Fon, Adja, Houéda, Popo, Mahi, Mina, Goun, etc.) dominates in the south and central regions. Yoruba is also widely spoken in these areas. Bariba and other languages are spoken in the north. To promote literacy, from 1975 to 1990 the government encouraged the use of major national languages in radio and television broadcasts. English, Spanish, German, and Russian are offered in secondary schools, and many Beninese can understand Nigerian Pidgin English.

Religion

Although Christianity has had a presence in Benin since the 17th century, indigenous belief systems permeate the country's culture. Most Beninese believe in a supreme God (*Mahu* among the Fon and *Olorun* or *Olodumare* among the Yoruba) and in a life after death. They attach great importance to worshiping ancestors who protect them against misfortune. Accordingly, death is regarded as an important family event, and in some cases, funeral rites are sophisticated. Divination is a central feature of local faith; people regularly consult an oracle about significant events they wish to undertake. People worship the supreme God through local divinities (*Voodoos* among the Fon and *Orisha* among the Yoruba). Most families have a fetish to which they pray and offer sacrifice to get help from these local gods.

Even Beninese who have adopted Christianity or Islam continue to practice fetish worship and other indigenous rites. They do not see the rules of organized religion as particularly binding or exclusive. Indeed, forms of Christianity that integrate African practices are developing quickly, and there is little religious conflict between groups. Twenty percent of Benin's population is Christian, mostly Catholic. Islam (15 percent) is practiced mostly in the north.

General Attitudes

Although attitudes and values differ between ethnic groups, some common traits are characteristic. For instance, few Beninese value privacy. Most wonder why anyone would actually want to be alone. They take life at a fairly casual pace and have a good sense of humor that allows them to laugh at life's trivial problems. Humor does not extend to sarcasm, however, which is viewed as insulting. The Beninese are proud of their heritage. Most value hard work and material success, but these come second to family priorities and friendship bonds. Although perhaps initially distrustful of individuals, Beninese are very hospitable. Once trust is established, relationships remain strong. Misconceptions between the north and south are partly due to the fact that northerners are more traditional and reserved than southerners, who have greater exposure to Western ideas and education.

Personal Appearance

Cleanliness and neatness are extremely important. People take great care to maintain and iron their clothing well, shower daily, and dress as well as possible. Urban residents wear anything from Western shirts, trousers, and suits to local fashions. Men's casual clothing often consists of a pair of loose trousers and a long-sleeved shirt that can reach to the knees. Formal outfits consist of three embroidered pieces: trousers, a long shirt, and a top usually called a *boubou* or *agbada*. Imported fabrics are used in addition to locally produced material. Rural men often wear a cloth about the waist and a small *dashiti* top or short-sleeved shirt, or they may wrap the waist cloth up to cover the chest and one shoulder.

Rural and urban women often wear a *pagne* (wraparound skirt). This can be long or short depending on one's age and marital status. A loose *boumba* (blouse) completes the outfit. Women wear a long *boubou* on formal occasions. A *boubou* is often ornately embroidered and quite colorful.

CUSTOMS AND COURTESIES

Greetings

A proper greeting always precedes conversation. When joining or leaving a small group, one greets each individual. Men usually shake right hands, with the oldest person initiating the handshake. Women only shake hands with men if the man initiates. To show special respect, particularly to an older person, one bows slightly and grasps one's right elbow with the left hand during a handshake. In cities, young men snap fingers when they shake hands. Many urban relatives and friends tend to kiss three or four times alternately on the cheeks. Some rural people do this and add a kiss to the mouth.

The Fon ask *A fon dagbe a?* (Did you wake up well?), while the Yoruba say *E Karo* (Good morning). Similar expressions are used in other languages. People of the same age and status address each other by first name or nickname. Titles are reserved for official functions. It is disrespectful to call older people by their first names. Instead, one uses "brother" or "sister" (*Fofo* or *Dada* among the Fon) and "uncle" or "aunt." If an eldest child is named Dossa, parents may be called "Dossa's mother" (*Dossanon*) or "Dossa's father" (*Dossato*).

Gestures

Everyday conversation is accompanied by many gestures and sounds. For instance, when women complain, they often hit the side of their thighs. Various verbal noises can express agreement or exasperation. It is considered offensive to beckon someone with the index finger; instead, one waves all fingers of the right hand with the palm facing down. Public displays of affection are unacceptable, but friends of the same gender often hold hands or touch when talking or walking. Using the left hand for gestures is unclean and considered bad luck.

Showing respect for elders is vital. One does not interrupt an older person in conversation, nor does one talk to an elder with hands in the pockets or while chewing gum or wearing a hat. Avoiding eye contact shows deference to elders. Among equals, eye contact can indicate frankness.

Visiting

Visiting friends and relatives is regarded as considerate, and it is not necessary to notify them in advance. Visitors are warmly welcomed and offered water to drink. The host may take a sip before offering it to guests, and in rural areas, guests often spill a bit on the earth to show respect for the dead.

If visitors arrive during a meal, hosts feel obligated to offer some food. Visitors should accept at least a bite, as it is rude not to taste the food, but they can politely decline to eat the entire meal. Visitors ask for permission to leave; when the host agrees, he walks them at least to the door and sometimes further. Reciprocity is an important part of relationships, so today's guest is expected to be tomorrow's host.

While most visiting takes place in the home, the marketplace is also a popular point of social contact. Every town or village has a market day once a week or so, where people enjoy meeting to chat.

Eating

Eating habits depend on one's activities. Rural peasants eat anytime in the morning, often in the fields. They have lunch at home later in the afternoon and dinner at night. Wage earners may have one, two, or three meals, depending on their financial means. Urban dwellers often have breakfast between 7:00 and 10:00 A.M., lunch between 1:00 and 3:00 P.M., and dinner between 7:00 and 10:00 P.M. Spoons and other utensils may be used for some foods, but the right hand is generally preferred, especially for okra, *eba* (see Diet), or pounded yam. At home, people eat from a common bowl (children share one and parents share another). The father usually is served first, and families eat together. In northern areas, however, when male guests are present, the wife eats separately.

LIFESTYLE

Family

The traditional family structure consists of an extended family living in a compound of separate houses. The compound is surrounded by a wall or fence and has a common courtyard with a well, space for animals, and a cooking area. Such a family expects to work hard together to meet basic needs, and all members expect to share the fruits of labor. Tolerance and support are key elements to family interaction, and it is considered a curse to have bad relations within the family unit. While this structure is preferred and remains mostly intact in rural areas, it is undergoing profound change in cities, where nuclear families are more common and where the idea of working together has become less important. Because the desire is still strong to share in what others have

accomplished, some conflicts have arisen and society is struggling to keep the system working.

Polygamy is legal and practiced across all ethnic groups and religions, but most families are monogamous. Northern men are more likely than southern men to have two wives. Women do much of the work in a family, but the father is its head. Nevertheless, women are respected for their role in raising children and for considerable success in agriculture and trade (retail and wholesale). Elderly women are highly regarded. Most families have more than two children and prefer to have at least one son to perpetuate the family name.

Dating and Marriage

While urban dating is becoming more of a casual affair, traditional dating is geared toward marriage. Depending on the area's customs, young people might socialize at local ceremonies, dance parties, dinners, or family functions like marriages or funerals.

Wedding traditions vary widely. Most Beninese attach a great deal of importance to customary and religious marriages. Christians and Muslims mix their respective customs with local ways. A common practice is negotiating the bride-price. Elder women from the bride's family preside over a ceremony where they accept the groom's gifts and officially agree to the marriage, which is considered an alliance between two families. This bride-price, which legislation has sought to discourage, and the cost of a proper wedding can be so high that the wedding might be postponed for months or years until sufficient finances are available. In such cases, couples may live together and have children as if married.

Diet

Beninese prefer hot and spicy foods. The basic daily meal is a spicy stew eaten with a stiff porridge made from corn flour (*wo*, *amiwo*) in the south, yam flour (*amala* or *loubo*) in Yoruba areas, or millet and sorghum flour in the north. Side dishes are pounded yam, fried or boiled yam and cassava, sweet potatoes, and fried bananas and *gari*, a kind of grits made from cassava. Beninese also eat *gari* with any kind of stew or soup or thin it and drink it like a porridge with sugar or milk. Boiled in water, *gari* is served as a side dish (*eba*) eaten with stew. Beans are popular. Rice, which is mostly imported, is increasingly consumed. Beninese stews have many ingredients: vegetables and leaves, okra, peanuts, palm nut pulp, and so on.

People eat a variety of tropical fruits (bananas, mangoes, oranges, papayas, avocados, tangerines, and pineapples) and snacks in the morning or late afternoon. They save meat for special occasions because it is so expensive; favorite types include chicken, goat, beef, and a special delicacy, *agouti* (sugarcane rat). The entire animal is eaten with no part being wasted. French cuisine is found in urban areas. Fresh seafood is plentiful in the south.

Recreation

Beninese enjoy getting together; visiting is a major form of recreation. Many social events are closely related to family or religious ceremonies. People also love soccer and other games like basketball, handball, and boxing. Wrestling is common in the north. Televisions are scarce, but people have access to one somewhere in the village, and large groups often get together to watch favorite programs or World Cup soccer. Only a few people can afford to go to a restaurant or on beach outings. The Beninese enjoy playing cards, checkers, or *adji* (a popular mathematical and probability game) outdoors. Traditional dancing to drums is popular.

Holidays

Official holidays are New Year's Day (1 January), Easter Monday, International Workers' Day (1 May), Independence Day (1 August), Christmas Day, *Odun Idi* (feast at the end of the holy Muslim month of *Ramadan*), and *Odun Lea* (Muslim Feast of Sacrifice). Rural people hold local celebrations.

Commerce

Government offices are open weekdays from 8:00 A.M. to noon and 3:00 to 6:30 P.M. Banks usually close by 4:00 P.M. Private businesses operate on their own schedules. Business should be initiated only after a greeting and social conversation. Shop prices usually are fixed, but bargaining is essential at open markets. Merchants respect a good bargainer and see the exchange as a game as well as a transaction. The most famous market, *Tokpa* or *Dantokpa* ("near the river"), is held every five days in Cotonou. Street hawkers informally sell their goods at crossroads. The first customer of the day is important because he or she brings either hard or good luck.

SOCIETY

Government

Benin is a multiparty democracy composed of six provinces. The president acts as chief of state and head of government and is directly elected for a five-year term. The National Assembly has 64 members, who are also freely elected. Every citizen may vote at age 18. More than 50 political parties are active in this young democracy, but only a handful have legislative representation. No one party has yet established dominance. Regionalism, a system of political clientelism based on ethnic origin that flourished prior to 1990, has not entirely disappeared, but the government is working to unite the country.

Economy

Benin is one of the poorest countries in the world. Real gross domestic product per capita is about $1,630, but most wealth is concentrated in the hands of a few. Two-fifths of all people live in poverty, relying on subsistence farming for their livelihood. In fact, 90 percent of all agricultural output comes from small farms. Agriculture accounts for 35 percent of export earnings. Major crops include corn, cassava and other tubers, groundnuts, sorghum, and millet. Cotton is the chief export crop, but cash crops like coffee, cocoa, peanuts, and tobacco are also produced in small quantities. Industry employs only 2 percent of the workforce. Crude oil is the country's most important export. Remittances from Beninese working abroad are vital to the economy.

Benin imports far more than it exports, and a great deal of illegal trade is conducted across Benin's borders, particularly with Nigeria. The government is implementing reforms and encouraging foreign investment to stimulate growth. Some success has been noted and annual growth is about 3 percent. The currency is the *CFA franc*.

Transportation and Communication

Benin's few roads are mostly unpaved. Urban public transport hardly exists, although inexpensive taxis do operate in large cities. Taxi-motorcycles called *zemidjans* have quickly become a substitute for taxis in Porto-Novo and Cotonou. Many people also have their own motorcycles and some have cars. Driving is unsafe, as traffic rules are minimal.

Private telephones are rare, but the number of public phones is increasing. Benin has one government-operated television station, and broadcasts from neighboring countries can sometimes be received. Abundant newspapers enjoy a wide urban readership. Rural people receive news from private radio stations and through village meetings.

Education

In 1974, the government tried to replace its French-based educational system, but it failed for a number of reasons. While it allowed people to learn written local languages (most languages are oral) instead of French, facilities and materials were lacking. Since 1990, more private and Catholic schools have opened, and the curriculum is reverting to the French model. Nevertheless, the challenges remain the same: to create a school system flexible enough to take into account changing national realities, to help reduce unemployment, and to absorb the vast majority of children younger than 15, who represent 48 percent of the total population. The drop-out rate is high. Reasons vary and often involve finances. Children are important members of the family labor pool and cannot be spared for many years of schooling, which begin at age six. Only about one in ten children gains a secondary education. Most students at all levels are boys. The adult literacy rate is 33 percent. Benin has a university in Abomey-Calavi with a medical school. Other professional schools (for nursing, administration, and teaching) are also available.

Health

Benin has no national health-care system. Preventive medicine is not widely practiced. For instance, some do not trust immunizations, food taboos for pregnant women cause malnutrition, and most people only seek medical attention when they get sick. Doctors are few, as most go abroad to practice. Many diseases afflicting Benin (yellow fever, influenza, river blindness, guinea worm, etc.) could be avoided if people accepted a more preventive approach. Indigenous (mostly herbal) medicines are more trusted, and the government is trying to integrate them with modern treatments. Training and modern equipment are badly needed. The infant mortality rate is 107 per 1,000; life expectancy is about 52 years.

FOR THE TRAVELER

A valid passport, visa, and proof of onward passage are required for U.S. citizens to enter Benin. Yellow fever and cholera vaccinations are mandatory. Malaria is common, so suppressants must be taken continuously. Eat only hot, well-cooked foods; wash and peel fruits and vegetables. Do not drink unboiled water. For information, contact the Embassy of Benin, 2737 Cathedral Avenue NW, Washington, DC 20008; phone (202) 232–6656.

A *Culturgram* is a product of native commentary and original, expert analysis. Statistics are estimates and information is presented as a matter of opinion. While the editors strive for accuracy and detail, this document should not be considered strictly factual. It is a general introduction to culture, an initial step in building bridges of understanding between peoples. It may not apply to all peoples of the nation. You should therefore consult other sources for more information.

Republic of
Botswana

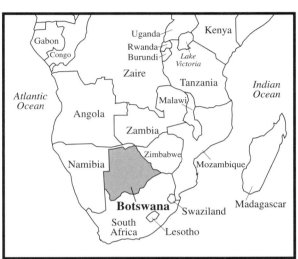

Boundary representations not necessarily authoritative.

BACKGROUND

Land and Climate

Botswana, a landlocked country in southern Africa, covers 585,370 square miles (600,370 square kilometers). It is about the same size as France or Texas. Eighty percent of its territory (west of most cities) is covered by the Kgalagadi (Kalahari) Desert, which consists of savanna grasses and shrubs but virtually no water. Gently rolling hills form the eastern border. The Okavango Delta, the world's largest inland delta, is found in the north. Its wetlands, as well as the country's many national parks, harbor a wide variety of animals and plant life.

Reservoirs provide water for major urban areas, but most water comes from wells. Small dams catch rain runoff for cattle, which far outnumber the human population. Drought cycles are common. An extended drought ended with abundant rains in 1995–96 (November–March).

Summer is from October to April, with temperatures often above 100°F (37°C). Winter (May–August) days are windy, sunny, and cool or warm. Temperatures may go below freezing at night in some areas.

History

Tswana ethnic groups began moving into eastern Botswana from the southeast in the early 1500s. They displaced and absorbed other peoples as they spread out to claim all land that had surface water or was suitable for grazing and agriculture. Various chiefdoms developed over the next several decades.

Ethnic disputes beginning in the mid-1700s left Tswana chiefdoms vulnerable to invasions by refugee armies from Zulu wars in Natal. These wars began in the early 1800s and caused great upheaval in southern Africa. Boer (white settler) encroachment from 1852 onward led major Tswana chiefs, under the direction of Khama III, to seek protection from the British government. The British, eager to secure a labor supply for their South African mines and a route to newly discovered gold in Matabeleland (Zimbabwe), established the Bechuanaland Protectorate in 1885.

In the 20th century, unrest in the Rhodesias and apartheid in South Africa led various groups to form political parties and demand independence from Britain. The Bechuanaland Democratic Party (BDP) led the way to independence in 1966. The founders of the BDP, Sir Seretse Khama and Sir Ketumile Masire, were declared president and vice president, respectively, of the new Republic of Botswana. Khama won three consecutive elections, but he died in 1980. Masire succeeded Khama and was reelected in 1984, 1989, and 1994. Today the BDP (now the Botswana Democratic Party) leads one of the most stable democracies in Africa.

THE PEOPLE

Population

Botswana's population is about 1.39 million, with half younger than age 15. It grows by 3 percent a year. Botswana's Human Development Index (0.763) ranks it 74th out of 174 nations. Adjusted for women, the index (0.696) ranks Botswana 55th out of 130 nations. For a developing nation, Botswana has done well in providing its people with the chance to improve their lives.

Descendants of the original Tswana peoples (Kwena, Ngwato, Ngwaketse, Kgatla, Tawana, Lete, Tlokwa, and Rolong) constitute about half of the total population. These groups essentially consider themselves one people because they descend from a common ancestor, but they tend to concentrate in different areas. The other half of the population is composed of the Kalanga, Kgalagadi, Birwa, Tswapong, Yei, Mbukushu, Subiya, Herero, and Khoesan groups. Whites, Indians, and other Asians compose small minorities.

While more than 70 percent of the population is rural, many are moving to cities for work and education. Gaborone, the capital, is one of the world's fastest-growing cities. Most people live in the eastern part of the country, where the railroad is located, soil supports agriculture, and rainfall can sustain life.

Language

Although English is the official language of government and secondary education, most people speak the national language of Setswana. Primary schooling is conducted in Setswana. But for many children, Setswana is a second language because each minority group speaks its own language. For instance, Tjikalanga (also called Ikalanga) dominates in the northeast. Like Setswana, these other languages are Bantu tongues and are related. In Bantu languages, the noun prefix is the key to grammatical connections. For example, the *mo* prefix can refer to a person. Thus, a *Motswana* is a Tswana person. The plural of *mo* is *ba*. So *Batswana* means "Tswana people" (and citizens of Botswana, regardless of ethnicity). There are seven other two-letter noun classes. Non-Bantu tongues are known collectively as Khosesan (or Sarwa).

The only languages in print are English and Setswana, but Bible publishers are trying to codify every language in Africa. Ikalanga is a written language in Zimbabwe.

Religion

Religious freedom is protected under the constitution, but Christianity is accepted as an official religion in the sense that the school day and official functions begin with prayer. School children also sing Christian hymns before classes begin, but religious instruction is not compulsory. Christianity was introduced in the early 1800s by missionaries (David Livingstone and others) traveling from South Africa. This opened the interior of Africa to exploitation by European hunters and slave traders. Because Christianity was often viewed as a means to Western technology, education, and health care, many chiefs allowed missions on their lands. During his reign (1835–1923), Chief Khama III, who converted to Christianity in 1862, tried to abolish many traditional practices (polygamy, initiation ceremonies, passing widows to a deceased man's brother, rainmaking ceremonies, and other rites) that conflicted with Christian teachings. But some outlawed traditions remain part of village life. Up to half of all people continue to exclusively follow other aspects of their indigenous beliefs. The other half are Christian; Catholics and Protestants comprise about one-fourth of the population.

Many local churches combine traditional beliefs with those of Western Christianity. The largest is the Zion Christian Church; another major congregation is the Spiritual Healing Church.

General Attitudes

Society is founded on traditional law, with the community as the core of Tswana life and the chief as the symbol of unity.

Traditionally, schools, roads, and health clinics were built through local organization. This practice of self-help, evident in such Setswana words as *ipelegeng* (carry yourselves), continues today, even though the government is now more responsible for infrastructure. Each individual is expected to benefit the community. The more a person does, the greater that person's status with the group. Anything that can benefit the group is valued, such as one's educational level, integrity, and generosity. Working family members are expected to support those without jobs, and people are expected to house traveling relatives for as long as necessary. Batswana value the lack of conflict. Public criticism is inappropriate, as is raising one's voice in anger.

Personal Appearance

Western dress is common in most areas. Despite the heat, urban men wear business suits and ties, and women wear fashionable dresses or a skirt and blouse. Some young urban women wear pants. Rural women often wear a wrap over their dresses to protect them from dirt. Mothers carry their babies on their backs in fabric slings. Older men wear overalls to protect their clothing. Many men wear hats, except in the *kgotla* (meeting place), and rural women cover their heads with a kerchief. Both sexes typically have short hair. Cleanliness and neatness are important. Smooth hands and longer fingernails are a status symbol for men, indicating they can pay someone else to do their farming or manual labor. For a rural woman, rough hands are considered honorable because they indicate that she works hard.

Batswana wear uniforms to church that distinguish their denominations, and they also display their political party's colors through clothing. Women of the Herero ethnic group, which migrated from Namibia in 1904, wear a long bouffant-skirted costume introduced in Namibia by German missionary wives. The heavy, colorful dress may require up to ten yards of fabric. A woman arranges a matching headdress to indicate her marital status.

CUSTOMS AND COURTESIES

Greetings

Greetings are important; failing to greet someone is rude. To show respect when greeting, particularly to an elder or superior, one shakes with the right hand while supporting one's elbow with the left hand. A slight head bow may also be added to lower one's eye level below that of an elder. Elders and those approaching greet first. A common adult greeting is *Dumela Rra/Mma, O tsogile jang?* (Greetings sir/madam, how did you wake?). The response is *Ke tsogile sentle* (I awoke well). At social gatherings, people greet those they know and are introduced to others. The handshake is less of a grasp and more a matter of palms and fingertips touching. Children and peers use informal greetings. For instance, the Setswana reply to *O kae?* (How are you?) is *Ke teng* (literally, "I am here," meaning "fine"). *Tsamaya sentle* (Go well) is said to one departing and *Sala sentle* (Stay well) to one staying.

Greeting customs vary for other ethnic groups. For example, among the Kalanga the younger person always greets first. Young children greet elders by extending both hands or clapping; the elder responds by kissing both hands and saying *Wa muka?* (Are you well?).

Children may be named for some circumstance related to their birth and also given a pet name by which they are known at home. Students often give themselves nicknames for use at school. Traditionally, the father's first name became the child's surname. Now, the child takes the father's surname. Upon the birth of her first child, a woman is thereafter referred to as the mother of that child (e.g., *Mma Jamey* in Setswana or *Bakajamey* in Tjikalanga).

Gestures

One may press the hands (palms and fingers) together in front of the chest before accepting a gift with both hands. Gifts are given with both hands or with the right hand supported by the left at the elbow. Batswana use a variety of gestures to suggest "no," "no thanks," or that something is all gone. One way is to rotate the wrist with fingers outstretched or pointing down. Hitchhikers rapidly wave their right hand with arm extended to hail a vehicle.

It is impolite to walk between two people in conversation. If passing through cannot be avoided, one bows below the level of the conversation and says *Intshwarele* (Excuse me). Respect for elders during conversation is best shown by looking down toward the ground rather than into their eyes. Public displays of affection are inappropriate.

Visiting

Relatives visit one another as often as they can. Because personal relationships are valued, unannounced visitors are welcomed into the home. Most visits cannot be arranged in advance due to a lack of telephones. Hosts offer guests water or tea to drink. Anyone who arrives at mealtime is expected to eat with the family. Guests who are not hungry are expected to try offered food and take some home. Urban relatives often bring staples and household goods as gifts, while people from the *lands* (fields) bring in-season crops. Acquaintances are not expected to bring gifts. Hosts accompany departing guests to the gate or even part of the way home (if walking) to show they were welcome.

Much socializing takes place at the standpipe (where people get water), general stores, and church activities. Men socialize at local *chibuku* depots (bars selling sorghum beer).

Eating

Eating habits vary between urban and rural settings, but sharing is the common denominator. For most, family meals involve eating from common bowls or plates. Visitors receive separate plates. Children share a bowl among them. Drinks are never shared; each person has a cup. Batswana use utensils, but eat some foods with their hands. They frequently eat outside in the shade of a nearby tree. Everyone usually leaves a little food behind to indicate the meal has been filling. Guests often say *Ke itumetse* (I am pleased) to thank the hosts. Smelling food before eating it implies something is wrong with it. Leftovers are kept for later or given to departing guests.

LIFESTYLE

Family

Batswana historically lived in large villages with their agricultural and grazing lands at a distance. With women at the *lands* and men at cattle posts, families were apart much of the time. In colonial times, many men worked in South African mines. Later, laborers moved to cities in search of work.

Families remained tied through an extended family network. Today, schooling and employment keep families apart. Women are primarily responsible for the family, agriculture, and entrepreneurial pursuits. They head most rural families with support from nearby relatives. Children take on chores at any early age.

A fenced family compound contains several *rondavals* (round thatched dwellings), a cooking area, and an outhouse. Animals are penned within the compound, which women keep clear of grass and debris. More modern homes are made of cinder blocks with cement floors.

Dating and Marriage

Living away from home villages has dramatically changed the way young people socialize. Interaction was once rather restricted, but the youth now meet at discos and other sites. School competitions and youth clubs also provide contact. Because of the expense and obligations involved in formal marriage, more than half of all couples live together rather than marry. Those who do marry may choose rites under either civil or customary law. Customary celebrations involve two or more days of eating, drinking, dancing, and speeches. The groom's family pays a negotiated *bogadi* (bride-price) to the bride's family.

Diet

Bogobe (porridge) made from *mabele* (sorghum), maize, or millet (in the northeast) is a staple food. It is served soft and often soured for breakfast and thick for the midday and evening meals. *Paleche* (white maize), although vulnerable to drought, is replacing sorghum as the primary grain. Many people have tea or *mageu* (a thick sorghum drink) instead of porridge for breakfast. Some enjoy *fat cakes* (deep-fried dough) with tea for breakfast or lunch. *Bogobe* is accompanied by a relish, such as a popular one made of onions, chicken stock, and tomato sauce. Batswana eat seasonal fruits and vegetables and raise goats and chicken for meat. *Phane* worms, a delicacy gathered from the *mophane* trees in the northeast, are dried in hot ashes and eaten. Men slaughter cattle for special occasions. Rice replaces *bogobe* at weddings.

Recreation

Batswana enjoy visiting, dancing, singing, and playing sports. Young men play football (soccer), often competing on village teams. Schools offer track-and-field as well as ball sports (soccer, softball, volleyball, and netball) to all students. Track-and-field competitions at local, regional, and national levels bring great prestige to a winning student and his or her school. Schools also sponsor choirs and traditional dance groups that perform at public events. Traditional dancing is popular in villages, where women play drums to provide the dancers with rhythm. Young urban professionals like ballroom dancing, and most Batswana enjoy African disco and *kwasa kwasa* dance music.

Holidays

Batswana celebrate the New Year (1–2 January), Easter (Friday–Monday), Ascension, President's Day (third weekend in July), Botswana Day (30 September–1 October), Christmas, and Boxing Day (26 December). Christmas is the most important holiday and people go to their home villages to be with relatives. Family members do not exchange gifts, but they usually receive new clothes. Boxing Day comes from the British tradition where service workers or the poor were given small boxed gifts on the day after Christmas. It is now a day to visit and relax. Batswana also go home for a four-day weekend on President's Day. On this weekend, government-sponsored programs begin with prayer and include traditional dancing, singing, speeches, and praise poems. Easter is a time for church and family.

Commerce

People exchange formal greetings before conducting business. Hours generally extend from 8:00 or 9:00 A.M. until about 5:00 P.M., with many offices and shops closing for an hour at 1:00 P.M. Wholesale and retail businesses are important, as there are few factories and most goods are imported.

SOCIETY

Government

Botswana is a parliamentary republic with a long democratic heritage. Villages are divided into *wards* (neighborhoods), each with a *headman* (an elder appointed by the village chief) and a *kgotla* (meeting place). Decisions at the ward and village levels are made in the *kgotla* by all adult males through a consensus process. Women may express opinions but remain in the back of the *kgotla*. The chief's *kgotla* is used to consider matters that cannot be settled at the ward level. Local councils govern schools and health clinics.

Members of the 40-seat National Assembly are directly elected, and the majority party's leader takes office as president. A 15-member House of Chiefs, representing major ethnic groups, advises Parliament on legislation pertaining to custom and tradition. Judiciary cases involving customary law are heard in the *kgotla* by local chiefs and headmen, while statutory cases are heard in Magistrate Court or the High Court. There is also an Appeals Court.

Botswana has never experienced a coup or been ruled by a dictator. This is partly due to five factors: Tswana cohesion and tolerance, a pastoralist heritage, traditional local democracy, well-educated and strong leaders before and after independence, and a stable economy based on diamond mining. Both main opposition parties, the Botswana National Front (BNF) and the Botswana People's Party (BPP) favor national unity over divisive politics.

Economy

With strong growth rates since independence and large foreign reserves, Botswana has enjoyed a stable economy. Diamonds account for 80 percent of export revenue. When world diamond prices fall, as they did in the early 1990s, Botswana's economy can be severely strained. The government is trying to diversify. Other exports include copper, nickel, and beef. The currency is the *pula* ("rain"). *Pula* is also used as a greeting or at the end of speeches to mean "good wishes."

Despite relative stability, problems exist. Unemployment is high, affecting half of the younger Batswana. A shortage of skilled labor keeps industrial growth low, and land deterioration hampers agriculture. Real gross domestic product per capita is $5,120. Poverty affects more than one-third of all residents. More than 60 percent of the nation's cattle, a tradi-

tional measure of wealth, is owned by less than 10 percent of the population. Hence, economic prosperity is enjoyed by a small percentage of people.

Transportation and Communication

A paved highway and a rail line parallel the eastern border, linking the major towns. The train is used for longer distances. Rural people often walk long distances or hitchhike. If given a ride, they pay bus fare to the driver. Some families use bicycles locally. A minority own cars, but more urban residents are buying them. Buses or *combies* (minibuses) run between towns and major villages. The "Trans-Kgalagadi Highway," begun in 1990, will eventually cross the desert and reach into Namibia.

Few people, even in towns, have telephones, but pay phones are located in post offices. Radio Botswana broadcasts in Setswana and English. Independent newspapers enjoy freedom of the press and wide circulation; the government sends free copies of the *Daily News* to schools.

Education

Botswana has the highest elementary completion rate in Africa and a literacy rate of 74 percent. The abolition of school fees (1987) marked the first step in offering primary and secondary schooling to all children. Increased construction was the next step, and helping young children learn English before junior secondary school is now a priority. Lack of English skills and lack of rural senior schools are two reasons why two-thirds of Junior Certificate (JC) holders cannot advance. The Brigades (units providing technical training) and other vocational programs accept some JC students. Senior secondary graduates qualify for higher education by earning the Cambridge Overseas School Certificate and performing one year of community service. There are six teacher-training colleges, a National Health Institute, the University of Botswana, a polytechnic institute, and an agricultural college.

Health

Clean water, infant immunization, and other factors combine to keep infant mortality relatively low (38 per 1,000). The average life expectancy is 64 years. Nurse-staffed primary-care clinics are within reach of most people. Doctors practice in cities and larger towns. Traditional "witch" doctors use herbal medicine and charms in providing a popular alternative to Western medicine. The most frequently diagnosed illnesses are related to poverty and malnutrition. AIDS cases have increased dramatically over the last decade. Malaria, schistosomiasis, and sleeping sickness are found in the north.

FOR THE TRAVELER

U.S. citizens do not need a visa for stays of fewer than 90 days, but a passport is necessary. National parks and game reserves provide ample opportunity for viewing wildlife. Islands of the Okavango Delta are accessible both by plane and *mokoro* (dugout canoe). A four-wheel-drive vehicle is necessary in remote areas. Take precautions against malaria and do not swim in freshwater ponds or lakes. For information, contact the Embassy of the Republic of Botswana, 3400 International Drive NW, Suite 7M, Washington, DC 20008.

Burkina Faso

Boundary representations not necessarily authoritative.

BACKGROUND

Land and Climate

Burkina Faso's name means "the land of upright and courageous people." This landlocked nation covering 105,869 square miles (274,200 square kilometers) of West Africa is somewhat larger than Colorado. The mostly flat northern quarter is characterized by sand dunes and a dry climate. Half the nation is covered by the central plateau, and forests are most common in the fertile south. Burkina Faso's highest elevations include Mount Tenakourou (2,300 feet or 750 meters) and Mount Naouri (1,372 feet or 447 meters). Formerly known as the Black, White, and Red Voltas, the country's main rivers are the Mouhoun, Nakambe, and Nazinon. Winter (November–March) is generally warm and dry, cooled by a consistent harmattan wind. March through May is typically hot and dry, but the rainy season follows in June to October. Daytime temperatures average 85°F (30°C) but can soar to 110°F (43°C) in the summer.

History

Before the colonial period, the region was dominated by several powerful kingdoms, the most important of which were the Mosse, Gurma, Emirat of Liptako, and Guriko. These kingdoms reached their zenith by the turn of the 11th century. Although Portuguese explorers named the three rivers, it was the French who conquered and colonized the land in the late 19th century. In 1904, the Burkinabè (Bur-keen-ah-BAY) territories became attached to the High Senegal–Niger French colony until it dissolved in 1919. The territories then became a colony called Upper Volta.

The French dissolved Upper Volta in 1932 and distributed its territory among Côte d'Ivoire (Ivory Coast), French Sudan (currently Mali), and Niger. However, the French reestablished Upper Volta in 1947 and a peaceful struggle for independence was waged throughout the 1950s. Two rival leaders emerged from that movement. One of them, Daniel Ouezzin Coulibaly, died in 1958 and his opponent, Maurice Yameogo, then reconciled himself to the African Democratic Rally (RDA), of which Coulibaly had been a prominent member. Yameogo was subsequently chosen as the country's first president upon independence on 5 August 1960.

Yameogo's regime was viewed as corrupt and undemocratic, and he was overthrown after a trade union uprising in a 3 January 1966 military coup. Lieutenant Sangoulé Lamizana took power as president. During the 1970s, Upper Volta's four trade unions were among the most powerful and independent in Africa and thus were often able to force political reform. For example, after a nationwide strike in 1980, Lamizana was overthrown in a coup. The coup leader was, in turn, ousted in 1982 by Commandant Jean-Baptist Ouedraogo. However, his supporting officers were divided in their opinions, which led to a 1983 coup by Captain Thomas Sankara.

For many, the charismatic Sankara soon became (and remains) a hero. He changed the country's name to Burkina Faso in 1984 and changed the flag colors from black, white, and red (for the three rivers) to red (blood of martyrs) and green (richness of agricultural potential) with a gold star (guide of the democratic and popular revolution). He made peace with Mali over a territorial dispute and espoused a socialist ideology. Sankara believed the people should be self-sufficient and not rely on Western aid, and he developed policies toward that goal. But in 1987, Sankara's closest associate, Captain Blaise Compaoré, staged a bloody coup in which Sankara and 12 other leaders were killed.

Despite Sankara's popularity, few Burkinabè protested the new coup in light of Compaoré's strength. Although some dissenters were punished, an armistice with opponents soon followed and a new constitution was issued in 1990. Presidential elections were held in December 1991 and legislative elections followed a few months later with 27 parties participating. Compaoré was elected president. Democratization then proceeded slowly but in a stable atmosphere.

PEOPLE

Population

Burkina Faso's population of 10.4 million is growing annually at 2.8 percent. Eighty percent of all inhabitants live in rural areas. The two largest cities are the capital, Ouagadougou (population 800,000), and Bobo Dioulasso (400,000). The capital's name is often abbreviated as Ouaga. Nearly half of the population is younger than age 15. In past years, many men went to work in neighboring countries and sent their wages home to relatives in Burkina Faso, but the migration trend has slowed considerably. Burkina Faso's Human Development Index (0.228) ranks it 169th out of 174 countries. Adjusted for women, the index is the same. The rank reflects the country's limited infrastructure, which contributes to the people's lack of access to resources that would allow for personal advancement.

The Mossi (about 55 percent of the population) inhabit the central plateau. A number of smaller groups comprise the remaining 45 percent of the population, including the Fulani (15 percent) in the north; the Gurmantche or Gurma (10 percent) in the east; the Bissa and Gourounsi in the southeast; the Lobi and Dagari in the southwest; and the Bobo, Bwaba, Samo, and Senoufo in the west.

Language

More than 60 languages are used in Burkina Faso, but the most widely spoken are Moore (by the Mossi), Diula (a trade language used by many different groups, including the Bwaba, Bobo, and Senoufo), Fulfuldé (by the Fulani), and Gurmantchéma (by the Gurma). French is the official language of government and education but is only spoken by 15 to 20 percent of the people. People use Diula and Fulfuldé to communicate with ethnic groups in neighboring countries. These languages and Moore are taught at the university level and are used in some television and radio broadcasts.

Religion

Both Muslims and Christians inhabit Burkina Faso, interacting on each others' holidays and respecting their traditions and beliefs. People from all ethnic groups belong to each religion, although Fulani are less likely to be Christians. Estimates differ as to how many people belong to each group, but Muslims comprise at least 30 percent of the population. Christians (15–20 percent) are most often Roman Catholic, but Protestant groups are also active. Christians tend to have Christian first names and Muslims use Islamic names.

Traditional animist belief systems are practiced exclusively by up to half of all people, who retain their Burkinabè names. Animist traditions act as unifying factors in Burkina Faso's tolerant religious climate, as many Muslims and Christians combine animist practices with their religion. It is not uncommon for them to consult a diviner or to participate in ritual dances. Masks play an important part in animist rituals. For example, dancers wear them to ward off bad luck or in performing agricultural rites. The shape and color of a mask depend on the ethnic group and purpose of the wearer.

General Attitudes

Burkinabè are warm, friendly, and generous. They have strong family values centered on respect for customs and tradition. A financially successful individual is responsible for the rest of the extended family. Humility and generosity are the most desired personal traits, while individualism and bragging are least tolerated. Although family ties are strong, people actually are quite independent. Moving into one's own home, even if it lacks running water or electricity, is an important goal; renting is considered a temporary situation.

Personal Appearance

Burkinabè wear both African and Western clothing. In rural settings, men wear a Muslim robe (*boubou*) while women wear a blouse (*camisole*) and a wraparound skirt (*pagne*). In cities, women wear elaborate, colorful African outfits made of locally designed or imported fabrics. Men usually wear the *tenue de fonctionnaire* (civil servant suit, with shirt and pants made of the same cloth). Both rural and urban dwellers buy used clothing imported from Europe, Asia, and the United States. Lately, however, with politicians and civic leaders calling for consumption of local products, embroidered traditional outfits have become more popular attire for social events.

Although on the decline, traditional face scarring is still practiced in rural areas by some (among the Mossi and Bwaba, for example) to distinguish between ethnic groups.

CUSTOMS AND COURTESIES

Greetings

Before engaging in any social activity, Burkinabè take time to greet each other and shake hands. Greetings include inquires about family, health, and work. Urban people who have not seen each other for some time may kiss each cheek and then the lips. One may show respect by bowing one's head. Or when shaking hands, one might touch the other person's right hand or arm at the elbow level with one's left hand. In the countryside, women may kneel to express respect. In Muslim settings, men often will not shake hands with women, as Islamic principles dictate minimal contact between unrelated men and women.

Acquaintances are addressed by first name, while the names of elders are preceded by *Monsieur* (Mr.) or *Madame* (Mrs.). French greetings range from the informal *Salut, Comment ça va?* (Hi, how are you?) to the more formal *Bonjour* (Good day) and *Bonsoir* (Good evening). In Moore, as in many of the national languages, greetings depend on the time of day or the activities performed by the person being greeted. Some common salutations include *Ne y yibeogo* (Good morning), *Ne y zaabre* (Good afternoon), *Ne y tuuma* (Greetings to you who are working), *Ne y kjena* (Greetings to you who are walking), or simply *Kibare* (Hi).

Gestures

Burkinabè use the right hand to greet people, eat, or pass items. Using the left hand, especially for greeting or eating, is offensive. Men and women hold hands in public with friends of the same gender, but displays of affection between men and women are inappropriate. Using the index finger to motion to someone is considered disrespectful; instead, one either calls the person's name or motions with the palm of the hand down.

To indicate the height of a human being, Burkinabè face the open hand up. They express disgust at events or actions by rounding the lips and making a noise by sucking air through the front teeth.

Visiting

Visiting friends and relatives is an important part of Burkinabè culture. Visits generally occur during the evening, sometimes during siesta time (1:00–2:30 P.M.) and at any time on the weekend. Most visits are spontaneous and visitors are allowed to stay as long as they wish. People announce their arrival by clapping their hands (instead of knocking); they wait to be invited in. In areas influenced by Islam, one announces oneself by saying *Salaam ale kum* (Peace be upon you), to which the host responds *Ale kum Salaam* (And peace to you) as a way of inviting the visitor in. Guests always are offered a place to sit and water to drink; refusing to drink is socially inappropriate, even if one is not thirsty. Burkinabè also enjoy inviting others over for a meal or evening socializing. In urban settings, guests rarely bring gifts on social visits, but rural people commonly give their hosts chickens, eggs, cola nuts, salt, or sugar.

Eating

Food is not treated casually and meals are eaten in general silence. Using the left hand to eat is forbidden. Rural men generally eat together in a circle on the floor, sharing a common platter and using clay or aluminum utensils. Women and children eat together in a different section of the compound. If offered food, guests must take a few bites or risk offending the host.

Urban families tend to eat together, and they use a dining table and utensils more often than their rural counterparts. Most single urban men eat their meals at street-side stands or in the numerous open-air bars where tasty meat kabobs (*brochettes*) and roasted chicken are sold; some hire young men or women to cook meals for them at home. Cities and villages usually have *dolo* cabarets (local beer stands), tended by women, where both men and women enjoy gathering for a drink, food, discussion of local events, and gossip.

LIFESTYLE

Family

Large families are the norm in Burkina Faso, especially in rural areas, where a family might have ten or more children. Children live with their parents until they get married. When elderly parents need care, they usually live with their eldest son. Burkina Faso's traditional social network is based on the extended family and guarantees that family members will help a relative in need.

Rural families often live in a compound, with separate sleeping quarters for men and women. A mother generally cares for her children until they are weaned at around age three. At this time, boys move from sleeping in the mother's house to sleeping in the father's house. Girls remain with their mother. Both boys and girls are cared for by their parents until they reach adulthood, but boys generally receive more support than girls. Once girls marry, they are perceived as having changed families.

In polygamous families, wives share weekly chores, including cleaning the courtyard and preparing family meals. Rural women have few property rights and can be sent back to their families if their husbands are unsatisfied with them. In matriarchal families within such ethnic groups as the Dagari, women have more rights. In urban settings, women are more often educated and able to find jobs. This gives them greater autonomy and, therefore, more decision-making power.

Dating and Marriage

Although casual dating is becoming the norm in urban areas, marriages in the countryside are still arranged. Often for women the only way out of an arranged marriage is to run away. Marriage expenses are shared by the groom, his parents, and the extended family. The average marriage age is 22 for men and between 18 and 20 for women. Women and men expect to marry and have children. Women are pressed to comply with this tradition by age 30 or risk not finding a husband. Old unmarried men are looked upon with suspicion. Islamic laws allow a man to have up to four wives if he can care equally for each. Polygamy is decreasing in urban centers due to the cost of raising and educating a family, but it is still practiced in rural areas.

Diet

Burkina Faso's main staple is sorghum or millet cooked into a hard porridge known as *tô*. People usually eat *tô* twice a day with a variety of sauces made from peanuts and indigenous plants and vegetables, such as sorrel and okra. Urban families with more financial means often eat rice with peanut or tomato sauce for lunch, reserving *tô* for the evening meal. A typical urban breakfast, when available, includes millet or corn porridge, or coffee or tea with buttered bread. A rural breakfast usually consists of leftovers from the previous night. People eat rice, *couscous*, and pasta cooked with meat on special occasions. Thanks to recent dam, fishery, and gardening projects, fresh fish and fruits are more plentiful in major cities.

Recreation

Burkinabè enjoy visiting each other and meeting at *dolo* cabarets to talk and enjoy card games; men play *pétanque* (French lawn bowling) or checkers. Women often meet to do each other's hair. On Saturdays, urban dwellers pack popular bars to dance to the rhythm of African, *Zouk* (Haitian), and reggae music. These bars are also known for their kabobs and broiled, spicy fish. Soccer is the most popular sport in Burkina Faso, followed by cycling, boxing, volleyball, basketball, and handball. On many Sundays in Ouagadougou, local businesses sponsor cycling races. During the harvest (October–November) and on holidays, villagers enjoy wrestling matches and traditional dances with drums and xylophones.

Holidays

Burkina Faso's national public holidays include New Year's Day, *Fête du 3 janvier* (commemoration of the 3 January 1966 uprising), Labor Day (1 May), Revolution Day (4 August, for the 1983 revolution), and Independence Day

(5 August). Political holidays are marked by speeches and parades. Other holidays include International Women's Day (8 March) and various religious celebrations. Important Muslim dates include a feast at the end of the holy fasting month of *Ramadan*; *Tabaski*, the feast that honors Abraham for his willingness to sacrifice his son; and *Mouloud*, the birth of Muhammad. Christians celebrate Easter, Ascension, Assumption (15 August), and Christmas. End-of-the-year festivities remain the most important, and Burkinabè of all creeds join together to celebrate the new year.

Commerce

A cash economy dominates rural and urban areas, although occasionally some people barter or use payment-in-kind. Still, most rural people provide for their own needs and have little cash. Each town has an open-air market where most business is conducted. Market days are held every day in big cities and every three days in small towns and villages. In the west, market days are held once a week. Due to the lack of refrigeration, most families shop for food every day, either in the market or at small neighborhood stores operated out of people's homes. Busy, informal roadside stands located near markets and taxi or train stations offer clothing, used books, and buckets and suitcases made of recycled material. The largest cities have a few department stores that are open from 7:30 A.M. to noon and from 3:00 to 5:00 P.M.

SOCIETY

Government

Burkina Faso's parliamentary democracy is led by a president as head of state and a prime minister as head of government. The president, Blaise Compaoré, was elected in 1991 to a seven-year term. The prime minister is Kadre Desire Ouedraogo. Delegates to the Assembly of Peoples' Deputies were directly elected in 1992 to a five-year term. The Organization for People's Democracy (ODPMT) has a majority 78 of 107 seats but has experienced some internal divisions. A second legislative chamber, which is not yet functional, is provided for by the constitution. The influence and power of local traditional chiefs began to decline in 1983 but is again on the rise.

Economy

The economy depends largely on agriculture and cattle raising. Most people are subsistence farmers. Real gross domestic product per capita is $810. Mining opportunities remain under-exploited, but manganese and limestone are found in the north, gold in the west, and copper in the east. Principal exports are crafts, cotton, shea nuts, cattle, and gold. Imports include manufactured products, cereals, petroleum, chemical products, vehicles, and machinery. France is the main trading partner. Burkina Faso's currency, the *CFA franc* is tied to the French *franc*. A 1994 devaluation of the *CFA franc* increased the price of imported goods and strained resources throughout the region. The economy is making progress but is not yet diversified enough to respond to weather irregularities, global market events, or rapid population growth.

Transportation and Communication

Due to the lack of a developed public transportation system, many Burkinabè own mopeds or bicycles. Some observers outside of the country have described Ouagadougou as the moped capital of Africa. A railway links Ouaga to Abijan (capital of Ivory Coast). A few paved roads, covering about 2,500 miles, exist inside the country; the best is between Ouaga and Bobo Dioulasso, both of which also have taxis and buses for intra- and inter-city travel. Unpaved roads (about 7,500 miles) may not be passable in the rainy season. Bush taxis can be taken from city to city, but the majority of people travel by foot, bicycle, or moped.

Phone service exists between major cities, and mail service is available where there is a post office. Three television stations (two are private) and four FM radio stations broadcast daily. There are several independent newspapers.

Education

The educational system is still based on the French model and is very elitist. Mastery of French largely determines one's success. Elementary school lasts six years; secondary has seven years (called "levels"). Primary enrollment is estimated at 37 percent; about one-third of these students go on to the secondary level. Adult literacy (in French) averages 17 percent. All rates are lower for girls and in rural areas. Entrance to one of the country's two universities is available to those who pass difficult exams.

The need for universal education has been the subject of various national conferences, and the government is exploring ways to improve the system by using national languages in instruction, emphasizing basic education, reducing the cost to families, and providing better access to schools.

Health

Burkinabè face several health problems, including dysentery, hepatitis, diarrhea, and malaria. The infant mortality rate (117 per 1,000) remains high due to malnutrition and malaria. Average life expectancy is 47 years. The government is trying to improve health conditions, and primary-care clinics recently have been built in all cities. All provinces have regional hospitals, but these are overburdened and underequipped. Most patients or families must pay for hospital stays and medicines; civil servants have some health benefits.

FOR THE TRAVELER

U.S. citizens need a valid passport and visa to enter Burkina Faso. Vaccinations for yellow fever and typhoid are required; prophylactics against malaria are strongly recommended. Tourist facilities are limited, but the country is safe and welcoming. Hotels are affordable. Sites and events of interest include the central market (*Grand marché*), biannual Art Festival, Nazinga and Deux Balé game parks, Arly game reserve, sacred crocodiles of Sabou, village of Laongo (for granite carvings), and caves of Borodougou and Arbinda. For more information, contact the Embassy of Burkina Faso, 2340 Massachusetts Avenue NW, Washington, DC 20008.

A *Culturgram* is a product of native commentary and original, expert analysis. Statistics are estimates and information is presented as a matter of opinion. While the editors strive for accuracy and detail, this document should not be considered strictly factual. It is a general introduction to culture, an initial step in building bridges of understanding between peoples. It may not apply to all peoples of the nation. You should therefore consult other sources for more information.

Kingdom of
Cambodia

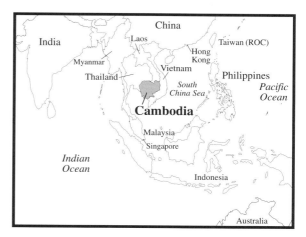

A
S
I
A

BACKGROUND

Land and Climate

Covering 69,900 square miles (181,040 square kilometers), Cambodia is just smaller than Oklahoma and is circular in shape. Its fertile soil is fed by the waters of the Tibetan-Himalayan glaciers, which flow to Cambodia by way of the Mekong River. There are mountains to the north and southwest. The center is basically flat, with a large lake, the Tonlé Sap, roughly in the middle. The lake swells to several times its surface area during the rainy season because excess water from the Mekong River is naturally diverted to it. More than 75 percent of the land was once covered with forests and woodlands. Today, due to rampant logging by foreign and local firms, less than 40 percent of Cambodia holds forests. Rapid deforestation threatens the fresh fish supply and other natural habitats and has increased the severity of floods. Without regulation, the forests could be decimated by the end of the century. Cambodia's climate is tropical, and annual temperatures average between 80°and 100°F (26–38°C). The dry season is from December to April; the rainy season is from May to November.

History

The word *Kampuchea* (the term used by Cambodians to refer to their land) comes from the Kingdom of Kambuja, an empire established by Indian settlers more than 1,800 years ago. From the ninth to the thirteenth centuries, the Khmer Empire flourished and reigned over much of Southeast Asia. The Angkor Wat (temple), built in the 12th century, is the largest religious building in the world and represents the glory of the Khmer Empire. Today, it is the national symbol of Cambodia. The area known today as Cambodia was colonized by France in the 1860s and remained under French control (except during Japanese occupation in World War II) until 1953, when Cambodia was granted its independence. In 1970, the monarchy under Prince Norodom Sihanouk was overthrown. In 1975, the Khmer Rouge began a violent, forced restructuring of the entire society. During the Khmer Rouge's four-year rule, more than one million people were killed or died of starvation and disease. The educated and business classes were all but eliminated, and the economy was completely destroyed. Pol Pot, leader of the Khmer Rouge, wanted to return the country to an agrarian, communal society.

After invading Cambodia in 1978, Vietnam forced Pol Pot to flee and installed a government with Heng Samrin as president. Hun Sen was later named prime minister. The invasion, while halting the genocide, was condemned by Western nations, who called for the withdrawal of Vietnamese troops. The Vietnamese remained and fought guerrillas opposed to the Hun Sen government until 1989, when they withdrew their troops. During Vietnam's occupation, the Hun Sen government was not recognized by the United Nations (UN). Instead, a coalition of three guerrilla groups (Khmer Rouge, Khmer People's National Liberation Front, and supporters of Prince Sihanouk) was recognized as a government in exile (as the Coalition Government of Democratic Kampuchea). After Vietnam withdrew, Hun Sen continued to run the country and sought to implement reform. The United Nations urged the guerrilla groups to enter into peace talks with Hun Sen.

Little progress was made until 1990, when the United States and other nations withdrew their support for the guerrilla coalition. All four parties agreed to adopt a UN plan that created a Supreme National Council (SNC) as an interim government. The United Nations sent troops and other personnel to take over the country's administration and organize national elections. Prince Sihanouk returned to Cambodia as head of the SNC. The United Nations began registering voters in 1992 for elections in May 1993. Violence between the government, Sihanouk's supporters, and the Khmer Rouge frequently threatened to halt the peace process. The Khmer Rouge promised more violence, but this did not deter the country's 4.5 million eligible voters from participating in peaceful, free, and fair elections on schedule.

Unfortunately, when the government saw it was losing to the Royalist opposition (loyal to Sihanouk), it threatened to reject election results. Sihanouk, who was not a candidate, stepped in to create a temporary copresidency between his son, Prince Ranariddh, and Hun Sen. The newly elected National Assembly then approved a new constitution that provided for Sihanouk's return to power as king of Cambodia. He was coronated in September 1993; he is greatly revered by nearly all Cambodians. King Sihanouk ratified the new constitution and named the crown prince, Norodom Ranariddh, as first prime minister. Hun Sen became second prime minister.

When UN peacekeepers left shortly after elections, the Khmer Rouge resumed its civil war in 5 of 21 provinces. By 1996, however, the guerrilla group had been nearly defeated by the government and Pol Pot was rumored dead. King Sihanouk became ill and had to spend considerable time in China for treatment, which kept him from exercising his authority and mediating conflicts. At the same time, the coalition government found it difficult to compromise on important issues, so Cambodia lost some economic and social advances achieved during the UN mission, such as lower crime and corruption, free speech, better utility services, and land reform. The inexperienced Royalists gradually lost control of many government functions to Hun Sen's Cambodia People's Party (CPP). By mid-1996, Hun Sen had consolidated enough power that he effectively controls the country.

THE PEOPLE

Population

Cambodia's population of 10.6 million is growing annually at 2.8 percent. The largest ethnic group is the ethnic Khmer, estimated to comprise more than 70 percent of the population. The second largest group (about 10 percent) is the Sino-Khmer (mixed Chinese and Khmer). In the past, the Chinese were powerful traders in Cambodia and many settled in the country. Because the Khmer and Sino-Khmer dominate the population, their customs and lifestyle are more fully explained here than those of smaller groups. In fact, some people use the terms Khmer and Cambodian interchangeably.

The Chams (perhaps 5 percent of the population) are descendants of the Champa Kingdom (eighth century A.D.), which was centered in present-day Vietnam and contained people of Malaysian origin. These people converted to Islam and are still Muslim today. There are also many Vietnamese

settlers and some Chinese in Cambodia. The ethnic Khmer and ethnic Vietnamese are historical enemies, and the Vietnamese minority has increasingly been subjected to violence. Women make up 64 percent of the population (a figure higher than in most countries) because of the large number of men killed in conflict since 1975. As a result of civil war (1978–89), 200,000 people became internal refugees, wandering from area to area because they had to leave their villages during fighting. An additional 375,000 settled in refugee camps on the Thai border. Repatriating these people was one of the United Nations's most important accomplishments, but up to 40 percent of these people cannot support themselves and have no land to farm.

Cambodia's Human Development Index (0.337) ranks it 153d out of 174 countries. Social and economic opportunities are found only in urban areas; for the 80 percent who live in rural villages, access to a better life is limited.

Language

The Khmer language is derived from an older language called *paali*, which developed as a successor to Indian Sanskrit. The closest languages to modern Khmer are Thai (Thailand) and Lao (Laos), both of which share several common words (though not necessarily equivalent meanings). Khmer has 26 vowels and 33 consonants. It is often difficult for Westerners to speak and write, even though it is not a tonal language. French is sometimes used to communicate with officials and traders because it was used during the French colonial period. English is understood in a few areas, such as the markets in Phnom Penh, and is becoming more popular in the cities.

Religion

Except for the Cham minority, which practices Islam, Cambodians are Theravada Buddhists. Christianity is often considered synonymous with Catholicism, which is not favored because of its connection to former Vietnamese settlers and past colonial powers. Most Buddhist records, libraries, monasteries, temples, and shrines were destroyed and the monks killed by the Khmer Rouge. Not until 1989 did the government again recognize Buddhism as the state religion. Only memories and a few books from educated survivors remain to restore Buddhist practices. But the people overwhelmingly favor rebuilding pagodas (places of worship and religious education), and they often take up collections on holy days to accomplish this. Private businesses are making Buddha sculptures and paintings, as well as other ornaments associated with worship, to help people regain their heritage. Traditional practices are being revived with government encouragement. It is a general belief that a man should have a monk's education for at least three months, if not several years, even if this is a drain on family and national resources. Monks generate no income.

General Attitudes

Although Buddhist monasteries were destroyed and religious worship banned during the Pol Pot regime in the 1970s, Buddhism generally shapes the lives and perspectives of Cambodia's people. Many believe that Buddhist teachings have helped the people survive the years of war and grinding poverty. Cambodians are traditionally known as optimists. Optimism was harder to find between 1975 and 1990, but the return of King Sihanouk and the chance for peace encouraged people's hopes for a better life. Although Pol Pot still lives and the Khmer Rouge is still a power to contend with, Cambodians today recognize that they have their greatest opportunity in decades for progress and peace. Unfortunately, the campaign for national renewal and democracy is complicated by remnants of war (specifically, millions of hidden land mines that kill or wound farmers and others on a regular basis), the internal refugee problem, and continued Khmer Rouge violence. Citizens are fighting back by joining mine-removal teams, pressing the government for greater reform, and reviving traditions.

The group or community (often defined as the extended family) is more important than the individual, as are ancestors and rulers. The individual generally lacks privacy and rights and expects to act for the good of the community. Difficult economic times spawned a segment of the population that ignores this principle, but that small group is acting against traditional behavior.

Personal Appearance

Western-style clothing is fairly common in Phnom Penh, although it is simple and not always the most modern. The *sampot* and *sarong* (for women) and the *sarong soet* (for men) are common pieces of traditional clothing. Each is a large, rectangular piece of colored cloth that is wrapped around the hips like a skirt or kilt down to the ankles. A *krama* is a large scarf that is used as a hat, a small blanket, or even a baby carrier. Young women may wear small, colored (red, pink, or bright yellow) hats.

CUSTOMS AND COURTESIES

Greetings

Cambodians greet one another by placing both hands together in a prayer position at chest level without touching the body. The higher the hands, the greater the sign of respect, although they should never be held above the level of the nose. This gesture is accompanied by a slight bow to show respect for persons of higher status or age. Persons holding or carrying something may simply bow their heads slightly. Shaking hands is not common in Cambodia; indeed, it embarrasses women if attempted. Although there are many greeting phrases, one common greeting is *Sok sebai*.

Gestures

Rules governing gestures come from Buddhism. While sitting, one should not point the feet toward a Buddha image or any person. To Buddhists, the head is the most sacred part of the body. One does not touch another person's head (even a child's), and one generally avoids sitting or standing on a level more elevated than that of an older person. Raising the voice is a sign of a bad personality. It is very improper to embarrass another person in public. Waving the hand is a friendly gesture, as is an "open" or friendly face, good eye contact, or a smile. In communication, one must be careful to clearly distinguish between a "yes" indicating a person is listening and a "yes" meaning the person understands.

Visiting

Among friends and relatives, visiting is frequent and usually unannounced. People remove shoes when entering a home or pagoda. Houseguests may be greeted with a bouquet of jasmine flowers placed on their desk or table. Cambodians are extremely hospitable and friendly in general, although they are cautious about inviting strangers into the home. Guests usually are offered something to drink and sometimes other refreshments. If a meal is provided, guests are given the best place to sit and the best portion of food.

Eating

Cambodians eat with chopsticks, spoons, and their fingers—depending on the food and family custom. Cambodians enjoy dishes that have been influenced by Indian, Chinese, and European cuisine. In general, Cambodian food is blander and consists of more fish and gravies than foods in Thailand or other neighboring countries.

LIFESTYLE

Family

The family is important to the Khmer people. The average family has four children and is often willing to adopt orphans or care for foster children on behalf of another family in need. Bonds formed through adoption are just as important as direct lineage. Multiple generations usually live together or near one another. The elderly are cared for by their children. Because so many men died at the hands of the Khmer Rouge, Cambodia has a large number of orphans, widows, and single-parent families. Single mothers try to remarry. Those who do not find another spouse tend to gather in small clans of women and children for mutual aid and companionship. Khmer tradition allows for a man to take more than one wife (including widows), but this is rarely practiced because of the economic burden involved.

Dating and Marriage

Khmer girls are shy and often lack self-assurance. Improved feelings of self-worth often come with marriage. While boys and girls generally are able to choose their spouses, dating is organized such that a girl's exposure is limited to certain choices. Khmer do not intermarry with other ethnic groups, although intermarriage was a common practice in the past. Wedding celebrations last a full day and are occasions for many guests, much food, and plenty of music.

Diet

There are two basic dishes in Cambodia: soup and rice. A bowl of soup may have any combination of fish, eggs, vegetables, meat, and spicy broth. Rice is the staple food of Cambodia. More than 20 years ago, Cambodia was known as "the cradle of rice" and grew a number of different varieties. Today, that number is much smaller and Cambodia is not as productive. Rice is prepared in many ways and is eaten at every meal. Bowls of rice may differ in flavor depending on which region the rice is from. In addition to soup and rice, Cambodians enjoy vegetables and a wide variety of fruits throughout the year. Seafood and fish are also common.

Recreation

There is a general lack of theaters and sports facilities because leisure activities were banned by Pol Pot and most facilities were destroyed or fell into decay during the 1980s. Still, the people enjoy soccer, table tennis, volleyball, and badminton. They also dance, play music, and sing. Video machines are becoming more accessible and are used to create small theaters in the villages. Other leisure activities include picnics, card playing, and Sunday rides on bicycles or motorcycles. Religious festivals and weddings are also opportunities for recreation.

Holidays

Cambodia's main national public holidays include Liberation Day (7 January), Revolution Day (17 April), King Sihanouk's Birthday (31 October), Independence Day (9 November), and The Front Day (2 December). The Chinese New Year is celebrated in February. The Buddhist New Year in April is celebrated for three days. In the last week of September, an important Buddhist festival, *Chun Ben*, is marked on behalf of the dead and one's own salvation. Before it begins, a person is supposed to accomplish a "seven pagodas" duty. This means one should either worship at seven pagodas or perform seven moral "good turns" (or a combination of both) to please one's ancestors. Six weeks after *Chun Ben*, large or wealthy families raise money to pay for the living expenses of the monks. Also in the fall, the Water Festival provides three days of fireworks, traditional dancing, canoe races, and other events. Funerals are an occasion for gathering. Attendees wear white (not black), and music is an integral part of the event.

Commerce

Nearly 90 percent of the population is engaged in agriculture, food processing, or forestry (logging and rubber processing). In addition, many people take extra jobs in town or work on roads to help make a living. Wages are low. Business hours are from 8:00 A.M. to 1:00 P.M. and 3:00 to 6:00 P.M. or dusk. During the UN mission, Phnom Penh, the capital, became a boomtown with bustling shops, plentiful food, and a good climate for conducting business. After the UN departure, conditions deteriorated, but the city is still the country's business and financial center.

SOCIETY

Government

Cambodia is a constitutional monarchy. King Sihanouk is head of state, and the two prime ministers are heads of government. With the king dying and Hun Sen controlling daily government, democracy may be in danger of failing. The National Assembly has 120 members. In addition to the ruling CPP and Royalists (FUNCINPEC—National United Front for an Independent, Neutral, Peaceful, and Cooperative Cambodia), important political parties include the Buddhist Liberal Democratic Party (led by Son Sann) and the Khmer Nation Party (led by Sam Rainsy). The voting age is 18. National elections are scheduled for 1998.

Economy

The economy has not yet been able to recover to its post-independence strength. Food shortages are common in rural areas. Industrialized nations extended loans to Cambodia in 1996 to help improve the agricultural infrastructure and output. The industrial sector is all but nonexistent. Timber is the major industry; mining for precious stones is conducted primarily by individuals. Rubber is an important export in addition to fish, rice, and pepper. Legalized smuggling has

allowed goods from Thailand to be made available on the market. Foreign investment and tourist receipts remain low despite efforts to attract visitors.

Real gross domestic product per capita is estimated at $1,250. Most Cambodians do not earn a cash income at all but are subsistence farmers. Wealth is still confined to a small elite class. The currency is the new *riel* (CR).

Transportation and Communication

The six national highways that radiate from Phnom Penh would provide a transportation network if in good condition. However, only limited repairs have been made during the past 20 years. Some roads are impassable while others may delay travel. It may take four hours to travel less than one hundred miles. People often traverse short distances on bike and motorcycle. Many rely on buffalo-drawn carts or walking. The communications system is not adequate outside the capital. Recent improvements to the transportation system include the renewed operation of Royal Air Cambodge in 1995, offering limited regional and domestic service, and a massive overhaul of the country's main port at Sihanoukville.

Education

The education system was destroyed under Pol Pot, and the majority of educated people were killed by the Khmer Rouge. Cambodians, however, are slowly regaining their education. Although books and other materials are lacking, especially in rural areas, literacy is rising. It is currently estimated at 38 percent. With the rebuilding of pagodas, many schools (which are adjacent to the pagodas) are reopening. Currently, Phnom Penh has many private "street schools" with self-proclaimed teachers who offer instruction in English and French to informal students.

Health

Sanitation is poor. Diseases from water and mosquitoes are common. Running water is available only in a few hotels. Otherwise, people must draw water from rivers or wells. Intestinal parasites, hepatitis, dengue fever, and malaria are all common ailments. Thousands of people suffer from wounds they received by stepping on hidden mines left over from the years of fighting. Adequate medical care is not available to many people, but the government has tried to establish a basic health-care system. International relief organizations work with government hospitals to provide care and improve the current system. The infant mortality rate is 110 per 1,000. Life expectancy is about 50 years.

FOR THE TRAVELER

U.S. citizens need a valid passport and visa to enter Cambodia. The political situation is not always stable. Call the U.S. Department of State for the latest travel warnings: (202) 647–5225. Be in good physical condition and have updated vaccinations. Prepare to pay cash for most transactions. The Angkor Wat was a great tourist attraction in the 1960s, and opportunities are again being made available for travelers to see this symbol of Khmer culture. For more information, contact the Royal Embassy of Cambodia, 4500 16th Street NW, Washington, DC 20011; phone (202) 726–7824.

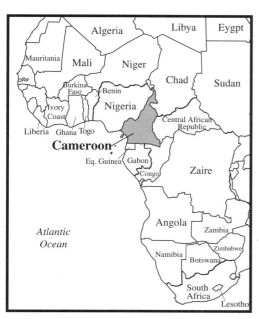

Boundary representations not necessarily authoritative.

Republic of
Cameroon

BACKGROUND

Land and Climate

Located slightly north of the equator, Cameroon (183,567 square miles or 475,440 square kilometers) is not much larger than California. The north is dominated from Garoua to Lake Chad by a dry plain where Sahara winds and hot temperatures are standard from October to May. Cooler winds and rain between June and September allow for large irrigated farms and grazing. A plateau of 2,000 to 4,000 feet (600–1,200 meters) covers much of central, southern, and eastern Cameroon. Here, dry-season daily heat is relieved at night and by occasional showers. Rains from May to October bring abundant water to the plateau's cities and farms. In wetter grassfields above 4,000 feet, the November to April dry season is cooler; rains are heavy and cool for several weeks after midyear. Rich volcanic soils provide for agriculture in this area. The narrow Atlantic coastal lowland is hot and humid all year. Douala's average temperature is 78°F (25°C). The region supports large areas of rubber, banana, cocoa, oil palms, and timber.

History

Various complex political structures, from bands and tribes to large kingdoms, were present in the area long before European colonization in the 1500s. The country's name comes from prawns (*cameros* in Portuguese) found in a river and along the coast. In the following centuries, southern Cameroon supplied the Atlantic slave and commodity trades, while northern peoples participated in the Muslim culture and economy organized by the Fulanis and Hausas south of the Sahara.

Germany united south and north into a colony between 1884 and 1916. Germany's defeat in World War I led to the partitioning of Cameroon; the east was administered by France and the west by Britain. The French area was ruled tightly from the capital, Yaoundé. The smaller British area (on the western fringe) was ruled more loosely from Nigeria. Anticolonialism grew after 1945 and independence was achieved in French Cameroon in 1960. British Cameroon elections in 1961 joined its south in a federation with Cameroon and its north with Nigeria. Former French and British areas kept separate educational, legal, civil service, and legislative structures until a 1972 referendum adopted a national, one-party system along French lines.

Cameroon has had only two presidents. Ahmadou Ahidjo, a northern Muslim, governed (1960–82), until he took ill and turned power over to his prime minister, Paul Biya, a southern Christian. Biya resisted a 1984 rebellion designed to reinstate Ahidjo and then dismantled the opposition. Under pressure, Biya instituted reforms in 1990, but unrest and strikes continue. For example, multiparty presidential and parliamentary elections in 1992 were boycotted in large numbers. Although 50 parties contested seats in Parliament, Biya retained his office as president. He faces another poll in 1997.

THE PEOPLE

Population

Cameroon's population of 13.5 million is growing at 2.9 percent annually. More than half the people live in rural areas, but cities are growing rapidly. Douala, center of commerce and industry, has more than one million residents and the capital, Yaoundé, has more than 700,000. Cameroon is often known as Africa's crossroads because of its many ethnic groups. The largest groups are the Bamileke (in the west), Fulani (north), and Beti (south). The Beti are also known as the Pahouin. No single group comprises more than 20 percent of the population, and most comprise less than 1 percent. Cameroon's more than two hundred ethnic groups have widely different backgrounds—from Fulani kingdoms to tiny bands of Pygmies that hunt in the southern forests. More typical are the farming and trading central and western peoples (half the population) with independent chieftaincies and rich cultural traditions.

Cameroon's Human Development Index (0.503) ranks it 127th out of 174 nations. Adjusted for women, the index (0.462) ranks Cameroon 90th out of 130 nations. These figures indicate that people, especially women, still lack access to resources that would improve their lives.

Language

Cameroon has some 240 languages; nearly 100 have written forms. Cameroonians commonly speak several local languages. French and English are official, and most urban residents can speak and read one of them. Most university graduates speak both. Rural people generally are not fluent in either. French is used primarily in the eight francophone provinces colonized by France. English is only common in the two anglophone provinces once governed by Britain. No local language is used widely enough to have official status. Some languages have regional dominance, such as Fulfulde in the north, Ewondo near the capital, and Duala on the coast. Pidgin English, an ever-evolving language with roots in English and other European languages, emerged during colonization to facilitate trade and communication between ethnic groups. Used primarily in anglophone provinces for common daily interaction, it is also sometimes used between Francophones and Anglophones who cannot communicate otherwise.

Religion

More than half the population is Christian, with about twice as many Catholics as Protestants. About one-fourth is Muslim (mostly Sunni). Most of the rest follow indigenous beliefs. Even Christians and Muslims often respect and practice these local beliefs. Indigenous practices are especially evident in certain ceremonies, traditional medicine, and family relationships. Merging religions does not create contradictions for the believers; they adopt the elements they believe enhance their religion's overall value.

General Attitudes

Complicated leadership patterns basically center on those with title and rank, either inherited or earned through education or wealth. Leaders often maintain a support base by providing favors to family members, village members, and those of the same ethnic group or social class. Cameroon is a group-oriented society; everyone has a place in the group and each group has a clear leader. Individualism is not encouraged. When one person of a group benefits from something (such as a high wage), the group expects to share the benefit.

Family and friendship ties are strong and obligations run deep. For example, even distant relatives or "junior" siblings (a half sibling or someone from the village) can expect a family to house and feed them, regardless of the hardship it might cause. Guests cannot be asked to leave except in rare cases. The practice is accepted because the host family assumes it will someday benefit from the same network. Deep, complex bonds also exist between fellow students or local residents of the same sex and age. These bonds mean that service, respect, and cooperation usually come before personal interest. Social change is disrupting this system, but it remains important.

Personal Appearance

Cameroonians consider a clean, well-groomed appearance and fashionable dress the marks of good character. All but the very poor have formal clothing for special occasions. The tall Muslim people in the north wear colorful, flowing robes. The shorter southern people also wear robes but more often wear Western clothing. Western clothing dominates in urban areas throughout the country.

Women often braid their hair and apply rich oils to their skin for a glossy appearance. Embroidery and appliqué, beads, shells, feathers, and ivory signify high or royal status for the wearer. Rural Muslim women do not wear pants, but other rural women sometimes do. Muslim women cover their heads in public, often wear a lot of jewelry, and color their hands and feet with patterns using henna (a plant) dye. More intricate designs are drawn on their legs and arms for special occasions, such as weddings.

CUSTOMS AND COURTESIES

Greetings

Men take handshakes seriously and use them to greet even friends or coworkers they see every day. In francophone areas, a brief handshake is preferred. Family or close friends may also brush alternate cheeks while they "kiss the air." In anglophone provinces, a slightly firmer handshake is most common. If one's hand is dirty, one offers the wrist. Hugs are reserved for family and close friends. Close male friends, as well as young people of the same age and gender, snap the middle finger and thumb while pulling the hands away from a handshake.

An informal anglophone greeting is *How na?* (pidgin for "How are you?"). *Good morning* (*Bonjour* in francophone areas) and *Good afternoon* (*Bonsoir*) are more formal. Different local greetings are used by different ethnic groups. Greetings are followed by inquiries about family welfare. People on the street may call to each other from a distance with "pssssst," but some don't consider this polite.

Most people recognize seniority (defined by gender, age, or prestige) by touching the right arm with the left hand during a handshake or by bowing the head. To show special respect, a man might bow from the waist (women curtsy); in the north, women may kneel. One avoids eye contact with respected individuals but does not turn one's back to them. To approach traditional royalty, one speaks through cupped hands, bows, and greets the chief with upturned hands; one never touches the chief, even to shake hands.

Gestures

Using the right hand for greetings, eating, or passing an object is always preferred. A person who uses the left accidentally or out of necessity apologizes. One points with head gestures or by puckering the lips. Legs may be crossed at the ankles, but not the knees; one does not cross the legs in front of those with higher authority. In some areas, it is considered indecent for women to cross their legs in front of men. For all, it is important to keep the soles of the feet from pointing at others. A quick head nod indicates agreement. In rural areas, people often display pleasure by dancing. Grief may be shown by placing the hand on one's opposite shoulder and bowing the head, or by resting both hands on top of the head (one hand on top of the other). People beckon by waving all fingers with the palm down. A hand extended and cupped upward is a request that something be shared.

Visiting

Visiting is a main form of entertainment in Cameroon. Social visits are casual and relaxed, except in more conservative homes where rank and gender distinctions are important. In such homes, women and children rarely appear; if they do, they are not introduced. Cameroonians enjoy visiting, especially on Fridays after mosque or Sundays after church. Unannounced visits are common, although strangers are expected to arrange visits in advance. At a small gathering, one greets each person individually.

A host is expected to offer guests something to eat and drink. Guests who drop in during a meal are asked to join in. Invited friends might bring food or drink as a gift. Food is not an acceptable gift from others because it may be interpreted as questioning the host's means or hospitality, but guests can present other gifts. A person offers gifts for children through the parents. One removes street shoes before entering a Muslim home. Business matters are not discussed during social visits. Northern Muslims show deference to a tribal chief by removing their shoes about 100 meters away before visiting him. Foreigners and government officials, considered on the same level as chiefs, do not remove their shoes.

Eating

Cameroonians eat the main meal in the evening after work. Food is not taken for granted or treated casually, so formal meals are often blessed, and elders are served first. In rural areas, women eat by the cooking fire with younger children, not with the men or older boys; women also serve the meal.

Water is made available before and after meals for washing hands; this is important because many people eat with the right hand from communal bowls. Bottles are opened in the drinker's view; the host leaves the cap loose and the guest pours. If given food, a guest must taste it. Smelling it first is an insult. Even if guests are not hungry, it is polite to eat a small portion and then say they have eaten recently. But in many areas, not being hungry is considered being sick, so guests are generally expected to eat plenty. Cameroonians would rather share a meal and eat less than eat alone. In restaurants, hosts expect to pay for everything.

LIFESTYLE

Family

Rural families often have as many as ten children. Urban families are smaller. Young children are cared for by their mothers until weaned. At that point, older siblings and other family members share in raising them. Often, a child is raised by grandparents or even a relative's family. By age ten, children are farming, herding, or doing domestic work.

The family structure is patriarchal. Children are raised almost exclusively by women, who may even be responsible for clothing and feeding them if the father does not provide enough money. Fathers become more involved with their sons regarding career choices, marriage, and property issues. Grandparents remain within family compounds, receiving basic needs and affection. People remember ancestors by drinking in their honor after pouring some of their drink on the ground.

Women basically lose their civil rights when they marry and can be sent back to their families by an unsatisfied husband. They seldom have property rights but do most of the farming and other productive work. Still, a growing number of urban women are getting an education and entering the job market.

Dating and Marriage

Although arranged marriages may involve months or years of negotiations that create obligations after marriage for relatives on both sides, many couples meet on their own and have simple court ceremonies. A church wedding and reception might follow sometime (even years) later, depending on finances. Women marry at the average age of 19, men at 27 (younger in rural areas, older in cities).

Men are expected to marry but may have many girlfriends in addition to one or more wives. Islamic law allows a man to have up to four wives if he can care equally for each. Polygamy is still common in rural areas but is decreasing for economic reasons. Marriage is often viewed more as a social contract than an affectionate relationship. Women are raised to be mothers more than wives. Educated women with jobs sometimes choose to have children but not marry. Their extended families help raise the children and provide financial support.

Diet

Staple foods include corn, millet, cassava, "peanuts" (groundnuts), yams, and plantains. Grains in the south are often cooked with palm oil, seasoned with hot pepper, and topped with a sauce made from fish, meat, or vegetables. *Fufu*, a common dish, is a stiff paste made by boiling flour (corn, millet, cassava, or sometimes rice). *Garri* is grated cassava that is dried over a fire until light and flaky. Meat and rice are luxuries for villagers. Northern people sometimes eat beef. "Bushmeat" (snake, monkey, porcupine, etc.) is a delicacy in the south. An urban breakfast might include tea or coffee, fruit, and bread. Rural breakfasts consist of the same foods eaten for the main meal. Energy snacks and street foods include raw sugarcane, boiled cassava, boiled eggs, roasted corn, fresh fruit, and nuts. Muslims usually prefer tea to coffee. Beer is popular on social occasions, but water is the main drink in the home.

Recreation

Team sports and individual athletics are sponsored by companies and urban social clubs. Soccer is the most popular sport. Cameroon's national soccer team competed in the 1994 World Cup. Men and women in schools and cities play team handball, volleyball, and basketball. In January, a marathon is run up and down Mount Cameroon (13,451 feet). Traditional board games played with seeds or pebbles are popular. Savings societies sponsor monthly feasts that provide recreation for many adults. Culture and Development Weeks bring urban migrants and students back to their home villages once a year, using feasts, dances, and athletic contests to raise funds for schools and community projects. Movies, videos, and television are popular in cities. Live music, dance, radios, and portable cassette players are popular everywhere.

Holidays

Cameroon's national holidays include New Year's Day, Youth Day (11 February), Labor Day (1 May), and Unification Day (20 May). Unification Day marks the 1972 union of the French and British zones. Some religious holidays have national recognition, including Easter, Assumption (15 August), and Christmas for Christians. For Muslims, the most important holidays include a three-day feast at the end of *Ramadan* (a month of fasting from dawn until dusk each day), and the *fête de mouton* (lamb feast), held 40 days later in honor of Abraham's willingness to sacrifice his son.

Commerce

The cash economy dominates in urban areas, but bartering and payment-in-kind still exist in rural areas. Most retailing is done curbside, from market stalls, in small shops, or out of converted cargo containers. Only Douala and Yaoundé have department stores. Multinational banks dominate trade and finance, but credit unions handle local savings and investments. In addition, people can form or join *tontines* (*njangis* in anglophone provinces)—savings societies of ten to twelve members (men, women, or both). Members pool their capital, provide loans to each other, and sponsor social activities. Doing business is considered a delicate matter, and taking one's time is essential. Stores are usually open from 7:30 or 8:00 A.M. to 4:00 or 5:00 P.M. Street vendors do business late into the evening. Stores commonly close on Saturday afternoon. Sunday is quiet except in the Muslim north.

SOCIETY

Government

Cameroon is a unitary republic. A president and cabinet form a strong executive branch. Several parties are represented in the 180-seat National Assembly, including Biya's Cameroon People's Democratic Movement. Main opposition parties are the National Union for Democracy and Progress and the Social Democratic Front. A strong autonomy movement has recently emerged among English speakers. Local courts for domestic and land law are maintained by hereditary kings in the north and west and appointed chiefs elsewhere. These rulers enjoy strong loyalty among many ethnic groups and are regularly consulted about national politics. The voting age is 21.

Economy

Economic prosperity depends largely on oil, coffee, and cocoa prices. Because oil reserves may run out by the year 2000, Cameroon is looking for ways to expand other industries. Agriculture employs a majority of the labor force in either growing or processing food. Most regions are able to feed themselves; some provide food for other areas; and some export cash crops such as coffee, cocoa, cotton, rubber, and timber. The currency, the *CFA franc*, is tied to the French *franc*.

Real gross domestic product per capita is $2,390. Economic growth is inhibited by poor management and corruption.

Transportation and Communication

Francophone provinces enjoy better transportation and communications systems than anglophone areas. For example, the North-West Province (anglophone) has more than one million people but few paved roads. This complicates the process of getting crops to market, especially during the rainy season. Throughout the country, vans or sedans provide local public transportation. Taxis are available in cities. Many people travel by foot, bicycle, or motor scooter. Trains connect five major cities. The domestic airline serves four provinces. Most telephones are located in large urban areas. Mail service is not reliable. Radio and television services are owned by the government. A free press is growing. Perhaps the most effective communication is by *radio trattoir* (pavement radio), a system of verbal relays that passes news and information with great speed.

Education

The education system is still divided between French and English patterns. Rural children enter school knowing neither French nor English, while urban children know at least one of them. Primary school enrollment is higher in the south than the north. More boys than girls actually finish school. The average adult literacy rate is 60 percent (48 percent for women, 72 for men). Secondary school enrollment is low due to exam failures, space shortages, higher fees, and parental choice. Muslim children memorize the *Qur'an* (Koran) at evening Koranic schools.

There is a full university in Yaoundé and smaller universities in four other cities. Informal education and apprenticeships provide vital vocational skills.

Health

Cameroon lacks an adequate health-care system. Hospitals, while able to provide emergency services, often cannot provide basic (especially long-term) care. Patients' families must supply food, medicine, and some care. Still, a low-cost rural health program has helped decrease the infant mortality rate to 75 per 1,000 and increase life expectancy to between 55 and 60 years. Cameroon confronts a full range of tropical and other diseases, including malaria, cholera, and AIDS.

FOR THE TRAVELER

U.S. travelers must have a valid passport and a visa to enter Cameroon. A departure tax is payable in *CFA francs* at the airport. Take precautions against malaria. Vaccination against yellow fever is required; it is recommended for cholera. Avoid swimming in freshwater lakes or ponds. Do not drink water unless it has been boiled or otherwise purified. Peel or cook all fresh fruits and vegetables before eating. Eat only well-cooked meat. Tourist beaches (Kribi and Limbe) and northern attractions (Waza for wildlife and Mandara for volcanic formations) are inviting. It is common for authorities to expect a "tip" to perform their duties. For more information, contact the Embassy of Cameroon, 2349 Massachusetts Avenue NW, Washington, DC 20008; phone (202) 265–8790.

Republic of
Cape Verde

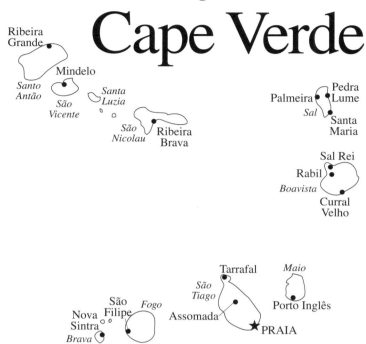

Boundary representations not necessarily authoritative.

BACKGROUND

Land and Climate

Cape Verde (also called Cabo Verde) is an archipelago of islands located some 278 miles (445 kilometers) off the West African coast. There are two island groups, consisting of a total of ten principal islands and eight smaller islands. Cape Verde's land area is 1,557 square miles (4,033 square kilometers). This is a bit larger than Rhode Island. The capital is Praia, located on São Tiago. The islands are of volcanic origin and are arid. Sahelian vegetation is prevalent, and the high rate of soil erosion does not favor plant life. However, the landscape is varied, with tropical valleys and coasts giving way to mountain forests. The average temperature is 75°F (25°C). The dry season begins in November and ends in July, while the rainy season spans August to October. Winds blowing off Africa's deserts send dust and dry air to Cape Verde. Rains fall irregularly and sometimes not at all for years.

History

Portuguese explorer Antonio Da Noli is credited with the discovery of Cape Verde in 1445. It is believed West African groups, such as the Wolor, Serere, and Lebou, inhabited some islands prior to his landing. Within ten years, Da Noli brought slaves to Cape Verde from the Guinea Coast in order to develop sugar plantations. The plantations proved unproductive given the inhospitable climate. Cape Verde came to be used by Portugal as a crossroads for trading slaves, gold, and other valuables.

The islands' more recent history began jointly with Guinea-Bissau. In 1955, the African Party for the Independence of Guinea and Cape Verde (PAIGC) was organized by Amilcar Cabral, Luís Cabral, Aristides Pereira, Pedro Pires, and others. After some 20 years of guerrilla warfare against Portugal, both Cape Verde and Guinea-Bissau gained their independence. Cape Verde became independent 5 July 1975. Amilcar Cabral, the movement's leader, was assassinated 20 January 1973 in Conakry, Guinea, presumably under orders from Portugal. Pereira was then elected president and Pires became prime minister. They led the government under a single-party system until 1990. In the nation's first multi-party elections in 1991, António Mascarenhas Monteiro was elected president and Carlos Veiga became prime minister. Their Movement for Democracy Party had won by a landslide over the PAIGC. Mascarenhas worked to strengthen democracy and improve living standards. When he ran for reelection in 1996, no one chose to oppose him. He was returned to office for another five years.

THE PEOPLE

Population

Cape Verde's population of about 435,000 is growing at an annual rate of 3 percent. The most populated islands include São Tiago (48 percent of all people), São Vicente (13 percent), Santo Antão (13 percent), and Fogo (10 percent). More than 52 percent of the population is comprised of women.

The largest cities are Praia (80,000 inhabitants) and Mindelo (40,000). The population is evenly split between rural and urban areas. People call themselves Caboverdians after the local name for their country. Most Caboverdians (71 percent) are descendants of a mixture of Black Africans and Portuguese, while 28 percent are Black African and 1 percent are European. Cape Verde's Human Development Index (0.536) ranks it 123d out of 174 countries. Adjusted for women, the index (0.502) ranks Cape Verde 85th out of 130 nations. Most people are poor and many lack access to the resources necessary to enjoy a decent standard of living.

Language

The official language is Portuguese. However, the national language, Crioulo, is most commonly used on a daily basis. Crioulo is a mixture of Portuguese and African and other languages. A project to publish a Crioulo dictionary is currently underway, but the language remains an unwritten tongue. Since the majority of people do not speak or write Portuguese well, many have difficulty understanding all the information in newspapers, on television, or on the radio. Realizing this, television and radio stations have recently added news programing in Crioulo. Many educated people speak English and French, which are subjects offered in secondary school.

Religion

Freedom of worship is allowed and religious differences are accepted. Nearly all Caboverdians are Christian. More than 80 percent of them belong to the Roman Catholic Church. About 12 percent are Protestant, with the rest belonging to other groups. People are very religious in Cape Verde, as shown by the large attendance at Mass and by the many sayings of a religious nature used in everyday conversation. On Sunday, churches are always crowded and one must come early to get a seat. The Catholic Church has a great deal of political and social influence. In fact, some people credit it for the Movement for Democracy's electoral win in 1991.

General Attitudes

Compared to those in the industrialized world, people in Cape Verde do things at a relaxed pace. For example, while going to work a person may stop and greet a friend, even though doing so may make that person a few minutes late. Caboverdians are also determined and do not give up easily. Farmers, for example, continue to plant crops every year hoping for rain, even if it has not come for many seasons.

To avoid confrontation, Caboverdians do not state opinions directly, and they are not at ease with a direct apology. People are hospitable, generous, and friendly. They are also open to the outside world, as twice as many Caboverdians live away from the islands (mainly in the United States, Netherlands, France, and Senegal) as on them. In general, individualism is not promoted among Caboverdians. One's success is to be used to help the less fortunate in the family and not simply to be enjoyed alone. The primacy of the group over the individual also means that there is a lack of privacy in Cape Verde.

Personal Appearance

Western clothing dominates in urban areas. Most people dress informally. Even highly ranked public officials wear shirts with short sleeves to work. Older people dress more conservatively than the younger generation, wearing longer dresses or darker colors, for example. People dress up in their finest clothing when going to church. Teenagers also dress up when they go to the *praça* (town plaza). Shirts with English inscriptions, such as the names of U.S. American sports teams and cities, are popular.

Rural people might mix Western clothing with more traditional styles, but their appearance is always neat and clean. Rural women favor dresses, or blouses with wraparound skirts, and a head scarf. Rural men wear lightweight shirts and pants and sometimes a wide-brimmed or other kind of hat. Adults usually do not wear shorts.

CUSTOMS AND COURTESIES

Greetings

Greetings generally involve a short handshake and a long greeting. It is always important to greet someone prior to talking. Women often kiss each other on each cheek. If acquainted, urban men and women might also kiss each others' cheeks. Parents or elders may be greeted with a kiss to one cheek. Most of the time, greetings are in Crioulo. Dialects vary between islands, but the most standard phrase is *Modi ki bu sta?* (How are you?). The response is *N'sta bom* (I am fine). After initial greetings, it is polite to ask how each other's family is doing. When conducting business, especially with strangers, one uses the Portuguese *Como estás?* (How are you?). In response, a person answers *Estou bem* (I am fine).

One respectfully addresses older people with a title before their name: *Senhor* (Mr.), *Senhora* (Mrs.), *Tio* (Uncle), or *Tia* (Aunt). It is also a sign of respect to address parents and relatives by familial titles: *Pai* (Crioulo for "father") or *Papa* (Portuguese for "father"), *Mae* or *Mama* (mother), *Tio*, or *Tia*. Friends address each other by first name.

Gestures

In Cape Verde, one beckons by waving all fingers with the palm facing up. It is not proper to beckon the elderly. When talking, people stand in close proximity and often touch each other during the conversation. This is an important part of communication. Hand gestures otherwise are not commonly used.

Eye contact during conversation is important among peers. However, it is a sign of respect to look down when talking to older people or to persons who are teaching. Caboverdians, who generally are music-oriented people, tend to whistle their favorite tunes in public.

Visiting

Caboverdians visit each other often. It is not necessary to call ahead, and most informal visits are unannounced. Hosts are hospitable and treat their guests well. Guests are offered a drink and some sweets in most cases. Guests arriving at mealtime are invited to eat. Declining a drink or a meal is not considered rude, but doing it consistently would probably be offensive. When invited to dinner, guests are not expected to contribute to the meal. Nevertheless, it is common practice to reciprocate a dinner invitation. Sometimes, a guest may bring a small gift to the host.

When invited to an event, guests say they will try to attend, even if they know it will not be possible. Saying "no" directly to an invitation may offend the inviting party, since it is interpreted as not valuing the invitation.

Caboverdians are not as conscious of time as people in industrialized nations. They are often late, even by an hour or more. This is especially true at dances. Although scheduled to start at 9:00 P.M., a dance may not begin before 11:00 P.M. (with guests beginning to arrive at 10:30 P.M.). Arriving late at a home does not insult a host. The host automatically assumes the guest had something to do prior to arriving.

People frequently socialize outside of their homes in Cape Verde. In fact, urban people gather daily at the *praça* between 5:30 and 8:00 P.M. to discuss their day, make plans for the weekend, or talk about issues affecting the country.

Eating

In general, Caboverdians eat breakfast between 7:00 and 9:00 A.M. and lunch between noon and 2:00 P.M. After lunch, many people take a short nap of about 30 minutes. The wealthiest have coffee or tea with cookies and cakes around 5:00 P.M. and eat supper around 8:30 P.M. For most people, however, supper is at about 7:00 P.M.

Due to the influence of Portuguese colonization, Caboverdians usually eat with forks, knives, and spoons. At a restaurant or café, it is not uncommon for the wealthiest person to pay for the entire meal, especially if others in the party have financial difficulties. Tips are not expected in restaurants, cafés, or taxis, but they are welcomed.

LIFESTYLE

Family

In Cape Verde, the average family has five or six children and is led by the father. The extended family unit is important to each person; group (family) success takes precedence over individual success. Some elderly parents live with their children. Adult children often live in their parents' house until they get married, even if they have a job. Many women work outside the home; they comprise 29 percent of the labor force. Three women have cabinet positions in the current government. Regardless of their responsibilities outside the home, women generally are expected to do all household cleaning and cooking and to care for the children.

Most households are modest. In fact, only about half of all rural homes have access to electricity. Rural homes are made of stone or brick, stone being plentiful in the islands. Urban homes are more commonly made of cement and other materials.

Dating and Marriage

Dating customs are similar to those in Western countries, with young people meeting through school, community events, and work. Couples enjoy going to movies, dancing, going to the beach, and having parties. Young people are free to choose their mates, but families often have input or play an integral role in planning the wedding and other celebrations. Some couples live together instead of marrying or until they can afford the expensive wedding celebrations. A religious ceremony typically is followed by an evening reception that may accommodate more than two hundred people. Fidelity is important in marriage, but male infidelity is somewhat tolerated.

Diet

The most commonly eaten foods in Cape Verde are rice and corn. Rice, although imported, is relatively inexpensive; corn is grown locally. Rice is often served with fish and beans (black or pinto). Corn is often served with beans, pork, manioc, and sweet potatoes. *Cachupa* is the national dish. It is a stew made of corn and meat with manioc that is cooked slowly in water. Since Cape Verde is an archipelago, fish and fish products are important to the diet.

To complement their diet, people eat fruits and vegetables, such as bananas, papayas, mangoes, tomatoes, lettuce, and others. Caboverdians enjoy sweets at any time of day, cakes and marmalades being among the favorites. Two popular sweets include *doce de leite* (made of milk, sugar, and lemon) and *doce de coco* (made of coconut and sugar, it looks like a table-tennis ball).

Recreation

In their leisure time, Caboverdians visit each other, go to the beach, read, and play *futebol* (soccer). Soccer is the most popular sport, and people watch or listen to soccer broadcasts with undivided attention. On Sundays, people can be seen on the streets with their ears "glued" to the radio. In recent years, basketball and some other sports have increased in popularity. In urban areas, television is gaining a wider audience.

Caboverdians like to spend time at the islands' beautiful beaches. They also enjoy music and dances. Three of Cape Verde's unique music and dance styles include *Morna*, *Coladeira*, and *Funáná*. Mazurka is also popular as dance music. *Morna* has a slow rhythm and mostly sad lyrics, while *Coladeira* is more upbeat and joyful. *Funáná* is even more lively and has a strong beat. It actually was forbidden before independence and only survived in the countryside. Now enjoyed throughout the country, it is the most popular dance music.

Holidays

Cape Verde's official holidays are New Year's Day (1 January), National Hero's Day (20 January), Women's Day (8 March), Labor Day (1 May), Children's Day (1 June), Independence Day (5 July), All Saints' Day (1 November), and Christmas (25 December). An additional holiday in February is added in some areas where *Carnaval* is important. National Hero's Day commemorates the death of Amilcar Cabral, who led the fight for independence. Other national heroes are also honored on this day. While every fifth of July is a holiday, an official celebration takes place only every five years to minimize the financial costs of celebrating Independence Day.

Commerce

Businesses are open from 8:00 A.M. to noon, and from 2:30 to 6:00 P.M., Monday through Friday. A pilot project currently is underway to determine if working hours can be changed using an 8:00 A.M. to 4:00 P.M. schedule, with a shorter (30-minute) lunch break. A few businesses use this alternate schedule, but it is unclear how popular it is. Cape Verde has stores where prices are fixed and open-air markets where prices are negotiable. The main open-air market, *Sukupira*, is in Praia. Staple goods are sold mostly in stores and are purchased less frequently, while fresh foods may be purchased several times a week.

SOCIETY

Government

Cape Verde is a republic administered through a parliamentary democracy. The National People's Assembly deliberates on, amends, and adopts national laws, plans, and budgets. The legislature has 82 directly elected members. According to the 1992 constitution, six of the legislators are elected by and represent emigrants living abroad. Previously, there were only three such representatives. Cape Verde's president is head of state, and the prime minister is head of government. Both serve five-year terms.

In opposition to the Movement for Democracy Party stands the African Party for Independence of Cape Verde (the former ruling party). The voting age is 18. There are 14 districts in the country, roughly representing each inhabited island. Because a multiparty democratic system was in place within 16 years of independence, Caboverdians point to their society as an example of genuine democracy in Africa.

Economy

Relatively speaking, Cape Verde is a poor country. Real gross domestic product per capita is $1,750. About two-thirds of the people are considered wage earners, but many do not earn enough to meet basic needs. Unemployment is high (25 percent). The country suffers from limited or underdeveloped resources. For example, the fishing and lobster harvesting industries are not well developed. In addition, the economy is not growing fast enough to keep up with population growth. Fish, bananas, hides, and skins are the main exports, while much of the country's food and many consumer items are imported. Most rural people work on road construction, fish, or are subsistence farmers. Urban residents mainly work for the government, are in the small retail business, or fish.

Without aid from the international community, as well as remittances from Caboverdians living abroad, the country's standard of living would be lower than it is. The currency is the Cape Verdean *escudo* (CVEsc).

Transportation and Communication

Most areas in Cape Verde are accessible by road, but many roads are not paved. Those that are paved are often in disrepair, but the government is trying to address the problem. Interisland transportation by sea is available for both passengers and freight, but most people do not travel much between islands. Locally, Caboverdians use a combination of transportation methods—going by foot, riding bicycles, or traveling by motorcycle and sometimes car. Some people ride animals, but most have access to the public bus system.

Telephone services are available in urban areas. Having service installed in a private home is expensive, and people are billed for each call, even local ones. The one national television station broadcasts to the entire country. On a clear day, television broadcasts from nearby countries can be received. There are three radio stations and a few newspapers. Postal delivery is slow and not always reliable, especially in rural areas.

Education

Enrollment in primary schools (ages seven to twelve) is compulsory, and 85 percent of children within this age group attend. About 48 percent of the school-age population attends secondary schools, while fewer than 1 percent of Caboverdians hold a college degree. Given that Cape Verde has no college or university, the country relies on overseas fellowships to provide its people with higher education. The government pays all educational costs. The official literacy rate is 66 percent.

Cape Verde's drop-out rates in primary and secondary schools are high for many reasons. First, classes are taught in Portuguese, creating a learning barrier for the majority of children, who speak Crioulo at home. Also, it is difficult for rural people to appreciate the value of or need for an education. It is not seen as necessary for earning a living. Economic constraints further compound the situation. For instance, the relatively high cost of transportation in rural areas, coupled with the need for children to help with work at home, can lead even eager students to drop out.

Health

Health care is provided by the government, free of direct financial costs to the patient. However, the waiting lines at the hospital are costly in terms of time, and the quality of care is not always adequate. This is due to the lack of equipment and to understaffing. Most people in urban areas, but only half of all rural residents, have access to safe drinking water, which is vital to good health. A 1995 cholera epidemic became difficult to control because of poor sanitation conditions. Cape Verde's infant mortality rate is 56 per 1,000; life expectancy ranges from 61 to 65 years.

FOR THE TRAVELER

A passport and visa are required for U.S. citizens to visit Cape Verde. Travelers coming from infected areas must have an inoculation against yellow fever. In addition, vaccinations against typhoid, cholera, and tetanus are recommended. Fruits and vegetables should be washed or cooked before being eaten. Cape Verde is appreciated by people who enjoy the beach, the sun, a slow pace of life, and dancing. One can surf, scuba dive, and practice other water sports in the islands. There are many historical sites of interest. For more information, contact the Embassy of the Republic of Cape Verde, 3415 Massachusetts Avenue NW, Washington, DC 20007; phone (202) 965–6820; or the Cabo Verde Mission to the United Nations, 27 East 69th Street, New York, NY 10021; phone (212) 472–0333. Travelers should also contact the Consulate General of Cape Verde, 535 Boylston Street, Second Floor, Boston, MA 02116; phone (617) 353–0014.

Central African Republic

Boundary representations not necessarily authoritative.

BACKGROUND

Land and Climate

The Central African Republic covers 240,533 square miles (622,980 square kilometers) and is a little smaller than Texas. The south is very green, with areas of dense rain forest. Farther north, the land becomes drier, but most of the country is covered by savanna. The Central African Republic is landlocked. Only one river, the Oubangui (on the southern border), can be used by large boats during the rainy season. But there are many small rivers.

Generally, daytime temperatures are hot, but nights cool off to 55°F (13°C) during November and December when cold winds blow off the northern desert. There is a rainy season, from May to November, and a second, shorter season in late February or early March. This precipitation is called the "mango rains" because it allows mango trees to produce fruit for the mango season in late March.

The Central African Republic government has been implementing a variety of conservation projects. Elephant hunting is banned, although poaching is a problem. Several preserves in the north and southwest protect wildlife and rain forests.

History

Central Africa has an ancient heritage, but prior to French control of the area in 1887, it was inhabited by the Aka (Pygmy) and peoples migrating inland to escape the coastal slave trade. The French established the area as the Ubangi-Shari territory in 1894 and united it with Chad in 1906 as the Ubangi-Shari-Chad colony. In 1910, the colony was united with the Congo and Gabon as the Federation of French Equatorial Africa. Ubangi-Shari became autonomous in 1958 and independent in 1960. At independence, the name was changed to Central African Republic.

David Dacko served as the country's first president but was overthrown in a coup led by Colonel Jean-Bedel Bokassa in 1966. In 1976, Bokassa created a monarchy and crowned himself Emperor Bokassa I. Dacko staged a coup in 1979 while Bokassa was out of the country and restored the republic. General André Kolingba overthrew Dacko in yet another coup in 1981. The military ran the government until 1985, when Kolingba appointed civilians to his new cabinet. Kolingba created the *Rassemblement Démocratique Centrafricain* (RDC) as the only legal party in 1986. Elections in 1987 were used to approve a new constitution and a six-year term in office for Kolingba. By the 1990s, however, in a climate of bleak economic conditions, other parties became active and posted candidates in 1993 elections. Bokassa ran for president, but Ange-Félix Patasse was elected. Despite his efforts to improve economic conditions, government payrolls were not met on more than one occasion. In protest, the army mutinied in 1996. At the request of President Patasse, French troops restored order to Bangui, sections of which were devastated by heavy fighting.

THE PEOPLE

Population

The population is about 3.2 million. More than 500,000 people live in and around the capital, Bangui. There are other urban areas, but more than half the people live in small towns and villages. Still, urban areas are growing faster (4 percent) than the overall population (2.1 percent). The country's Human Development Index (0.361) ranks it 149th out of 174 nations. This reflects the fact that few people have access to basic resources that would allow them to improve their lives.

Eighty-plus ethnic groups inhabit the Central African Republic, although two account for more than half of the total population. In addition to the Gbaya (34 percent) and Banda (27 percent), there are the Mandjia, Sara, Mboum, M'Baka, Sango, and others. A significant Aka (Pygmy) population lives along the southwest border. The Mbororo, descendants of the Fulbé (or Fulani), are migratory herding people who do not consider themselves Central Africans; others also recognize them as distinctly different. In addition to local peoples, a significant population of Portuguese-, Greek-, and Arabic-speaking merchants live in urban areas.

Language

Sango and French are the two main languages, but each ethnic group also has its own language. Sango (a Bantu tongue) is the national language. It was spread years ago as a trade language. French is the official language but is used mostly in government. Most people are fluent in their own tongue and Sango. French is spoken only by the more educated (about 10 percent).

The government promotes Sango because the language reinforces national identity. It recently introduced Sango as the language of instruction in primary school. Many official speeches are made in Sango rather than French, especially if the audience is primarily Central African. The national radio, *Radio Centrafrique*, broadcasts in both Sango and French.

Religion

Several religions are practiced in the Central African Republic. About half of the population is Christian, mainly Catholic and Baptist. About 15 percent of the population is Muslim. The rest practice local religions. Even Christians and Muslims maintain traditional beliefs or combine local practice with Christianity or Islam. For example, funerals may be less Catholic and more African. A belief in magic is widespread. People also seek the services of local charmers for guidance.

General Attitudes

Central Africans are friendly, gentle, and generous. Strangers are greeted with smiles. There is a strong sense of community among the people, including a deep commitment to the family and loyalty to one's ethnic group. Young people attending school away from home can expect to live with relatives, no matter how distant the relationship.

Central Africans tend to live in the present. Because there are many immediate daily concerns and limited resources, money is usually spent when obtained. Savings are not common. Those with money left over are expected to share it with family members who need it; saving money is considered a sign of greed. There is a degree of uncertainty about the future, so people are fatalistic about their lives. At the same time, they have a genuine appreciation for and enjoyment of the present.

Ethnic groups have strong internal bonds and often have identifying characteristics like specific trades, customs, or facial features (tattoos, scars, henna leaf designs, etc.).

Personal Appearance

Central Africans take pride in being clean and well dressed. Wealthier urban men may wear a shirt and slacks or a Western-style suit. A *complet*, also popular, consists of pants and a matching shirt jacket that buttons to the collar. A common traditional outfit consists of pants and a matching *boubou* made from bright, locally produced fabric. A *boubou* may be cut as a pullover-style shirt, but a *grand boubou* is more like a robe that reaches the man's knees or feet. Embroidery on the front is popular.

Urban women commonly wear traditional styles. One outfit is a tight-fitting, short-sleeved blouse with a matching *pagne* (long, wraparound skirt). Wealthier women might wear a short and a long *pagne* at the same time. The way a woman ties her *pagne* and allows the cloth to drape over her body conveys a number of unspoken messages, such as marital status. Women usually wear some sort of head wrap; a scarf is required to enter a church. Gold jewelry is a status symbol. Hairstyles can be elaborate. Girls learn at an early age to braid and weave hair.

Rural people and the urban poor dress modestly. They often wear secondhand Western clothing or a combination of local styles with Western T-shirts. Villagers often go barefoot to save their shoes for special occasions.

CUSTOMS AND COURTESIES

Greetings

A handshake is used in formal and social settings, along with verbal greetings. If close male friends meet informally, they might begin a greeting by slapping right hands together. Then, each would grasp the other person's middle finger with the thumb and middle finger and "snap." Women sometimes kiss each other on alternating cheeks. After these physical gestures, inquiries about one's health, family, and crops usually follow. This is true even when people meet by chance; just a passing "Hello" to a friend or coworker is not polite.

A common Sango greeting is *Bara ala!* or *Bala mo!* (Greetings to you), followed by *Tonga na nyen?* (How's it going?) or *Ala yeke senge?* or *Mo yeke?* (Are you okay?). French greetings include *Bonjour* (Good day) or *Salut!* (Greetings), followed by *Ça va?* (Everything okay?). French is not used in villages.

How one addresses a person depends on the situation. Formally, one uses titles alone or with the last name. Respected older men may be addressed as *baba* (Sango for "father"), and women as *mama* (mother). Informally, one may use first or last names, nicknames, or family affiliation (cousin, brother, sister). A very close friend may be called *ita* (brother or sister) or *cousin* (cousin). When meeting a small group, one greets each person individually. To greet a larger group, one might raise both hands, palms facing the group, and say *Bara ala kwé* (Sango for "Greetings, everyone").

Gestures

People beckon by extending the hand, fingers out and palm down, and waving the fingers inward. During conversation, one can indicate "yes" by raising the eyebrows. This gesture is sometimes accompanied by a quick inhalation or a glottal clicking sound. One might ask, "What?" or even "How are you?" by holding the hand out next to the body, palm open and down with the fingers relaxed, and flipping the hand over. Surprise or shock may be expressed by slapping the forehead with an open hand, sometimes saying "Aye!" or "Mama!" A hissing sound may be used to attract attention. Children often cross their arms over their stomachs as a sign of respect when speaking to a person of authority. Pointing with one finger is impolite. Forming a circle with the thumb and index finger means "zero." One may show respect when shaking hands by supporting the right wrist with the left hand and bowing slightly. Young friends of the same age and sex often hold hands while walking and talking.

Visiting

Visiting is a popular way to spend free time; it is common for a person to "drop in" uninvited at a friend's home. After greeting those present, the visitor is offered a chair or stool (*barambo*) and something to drink. Hosts may ask visitors to sit inside the home, but it is more common to sit outside on the porch or in the shade of a nearby tree. The visitor usually is given the nicest place to sit. During the visit, everyone might talk or listen to the radio. Sometimes very little is said and everyone just relaxes. Visitors arriving at mealtime are asked to share the meal. It is impolite to refuse offers of food, drink, or a seat.

Invited guests are not necessarily expected to be prompt. Hosts are patient with late guests and accomodating of those who arrive early. The host will often accompany a departing guest for a short distance.

Eating

The number of meals eaten in a day depends on family income. At mealtime, people (especially children) may sit on the ground or on low stools around the food, which may be on a mat or a low table. Townspeople often have Western-style tables and chairs. While people might use plates and utensils, they generally eat food with the hands from a common bowl. The right hand is used unless the type of food requires both hands. Before and after the meal, soap and water are passed around to wash the hands. In villages, men and boys eat together. Girls and young boys eat near their mother by the cooking fire. The mother eats last because she usually is still preparing food while others are eating. People generally snack throughout the day. Popular snack foods include peanuts, small pieces of grilled meat, *makala* (fried dough), fried sweet potatoes, hard-boiled eggs, *mangbele* (cassava dough wrapped and boiled in leaves), and *kanda* (meat, fish, fruit, or termites wrapped in a leaf and steamed).

The average person rarely eats at a restaurant, but when one is invited to do so, the host expects to pay for the meal. Friends who decide together to eat out pay for their own meals.

LIFESTYLE

Family

The extended family is the basic social unit; it includes the mother, father, children, grandparents, aunts, uncles, and cousins. They may live together in one home, and great emphasis is placed on taking care of elderly relatives. Adults often consider nieces and nephews as daughters and sons. Families are relatively large and can seem larger because men may have more than one wife (or girlfriend). Each wife or girlfriend lives apart from the others. Women are responsible

for raising their children and providing the family with food. The man provides money for school, clothing, and the home.

Special pride is taken in introducing someone as, for example, *mon frère, même mère, même père* (my brother, same mother, same father). *Un frère* (a brother) might be a half brother or other relation. *Un cousin* could be a very distant relative. *Ita ti mbi* (in Sango) can mean "brother," "sister," "half brother," "cousin," or even "close friend."

Depending on the family's income, a home may be made of mud or cement bricks, a dirt or cement floor, and a thatched or tin roof. The kitchen may be a thatched hut away from the home where women cook over an open fire; outhouses are also located away from the home. The wealthy might have structures for a kitchen and bathroom attached to their homes. People don't spend much time in the home but are busy with daily activities.

Dating and Marriage

Rural inhabitants follow traditional customs. Parents sometimes arrange a marriage, and older men sometimes take young women as wives. In larger urban areas, men and women usually choose their own spouse. Although illegal, the practice of paying a bride-price to the bride's family is common. Depending on the groom's financial status and reputation, the bride-price can be quite high. It consists of money, clothing, animals, jewelry, household items, food for the wedding party, and other items. A wedding party can last for days. Men are allowed, by custom, to have relationships outside of marriage, but women are not. Polygamy is common but less so than in the past. The poorest can afford only one wife.

Diet

Lunch is the main meal of the day; dinner consists of leftovers or fruit. A traditional meal is *ngunza* with *gozo*. *Ngunza* is a thick sauce made from ground cassava leaves, tomato paste, and peanut butter. A *kpu* (similar to a giant mortar and pestle) is used to grind the leaves and prepare many other foods. *Gozo* is a thick paste made by soaking cassava root in water, drying it in the sun, grinding it into flour, and mixing it with boiling water. The *gozo* is formed into balls and dipped into *ngunza*. Meals may also include sauces with fish or meat (beef, chicken, goat, gazelle, monkey, snake, even elephant). The country produces a variety of fruits and vegetables, including sweet potatoes, tomatoes, avocados, bananas, oranges, grapefruit, guavas, papayas, pineapples, and mangoes. The Central African Republic imports powdered milk, noodles, rice, and other items.

Recreation

Because girls and women do household work, tend the fields, and do the shopping, recreation mostly applies to men and boys. They enjoy playing and watching soccer and basketball. Several amateur teams compete in the capital and in each large town. Some towns sponsor scout troops.

Schools provide all students with some recreation. Basketball, soccer, handball, and track-and-field are popular. Children also like to sing and play games at recess. Some schools have other extracurricular activities, such as theater. Church groups provide social activities, too.

Music is important. Each ethnic group has a distinct style and ensemble of instruments (skin drums or log drums). Specific drumming rhythms are used for certain events.

Holidays

Central Africans observe "official" and religious holidays. Official days include New Year's Day (1 January), *Fête du Travail* (Labor Day, 1 May), *Fête des Mères* (Mother's Day, end of May), Independence Day (13 August), and the Declaration of Independence from France (1 December). The latter is the biggest holiday, celebrated countrywide with parades and festivities. Schoolchildren practice for months to perform on this day. For Mother's Day, men stay home to cook and women get together to socialize, play sports, and dance.

Religious holidays include Easter and Christmas for Christians. Muslims celebrate the end of *Ramadan* (the month during which Muslims go without food or water during the day) with a feast, and *Tabaski* (Feast of the Sacrifice), which commemorates Abraham's willingness to sacrifice his son.

Commerce

Offices are generally open Monday through Friday until early afternoon. Shops are open Monday through Saturday from early to late, with a couple of hours' break in the afternoon. Some outdoor markets are open only in the morning or afternoon. Many open on Sunday, a popular day for shopping and socializing. Prices in open markets are negotiable, but some staple foods are sold at fixed prices. Post offices sell stamps in the morning; those with public telephones stay open later so people can make calls. Business meetings are usually preceded by socializing, which is important for good relations.

SOCIETY

Government

The Central African Republic's president serves as chief of state and head of government. The National Assembly has 85 deputies. That body is advised by an Economic and Regional Council. When the two bodies are in session together, they are called a congress. There is a separate judicial branch. The country is divided into 16 prefectures, each of which is divided into sub-prefectures. Each town has an elected mayor. In addition, a *makunji*, or village chief, is elected in each village. The responsibilities of the *makunji* depend on the strength and popularity of the mayor. All citizens have the right to vote at age 21. President Patasse's party is the Movement for the Liberation of the Central African People (MLPC). It and Kolingba's RDC are joined by more than 20 others.

Economy

The economy is based on agriculture, and most people are subsistence farmers. Coffee, cotton, tobacco, peanut and palm oils, and wood are exported and used locally; food crops and livestock are raised for domestic consumption. Industry usually centers on food processing and textiles. France is an important trade partner. It also provides loans and grants to the country. The currency is the *CFA franc* (Fr).

The Central African Republic's real gross domestic product per capita is $1,130. This reflects the wealth of a small number of people rather than the great poverty among the vast majority of people (e.g., subsistence farmers) who do not earn an income or do not earn enough to meet basic needs.

Transportation and Communication

The main form of intercity transportation is the *taxi brousse* (bush taxi); this can be a small pickup or a van. They are crowded and overloaded with luggage but affordable. People also hitchhike, while some have mopeds or bicycles. Short trips (up to 30 miles) are sometimes made on foot. Very few roads are paved. Post offices handle mail and telephone services. The government runs radio and television facilities. Radio programs are broadcast in French and Sango.

Education

Children begin primary school at age seven. Attendance is mandatory, but only about two-thirds of eligible students are enrolled. Although school is free, students may not have enough clothing or food to stay in school. Books are scarce, so teachers write lessons on the board and students copy them in their notebooks. About 10 percent go on to secondary school. Successful graduates (about 2 percent) may go to the university in Bangui or to a technical school. Some study abroad. The literacy rate is 38 percent, although it is lower for women.

Health

The country lacks adequate health care. Health-care professionals are often dedicated but underpaid. Public clinics exist in cities, but equipment is usually outdated and patients are required to provide their own anesthetics and medicine (available at pharmacies). Public facilities are virtually nonexistent in smaller towns and villages. Private clinics are found in the capital, and missionaries run rural clinics. Traditional healers in rural areas treat illness with organic medicine and rituals. The infant mortality rate is 136 per 1,000. If children survive to age six, they have a good chance of living to adulthood. Women often have children in their late teens and many die in childbirth. The average life expectancy is 45 years. Malaria, hepatitis, polio, intestinal parasites, and river blindness are common.

FOR THE TRAVELER

U.S. citizens need a valid passport and visa to travel to the Central African Republic. Professional photographers need special permits. A yellow fever vaccination is required; cholera, rabies, polio, typhoid, and hepatitis vaccinations are recommended. Malaria is endemic. Avoid swimming in rivers or pools of water because of the threat of schistosomiasis. Peel or cook fruits and vegetables before eating them, and purify or boil all drinking water. Eat only meat that is hot and well cooked. Because of unrest, check with the State Department for travel advisories: (202) 647–5225. Visitors leaving by air must pay an airport tax of 3,000 *CFA francs* (or 60 French *francs*). Tourism is not actively promoted, but there are many interesting sites to visit. For more information, contact the Embassy of the Central African Republic, 1618 22d Street NW, Washington, DC 20008.

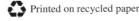

People's Republic of

China

Ürümqi

Harbin

Shenyang · Changchun

Yellow (Huang He) BEIJING ★

Taiyuan · Tianjin · Dalian

Lanzhou

Xi'an Zhengzhou · Zibo

QINGHAI-TIBET PLATEAU

Mekong

Chengdu

Grand Canal

Wuhan

Shanghai

HIMALAYAS Lhasa

Yangtze (Chang Jiang) Chongqing

Guiyang Changsha

Boundary representations not necessarily authoritative.

Kunming

Guangzhou (Canton)

ASIA

BACKGROUND

Land and Climate

At 3,705,751 square miles (9,597,905 square kilometers), China is just larger than the United States. Because much of the country is covered by mountains or desert, the majority of people live in the fertile east, where rivers and plains allow for productive agriculture. While summers are warmer and winters colder, China's climate is much like that of the United States. Monsoons cause frequent summer floods. China experiences several climates and has many geographical features, from the Himalaya Mountains to the Qinghai-Tibet Plateau (known as the "roof of the world") to subtropical islands. Some of the world's longest rivers are in China; the Yangtze River is 3,900 miles (6,300 kilometers) long. The Great Wall of China stretches 1,500 miles (2,400 kilometers).

History

The Chinese have one of the world's oldest continuous civilizations, spanning some five thousand years. From its earliest history, China was ruled by a series of dynasties—some were native (such as the Ming Dynasty) and some were nomadic tribes (the Qing Dynasty)—that were eventually absorbed into Chinese culture. A revolution inspired by Sun Yat-sen overthrew the Qing Dynasty in 1911. In the 1920s, with the country fragmented by opposing warlords, Sun Yat-sen established the Kuomintang (KMT) political party in an effort to unify China.

After Sun's death in 1925, Chiang Kai-shek took control (1927) and ousted the once-allied Communist Party. The Communists, led by Mao Zedong, are famous for their Long March across China to regroup and fight the KMT for control of China. After the Japanese were defeated in World War II, the civil war ended with Mao's forces in control and Chiang's army fleeing to Taiwan to regroup and return. They never did. Mao ruled from 1949 to 1976.

While the Chinese initially welcomed communism, the periods of the Great Leap Forward (1958–61) and the Cultural Revolution (1966–76) had disastrous effects on the country. More than 40 million people starved or were killed during Mao's rule. Policy makers after him have been more pragmatic, and Mao is not the hero he once was. Deng Xiaoping, a more moderate leader, dictated policy during the 1980s. His policies led to foreign tourism, a more liberal economy, growth, trade, and educational exchanges. Unfortunately, the Tiananmen Square massacre in 1989 and a subsequent government crackdown slowed China's open-door policy.

In 1992, Deng and his moderate supporters won a quiet power struggle to bring China back on track toward economic reform. China quickly became one of the world's fastest growing economies; by the year 2000, it is expected to be the largest economy (the United States currently holds that position). Political liberalization is nevertheless resisted by certain leaders, partly out of the natural tendency of authoritarian societies to conserve power. But even moderate leaders contend that socialism can be maintained in an era of prosperity. Improvements in material welfare, others say, will eventually bring social and political change. For the majority of people, the issue is not who governs but whether the standard of living rises. And the majority of people desire any change to occur peacefully, rather than through uprisings and distress.

THE PEOPLE

Population

China's population is the largest in the world, with 1.2 billion people. To reduce the 1 percent annual growth rate, the government officially sponsors family-planning programs and offers incentives (money, housing, and educational advantages) to families that have only one child. This policy applies mainly to the Han Chinese (92 percent) and not necessarily to minorities. Fifty-five minorities make up 8 percent of the population; 15 of these groups include more than one million people. These are the Zhuang, Mongolian, Hui, Tibetan, Uygur, Miao, Yi, Buyi, Korean, Manchu, Dong, Yao, Bai, Tujia, and Hani nationalities. While 72 percent of all Chinese live in rural areas, urban population density often rises to more than three thousand people per square mile. China's Human Development Index (0.594) ranks it 111th out of 174 countries. Rural people generally have little access to the resources necessary to enjoy a decent standard of living.

Language

Standard Chinese (Putonghua), based on the Mandarin dialect, is the national language and is spoken by more than 70 percent of the population. Other dialects include Wu (spoken in Shanghai), Min, Yue (Cantonese), and Kejia. Each of the 55 minorities speaks its own language or dialect. In some places, education and all official transactions may be conducted in the local minority language. Chinese does not have a phonetic alphabet; it uses characters to express words, thoughts, or principles. A romanized alphabet (pinyin) is used to help teach Chinese in school and for international communication. While up to 50,000 characters exist, only about 8,000 are currently in use. Chinese requires a knowledge of 1,500 to 2,000 characters for basic literacy.

Religion

While the government officially encourages atheism, the people may exercise religious beliefs within certain guidelines. Buddhists, Taoists, Muslims, and Christians all practice their religion. Temples and churches are open to the public, but since public worship is frowned upon, people often worship at home. While the government allows domestic religious groups to print materials, hold meetings, and worship, they are carefully monitored. Unauthorized activities can lead to imprisonment or other restrictions. Christianity is growing, and unofficial estimates claim that up to 5 percent of the population is Christian.

General Attitudes

The Chinese are noted for good manners, hospitality, and reserve. Confucianism, the ancient philosophy of social order, still has a great influence on attitudes and actions. The elderly are respected. The Chinese are very proud of their nation's long history and of past Chinese achievements. Foreign visitors should respect this and refrain from negative comments about China. Authority is respected and obedience emphasized; this keeps open political debate to a minimum.

The principle of *guanxi* binds friends and associates in committing them to do what they can for each other when called upon. To violate *guanxi* is to "lose face" (to lose reputation or honor), another principle in Chinese society. "Keeping face" means avoiding embarrassment, failure, defeat, or contradictions. Children are expected to uphold the family "face," or its social respect. This has had different meanings in different eras. For today's urban children, it means being well educated, dressing well, earning money, and practicing traditionally valued traits like loyalty, politeness, and kindness.

Society is changing in China as economic opportunities expand. The goal of many families, for which they generally save for many years, is to build or have a nice home. Owning a house is a symbol of a better life. Most people want their children to have greater prosperity than themselves.

Personal Appearance

Chinese attire is traditionally conservative and simple. In the past, most wore the same style pantsuits because of government policy. Reforms and economic modernization have made Western styles the most popular in urban areas. Many women wear dresses. Bright colors, Western suits, jeans, and jackets are increasingly popular. Nevertheless, styles are not always as modern as in other nations and "Mao suits" are still worn by the very conservative. Ethnic minorities wear clothing reflective of their cultural past and the climate in which they live. Throughout China, people strive to keep themselves and their surroundings clean.

CUSTOMS AND COURTESIES

Greetings

The Chinese nod politely or bow slightly when greeting. A handshake is also acceptable, especially in formal situations or to show respect. A greeting common to foreigners is *Ni hao ma?* (How do you do?). While many Chinese accept this term and use it, there are also various, more traditional terms. A common informal greeting is *Chi le ma?* (Did you eat?). The response is either *Chi le* (Yes) or *Mei you* (Not yet).

The Chinese tend to be formal in their introductions; they use the full titles of their guests but are less precise in identifying themselves. Chinese names usually consist of a one-syllable family name, followed by a one- or two-syllable given name. A person is addressed either by full name or by title and family name. In lieu of professional titles, the Chinese equivalents of "Mr." and "Mrs." are used. Thus, Wang Jian-Jun can also be called Mr. Wang, but never simply Wang and rarely ever Jian-Jun. To show special respect, friends might use the terms *Lao* (old) and *Xiao* (young) in place of titles.

Gestures

Except in crowds when physical contact is unavoidable, Chinese do not like to be touched by people they do not know. A smile is preferred to a pat on the back or a similar gesture. This is important when dealing with older people or those in important positions. Chinese point with an open hand rather than one finger. To beckon, they wave all fingers with the palm of the hand facing down. In some regions, it is common for people to spit in public after clearing their throat. Government fines have tried to curb this behavior, but because it is necessitated by health conditions, it remains common.

Visiting

Invitations are usually extended for formal events, but otherwise people commonly drop by unannounced. When invited, they are generally prompt; being more than a few minutes late is impolite. Guests conduct themselves with restraint and refrain from loud, boisterous speech and actions. Valuable gifts usually are not accepted from strangers, but small gifts may be given by friends. Friends often bring gifts such as tea, cigarettes, fruit, chocolates, cakes, or wine when they visit. Hosts rarely open wrapped gifts before visitors leave. They usually offer refreshments, but declining them is not impolite. A host will probably insist several times before accepting a guest's refusal. People enjoy gathering for discussion or playing card and table games. Many ancient and popular games originated in China, including *Majiang* (mahjongg), Chinese chess, and various card games. Conversation topics generally include personal experiences, family, business, or a mutual interest.

Eating

The Chinese use chopsticks for all meals. Food is placed at the center of the table and may include more than one type of main dish to be eaten with rice. Diners place some food in their individual rice bowls, which they hold close to the mouth while eating. They place bones and seeds on the table or a dish but never back in the rice bowl. When finished, a person places the chopsticks neatly on the table; they are not left in the rice bowl.

At restaurants, a revolving tray at the center of the table allows guests to sample from several dishes. Toasts are offered to the whole table and sometimes even to a neighboring table. At formal banquets, guests have a short, friendly speech prepared to respond to a host's remarks. Tipping in restaurants is traditionally considered an insult—something a superior does for an inferior—but with economic change, it is now popular in the Guangdong and Fujian provinces and is spreading elsewhere.

LIFESTYLE

Family

Historically, loyalty to the family unit has always been important to the Chinese. During the Cultural Revolution, the state tried to shift loyalty to the government, and families were often split by work or study assignments. Family-planning policies limited couples to one or two children, imposing fines or sterilization on violators. This practice continues in many areas, but not to the extent of the past. Less than 10 percent of all families have more than two children. Housing is generally poor and in short supply. Small apartments without bathrooms are the norm in cities, while simple, dirt-floor homes are common in rural areas. Most housing is owned by the government or a person's work unit. In an effort to improve housing conditions and availability, the government is encouraging people to buy their own homes or apartments. It is also raising rents gradually to provide companies with the incentive to build more and better houses and apartments.

Dating and Marriage

Chinese customs stress moral purity. Intimate relations and public displays of affection are discouraged. To help the family-planning program succeed, young people are encouraged to marry late. In fact, college students are forbidden to marry until after graduation. The sanctioned age for marriage is 22 for men and 20 for women. Those who marry before that

age are not eligible for some of the same benefits as those who wait. To marry, a couple first seeks permission from the local governing unit. If granted, a legal contract is recorded without a wedding ceremony. The couple then joins family and friends in a marriage celebration. While simple festivities are common, many urban couples are spending large amounts of money on Western-style receptions/parties, a large feast, and in buying household items. This is a matter of "face," so considerable attention might be paid to the celebration. Wedding rings traditionally are not a part of marriage, but they are becoming more common. The bride retains her maiden name and does not take the family name of her husband.

Diet

Except where private enterprise is encouraged, a wide variety of food is not available in China. What people eat largely depends on what is produced in the region where they live. Dishes with rice, potatoes, cornmeal, tofu, and other grains are staple meals. Dishes made with pork, beef, chicken, or fish are popular but expensive. Specialties vary from region to region, from duck in Beijing to spicy dishes in the Sichuan province. Fruits and vegetables are eaten in season; few dairy products are available or eaten. Sauces are mixed with vegetables and meats and eaten with rice. Noodles are also common. *Man tou* (steamed bread) is a staple in northern China.

Recreation

Theaters, operas, ballets, films, and cultural monuments all provide recreation in cities. Imported movies are popular; the average Chinese attends more than ten each year. Traveling cultural groups perform in rural areas. Travel restrictions have been eased and people enjoy visiting other parts of China. Sports are popular and most cities have facilities. Favorites include table tennis, swimming, and soccer. People play table and board games in homes and parks. *Majiang* is the most popular table game in China; probably 90 percent of the people play it. *Wei qi* (known as *Go* in other countries) is a strategy game played in more educated circles. Chinese chess is another favorite. Parks and courtyards are often filled in the morning by those practicing *taijiquan*, a traditional form of shadowboxing that provides exercise and therapy.

Holidays

Official public holidays are 1 January, Labor Day (1 May), National Day (1–2 October), and Chinese New Year (also called Spring Festival), which is held for three days in January or February, according to the Chinese lunar calendar. As the most important holiday, the Spring Festival is marked by banquets, family gatherings, carnivals, and dragon dances. Extra food provided by the government includes fish (a symbol of abundance), meat, prawns, rice, and Chinese dumplings (*jiaozi*). Festivals are also celebrated around the country, including the Lantern Festival (15th of the first lunar month), the Dragon Boat Festival (fifth of the fifth lunar month), and Tibet's Fruit-Expecting Festival (August).

Commerce

Office hours are generally from 8:00 A.M. to noon and 2:00 to 6:00 P.M., Monday through Saturday. Shops are open from 9:00 A.M. to 7:00 P.M. every day. State-run restaurants often close by 8:00 P.M. It is improper to be late for business appointments. Until recently, the state determined what career one would have and where one would work. This is changing with the increase in private ventures, as more people are being allowed to seek their own jobs. Private firms do not operate like assigned work units, which have customarily provided housing, day care, health care, and other benefits.

SOCIETY

Government

The People's Republic of China has a Communist government. National policy is determined by a 20-member Politburo and, more importantly, its 7-member Standing Committee. Jiang Zemin is president and the general secretary of the Chinese Communist Party (CCP), which is the only legal party in the country. Li Peng is premier. Deng Xiaoping, while no longer officially head of state, is still considered China's most powerful individual and is the de facto leader of China's government. The National People's Congress has nearly three thousand members, indirectly elected at local levels. The last elections for that body were in 1993.

Economy

China's large economy is offset by its population, meaning the real gross domestic product per capita is just $1,950, a level that reflects China's status as a developing country. While the figure is rising, wealth is not equally distributed. In a state accustomed to equal wages for all, this has caused no small amount of contention between average people. Still, a vibrant and growing private sector and government policies designed to liberalize the economy are improving living standards for many people. Leaders note that their "socialist market economy" means communism does not have to be synonymous with poverty. Urban areas are experiencing a growth in the middle class. Private enterprise is encouraged, and Western institutions like the stock market are beginning to thrive. While the economy is growing at more than 10 percent, inflation, corruption, and crime are also on the rise. A large government budget deficit threatens the social security network and other institutions.

A better economy has improved life in many villages: diets are better, health is better, and people are generally content. The prevalence of absolute poverty has been cut in half since 1980. Once-common shortages for consumer goods are rare in today's economy. Nonetheless, 100 million people are still very poor; many still live in inadequate housing (even caves in some regions) and few have any say over what happens to them in their lives. This contradictory situation is hard for foreigners to understand and is becoming harder for the Chinese to accept.

China produces manufactured goods, oil, minerals, coal, and steel. While only one-tenth of China's land is arable, the country is a world leader in the production of rice, tobacco, corn, barley, soybeans, peanuts, eggs, and pork. Wheat, fish, and potatoes are also important agricultural products. About 61 percent of the population is employed in agriculture. The currency is called *renminbi*; the standard unit is the *yuan* (¥).

Transportation and Communication

All major transportation facilities are state owned. Individuals travel by train, bicycle, or bus. Domestic air travel is also available, but expensive, and not always reliable. In some areas, people travel by river barge or ferry. Roads between cities are often in poor condition. Few people have cars. Communication systems are getting better. The government controls radio and television broadcasts and there is only one officially sanctioned television station (CCTV). However, an information revolution has brought satellite disks, fax machines, and electronic mail to China, making it nearly impossible for the government to control what people read and hear.

Education

China's goal for the 1990s is to provide an elementary education to every citizen. While 96 percent of first-grade-age children are enrolled, only about 65 percent of children finish elementary school. Rural girls are least likely to be enrolled. The government eventually plans to extend mandatory schooling to nine years in all areas. To increase adult literacy, a TV university was established to give instruction over radio and television. Only a small fraction (5 percent) of all people attend college; these students often receive the best government or management positions after graduation. Tuition fees are being charged at the undergraduate level and may eventually extend to the graduate level. College students must work at least five years after graduation before they can apply to study abroad. The adult literacy rate is 79 percent.

Health

While malaria and cholera are problematic in China, the people are generally healthy. The average life expectancy is 68 years. Medical care is usually free for urban Chinese and subsidized for rural people. The health-care system concentrates on prevention. The extensive network of programs emphasizes immunizations, prenatal care, pediatrics, and sanitation. Facilities are simple, but the system has greatly improved the basic health of the people and lowered infant mortality to 52 per 1,000. It is much lower in the cities. Water usually is not potable, and open sewers are common. Traditional Chinese medicine (use of medicinal herbs and acupuncture, among other things) is combined with Western medical techniques in treating illness and injury.

FOR THE TRAVELER

A visa and valid passport are required of all visitors. Some areas are closed to tourists, but one can see most major cities. Visas are more easily obtained by tour groups, which also receive the best accommodations. Individuals traveling without prior arrangements or itinerary may encounter some difficulties. Visas are often sold at various locations in Hong Kong. Those not traveling in groups should have some understanding of Chinese. Malaria pills are recommended, as are gamma globulin shots. Clean and peel fruits and vegetables before eating, and do not drink unboiled water. Wash-and-wear clothing is best to take, as modern cleaning facilities are not always available. For more information on travel opportunities, contact the China National Tourist Office, 350 Fifth Avenue, Room 6413, Empire State Building, New York, NY 10108. China's embassy is located at 2300 Connecticut Avenue NW, Washington, DC 20008–0163.

A Culturgram is a product of native commentary and original, expert analysis. Statistics are estimates and information is presented as a matter of opinion. While the editors strive for accuracy and detail, this document should not be considered strictly factual. It is a general introduction to culture, an initial step in building bridges of understanding between peoples. It may not apply to all peoples of the nation. You should therefore consult other sources for more information.

CULTURGRAM '97

Federal Islamic Republic of the
Comoros

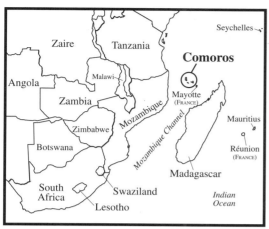

Boundary representations not necessarily authoritative.

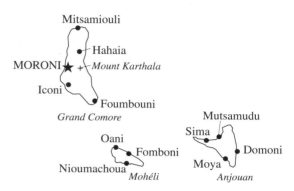

BACKGROUND

Land and Climate

Comoros is located in the Mozambique Channel of the Indian Ocean. Its three islands, Anjouan, Mohéli, and Grand Comore, together are about the same size as Delaware, covering 838 square miles (2,171 square kilometers). These volcanic islands were formed in succession from east to west, Grand Comore being the youngest. It has less-evolved soil than the other islands and so lacks their ability to support agriculture. All the islands are mountainous, with Grand Comore being dominated by Mount Karthala (7,800 feet or 2,400 meters), which has a large active volcanic crater. Mayotte Island to the southeast is geologically the oldest member of the Comoros Archipelago, but it is currently a French territory.

The hot, humid rainy season (*Kashkazi*) runs from November to March, but it varies annually. The pleasant season of *Kusi* (April–September) has warm, clear, breezy days and cool nights. Comorian waters are home to the ancient coelacanth fish, thought to be long extinct before one was seen in South Africa in 1938.

History

Africans arriving in the 13th century were thought to be the first inhabitants, but discoveries in 1990 led to theories that Persians may have actually settled the islands in the 800s. Malagasy people from Madagascar came in the 16th century, but the population remained small until the islands were used by Arab slave traders as holding areas.

Arab slavers set up towns and mainland Africans formed their own communities. Over time, the islands were divided into various opposing sultanates. Except for pirates and a few other sailors, Europeans paid the islands little attention until the 19th-century "scramble for Africa." The French, having occupied Madagascar, became interested in the Comoros to counter a British presence in East Africa and the Seychelles.

A sultan on Grand Comore allied with the French in the 1870s, and by 1886 the entire four-island archipelago was proclaimed a French protectorate.

In 1958, Comorians voted to remain a French overseas territory while assuming responsibility for internal affairs. Saïd Mohammed Cheik became president of the Council of Government. Though he served mostly as a figurehead, he gave Comorians their first idea of self-determination. Cheik moved the capital from Mayotte to Moroni on Grand Comore (1962–64). As part of the global decolonization effort, a referendum for independence was held in 1974. Of the total population, 94 percent voted for autonomy, but 64 percent of Mayotte's residents voted to remain under French control. Hence, when the Federal Islamic Republic of the Comoros became independent in 1975, France maintained possession of Mayotte. Comoros still has an internationally recognized claim to the island, on which France supports a large naval base, because of the overall popular vote for independence.

Ahmed Abdallah, elected as the first post-independence president, was overthrown after only a few months in office by a socialist visionary named Ali Soilihi. Soilihi was assisted by European mercenaries led by Bob Denard. Soilihi's austere policies managed to boost agricultural production and increase the number of schools. However, his strict approach alienated Comorians, his economic policies were not appreciated by Western donors, and his criticism of many Islamic traditions offended Muslim nations. Having little foreign or domestic support, Soilihi was overthrown in 1978 by Abdallah (with Denard's help).

Abdallah led the country away from the socialist economy, but he faced the challenges of a 1977 volcanic eruption and a 1978 influx of Comorian refugees from Madagascar. He was only able to maintain order with Denard's assistance. Comorian resentment of the mercenaries grew and, by 1989, Abdallah had planned to oust Denard with help from France and

South Africa. In November 1989, Abdallah was murdered at home and Denard took control for several weeks until France forced his departure.

The head of the Supreme Court, Saïd Mohammed Djohar, was elected president in 1990. Economic crisis and political unrest soon gripped the country and Djohar was targeted in several coup attempts. Violence and instability continued in the 1990s, despite efforts in 1994 to reconcile political rivalries. Bob Denard returned to lead a coup in 1995 against the unpopular Djohar, but France invaded and captured him. Elections in 1996 brought Mohamed Taki to office as president.

PEOPLE

Population

The population of 550,000 is growing annually at 3.5 percent. Nearly half is younger than age 15, and 74 percent lives in rural areas. The capital, Moroni, and Mutsamudu are the largest cities. Grand Comore has the most residents, followed by Anjouan and Mohéli. The country's Human Development Index (0.415) ranks it 139th out of 174 nations. A minority of people enjoy opportunities for personal advancement.

There are no true ethnic divisions, but Comorians are divided by language and other factors. Most Comorians are descendants of both Arab slavers and the African mainlanders they brought as slaves to be shipped north to the Arabian Peninsula and Nile Basin. Those with more Arab blood tend to enjoy higher social status than darker-skinned people (such as the Mohélians). A few families have Malagasy or Asian ethnic backgrounds.

Language

French and Arabic are official languages. French is used for official business. Indigenous languages are Bantu tongues derived from Swahili. Shingazidja is spoken on Grand Comore (locally called *Ngazidja*). Shinzduani is Anjouan's (*Nzduani*) language, and Shimwali is spoken on Mohéli (*Mwali*). People understand each other's languages, as well as the Shimaore spoken on Mayotte. Comorians traditionally use the Arabic script, but the Roman alphabet is being promoted.

Four- and five-year-olds attending *Qur'anic* schools learn Arabic, and while few adults speak it, most read the alphabet. Many Comorians know some French. Since French is the language of school instruction, anyone with a secondary education will be fairly fluent. English is offered in school, but usually only workers connected to travel can speak it.

Religion

Nearly all Comorians are Sunni Muslims, and Islamic traditions play a key role in daily life. Muslims accept the *Qur'an* (Koran) to be the final word of *Allah* (God) as revealed to the prophet Muhammad. Muhammad is revered as the last and greatest in a long line of prophets, from Adam and Abraham to Moses and others. Devout Muslims pray five times daily; the call to prayer is heard regularly from mosques in even the smallest villages. On Friday, all men (even less devout ones) go to their town's largest mosque for the noon prayer. Comorians have little sympathy for Islamic fundamentalism.

Non-Islamic (mostly African) beliefs are present, but they have largely been incorporated into Islamic practices. Many people maintain a belief in good and evil spirits and use *gris-gris* (charms) to ward off the evil ones. Some attend special ceremonies to bring out spirits. Other religions are tolerated. Most foreigners are Christians; large towns have both Catholic and Protestant churches.

General Attitudes

As Muslims, Comorians believe all events occur according to *Allah's* will. This faith is expressed as fatalism and people often feel they do not control their conditions. Comorians have a wonderful sense of humor. They enjoy a good joke and often exchange humorous light insults with friends.

Individual needs are subordinate to the family. People expect to share in both the successes and failures of family members. Within the larger community, sharing one's wealth is a way to increase social standing and influence, both of which are highly desired. Comorians also desire material possessions, the acquisition of which is seen as the will of *Allah*. Gifts from relatives working in France are particularly prized.

Personal Appearance

Quite conscious of their appearance, Comorians dress well in public. The traditional Islamic emphasis on cleanliness is not taken lightly. Urban men usually wear Western shirts and slacks. They have a nice suit for formal occasions. Elders, rural men, and urban men going to mosque more often wear the traditional white robe (*kandu*). Regardless of their outfit, men usually wear an embroidered cap (*kofia*). Shorts and a sloppy appearance are frowned upon. Most adults wear plastic flip-flops on their feet, although professionals wear shoes to work.

Women rarely wear pants except in cities. They wear Western dresses with colorful patterns and nearly always carry a printed shawl (*leso*) that often serves as a head covering. Anjouan women often wear a *shiromani* (traditional cloth) over their dresses (or skirt and blouse) and pulled up over their heads. Women on all islands occasionally wear a face mask made of ground sandalwood that is considered a cosmetic and skin lightener.

CUSTOMS AND COURTESIES

Greetings

Comorian men shake hands at every opportunity. They offer a verbal greeting to women, as touching women in public is considered improper. In private, among relatives, men and women may kiss on the cheek. Women might also greet female friends with a kiss.

Comorians exchange several standard greeting phrases, depending on the level of formality. The Shingazidja version of an exchange between social equals is *Edje?* (an informal "Hello") followed by *Ye yapvo?* (What's up?). More formal terms are required for greeting elders, professionals, or strangers. *Bariza husha* (Good morning), *Bariza hazi?* (How's work?), and *Bariza masihu* (Good evening) are all common Shingazidja phrases. In fact, *Bariza* can precede anything to form a greeting.

On Anjouan, *Djedje?* (How how?) is the most common informal greeting, followed by *Habari?* (News?). Mohéli has similar greetings. Comorians also use traditional Muslim Arabic terms like *Asalaam alaikum* (Peace be unto you). A positive response to something is often followed by the Arabic expression *Insha'Allah* (God willing) or *Alhamdul'illah* (Thanks be to God).

When calling out to someone, Grand Comorians often precede the addressee's name with *Bo* (e.g., "Bo Mbaraka!"). Titles are used to address people. Some are *mwana hangu* (my child/brother) for good friends, *coco* for a grandmother, *fundi* for a teacher or craftsman, and *mzé* for an elder man.

Gestures

Comorians beckon by opening and closing a hand, palm facing down or out. They indicate direction with the index finger. Members of the same sex often hold hands while walking, but members of the opposite sex do not touch in public. After a shared joke, it is common to slap each other's hands and laugh. One expresses polite refusal by placing a hand on the chest while verbally thanking the offerer. Various other hand gestures are used in the course of conversation.

A child respectfully greets an elder with both hands cupped and extended while saying *Kwezi*. In response, the elder clasps the child's hands and says *Mbona*. The exchange is like asking for and receiving a blessing. On Anjouan, the elder raises the cupped hands to the child's forehead before saying *Mbona*.

Visiting

Comorians make informal daily visits to close friends; it is impolite to lose contact with any friend or family member for more than a few days. Extended families are large, so social obligations are numerous. People enjoy having guests in their homes. It is a special honor to host a foreigner.

Within a village, Comorians visit freely without prior arrangement. Time for visiting is usually set aside from 4:00 to 6:00 P.M. When visiting someone in another town, it is more polite to give advanced notice (*Oulaha*) and thereby allow the hosts time to prepare. Hosts offer guests food and drink; refusing these refreshments is impolite. Weekday visits are short (an hour or less) but weekend visits can take the entire afternoon and include at least one meal. Visitors usually take gifts only when returning from foreign travel.

Eating

Comorians eat cold leftovers, if anything, for breakfast, along with hot, sweet tea. The afternoon meal includes a sauce-covered starchy food, like cassava or green bananas, and some meat. *Putu*, a hot pepper sauce, is served to season all types of food. Dinner features a rice dish and is the main meal.

Affluent urban families eat at a table with Western utensils. Otherwise, families eat on a mat on the floor, everyone sitting cross-legged around several shared plates of food. Rural women usually eat separately from men, especially if guests are present. If a guest eats with the entire family, he or she is considered a very close friend.

Comorians wash hands in a dish of water before and after eating. Utensils (generally spoons) are not uncommon, but people eat most often with the hand (right only). At large gatherings, food is served buffet-style and guests stand and eat from many plates. They take a handful of rice from a large common bowl and compress it with sauce before putting it in their mouths. No one eats until a short blessing has been offered.

Some urban men eat at restaurants when they cannot go home for lunch, but most Comorians (especially in rural areas) consider eating out embarrassing; it implies a person is poorly fed at home, has no family, or has marital problems.

Family

Comorians have little concept of the nuclear family. The extended family is large, especially in villages where polygamy is common. Men are in charge of family finances and property, while women control the household. Men do little domestic work; they farm or fish for the family's subsistence. Women seldom leave home except to do chores or for holidays, although some urban women do have outside jobs. Comorian women are not submissive and are proud of their traditional role.

Children use their father's given name as their own surname. At about age 18, sons might build themselves a *paillotte* (thatched hut) near the family home. They still eat at home and take part in family activities, but they sleep and entertain guests in their own dwelling. Daughters live at home until they marry. Small children are cared for by older sisters, and elders live with the adult children when they can no longer live alone.

Dating and Marriage

In Comoros, there is little open dating. A man and woman seen together are assumed to be romantically involved. Wealthy urban youth might go to dance clubs, but most socializing is discreet.

The most conspicuous social "statement" in Comoros is the Grand Marriage. Any man who wishes to be a full-fledged member of the community's group of elders, or *Notables*, must marry off at least his eldest daughter in a Grand Marriage. Maternal uncles can also give a Grand Marriage for nieces. This highly expensive, multi-ceremony event lasts more than a week. Families save for it for years and can expend their life's savings hosting the entire village for dances and meals. Guests offer expensive gifts, which are recorded so the recipients can properly reciprocate in the future. A Grand Marriage that involves much local purchasing benefits the community and so brings greater status to the host. The groom and both families also gain greater status for their roles in the wedding. The bride's father builds the newlyweds a house. If any problems occur, the husband must leave and the woman keeps the house.

The Grand Marriage began simply as a celebratory event, but it has taken on great social importance. On Grand Comore, rising competition between families to host better ceremonies has serious implications. Families save so much for the event that they spend less on basic needs. Some go into debt, which is passed on to future generations. Couples can marry without a Grand Marriage, and many do, but the respective families will not join the highest social class until a Grand Marriage is held.

Diet

Comorians eat mostly imported rice, usually topped by a fish or meat sauce. Plentiful local fish (tuna, barracuda, wahoo, and red snapper) are the main source of protein. Cassava (manioc root) is eaten fried, boiled, or grilled. Taro, green bananas, breadfruit, and potatoes (both white and sweet) are often served. Chicken, goat, and imported beef are popular meats. Pork is forbidden by Islam. Comorians love to spice their foods with *putu*. Most people have access to bread, and fruit is plentiful. Oranges, bananas, pineapples, papayas, mangoes, passion fruit, litchis, and others are eaten seasonally. Coconut is used in some sauces. Urban markets sell tomatoes, onions, cucumbers, and green beans. Cloves, cinnamon, saffron, and cardamom are indigenous spices. People drink water, tea, and fruit juice with meals.

Recreation

Soccer is the most popular sport and each town has a team to compete at the national level. Young men enjoy basketball and volleyball. There are no real movie theaters, but most villages have a video hut that plays VCR tapes for a small admission price. Television is available in towns with electricity, but only a French overseas broadcast is receivable. Comorian youth like to organize village dances. Musical tastes range from Western pop to reggae to traditional wedding dance music. Men spend free time walking, visiting, and playing games such as cards, dominoes, or *mdraha* (a pebble-and-board game). On weekends, families and friends might take a picnic to the beach.

Holidays

National holidays include New Year's Day (1 January), the Lunar New Year, Labor Day (1 May), and Independence Day (6 July). Islamic holidays are based on the lunar calendar and so vary every year. During *Ramadan*, the holy month of fasting, people do not eat or drink from dawn to dusk, but nights are filled with activity and eating. At the end of the month is the most celebrated and holy day, *Id-al-Fitr*. Comorians visit, share gifts, and feast all day long. Forty days later, *Id-al-Adha* honors Abraham for his willingness to sacrifice his son. Comorians celebrate Muhammad's birth for a month, and *Maulid*, his actual birthday, is a national holiday.

Commerce

Business hours are 8:00 A.M. to 6:00 P.M., but most offices close at least two hours for lunch. Stores are closed Friday afternoon and Sunday. Asian (Pakistani and Indian) merchants operate on a large commercial scale and have considerable economic influence. Open markets offer produce and meat, and stores have basic supplies; specialty items are only available in larger cities. Store prices are set, but market prices are negotiable. Business is conducted in the home only if the people are well acquainted.

SOCIETY

Government

Comoros is a democratic republic; its constitution combines French and Islamic law. The country's president is chief of state and head of government. The Federal Assembly has 42 seats. More than 20 parties are represented in the legislature and none has a majority. Each island has an appointed governor and each prefecture has an elected prefect. All citizens may vote at age 18.

Economy

Comoros is called the "Perfume Islands" because it is the world's leading exporter of ylang-ylang, the oil base of many French perfumes. Comoros also exports vanilla, cinnamon, and cloves. With the once-valuable world market in these commodities rapidly shrinking, the country finds itself in a difficult situation. There are no factories or other productive industries, although some small businesses have emerged since 1991 to generate more than 3 percent growth. France's 1994 devaluation of the Comorian *franc* (CF) led to panic and instantly higher prices. The economy relies on foreign aid and remittances from Comorians who work abroad. Foreign investment in a hotel resort on Grand Comore has opened tourism as a possible source of revenue. Real gross domestic product per capita is $1,350. However, most people are subsistence farmers and do not earn a wage.

Transportation and Communication

Comoros has few roads, but most are paved. Private, unregulated *bush taxis* connect all villages on each island. Moroni and Mutsamudu have city taxis. Boats ferry passengers and cargo between islands. Air Comoros also connects the islands and flies to Madagascar. Grand Comore's international airport receives traffic from Europe and neighboring countries. Mutsamudu boasts a deepwater port for large ships.

A few private radio stations broadcast in addition to the main government station. The national weekly newspaper, *Al-Watwan*, is found in cities. Private homes rarely have telephones, but each island has public pay phones. All international mail must go through Paris.

Education

The educational system is based on the French model, but it does not function effectively. Schooling is free and every village has an elementary school (*école primaire*), but teachers are poorly trained and often not paid. Only about 30 percent of all students finish elementary school, and even fewer go on to junior high (*collège*). A small number continue to high school (*lycée*) and sit for the graduation exam. There is a teacher-training college but no universities. Formal education is geared toward academics. Because there are no state-funded technical training schools, many youths take apprenticeships with craftsmen instead of going to school.

Health

Malaria is the greatest health problem in Comoros, but diarrhea and intestinal parasites are also common. Although cities and towns have hospitals, basic supplies and equipment are lacking. Patients provide their own medications and food. A new public hospital in Mitsudjé (south of Moroni) does offer better care. The infant mortality rate is 77 per 1,000; life expectancy averages 59 years.

FOR THE TRAVELER

U.S. citizens may enter Comoros with a passport, but they must purchase a visa on arrival. Various vaccinations and measures to protect against malaria are recommended. Drink only bottled water (although Moroni's water supply is considered safe). Wash and peel fruits and vegetables. Dress modestly in light fabrics. Women should cover their knees and tie loose hair; loose hair is equated with loose morals. Visitors enjoy beaches, diving and fishing, and climbing to the Karthala crater. For more information, contact the Comorian Permanent Mission to the United Nations, 336 East 45th Street, Second Floor, New York, NY 10017; phone (212) 972–8010.

A Culturgram *is a product of native commentary and original, expert analysis. Statistics are estimates and information is presented as a matter of opinion. While the editors strive for accuracy and detail, this document should not be considered strictly factual. It is a general introduction to culture, an initial step in building bridges of understanding between peoples. It may not apply to all peoples of the nation. You should therefore consult other sources for more information.*

Arab Republic of
Egypt

A
F
R
I
C
A

Boundary representations not necessarily authoritative.

BACKGROUND

Land and Climate

Covering 386,650 square miles (1,007,258 square kilometers), Egypt is just larger than Texas and New Mexico combined. Most of it is dry and arid desert, spotted with small, inhabited oases. Part of the Sahara Desert is in southwestern Egypt. The Nile River, the longest in Africa, runs north through Egypt into the Mediterranean Sea, providing a fertile delta area and the lifeblood for the country. Before the Aswan Dam was built, this area was subject to seasonal flooding. Now the dam regulates water flow and allows for more predictable crop planting, although it has also caused some environmental problems. Summers are hot and humid, with temperatures reaching 100°F (38°C). Winters are moderate, with lows near 40°F (4°C). Annual rainfall ranges from virtually nothing in the desert to about eight inches in the Nile Delta. In the spring, the *Khamasiin* (a hot, driving, dusty wind) blows.

History

The earliest recorded Egyptian dynasty united the kingdoms of Upper and Lower Egypt around 3110 B.C. Today's Egyptians are proud of the Pharaonic heritage that followed. In 525 B.C., Egypt came under Persian control. Alexander the Great's conquest in 332 B.C. brought Greek rule and culture to Egypt. As one of the first nations visited by Christian missionaries (the apostle Mark), Egypt was Christianized within three centuries and followed a Coptic patriarch. Because of Byzantine religious persecution, Egyptians welcomed the Muslim invasion that began in A.D. 642. By the eighth century, Egypt had become largely Muslim. For centuries, Egypt was ruled by successive Islamic dynasties, including the Ottoman Turks in the 16th century. France's Napoleon invaded in 1798, but Egypt was still associated with the Ottoman Empire until World War I.

France and Britain vied for influence over Egypt throughout the 19th century, during which time Viceroy Muhammad Ali successfully governed and reformed Egypt (1805–48). France and Britain exerted increasing control over Egyptian affairs after the completion of the Suez Canal in 1869, and Britain made Egypt a protectorate in 1914. Although given official independence in 1922, the Egyptians regard 1952 as the beginning of real independence. In that year, a revolution overthrew the British-supported monarchy. Gamal Abdel Nasser ousted the first president of Egypt in 1954 and became a popular and influential leader and statesman. Nasser was responsible for a number of reforms, including universal education, land reform, nationalization of major industries and banks, and Egyptian leadership of the Arab world. He governed until his death in 1970.

During Nasser's tenure, Egypt fought two wars that involved Israel (1956 and 1967). The Sinai Peninsula was taken by Israel in the 1967 war, a crushing blow to Egypt's pride. Upon Nasser's death, his vice president, Anwar el-Sadat, succeeded him. His government orchestrated a war (1973) in which Egypt restored its national honor by crossing the Suez Canal and regaining a foothold in the Sinai. Sadat liberalized economic policy, greatly reduced relations with the

Soviet Union, and signed a peace treaty with Israel (1979) that returned the Sinai to Egypt. In 1981, Sadat was assassinated by Muslim fundamentalists who disagreed with his policies. Vice President Hosni Mubarak succeeded him and became an important leader of moderate Arab nations.

Islamic fundamentalists, led by the Islamic Group, began pressing in 1991 for an Islamic state that shuns Western art, music, literature, and values. Their quest to overthrow the secular state has included pressing the government to restrict freedom of expression, liberal education, and secular law; committing violent acts against Coptic Christians, Western tourists, and government installations; and making assassination attempts. A government crackdown has been harsh, but voters reelected Mubarak to a third presidential term in 1993. Parliamentary elections at the end of 1995 brought a new prime minister, Kamal Ganzoury, to office. His main priority is the economy.

THE PEOPLE

Population

Egypt's population of 60.5 million is growing annually at 2.1 percent. The majority (90 percent) are descendants of both native Egyptians and Arabs that conquered Egypt in the seventh century. The rest of the population is composed of Nubians (southern Egypt), Bedouin nomads, Greeks, Italians, and Syro-Lebanese. Nearly all Egyptians live on the arable land along the Nile River, because the rest of the country is mostly desert. Cairo, the capital, has between 12 and 14 million inhabitants. An exact count is impossible due to migrants, informal residents (up to five million), and other factors. Alexandria claims three-million-plus residents. More than 65 percent of the people are younger than 20 years old. Egypt's Human Development Index (0.613) ranks it 107th out of 174 nations. Adjusted for women, the index (0.453) ranks Egypt 92d out of 130 countries. These figures reflect the disparity between men and women; the latter earn only 8 percent of the nation's income. Egypt has yet to provide most individuals with the resources necessary to direct the course of their lives.

Language

Arabic is the official language in Egypt, although English and French are used in business and education. Written Arabic differs from the standard Egyptian dialect (Cairene) spoken in daily life. Egyptians are enormously proud of Cairene and its rich expressions. They like to use it for wordplay, jokes, clichés, and riddles. Cairene is therefore an integral part of Egyptian culture.

Religion

More than 90 percent of all Egyptians are Sunni Muslims. Islamic philosophy is deeply rooted in the minds, hearts, and behavior of the people. Islamic scripture, the *Qur'an* (Koran), is considered the final, complete word of *Allah*. Muslims accept and revere all major Judeo-Christian prophets from Adam to Jesus, but they proclaim Muhammad to be the last and greatest. Although Egypt is offically a secular state, Islamic principles are very much a part of its laws, business relations, and social customs. The Islamic day of worship is Friday, a day for men to pray at the mosque (as opposed to other days, when they pray at home or at work) and hear a sermon. Women pray at home or in a separate part of the mosque. Islam is practiced every day through dress and dietary codes, prayers, and constant references to *Allah's* will or blessings. Muslims pray five times daily, always facing Makkah, Saudi Arabia. Other religious groups are also found in Egypt, including a significant minority of Coptic Christians (more than seven million), whose religion dates to its separation from Rome in the fifth century.

General Attitudes

Egyptians generally prefer a relaxed and patient life, characterized by the phrase *Ma'alesh*, meaning roughly "Don't worry" or "Never mind." This term is used to dismiss concerns or conflicts that are inevitable or not serious. Both business and leisure activities are governed by the concept of *Insha'allah* (If *Allah* wills), which dominates all aspects of Muslim life. Patience also influences life, as the people view events in an expanded time frame. Egyptians are expressive and emotional. In addition, they are well-known for their marvelous sense of humor, which has helped them endure difficult living conditions with great composure. Part of Egyptian humor is a love for riddles (especially during the month of *Ramadan*), jokes, sarcasm, and wordplay. Egyptians often identify with community groups to the point that personal needs become secondary to those of the group. Generosity goes hand in hand with this sense of community, and homelessness is fairly rare even in crowded Cairo.

Society is engaged in a serious debate over its future course; that is, both secularists and Islamists are battling for the hearts of Egyptians. Secularists desire Egypt to remain a secular state in which multiculturalism, a free press, and diversity can flourish. The Islamists see greater devotion to Islamic principles in schools, government, and the arts as the answer to Egypt's problems with poverty, government corruption, and other social ills. Both sides of the debate have strong followings throughout the country.

Personal Appearance

Dress standards in Egypt follow traditional patterns. In public, most women completely cover their hair and bodies, except their faces and hands. Men wear modest clothing and skullcaps and sometimes grow a beard. A beard can be a sign of religious faith, but it can also express membership in certain political organizations. In large cities, modest Western-style clothing has been popular, although trends toward fundamental Islamic practices have led many women to return to stricter observance of Islamic dress codes. Business representatives wear business suits.

CUSTOMS AND COURTESIES

Greetings

Warmth in personal relations is important to Egyptians, and greetings are often elaborate. Because social classes play a key role in society, phrases used for greetings depend largely on the differences between the individuals' social classes. Generally, however, friends of the same sex shake hands and kiss on the right and left cheeks. If the greeting comes after a long absence, the kisses may be repeated more than once and even end with a kiss on the forehead. A man greets a woman with a handshake only if the woman extends her hand first. Otherwise, the greeting is verbal. One does not use first names unless invited to do so. Good friends exchange first names in informal settings, but they may add a title to the first name in formal settings. To thank someone for a compliment, one responds with an equally respectful compliment on the same subject or wishes *Allah's* blessings.

Gestures

Physical distance between members of the same sex is closer than in the United States and much farther apart between members of the opposite sex. In fact, good friends of the same sex may walk hand in hand in public. Yet, except for married or engaged couples that walk arm in arm, a man does not touch a woman in public. It is impolite for the bottom of one's foot to point at another person, and feet should not be propped on a table or chair in the presence of others. Pointing at a person is impolite, as is walking in front of a praying person.

Visiting

Because personal relationships with friends and relatives are so vital, visiting is one of the most important pastimes in Egypt. Not visiting for a long period is a sign of the relationship's insignificance. Married children often visit parents on Fridays and holidays. One passes and receives gifts with either both hands or only the right hand, not the left. Alcohol is prohibited by the Islamic religion, so it is not given as a gift to a Muslim. Business visits usually begin with light conversation over coffee or tea to establish trust and confidence. Visitors to a mosque remove shoes before entering and wear clothing that covers the entire body.

Eating

Egyptians prepare elaborate and expensive meals when they have guests. Sometimes a person will not eat everything on the plate because leftover food is a symbol of abundance and a compliment to the host for providing so well. Or, in restaurants, food is left as a sign of wealth (one can afford to leave food behind). Egyptians eat finger food with the right hand. When they use Western utensils (mostly in large, urban areas), they eat in the continental style, with the fork in the left hand and the knife remaining in the right.

LIFESTYLE

Family

Families are extremely important in Egypt. In most homes, a young woman is protected by her brothers and may even be accompanied by them in public. Traditionally, a man's honor is based on how well he protects the women in his care. In rural areas, a young woman may discontinue her schooling when she comes of age. It is customary for extended families, including families of brothers and sisters, to live under the same roof. Increased urbanization, however, is changing this tradition toward a home with only a nuclear family. Still, families maintain close ties, and cousins are often as close as siblings. The thought of putting the elderly in a rest home is repulsive to Egyptians; children expect to support their parents in old age. Parents often play a key role in planning the future of their children; their influence ranges from the choice of profession to the selection of a mate. Egyptians value this support as a source of emotional security.

Dating and Marriage

Although attitudes toward dating are changing in Westernized circles, dating is not widespread. Public displays of affection are frowned upon. Moral purity is highly valued in a woman and is usually a key requirement in the marriage contract. Traditionally, marriages were arranged between heads of families, often with little input from the couple involved. Now individuals have more say as to whom they wish to marry. Because marriages join not just two people but two families, both families are heavily involved in wedding preparations. Housing is expensive and hard to acquire, given the large urban population and number of migrants. Therefore, engagements may last until the couple saves enough money for their own apartment.

Diet

Egyptians eat rice, bread, fish, lamb, chicken, turkey, and stuffed vegetables. *Tahina* (sesame seed paste), tomatoes, yogurt, and cucumbers are also eaten with meals. The *Qur'an* prohibits the consumption of pork and alcohol. Traditional foods include flat Egyptian bread and fava beans prepared as *foul* or *ta'miyya*. Meat is expensive and eaten only occasionally, sometimes just once a month. Bread is eaten with every meal.

Recreation

Soccer is the national sport, but sport clubs also offer tennis, swimming, and horseback riding. Many enjoy going to the movies in urban areas; a wide variety of Egyptian and foreign films are shown. In the Middle East, Egypt is well-known for its dedication to cultural arts—evident in its cinema and television programming. Many enjoy watching television, even in rural areas. While the wealthy socialize in private clubs, men of all other classes go to coffee shops for recreation. At a coffee shop, men play table games like backgammon and dominoes, have refreshments, and relax with friends. Many coffee shops cater to specific groups or professions (barbers, plumbers, etc.). Even the smallest village will have at least one coffee shop. Women socialize in the home.

Holidays

The Western (Gregorian) calendar is used for all business and government purposes, but the lunar calendar is used to calculate the dates of Muslim holidays. The lunar year is about 11 days shorter than the Western calendar year, so holidays vary each year. During the month of *Ramadan*, Muslims go without food or drink from sunrise to sundown and eat only in the evening. *'Aid al Fitr* is a three-day feast held at the end of *Ramadan*. Another major religious holiday is *'Aid al Adha* (Feast of the Sacrifice), which commemorates Abraham's willingness to sacrifice his son. The prophet Muhammad's birthday (*al-Mawlid*) is also celebrated. National holidays include Labor Day (1 May), Anniversary of the Revolution (23 July), and Armed Forces Day (6 October). *Sham el-Nasseem* is celebrated at the beginning of spring. The lunar New Year is also an official holiday.

Commerce

Business hours are generally from 8:30 A.M. to 1:30 P.M. and from 4:30 to 7:00 P.M., Saturday through Thursday. Government offices are open from 8:00 A.M. to 3:00 P.M. In the summer, many workers take a longer lunch break because of the heat, then work later in the cool evening. Shops are generally closed on Friday afternoon, but work is not prohibited. Street vendors are common, and people in high-rise apartments will often lower a basket from balconies to purchase something from a passing salesman. Also common are outdoor *souks* (markets), where businesses sell their products. This encourages barter trade. Prices in tourist shops near hotels are fixed. During the month of *Ramadan*, business hours are often cut back by an hour, and work slows down in many areas. However, many shops open again in the evening.

SOCIETY

Government

The Arab Republic of Egypt is divided into 26 governorates. The president is chief of state, and a prime minister is head of government. The legislative branch consists of a 454-seat People's Assembly and a 258-seat *Shura* Council. All but ten representatives in the assembly are elected, but more than eighty council members are appointed by the president. The *Shura* Council acts as a consultative body, so the assembly is the main legislature. Citizens are required to vote at age 18. Mubarak's party (National Democratic Party) dominates the assembly, but some opposition parties and independents also hold seats. Religious-based political parties are banned.

Economy

More than one-third of the people are employed in agricultural pursuits, such as growing corn, wheat, cotton, rice, barley, and fruit. Egypt also produces cheese and dairy products. Chief industries include food processing, textiles, chemicals, cement, petroleum, and metals. Egypt exports cotton, petroleum, yarn, and textiles. Important natural resources are oil, natural gas, lead, and other minerals. The Suez Canal is a vital source of income. Tourism is usually a leading industry, but threats of violence have kept travelers away. The currency is the Egyptian pound (£E).

Egypt's real gross domestic product per capita is $3,540, which has more than tripled in the last generation. In the 1990s, Egypt has made progress with long-term economic reform; this has lowered inflation to less than 5 percent and improved the climate for international investment. However, economic growth was stagnant for 1995. A new government policy in 1996 allowing for more rapid privatization of state-owned enterprises significantly boosted confidence in the economy and opened the way for more rapid growth.

Transportation and Communication

In urban areas, people travel by car, bus, and taxi. Cairo has a modern, efficient subway, the first in the Middle East. Unfortunately, with such a large urban population, the transportation system is still overburdened. Between cities, travel is by train, bus, and even taxi. There is also a domestic airline. In rural areas, a few still travel by donkey and camel. Water taxis use the Nile River. Many improvements have been made in the phone system in recent years. While getting a phone takes a long time and is expensive, the system is efficient; people without phones make calls from a central phone office. There are five main television stations and seven radio networks.

Education

The government subsidizes free education through the university level, although not all are able to take advantage of it. Recent programs aimed at building schools in rural areas have succeeded in bringing some educational opportunities to the poor. The adult literacy rate of 49 percent—lower for women and rural inhabitants, but higher for men and urban youth—will increase significantly in the next generation. Most children who begin primary schooling now also complete it. A significant number go on to secondary school. Universities are located in most urban centers, and nearly half of all students are women. Education is viewed as the key to a better life, and parents will sacrifice much to hire private tutors so their children can excel in school. Parents often measure their personal success by that of their children, and they work their entire lives to provide them with a better life than their own.

Health

Egypt has many excellent doctors, but medical facilities are limited, especially in rural areas. The infant mortality rate is 74 per 1,000 and life expectancy averages about 61 years. A United Nations program sends doctors and volunteers into villages for one-week clinics ("medical caravans") to provide hygiene education (such as how to brush teeth), examine children, dispense medicine, give shots, administer first aid, and teach family planning. The government has expanded this program by establishing a hospital in every small city. Private hospitals for the wealthy are equipped with the latest medical technology.

FOR THE TRAVELER

In addition to valid passports, visas are required to visit Egypt, but they can be obtained on arrival or through the consulate. Bottled or boiled water is recommended. Be wary of unprocessed dairy products and avoid all fruits or vegetables that cannot be peeled or cooked. Eat only well-cooked meat. Do not swim in freshwater ponds or lakes. Typhoid, tetanus, and hepatitis vaccinations are recommended. Dress conservatively in respect for cultural norms. Tipping, or *Baksheesh*, can be important and it is wise to carry plenty of small change to reward personal services. For travel information, contact the Egyptian Tourist Authority, 630 Fifth Avenue, Suite 1706, New York, NY 10111; phone (212) 332–2570. Offices are also located in Los Angeles and Chicago. You may also wish to contact the Egyptian Educational and Cultural Bureau, 1303 New Hampshire Avenue NW, Washington DC 20036; phone (202) 296–3888.

A *Culturgram* is a product of native commentary and original, expert analysis. Statistics are estimates and information is presented as a matter of opinion. While the editors strive for accuracy and detail, this document should not be considered strictly factual. It is a general introduction to culture, an initial step in building bridges of understanding between peoples. It may not apply to all peoples of the nation. You should therefore consult other sources for more information.

MALABO
Luba
Riaba
Bioko

Republic of
Equatorial
Guinea

Mali
Burkina Faso
Niger
Benin
Chad
Guinea
Ivory Coast
Ghana
Nigeria
Sierra Leone
Liberia
Togo
Cameroon
Central African Republic

Equatorial Guinea
Annobón Island

Congo
Gabon
Zaire

Atlantic Ocean

Angola
Namibia
South Africa

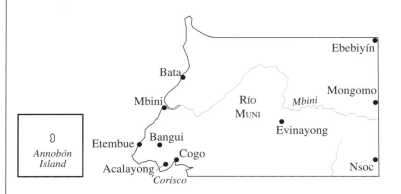

Ebebiyín
Bata
Mbini
RÍO MUNI
Mbini
Mongomo
Evinayong
Etembue
Bangui
Cogo
Acalayong
Corisco
Nsoc

Annobón Island

Boundary representations not necessarily authoritative.

BACKGROUND

Land and Climate

About the size of Maryland, Equatorial Guinea consists of a small continental portion and several small islands. It covers 10,830 square miles (28,050 square kilometers). Río Muni, the continental portion, lies between Gabon and Cameroon on Africa's west coast just north of the equator. The country's largest river, Río Mbini, divides it in half. The largest island, Bioko, is the site of the nation's capital, Malabo. The island is about 19 miles (30 kilometers) from the Cameroon coast, far enough north of Río Muni (about 95 miles or 153 kilometers) to make transportation and communication difficult. Bioko has fertile volcanic soil and a 10,000-foot peak (3,008 meters). Annobón Island lies 370 miles (592 kilometers) southwest of Bioko. The entire country is covered by dense rain forest and has a humid climate. The average temperature is 80°F (27°C). Bioko is generally hotter and wetter than Río Muni.

History

The histories of Bioko and Río Muni are strikingly different. Río Muni remained isolated from contact with the West until the 20th century. The Bubi on Bioko, however, retreated upland as the natural harbor of Malabo changed from Portuguese to Spanish to British and then back to Spanish hands between the late 1400s and early 1900s. During this time, Malabo was primarily a slave-trading center, except during the British occupation of 1827 to 1843. During the first half of the 1900s, Spain developed the infrastructure to support cocoa plantations on the island. Because of that system, Bioko has a relatively high per capita income, a high literacy rate, and better health care.

Conflicting claims to the mainland were settled in the Treaty of Paris (1900), which set the borders for Río Muni and gave it to the Spanish. The lives of the indigenous people of Río Muni were not really affected until the 1920s when Europeans established coffee production there. Río Muni and Bioko were artificially joined by the Spanish as Spanish Guinea.

In 1959, Spanish Guinea was made part of Spain, with all indigenous peoples gaining full citizenship. Representatives were sent to the Parliament in Madrid. In 1963, a measure of autonomy was granted and a joint legislative body was set up. On 12 October 1968, full independence as Equatorial Guinea was granted peacefully, and Francisco Macías Nguema became the first president in a multiparty election.

An attempted coup and an antiwhite incident in Malabo were among events that led to tighter political controls. In 1972, Macías assumed complete control over the government and presidency for life. He deteriorated into a brutal ruler, and all government functions completely eroded except for internal security. The economy existed only due to Spanish, Cuban, Soviet, and Chinese assistance. Under Macías, about one-third of the population was either exiled or executed. Twenty thousand Nigerians left, which greatly disrupted

Bioko's cocoa production, the nation's primary source of income. Churches, banks, and schools ceased to operate.

On 3 August 1979, Teodoro Obiang Nguema Mbasogo, the commander of the national guard and a nephew of Macías, staged a successful coup and Macías was executed after a trial attended by international observers. Obiang Nguema assumed the presidency but also ruled with tight control. The country struggled to overcome the darkest years of trouble. In a single-candidate election in 1989, Obiang Nguema was elected to a seven-year term as president. The country legalized a multiparty system in a new 1992 constitution, but elections were not held until 1996. Opposition parties had posted presidential candidates but withdrew in protest over polling irregularities. Obiang Nguema was therefore reelected to another seven-year term in a landslide victory.

THE PEOPLE

Population

The population is about 420,000 and is growing at 2.6 percent annually. The predominant ethnic group is the Fang (80 percent), whose traditional territory is Río Muni. The Fang, a Bantu people, migrated from what is now southern Sudan over a 250-year period and have inhabited Río Muni and surrounding areas for about 150 years. The traditional territory of the Bubi (15 percent) is the island of Bioko. The Bubi came to Bioko from the shores of Cameroon and Río Muni. Annobón Island is inhabited by Angolan people, brought there by the Portuguese. Eighty percent of Equatoguineans live in rural areas. The country's two largest cities, Malabo and Bata, each have about 40,000 residents.

Equatorial Guinea's Human Development Index (0.399) ranks it 142d out of 174 nations. This reflects the fact that very few people have access to resources that would allow them to pursue personal goals.

Language

Because Equatorial Guinea was colonized by Spain, Spanish is the official language and the primary language of business, government, public schools, and urban life. However, it usually is not spoken in the home. French, spoken in surrounding countries, is increasingly influential and Pidgin English is common in the markets. Local languages prevail in villages, none of which are written. If a transaction requires writing, Spanish is used. However, most traditional transactions do not require writing and people have extensive mental skills for keeping track of such dealings. Fang is spoken in Río Muni, and Bubi is spoken in rural areas of Bioko. Annobónese is spoken on Annobón and Coriscan on the island of Corisco. Ndoe and Kombe are spoken by their respective groups.

Religion

Due to colonization, the population is 83 percent Roman Catholic. While people actively honor the Catholic calendar (celebrating holidays and saints' days), they commonly mix traditional African practices with Western rites. An example is the Fang *defunción*, a three-day celebration to honor the passing of the dead, which occurs four to six months after the death. Clan members may come from all over the country to take part in the traditional dancing and feasting and to hear the *nvet* (a traditional stringed rhythm instrument) player create a bridge to ancestors through his song, which assists the soul's passage to the beyond. Traditional healers continue to play a religious role, and polygamy is accepted among many who profess Catholicism. Other Christian denominations do exist, and some Muslims and Baha'is live in the country as well.

General Attitudes

Equatoguineans are warm, friendly, and generous. Mainlanders generally are known as being more gregarious than islanders. All ethnic groups, however, love a celebration. Village life, in particular, revolves around the celebration of life's passages (birth, marriage, death) and the Catholic calendar.

Generosity is both in the people's nature and part of clan obligation. This provides for a type of social security for the elderly and disabled, but it also makes improvement of an individual's economic situation difficult. One is expected to share gains with the extended family.

Traditional religious beliefs, mixed with Catholicism, focus heavily on the unexplainable and the mysterious. Fate is accepted without question. Equatoguineans highly respect elders, village officials, and political figures. They take pride in the clan, village, and nation.

Personal Appearance

The average person commonly wears secondhand Western clothing, sold at low cost by Christian missionaries or in the market. Dress in urban areas is more formal than in villages. Traditional dress is highly valued but too expensive for most people. Rural people reserve their best colors, fashions, and mended clothing for celebrations and church. Women generally wear dresses rather than pants or shorts, even when working their fields in the rain forest.

CUSTOMS AND COURTESIES

Greetings

Greetings are accompanied by enthusiastic handshaking and sometimes a bit of a bow. People greet each person in a small group. If the hand is dirty, one extends a wrist or forearm. In cities, Spanish greetings such as *¡Buenos días!* (Good day!) and *¡Buenas noches!* (Good evening!) are common. A light kiss on each cheek may be used to greet women.

In villages, handshakes with local greetings are more common. For example, *Mbolo* (Hello) is common on the continent. Rural Fang women often greet each other by joining both forearms to the elbow, bowing slightly at the hips and knees, and issuing a long, low, guttural *sah* (Hello). The Fang, who consider their ethnic group a family, also ask each other where they are going or have been. This custom of keeping track of family members is such a habit that the Fang often ask the question of non-Fang people.

In cities, the use of titles and proper honorifics is important when addressing someone. People commonly use *Señor* (Mr.), *Señora* (Ms. or Mrs.), or an official title with a person's last name. Respected older people may be addressed as *Don* or *Doña* with their first name. Rural people use first names, which often have a Spanish origin, or African nicknames when addressing one another.

Gestures

People use hand gestures during conversation and for many of life's situations. For example, the hands pressed together in prayer position and opened up as if empty can mean anything from "nothing left" to "such is life." Drawing the fingers closed with the palm facing down indicates "come here." In Fang, *ka* means "no" and is often accompanied by a finger wagging back and forth close to the face. People stand close to one another, often touching while they talk. Holding hands or locking arms while talking or walking is common for men and children. Such physical contact is not appropriate for members of the opposite sex. Even husbands and wives do not display affection in public.

Visiting

Equatoguineans are very social, and visiting is an important way to establish and maintain social contacts. A visit is considered a gift in itself, but people might also take fruit or bread to their hosts. Visits are usually returned. People drop by unannounced in villages but might make prior arrangements in the cities. Arranged visits rarely begin on time, as the concept of time is more flexible than in the West. Hosts may offer visitors offered water, beer (in the city), *tope* (palm wine), *malamba* (cane alcohol), or a meal. Although one may refuse refreshments, it is polite to at least taste some of the food offered. However, since Equatoguineans often have personal taboos concerning a particular food, hosts are not offended by a refusal to eat a certain item.

When one enters a village, it is polite to visit the *abaa*, a hut made of bamboo and palm leaves, and greet the elderly men who socialize there and work on crafts.

Eating

Urban people tend to follow Spanish eating customs, with a light breakfast of coffee or tea and bread, a main meal at midday, and a light dinner between 8:00 and 10:00 P.M. In rural areas, people often eat only a light mid-morning meal and supper just before dusk. When invited for dinner among the Fang, guests might eat alone in a reception room reserved for the male head of household, or senior male family members may eat with the guests. Women serve the meal and then eat in the kitchen with the children.

People use western utensils for most meals. Only in very informal settings do they eat food with the hands. Then, even peanut pastes and sauces, bundled in banana leaves and tied with melango fiber, become finger foods. It is improper to drink from a common container; therefore, when glasses are not available, individuals pick an appropriate type of leaf and form a leaf cup.

LIFESTYLE

Family

As in much of Africa, polygamous extended family structures still dominate rural life, while nuclear families are more common in cities. "The family" actually refers to the entire clan, which once also implied a village. The power structure revolves around gender, age, and clan status. This system leaves women with limited power, although they do control the production of food. Each wife in an extended family has her own kitchen (used for both sleeping and cooking) or her own cooking-fire area, where she is the authority figure. The kitchen is the center of family life. The husband has his own building, and wives take turns spending time with him there. Wives also share child care and household chores.

Cousins are considered siblings; aunts and uncles are considered mothers and fathers. Children must obey their elders, even older siblings, but especially their various mothers and fathers. It is not uncommon for children to be sent to live with other family members. Large families are prized as a sign of wealth, health, and virility; having six or more children is common. Women grow the food, cook, clean, serve, haul water and firewood, and raise the children. Men are responsible for hunting, building and maintaining houses, making tools and baskets, and clearing the *fincas* (agricultural plots in the forest) twice a year.

Dating and Marriage

Young urban people like to date by going to late-night discos. Young rural people more commonly meet at large celebrations that involve other clans, but discos are becoming popular for them as well. Many marriages are still arranged. When two people marry, a three-day wedding celebration of dancing and feasting marks the woman's acceptance into her husband's clan. This celebration is preceded by negotiations between the two families on the bride-price (paid to the bride's family), which can be extremely high. Because of the expense, young people often enter into a common-law relationship and begin having children before they are actually married. Any children born before the wedding technically belong to the woman's father, but the groom can take the children when he pays the bride-price and formally marries. In the rare case of divorce, the bride-price must be returned to the husband, who retains the children, while the woman returns to her family.

Diet

Cassava and other starchy roots, which adapt well to rain forest agriculture, are the main staple foods. Fermented cassava (*yuca* in Spanish, *mbo* in Fang) sticks are eaten with nearly every meal. Meat is the preferred source of protein when available and may include anything from goats and chickens to rodents, monkeys, and snakes. Fish is also a traditional favorite. Peanuts, another staple, are prepared in many different ways, such as peppery leaf-roasted rolls, peanut brittle, or sauce. A favorite dish is ground squash seeds made into a curd similar to tofu. Papayas, pineapples, bananas, and plantains are abundant. The cities are more influenced by Spanish cuisine and have access to seafood, bread, and pasta.

Recreation

Social visiting is a primary leisure activity. *Voy a pasear* (I am going visiting) is a common weekend pastime. Drumming, dancing, and singing surround holidays and family events. Soccer is the only group sport, but it is very popular and every village has a soccer field. A traditional strategy board game is played with rocks and seeds. Bata and Malabo have cultural centers, sponsored by the French and the Spanish, where art exhibits and occasional music and theater performances occur.

Holidays

National holidays include New Year's Day (1 January), Easter (including Good Friday), Labor Day (1 May), Corpus Christi, the President's Birthday (5 June), Armed Forces Day (3 August), Constitution Day (15 August), Independence Day (12 October), Immaculate Conception Day (8 December), and Christmas (25 December). Easter is the most important holiday, with a week of celebrations from Palm Sunday to Easter Sunday. Independence Day is marked by large gatherings, singing, and food.

Commerce

Generally, hours for businesses, banks, and government offices are 7:30 A.M. to 2:30 P.M. Stores operate from 8:00 A.M. to 1:00 P.M. and from 4:00 to 7:00 P.M. Even in the open-air market, bargaining is uncommon. In rural areas, traditional patterns such as clan obligations have a substantial impact on business negotiations.

SOCIETY

Government

The country is a unitary republic. The constitution provides the president with extensive powers; he is commander in chief of the military and minister of defense. He also appoints all cabinet members. The unicameral House of Representatives of the People has 60 representatives. Fifteen are appointed by the president and the rest are elected. Major opposition parties include the Social Democratic Popular Coalition (CSDP), Progress Party (PP), Popular Union (UP), and others. Each of the seven provinces has a governor appointed by the president. When not in conflict with constitutional law, tribal laws and customs usually are honored by the judicial system.

Economy

Most people (90 percent) are engaged in subsistence agriculture. The main exports are cocoa beans, timber, and coffee. Cocoa production, which dropped in the Macías years, is now beginning to revive, but it is still well below capacity. Conversion in 1985 to the *CFA franc*, which is a hard currency tied to the French *franc*, provided a much needed stepping-stone out of isolation. Timber harvesting is increasingly relied upon to attract foreign capital. Most timber is shipped out as raw logs, however, with very little manufacturing taking place in Equatorial Guinea. Some success has been achieved with petroleum production, and major international firms announced in 1996 they would begin offshore drilling soon. The potential for increased trade with neighboring countries exists for local food crops such as cassava, taro, pineapples, and coconuts. Spain is the main trading partner. Real gross domestic product per capita is estimated to be $700. Two-thirds of all people live in poverty. Most people either do not earn an income as subsistence farmers or their income is insufficient for their basic needs. Nevertheless, economic growth for 1994 was more than 7 percent, and new jobs may be created in the petroleum and logging industries.

Transportation and Communication

For common people, the accepted mode of transportation is walking. Few can afford bicycles. *Bush-taxis*, which are privately owned cars for hire, are the only transportation to rural areas. They collect passengers at the market and leave when full; there are no schedules. For many, a ride in a *bush-taxi* is a special event for which to save. There are two or three weekly flights between Bata and Malabo, as well as out of the country. There is also a weekly flight to Spain.

A radio-phone system connects district capitals, but people otherwise do not have access to telephones. There is one government-owned television and radio station. There are no national or private newspapers or magazines.

Education

While the majority of all children attend primary school, only about 11 percent are enrolled in secondary schools. Malabo offers an academically oriented agricultural vocational school. Bata has a post-secondary vocational program that offers courses in agriculture, metalworking, and carpentry, but placement is limited. The Catholic Church has made important contributions to primary and secondary education, as well as to health. About half of the population is literate.

Health

The population's primary health problems are malaria, diarrhea (among young children), and intestinal parasites. Availability of Western health resources is generally poor, with very few doctors and clinics. In most parts of the country, people still rely on traditional tribal medicine to provide effective care for many health problems. The infant mortality rate is about 100 per 1,000; life expectancy averages 53 years.

FOR THE TRAVELER

U.S. visitors need a valid passport and visa to enter Equatorial Guinea. Visas are easiest to obtain at the embassy in Douala, Cameroon. As health care is unavailable, visitors should arrive in good health. Malaria prophylactics are necessary and some vaccinations are required. Contact your county health office for information, or call the U.S. Centers for Disease Control and Prevention International Travel Hotline at (404) 332–4559. Water is not safe to drink, and fruits and vegetables should be peeled or cooked before being eaten. Do not swim in freshwater ponds or lakes due to the presence of bilharzia. Running water and electricity are available daily on a limited basis in Malabo and Bata. Declare any cash in excess of $40 upon arrival to avoid forfeiting it upon departure. Registration with the U.S. embassy in Cameroon is advised; the embassy in Equatorial Guinea closed in November 1995. For additional information, contact the Equatorial Guinea Embassy, 1511 K Street NW, Suite 405, Washington, DC 20005; phone (202) 393–0525.

CULTURGRAM '97™

State of
Eritrea

Boundary representations not necessarily authoritative.

BACKGROUND

Land and Climate

Eritrea sits on the Horn of Africa bordering the Red Sea. It consists of the mainland and the Dahlak Archipelago. Covering 46,842 square miles (121,320 square kilometers), it is a bit larger than Pennsylvania. Central highlands rise to an elevation of more than 8,000 feet (2,500 meters) near the east coast, forming an escarpment of the Great Rift Valley. Western elevations are lower. The hot Danakil Depression lies below sea level.

The semiarid highland climate is mild and dry; temperatures rarely fall to freezing. Precipitation in the rainy season (June–September) varies by elevation and is not always dependable. Dry conditions have cut crop production in recent years. Rain falls between October and February on foothills and lowlands east of the northern escarpment. This allows for an extra growing season. Given a history of recurring drought in some areas, officials expect sustainable agriculture to be possible only with proper irrigation.

History

Eritrea's original inhabitants were joined successively by people from the Nile River area and by Egyptians, Cushites, and Semites. The region was later influenced by Greeks, Turks, Egyptians, and Persians. The name *Eritrea* comes from the Greek *erythrea* (red).

After 1885, Italy colonized the region, establishing some industries and confiscating arable land. Asmara, the colonial and current capital, still displays a distinct Italian influence. Italian forces pressed south and eventually conquered Ethiopia in 1935. Ethiopia's Emperor Haile Selassie I requested intervention from the League of Nations. In response, the Allied Powers of World War II eventually halted Italy's advances and forced its surrender at Asmara in 1941.

Britain then governed Eritrea as a protectorate until 1952, when the United Nations–recommended federation with Ethiopia took place. Ethiopia moved to assert greater control over Eritrea by annexing it as a province in 1962. The Eritrean Liberation Front organized initial resistance, and the Eritrean People's Liberation Front (EPLF) later led the movement. After Haile Selassie I was deposed in Ethiopia by Marxists in 1974, the liberation movement gained popularity. Over the next two decades, the EPLF steadily captured territory as it received financial support from Eritreans outside the country and as it took arms and vehicles from the Ethiopian army. Over time, the EPLF set up schools, industries, and a hospital. By 1990, it occupied the strategic port of Massawa.

Ethiopia's Marxist dictator, Mengistu Haile-Mariam, was opposed by many ethnic groups and, by 1990, had lost support from former Communist countries. When he was about to flee, the EPLF took Asmara on 24 May 1991, forcing the Ethiopian army to abandon Eritrea. In an April 1993 referendum, 98 percent of all Eritreans voted for independence, which was declared 24 May 1993. Eritrea quickly joined the United Nations and other organizations and established diplomatic ties with many countries. In July 1993, Ethiopia (under a new government) and Eritrea signed an Agreement of Friendship and Cooperation to establish good relations and grant Ethiopia access to the Red Sea.

Eritreans were soon working to repair war-damaged institutions, feed the hungry, establish a free-market economy, and draft a new constitution. By 1996, Eritrea was being billed as an African phenomenon because of enormous strides in revitalizing the economy, cleaning up cities, cracking down on crime, and establishing a democratic society. The accomplishments are most noteworthy because of the general lack of Western aid or skill that is involved.

PEOPLE

Population

Of Eritrea's 3.5 million people, the vast majority (85 percent) live in rural areas. The largest ethnic groups are the highland Tigrinya (50 percent) and the Tigre (33 percent) of both highland and lowland areas. The remaining population is composed of Saho, Bilen, Afar, Hadareb, Kunama, Nara, and Rashaida minorities. Asmara's population is 400,000.

The population figure includes more than half a million Eritreans who fled during the war. Nearly two-thirds are returning from Sudan refugee camps. Of those living abroad, many are waiting for housing and jobs before they return.

Language

Eritrea has no official language. Tigrinya, Arabic, and English are all government working languages. Tigrinya is spoken by highlanders and is closely related to Tigre, spoken in the western and eastern lowlands. Tigrinya and Tigre use an ancient Ge'ez script. Like Arabic, they are both Semitic tongues. Arabic, native to the Rashaida, is widely used in commerce. Minority groups speak their native languages but are familiar with Tigrinya or Arabic. Except for the Rashaida and Hadareb (whose language is called To Bedawi), the language name is the same as the ethnic group name.

Religion

Some Eritreans follow traditional practices usually classified as animism, but nearly equal portions (roughly 40 percent each) follow Islam and Christianity. Although Roman Catholics and Protestants are found among the more affluent and Westernized Eritreans, most Christians are Orthodox. The Eritrean Orthodox Church has its own bishop but maintains ties to Ethiopian Orthodox Church. The church is conservative, uses the Ge'ez language, and incorporates both monks and married priests in its clergy.

Whereas most Christians reside in the highlands, Sunni Muslims tend to inhabit the lowlands. They include nearly all of the Saho, Nara, and Rashaida, as well as many Tigre and Kunama. During the war, fighters (30 percent were women) of different religions often married. These intermarriages and the unity of religious leaders in a common cause are factors in the country's religious freedom and tolerance. By law, neither religion nor ethnicity can be the basis of a political party.

General Attitudes

Eritreans are optimistic, hardworking, committed people who love their country and their independence. They are grateful to the EPLF, whose leaders genuinely want to maintain the respect it worked to establish for cooperative effort, manual labor, equality among ethnic groups, and equal participation by women. People are well disciplined. Whereas crime is often a major problem for societies in transition, it is almost nonexistent in Eritrea. Eritreans believe in self-sufficiency, community cooperation, and friendliness. They are aware of challenges they face in building a nation anew, but despite poverty and other hardships, they are confident they can succeed.

Personal Appearance

Eritreans have dark skin, black curly hair, and narrow facial features. Western-style clothing is popular in urban areas, with even girls and women often wearing trousers. Rural dress is more traditional. Highland Christian women wear white cotton dresses with a woven border at the hem, or embroidery on the bodice and skirt, and a shawl with a matching border. Their hair is customarily braided in tight, narrow rows up front, but is left free and fluffy behind. Highland men wear a long-sleeved, knee-length white shirt over white trousers. They also wear white cotton shawls with colored borders. Work clothing or "daily dress" is less decorated and is made of heavy, off-white cotton.

Muslim men wear *jalabiyas* (long gowns) and embroidered caps with turbans. Women usually cover their dresses with black or colorful cloth called *luiet*. The cloth can be loosely draped or sewn to be more tailored. Some Muslim women wear veils that cover all but their eyes. Throughout Eritrea, women use henna as a skin conditioner, hair tint, or dye to decorate their hands and feet.

CUSTOMS AND COURTESIES

Greetings

Greeting styles vary by region and ethnic group. Highlanders greet with a handshake. Nudging right shoulders at the same time is common between male former fighters and villagers. Urban dwellers (opposite or same sex, relatives, and acquaintances) shake hands and kiss the air while brushing alternate cheeks three times. Verbal greetings depend on the time of day but nearly always involve an inquiry about well-being. *Salaam* (Peace) is a general greeting or leave-taking phrase. Muslims grasp and kiss each other's right hands, ask *Kefelhal?* (How are you?), and answer *Hamdellah* or *Marhaba* (both roughly mean "Fine").

Friends call one another by nickname. Eritreans address older people by title (equivalents of "Mr.," "Mrs.," "Miss," "Aunt," "Uncle") and name. They use professional titles in formal situations. The use of second-person plural shows respect. A person's given name is followed by the father's name, so that Mhret, the daughter of Tesfai, is called *Mhret Tesfai*.

Gestures

Eritreans use the right hand for eating and making gestures. They also use it alone or together with the left hand to pass or receive items. A hand held high is a greeting, whereas a hand waved back and forth indicates a negative response. Snapping fingers shows agreement. To beckon, one waves all fingers with the palm facing out. Pointing with a finger to indicate location is fine, but pointing at people is impolite. In discussion, old men often gesture with their fly whisks to emphasize a point or indicate direction. Seated girls keep their legs uncrossed—knees touching and covered—with elbows on their knees as a sign of respect.

Visiting

Relatives and good friends visit each other often and without invitation. Guests may be offered food or asked to join the family for an upcoming meal, which they may accept or politely decline. They are always served tea or coffee. The latter involves a prescribed sequence of roasting and pounding the coffee beans. The coffee is then boiled, heavily sweetened, and served in small cups. Three customary rounds might be accompanied by fresh popcorn. People enjoy the prolonged conversation encouraged by this coffee ceremony.

When visiting on special occasions, townspeople often take villagers gifts of coffee or sugar; villagers take urban dwellers local produce or food (such as bread), a chicken, or firewood (which is precious due to soil erosion and deforestation).

Special events require invitation and involve women and men socializing separately. Wedding guests take *ingera* (sour bread) for the feast or they contribute its cost. *Ga'at*, a thick barley porridge, is served at gatherings to welcome new babies. When someone dies, friends and relatives gather for the burial. For at least 12 days, they attend the bereaved family, cook their meals, divert their attention with games and entertainment, help receive many visitors, and collect money for the family.

Eating

Among highlanders, adults and children eat separately. Among other Eritreans, families eat together, although children eat separately when guests are present. In such cases, the hostess serves the guests and eats later with the children.

To begin each meal, the oldest man takes a piece of bread, blesses it, and offers some to each person. Diners eat with the right hand from a large communal tray set on a low table. Each person eats only the portion directly in front of him or her. In Christian homes, mealtime etiquette is stressed because heaven is watching. Restaurants offer traditional and Italian foods. Tipping is common only in hotel restaurants.

LIFESTYLE

Family

The family is more important than any of its individual members, who will sacrifice as necessary for the good of the group or for future generations. A family unit typically consists of parents, four or more children, and frequently grandparents. Respected for their wisdom, the elderly are always cared for by adult children. After marriage, a son and his wife usually live with his parents for at least two years before establishing their own home.

Village men are farmers. Women work on the farm and do all household work. Chores, especially food preparation, can be lengthy. Some urban women work outside the home and employ house servants.

Village homes, usually made of stone, have thatched or metal roofs and concrete or dirt floors. City dwellings, made of stone or brick, have metal roofs, tiled floors, and water and electricity. Nomadic and seminomadic peoples (Afar, Hadareb, Rashaida, and Tigre) have different lifestyles than the settled population. Accordingly, their homes are portable or built with whatever materials they find when they settle temporarily. Regardless of the style, homes are kept clean and neat.

Dating and Marriage

In Eritrea, nearly all marriages are arranged by families. Among the monogamous Tigrinya, parents suggest marriage partners to establish family alliances. The couple involved usually makes the final decision to marry, although some rural couples may not be acquainted before they wed. The bride is often some ten years younger than the groom; in cities she will have completed secondary school before getting married.

The wedding celebration involves at least a week's food preparation and requires a month to brew *suwa*, a beer, and *miyess*, a honey mead. Both families provide banquets following the morning church ceremony. After a display of gifts, the couple enters the banquet to share a meal with their attendants. Some urban couples also cut a tiered wedding cake. For two or three weeks, the couple stays at home while relatives provide their meals.

Among Muslims, wedding festivities include the bride's arrival on a camel and a feast where guests sit on floor mats to eat from bowls. Muslim men may have up to four wives if they can provide for each equally. Due to the economic burden, this practice is diminishing.

Diet

Eritreans traditionally enjoy a wide variety of foods, but culinary skills and food levels are not yet what they were before the war. The preferred meal is meat (chicken, goat or sheep mutton, or beef) cooked with onion, garlic, red pepper, spices, and clarified butter. *Shuro*, a typical meal of garbanzo bean flour and spices, is similarly cooked. Lentils or other vegetables are served. Spicy main dishes, eaten for lunch or dinner, are complemented by *ingera* (also called *taitah*), a sour pancake bread made of *teff* (a local grain), millet, or corn flour fermented in water. Breakfast may be tea served with honey and unleavened *k'itcha* bread, bits of bread (*fit fit*) and yogurt, *ga'at* (porridge) and yogurt, or leftovers.

Orthodox Christians eat no animal products on Wednesdays and Fridays and during Lent. Muslims abstain from pork and alcohol.

Recreation

Whole families participate in annual church festivals, make social visits, and help relatives prepare food for weddings or babies' baptisms. Urban dwellers often return to their home villages for such celebrations.

In Asmara, espresso coffee bars are popular meeting spots, especially for men. Villages have tea shops. Women visit mostly in each other's homes. They also get together to weave baskets used to store and serve food.

Boys enjoy soccer, bicycle racing, a game similar to field hockey, and another game that is like horseshoes but uses stones. Boys and girls play *gebetta*, a strategy game played with pebbles on a playing surface they create by making depressions in the ground. Girls enjoy drumming and dancing.

Holidays

Eritrea's holidays include New Year's Day (1 January), International Women's Day (8 March), Independence Day (24 May), Martyr's Day (20 June), and the Anniversary of the Start of the Armed Struggle (1 September). Christian holidays include Christmas (7 January); *Timket*, the baptism of Jesus, also in January; *Fasika (*Easter); and *Meskel*, the finding of the true cross by St. Helena, in late September.

Muslims celebrate *Eid el Fitr* at the end of *Ramadan*, the holy month of fasting in which they go without food and drink each day from dawn to dusk. Forty days later, they observe *Eid el Adha* to mark the completion of the pilgrimage to Makkah, Saudi Arabia, and to honor Abraham for his willingness to sacrifice his son. *Eid Milad el-Nabi* honors the prophet Muhammad.

Commerce

Government offices and businesses are open weekdays, 8:00 A.M. to 5:00 P.M., with a two-hour closing for lunch. Most are also open Saturday morning. Shops and markets are open mornings and late afternoons. Bargaining is officially discouraged in favor of posted prices. Before people conduct office business, they converse socially for several minutes.

SOCIETY

Government

After independence, the EPLF installed the Provisional Government of Eritrea (PGE). In 1997, elections will determine the successive government.

In 1994, the EPLF separated from the PGE and became a political party, the People's Front for Democracy and Justice (PFDJ). Mandated until 1997, the provisional government consists of legislative, executive, and judical bodies. The National Assembly has the highest legal power. It consists of the PFDJ's 75-member Central Committee and 28 members nominated from the ten provinces that existed before 1995, when they were reorganized into six regions. The assembly outlines and regulates policy, approves the government budget and ministerial appointments, and elects a president to be head of government and commander-in-chief of the army. President Issaias Afwerki has 30 cabinet ministers. When the legislature is not in session, the president holds the highest legal authority. The judiciary functions independently.

In late 1996, a constitution will be adopted that guarantees basic personal rights and sets forth a multiparty democracy. It is being drafted by an appointed commission that is consulting extensively with Eritreans from villages, cities, and expatriate communities all over the world.

Economy

Eritrea, though poor, has great economic potential. Statistics are not yet available for many economic indicators, but per capita income is estimated to be about $150. Eighty percent of all people depend on subsistence agriculture for their living. Rural food levels are often inadequate. The government is trying to develop long-term solutions to poverty. Solar and other technology is being explored as an alternative to wood and charcoal. A steel plant makes steel with melted down tanks. Eritreans are building their own roads rather than having foreign firms do it. And people are being patient while they wait for jobs and better incomes. Even the president does not receive his actual salary.

A liberal investment code has allowed foreign investment to steadily increase. Private enterprise is beginning to flourish. Industries once nationalized by Ethiopia are being privatized and new ones are opening. Eritrea's potentially most productive economic sectors include tourism, thanks to a long coastline; marine resources, including fishing and petroleum; trade, as Eritrea is situated on the world's busiest shipping lane; and mining for gold, copper, silver, marble, potash, and iron ore. Current exports include sesame seeds, gum arabic, leather shoes, beer, and refined petroleum. The currency is the Ethiopian *birr*, but a national currency is expected.

Transportation and Communication

Major roads crossing the country are under repair; most city streets are paved, while country roads are not. Public buses serve even remote villages and are the most common transport within cities. Taxis are available. Telephones are used mostly by government and business offices. Public phones are found at central urban locations. The government administers the postal system and provides radio and television broadcasts. It also prints weekly English and semiweekly Arabic and Tigrinya newspapers.

Education

Because of the war's destruction, few children (about 100,000) are presently attending school. Of those who do attend, 23 percent finish grade six and only 6 percent complete all 11 years. The literacy rate is 20 percent. Nevertheless, education is highly valued in Eritrea. The national goal is to have mandatory free education up to seventh grade that will emphasize skills needed to develop rural areas. To that end, schools are under repair or construction, teachers are in training, and instructional materials are in development. For the first several years, students are taught in their native tongue but can study English and Arabic or Tigrinya. From the sixth grade on, instruction is in English. Adult literacy and education classes are available for adults who wish to finish elementary and secondary school.

Health

Maternity and child care are high priorities of the Primary Health Care Programme (PHCP) because more than 21 percent of Eritreans are women of childbearing age, 18 percent are children under age five, and the population is growing at 3 percent. The infant mortality rate is 121 per 1,000. Common health problems include malnutrition, malaria, parasitic and upper respiratory infections, diarrhea, and other diseases. The PHCP plans extensive education in preventing disease and malnutrition.

Currently, comprehensive medical services are centralized in a few hospitals. The plan is to have a hospital in each of the eight provinces, with health-care centers at the sub-provincial, district, and village levels. By 1993, more than 30 clinics were under construction. Doctors and nurses are in short supply, but by 1994 the PHCP had trained and posted nearly 1,500 health workers to various communities. In 1995, the University of Asmara opened the College of Health Sciences to train nurses.

FOR THE TRAVELER

U.S. citizens need a passport and visa to visit Eritrea. A yellow fever vaccination certificate is also required. Travelers enjoy the mild climate, people's enthusiasm for building their country, and numerous historical sites. Accommodations range from first-class hotels to small *pensiones*. Modest clothing is a must (no shorts or sleeveless dresses). Water is purified, but underground pipes are unreliable, so visitors should treat their drinking water. For more information, contact the Embassy of Eritrea, 1708 New Hampshire Avenue NW, Washington DC 20009; phone (202) 319–1991.

A *Culturgram* is a product of native commentary and original, expert analysis. Statistics are estimates and information is presented as a matter of opinion. While the editors strive for accuracy and detail, this document should not be considered strictly factual. It is a general introduction to culture, an initial step in building bridges of understanding between peoples. It may not apply to all peoples of the nation. You should therefore consult other sources for more information.

Federal Democratic Republic of

Ethiopia

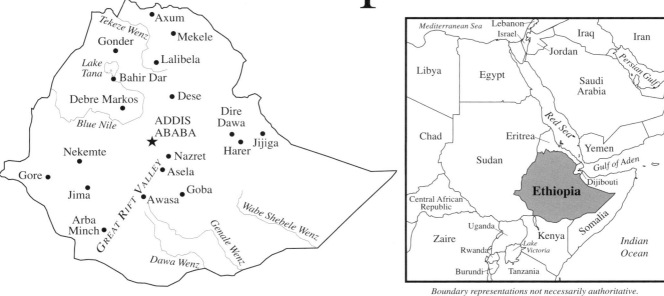

Boundary representations not necessarily authoritative.

BACKGROUND

Land and Climate

Ethiopia, a landlocked country on the Horn of Africa, covers 435,184 square miles (1,127,127 square kilometers). It has access to the Red Sea through Eritrea's southern port at Aseb. Ethiopia has a variety of climates and terrains. The Great Rift Valley, which is subject to earthquakes, separates the northwest highlands from the southeast mountains. Addis Ababa, at 8,000 feet (2,400 meters), has a moderate climate. Most lakes are situated along the Great Rift Valley. The largest, Lake Tana, is the source of the Blue Nile. Many rivers originating in Ethiopia flow to neighboring countries.

In western lowlands, the hottest days average 95°F (35°C), but can rise to 120°F (49°C). Temperatures in the highlands average between 60°F (16°C) and 74°F (23°C). The rainy season is from mid-June to mid-September in the highlands, and the period from October to February is extremely dry. Rainfall varies widely from year to year, a factor that causes extreme problems for agriculture and animal husbandry, the two main sources of sustenance for Ethiopians.

History

Ethiopia is the oldest independent country in Africa. For centuries, the coast (now part of Eritrea) was important to regional trade. Legend has it that Ethiopian monarchs are descendants of Solomon and the Queen of Sheba.

By far, the most important period of consolidation was the Kingdom of Axum in the first through seventh centuries A.D.

A strong monarchy established in this era lasted until a 1974 Marxist coup. During the Axum period, the monarchy and most people embraced Orthodox Christianity. In following centuries, Ethiopia had periodic contact with Western nations, who were intrigued to find Christianity in Africa. Islam began to have influence in the 17th century.

Around 1885, Italy colonized the coast and tried to move inland. They were defeated at Adwa in 1896 by the Ethiopian army under Emperor Menilek II. That victory spared Ethiopia further aggression until the 1930s. Mussolini's Italian Army invaded and occupied Ethiopia from 1935 to 1941, when the British helped exiled emperor, Haile Selassie, regain control. He had been Ras Tafari Makonnen, regent to the Empress Zauditu (daughter of Menilek II) during the 1920s. He gained power and took the throne from the empress, declaring himself Emperor Haile Selassie. After his return in 1941, he ruled autocratically. General economic and political unrest led to his fall in 1974; when he died a year later, a socialist state was proclaimed. The country was named the People's Democratic Republic of Ethiopia.

Mengistu Haile Mariam came to power in 1977 as leader of the provisional government. A 1987 constitution established a national assembly, which elected Mengistu president. He ruled as a dictator. Mengistu faced several problems, including an ongoing civil war (that began 1961) with the Eritrean People's Liberation Front (EPLF), which sought Eritrea's independence. Other ethnic groups were also fighting for control of the government. Famine in the 1980s became all the more difficult to deal with because of the fighting and the Marxist economy.

An attempted 1989 coup prompted Mengistu to announce economic reforms in 1990, but rebel groups were not satisfied. Fighting intensified in 1991 and Mengistu left the country. An assault on the capital by the Ethiopian People's Revolutionary Democratic Front (EPRDF) led to the government's collapse. At the same time, the EPLF took control of Eritrea and eventually (1993) formed an internationally recognized independent country. Eritrea granted Ethiopia access to the sea, and the two nations established peaceful relations.

The new Ethiopian leader, Meles Zenawi of EPRDF, set up a provisional government to sponsor fair elections with all ethnic groups represented for the first time in history. A 1994 elected constituent assembly revised a draft constitution put forth by Meles. The constitution was ratified and full national multiparty elections were held in May 1995. Several parties posted candidates, although many boycotted the polling, protesting EPRDF's domination of the electoral process. Nevertheless, Meles won a parliamentary seat in a landslide victory. As leader of the majority party, he became the new prime minister. Ethiopia became the Ethiopian Federal Democratic Republic. The country's focus since that time has been to establish a democratic society, repatriate thousands of refugees stranded in Sudan, and develop a viable economy.

THE PEOPLE

Population

Ethiopia's population of 55.9 million is growing at 3.1 percent a year. The Amhara of the northwest account for about 25 percent of the population, and they were politically dominant for many years. The Tigreans in the north comprise almost 12 percent of the population. The Oromo (40 percent) live in central Ethiopia, while the Somali (6 percent) live in the southeast. Other larger groups include the Sidamo (9 percent), Shangul (6), Afar (4), Guraghe, and Walyta. At least another 65 smaller ethnic groups live in Ethiopia.

Historical tensions between various ethnic groups remain a problem, with small guerrilla movements still fighting for separation. Some groups oppose the government's demarcation of state boundaries based on ethnic majorities. These factors contribute to a difficulty leaders are having in creating unity or encouraging a shared identity among people as Ethiopians.

Addis Ababa, the capital, has 1.4 million residents. Most (85 percent) live in rural areas. Ethiopia's growth rate is subject to periodic famines. The country's Human Development Index (0.207) ranks it 171st out of 174 nations. This reflects the fact that nearly all Ethiopians (95 percent) are subsistence farmers with little or no access to the resources necessary to pursue personal goals beyond feeding and clothing a family.

Language

Amharic, a Semitic language related to Hebrew and Arabic, is the official national language and is used in commerce and administration. It and Tigrinya are written in a Sabian script. Oromifaa, written in a Latin script, joins Amharic and Tigrinya as a widely spoken language. Guaraginga, Somali, Arabic and more than 80 other tongues are spoken in Ethiopia. With dialects, the figure rises to more than two hundred. No one language is spoken by a majority of people. Rural people often speak only their own ethnic tongue. Residents of towns and cities might speak two or three.

Ge'ez is the language of the Ethiopian Orthodox Church and is used in prayers and worship. A Sabian language of Semitic origin, its significance diminished in the 20th century, but Ge'ez is still used by clerics and sometimes taught in church schools. English is taught in secondary schools, making it the most widely understood foreign language.

Religion

About 45 percent of the population belongs to the Ethiopian Orthodox Church, a leading influence in the culture since the fourth century. Indeed, Ethiopian Christians stress that, while Christianity was introduced by European colonizers in other African countries, it was adopted by Ethiopian rulers in A.D. 332—before many Western nations were exposed to it. Ethiopian Orthodox doctrine is most similar to Roman Catholicism in its emphasis on celebrating mass, reverencing icons and patron saints, and following other traditions. Some living in the Axum Tsion area claim that the Biblical Lost Ark of the Covenant is in their hands, but they have not permitted anyone to see it. The average Ethiopian has little knowledge of this Lost Ark, but there are many arks of covenant (called *tabots*) in the country's various churches. During religious holidays, arks in the region are gathered together for a celebration. There are feast days in each month when certain saints, angels, and religious fathers are remembered by those Christians who have chosen them as patrons.

Christianity's legacy can be seen in many ancient structures, including 11 churches in Lalibela carved from stone in the 12th and 13th centuries. Muslims account for 40 percent of the population, mostly among the Oromo. Much of the remaining population follows traditional religious beliefs that stress a reverence for all living things.

General Attitudes

Although attitudes vary widely among Ethiopia's many ethnic groups, one common trait is friendliness toward foreigners. Also of utmost importance is a source of income. People will do whatever is necessary to provide for their families. Ethiopians generally appreciate others who are humble and pleasant. Agressive, loud, or demanding behavior demonstrates poor character. Stoicism developed in years of hardship pervades the Ethiopian personality, as do courtesy and concern for others. Despite many years of civil conflict, most individuals favor peaceful solutions to problems and look forward to greater prosperity and harmony.

Personal Appearance

For the most part, men and women working as professionals or in offices wear Western-style clothing. Most other women wear traditional dresses. People may change clothing depending on whether they are at home, working in the fields, or attending a community meeting. Rural people often are performing agricultural tasks and do not have the time to concentrate on their physical appearance. Thus, only a few people in a village will appear neat and clean. Villagers who are always well dressed are held in derision.

For holidays and other important occasions, Ethiopians of the northern and central regions wear traditional white cotton clothing decorated with various designs. Some are embroidered in bright colors; other are bordered in handwoven silk. A matching cloth covers women's heads. This cloth is also used as a shawl by both men and women.

CUSTOMS AND COURTESIES

Greetings

Greetings are courteous and warm in Ethiopia. Relatives and friends often kiss on each cheek. New acquaintances shake hands gently with one or both hands. Phrases vary among ethnic groups, but some form of "How are you?" is typical. In Amharic, one says *Ndameneh?* to a male or *Ndamenesh?* to a female. In Oromifaa, one greets members of either sex with *Akam jirta?* The Tigrinya form is *Kamelaha?* for a man or *Kamelehee?* for a woman.

In all areas, one greets an elderly person by lowering or bowing the head to show deference. The elderly greet grandchildren by kissing them on the forehead; in return, they receive kisses on their knees. People are addressed by their titles (Mr., Mrs., Miss, Doctor, etc.) and surnames, although parents can be greeted by the name of their first child (e.g., "How are you, Mary's father?" or "Hello, Solomon's mother.").

Gestures

Pointing with the finger or foot is not appropriate in Ethiopia. One uses the entire hand for gestures. Ethiopians avoid passing items or food with the left hand. They smile to resume a discussion. Trilling the tongue is an expression of excitement or happiness. Walking between two or more conversing people is considered rude.

Visiting

Visiting is an important social function. Rural dwellers visit friends and family frequently and without advance notice. They are always warmly welcomed. Hosts generally offer locally brewed beverages to their guests. In most cases, men and women chat freely and enjoy a relaxed visit. In some Muslim homes, men and women do not socialize together. Many people in the east meet to chew *chat*, a leafy plant that produces a mild stimulating effect when chewed. One removes the shoes when chewing *chat* or when in a Muslim home.

Urban visits may also occur unannounced between family and friends, but advance invitation or notice is generally required of others. Ethiopians enjoy inviting friends over for an evening of socializing, although the Amhara consider the home to be highly private.

Eating

Ethiopians eat three meals each day. Children eat separate from or before their parents, except on holidays or on special occasions. People wash hands before the meal is served; the father, the oldest person, or any guest washes first. Everyone eats from a common platter, taking food with the fingers of the right hand from the space on the platter directly in front of them. In most areas, hosts expect guests to eat and drink without reservation. Hosts may occasionally say, "Please eat," until the food is finished. After the meal, people enjoy coffee, which is often served with elaborate ceremony. Ethiopians frequently go to a community teahouse or restaurant after market day. A tip may be included in the bill or left at the table.

LIFESTYLE

Family

The extended family is strongly patriarchal throughout Ethiopia. Sons usually bring their brides to live with or near their father's family, and three or more generations in the male line frequently live under one roof or in one family compound. Polygamy is common in many areas. Age is highly respected in Ethiopia, and adult children care for their elderly parents. Only 2 percent of the population is older than age 65.

In rural areas, a father builds a separate house in the compound for each son before a wedding. He also gives each son a plot of land to farm. In the absence of the father, the eldest adult son leads the family. Women are responsible for household and compound upkeep and for child care. Their duties and privileges are well-defined and they often lead sheltered lives. While women may have certain legal rights, such as property inheritance, cultural practice often overrides these rights. Many men died during the years of fighting. The resulting female-headed households tend to be the poorest and most marginalized in the country.

Dating and Marriage

Western-style dating is not common in Ethiopia. Because marriage represents the union of two families, the choice of spouse is most often arranged by the families. While individuals have some freedom in the decision, most abide by traditional methods of finding a mate. Marriages tend to last long and divorce is not common.

Diet

Porridge made from corn, barley, oats, or sorghum flour boiled with milk is the most common food in nearly all states. One adds butter and eats it with a wooden spoon. The Guraghe enjoy *kitfo*, a finely chopped, raw red meat mixed with butter, cheese, and cabbage. *Kitfo* is served with *koocho*, a bread prepared from the stem of a plant called *inset*. *Injera* and *wat* are popular Amhara dishes. *Injera*, used as bread, is made from a native grain known as *teff*, while *wat* is a stew made with chicken, beef, or vegetables. *Berbere*, a red hot pepper, is often used to spice *wat* or is served separate with raw meat. Available fruits include oranges, bananas, mangoes, papayas, avocados, grapes, tomatoes, and lemons. The most common vegetables are potatoes, carrots, cabbage, and onions.

Strict religious dietary and fasting customs affect the menu. For example, Orthodox Christians do not eat pork or meat from closed-hooved animals; they also abstain from dairy products and meat on Wednesday, Friday, and during Lent. Muslims do not eat pork. During the holy month of *Ramadan*, Muslims fast from sunrise to sundown each day.

Recreation

Urban residents enjoy different leisure activities than do rural Ethiopians. They watch television, go to sporting events, eat at restaurants, go to movies, take their children out for sweets, and so forth. Rural people rarely have access to electricity. They go to community meetings, attend their local burial society meeting (*idir*) or savings club (*equib*), and play with their children. One activity common for all Ethiopians is visiting friends and relatives. Chess, checkers, and cards are popular games. Soccer is the most popular sport for men and boys, along with track-and-field. Women usually do not play sports, but socialize at home.

Holidays

Major public holidays include the Victory of Adwa (2 March), Victory Day (5 May), Downfall of the Communist Regime (28 May), Ethiopian New Year (in September), and *Meskel* (Finding of the True Cross; end of September). In addition to the various holidays for saints and angels, Christians celebrate Christmas (7 January), Epiphany (20 January), and Easter (Friday–Sunday). Muslims mark *Id al-Fatar* (three-day feast at the end of *Ramadan*), *Id al-Adha* (Feast of Sacrifice, also called *Arefa*), and *Moulid* (Birth of the Prophet Muhammad).

Meskel is the most significant holiday. It was celebrated before the advent of Christianity and Islam but has been adapted by all faiths. *Meskel* comes at the end of winter when the land is green. Each religion or culture celebrates it in different ways, but some customs are similar. People in towns visit their friends and relatives in the countryside. One the eve of *Meskel*, each person places a tree branch vertically with others. There is a dance around the pile, and a community elder then lights the branches on fire. In the morning, most families slaughter a sheep or goat to eat; some people pool their money to buy a bull. Families and neighbors gather to eat, sing, and dance.

Ethiopia follows the Coptic calendar. Each of 12 months has 30 days and a 13th month has 5 or 6 days. There is a seven-year difference between the Coptic and Gregorian calendars. Therefore, 1997 in Western societies is 1990 in Ethiopia. Also, the 24-hour day begins at sunrise, not midnight, so 7:00 P.M. is popularly called "one o'clock."

Commerce

Business is conducted using Western time and calendar standards. In large cities, offices are open from 8:30 A.M. to 1:00 P.M. and from 3:00 to 8:00 P.M., Monday through Friday. Saturday hours are 9:00 A.M. to 1:00 P.M. Government offices close at 6:00 P.M. on weekdays. Rural people generally produce their own food and rely on open-air markets for products like soap, sugar, clothing, and so on. Urban wage earners purchase most items from markets.

SOCIETY

Government

Ethiopia is divided into eight states and two autonomous cities (Addis Ababa and Harer). Each state has its own parliament and council of ministers, but leaders are ultimately responsible to the federal government.

The 1994 constitution provides for a president (Nagaasoo Giidaadaa) as head of state. Elected by Parliament, he has mostly ceremonial duties. The prime minister (Meles Zanawi) is head of government and has strong executive authority. Parliament has two chambers: an upper Federal Council and a lower Council of Peoples Representatives.

The EPRDF dominates Parliament, and no strong opposition parties have yet formed to challenge its control. Opposition groups are fully legal but some allege the EPRDF has suppressed their organization. Meles contends the situation is best for eventually developing a stable democracy.

Economy

Ethiopia's economy is based almost entirely (90 percent) on subsistence agricultural and animal husbandry, although only 12 percent of the land is arable. Rural wealth is often measured in the size of a person's herds. Coffee is the main cash crop, accounting for 60 percent of all export earnings. Other important crops include *teff*, wheat, millet, pulse, and barley. Ethiopia also exports animal hides. Drought, soil erosion, and civil war have all contributed to the poor economy and periodic famines. Still, the country has the potential for self-sufficiency. Improvements are already visible. Areas of focus include mining and gold exploration.

Ethiopia is a very poor country with a real gross domestic product per capita of $330. Nevertheless, Ethiopians are skilled, industrious, and capable of rebuilding their nation. The currency is the *birr* (E$).

Transportation and Communication

In cities, transportation is relatively easy to find and is affordable for the majority of Ethiopians. Taxis, buses, and a train that travels between Addis Ababa and the country of Djibouti are available. Ethiopian Airlines operates with relative efficiency. Outside of major towns, people travel on foot, horseback, camels, donkeys, or mules.

The telephone network in major cities and towns is fairly good, although public phones are in short supply and direct-dial services are not always available. Rural residents rely on the mail and word of mouth for communication. One television station and four radio stations broadcast in the country.

Education

Education is not yet compulsory in Ethiopia, and the literacy rate is about 33 percent. Less than half of all school-aged children are enrolled. About one-third of all students finish primary schooling, which begins at age seven, and go on for secondary school at age thirteen. Until 1991, many children fought in the civil war. The government allotted more funds to education in 1995 and established a policy to allow primary school instruction in the chief language of each region.

Health

Addis Ababa has some medical facilities, but most Ethiopians do not have access to proper medical care. There is approximately only one physician for every 100,000 people. Life expectancy averages 50 years, and infant mortality is 120 per 1,000. Malnutrition and diseases such as meningitis, cholera, and yellow fever are common. Water is not potable.

FOR THE TRAVELER

Passports and visas are required of U.S. citizens. Proof of yellow fever vaccination is required, and one should take precautions against malaria. Travelers must arrive by air; overland entries are not permitted. An exit visa and departure tax are required. For tourist information, contact the Ethiopian National Tourist Organization, PO Box 2183, Addis Ababa, Ethiopia; or Ethiopian Airlines, 405 Lexington Avenue, New York, NY 10174; phone (212) 867–0095. You may also wish to contact the Chancery of Ethiopia, 2134 Kalorama Road NW, Washington, DC 20008; phone (202) 234–2281.

CULTURGRAM ™ '97

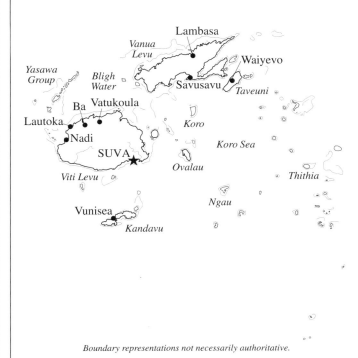

Boundary representations not necessarily authoritative.

Republic of
Fiji

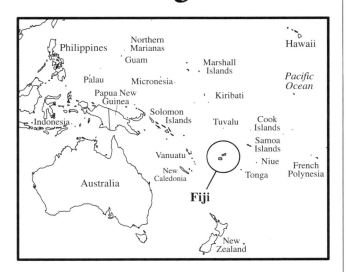

BACKGROUND

Land and Climate

Fiji is located in the southwestern Pacific, north of New Zealand. More than 300 islands make up Fiji but only about 110 are inhabited. Covering 7,054 square miles (18,270 square kilometers), Fiji's total size is about the same as Hawaii or just smaller than New Jersey. Three main islands, Viti Levu, Vanua Levu, and Taveuni, are home to the majority of the population. The larger Fijian Islands are volcanic, mountainous, and surrounded by coral reefs. The windward sides are covered with dense tropical forests. The leeward sides consist of grassy plains that receive less rain. The climate is humid and tropical. The rainy season is from November to April, when violent hurricanes are possible. Annual temperatures change little and range from 72°F to 86°F (22–30°C).

History

The islands of Fiji were first settled some 3,500 years ago by what are now known as the Lapita people, perhaps from Asia. Various Pacific peoples migrated to the Fijian Islands, which they called *Viti*; Western explorers used the Tongan word *Feejee* to name the islands and the people. Although the Dutch had a brief encounter with Fijians in 1643, it was Captain James Cook of England who spent more time with them in 1774. Later, trade vessels came for sandalwood, which was used in ornamental carving and cabinetmaking. The islands were known by many as the Cannibal Islands because of the Fijians' reputation as fierce warriors and ferocious cannibals. After years of tribal warfare, Chief Ratu Cakobau converted to Christianity in 1854, united rival tribes under the new religion, ended cannibalism, and became King of Fiji in 1871.

Cakobau was aware of European competition for territory in the Pacific and, in 1874, offered to cede the islands to Great Britain (after the United States refused the same offer). Britain brought in laborers from India, whose descendants now make up nearly half the population. Exactly 96 years to the day after cession to Britain, Fiji gained its independence (10 October 1970). Ratu Sir Kamisese Mara became the first prime minister and his Alliance Party (mostly ethnic Fijians) governed until 1987, when a coalition led by the National Federation Party (mostly ethnic Indians) won a majority in parliamentary elections.

Two weeks after the elections, however, General Sitiveni Rabuka led a military coup to restore control to native Fijians. The coup was halted because Britain's governor general (Queen Elizabeth's representative) assumed executive control and negotiated a settlement between the Indians and Fijians. Rabuka then staged a second coup, establishing a civilian government dominated by Fijians. Fiji was subsequently voted out of the Commonwealth by its member nations. Rabuka appointed Mara (the first prime minister in 1970) prime minister. A new constitution was ratified in 1990 favoring indigenous Fijians over Indians. As a source of tension between these two groups, it came under review and is expected to be revised in 1997. In 1992 elections, Rabuka was elected prime minister. Mara became vice president and, after the 1993 death of President Ganilau, was elected president in 1994 by the country's Great Council of Chiefs.

THE PEOPLE

Population

There are about 773,000 people in Fiji, a population that is growing at 1 percent annually. Relatively few people live in urban areas. There are only nine towns, and six of them are on the main island, Viti Levu. The two largest towns are Suva, the capital, and Lautoka. Indigenous Fijians and Fijian Indians have nearly equal numbers, together forming 95 percent of the total population. The Indians are descendants of Asian Indians brought as laborers by the British in the 1800s to work on sugar plantations. They live mostly on Viti Levu. About 5 percent of the total population is made up of other Pacific Islanders, Chinese, and Europeans.

Fiji's Human Development Index (0.860) ranks it 46th out of 174 nations. Adjusted for women, the index (0.722) ranks Fiji 48th out of 130 nations. This reflects a gap in income between men and women. Most people have access to basic resources that afford them opportunities to pursue personal goals.

Language

English is the official language. Fijian and Hindustani are widely spoken. Fijian can be written in two different ways, one of which is more phonetic than the other. For instance, the letter *b* is pronounced with an *m* sound before it, as in the case of the town Ba. Its name can be written *Ba* or *Mba*, but it is pronounced MBAH. Also, a *q* is usually pronounced NGG. That is, *yaqona* is pronounced YANGGONA. In this text, most words are written in the more standard, less phonetic spelling. Hindustani is an Indian language. However, the Hindustani spoken in Fiji is called *Fiji Bat* or Fiji Talk and differs slightly from the Hindustani spoken in India. English spoken among the people often includes words and phrases from Fijian, Hindustani, and other languages.

Religion

Fijians are mostly Christian, belonging to various churches. Methodists and Roman Catholics predominate. Indians are either Hindu or Muslim and the Chinese are either Christian or Buddhist. There are also some Sikhs and Christian Indians. The people often celebrate festivals of other religions. Freedom of religion is guaranteed by the constitution. Religion plays a major role in the lives of all Fijians.

General Attitudes

Fijians are generous, friendly, and easygoing. Daily life in Fiji is relaxed and casual. Some call it the "Pacific Way." People enjoy life. The community is important, as is evident in community ceremonies, cooperative building projects, and community pride. The custom of *kerekere* dictates that a relative or neighbor can ask for something that is needed, and it must be given willingly, without expectation of repayment. An exception is if the requested item was a gift from someone else, in which case a person does not have to give it away.

Although Fijians have abandoned their tradition as fierce warriors for a more peaceful life, they remain proud of their cultural heritage and traditions. Ethnic tensions exist between Fijians and Indians. The two groups rarely mix and are political opponents. Indians often feel discriminated against by the Fijian government. They point to such inequalities as land ownership to argue their case. More than 80 percent of all land is owned by Fijian clans, and Indians do not have access to it. These tensions have increased since 1987, when Indians gained political power through elections and were then overthrown by the Fijian-dominated military.

Personal Appearance

The people of Fiji wear light, casual clothing throughout the year, but public attire is fairly conservative (no bathing suits), especially for women. In traditional villages, women do not wear shorts or pants. Daily clothing for Fijian men and women is most often the *sulu*, a medium-to-long wraparound cloth made of colorful cotton. Businessmen, clergy, and civil servants (such as police officers) wear a tailored *sulu* made from suit material. This *sulu*, called a pocket *sulu*, is worn with a short-sleeved shirt and sometimes a tie. Indian men wear long pants and shirts. Indian women wear a *sari* (wraparound dress) or a *salwaar kameez* (pants with a matching, long tunic). Fashions in the larger urban areas are changing due to Western influence.

CUSTOMS AND COURTESIES

Greetings

The most common way to say hello among indigenous Fijians is *Bula!* (pronounced MBOOLA, meaning "health"). For formal meetings, they use a handshake and the more formal *Ni Sa Bula!* The Fijian handshake can last a little while, as the greeters continue polite conversation before they let go. Fijian Indians often use shorter handshakes and say *Namaste* when they greet. Fijians are friendly and will go out of their way to greet whomever they meet. When passing a rural Fijian house, a person is greeted with *Mai kana* (Come eat). In this casual society, it is common to address most people by their first names. When people are related or have an established relationship, they may greet by reference to that relationship rather than using first names. For example, close friends may address each other by *itau* (a traditional friendship), and male cousins might use *tavale* (cousin). People address chiefs by the title *Ratu* before their first names.

Gestures

Among Fijians, tilting the head down and avoiding eye contact while speaking to someone shows respect. Staring is offensive. One indicates agreement by raising the eyebrows, closing the mouth, and making an "mm-mm" sound (similar to a sound that would mean "no" in the United States). A "thumbs up" gesture means "good" or "okay." Pointing directly at someone while speaking to them is considered rude. Standing with hands on hips is thought to be aggressive or brash. Pointing the bottom of one's foot at another person is impolite. Among Fijians, it is especially offensive to touch someone's head (except for a child's). One beckons by waving all fingers of the hand with the palm facing down. Physical displays of affection, even between married couples, are frowned upon. People practice a custom called *cobo* (pronounced THOMBO) when accepting a gift, presenting *yaqona* (see Visiting below), or excusing oneself when reaching above a person's head. *Cobo* involves clapping cupped hands three or more times.

Visiting

Visiting is an important part of social relations. Most people visit unannounced, and guests are welcome.

Removing one's shoes when entering a home is customary. Sitting cross-legged on a mat-covered floor is common in a Fijian home, but Indian homes have furniture. A chief or guest sits in a place of honor. It is impolite to stand higher than those who are sitting, so one takes care to also be seated or to walk in a stooped position when others are seated. The people of Fiji are hospitable; they enjoy sharing a visitor's company and visits may last a long time. Hosts nearly always offer refreshments, including tea, juice, or food. It is impolite to refuse them. Instead, one accepts the offering and says *Vinaka* or *Dhananbaad*, the respective Fijian and Hindustani words for "Thank you."

An important symbol of social relations is *yaqona*, which is made from the root and lower stem of a shrub in the pepper family. The powdered root, when combined with water, is Fiji's national drink. It is sometimes called *kava*. It may be offered to guests as a special sign of goodwill. The bitter-tasting drink numbs the tongue and, drunk in large enough amounts, can bring a mild sense of well-being. People use *yaqona* to mark special occasions and end disputes and drink it at all official ceremonies. Both ethnic Fijians and Indians use the drink socially. *Yaqona* is prepared in a *tanoa* (a special wooden bowl) and drunk from a *bilo* (coconut shell). When a stranger enters a Fijian village, he seeks out the chief or village headman to ask for permission to enter and visit and is expected to present some unpounded *yaqona* to him.

Eating

Traditionally, neither Fijians nor Indians used eating utensils, but spoons and forks are becoming more common in urban areas. In Fijian villages, breakfast consists of tea drunk from tin bowls and possibly rice or any leftovers from the previous night's dinner. For all meals, Fijians spread a cloth on the mat-covered floor, sit cross-legged, pray, pass a bowl of water around for washing hands, and eat from tin plates and bowls. They pass the water bowl again after the meal. Women and girls usually eat after the men and boys. Food is shared in Fijian villages, due not only to communal obligations but also to the fact that most homes do not have refrigerators to keep leftovers. For large feasts and special meals, Fijians still cook food in the traditional manner in a *lovo* (ground oven).

Indian homes generally have a small wash basin in the dining room for washing hands. Indians eat with the right hand. Their meals consist of curries, rice *dhal* (lentil soup), and *roti* (round, flat bread used for scooping up the curry). Tipping is not expected in restaurants.

LIFESTYLE

Family

The Fijian people are family oriented, and the father acts as head of the home. Families can be large. The elderly are usually cared for by their children. Villages are composed of families that form clans or *mataqali* (land-holding units). In this extended family system, Fijians live in a collective or communal way. *Kerekere* plays an important role in family relationships. Subsistence chores are shared between men and women. Men are engaged in spearfishing, gardening and construction, while women do line and small-net fishing, as well as cook, weave *ibe* (pandanus mats), and collect wild food.

The traditional Fijian home is called a *bure*. It usually is built of local hardwoods, a thatched roof, and woven floor covers. The four doors generally are kept open for circulation and are used by different people. Visitors enter through the front door, except for the village chief, who enters at the side. A *bure* is one large room and typically is built by the entire community. Other than beds and sometimes a dresser, furniture is not considered necessary. Women cook in a smaller, separate structure.

Indians usually live in furnished tin, cement, or wood homes. Urban dwellers of any ethnic group often live in Western-style homes. Some rural Fijians have adopted the tin, cement, and wood homes.

Dating and Marriage

Dating is traditionally nonexistent in Fijian culture, but Western influences are changing society so that dating is found in some areas. People do not show affection in public. The ethnic Fijian man chooses his own wife and a grand wedding ceremony is held, accompanied by a *solevu* (great feast). In high chiefly Fijian families, parents must still approve their children's future spouses. Indian parents have customarily arranged their children's marriages, but this practice is also changing with Western influence.

Diet

The mainstays of the Fijian diet are boiled taro and cassava, starchy roots often grown in the family garden. There are some leafy vegetables and many tropical fruits (papayas, mangoes, pineapples, bananas). Many dishes are prepared in *lolo* (coconut milk). Seafood, chicken, pork, and beef are eaten in Fiji. Foods are rarely deep-fried, but are steamed, boiled, or roasted. Indian cuisine is often made with curry and is spicy. *Roti* is a daily Indian staple. Hindus do not eat beef; Muslims do not eat pork. Many Indians are vegetarians.

Recreation

Fijians are sports enthusiasts. The most popular team sports are rugby, soccer, and cricket. Fiji's national rugby team is among the best in the world. Visitors enjoy the beaches, golf, many water sports (snorkeling, wind surfing, scuba diving, etc.), and game fishing. Festivals are also a time of recreation for many people. Women in villages play the traditional Fijian game of *veicaqe moli* (kick the orange) during January to celebrate the new year. The winning team must present the losers with clothes, while the losers are responsible for mixing and serving *yaqona* to the winners that night.

Holidays

Official public holidays include New Year's Day, Easter, the Queen of England's Birthday (13 June), a Bank Holiday (1 August), Fiji Day (or Independence Day, 10 October), the Prophet Muhammad's Birthday (26 October), Prince Charles's Birthday (14 November), Christmas, and Boxing Day (26 December). Boxing Day comes from the British tradition of presenting gifts to tradesmen and service persons. It is now a day for relaxing and visiting friends and family. Many festivals throughout the year celebrate different events. The largest, held in Suva for a full week in August, is the Hibiscus Festival. Also popular is *Diwali*, the Hindu Festival of Lights, held in either October or November.

Commerce

Businesses are open Monday through Friday, usually 8:00 A.M. to 4:30 P.M., with an hour break for lunch. Restaurants and stores remain open during lunch but are closed Saturday after 1:00 P.M. All stores close on Sunday, with the exception of some restaurants that are permitted to remain open. Nearly all businesses in Fiji are owned by Indians and Chinese.

SOCIETY

Government

Fiji's government is comprised of three branches. The executive branch is led by the president as head of state, the prime minister as head of government, and the Great Council of Chiefs (highest ranking members of the traditional Fijian chief system). Parliament has two houses, a 34-seat Senate and a 70-seat House of Representatives. Senators are appointed; 24 seats are reserved for Fijians. Representatives are technically elected (the next vote is in 1999), but 37 seats are reserved for Fijians and 27 for Indians. The two main political parties are the Fijian Political Party and the National Federation Party. A number of smaller parties operate but have little power. The judicial branch is headed by a Supreme Court.

Economy

Subsistence farming is the key economic activity for most Fijians. Primary cash crops include bananas, rice, taro, cassava, pineapples, coconuts, and copra (a coconut product). Until recently, sugar was the most important industry and major source of revenue. Tourism is gaining rapidly, however, and now equals sugar in economic importance. Fiji also exports ginger, gold, lumber, and processed fish (mostly tuna). It has started to manufacture clothing and furniture on a small scale.

The economy suffered dramatically following the 1987 coups, but it regained its strength by 1990 and has been growing steadily since then. Growth in 1994 was 5 percent. Real gross domestic product per capita is $5,410, which has more than doubled in the last generation. While poverty still affects up to 30 percent of rural families, the rising generation is already benefiting from increased economic opportunities. The currency is the Fijian dollar (F$).

Transportation and Communication

Most people travel by bus (open-air) because service is regular and inexpensive. Taxis and private automobiles are also used but are more expensive. Relatively few people own cars. Following the British tradition, traffic travels on the left side of the road. A ferry service and two airlines provide travel between more populated islands. Fiji has a modern communications system, with satellite links to other countries. There are about 60,000 phones in the country. There are eight radio stations, which broadcast in English, Fijian, and Hindustani. Limited television broadcasts, now available in Suva and Nadi, are slowly expanding. There are two daily English newspapers, one weekly Hindustani paper, and two weekly Fijian papers.

Education

For the past 15 years, the government has worked to provide free education for grades one through eight, and it hopes to extend this in the future. Many schools are operated by religious groups such as the Catholics, Hindus, Latter-day Saints (Mormons), Methodists, and Muslims. Each school has its own uniform, and most accept both boys and girls. The University of the South Pacific is a joint effort by several small Pacific Island nations to provide their people with higher education. It receives substantial funding from Fiji's government, and one of its many campuses is located in Suva. Fiji also has a medical school, an institute of technology, and a college of agriculture. The adult literacy rate is 90 percent.

Health

There is usually very little disease in Fiji and the water supply is safe to drink. An influenza epidemic occurred after a cyclone in 1993. The government provides most medical care through local clinics. The infant mortality rate is 18 per 1,000; life expectancy averages between 63 and 68 years. Life expectancy rates are rising steadily and infant mortality rates are falling.

FOR THE TRAVELER

Due to the general lack of disease, no inoculations are required for travel to Fiji. U.S. travelers must present a valid passport and proof of onward passage upon arrival to receive a 30-day visa. There is a F$20 departure tax. Taxi fares are reasonable and fixed, but one should agree on the price before taking longer trips. Water is safe in hotels and urban areas, but precautions should be taken in rural areas. For information on travel opportunities, contact the Fiji Visitors Bureau, 5777 West Century Boulevard, Suite 220, Los Angeles, CA 90045. You may also wish to contact the Embassy of Fiji, 2233 Wisconsin Avenue NW, Suite 240, Washington, DC 20007; phone (202) 337–8320.

Gabon

(Gabonese Republic)

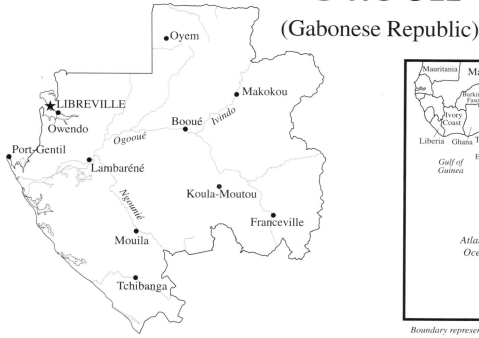

Boundary representations not necessarily authoritative.

BACKGROUND

Land and Climate

Gabon lies on Africa's west coast and straddles the equator. It is about the same size as Colorado, covering 103,347 square miles (267,670 square kilometers). It comprises the drainage basin of the Ogooué River. About three-fourths of the country is low-lying equatorial rain forest, which is harvested for timber. Forests are dotted with small towns and villages. Although the Gabonese practice a sort of slash-and-burn agriculture, their small population has thus far left the forests mostly intact. It is only the larger-scale logging that can threaten the virgin forests. Although laws are supposed to ensure that logging is conducted only at sustainable levels, 1996 reports indicated that vast stretches of pristine forests are being destroyed by European (mostly French) logging firms. The east is slightly higher in elevation and is covered with grasslands. Gabon's climate is moderate in the dry seasons (May–September and December–February) and hot in the rainy seasons (September–December and February–May). Libreville has an average temperature in January of 80°F (27°C) and in July of 75°F (24°C). It receives about 99 inches (251 centimeters) of rain each year.

History

The earliest inhabitants of Gabon were the Pygmies. Migrations of Bantu peoples (A.D. 1000) resulted in Bantu domination of the area. The southern-most part of Gabon was ruled by the powerful Bantu Bakongo Empire, centered at the mouth of the Zaire River. When the Portuguese arrived in the 1400s, the rest of Gabon was made up of small migratory villages of hunting and farming Bantus. Soon, the export of slaves and ivory to Europe began. These exports were replaced with timber and rubber by the early 1800s. Trade was dominated by coastal peoples who eventually allied themselves with France. Interior people first resisted French colonization, but Western explorers, traders, and missionaries opened the area in the 1800s to eventual incorporation into French Equatorial Africa (present-day Gabon, Congo, the Central African Republic, Cameroon, and Chad).

Gabon was not developed much during the colonial era because of its small population and dense forests. This minimized contact with colonial rulers. Independence came in 1960. Borders were based on French Equatorial Africa's artificial internal boundaries rather than natural ethnic groupings. The first president of Gabon was Leon M'ba. He died in 1967 and was succeeded by Albert-Bernard Bongo, who has been reelected to several successive seven-year terms.

Bongo instituted a relatively tolerant one-party rule that lasted until 1990. In the 1970s, Gabon joined the Organization of Petroleum Exporting Countries, and Bongo adopted Islam, changing his first name to El Hadj Omar. Protests and strikes in 1990 and 1991 forced the president to loosen political restrictions and legalize opposition parties. Gabon's subsequent transition to multiparty democracy has been slow. In 1991 free elections, more than 40 parties ran for seats in the national assembly. Bongo's party won a majority. Multiparty presidential elections were held in 1993 and Bongo was re-elected president. He is more powerful than popular and faces polls again in 1998.

THE PEOPLE

Population

The current population of Gabon is about 1.2 million, but an accurate count is not available. All Gabonese, except Pygmies, belong to one of Africa's many Bantu-speaking groups. Gabon's largest is the Fang, comprising 30 percent of the population. Others include Eshira, Adouma, Mbeda, Bakota, Omyene, Okande, and Bateke. There are more than 40 different ethnic groups, but most are small. The country is also home to many immigrants, especially from other French-speaking African nations, who work as shopkeepers, tailors, dressmakers, teachers, cabdrivers, and laborers. A large number of Western workers manage many of Gabon's export industries. Gabon's largest city and capital, Libreville, is home to about one-third of the total population. Other cities are Port-Gentil (100,000), Franceville (30,000), and Lambaréné (20,000). More than half of the people live in towns and villages.

Gabon's Human Development Index (0.579) ranks it 114th out of 174 nations. Many people have access to resources that can help them pursue personal goals, but many more still lack such opportunities.

Language

French is Gabon's official language. Nearly all publishing and broadcasting occurs in French, and it is the most commonly heard language in cities. Taught in schools, it is the only language the Gabonese have in common and is basically the only written language. Local languages are oral. Most Gabonese speak both French and their ethnic group's native tongue. People usually are not fluent in another ethnic group's language, even though many different groups live close to one another. In the north, Fang is more common than French.

Religion

About 60 percent of the population is Roman Catholic, 20 percent is Protestant, and the remaining people practice local animist beliefs or are Muslim. Most Muslims are immigrants from other countries. Going to church is a popular social occasion, especially for women and girls. Most Christian clergy are from the West, but meetings are influenced by African music and are conducted in the local language by village elders. In their daily lives, people mix local beliefs with Christianity, often turning to tradition in times of emergency rather than to Western religion.

General Attitudes

The Gabonese are generally polite and kind. Although they get loud and angry in disputes, they quickly resolve problems and rarely harbor hard feelings. The Gabonese are considered outspoken and even argumentative among some West African neighbors. Certain ethnic groups do not often say "please" and "thank you" because there is no tradition for these words in their languages. Regardless of whether the words are used, kindness and consideration are acknowledged and favors are usually repaid.

Gabonese tend to accept life as it is. They see themselves as members of a family (including the extended family and, in rural areas, the village), then as part of an ethnic group, and finally as Gabonese and Africans. They are proud of Gabon's accomplishments since independence and of its status as a relatively prosperous African country.

Personal Appearance

The Gabonese wear both Western and African clothing. All people like to be neatly groomed and dressed as well as possible. Modesty and cleanliness are important. The Gabonese borrow their fashions from neighboring countries. Women like elaborate, braided hairstyles—some sticking straight out, others in intricate loops, and others tied in bunches—and they change them often. Women might wear loose-fitting dresses made of colorful, embroidered fabric or a colorful *pagne* (wraparound skirt) with a blouse. Urban men might wear Western suits or, more often, just shirts and pants. Muslims might also wear a *boubou*, a loose-fitting, long-sleeved, embroidered cotton shirt extending to mid-calf that is worn over loose-fitting pants. Fabrics are colorful and designs often bold. The youth wear shorts or other casual attire.

CUSTOMS AND COURTESIES

Greetings

The Gabonese shake hands and smile each time they meet, even if several times a day. If the hand is dirty, one extends a closed fist (palm down) so the greeter can "shake" the wrist or forearm. Urban friends might hug and brush alternating cheeks while "kissing the air." In small groups, one greets each individual. In larger gatherings, one can raise both hands to the group and say, *Bonjour tout le monde* (Hello, everyone). People of the same sex, especially men, often hold hands while talking or walking. It is improper, especially in rural areas, for members of the opposite sex to do this. Rural women might clasp forearms when greeting. Older rural men often shake another person's hand with both of their hands.

Urban greetings include the French *Bonjour* (Good day) and *Bonsoir* (Good evening). Common throughout Gabon is the Fang *Mbolo* (Hello). Greetings include asking about one's family and health. Older people may be addressed as *mama* or *papa*. People of about the same age may address each other by first name or as *mon frère* (my brother) or *ma soeur* (my sister). At work, *monsieur* (Mr.), *madame* (Ms. or Mrs.), or a title is used with the last name.

Gestures

A closed fist with the thumb extended up means "good." Rubbing the thumb against the index finger means "money." Hitting a raised, closed left fist with the right palm open means *beaucoup* (many, much). Hooking one's right thumbnail behind a front tooth and snapping it to make a loud clicking sound indicates a statement is true. One may express enthusiasm by shaking the wrist rapidly to make the fingers slap together. A person points by quickly extending puckered lips. One indicates "come here" by holding the hand vertical, palm facing out, and waving the fingers. To hail a taxi, one waves an extended arm, palm down, from shoulder to waist. Muslims object to contact with one's left hand. It is impolite to touch someone's head.

Visiting

Visiting is common after work or on weekends in urban areas and anytime one is home in villages. Most rural socializing takes place Sunday after morning church services. Hospitality is important, and hosts frequently offer food to guests, especially if a meal is in progress. They always offer a drink and quickly refill an empty glass. A guest who is not hungry should at least taste offered food. Guests usually are not expected to bring gifts, but friends might bring food or drink. In urban areas, a new acquaintance might make a vague appointment ("I'll drop by next week") before visiting, but most visits are unplanned. Rural people might invite passing friends in for a drink; it is impolite to refuse, even if one has something else to do. Rural women socialize in the *cuisine* (kitchen), where much of daily life usually takes place. Kitchens generally are separate from the living quarters (*salon*), as open cooking fires are often used. The *salon* consists of a living room and bedrooms. Rural men often socialize and work together in open-air structures called *corps de gars*.

When guests are invited, promptness is unimportant and time is a formality. Guests customarily return the favor of an invitation at a later date. It is polite to knock before entering a home. If the door is open, the visitor imitates the knocking sound by saying *kokoko*. One does not enter without announcing one's presence.

Eating

An urban breakfast, eaten around 7:00 A.M., may include bread, croissants, butter, marmalade, eggs, yogurt, and coffee. Lunch might be around noon; dinner is after dark, even as late as 9:00 P.M. Most people use utensils but eat certain foods with the hand.

In villages, breakfast may consist of leftovers from the day before, but adults might also have bread and coffee or hot chocolate. Adults usually are working around lunchtime, so children returning from school eat a light meal or leftovers. Adults also eat light; they might harvest fruit for a snack. The main meal is eaten in the evening (usually after 7:00 P.M.) when work is done. People eat snacks throughout the day. They often eat with the right hand or a spoon. Rural Gabonese men and older boys usually eat in the *salon*, with women and young children eating in the *cuisine*. The father often has his own bowl. Small families might eat together in the *cuisine*, with adults sharing a bowl and children sharing another. Guests are given a separate bowl.

LIFESTYLE

Family

The Gabonese feel great loyalty toward family members. Family obligations require the Gabonese to extend hospitality (food, lodging, and expenses) to any member of the extended family who asks for it, even for a prolonged period of time. Traditionally, an extended family lives in a large compound of several buildings, usually sharing cooking, child care, and other chores. A man, his wife (or wives), their children, and often cousins or other relatives live in the compound. A man with more than one wife provides each with a separate home and kitchen whenever possible. Since this is expensive, the trend is to have only one wife. Still, an unmarried man may have children by more than one woman, and married men often have mistresses.

A village functions as an extension of the family. Villagers who move to cities have a spirit of unity with fellow villagers they meet there. They make regular visits back home; students might return on weekends or holidays to work and visit.

Dating and Marriage

Western-style dating occurs mostly among the urban educated. Rural courtship involves the boy visiting the girl at her parents' home. An engaged couple may date outside the home. The family often has great influence in the choice of a marriage partner. Girls are sometimes promised at a very young age, although the wedding does not take place (if at all) until after puberty. A groom must often give gifts (*dot*) to the bride's family when they get engaged and when they marry. The Gabonese generally marry within their ethnic group but outside of their village to avoid marrying relatives. Women are often encouraged to have a child or two before marriage to prove fertility. These children frequently are raised by the woman's mother and are not taken into marriage. If a marriage fails, the *dot* must be repaid and children born in wedlock remain with the father.

Diet

The most widely grown food is cassava (*manioc*). A typical meal consists of either plantains (boiled and mashed) or *bâton de manioc*, a dough-like paste made from cassava. It is served with meat or fish in urban areas and with fresh meat among villagers who have had a successful hunt. People might eat imported sardines or locally caught small fish when meat is unavailable. The main course is often a stew in peanut butter or palm oil sauce. Hot peppers (*piment*) are frequently used. A green-leaf vegetable, cut into strips and boiled, is usually served. Water is the most common drink, but beer is also popular.

Yams, taro, peanuts, and corn are grown in Gabon. Coffee, cocoa, sugarcane, and palm oil are produced for commercial purposes. There are many tropical fruits: papayas, bananas, pineapples, mangoes, avocados, and *atangas* (a violet, bitter fruit about the size of a golf ball). *Atangas* are often boiled until soft and then spread on bread or rice. Some non-Gabonese call this fruit "bush butter."

In remote areas, people hunt wild animals (gazelles, anteaters, snakes, crocodiles, boars, etc.) and grow food for themselves. Insects, like termites, are not an uncommon part of the diet.

Recreation

In the capital, Western forms of recreation are common, including going to movies, dancing, and swimming. Visiting is the most common leisure activity everywhere. Soccer is Gabon's most popular sport. Basketball is also popular. Television is available in much of the country. Dancing to drums and local music is common and usually a part of weddings, religious ceremonies, and other occasions. A traditional strategy game for two players called *songo* (in Fang) is popular. It is played on a wooden board with pebbles or seeds. People also enjoy tag and tug-of-war.

Holidays

Official public holidays are given for major Christian holy days, including *Pâques* (Easter), *Pentecôte* (Pentecost), *Toussaint* (All Saints' Day, 1 November), and *Noël* (Christmas). The Islamic holy days of *Fin du Ramadan* (a feast at the end of *Ramadan*, a month of fasting) and *Fête de Mouton* (a feast to honor Abraham's willingness to sacrifice his son) are observed according to their dates on the lunar calendar. The Gabonese celebrate *Jour de l'An* (New Year's Day) and *Fête du Travail* (May Day, 1 May). *Fête National* commemorates independence on 17 August.

Commerce

A few minutes of greetings and small talk precede discussions of business. Businesses generally open between 7:00 and 9:00 A.M. and close for lunch at noon. Lunch lasts until 2:00 or 3:00 P.M. to allow for a break from the hot weather. Businesses are then open until sometime between 5:00 and 7:00 P.M. Many offices open on Saturday morning. Small food shops are open through lunch, late in the evening, and on weekends. In these shops, and in open-air markets, prices are negotiable. A majority of small and medium-sized companies and shops are owned by non-Gabonese (usually from other West African countries).

SOCIETY

Government

Gabon is a multiparty democracy with a president, a prime minister, and a 120-seat national assembly (*Assemblé National*). Everyone older than age 18 must vote. To limit the president's traditional dominance, his term has been reduced from seven years to five, the national assembly and prime minister have more constitutional authority, and the government is becoming more balanced. Major parties include the Gabonese Democratic Party, two factions of the National Recovery Movement, and the Gabonese Party for Progress.

Economy

During the last century, Gabon's major exports were *okoumé* (a hardwood) and soft woods used to make plywood. Timber exports continue, but they have been exceeded by oil exports since the 1970s. Manganese and uranium are also exported. Export industries are mostly owned by Western companies.

Because of the value of Gabon's exports, the country has one of the highest per capita incomes in Africa. However, most wealth is in the hands of a small minority and the average person does not necessarily earn a decent income. Real gross domestic product per capita is $3,913, a figure that has tripled in the last generation. The country has the potential to extend economic opportunities to its people. Progress is hindered by corruption, the instability of oil prices, lower demand for uranium, and a 1994 currency devaluation. The currency (*CFA franc*) is tied to the French *franc* and France cut the value of the *CFA franc* in half. Gabon is trying to diversify its economy to reduce dependence on oil and create more jobs. Most people (65 percent) are engaged in subsistence agriculture. Thirty percent of the labor force works in industry or commerce.

Transportation and Communication

Roads between major cities are not paved and are difficult to travel during the rainy seasons. A domestic airline provides service to many areas, but flights are expensive. The Trans-Gabonais railway (one of Bongo's major accomplishments) provides daily service between Libreville and Franceville. Only government officials and the wealthy have access to private cars. Animals are not used for transportation, and bicycles and motorcycles are rare, so people walk a lot. They may get from one town to another by way of an *occasion* (bush taxi), which is often crowded. Passengers pay a commonly understood fare and take their luggage, food, and animals with them. Goods are transported by rail to Franceville and by truck or air everywhere else, making imports much more expensive in the interior than in the capital. The post office provides reliable mail and phone service between many locations. Mail moves slowly because it is all sorted at the capital, regardless of its origin or destination.

Education

Gabon follows the French system of education, with students attending school for up to 13 years and ending with a *bac* (baccalaureate) exam. Free education is guaranteed to all, even though the government reduces education spending when oil revenues fall. The system has produced a literacy rate of 59 percent, high by African standards. In the past, many schools were run by churches. But the government, which sets curriculum and appoints teachers, is replacing cleric administrators with government officials.

Nearly all children are enrolled in and finish primary school, which lasts six years (to age 11). Only one-fifth continue on for seven years of secondary school. Students who pass the *bac* may attend one of Gabon's two universities free of charge. Living expenses are paid for those with passing grades. College graduates often work for the government.

Health

Gabon has a relatively good national health-care system. Doctors' services are free, but medicine is not. Small towns have clinics, although sometimes not well equipped, and cities have hospitals. People in villages must travel to the nearest town or city for medical care. Traditional methods of healing are popular. Villagers might visit a local "healer" as well as, or instead of, a town doctor. Serious medical problems can only be treated in Libreville. The average life expectancy is between 53 and 58 years. Infant mortality is estimated to be 93 per 1,000. In 1913, French humanitarian Albert Schweitzer built a hospital in Lambaréné and expanded it in 1952. It still functions and is supported by the government.

FOR THE TRAVELER

U.S. citizens need a valid passport and visa to visit Gabon. There are few tourists in Gabon; most foreigners are expatriate workers and their families. Hotels and restaurants are expensive. A vaccination is required for yellow fever and recommended for cholera. Take precautions against malaria. Water is safe to drink in cities, but one should drink only bottled beverages elsewhere. Avoid eating unpeeled fruits and vegetables, and eat only well-cooked foods. For more information, contact the Embassy of the Gabonese Republic, 2034 20th Street NW, Washington, DC 20009; phone (202) 797–1000.

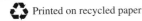 Printed on recycled paper

July 96

Republic of
The Gambia

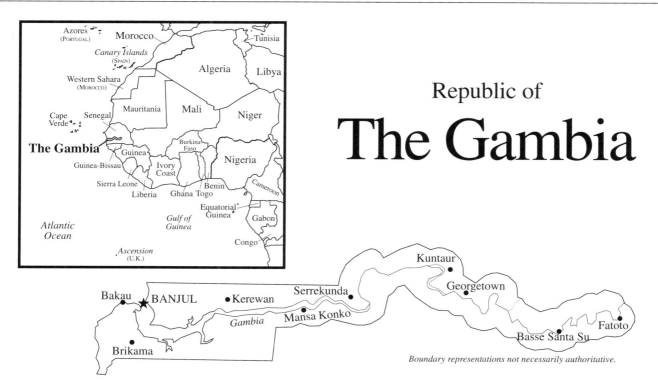

Boundary representations not necessarily authoritative.

BACKGROUND

Land and Climate

The Gambia is located on the coast of West Africa, about 10 degrees latitude north of the equator. It is one of Africa's smallest countries, occupying a narrow strip of land on both sides of the River Gambia, about 250 miles (400 kilometers) in length. Covering 4,363 square miles (11,300 square kilometers), The Gambia is slightly larger than Maryland and is surrounded on three sides by Senegal. The River Gambia provides excellent transport from the Atlantic coast to points inland. The capital, Banjul, is an island that is connected to the mainland by bridge. Surrounding Banjul are various urban areas that collectively make up the Kombos.

The Gambia experiences two seasons: a humid, rainy season from June to October and a dry season from November to mid-June. The average daily high temperature is 88°F (31°C); nights are hotter in the summer than during the rest of the year. Temperatures are somewhat cooler upriver.

History

The Gambia was once part of various large African empires, including the Serrahule and Mandinka Empires of the fifth and sixth centuries. The country's modern history is closely linked to the River Gambia. It is believed the Portuguese were the first Europeans to navigate the river in 1455, but it was not recognized as a European possession until 1783 when the British claimed the river and its surrounding territory. The British remained in the area until 1965 when The Gambia became an independent state and a member of the (British) Commonwealth. In 1971, the country became a republic and enjoyed relative peace and multiparty democracy under the leadership of President Dawda K. Jawara.

In July 1981, political turmoil led to an attempted coup while Jawara was in England for Prince Charles's wedding. The coup ended when Senegalese troops intervened at Jawara's request. As a result of Senegal's involvement, the two countries accepted an old idea and joined together in closer union, establishing a Senegambia confederation in September 1981. Close diplomatic relations and the loose confederation continued until 1989 when Senegal withdrew. Jawara, who had been reelected several times and was considered personally popular, faced strong opposition in the 1992 elections but still won with a majority.

In July 1994, Lieutenant Yahya Jammeh seized power in a bloodless coup, forcing Jawara to flee to Senegal. Jammeh suspended the constitution, banned political activity, and detained top military and government officials. Although he promised a swift return to civilian rule—as soon as corruption had been cleaned up—his government quickly settled in for a long tenure. Western nations withdrew aid, business (international trade) suffered from the uncertainty, and Jammeh announced in October 1994 that he would remain in power until 1998. Gambians did not welcome the news, despite Jammeh's promises of a new constitution and free-market economy. The international community also denounced Jammeh's announcement, and he eventually promised to reschedule elections for 1996. Set originally for May, they were twice delayed. A referendum on a new constitution was set for August, with parliamentary elections to follow in

September. Assuming the schedule is maintained, presidential elections would then be held in December 1996.

THE PEOPLE

Population

The current population is estimated at 989,000. The Gambia is inhabited by five major ethnic groups: the Mandinka (42 percent), Fulani or Fula (18), Wolof (16), Jola (10), and the Serrahule (9). About 5 percent of the population is comprised of a community of Europeans, U.S. Americans, Mauritanians, Lebanese, Syrians, and people from neighboring countries.

The Mandinkas are descendants of the Mali Empire, whereas the Fulanis migrated from the Guinea highlands. There are larger Mandinka settlements upriver (east of the capital), but a few are found in the Banjul area. Wolofs are from the Senegambia area; it is believed that they and the Jolas have always lived in the region. The Serrahules, who are basically traders and live in the Banjul area, migrated from Mali and Mauritania. About 80 percent of Gambians live in rural areas. The largest cities are Serrekunda, Banjul, Brikama, and Bakau, a suburb of Banjul, respectively.

The Gambia's Human Development Index (0.299) ranks it 161st out of 174 nations. Adjusted for women, the index (0.277) ranks The Gambia 119th out of 130 countries. These figures reflect a general lack of opportunities in the country for people to pursue personal goals or enjoy a decent standard of living.

Language

Although English is the official language, most Gambians speak Wolof and/or Mandinka on a daily basis. Official business and school instruction is conducted in English. Most Gambians who have attended school speak English, and Gambians with contacts in Senegal also speak French. French is encouraged in the high school curriculum. Wolof is the commercial language. Informal conversations are conducted in the respective local languages, which include Fula, Creole, Jola, Serere, and Serrehule. None of these languages is written, although members of the religious elite sometimes use Arabic characters to "write" in Wolof or Mandinka.

Religion

About 85 percent of Gambians are Muslim, 13 percent are Christian, and 2 percent are animist. Religious differences are not emphasized; intermarriage and tolerance between people of different backgrounds are common. Religious freedom is guaranteed. Most Christians live in Banjul, Bakau, and Serrekunda, whereas Muslims reside throughout the country.

Muslims basically believe in *Allah* as God and Muhammad as his prophet. They accept Jesus as a prophet but not as the son of God, as Christians believe. Muslims pray five times daily, give alms to the poor, and try to make a pilgrimage to Makkah, Saudi Arabia, at least once in their lifetime. Muslims also fast each year during the month of *Ramadan*, going without food or drink from sunrise to sunset each day. Most entertainment is temporarily suspended during *Ramadan* because of the fast, which commemorates *Allah's* revelation of the *Qur'an* to Muhammad.

General Attitudes

Gambians are generally self-confident, outgoing, and positive about life. They are usually open and hospitable toward strangers because sharing and openness are valued over secrecy and individualism. People eat and spend what they have today, hoping *Allah* will provide for tomorrow. Most lead lives of great simplicity.

Gambians are proud of their heritage, but many are also curious about Western civilization. Westerners are often approached by young people interested in going to a Western nation. Most Gambians are pleased to host international guests; this is known as *Tarranga*. The Gambia's social value system includes a belief in strong family bonds, honesty, friendliness, sharing, respect, and communal effort. These values are changing as Western ones are introduced. For example, elders (especially those with gray hair) are traditionally considered wise and irreproachable—one should not speak boldly to elders but rather listen carefully to their advice. Yet the Western concept of children standing up to their parents has led some Gambians to do the same, and now it is not uncommon to see a child talk back to a parent.

Time is perceived differently in The Gambia than in the West. Gambians prefer to take their time with activities. Appointment times are given in general terms ("around lunchtime"). Further, if something cannot be done today, it will be done tomorrow or the next day. This attitude is not as prevalent in farming communities, since work must be done according to the seasons.

Personal Appearance

Most Gambians value neatness. Shorts are worn only by children up to the high school level. Men usually wear dress pants and shirts. Many people mix Western and African clothing (Western pants with an African shirt, for example). Some men may also wear an "ambassador suit" (also called a safari suit). Suits and ties are common in offices. School children wear uniforms.

While most older women wear a traditional colorful dress called a *Deppeh* or *Grandmbuba*, older men wear *Haftans* (tailored, long robes) or *Warambas* (shorter, more flowing robes). Younger women often wear a *Dagit* (skirt-and-blouse outfit).

CUSTOMS AND COURTESIES

Greetings

Gambians consider greetings to be important before beginning a conversation or conducting formal business. The younger person usually initiates a handshake and the greeting process. The initiator follows the handshake with *Salama lay kum* (May peace be upon you), to which a person responds *Wal lay kumma salam* (May it be upon you, too). When greeting an elder, one may start by saying the elder person's first name once and his last name several times. As part of a greeting, inquiries are made about an individual's health and that of his or her family. Greetings may last a minute or two. If a girl greets an elder, she might shake hands, but she may also dip her knees toward the ground to show respect. Traditionally, the girl would actually kneel, but the gesture is more of a curtsy today. Boys do not kneel or curtsy when they greet elders.

A person of the same age group as one's parents is greeted as "mother," "aunt," "father," or "uncle," regardless of their relation to the greeter; these titles are combined with the first names (Aunt Marie). This greeting is especially common in and near Banjul, Serrekunda, and other cities. In some other towns, especially in the east, the Mandinka greeting *Summo lay* (How are people at your house?) is common. The customary response is *Ibbi jay* (They are fine; they are there). The Wolof also use *Na ka nga def* (How are you?) and respond *Ma ngi fi rek* (I am alright; I am here).

Gestures

To beckon, Gambians wave all fingers inward with the palm facing down. They avoid using the left hand for most activities (shaking hands, passing items, eating), but it is used to shake hands with someone departing on a long trip as a sign of wishing a safe journey. Direct eye contact with older people is disrespectful. The index finger is a sign of good luck and safety. For instance, a Gambian might dip the finger in food to taste before eating; it is believed this can prevent food poisoning. Dipping the index finger is also a substitute for saying prayers before a meal.

While eating on the streets is uncommon for adults, people might eat peanuts or oranges sold at street stands. Children might eat on the street and elders may chew kola nuts or bitter kola. Kola nuts are round and have a caffeine effect; bitter kola is elongated and bitter but is not a stimulant. When one yawns, one must cover the mouth and then touch the forehead. Burping after a meal is not rude; it is a positive comment on the food and is often followed by a word of thanks to the cook or *Allah* for providing the meal.

Visiting

Visiting friends and relatives is common and is a way to maintain strong relationships. People normally visit friends and relatives without prior notice. Guests are always welcome and should never be turned away. Even if the host is about to leave, he will stay a while to talk with the guest. Visits are most common in the late afternoon or evening when the sun is mild and there is enough shade to be outside. The normal greeting takes place first with both parties standing. The host then offers a drink or food. It is also common for people to visit during mealtime, in which case the guest is expected to at least taste the food.

Gifts are not an obligation when visiting, but it is not unusual for people with a mango or other fruit tree to bring some fruit to the host. Visitors from other towns normally bring gifts, which may range from vegetables to chickens. People chat about local developments: who is marrying whom, who has died, when the next naming ceremony will be, and so on. When a guest leaves, a host may offer a gift in the form of taxi fare. Although most visiting is done at home, some is done at work or in public places.

Eating

Most Gambians eat three meals a day. Breakfast is usually from 7:00 to 9:00 A.M., lunch from 1:00 to 3:00 P.M., and dinner from 7:00 to 9:00 P.M. Many wage earners, however, do not have lunch until after 4:00 P.M., when government offices close. Schedules are different in farming communities. Lunch is the most important and largest meal of the day. Most Gambians sit on a floor mat to eat; elders may sit on a low stool or bench. Although some urban Gambians eat with utensils, most prefer to eat with their hands from communal bowls. The left hand steadies the bowl while the right is used to eat. Conversation is limited. Food does not have to be finished. It

is impolite for children to reach for meat in a bowl; they must wait to be given a portion. Children also look down while eating and do not engage in conversation with their elders. Leftovers are divided equally among the children. Since eating and drinking at the same time is not acceptable, drinks usually are served only after a meal. If soft drinks are served, water will be served first.

Few Gambians eat in restaurants because each family usually prepares three meals a day at home. Tourists often eat in restaurants, where tips are expected.

LIFESTYLE

Family

The Gambian family structure is not limited to the nuclear family but is based on the extended family. Three generations may live together in one household. Most Gambians refer to one another by their family title. For example, one is a "brother," "sister," "aunt," "grandfather," and so forth. It is common to call more than one person father or mother, and there are various kinds of "relatives." If not related by blood, people may become related by long years of friendship, comingling, or working together.

Families, usually headed by the father, are generally large by Western standards. The family is the nucleus and pillar of the community, as well as the source of individual strength, recognition, and social standing. The concept of marriage goes beyond two people to extend to the community, especially when a son marries and introduces his new wife to the family compound. Although women of the younger generation often work outside the home, most older women remain in the home as housewives.

Dating and Marriage

Boys and girls normally do not socialize together. "Boys with the boys and girls with the girls" is a popular Gambian phrase. Young boys generally are not welcome to visit a girl's house and can only court a girl with parental permission. Although dating is not accepted, some dating occurs at night without the knowledge of parents. This may include meeting at parties, soccer games, or on the street. The youth also meet at marriage ceremonies or school. It is not unusual for a boy to tell a girl "I love you" at first sight.

While the practice of arranged marriages is rapidly diminishing in urban areas, it is still common among rural families. Men and women share family responsibilities, but women are responsible for household chores while men provide the family income. Although polygamy still exists, especially in rural areas, only a few men have more than one wife.

Diet

For breakfast, bread with butter or jam and hot tea are popular in urban areas. People might also eat *Rui/monno* (pap), *Chura* (porridge), or *Accara* (fried bean flour). These breakfasts can be purchased from street vendors or prepared at home. Rice is the main staple and most Gambians eat rice and stew for lunch. The stew, which always includes spices and vegetables (eggplant, cabbage, cassava, and/or okra), varies from a fish, chicken, or beef base to a peanut butter base. Pork is forbidden for Muslims but is still sold in some urban markets. Other popular lunch dishes include *Benachin* (jollof rice), *Superkanja* (okra soup), and *Domoda* (peanut butter stew). Dinner may be leftover rice from lunch, *Chereh* (a form of millet couscous), fried fish, beef sauce with bread, or salad with potatoes and chicken or beef. Gambians eat more fish than beef, but couscous with a special beef sauce is popular for certain festivals.

Recreation

Gambians spend their leisure time at festivals or ceremonies, such as weddings, burials, or naming ceremonies. People also visit friends and relatives as a form of recreation. Although The Gambia has beautiful beaches, most Gambians rarely use them, except for young men who may play beach soccer or go swimming. While soccer is the most popular sport, Gambians also wrestle, run track, and play tennis, basketball, and cricket. Family outings are not common. Playing cards or checkers is popular.

Television programming is provided only at night. There are movie theaters in Banjul, Serrekunda, and Bakau, but going to movies is not popular among Gambians. Some are able to watch videos at home.

Holidays

The Gambia's official public holidays include New Year's Day, Independence Day (18 February), Easter (including Good Friday), Labor Day (1 May), and Christmas. Most holidays, except Labor Day, are celebrated with festivals, which include ethnic dances, house parties, dances, and local wrestling competitions. Muslim holy days that also have official recognition include *Eid-el-Fitre* (three-day feast at the end of *Ramadan*), *Eid-el-Kabir* (Feast of the Sacrifice, held in conjunction with the summer pilgrimage to Makkah), and *Mauloud-el-Nabi* (Muhammad's birthday). Muslim festivals fall on different days each year because they are set by the lunar calendar.

Commerce

Offices are open from 8:00 A.M. to 4:00 P.M., Monday through Thursday. Shops remain open until 6:00 or 7:00 P.M. Businesses close on Friday by 1:00 P.M. for afternoon (Muslim) prayers. Almost all buying and selling, except in a few large or well-established stores, is subject to barter. Goods are sold in the market, in stores, and on side streets.

SOCIETY

Government

The Gambia has five divisions (Lower River, MacCarthy Island, North Bank, Upper River, and Western) and one major city, Banjul. Before the coup, the democratic system included an elected president and Parliament. Until new elections, Lieutenant Jammeh rules by decree and is advised by a handful of junior military officers.

Economy

Agriculture employs 75 percent of the labor force. The Gambia exports peanuts, but cotton, rice, millet, maize, and sorghum are also key crops. Trade with neighboring countries, especially Senegal, is vital to economic growth. A growing number of people are involved in the fishing industry. Seafood is exported to Europe. Tourism is a vital source of revenue, and The Gambia has been a favorite destination for British and other tourists because of its nice beaches and pleasant weather. Violence in a 1994 counter coup prompted tourists to stay away in 1995, but the tourist industry recovered somewhat in 1996.

Real gross domestic product per capita is estimated at $1,260, which has improved substantially in the past generation. Still, 40 percent of rural people live in poverty. Indeed, most people do not earn a wage and find it difficult to meet basic needs. Economic opportunities are limited to the few who are educated or wealthy. The currency is the *dalasi* (D).

Transportation and Communication

The Gambia's main road to major cities, which leads upriver, is paved, but only major streets in other cities are paved. Public buses run from Banjul to other cities, but they are very crowded. People usually walk in the cities and take the bus from one city to the next. Taxis are usually available.

The Gambia has a modern telephone system, but most Gambians do not own a phone. Public phones are available for use at a fee. There are several newspapers and two radio stations. Radio Gambia is controlled by the government, but the other station (Radio Syd) is private.

Education

Although there are no tuition fees at the primary education level, only about 35 percent of adult Gambians are literate. Preschools and kindergartens are available. Beginning at age eight, students spend about six years in primary school. Approximately one-fifth proceed to high school for five years, provided they pass the Common Entrance Exam. Those who do not pass may go to secondary technical school for four years. High school graduates may spend two years in Sixth Form as preparation for college. While there is a highly specialized technical institute (Gambia Technical Training Institution) and a college for teachers (Yundum College), The Gambia has no university. More men than women tend to be educated or enrolled in school.

Health

The Gambia's health-care system includes some facilities in Banjul and the Kombos and regional health centers at upriver locations. Government doctors and nurses staff these clinics. Private doctors are also available. The Jawara administration failed to invest in health programs in general and did not build any much needed hospitals. The immunization program is fairly extensive, but infant mortality remains high (121 per 1,000) due to poor hygiene and nutritional deficiencies. Life expectancy ranges from 48 to 53 years.

FOR THE TRAVELER

U.S. citizens need a passport and visa to visit The Gambia. A yellow fever vaccination is no longer required. Malaria precautions are recommended. There are a number of interesting places to visit, including the Stone Circles that date from A.D. 750, James Island, Abuko Nature Reserve, and Tendaba Camp. The potential for violence during the elections is remote, but prospective travelers should monitor events closely. For information, contact the Embassy of The Gambia, 1155 15th Street NW, Suite 1000, Washington, DC 20005.

A *Culturgram* is a product of native commentary and original, expert analysis. Statistics are estimates and information is presented as a matter of opinion. While the editors strive for accuracy and detail, this document should not be considered strictly factual. It is a general introduction to culture, an initial step in building bridges of understanding between peoples. It may not apply to all peoples of the nation. You should therefore consult other sources for more information.

Republic of
Ghana

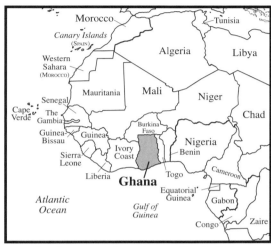

Boundary representations not necessarily authoritative.

BACKGROUND

Land and Climate

Ghana lies in the tropic zone on the Guinea Coast of West Africa. Covering 92,100 square miles (238,540 square kilometers), it is about the same size as Oregon. The south is dominated by low-lying plains that alternate between grass cover and mangroves. The west and southern interior are primarily tropical forests. About 5 percent of Ghana is arable. Forests and woodlands cover 37 percent of the total land area. The Volta River country is covered with savanna woodlands and swamps. A dam on the Volta River has created the largest man-made lake in the world: Lake Volta. The north is primarily dry grassland.

Ghana has two seasons: rainy from April to October, and hot and dry the rest of the year, with temperatures reaching 100°F (38°C). The Harmattan subseason (two months between late November and early January) brings hot, dry, and dusty winds to the north. In the south, rain is expected between April and June and again in September and October. Temperatures in the southeast range from 74°F (23°C) in October to 86°F (30°C) in June.

History

Ghana takes its name, though not its modern boundaries, from one of the great inland trading empires that flourished in West Africa from the fourth to the eleventh centuries A.D. The fabled university city of Tombouctou (Timbuktu—now in Mali) was part of ancient Ghana. Because of the diversity of ethnic groups, the country's history is quite varied. Modern history began when Portuguese traders arrived in the 16th century. They mined gold and established headquarters for the slave trade. The area became known as the "Gold Coast," and several European powers established forts there. In 1874, Britain took control of the Gold Coast. After several years of battles with the Asante of the interior, the British gained control of present-day Ghana in 1901.

The Convention People's Party (CPP), under the leadership of Kwame Nkrumah, won legislative elections in 1951, and for the first time the black majority controlled the government. On 6 March 1957, Ghana became the first Black African colony to gain independence from Britain. Three years later, the country became a republic and Nkrumah was elected president. Unfortunately, his socialist policies led to a significant drop in the standard of living. While he was on his way to Vietnam in 1966, Nkrumah was deposed by a military coup. General A. A. Afrifa ruled until general elections were again held in 1969. But after three years of civilian rule, the military again took over in 1972, and Prime Minister Kofi Busia was dismissed.

In 1979, Flight Lieutenant Jerry Rawlings, with a group of junior officers and enlisted men, overthrew the government, arrested dozens of government officials, and executed eight of them, including three former heads of state. Rawlings drafted a new constitution, held elections, and just six months after gaining power turned the government over to newly elected Dr. Hilla Limann and the new national assembly. However, Rawlings was not satisfied with government performance and again seized power in December 1981. He outlawed all political parties, suspended the constitution, and appointed a seven-member Provisional National Defense Council (PNDC).

In 1988, a national assembly was established, but members could not belong to political parties. The assembly was to represent different walks of life rather than political views. It was eventually determined that Ghana would return to democratic rule. A constituent assembly, composed of elected and appointed officials, helped draft a constitution to legalize political parties and provide for elections. National elections were held in November 1992. Rawlings won the presidential race to remain leader of the country. His term expires in December 1996.

THE PEOPLE

Population

The population of Ghana is more than 17.8 million and is growing rapidly at 3 percent a year. While 99.8 percent of the population is Black African, it is divided into more than one hundred different ethnic groups, each with its own language and cultural heritage. Some major groups include the Fante in the coastal areas, the Asante in the south-central area, the Ga-Adangme and Ewe in the south, and the Hausa and Moshi-Dagomba in the north. The 0.2 percent nonblack population is mostly European, with some Lebanese merchants and communities of Indians and Chinese. The largest city is the capital of Accra, with more than one million people. Kumasi, a bustling trade center for the entire country, is also home to a large population. However, two-thirds of Ghanaians live in rural areas.

Ghana's Human Development Index (0.482) ranks it 129th out of 174 nations. The index is only slightly lower for women, although women tend to be less literate than men. Most people lack opportunities for economic prosperity and personal advancement.

Language

English is the official language of Ghana, partly because of the country's colonial association with Great Britain and partly because there are so many ethnic languages that just one of them could not effectively serve as the official language. English is used in school, business, and government. There are movements to make several local languages official as well. Widely spoken as primary languages are Akan (44 percent of the population), Mole-Dagbani (16 percent), Ewe (13 percent), and Ga-Adangme (8 percent). The Twi dialect of Akan is the language most commonly used on a daily basis to communicate between ethnic groups. Most Ghanaians are at least bilingual.

Religion

Traditional African beliefs and practices still play a major role in the lives of the people of Ghana. These are inseparable from the life and culture of Ghanaians and are retained regardless of any other religious affiliation. About 24 percent of Ghanaians belong to various Christian churches, 30 percent are Muslim, and 38 percent completely maintain their traditional beliefs.

This traditional faith is characterized by a belief in a Supreme Being who has created all things and has given various degrees of power to all living (animate) and nonliving (inanimate) things. Out of respect for the Supreme Being, who cannot be approached directly, traditional Ghanaians often communicate with him through intermediaries. Intermediaries can include animate or inanimate objects, as well as the spirits of ancestors. People especially seek guidance through their ancestors. Because of this, ancestor veneration is an important aspect of the culture and worship. These traditional beliefs are often referred to by outsiders as *animism*, because of their emphasis on showing reverence for living things. Many Ghanaians would not accept the term *animism* to describe their worship. Traditional faith also includes a belief in wizards, witches, demons, magic potions, and other supernatural phenomena.

General Attitudes

Ghanaians are warm, friendly, and sociable people. They are polite, open, and trusting—even with strangers. They tend to take life at a more relaxed pace, viewing time as a series of events rather than a matter of hours or minutes. People are more important than schedules. Tolerance and acceptance are typical individual characteristics. The group is valued over personal needs.

Ghanaians are proud of their status as the first sub-Saharan colony to gain independence from a European power. Although greatly influenced by Western civilization, the people are striving to develop a nation and culture that is uniquely African. Western visitors should take care not to act, or give the impression of being, superior just because they come from industrialized nations. This is offensive to Ghanaians.

Personal Appearance

Ghanaian dress is modest, neat, and generally conservative. Casual dress is the rule for most occasions, although a suit and tie or dress are required for more formal occasions. Shorts are not acceptable public attire. Western dress is normal in urban areas, but officials often wear traditional *kente* cloth robes on ceremonial occasions. Non-Western attire for men varies by region and ethnic group. For example, in the south men may wear long, colored cloth wrapped around the body somewhat like a toga. Northern men wear long tunics made of wide strips of rough cotton cloth that are sewn together. Muslim men wear robes similar to those worn by Arab Muslims, except that the Ghanaian version is colorful. Regardless of what one wears, the design of the cloth can reflect one's status. Women usually wear a traditional, long, wraparound skirt; a separate top; and a head scarf. Women prefer bold colors and large prints. They wrap extra cloth at the hips or add it to the sleeves. A woman's head cloth generally matches her dress.

CUSTOMS AND COURTESIES

Greetings

Because of pronounced differences between ethnic groups, greetings vary from area to area. English handshakes and greetings are common. Indeed, a handshake is important when greeting most people. Before beginning a conversation, a general greeting such as *Good morning*, *Good afternoon*, or *Good evening* is necessary. Most greetings are in the dominant local language and are followed by questions about one's health, family welfare, journey, and so forth. People address new acquaintances by title and family name. Friends and family members often use given names. Children refer to any adult that is well-known to the family as *aunt* or *uncle*, even when they are not related. By the same token, adults of the same age might refer to each other as brother or sister, regardless of their relationship, and will use *auntie* and *uncle* for respected older people.

Gestures

Courtesy is important. Gesturing with the left hand is impolite. Some Ghanaians, especially Muslims, may consider it improper to pass or receive items with the left hand. Either the right hand or both hands should be used. When yawning or using a toothpick, a person covers the mouth. Among Muslims, and some other groups used to sitting on the floor, it is improper to allow the sole of one's foot to point at another person. Generally, one does not place feet on chairs, desks, or tables—especially those being used by another person. It is impolite and an act of defiance for a child to look an adult in the eye. Friends of the same gender may often and appropriately hold hands while walking or speaking. However, members of the opposite sex (except relatives) do not hold hands or show any affection in public.

Visiting

In a society where friendly social relations are important, visiting plays a key role in everyday life. Friends and relatives visit one another frequently, often unannounced, and appreciate the visits of others. Ghanaians work hard to accommodate their guests. Most visits occur in the home. Guests might take a small gift for the children. Some hosts prefer that guests remove their shoes when entering the home. Guests are nearly always served drinks and often other refreshments. Refusing these offers is impolite. Visitors are usually welcome to stay as long as they wish. People generally avoid visiting during mealtime, but an unexpected guest would be invited to share the meal. Visiting is most popular on Sunday, and many people like to dress up for the occasion. When a visit is over, guests are accompanied to the bus stop or taxi stand or given a ride home. Leaving them on their own is considered impolite.

Eating

Ghanaians usually eat meals with their right hand. At the beginning of the meal, hosts provide a bowl of water in which each person washes the hands. To eat, one scoops food and forms it into a ball with the right hand before eating it. Water is passed around at the end of the meal for diners to wash their hands. Foreigners may need to become accustomed to the food, which is often spicy.

Most larger restaurants serve Western and native Ghanaian food. While the bill often includes a service charge, it is customary to leave a small tip.

LIFESTYLE

Family

Family structures vary from one ethnic group to another, but the extended family is strong and vital in most areas. Some groups have a matriarchal family organization, in which inheritance is passed down through the wife's family. In these groups, the chief responsibilities for the family fall on the women. Others have male-dominated structures. Polygamy (having more than one wife) is also practiced by some Ghanaians. Extended families of three or four generations often share one household. The entire community looks after children, who can move about by themselves without direct supervision.

All elderly members of the family are deeply respected and exercise a great deal of influence on family decisions. Ghanaians normally sacrifice personal desires and ambitions for the sake of the family unit. Funerals are very important and last three days. For those people involved, everything else comes to a stop and all attention is directed toward funeral-related activities.

Dating and Marriage

Families still arrange many marriages, although the children have the right to reject undesirable arrangements. Westernized dating practices are found among a growing number of urban youth. Marriage in rural areas (and to some extent in urban areas) may also follow tradition, which allows a man to take more than one wife. Still, the Christian marriage with its monogamous restrictions is becoming prevalent. Traditionally, the groom pays the bride's family a *bridal token* to indicate responsibility for the new bride.

Diet

The diet consists mainly of yams, cassava (a starchy root), maize, plantains, and rice. Ghanaians enjoy hot and spicy food, and most of their meals are accompanied by a pepper sauce made with meat, fish, or chicken. Fish is most common due to cost. Popular dishes include *fufu* (a dough-like combination of plantains and cassava), *ampesi* (a green vegetable dish), and palm or peanut oil soups and sauces. Ghana also produces a variety of tropical fruits and vegetables to supplement the diet.

Recreation

Soccer is the national sport to which most people are highly devoted. Ghanaians are also fond of boxing, field hockey, horse racing, and track-and-field. Where available, people enjoy the theater, movies, cultural presentations, and music and dance festivals. Ghana has its own movie industry. Various ethnic group festivals are celebrated throughout the country.

Holidays

Holidays include Independence Day (6 March), Good Friday (Friday before Easter Sunday), Easter Monday, Republic Day (1 July), Christmas, Boxing Day (26 December), and 31 December (to celebrate the 1981 revolution). Boxing Day comes from the British tradition of giving service personnel and tradesmen small boxed gifts. Today, people generally spend the day visiting friends and relatives.

Commerce

Most businesses are open from 8:00 A.M. to noon and 2:00 to 4:30 P.M., Monday through Friday. Some are open on Saturday morning. Business dress is conservative. *Dash* is a common Ghanaian form of compensation in money, goods, or favors for personal services performed. Except in restaurants and for bellhops in hotels, *dash* is normally paid before the service is given. While the system of *dash* is discouraged by the government, it is widely practiced and includes anything from watching a car to expediting the movement of goods in and out of the country.

SOCIETY

Government

Ghana is a constitutional democracy, although in practice the country is still in transition from a dictatorship to a multiparty democracy. The president is head of state and head of government, but he works with the National Assembly in establishing laws and policy. The governing National Democratic Congress dominates the assembly, but opposition parties are becoming more organized and stronger. They include the New Patriotic Party and the People's Heritage Party, among others. The voting age is 18. Ghana is divided into ten regions.

Economy

The Ghanaian economy is based primarily on agriculture, which employs more than 50 percent of the labor force. Cacao (from which cocoa is made) is the most important cash crop, accounting for about 45 percent of all exports. Other crops include corn, root crops, sorghum, millet, and peanuts. With gold, bauxite, aluminum, and diamonds as natural resources, mining is also important to the economy. Fishing, light manufacturing, and timber are key industries. Economic growth is dependent on world prices for Ghana's exports, of which gold is the most important. World price fluctuations can cause great financial strain and economic difficulties at times. Growth in 1994 was 5 percent.

Government policies have successfully reduced inflation to manageable levels. Ghana has been privatizing and modernizing its economy for several years. A stock market has existed since 1990. Ghana remains an essentially poor country, as poverty affects more than 40 percent of all people. Real gross domestic product per capita is $2,110, which is now improving for the first time in years. The currency is the new *cedi* (¢).

Transportation and Communication

While the transportation system is underdeveloped, a rail system connects Accra with Kumasi and Takoradi. A fairly good system of buses connects major cities. There are also some domestic flights available. Most people do not own cars but rely on public transportation or other means of travel. The *tro-tro* is a crowded, but efficient and inexpensive, minibus used for short-distance public transport. Taxis are also available. Communications systems are equally underdeveloped, although the government is seeking to upgrade facilities and networks. Mail and phone services are often unreliable, but the informal method of passing information works rapidly and well: letters or messages are passed to a driver or passenger traveling in the intended direction until they reach their destination.

Education

Ghana is striving to increase the availability of primary education, but efforts have so far not improved conditions of overcrowding or underfunding. Schools are organized on three levels: primary (six years), junior secondary (three years), and senior secondary (three years). Today, every administrative district has at least one high school. The average adult literacy rate is 61 percent: 73 percent for men and 49 percent for women. About 30,000 students study above the secondary level, including students at the four universities in Ghana (at Legon, Kumasi, Cape Coast, and Tamale).

Health

Although the government is working to increase the quality and availability of medical care, standards do not equal those in the West. Medical facilities are limited outside of Accra and other major cities. Malaria and other tropical diseases are still present in Ghana. Ghana lacks a clean water supply and modern sewer system, which presents a serious health hazard to even urban residents. Intestinal disorders are common. Many people rely on various forms of herbal medicine and traditional healing. The infant mortality rate is 82 per 1,000, which is lower than in the past but still very high. The average life expectancy is 54 to 58 years.

FOR THE TRAVELER

A tourist visa is required with a valid passport and can only be obtained with proof of finances, a letter from one's employer, and an onward ticket. Vaccinations against yellow fever are required. Cholera vaccinations and malaria suppressants are recommended. Water is not potable, and bodies of fresh water are not safe for swimming. One should peel all fruits and vegetables before eating.

Visitors should not use the word *tribe* when referring to a Ghanaian's ethnic background. This word has negative connotations, and Ghanaians may be offended by its use or question the visitor's intentions. The term *ethnic group* is a suitable substitute, but one should reserve questions about a person's ethnic background until well acquainted with him or her.

U.S. American travelers should consider contacting the U.S. Embassy on arrival (in Accra, on Ring Road East) for any advisories on Ghanaian law, which can differ substantially from U.S. law. Getting arrested for breaking a law can cause many difficulties. Any visitor staying more than seven days must register with the Ghana Immigration Service within 48 hours of arrival. For more information, contact the Trade and Tourism Department of the Embassy of Ghana, 3512 International Drive NW, Washington, DC 20008; phone (202) 686–4520.

Republic of
Guinea

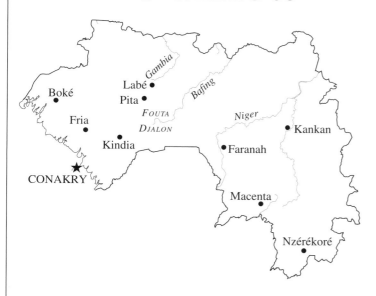

Boundary representations not necessarily authoritative.

BACKGROUND

Land and Climate

Guinea covers 94,000 square miles (243,460 square kilometers) and is somewhat smaller than Oregon. The nation is divided into four regions: the coast of lower Guinea; the central, mountainous Fouta Djalon; the savanna of upper Guinea; and the forest in the southeast. Numerous major rivers, including the Niger, Bafing, and Gambia, have their sources in Guinea.

Guinea has two distinct seasons: the rainy season, or *hivernage* (May–October), and the dry season (November–April). As much as 170 inches (67 centimeters) of rain may fall on the coast annually, while the savanna region receives only about 60 inches (24 centimeters) each year. Average temperatures range from 80°F to 90°F (26–32°C), but temperatures above 100°F (38°C) are not uncommon. Nighttime temperatures in the Fouta Djalon may fall to as low as 50°F (10°C).

History

For thousands of years, Guinea was populated by various peoples. In the tenth century A.D., Soussou and Malinke groups began to move into the area, pushing the former inhabitants into smaller regions. Upper Guinea was part of the Ghana Empire in the 10th and 11th centuries, then the Mali Empire until the 14th century, and the Songhai Empire until the 19th century. The Fulani moved into Guinea in the 17th century and brought Islam with them. They pushed the Soussou to coastal areas, where the Soussou established trade with Europeans. While not a major slave trade area, Guinea was affected by that trading as well as by disputes among European groups. In the 19th century, El Hadj Umar came from Senegal to reform the practice of Islam in Guinea. His fundamentalism was accepted by the Fulani and the Malinke, and his influence accounts for Guinean Muslims' devotion to Islam today. Almamy Samory Toure, a follower of Umar, was a great leader in the late 1800s; he was so powerful that France did not capture him and complete their conquest of the region until 1904.

French rule, which began in the 19th century, brought private ownership of communal land and the expansion of commercial and service jobs. An urban elite that adopted the French language and culture evolved, but most of the area's people continued to live a subsistence agriculture lifestyle until the 1940s.

After World War II, several labor parties were established, including the *Parti Democratique de Guinee*, led by Ahmed Sekou Toure. In 1958, this party organized support to vote against Charles de Gaulle's proposed French community and then declared independence. Guinea was the only French colony to vote "no" on the issue. Thus, unlike other francophone African states, it was cut off from France's financial aid and other assistance programs. Guinea was also shunned by other Western nations and, in this relative isolation, developed a strong national identity.

Toure, once loved by the people for his leadership, never allowed elections and governed a one-party state. He deteriorated into a dictator and began facing opposition from various groups. Nevertheless, Toure survived several attempted coups and continued to rule Guinea until his death in 1984. Two weeks later, the military took control of the government and established the Second Guinean Republic under Lansana Conte. In 1990, a committee was established to oversee Guinea's transition to a multiparty system. A constitution providing for a democratic government was drafted and accepted in 1991. Presidential and parliamentary elections took place in late 1993. Lansana Conte was declared president.

THE PEOPLE
Population
Guinea's population of approximately 6.5 million is growing annually at about 2.4 percent. Guinea's Human Development Index (0.237) ranks it 168th out of 174 countries. This reflects not only a lack of economic development but also of access to opportunities for personal advancement. The country's resources are further strained by the presence of at least 400,000 refugees from fighting in Sierra Leone and Liberia.

More than one million people live in the capital, Conakry. Another 250,000 live in each of the regional capitals of Labé, Kankan, and Nzérékoré. Almost three-fourths of the population lives in rural areas. The major ethnic groups include the Fulani (35 percent) in the Fouta Djalon, the Malinke (30 percent) in upper Guinea, and the Soussou (20 percent) in the coastal region. There are numerous other ethnic groups, sometimes comprising only one village.

Language
French is the official language of Guinea, but most rural people do not understand it. Various African languages are spoken in different regions. On the coast, the language is Soussou; in the Fouta Djalon, it is Pular; in upper Guinea, it is Malinke; and in the forest, numerous languages intermingle, including Guerze, Kissi, and Toma. Except for a few religious phrases, Arabic is only spoken by those who have learned to read the *Qur'an* (Koran).

Religion
Guinea's government promotes religious freedom. About 85 percent of the population is Muslim. Most other Guineans are Christian. Animism is still practiced by certain rural groups and by some Muslims and Christians. For example, people remain superstitious and buy *gri gri* (good-luck charms) for their children. Animists in the forest do not trust people of other religions or races because these groups have destroyed or otherwise violated sacred forests.

Guinean Muslims are devout and follow the traditional worship practices of praying five times daily, avoiding alcohol, professing the name of and attributing all to *Allah* (God), fasting during the holy month of *Ramadan*, and giving alms to the poor. They accept the *Qur'an* as scripture that was revealed to Muhammad, Islam's last and greatest recognized prophet.

General Attitudes
Guineans identify strongly with their families and ethnic groups. Although various groups coexist without serious strife, there is a tendency to reserve help and trust for one's own group. Tensions exist between ethnic groups, religions, and social classes in some areas, but they have not yet seriously threatened stability.

People speak often of religion in discussing how one should act. Most Guineans strongly believe that whatever happens is *Allah's* will, and they accept disappointment or sorrow with this attitude. Such fatalism also means people live more for the present, assuming the future will take care of itself. Daily living and interpersonal relationships are often more important than material goods. The Guinean sense of time is relaxed, and people may arrive hours late for an appointment or event with little explanation.

Personal Appearance
Guineans wear Western styles as well as traditional Muslim and West African clothing. To work, men may wear a short-sleeved suit coat and matching pants, or they may wear a Western-style shirt, a tie, and pants. Muslim men may wear long robes called *boubous* over loose pants and a shirt. Women often wear brightly patterned, locally tailored blouses or Muslim-style robes called *petits boubous* with a matching *pagne* (length of cloth wrapped around the waist). Some women also wear Western-style dresses. No matter what style a person wears, it is extremely important in Guinea that clothing be clean, well pressed, and in good repair.

CUSTOMS AND COURTESIES
Greetings
Greetings are an important part of everyday interaction. To fail to greet someone or to skip a greeting in favor of conversation is an insult. Guineans most often greet others in French, Arabic, or the language of the particular region or individual to whom they are speaking. *Bonjour* (Good day) and *Bonsoir* (Good evening) are the common French greetings. Greetings are usually followed by inquiries about the other person's family.

When walking along the road, a person might call out greetings rather than stopping. Even strangers are greeted, including store clerks, taxi drivers, or anyone with whom one is about to interact. Upon arrival at a gathering, Guineans greet every person with a right-handed handshake. When the right hand is not clean, one extends a closed fist and the other person shakes the wrist. Raising both hands, palms out, is a common way to greet a larger group or someone who is a bit distant for a handshake. Some older men also use this greeting rather than shaking hands with women. If seated, a person shows respect by standing up to shake hands. Respect is also conveyed by grasping one's own right forearm with the left hand while shaking hands. Good friends who are parting for a long time might use a left handshake.

When addressing others, Guineans use titles, such as *Doctor*, *Madame* (Mrs.), or *Monsieur* (Mr.), instead of names. They also use familial titles, such as *Frere*, *Tanti*, and *Cousin* (Brother, Aunt, and Cousin), with strangers as well as within the family.

Gestures
Guineans hand objects to or accept them from others with the right hand. They beckon by waving all four fingers with the palm down. A taxi is hailed by extending the arm, palm down, and waving the hand. To show respect, one avoids eye contact, especially with older people. Men and women do

not show affection in public, but friends of the same gender often hold hands or walk arm in arm. People avoid pointing the soles of their feet at others.

Visiting

To visit someone is to honor them, and Guineans are gracious hosts. They frequently invite friends over for a meal, but invitations are not necessary for one to visit. People sometimes visit simply to exchange greetings. To pass by a friend's home without stopping briefly is an insult. Proper greetings are exchanged at every visit, regardless of the purpose. A visitor usually does not bring a gift; rather, a visit is reciprocated with a return visit. The exception is when a person returns or arrives from out of town; then food (fruit, vegetables, or rice), fabric, or a specialty of the region from which the person traveled is an appropriate gift.

Guests may be offered fruit or a beverage if the visit is not during mealtime, but otherwise they are often invited to eat. It is not impolite to say one has just eaten. However, the host usually insists the guest eat something, and it is rude to refuse entirely. Generally, the guest eats at least a small portion and thanks the host and the person who prepared the meal.

During visits, there are often several-minute gaps in conversation, filled only by a repeat of the greetings and inquiries about the family. When guests are ready to leave, they say they must go, shake hands, and thank the host and family for their hospitality.

Eating

Most Guineans eat with the right hand from a common platter that is often placed on the floor or a mat. In some families, people eat separately according to age and gender. Before and after any meal eaten with the hands, a bowl of water is made available for washing hands. Individuals eat only from the part of the dish that is immediately in front of them. The oldest person or the woman who prepared the meal may divide the meat and vegetables among those eating. Most Guineans do not drink during a meal because it implies the food is not good enough to satiate the appetite. Most drink water after the meal. Conversation is minimal, but guests always thank the host at the end of the meal. The host often replies with *Albarka*, an Arabic term used to credit *Allah* for providing the food.

Eating patterns differ for each family. Many Guineans living in nonagricultural settings eat the main meal at midday and another meal or leftovers in the evening. Breakfast may include coffee and bread, as well as any leftovers from the previous day. In agricultural settings, people working in the fields eat a larger breakfast, which may include hot cereal. They then eat their main meal upon returning from the fields in the evening.

LIFESTYLE

Family

The family is the most important social unit in Guinea. Extended families living together—and sharing child care, domestic chores, and meals—are common in rural areas. While extended families are also common in urban areas, the number of nuclear families living in individual homes is increasing. Obligations to one's extended family run deep and can involve giving money, lodging, or other favors to distant relatives. In general, the eldest male presides over the household.

Large families share a common compound with separate homes or rooms for individuals or nuclear family members. Sturdy homes made of thick mud and thatched roofs are common in rural areas, while urban homes may be single- or multi-family cement block structures.

Dating and Marriage

Urban youth may date as in Western cultures, but they more often associate in groups. The choice of a mate may be influenced by the family. Women usually marry before they are 20 and men usually wait until they are 25 or older. Traditionally, the man presents ten kola nuts to the woman's family to propose marriage. The head of the woman's family cracks the nuts to signal his approval. The groom offers fabric, jewelry, or cattle to the bride and her family. Muslim men are allowed to marry more than one wife (up to four total), but they must be able to financially support each one.

Diet

The main meal usually consists of rice with a sauce made from palm oil and tomato paste, peanut butter, or ground leaves. Meat or fish and vegetables, such as manioc, sweet potatoes, or squash, may be cooked with the sauce. Millet is a popular grain in the Sahelian region near Mali. The Malinke eat *too* (pronounced TOE), made from cassava or rice powder. Avocados, peanuts, mangoes, papayas, bananas, oranges, pineapples, and sometimes watermelons are eaten in season. Muslims do not drink alcohol or eat pork.

Recreation

Soccer is the most popular sport in Guinea. Basketball and volleyball are also favorites. Sports are mostly for boys, but urban girls participate through school. Many urban areas have facilities and organized sporting competitions. Guineans also love music and dancing. Traditional musical instruments include the *kora*, a lute-harp (made from half of a large calabash) with metal or fiber strings; the *balafon*, a wooden zylophone; and a wide variety of drums and other percussion instruments. Family gatherings, visits, and local festivals provide recreation for many people, especially in rural areas. Dancing is popular at weddings and other celebrations.

Family celebrations held for Christian baptisms and traditional Muslim and Christian weddings are important. It is customary at these events for *griots* (traditional singers) to sing about individual guests (their name, appearance, character), and the honored person is expected to give the *griots* a small sum of money in return.

Holidays

Guinean holidays include New Year's Day, Easter, *Tabaski* (a Muslim holiday commemorating Abraham's willingness to sacrifice his son to God); a feast at the end of *Ramadan*, a month in which Muslims do not eat or drink from sunrise to sunset; Labor Day (1 May); *Mawloud* (the prophet Muhammad's birthday); Independence Day (2 October); All Saints' Day (1 November); and Christmas. Muslim holidays involve people attending a mosque, visiting friends and family, and eating large meals.

Commerce

Government offices and businesses are open 8:00 A.M. to 4:30 P.M., Monday through Thursday. They close by 2:00 P.M.

on Friday. Offices are closed Saturday and Sunday. Urban markets are open all day, every day, but many merchants close Friday afternoon and Sunday. In rural areas, market day may be only one day a week. Business transactions can take some time to complete in Guinea, and patience and persistence are vital.

SOCIETY

Government

Guinea is officially a multiparty democracy consisting of 33 administrative regions. The elected president is head of state and head of government. President Conte began his five-year term in 1994. The 114 members of the new National Assembly also began serving in 1994. The voting age is 18. A few small parties stand in opposition to the governing Party for Unity and Progress (PUP), including the Rally for the Guinean People (RPG) and Union for a New Republic (UNP).

Economy

Guinea has abundant natural resources, including 25 percent of the world's known reserves of bauxite, along with diamonds, gold, and other metals. The country also has great potential for hydroelectric power. While bauxite and alumina are currently the only major exports, the Guinean government plans to encourage the mining of other resources. Other industries include processing plants for beer, juices, soft drinks, and tobacco. The government encourages a free-market economy and is working hard to promote foreign investment. A continued privatization effort is expected to help the economy and encourage more growth.

Agriculture employs 80 percent of the nation's labor force. Under French rule, and at the beginning of independence, Guinea was a major exporter of bananas, pineapples, coffee, coca, peanuts, and palm oil. Unfortunately, isolation and insufficient capital caused these exports to decline under Toure. If democracy brings an infusion of new investment, exports may be revived. The currency is the Guinean *franc* (GF), which is not tied to any international currency and cannot be converted. It is not allowed outside Guinean borders.

Guinea is one of the poorest countries in the world. Real gross domestic product per capita is $592, a figure that has barely increased in 30 years. Most people do not earn a sufficient income or have no income at all.

Transportation and Communication

Guinea is working to pave roads that link major cities in each of its regions. But most roads, especially in rural areas, are unpaved and not maintained well. Air Guinea flies from Conakry to regional capitals. Guinea also has an intercity bus service (*Sogetrag*) that serves most of the nation's regions. Taxis and trucks are the main means of public transportation for most people, few of whom own cars. Many Guineans travel within their regions by motorcycle or bicycle. Short-distance travel is by foot.

The government sponsors a weekly newspaper, *Horoya* (Liberty), which is available in Conakry. National radio and television programs are broadcast from Conakry. In each region, a radio program in the local language is also broadcast. Domestic and international telephone service is available, but most people do not have phones.

Education

Guinean education is based on the French system and includes six years of primary school, four years of middle school, and three years of high school. Students follow one of three tracks: social science, mathematics, or natural sciences. National tests are required for graduation. Enrollment levels are low; only about one-third of all children attend primary school and the number drops to 15 percent for secondary school. Guinea's officially reported adult literacy rate is 33 percent (less than 20 percent for women). In reality, only about 15 to 30 percent of the population is functional in French, partly because school is sometimes taught in local languages rather than French. This is necessary because children begin school without knowing any French. French was not used as the language of instruction under Toure, but it was reintroduced in the Second Republic. Guinea has four universities and several trade and vocational institutions.

Health

Despite efforts to improve health conditions, the national health-care system is weak. Half of all doctors are in Conakry, and they are scarce in the rest of the country. Only the wealthy can afford quality care. However, many *Centres de Sante* (health centers) are opening in rural areas, providing low-cost care and essential medications. Traditional healers practice in nearly every village and are often the first source of rural care. Childhood diseases and malaria are widespread. Waterborne diseases are common. The infant mortality rate is 137 per 1,000. Life expectancy averages 45 years.

FOR THE TRAVELER

U.S. visitors need a valid passport and visa to enter Guinea. A yellow fever vaccination is required. Immunizations for hepatitis, tetanus, polio, typhoid, meningitis, and rabies are recommended, as are malarial suppressants. For more details, call the Centers for Disease Control and Prevention International Travel Hotline: (404) 332–4559. Electricity is available only part of the time in villages and towns. Visitors should travel with their own drinking water (either bottled or treated).

Guinea's geographical beauty is a great attraction for visitors. The Fouta Djalon region has several waterfalls, including Kin Kon near Pita and *La voile de la mariee* (Bridal Veil) near Kindia. Accommodations and transportation, especially outside Conakry, are somewhat lacking, but Guinea offers a glimpse of West Africa unspoiled and less commercialized than the region's more popular tourist sites. For more information, contact the Embassy of Guinea, 2112 Leroy Place NW, Washington, DC 20008; phone (202) 483–9420.

Republic of

Guinea-Bissau

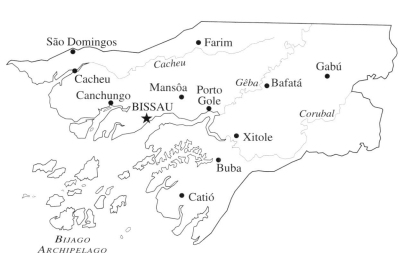

Boundary representations not necessarily authoritative.

BACKGROUND

Land and Climate

Guinea-Bissau is a small West African country that includes the Bijago Archipelago. About the same size as Massachusetts, Rhode Island, and Connecticut combined, it covers 13,946 square miles (36,120 square kilometers). A low-lying coastal plain rises to savanna in the east. Guinea-Bissau is cut by three rivers that flow into the Atlantic Ocean. Mangrove swamps are common along the coast. The climate is tropical and temperatures average near 80°F (27°C). The rainy season is hot and humid; the dry season is hot and dusty. Rainfall differs dramatically from north to south, with the south getting twice as much. Thus, the northern third of the country may be dominated by savanna, but the southern third features canopied gallery forests. The country's coolest months are December and January. Bissau is the capital city.

History

The Portuguese began exploring the region around present-day Guinea-Bissau in the 15th century, first establishing themselves on the islands of Cape Verde, about 350 miles (560 kilometers) northwest of Guinea-Bissau. They claimed the area around current Guinea-Bissau as Portuguese Guinea. The Portuguese established trading posts and, in the 1600s, began exporting slaves from the territory. As the slave trade diminished in the 1800s, Bissau became an important commercial center. The Portuguese did not begin to conquer inland territory until this time.

Initially helped by the Muslims, the Portuguese subdued animist groups and by 1936 had gained control of the entire area. In 1952, the colony of Portuguese Guinea became a province of Portugal. In 1955, Amilcar Cabral and others formed the African Party for the Independence of Guinea and Cape Verde (PAIGC) and led most ethnic groups in a guerrilla war against the Portuguese, beginning in 1961. By 1972, the PAIGC controlled most of the country (including the Cape Verdean islands) and held national elections. It declared the independence of Guinea-Bissau in September 1973; Portugal officially granted independence one year later. Luis Cabral became president. In 1980, he was overthrown and the union between Cape Verde and Guinea-Bissau was dissolved. João Bernardo Vieira assumed control after the coup. As the new leader of the PAIGC, Vieira was elected president of the Council of State in 1984 and reelected in 1989. In both cases, he was not opposed because the PAIGC was the ruling and only official party.

In 1990, a committee was formed to recommend changes in the constitution and electoral process so a multiparty system could gradually be established. The nation's first free elections were held in July 1994, but opposition parties (which had become active as early as 1991) were not well organized. The PAIGC retained its dominance by gaining 62 of 100 parliamentary seats. Vieira faced a closer race for president but won in the second round of voting. Manuel Saturnino Costa, national secretary of the PAIGC, was appointed prime minister. In January 1995, he negotiated substantial financial support from international lenders to fund a three-year economic reform program designed to help Guinea-Bissau create sustainable growth.

THE PEOPLE

Population

Guinea-Bissau's population of 1.1 million is growing annually at 2.4 percent. Only 20 percent of the people live in urban areas, as the majority are farmers and fishing families living in small villages. Guinea-Bissau's Human Development Index (0.293) ranks it 163d out of 174 nations. Adjusted for women, the index ranks the country slightly lower. These figures indicate few people have access to the resources that allow them to expand their options for personal development and prosperity.

Most of the population is Black African. The country has been described as a melting pot of West African ethnic groups. There are at least 13 major groups with distinct languages, customs, religious beliefs, and forms of social organization. The largest of these groups include the Balanta (27 percent), Fula (23), Mandinga (13), Manjaco (11), Papel (10), Beafada (3), Mancanha (3), and Bijago (2.5). Some Cape Verdeans, Senegalese, and Mauritanians also live in Guinea-Bissau. More than 40 percent of the people are younger than age 15.

Language

Although Portuguese is the official language of Guinea-Bissau, it is reserved mostly for business and government use. The language of daily interaction is Kriolu, a mixture of Portuguese and various African languages. Nearly everyone in Guinea-Bissau speaks Kriolu. It is the native tongue of those raised in Bissau and a second language for most other people. Some people speak French because of contact with neighboring, French-speaking countries, and many different African languages are spoken in rural areas.

Religion

While 30 percent of the people are Muslim and 5 percent are Christian, the rest follow traditional beliefs—sometimes called animism. Religious preference is tied to ethnic grouping. The Fula, Mandinga, and Beafada, among others, are Muslims. The Balanta, Manjaco, Papel, Mancanha, Bijago, and others are animists. Many animists believe in a creator-god that can be contacted only through other gods or supernatural beings (*iran*). The *iran* reside in shrines usually built near large trees. Persons considered "spiritual advisors" or intermediaries perform ceremonies to the *iran* and services for people (casting spells, telling fortunes, and treating illness). Animists who convert to Christianity and Islam often mix their old and new beliefs rather than abandon their animist traditions. Seeking advice from spiritualists and using amulets and charms are common throughout the country.

General Attitudes

Guinea-Bissauans are friendly and hospitable. They are also peace loving and nonaggressive. They generally try to avoid confrontation and therefore also refrain from making direct or assertive statements. Although some tensions exist between various ethnic groups, most are united because of their struggle for independence against the Portuguese. This feeling of unity has helped Guinea-Bissau avoid major internal conflict.

Guinea-Bissauans are ready to help one another and, although the country is poor, there are relatively few beggars or homeless people. People love to socialize with friends; a desire for privacy may be considered antisocial. Most Guinea-Bissauans believe that nature is controlled by gods and spirits and that people have relatively little power over nature. They tend to be fatalistic about their individual conditions and may seem less motivated to change them. However, such acceptance of one's condition helps one cope with the difficulties of life. This is obvious in the fact that Guinea-Bissauans value patience, perseverance, and even resignation.

Personal Appearance

Western-style clothing is common in urban areas. Clothing is informal but not immodest. In offices, people wear short-sleeved shirts more often than suits and ties. However, adults do not wear short pants or other less-conservative attire in public. In rural areas, many people prefer traditional clothing. For example, Bijago women wear short straw skirts, Muslims wear long robes that cover their bodies (but women do not wear veils), and many women wear long, colorful, wraparound skirts with loose-fitting tops. Intricately braided hairstyles are popular with women.

CUSTOMS AND COURTESIES

Greetings

Greetings are an important way to show respect for others. It is rude to start speaking without first greeting a person. Traditional, ritualized greetings, especially those exchanged among rural Muslims, can last several minutes and involve polite inquiries about the person's health, family members, and work. At a minimum, people ask each other, "How are you?" and respond, "I am fine." People greet each other in either Portuguese or a native language such as Kriolu. Portuguese for "How are you?" is *Como está?* Kriolu is *Kuma di korpu?* (How is your body?) or simply *Kuma?* In Portuguese, "I am fine" is *Estou bem* (esh-TOE BAIN); in Kriolu it is *Sta bon.*

People shake hands when they greet. Some hold on to the hand for a while after the initial handshake. One offers a closed hand if it is dirty, and a person shakes the wrist instead. In urban areas, the Portuguese tradition of kissing alternate cheeks (first right, then left) is common. Except at large gatherings, it is polite to greet each individual in a group rather than the group as a whole. The same applies when a person leaves; he or she should address each individual. Good friends may call each other *Primo* (cousin) or *Mano* (brother); strangers are often addressed as *Amigo* (friend). In more formal situations, titles, such as *Senhor* (Mr.) or *Senhora* (Mrs.), are appropriate. To address an older person, many Guinea-Bissauans use the term *Tio* (uncle) or *Tia* (aunt).

Elders are highly respected and are not called by their first names. First names are also avoided in business and government circles, but they are commonly used among friends in rural areas.

Gestures

One beckons by waving all four fingers with the palm facing down. Some rural Guinea-Bissauans may point directions with their tongues. Personal space is smaller than in the West; people stand close together when conversing, and touching is an important part of communication. Friends of the same sex often walk hand in hand, but this does not suggest anything beyond friendship. Stretching in public is rude. A common gesture is associated with the Kriolu word *nega*, which means to refuse, negate, or deny something. When someone says *Nega*, he or she bends one or both arms and quickly flaps them once against the side of the body (like a bird). This signifies the person definitely means "no." As a sign of respect, children are taught not to look elders or superiors in the eye. Muslim elders addressing each other often look sideways. Women are supposed to avoid eye contact with men unless they are romantically involved.

Visiting

Because visiting is considered a generous and thoughtful act, visitors are treated with great hospitality. Most Guinea-Bissauans offer guests something to drink. Unless the drink has been bottled (especially water), foreign visitors should politely decline the offer or let the drink sit; this is not improper. If visitors arrive while the hosts are eating, they are invited to share the meal. It is rude to refuse this offer, even if a person is not hungry. Guests should at least take one bite before saying *N justa* (NG JUICE-ta), Kriolu for "I've had enough."

It is not necessary to make appointments before visiting, although they are sometimes made in urban areas. Invited guests may arrive up to two hours later than a scheduled time without offending the hosts. Guests show appreciation to hosts with gifts of tobacco, kola nuts, bread, sugar, fruit, or *cana* (cane alcohol). Some topics of discussion—poverty (of the hosts), sickness and death, marital status, and one's educational background—are not appropriate. Discussing these topics could lead to embarrassment for the hosts. It is also inappropriate to criticize or joke about the ethnic group of anyone present. Likewise, the use of the word "tribe" is offensive. It is better to use the term "ethnic group" (*etnia* in Portuguese; *rasa* in Kriolu).

Eating

In urban areas, breakfast might be eaten between 7:00 and 9:00 A.M., lunch between noon and 3:00 P.M. (including time for rest or a nap), and supper between 8:00 and 10:00 P.M. People in rural areas eat at varying times, depending on ethnic group, season, and personal habits. Some eat only once or twice a day. Except in urban areas, the main dish typically is served in large bowls placed on mats on the floor or ground. An older person usually divides the food into portions. Individuals eat only from the portion that is directly in front of them. It is impolite to move the bowl while others are eating. In many parts of the country, family members eat separately according to sex and age. Most ethnic groups eat only with the right hand; the left is used for personal hygiene. Others, especially in urban areas, eat with utensils in the continental style (fork in the left hand, knife in the right).

Family

The value placed on the extended family has a great impact on society and individuals. Conformity and contribution to the extended family are considered more important than individual interests. In return for conformity, individuals enjoy a sense of belonging and security. Most Guinea-Bissauans desire large families. Most ethnic groups have a male-dominated family and political structure. Intricate rules govern which tasks belong to men and women. Most rural families engage in agriculture and have rudimentary living conditions; they do not have electricity, running water, or other modern conveniences. Urban families enjoy somewhat higher living standards.

Dating and Marriage

Traditions related to dating and marriage vary widely. Muslims are generally stricter about moral behavior and interaction between boys and girls, but young women often marry in their teens. Arranged marriages are common in rural areas. Social norms in urban areas are less rigid than in rural villages, and some urban youth prefer to live together without legally getting married. Marriage can be very expensive because the bride's family often requires the groom to provide costly gifts or to farm family land for many years. In addition, a communal feast must be furnished at the wedding. Many men marry late because they have to save money for the event. Polygamy is a common practice, especially among Muslims (Islamic law allows a man to have up to four wives). The more wives a man has, the more respected he is.

Diet

Rice is important to a person's diet. Guinea-Bissauans often say that if they haven't eaten rice at a meal, they haven't eaten at all. In rural areas, a normal meal consists of rice or millet and some type of sauce (made of palm oil or peanut paste, for example) served with fish or meat, if available. Among some groups, cattle are only killed for ceremonial feasts, although their milk is used for food. While fish is plentiful in coastal areas, people who live farther inland do not often eat it. Tropical fruits (mangoes, papaya, and bananas), vegetables (manioc, sweet potatoes, corn, and squash), and peanuts are eaten in season. Muslims do not drink alcohol or eat pork. Throughout much of Guinea-Bissau, malnutrition is a serious problem.

Recreation

Soccer is the most popular sport in Guinea-Bissau. People take advantage of the rainy season work schedule to attend local soccer matches or listen to World Cup broadcasts. Some urban dwellers enjoy basketball and tennis, while traditional wrestling (*luta livre*) is popular in rural areas. The people love music and dance, both of which are an integral part of traditional ceremonies. Visiting friends is a common activity. Many urban dwellers socialize late into the night. Discos are popular. Television broadcasts, which began in 1989, reach more people each year.

Holidays

Official holidays include New Year's Day (1 January), National Hero's Day (20 January), Women's Day (8 March),

International Worker's Day (1 May), Martyrs of Colonialism Day (3 August), Independence Day (24 September), Readjustment Day (14 November), and Christmas. *Carnaval* is usually held in February (before Ash Wednesday). Traditional dancing, parades, and papier-mâché masks are combined in several days of frenzied activity.

Two major Muslim holy days are also national holidays: a feast at the end of the Islamic month of *Ramadan* (a month in which Muslims fast from sunrise to sundown) and *Tabaski* (40 days later). In rural areas, various ethnic groups also maintain their own calendars and holidays.

Commerce

During the rainy season (May–October), government offices are open from 8:00 A.M. to 3:00 P.M., with no lunch break. This is a "short" schedule because of an increased demand for labor in the rice fields and because traveling on muddy roads is difficult. During the dry season (October–May), office hours are from 8:00 A.M. to noon and 3:00 to 6:00 P.M. Private merchants use the dry season schedule all year.

SOCIETY

Government

Guinea-Bissau is a democratic republic divided into nine regions. The president is chief of state and is elected in a national vote. The prime minister (a new office in 1994) is head of government and is appointed by the president on recommendation of the majority party in Parliament. The National Assembly's one hundred members are all elected. All citizens are eligible to vote at age 15.

Economy

Guinea-Bissau is one of the poorest countries in the world. Real gross domestic product per capita is $820. Most people do not earn a wage, being subsistence farmers, or their wages are not sufficient to meet basic needs. Guinea-Bissau must import much of its food and fuel, as well as manufactured goods. It exports cashews, fish, peanuts, and palm products. With about 85 percent of the labor force working in agriculture, greater agricultural productivity and industrial development are top priorities. Many natural resources are underdeveloped. Before they can be utilized, however, the government must implement structural and fiscal reform. With the three-year (1994–97) economic plan, officials hope to achieve growth at more than 3 percent and inflation at less than 15 percent (it was 50 percent in 1993). They are targeting land and property reform, tighter business regulations, and agricultural self-sufficiency, in addition to fiscal measures. The currency is the Guinea-Bissauan *peso* (PG).

Transportation and Communication

Most roads are not paved. Therefore, travel is difficult during the rainy season. Rivers are used for major transportation. Public transportation is minimal, although *kandongas* (bush taxis—pickup trucks with seats and a roof for baggage) are used for long-distance travel. Otherwise, people walk. Phone service is adequate in Bissau but underdeveloped elsewhere. Mail service is unreliable. The national radio station broadcasts mostly in Portuguese and Kriolu. There is one national weekly newspaper.

Education

Educational opportunities are limited and the adult literacy rate is less than 40 percent. School facilities are inadequate. The national goal is to provide four years of compulsory education, but attendance is low. Drop-out rates are high because of family needs. The fact that all school instruction is conducted in Portuguese also causes problems. Because children do not learn Portuguese at home, they are essentially taught in a foreign language. Moreover, using Kriolu as the language of instruction is difficult because its written form was only recently developed and few printed materials in Kriolu are available. The nation has secondary schools, but students must move to Bissau to complete their last two years of high school. This is nearly impossible for some people. Fewer than one-third of all eligible students, ages six through twenty-three, are enrolled in school. The country has a few vocational and teacher-training schools, a law school, and a medical school. While Guinea-Bissau has no universities, plans have been proposed to create one from existing post-secondary institutions.

Health

Medical facilities are generally inadequate. Life expectancy is low, averaging between 45 and 49 years. The infant mortality rate is 118 per 1,000. Major causes of death include malaria and gastrointestinal infections. Bilharzia and tuberculosis are widespread. A cholera epidemic in 1994 and 1995 threatened coastal villages. Only about one-third of all people have access to safe water and proper sanitation.

FOR THE TRAVELER

A passport and visa are required for U.S. citizens to enter Guinea-Bissau. An exit visa is required to leave. The yellow fever vaccination, although no longer required, is still recommended. Other vaccinations and malarial suppressants are also strongly recommended. Uncooked or unpeeled fruits or vegetables should not be eaten; all food should be well cooked and served hot. Visitors should not swim in freshwater ponds or streams. Water is not potable. Tourism is not well developed, but some beach resorts have been and are being built. It is appropriate to stand still when the national flag is raised or lowered; traffic stops and people stand outside their cars when it is lowered in the evening.

For travel information, contact the Permanent Mission of Guinea-Bissau to the United Nations, 211 East 43d Street, Suite 604, New York, NY 10017; phone (212) 661–3977; or the Embassy of Guinea-Bissau, 918 16th Street NW, Mezzanine Suite, Washington, DC 20006; phone (202) 872–4222.

CULTURGRAM ™ '97

Territory of
Hong Kong

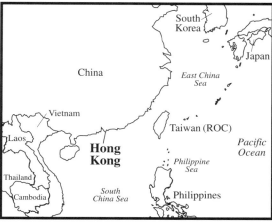

Boundary representations not necessarily authoritative.

BACKGROUND

Land and Climate

Hong Kong is a British territory located on the south coast of China. Occupying an area about half the size of Rhode Island, Hong Kong covers 421 square miles (1,092 square kilometers). It includes the New Territories (adjacent to China's Guangdong Province), the Kowloon Peninsula, two large islands (Hong Kong and Tai Yue Shan), and two hundred smaller islands. The peninsula and islands are mountainous. Only a fraction (7 percent) of Hong Kong's land mass is arable, and natural resources are scarce. Hong Kong Island and the tip of the Kowloon Peninsula form the natural harbor that has made the colony such an important center for commerce. The climate is tropical with seasonal monsoons. Hong Kong experiences more seasonal change than most tropical areas. From October to March, the weather is generally dry and cool (50–65°F or 10–18°C). Hot, rainy weather prevails the rest of the year, when temperatures range from 80°F to over 90°F (26–34°C).

History

The British East India Trading Company began using the Hong Kong Harbor for trade with China as early as 1699. The Chinese ceded control over Hong Kong Island to Great Britain in 1842, following the so-called Opium War, in which the Chinese tried to halt British opium shipments to China. Kowloon was ceded after the Arrow War in 1860, and the New Territories were acquired on a 99-year lease in 1898, which effectively extended Kowloon to the Chinese border. Hong Kong's importance as a free port was not established until after World War II, when it became a leading commercial port and tourist center. It also became a point of refuge for Chinese fleeing changes in China.

With the lease on the New Territories due to expire in 1997, the British and Chinese governments began meeting in 1982 to determine Hong Kong's future. The resulting 1984 agreement states that Hong Kong will become a Special Administrative Region (HKSAR) of China on 1 July 1997. The agreement (Sino-British Joint Declaration on the Question of Hong Kong) provides for the continuation of Hong Kong's unique social, economic, legal, and other systems for 50 years after 1997 and for Hong Kong's smooth transition to its new status as part of China. A Basic Law, drafted in 1990, is to serve as the HKSAR constitution for those 50 years. As the transfer date approaches, China has been increasing its activity in and exercising influence over the colony. In 1991, it negotiated certain concessions, including a voice in an important new airport project.

The transition process became tense in 1992 when Hong Kong and British officials supported a plan that would increase democratic political participation in the colony before 1997. China strongly opposed any strengthening of democratic institutions and sought to derail the effort by threatening to dismantle any system created outside of the 1984 agreement. But citizens of Hong Kong strongly favored greater democracy, so Governor Christopher Patten pressed ahead. In 1994, Hong Kong's 60-member Legislative Council passed a reform package that lowered the voting age from 21 to 18, eliminated appointed local council seats (replacing them with elected seats), and introduced other measures. The historic elections in 1995 were the first in which all 60 members of the Council were elected. China vowed to dissolve the Council in 1997. It formed a 150-member Preparatory Committee to handle the transition. The Committee, comprised of both mainland Chinese and Hong Kong Chinese, will choose a 400-member group to elect a post-colonial governor and set up a provisional legislature, among other things.

THE PEOPLE

Population

Hong Kong's population of 6.3 million grew by 2.6 percent in 1995. Emigration rates declined in 1995, such that more people came to Hong Kong than left it. Whereas 62,000 people left in 1994, only 43,000 left in 1995. And of the thousands who left between 1984 and 1994, 12 percent have returned to the colony.

Following political upheaval on the Chinese mainland, large numbers of people began to flow into the colony. Most settled on the peninsula or Hong Kong Island, transforming the two areas into a highly urbanized, densely populated metropolis. There are more than 14,000 people per square mile (5,900 people per square kilometer) on the entire territory, but few people actually live outside the main urban area. Hence, Hong Kong is one of the most densely populated areas in the world. Hong Kong is ethnically homogeneous; nearly 98 percent of the people are Chinese, mostly Cantonese with roots in Guangdong Province. Only about 57 percent of all residents were actually born in Hong Kong. The small number of non-Chinese Hong Kong residents who will have no citizenship rights after July 1997 have applied for assistance from Great Britain.

Hong Kong's Human Development Index (0.905) ranks it 24th out of 174 political entities. Adjusted for women, the index is slightly lower. Nearly all people have access to resources and social services that allow them to achieve personal goals and enjoy economic prosperity.

Language

Hong Kong has two official languages—Chinese and English—but English will lose its official status in 1997. Street signs, telephone directories, and government documents are written in both. Although dialects from all provinces of China can be heard in Hong Kong, the Cantonese dialect from Guangdong Province dominates and is officially recognized. More people are learning the Beijing dialect, *Putonghua* (Mandarin). Chinese dialects can be very different, but the written script has been standardized for centuries. Most people learn English in school.

Religion

The Chinese have a heritage of diversity with respect to moral philosophy and formal religion. Strong elements of Taoism and Confucianism, both of which originated in China, and Buddhism, with roots in India, form part of the religious life of many Hong Kong residents. Folk religious practices and ancestor veneration are also widespread. Many homes contain brightly decorated boxes with pictures of deceased relatives, smoldering incense sticks, or symbolic offerings of fruit, which are all part of the custom of honoring ancestors. Marriages and funerals are special ceremonial events. There

is little congregational worship in the Western sense. The faithful observe special occasions with visits to shrines and temples or perform informal rites on the sidewalks near their homes. Nearly all major Christian denominations are represented in Hong Kong, and about 10 percent of the population is Christian. It is not yet clear how Hong Kong's current climate of religious freedom will be affected in 1997.

General Attitudes

Hong Kong is referred to as the "Pearl of the Orient." The name not only describes its scenic beauty, impressive modern structures, and magnificent natural harbor but also the energetic, hardworking people who have built Hong Kong into a major trade center. The Confucian ethic of proper social and family relationships forms the foundation of Chinese society. The Chinese are very conscious of their social position in relation to the people with whom they interact. An individual's actions reflect on the entire family. Likewise, a child's achievements honor the entire family. "Saving face" or avoiding embarrassment, shame, or dishonor is very important. In social interaction, the Chinese are careful to allow others to escape from potential embarrassment with dignity; causing someone to "lose face" is improper. The Chinese value modesty and patience over aggressive behavior. Humility or self-demeaning comments are normal in describing oneself or one's accomplishments. The Chinese give and receive sincere compliments, but they try to deny praise.

Social attitudes, traditions, employment patterns, and daily culture have been disrupted by the prospect of Hong Kong's future in a "one country, two systems" arrangement. For most Chinese, feelings are mixed. On one hand, they feel proud to rejoin the Chinese nation; on the other hand, many fear China's hardline reaction to the colony's democracy movement. The disagreements between Beijing and Hong Kong have politicized society in a way that has created deep divisions between pro-China groups and liberal democrats. People's greatest worries are over the possibility of losing fundamental rights and individual freedoms. But these are balanced by great optimism for a surge in economic growth as Hong Kong interfaces with China's vast market.

Personal Appearance

People in Hong Kong wear all styles of clothing, from traditional to modern, from European to Asian. Modesty is important in public, as is cleanliness. Businesspeople wear suits. Casual clothing is worn more at home than in public.

CUSTOMS AND COURTESIES

Greetings

Both English and Chinese greetings are common in Hong Kong. Ethnic Chinese shake hands with non-Chinese. *Neih hau ma?* (How are you?) and *Neih sik msik a?* (Have you eaten?) are typical Chinese greetings. Upon greeting, people politely inquire about each other's health, business affairs, or school activities. Friends address one another by given name. Relatives and close friends may use nicknames. Titles and family names are used in formal situations.

The Chinese family name traditionally comes first. However, Hong Kong Chinese often adopt Western "first" names even if they are not Christian. In this case, the family name may come last—or it may remain first, with the Western name used phonetically as if it were Chinese. These adopted names are unusual, or people may change them from time to time.

Gestures

The most proper way to sit is with one's hands in the lap and one's feet on the floor. Although traditional Chinese will not cross their legs, one may do so without offending. Winking at someone is impolite and can have bad connotations. An open hand is usually used for pointing. Chinese beckon with the palm down and all fingers waving. Talking loudly is inappropriate.

Visiting

People in Hong Kong enjoy socializing with friends and relatives as often as their busy schedules allow. They commonly entertain in restaurants, as homes are small and many working people are unable to prepare the culinary delicacies they would like to serve. Very close friends and relatives do visit in the home and without prior arrangement. Calling ahead is the norm, however, as people are often not home. Guests in the home are offered hot tea or a cold soda or juice. Hosts might also provide snacks. Visitors are treated with special consideration: food is prepared to their liking and conversation geared to their interests. Invited guests take a gift, usually something consumable (wine, fruit, candy). First-time visitors also present gifts to their hosts. People offer and receive all gifts with both hands. A final round of tea signals the end of a visit.

Contrary to those in other Asian societies, people usually do not remove shoes when entering a home. Visitors sit when invited to do so and maintain good posture. People make an effort to greet and show respect to older people. Correct manners in social situations include generosity. This means one does not take the best portion of food first but rather serves it to others. One pours tea for others first and then for oneself. People decline the best pieces of food or refreshments, even as a guest, encouraging the hosts to eat these themselves.

Eating

Chinese families eat together whenever possible, but work schedules make it difficult for some. They maintain a Chinese diet at home and usually eat with chopsticks. Dishes of food are typically placed in the center of the table. Diners help themselves by taking portions with chopsticks from the central plates and placing them in their individual bowls of rice. It is proper to hold the rice bowl close to one's mouth when eating. The host or parent refills bowls with more rice until politely refused. It is considered impolite to make noise or talk too much during the meal.

People enjoy international cuisine when dining out. Because of the cosmopolitan nature of Hong Kong, restaurants offer many types of food, including most U.S. American foods. Eating habits follow the custom most associated with the type of food being eaten. The bill often includes a service charge, but leaving a tip is still customary. Eating food on the street traditionally is inappropriate.

LIFESTYLE

Family

Chinese family members are bound by a strong tradition of loyalty, obedience, and respect, as reflected by one of the lowest divorce rates in the world. Couples usually have one or two children. While the concept of nuclear households is gaining ground, it is not unusual for households to consist of extended families. This could mean three generations living under one roof or sometimes even distant relatives (e.g., an elderly aunt with nowhere else to go, a niece or nephew whose parents are overseas, etc.) living together for convenience. Financial constraints frequently contribute to the existence of the extended family system. A source of stress for many families in Hong Kong is the sharp difference between traditional values and more modern, or Western, practices. Emigration is also straining family ties. Families sometimes have had to leave the elderly and disabled behind.

Gender roles are clearly defined within the home. Men are breadwinners and women are housekeepers and mothers. Even if women work outside the home, they are responsible for the household. Working-class women depend on relatives, neighbors, or public agencies for child care. Professional or white-collar families often have live-in domestic help to do chores and watch children. More than 140,000 Filipinas and other foreign nationals work as domestic helpers in Hong Kong. Most people live in high-rise apartments, the average size of which is 700 square feet for a family of four.

Dating and Marriage

Dating couples enjoy movies, picnics, beach outings, outdoor sports, dining out, and cruising shopping malls. Young people often wait to marry until they have job security or the means to live in "married quarters" (their own apartment). All weddings must include a civil ceremony through the Marriage Registry. Couples try to reserve the "best" dates according to the Chinese calendar, as space on each day is limited. Brides wear white and grooms wear tuxedos. After the civil ceremony, a traditional wedding celebration includes a large restaurant or hotel banquet for family and friends. The bride wears a traditional *cheong sam* (red and gold Chinese wedding dress) but changes her outfit two or three times in the course of the evening. The groom wears a Western suit. Christians also have church ceremonies.

Diet

Rice and some vegetables are grown in Hong Kong's rural areas and the New Territories, but most food is imported and rather expensive. Rice is the main staple. Fried rice often incorporates fish, pork, chicken, and vegetables. *Congee* is a porridge-like rice dish. Chinese noodles are boiled or fried. *Dim sum* (dumplings) are served in several varieties. Oranges and watermelon are the most popular fruits, but people also eat tropical fruits from nearby countries. Fresh-squeezed oranges make the most popular juice.

Recreation

Favorite sports include table tennis, soccer, skating, squash, tennis, swimming, horse racing, basketball, and boating. People enjoy beach outings and picnics, movies and television, and theater. Traditional Cantonese Opera remains popular for some. For evening entertainment, many enjoy karaoke singing. During the day, older men often play *mah-jong* (a cross between dominoes and cards, played with tiles). Children learn traditional dances in school.

Holidays

Holidays are based on the lunar calendar and fall on different days each year. The Chinese New Year, in winter, is the most important holiday. Weeklong festivities include parades, visiting relatives, paying debts, and displaying messages of prosperity and longevity on doorways. The two most important traditional festivals are for honoring the dead. One occurs in the spring (*Ching Ming*) and the other in the fall (*Chung Yeung*). In June, the Dragon Boat Festival is celebrated with colorful dragon boat races. The Mid-Autumn Festival is a harvest holiday celebrated with lanterns and moon cakes. Other holidays include Easter, Liberation Day (last Monday in August), and Christmas.

Commerce

Hard work is the basic element of life for most. A six-day, 48-hour workweek is common. Business hours are from 9:00 A.M. to 5:00 P.M. five days a week, and from 9:00 A.M. to 1:00 P.M. on Saturday. However, shops usually are open from early in the morning until late at night, especially if the owner lives in an apartment above the shop. The evening streets are very busy with people enjoying Hong Kong's night life.

SOCIETY

Government

Until midnight on 30 June 1997, Hong Kong is a British colony. External affairs are the responsibility of the United Kingdom, but Hong Kong administers local affairs. China has a consultative role in policy matters. Hong Kong's governor (Christopher Patten) represents the British queen and is assisted by an Executive Council. The Legislative Council enacts laws and controls finances. All those older than 18 who have lived in Hong Kong for at least seven years were eligible to vote in 1995 for the Legislative Council. When Hong Kong becomes the HKSAR, the Preparatory Committee will disband the Council and replace it with an appointed provisional legislature.

Economy

Hong Kong relies on shipping, commerce, and manufacturing for its survival and success. *Hong Kong* means "fragrant harbor," and the busy harbor is the key to its business. It is a free port; no tariffs are levied on imports or exports. Duties are placed only on tobacco, liquors, cosmetics, and a few other items. More than 35 percent of the population is employed in manufacturing. The chief industries are textiles, clothing, toys, electronics, and plastics. Tourism is also a significant source of income.

Economic growth in the past two decades averaged 7.5 percent; for 1995, the rate was 4.6 percent. Joint ventures with Chinese firms in Hong Kong and southern China are adding to a robust economic performance. Indeed, investments in Guangdong Province have already blurred the border between China and Hong Kong. Real gross domestic product per capita is $20,340, which has increased dramatically in the last generation. Although income distribution is somewhat unequal, most people enjoy a comfortable standard of living. The currency is the Hong Kong dollar (HK$).

Transportation and Communication

A subway system offers rapid transit to major locations on Hong Kong Island and Kowloon. Trains connect Kowloon and the New Territories. A ferry connects the islands and the mainland. The new airport under construction is scheduled for completion by July 1997. Hong Kong has an extensive bus and minibus system. In the New Territories taxis are green, but on Hong Kong and in Kowloon they are red. Many people own private cars, and traffic can be heavy. All traffic travels on the left side of the road.

Hong Kong has all the modern communications systems necessary for excellent domestic and international service. Fifteen radio stations and four broadcast television stations combine with a number of satellite and cable channels to provide Hong Kong with comprehensive media services.

Education

Education is considered the stepping stone to success, and parents try to provide their children with the best schooling. A free, nine-year education program is required for all children. During the nine-month school year, primary students attend weekdays for six hours; secondary students attend for eight hours. Nearly all pupils complete the primary level; three-fourths proceed from primary to secondary school. Entrance to the better secondary schools is based on competitive examination. The adult literacy rate is 91 percent. Hong Kong's two universities offer a full variety of traditional degrees. In addition, vocational-training colleges prepare people for careers in applied sciences, business, construction, tourism, and other fields.

Health

All citizens have access to comprehensive public care, regardless of their ability to pay for services. Private care is widely available, and most people have private insurance to pay for it. Hong Kong residents enjoy one of the highest life expectancy rates in the world, averaging 77 to 84 years. The infant mortality rate is 6 per 1,000. Success is credited to health education and the availability of preventive care to all.

FOR THE TRAVELER

No visa is required of U.S. visitors staying less than one month, but a valid passport and proof of onward passage are required. English-speaking policemen have red shoulder tabs on their uniforms. If visiting mainland China, unless with a guided tour, one should carry some Hong Kong dollars to pay for transportation from the border back to one's hotel. The airport tax must also be paid in Hong Kong dollars. When departing, arrive earlier than usual for an international flight, since check-in can take longer; there are strict limits on the size and weight of carry-on luggage.

Visitors will enjoy not only shopping in Hong Kong but viewing art, visiting old temples, and exploring the colony's culture. For information, contact the Hong Kong Tourist Association at 590 Fifth Avenue, Fifth Floor, New York, NY 10036; phone (212) 869–5008; or at 10940 Wilshire Boulevard, Suite 1220, Los Angeles, CA 90024. For visa information, contact the Consular Section of the British Embassy, 19 Observatory Circle NW, Washington, DC 20008; phone (202) 986–0205.

Republic of
India

Boundary representations not necessarily authoritative.

BACKGROUND

Land and Climate

Covering 1,269,338 square miles (3,287,590 square kilometers), India is roughly one-third the size of the United States. A small section of the Himalaya Mountains lies in the disputed territories of the north. The Ganges Plain below is fertile and densely populated. South of the plain is the Deccan Plateau. About half of the country is under cultivation and one-fourth is forested. Most of the country experiences three basic seasons: hot summer (March–May), rainy (June–September), and cool winter (October–February). Temperatures rarely go below 40°F (4°C) in January and will reach 100°F (38°C) during the summer. Variations exist according to region and elevation.

History

The Indus Valley civilization dates back more than five thousand years. Around 1500 B.C., Aryans arrived from central Asia and gradually pushed the native Dravidians to the south. Buddhism flourished during King Asoka's reign in the third century B.C. but declined afterward. The northern Gupta Kingdom, from the fourth to sixth centuries A.D., was a golden age of science, literature, and the arts. Southern India also experienced several great empires. Arab, Turk, and Afghan Muslims ruled successively from the eighth to eighteenth centuries, providing some basis for the historical animosity between Hindus and Muslims. Then Portuguese and Dutch traders entered India. The English eventually assumed political control of the area.

After World War I, Mahatma Gandhi led a continuing nationalist movement, advocating civil disobedience and passive resistance in a campaign to gain autonomy from Great Britain. Gandhi's goal was realized in 1947, when India was granted independence. Religious rivalry and violence led to the establishment of Pakistan as a Muslim state. India became a republic within the British Commonwealth; Jawaharlal Nehru was the first prime minister. Gandhi was assassinated in 1948. Nehru's daughter (Indira Gandhi) was prime minister twice (1966–77 and 1980–84). She was assassinated by her own Sikh bodyguards after Indian troops stormed the Sikhs' Golden Temple in a violent clash with separatists. Violence marked the Sikh movement for independence in Punjab Province through the early 1990s. While violence has subsided, the desire for independence remains strong. Muslims also desire secession in the far north area of Jammu and Kashmir, where fighting has cost 20,000 lives since 1990.

Indira Gandhi's son, Rajiv, was elected prime minister in 1984. He lost the 1989 election to V. P. Singh. Two years of economic troubles, tensions between castes, a rise in Hindu fundamentalism, and violence between religious groups caused both Singh and his replacement to resign. During elections in 1991, Rajiv Gandhi was assassinated as he campaigned for the premiership. Congress Party leader P. V.

Narasimha Rao then became prime minister. Riots sparked by the 1992 Hindu destruction of a treasured Muslim mosque left hundreds dead and again threatened government stability. Rao remained in office, however, and worked to improve economic and social conditions throughout India. His economic liberalization program attracted large amounts of foreign investment by 1995 and earned international praise, but it angered some political elements in India who did not agree with the program's social cuts.

That and continued religious divisions led to the Congress Party's defeat in 1996 parliamentary elections. The election was so indecisive that the party with the most (160) seats, Bharatiya Janata (BJP, a Hindu nationalist party), was unable to form a viable government. It took three weeks before a 13-party United Front coalition of centrist and leftist parties was able to form what is expected to be a stable and progressive government. The Congress Party is part of the coalition but does not hold the power it previously did. The new prime minister, H. D. Deve Gowda of the Communist Party of India (CPI), pledged to continue with economic liberalization while addressing some of India's most pressing problems.

THE PEOPLE
Population
India has the second largest population (936 million) in the world behind China. It grows annually at 1.8 percent. India is one of the most ethnically diverse countries in the world, but factors other than ethnicity are more likely to separate people. These include rural/urban, religious, and socioeconomic differences. The Indo-Aryans make up the largest ethnic group (72 percent), while the Dravidians account for 25 percent of the population. The remaining 3 percent is made of a myriad of other groups, including Mongoloids.

India's Human Development Index (0.439) ranks it 134th out of 174 nations. Adjusted for women, the index (0.401) ranks India 99th out of 130 nations. These figures reflect the fact that nearly 20 percent of all people are unable to provide for their basic needs, that up to 70 percent are subsistence farmers, and that most people still lack access to resources that would allow them to pursue personal goals. Women are less likely than men to be literate or to earn a decent wage.

Language
India is home to at least three hundred known languages; twenty-four of these have one million or more speakers each. Besides Hindi and English, there are 14 other official languages, including Bengali, Urdu, Punjabi, and Sanskrit. At least 30 percent of the population speaks Hindi. English is important for business and government and is the language of national communication. Hindustani, a blend of Hindi and Urdu, is spoken widely in northern India.

Religion
India is the birthplace of Hinduism, Buddhism, Jainism, and Sikhism—all of which believe in reincarnation. It is also the adopted home of most followers of Zoroastrianism. Slightly more than 82 percent of the people are Hindu. Hinduism is extremely diverse, polytheistic, rich in ceremony, and associated with the caste system. Hinduism has no supreme authority, but the caste system provides structure for the Hindu doctrine that dictates individuals must work their way to the highest caste through reincarnation before they can exit life on earth to a better existence. Below the fourth caste (laborers) are the "Untouchables," who are usually poor and powerless and with whom other Hindus are to have no contact. The caste system has been constitutionally abolished but continues to be practiced. It limits social and economic mobility for millions of Indians and maintains the status of the privileged few.

Almost 12 percent of the people are Muslim, who follow scriptures (the *Qur'an*) revealed by *Allah* to the prophet Muhammad. The Sikh religion (2 percent, mostly in Punjab) began around the 16th century, drawing on principles from both Hinduism and Islam. It stresses simple teachings and devotion. The Sikh practice of tolerance is reflected in offers of free food and shelter to anyone who comes to their places of worship. Buddhism, although it began in India and flourished for a time, did not maintain a following in India. Less than 1 percent of the population is Buddhist. Jains, though powerful in India, also make up less than 1 percent. Jains practice a reverence for life (*ahimsa,* literally "nonviolence"), self-denial (especially monks), and follow a vegetarian diet. Less than 3 percent of the population is Christian.

General Attitudes
Indian people are religious, family oriented, and philosophical. They believe strongly in simple material comforts and rich spiritual accomplishments. Physical purity and spiritual refinement are highly valued. Fatalism is widespread, meaning one accepts one's course in life as the will of God or fate. The ideals of humility and self-denial, as encouraged by Mahatma Gandhi, are highly respected. Abundant expressions of gratitude are reserved for real favors rather than routine courtesies. Indians are proud of a rich heritage that has produced numerous architectural and artistic masterpieces.

They are equally proud of being the world's most populous democracy—where free elections have been held since 1947. But it is a complex democracy. The tensions between Hindus and Muslims, social classes, rural and urban areas, and traditional and modern values were clearly visible in the 1996 election results. While this challenges India's people to seek common ground amid diversity, it also opens up great opportunities to build a stronger society.

Personal Appearance
Women generally wear a *saree*, a long length of fabric draped in variations that can represent socioeconomic status and religious affiliation. Or they wear a colorful pantsuit with a long shirt that extends to the knee. Women also wear considerable jewelry. Hindu women may wear a *bindi*, or red dot, on their foreheads. Traditionally, this was a sign of femininity, gracefulness, and marital status, but in modern times it has become more often an optional beauty aid, with the color of the *bindi* frequently matching the wearer's outfit. After marriage, the *bindi*, accompanied by white powder on the upper forehead (or vermilion powder in the part of her hair), signifies the woman's husband is alive; widows do not wear a *bindi*.

Men wear Western-style suits or more traditional clothing, such as the *dhoti* (large piece of cloth wrapped around the waist). As with women, this varies with region and religion. Sikhs wear turbans and specific items with religious significance, while Hindus and Muslims may wear a long shirt with pants, sometimes accompanied by a jacket or a vest.

CUSTOMS AND COURTESIES

Greetings

The *namaste* is the traditional greeting used in India. One presses the palms together (fingers up) below the chin and says *Namaste* (in the south, *Namaskaram*). For superiors or to show respect, a slight bow is added. Indians usually do not shake hands with or touch women in formal or informal gatherings. This is a sign of respect for a woman's privacy. Indian men will, however, shake hands with Westerners, and educated women may do so as a courtesy. "Hello" and "Hi" are acceptable greetings among equals, but more formal terms like "Good morning" or its equivalent are necessary for superiors. It is polite to use titles such as *Professor*, *Doctor*, *Mr.*, *Shri* (for men), *Shreemati* (married women), *Kumari* (single women), or the suffix *-ji* with a last name to show respect. Muslims use the right hand for a *salaam* gesture of greeting and farewell. Indians usually ask permission before taking leave of others.

Gestures

Excessive hand gestures or verbal articulation are considered impolite. People beckon with the palm turned down; they often point with the chin. It is impolite to sniff or handle flowers displayed at bazaars. Grasping one's own ears expresses repentance or sincerity. One's feet or shoes should not touch another person, and if they do, an immediate apology is necessary. Whistling is very impolite. Women do not wink or whistle; such behavior is considered unladylike. Public displays of affection are inappropriate. Postage stamps are not licked, but water is provided to moisten them. All people cover their heads when entering a Sikh shrine. Women also cover their heads in temples.

Visiting

Visits in the home between friends or family are often unannounced. The need for prior arrangements is increasing in large cities. It is impolite to say "no" to an invitation; if one cannot attend, one more likely says "I'll try." Among traditional families, women may not be involved in social functions. At certain gatherings, guests may be adorned with a garland of flowers, which they immediately remove and carry in the hand as an expression of humility. Guests repay the host's hospitality by giving gifts, such as flowers, specialty foods (fruits, sweets) from other areas of the country, or something for the children.

Many Indians do not wear shoes inside the home. Most at least remove shoes before entering the living room. Hosts offer their guests water, tea or coffee, and fruits or sweets. It is polite for a guest to initially refuse these refreshments but to eventually accept them. When visitors are ready to leave, they often indicate it by saying *Namaste*. In temples, saffron powder, holy water from the Ganges River, and sometimes food are offered to visitors as *prasad*, or blessings from the gods; refusing these gifts is discourteous.

Eating

Eating habits vary sharply between traditional and modern settings. Modern (most often urban) families will eat together and follow many Western customs. Traditional families may eat their food with the right hand instead of utensils. Also, women may eat after other members of the family and any guests. Diners might drink from a communal cup; if so, the lips never touch it. A gesture of *namaste* can indicate one has had enough to eat. Some Hindus object to having their food handled by members of lower castes.

LIFESTYLE

Family

The basic social unit in India is the family, which takes precedence over the individual. Families are generally large, but the government is actively encouraging family planning to curb rapid population growth. Extended families often live together or near each other. The elderly are respected and cared for by their families. The father is head of the household. A middle- or upper-class father expects to provide financially for his children until they finish their education and take a job—regardless of how long it takes. Few women work outside the home. However, a growing number of urban women are part of the workforce, making important professional contributions to Indian society.

Dating and Marriage

Dating practices of Western countries are not common in India, although urban residents are affected by Western standards. Traditional marriages are still arranged by parents, often with the consent of the bride and groom. Marriage is sacred to most Indians and is considered to endure beyond death. Chastity is the most treasured virtue of womanhood. Weddings are times of great celebration, expense, and feasting. Ceremonies are often elaborate and vary widely from region to region. In many, the bride and groom exchange garlands and/or words before they circle around a fire three to seven times to solemnize the marriage. Bright clothing, jewelry, and flowers are part of nearly every type of ceremony. Giving a dowry (money, land, etc.) to the groom is still common for the bride's parents, even though the practice is illegal. Divorce rates are very low.

Diet

Foods vary widely in India, depending on the culture and region. For example, rice is a staple in the south, while wheat bread *(roti)* is the staple in the north. Indian meals are usually very spicy. Different types of curry (eggs, fish, meat, or vegetables in a spicy sauce) are popular. Vegetarianism is widely practiced, often for religious reasons. All castes have different food laws and customs, as does each religion. The Hindus consider cows to be sacred and will not eat beef or even use anything made of leather. Muslims do not eat pork or drink alcohol. Betel leaves and nuts are commonly eaten after meals to aid digestion.

Recreation

Soccer, cricket, and hockey are favorite sports. India's motion picture industry is one of the world's largest. Every major city has more than one hundred modern theaters, some equipped with elevators and restaurants. Musicals and romance films are typical and are the source of India's pop music. Dance and music performances are also popular. India's classical music has two styles, northern and southern, both of which follow rigid rhythm rules. Many religious and folk festivals are held throughout the year.

Holidays

India's national holidays include International New Year's Day (1 January), Republic Day (26 January), Independence Day (15 August), and Mahatma Gandhi's Birthday (2 October). Numerous spring and harvest festivals are common between January and March, celebrated with dancing and many colorful events. One such festival is *Holi*, a celebration to mark the end of the cold season, during which people toss colored water and powder on each other. *Baisakhi* is the Hindu New Year, a time for feasts, fireworks, and dancing; it also marks the beginning of Punjab's harvest season. Muslims celebrate *Id-ul-Fitr* with prayers and greetings at the end of *Ramzaan*, the month of fasting. Snakes are venerated during the summer festival of *Naag Panchami* because of their association with Hindu gods. The Hindu Lord Krishna's birth is celebrated in August or September during *Jan mashtami*. *Dussehra* (under different names in various regions) is held around October to celebrate the triumph of good over evil. *Diwali* (Festival of Lights) is a Hindu holiday celebrating the triumph of light over darkness. Thousands of lights decorate stores and homes at this time of goodwill. Christians celebrate Christmas and Easter.

Commerce

Normal business hours generally run from 9:30 A.M. to 1:00 P.M. and 2:00 to 5:00 P.M., Monday through Friday. However, many people must work far more than a 40-hour week to buy basic necessities. Government offices open at 10:00 A.M. These hours are mostly for urban areas; hours in rural areas vary. Bazaars and fairs are popular in India. Rural areas may have a fair every week—some for trading animals, others for selling farm produce and handicrafts, and others as part of a festival.

SOCIETY

Government

A democratic republic, India is divided into 26 states. President Shankar Dayal Sharma, elected by members of Parliament and the state assemblies, has mostly ceremonial duties. The prime minister is head of government. India's parliament has two houses: the *Rajya Sabha* (Council of States) and the *Lok Sabha* (House of the People). No more than 250 members, elected by the legislatures of each state, serve in the *Rajya Sabha*. All but two of the 545 members of the *Lok Sabha* are directly elected by the people. All citizens may vote at age 18. The 1996 elections marked a new era of multiparty politics in India, since the Congress Party had governed for all but four years since 1947.

Economy

Despite increased industrial development, India remains primarily an agricultural nation. It is self-sufficient in food, and agricultural production is expanding. India is a leading world producer of peanuts, rice, cheese, tobacco, wheat, cotton, milk, sugarcane, and rubber. Other important crops include cereals, oil seed, jute, tea, and coffee. Export earnings come mainly from tea, coffee, iron ore, fish products, and manufactured items. Textiles are a principal domestic product and also a profitable export. India is rich in natural resources, with coal, iron ore, natural gas, diamonds, crude oil, limestone, and important minerals. High-technology industries lead the way for industrial growth. The expanding middle class is consuming new products. Tourism is also increasingly vital for income. Economic growth for 1995 was more than 5 percent.

Despite India's booming economy, serious gaps between rich and poor remain. The government's most delicate challenge is to balance modernization with meeting social needs and to see that economic prosperity becomes available to more people. Real gross domestic product per capita is $1,230. The currency is the *rupee* (Re).

Transportation and Communication

Roads in urban areas are generally well developed, but those in rural regions may be unpaved and impassable in heavy rains. Buses, which are often crowded, serve as the main source of public transportation in cities. Taxis are also plentiful, but meters are not always used and rates change often. Trains connect major cities. Other common forms of transportation include rickshaws (bicycle driven), motor scooters, and horse-drawn *tanga*. Traffic travels on the left side of the road. Many people own televisions, especially in urban areas. Radios are even more widespread, as they are more affordable. Newspapers are also plentiful. Domestic telephone service is not well developed.

Education

Education is a primary concern in India. Although schooling is free and compulsory from ages six to fourteen, facilities are often inadequate and many children do not attend. Government programs are trying to meet the increasing demand for education. Some progress has been realized because the literacy rate has risen to 52 percent in the past few years. India has more than one hundred universities, three thousand colleges, and at least fifteen institutes dedicated to research in the arts and sciences.

Health

The people of India face health challenges stemming from poverty, malnutrition, and poor sanitation. Religious beliefs (such as Hindu rat worship, which allows rats to breed freely) also pose certain threats. Diseases such as cholera, yellow fever, malaria, typhoid, and hepatitis endanger many, especially rural inhabitants who lack access to medical care. Health-care workers are trying to teach people better hygiene, nutrition, and family planning. The infant mortality rate is 76 per 1,000, while life expectancy is about 59 years.

FOR THE TRAVELER

A visa and a valid passport are required of U.S. travelers. Yellow fever vaccinations are necessary and others are recommended. Drink only treated or boiled water. Eat only well-cooked meats served hot and thoroughly washed fresh produce. For travel information, contact the Government of India Tourist Office, 30 Rockefeller Plaza, Suite 15, North Mezzanine, New York, NY 10112; phone (212) 586–4901; or the Embassy of India, 2536 Massachusetts Avenue NW, Washington, DC 20008; phone (202) 939–9839.

CULTURGRAM ™ '97

Republic of
Indonesia

Boundary representations not necessarily authoritative.

BACKGROUND

Land and Climate

Indonesia is made up of 13,670 islands that stretch some 3,200 miles (4,800 kilometers) along the equator, south, east, and west of Malaysia. It shares the island of Borneo with Malaysia and Brunei. Its portion is called Kalimantan. It also shares the island of New Guinea with the independent country of Papua New Guinea. Indonesia's province there is Irian Jaya. The largest unshared islands include Sumatra, Java, Celebes, and Timor. Only six thousand islands are actually inhabited. Covering 741,096 square miles (1,919,400 square kilometers), the islands total about one-fifth the size of the United States, or three times the size of Texas. The popular island of Bali is also in Indonesia. The dry season extends from June to November, with temperatures ranging from 80°F to 90°F (26–32°C) or more. The wet monsoon season is from November to March or April. Rainfall is heavy. The climate is hot and humid year-round, although it is somewhat cooler in the mountains of the larger islands.

History

When Christopher Columbus reached the Americas, he was looking for the East Indies to get access to the rich spice trade. Most of the islands he sought but never found are part of present-day Indonesia. Early Indonesian culture was influenced by India in the first century B.C. Islam was introduced through Muslim traders in the 15th century. Western traders were active in the region during the 16th and 17th centuries.

In fact, Indonesia became a Dutch colony in 1816 and remained so until the 1940s.

The Japanese occupied the islands during World War II. Upon Japan's defeat, Indonesian nationalists proclaimed independence from the Netherlands in August 1945. A republic was formed under President Sukarno. A Communist coup attempt, supported by China and led by Indonesia's large Communist Party, was suppressed in 1965 by General Suharto. Thousands died in the rioting and violence surrounding the coup. Suharto banned the Communist Party and became president; he continues to lead Indonesia today.

When Suharto loosened control on the press and opposition groups in the early 1990s, many people demonstrated for greater democracy and a change of leadership with the 1993 elections. These people felt Suharto's government had denied certain civil rights (such as freedom of speech) for too long. However, Suharto was the only candidate on the 1993 ballot and, therefore, was reelected to a five-year term. He is expected to retire in 1998, when the next presidential elections are scheduled. Although accused of human-rights abuses (particularly against rebel groups), giving special treatment to relatives, and being an authoritarian ruler, Suharto is credited for creating Indonesia's vibrant and growing economy. He is appreciated by the people for the more prosperous life they now enjoy. As a strong figure, he is also seen as the only man who can hold Indonesia's rich diversity of peoples together.

THE PEOPLE
Population

There are some 204 million people in Indonesia. The population is growing annually at 1.5 percent and is the fourth largest in the world. Indonesia's ethnic makeup is diverse, consisting of approximately 350 distinct ethnic groups; many have their own language and most have their own customs and heritage. The largest groups are Javanese (45 percent of the population), Sundanese (14), Madurese (7.5), and Coastal Malays (7.5). The remaining 26 percent belong to various, smaller groups.

Java is the most densely populated island. Although it comprises just 7 percent of Indonesia's land, it holds 60 percent of the country's people. Since the late 1960s, the government has carried out a transmigration program to resettle people (mostly Javanese) to other islands in order to ease population growth problems on Java. Millions of people have been moved; some have had success but others have been sent to isolated or unsuitable areas. Reforms have addressed those problems, and the program continues with the intent to make life better for the migrants and for the people on Java.

The farmers of Java and Bali form the largest cultural group. They are predominantly Muslim and have strong social and spiritual values. They are skilled in the arts of native dance, music, and drama. The commercially oriented traders of the coastal region, mostly Muslim, have a high regard for religious learning and law. Some northern areas are strongly Christian. The tribes on Kalimantan and Irian Jaya maintain tight kinship bonds, practice animistic religions, and have a clan-oriented economic and social life. The people on Bali are mostly Hindu and belong to traditional kingdoms. Ancient cultural practices are being lost to Westernization, but some Balinese leaders are working to save them.

Language

The official language is Indonesian (a variety of Malay). However, some three hundred other languages are also spoken in the country. Of them, Javanese is the most common with more than 70 million speakers. More than half the population speaks some Indonesian or Malay. Because Dutch was the official language until 1942, some older adults still speak it. English is the leading international language and is taught as a third language in the schools (after the main ethnic language and Indonesian).

Religion

At least 87 percent of the population is Muslim. In fact, Indonesia is home to the world's largest Muslim population. Muslims believe in *Allah* as God and that Muhammad was *Allah's* last chosen prophet (following a long line of biblical prophets). They accept the *Qur'an* (Koran) as scripture, which they believe was revealed to Muhammad by *Allah* through the angel Gabriel. Muslims show their devotion by professing the name of *Allah* and the prophet; fasting during the holy month of *Ramadan*; donating to the poor; making a pilgrimage to Makkah, Saudi Arabia; following dietary codes, such as not drinking alcohol or eating pork; and praying five times daily.

Nine percent of the population is Christian (mostly Protestant) and 2 percent is Hindu. There are also some Buddhists, mostly among the Chinese population. Regardless of their religion, most Indonesians venerate their ancestors. Freedom of religion is guaranteed and religious tolerance is important, but proselyting has been banned by the government to avoid religious conflict.

General Attitudes

Indonesians value loyalty to family and friends more than their own concerns. They rarely disagree in public, seldom say "No" (they say *Belum,* "Not yet"), and generally have time for others. Punctuality, while important, is not emphasized at the expense of personal relations. Indonesians appreciate a quiet voice, an unassuming attitude, and discretion. To embarrass someone is a terrible insult. Indonesians often view Westerners as too quick to anger, too serious about themselves, and too committed to the idea that "time is money." Patience is the key to interaction.

Accompanying Indonesia's growing prosperity is an increasing desire for democracy. More people, though still a minority, are demanding that the people have a voice in government and that political opposition be allowed. Should Suharto retire, there is speculation the transition might include some democratization but also some instability. Fear of possible instability is keeping many Indonesians from becoming involved in politics.

Personal Appearance

Indonesians prefer modest dress, whether they wear Western styles or more traditional clothing. Businessmen wear a shirt and tie; a suit jacket is not necessary. The traditional dress for a woman is called a *sarong*, a long wraparound dress with an intricate *batik* pattern. *Batik* is the national handicraft and has been part of Indonesian culture for centuries. It traditionally is made by creating designs on cloth with molten wax. When the cloth is dyed, the wax preserves a white pattern. Authentic *batik*, made by hand, is being replaced with mass-production imitations. Both men and women may wear authentic *batik* clothing for formal occasions.

CUSTOMS AND COURTESIES
Greetings

Indonesian culture is based on honor and respect for the individual. Letters begin with *Dengan hormat* (With respect), and respect is also important in greeting others. When introduced for the first time, men and women usually shake hands and bow the head slightly. In Indonesian, they ask *Apa kabar?* (How are you?) and the response is usually positive. After an initial introduction, people usually do not shake hands in greeting; a nod or slight bow is most appropriate. Indonesians shake hands when congratulating someone or when saying good-bye before a long trip. Muslims follow a handshake by touching their right palm to the heart in a show of friendship.

Older individuals are greeted with a slight bow. They are respectfully addressed as *Ibu* (mother) or *Pak* (father). Unless married or engaged to a woman, a man usually does not touch her in public, except to shake hands, even if he knows her well. If a person has a title, it is used in greeting and general conversation. Many Indonesians, especially the Javanese, have only one name and are addressed both formally and casually by that name. Business representatives often exchange calling cards when greeting each other.

Gestures

One should avoid using gestures to beckon another person, except for children or a *becak* (pedicab) driver. One beckons by waving all fingers with the palm facing down. Indonesians sometimes show approval by a pat on the shoulder, but they never touch the head of another person. They do not use the left hand to shake hands, touch others, point, eat, or give or receive objects. Standing with one's hands in the pockets or on the hips is a sign of defiance or arrogance. Crossing the legs usually is inappropriate, but if crossed, one knee should be over the other (never an ankle on the knee). The bottom of one's foot should never point toward another person. Yawning in public is avoided, but one must yawn, one places a hand over the mouth. Laughing at another's mistake is offensive. People on public transportation should offer their seats to the elderly.

Visiting

Indonesians believe visits bring honor to the host, and they warmly welcome all guests. Unannounced visits are common between friends and relatives. Visitors sit when invited to, but they will also rise when the host or hostess enters the room. Hosts often serve a drink, but a guest does not drink until invited. They also serve refreshments, and the guest eats at least a little bit to avoid offending the hosts. If the host or hostess is not wearing footwear, it is polite for visitors to remove theirs. People remove shoes before entering carpeted rooms, feasting places, places of funeral viewings, or holy places (especially mosques). More Westernized Indonesians appreciate flowers from guests invited to dinner, but traditional Indonesians do not expect gifts. Any gift given is accepted graciously because it is impolite to refuse anything. Recipients do not open gifts in the giver's presence.

Eating

Although many restaurants line the streets, eating while standing or walking on the street is inappropriate. Finishing a drink implies the desire for the glass to be refilled. Many Westernized Indonesians eat with a spoon and fork, but more traditional families eat with their hands. Generally, Indonesians hold the fork in the left hand and the spoon in the right. It is impolite to eat or drink until invited to do so by the host. One keeps both hands above the table while eating. The hostess appreciates compliments about the food. At restaurants, the bill usually includes a service charge. Tipping is not common. Public use of toothpicks is avoided; if toothpicks must be used, one hand should cover the mouth during use.

LIFESTYLE

Family

Traditionally, Indonesians have had large families, but couples now typically have two children. Members of the extended family often live under the same roof or near one another. Loyalty and cooperation among family members are highly valued. The home traditionally is dominated by the father, and the mother is responsible for raising children and caring for the household. The trend today is for many urban women to work outside the home, and they comprise 40 percent of the labor force. Women comprise 12 percent of Parliament and generally have equal access to education. Indonesian women also have more rights than women in other predominantly Muslim countries, including rights in property settlements, inheritances, and divorce.

Dating and Marriage

Conventional, Western-style dating is uncommon, except in urban areas. Even in a city, in order to date someone, a boy must visit a girl's home several times to get acquainted with the family. After a while, the two can go on a date. If the girl does not want to go, she may tell the boy to stop coming to the home. Arranged marriages have given way to marriages of individual choice only in urban areas. They are still common in rural areas. Rural women often are married by the time they are 20 years old. As in other predominantly Muslim countries, a man may have as many as four wives if he can provide for each equally. Yet it is rare to find a man who has more than one wife; women generally oppose polygamy, and men usually cannot afford it.

Diet

Rice is the main staple food, and *nasi dan tempeh* (rice with fermented beans) is a typical daily meal. Now nearly self-sufficient, Indonesia once imported large amounts of rice to feed its growing population. Vegetables, fish, and hot sauces often are served with rice. Tea and coffee are the most common drinks. Fresh fruits are widely available and are often eaten as dessert. Popular meats include beef and chicken. Muslims do not eat pork. Chilies frequently are used (sometimes in large quantities) in cooking, as are other spices. Coconut milk is used to cook particularly spicy food known as *padang,* which is named after the city on Sumatra where it originated.

Recreation

Indonesians participate in or watch sports of all types. Soccer is very popular among the youth. Indonesians are consistently among the best in the world in badminton. They also enjoy volleyball and tennis. Bicycling serves not only as transportation but also recreation. Watching television and going to movies are popular nonathletic recreational activities. People prefer films from the United States and Hong Kong, but Indonesia does have its own successful film industry.

Holidays

Indonesians celebrate International New Year's Day (1 January), Easter, Ascension, *Idul-Fitr* (celebrating the end of *Ramadan*), Independence Day (17 August), *Idul-Adha* (11th day of the 12th lunar month, celebrating the end of the Muslim pilgrimage to Makkah), and the Muslim New Year. During the Islamic month of *Ramadan*, Muslims do not eat or drink from sunrise to sundown; they eat a family meal in the evening. Some Hindu religious festivals are also commemorated. Christians celebrate Christmas. A variety of festivals common to certain islands or ethnic groups are also held throughout the year.

Commerce

Businesses generally are open from 8:00 A.M. to 5:00 P.M., but many close for an hour or two in the afternoon. Some, including government offices, close at midday on Friday for Muslim worship. Some open on Saturday mornings, but most are closed on Sunday. Restaurants close between 10:00 and 11:00 P.M., except for those serving *padang*, which are often open 24 hours. Except in large stores, where prices are fixed, bartering is frequently practiced in purchasing goods.

SOCIETY

Government

The Republic of Indonesia is composed of 24 provinces, two special regions, and one special capital city district. The president is elected by the People's Consultative Assembly (MPR), which is made up of the unicameral legislature (five hundred members) and five hundred other people chosen through a variety of processes. One hundred members of the *Dewan Perwakilan Rakyat* (House of Representatives) are appointed from the military. For the other four hundred seats, free elections occur in theory, but issues and candidates are carefully screened and controlled by Suharto's ruling party, GOLKAR. There are two nominal opposition parties, but they are influenced by and essentially allied with GOLKAR. The president holds most of the power in the country and has been reelected six times without opposition. All Indonesians who are married or older than age 17 are eligible to vote.

Economy

Indonesia is rich in natural resources, but many of them remain undeveloped. Agriculture still employs 55 percent of the labor force and accounts for 25 percent of Indonesia's production. Important crops include rice, rubber, soybeans, copra, tea, cassava, and peanuts. The government promotes increased natural rubber production by planting new trees. Forestry and fishing are also important. Currently, petroleum and liquid natural gas account for about 30 percent of all export earnings. That is, however, substantially lower than it was only a few years ago. When oil revenues were at their highest, the government invested money in manufacturing and other enterprises. This allowed Indonesia to diversify and be protected against wide fluctuations in the price of oil. It also gave jobs to millions of people, and tens of millions of people have benefited from antipoverty programs and economic reforms.

The country's Human Development Index (0.637) ranks it 104th out of 174 countries. Adjusted for women, the index (0.591) ranks Indonesia 68th out of 130 countries. This reflects mostly a gap in incomes. Real gross domestic product per capita is $2,950, which is certain to show substantial gains as the growing middle class becomes more established. Indonesia's rank is also expected to improve in the next few years. Monthly wages are rising. The gross domestic product is growing strongly at about 7 percent.

Inflation is relatively low, as is unemployment. Underemployment is still a problem to be addressed. One of Indonesia's successes is its economic base. Many cottage industries produce consumer items such as clothing and shoes for markets in the industrialized world, including the United States. The number of employees per enterprise is relatively small, so market shocks are less painful to large groups of people. Many corporations inhabiting skyscraper offices in Jakarta are domestic firms, not foreign ones. Indonesia is also looking to the future of more advanced industries that will further expand revenues. Economic deregulations announced in 1995 are expected to further boost the country's regional and global competitiveness. Observers are calling Indonesia an "emerging Asian tiger." The currency is the Indonesian *rupiah* (Rp).

Education

Education is free and compulsory between ages six and twelve, although facilities in rural areas are often not adequate to allow all students to attend. Still, nearly 80 percent of all students complete the six years of primary schooling. About half of them go on to secondary schools, which are divided between junior and senior levels, each lasting three years. The adult literacy rate is 83 percent and is steadily improving. Each of Indonesia's 24 provinces has at least one university or academy for higher education.

Transportation and Communication

Indonesia is easily reached by international flights; domestic flights connect major islands. There are rail systems in large urban areas. Taxis and pedicabs are readily available. A passenger agrees with the driver on the fare before getting into the cab, especially in taxis without meters. Buses are crowded and roads outside urban areas are not very good. Ferries connect islands. Many people travel by bicycle and foot. Traffic travels on the left side of the road.

Health

Medical facilities are best in urban areas, but the government is striving to improve conditions in villages as well. Significant improvements have been made to the health-care system, especially regarding the accessibility of rural clinics and sanitation. The infant mortality rate has dropped by more than 50 percent since the 1970s. It is now 65 per 1,000. Most infants are immunized. Life expectancy rates have also risen substantially to an average of about 61 years. Family-planning programs, promoted under the slogan "Two children is enough," have slowed population growth and contributed to the healthier lives of most families. Despite the progress, problems remain. Malnutrition, diseases such as cholera and malaria, lack of extensive prenatal care, and unsafe drinking water all affect Indonesia's people (especially in rural areas).

FOR THE TRAVELER

U.S. travelers do not need a visa for visits of less than two months, but a valid passport is necessary, along with proof of return ticket or onward passage. The U.S. State Department warned in January 1996 that travel to remote areas of Irian Jaya could be dangerous because of recent abductions there. For recorded updates, call (202) 647–5225. All travelers should have a yellow fever vaccination and consider taking precautions against cholera and malaria. Water is not potable. Indonesia offers a variety of out-of-the-way vacations as well as luxury hotels. Beautiful beaches, charming villages and people, and fascinating culture draw many tourists each year. For information on travel opportunities, contact the Indonesian Tourist Promotion Office, 3457 Wilshire Boulevard, Suite 100, Los Angeles, CA 90010. You may also wish to contact the Embassy of Indonesia, 2020 Massachusetts NW, Washington, DC 20036; phone (202) 775–5200.

CULTURGRAM '97

Islamic Republic of
Iran

Boundary representations not necessarily authoritative.

BACKGROUND

Land and Climate

Iran is just larger than Alaska or about one-fifth the size of the continental United States. It covers 636,293 square miles (1,648,000 square kilometers). Most of Iran is a mountainous plateau, 4,000 feet (1,200 meters) above sea level, rimmed with two major mountain chains. The desert to the east is largely uninhabited, as are the mountains. There are narrow coastal plains in the north (along the Caspian Sea) and south (along the Persian Gulf). The highest mountain is Mount Damavand at 18,386 feet (5,604 meters) in the northeast. The central plateau is very arid, and long, hot, dry summers prevail. Winters are cold in the north except for along the Caspian Sea. Fall and spring are relatively short. The country is subject to earthquakes; a northern quake in 1990 killed 40,000 people and injured many more.

History

The area of present-day Iran was known anciently as Persia and was ruled by such powerful emperors as Darius and Cyrus the Great. The Arabs conquered the area in the seventh century, introducing the people to Islam. Both the Seljuk Turks and the Mongols (Genghis Khan) ruled in Iran at one time. Persian dynastic rule was revived when the Safavid Dynasty essentially set up the first national government in the 1500s. The Safavids also established Shi'ism as the state religion, linking it with nationalism. They were interested in preventing further expansion of the Ottoman Empire, whose rulers were Sunni Muslims. The Qajar Dynasty took over in the 1800s, followed by the Pahlavi Dynasty of the 20th century.

This dynasty was created when a military officer, Reza Khan, seized control of the government in 1921 and reigned (from 1925) as Reza Shah Pahlavi. He did much to modernize the country. His son, Mohammed Reza Pahlavi, continued the modernization when he took power in 1941. Known as the Shah, he sponsored literacy campaigns, voting rights for women, and industrialization. Despite these goals, his neglect of basic social problems and his lack of emphasis on Islam made his reign unpopular.

In 1979, the Shah fled the country in response to popular unrest. The Ayatollah Ruhollah Khomeini, exiled leader of the movement against the monarchy, returned at that time to establish the Islamic Republic of Iran. Khomeini ordered that all laws and practices follow strict Islamic principles. When the Shah was admitted to the United States for medical treatment, Iran's revolutionaries responded by seizing the U.S. embassy in Tehran and holding its personnel hostage until January 1981. The Shah moved to Panama and then to Egypt, where he died in 1980. The United States severed ties with Iran and still has no diplomatic relations with the government. Many Iranian policies, including the sponsorship of terrorism, has alienated Western nations. A war with Iraq in 1980 over the disputed region of Shatt-al Arab drained the economy and crippled many industries. A 1988 cease-fire led to a 1990 peace treaty.

Khomeini died in 1989 and was succeeded as the supreme leader (*Valli-e-faghih*) by the Ayatollah Ali Hoseini-Khamenei, who had been president. The *Hojatolislam* (a religious title) Hashemi Rafsanjani became the new president. He liberalized some policies, such as strict public dress requirements, and was reelected in 1993. Hopes for further policy moderation and better relations with the West (particularly the United States) darkened in 1995 when Washington, D.C., condemned Iran for seeking to obtain nuclear weapons and for sponsoring terrorism. A subsequent U.S. trade embargo hindered Iran's international trade. In the midst of food shortages and 50 percent inflation, voters were apathetic about 1996 parliamentary elections in which conservative leaders retained power.

THE PEOPLE

Population

Iran's population of 65 million is growing at 2.3 percent. Tehran, the capital, is the largest city, with more than six million inhabitants. The rest of the urban population (about 57 percent of the total) is divided among various other large cities, including Mashhad (1.5 million people), and four cities with about 1 million inhabitants each: Tabriz, Esfahan, Ubadan, and Shiraz. While urbanization was the trend during the 1970s, the opposite was encouraged in the 1980s. Nomadic life has always played a role in traditional Iranian society and more than 10 percent of the population is nomadic or seminomadic, including the Lur, Bakhtiari, and Qushqa'i. Most Iranians are ethnic Persians (51 percent). Smaller groups include Azerbaijanis (24 percent), Gilakis and Mazandaranis (8), Kurds (7), Arabs (3), Lurs (2), Balochs (2), and Turkmen (2), among others. Iran's Human Development Index (0.770) ranks it 70th out of 174 nations. Adjusted for women, the index (0.611) reflects the fact that women are less likely to earn an income or be literate.

Language

The official language is Persian Farsi, but many other languages and Persian dialects are spoken by the different ethnic groups in Iran. Turkic, Kurdish, Luri, and Arabic are among the major languages spoken. Turkic is the most widely spoken language after Farsi, as it is the language of the Azerbaijanis and Turkmen. All school instruction is in Farsi.

Religion

Shi'ite Islam is the state religion and has been since the 1500s. Before that time, most Persians were Sunni Muslims. About 95 percent of the population is *Shi'a* (Shiite) Muslim, while some 4 percent belongs to the Sunni branch of Islam. Shi'ism adds a strong nationalist element to the religious principles of Islam. Iran is the most populated Shiite Muslim country. Muslims believe in a monotheistic God (*Allah*) who chose Muhammad to be his prophet and in a day of judgment. Shiism reveres Fatima, the daughter of the prophet Muhammad; her husband, Ali; their two sons, Hassan and Hussein; and their descendants (*Imams*). Shiite Muslims, unlike the Sunnis, believe Ali was selected by Muhammad as his successor. Shiites consider the *Imams* to be holy men who have the right to leadership. The 12th *Imam* disappeared; it is believed he will reappear as a messiah to guide Muslims in the future.

The *Qur'an* (Koran), the scripture of the Muslims, is composed of God's revelations to Muhammad through the angel Gabriel. Revelations to other prophets (Adam, Noah, Abraham, Isaac, Jacob, Joseph, Moses, and Jesus) from the Bible are also acknowledged by Muslims. They accept Jesus as a prophet but not as the son of *Allah*, since they do not believe *Allah* begets children. Since the 1979 revolution, the clergy (*mullahs*) has carried out a strong conservative and fundamentalist interpretation of Islam. Persons belonging to another religion are allowed to maintain their beliefs, but they are subject to civil law as established on Islamic principles. There are about 350,000 Baha'i in Iran, along with 80,000 Christians, and 30,000 Jews. Zoroastrianism, the religion displaced by Islam in the seventh century, is also officially recognized and has some followers. With the exception of the Baha'i, each minority group has representation in the *Majles* (see Government). The Baha'i faith is outlawed because the Shiites consider it an apostate branch of Islam.

Muslims show devotion through the "Five Pillars of Islam." These include *shahada*, professing that there is no God but *Allah* and Muhammed is his prophet; *salat*, praying five times daily while facing Makkah, Saudi Arabia; *zakat*, giving money to the poor; *saum*, fasting during *Ramadan*; and *hajj*, making a pilgrimage to Makkah once in a lifetime.

General Attitudes

Iran has a rich cultural heritage, including the great Persian Empire. Although radicalism prevailed in the politics of the 1980s, Iranians remained hospitable and open to others. They like foreigners as a whole, even U.S. Americans. Official statements condemning Western nations express contempt for foreign policy choices rather than hatred toward other people. Iranians value education, culture, cleverness, and wisdom. Their perception of time is more flexible than in the West. Iranians do not stress punctuality over the needs of individuals, who are more important than schedules.

Personal Appearance

Iranians dress formally and conservatively in public. Men usually wear Western-style clothing, although some, especially religious leaders, wear traditional robes and turbans. Women must be covered from head to foot in public. During the 1980s, a veil and a black *chador* (long dress) were required as well. However, moderations have allowed women to go without the veil and to wear other clothing if it is loose fitting. Even so, only a woman's hands and face may be visible in public. The traditionally legal black head covering (*maghna-eh*), while still worn, is being replaced by more colorful scarves. Younger women may even let a little hair show on the forehead, although this is still illegal. Some women are also wearing makeup again at private gatherings. Black *chadors* cover stylish, modern clothing. Islam generally requires men to wear long sleeves. Bright colors are not worn. Personal cleanliness is important. Most men have beards. At home, Iranians often dress in comfortable pajamas. They may also receive guests while dressed in pajamas, which are for relaxing as well as sleeping.

CUSTOMS AND COURTESIES

Greetings

A handshake is the customary greeting in Iran. A slight bow or nod while shaking hands shows respect. A man does not shake a woman's hand unless she offers it first. Iranians of the same sex will often kiss each other on the cheek as a greeting and sign of affection. Proper etiquette is essential when greeting another person and one will often ask about the family and health of the other. A typical Farsi greeting is *Dorood*

(Greetings); an appropriate response is *Dorood-bar-to* (Greetings to you). People often use Arabic greetings such as *Salam* (Peace). A common parting phrase is *Khoda hafiz* (May God protect you). People use formal titles and last names in greetings to show respect. Iranians generally stand when someone (especially an older or more prominent person) enters the room for the first time and when someone leaves. Shaking hands with a child shows respect for the parents.

Gestures

Iranians pass objects with the right hand or both hands but not with the left hand alone. They do not allow the soles of the feet to point at any person. Crossing the legs is generally not acceptable. Slouching or stretching one's legs in a group is offensive. Out of respect and to maintain proper distance between genders, men and women do not always make eye contact during conversation. Men and women do not display affection in public, even if married. However, friendship and affection is often shown between members of the same sex. To beckon someone, one waves all fingers with the palm facing down. Tilting the head up quickly means "no" and tilting it down means "yes." Twisting the head means "what?" Extending the thumb is vulgar.

Visiting

Hospitality is a cherished tradition in Iran. Iranian philosophy claims a guest is a gift from (or friend of) *Allah*. Respecting the guest is a way of respecting *Allah*. Guests therefore are the center of attention in an Iranian home and everything is done to make them feel comfortable. Visitors remove their shoes before entering carpeted areas of a home, although this is not often practiced in larger cities. A polite guest compliments the host generously and accepts compliments in return. However, one should avoid complimenting objects; the host may feel an obligation to offer the object to the guest.

Dinner guests customarily take a flowering plant, cut flowers, or candy to the host. Iranians do not open gifts in front of the giver. If one is offered gifts, refreshments, or invitations from a friend, it is polite to decline a few times before graciously accepting and thanking him or her several times. The oldest man present receives the greatest respect. Because visiting is so much a part of the culture, families and friends visit one another often, even several times a month if they live close by. Iranians enjoy getting together for conversation, picnics, or just to enjoy each other's company. The common term for visiting is *did-o-bazdid*.

Eating

The midday meal is the most important meal of the day. Dinner usually is served after 8:00 P.M. Elaborate Persian meals are often prepared for guests, and a host may insist they eat several helpings. Food is eaten with the right hand only. Hosts usually offer tea to guests. During the month of *Ramadan*, Muslims do not eat or drink from dawn to dusk; in the evenings, families eat together and visit friends and relatives.

LIFESTYLE

Family

The family unit is strong in Iran and provides its members with identity, security, and social organization. The father is the undisputed head of the household. Large families with many children, especially boys, are preferred. It is legal for a man to have up to four wives if he can provide for each equally and if he has permission from his other wife or wives; permission from the government is also necessary. Most men, however, choose to have only one wife. The elderly are respected and cared for by younger members of the extended family. Relatives remain close. Parents feel a lifelong commitment to children, often providing them with financial support well after marriage. Regardless of their age, unmarried persons live with their parents until they marry. Most families are able to provide for their own basic necessities, and there is a growing upper class that enjoys many modern amenities.

If someone has two family names, the second one is the official surname. It is often based on the person's hometown.

Dating and Marriage

Dating as practiced in the West is not common; members of the opposite sex are rarely alone with each other unless married, related, or engaged. Daughters usually are protected by their families to the point that they do not speak to strangers until married. More traditional families will limit a daughter's education to keep her home. Marriage is highly valued. Most people expect to marry and have a family. Divorce is very rare. Most marriages are arranged by families. In the past, this meant that many girls married their cousins. But new attitudes have developed in some areas regarding education, work, and freedom in selecting marriage partners.

Girls marry between the ages of 18 and 25. Men marry somewhat later because of military service or because they are not earning enough money to start a family. A couple may choose to have a temporary marriage (*sigheh*) that can last between a few days and 99 years. A woman marrying in this arrangement and any children born in the marriage do not have the same rights and privileges as conventional wives and children, but they are accepted as legitimate. Both a man and woman must consent to a *sigheh*, and women marrying for the first time must have parental consent. Couples might choose the *sigheh* as a trial marriage or because the wedding is much less expensive than a conventional wedding. When a *sigheh* is terminated, or if a regularly married couple divorces, the woman may not marry again for at least one hundred days. Weddings are elaborate celebrations.

Diet

The diet varies throughout the country. Muslims do not eat pork or drink alcohol. Under current law, alcohol consumption is forbidden. Rice and wheat bread are the most common staple foods. Rice is often served with a meat and vegetable stew. Yogurt is generally served with rice or other foods. Fresh vegetables are important in the diet, and fresh fruit is a favorite dessert. White cheeses are also popular.

Recreation

Iranians enjoy soccer, wrestling, the martial arts, basketball, volleyball, and ping pong. The urban population enjoys going to the movies. Socializing, however, provides the greatest opportunity for relaxation. Iranians also visit teahouses, shop in bazaars, and stroll through the streets.

Holidays

The lunar calendar is used in Iran to determine religious festivals and the new year; the solar (Gregorian) calendar is used to set official public holidays. The Iranian New Year (*Naw Ruz*) is celebrated around the end of March in connection with the spring equinox. This is the biggest holiday of the year and is marked with visits, gifts, and feasts. Businesses close and the celebrations last four days. National holidays include Revolution Day (11 February), Oil Nationalization Day (20 March), Islamic Republic Day (1 April), National Picnic Day (2 April), Armed Forces Day (18 April), Anniversary of Khomeini's Exile (4 May), and Anniversary of Khomeini's Death (5 May). Religious holidays occur on different days each year. They include feasts for *Aid-e-fitr* to end the month of *Ramadan* and *Aid-e-adha* to commemorate Abraham's willingness to sacrifice his son and to mark the end of the *hajj*. Other holidays mark the birth and death of the prophet Muhammad and the *Imams*. *Aid-e-khadir* celebrates Muhammad's choosing of Ali (Fatima's husband) as his successor.

Commerce

Iranians conduct business Saturday through Thursday. Office hours are usually from 8:00 A.M. to noon and 2:00 to 6:00 P.M. Summer hours may differ; businesses often close in the hot afternoon and reopen for a short time in the evening. Many businesses are only open until noon on Thursday and most close on Friday, the Muslim day of worship. Shops and retail stores are often open from 8:00 A.M. to late in the evening, with a break from noon to 3:00 P.M. Bartering, especially in the bazaar, is a way of life. Keeping a client waiting is not an insult; clients are often served refreshments while waiting.

SOCIETY

Government

A Council of Guardians (made up of religious and lay leaders) holds power over the constitution, appoints judicial authorities, and approves candidates for president. Twelve of the members are elected; twelve are appointed. The council must approve all legislation passed by the Islamic Consultative Assembly (*Majles*). All laws must be in harmony with the doctrines of Islam, as interpreted by the country's religious authorities. The head of government and official chief of state is President Rafsanjani. The supreme leader, the Ayatollah Ali Hoseini-Khamenei, often functions as head of state. The voting age is 15. Voters receive a stamp on their identity papers verifying they have voted. This makes it easier to get government employment or assistance and to qualify for a passport.

Economy

Oil reserves allowed Iran to prosper in the 1970s and early 1980s. Energy production is still the most important economic activity in Iran; oil exports account for 90 percent of all export earnings. After the 1979 revolution, major industries were nationalized, but these became inefficient at producing enough goods for the country's needs. The Rafsanjani government tried to liberalize the economy but met with stiff opposition from conservative politicians. Still, some progress was realized, and conditions improved slightly before 1995. Iran hopes to attract increased tourism to earn more hard currency. Real gross domestic product per capita is $5,420. This figure may decline before it rises, since more people find it difficult to meet basic needs, 30 percent still live in poverty, and the economy registered negative growth for 1994 and 1995. The currency is the Iranian *rial* (IR).

Transportation and Communication

Iran has a well-developed transportation system with railroads, highways, ports, and several airports. Buses and minibuses provide most public transportation in the cities. A metro rail service operates in Tehran. The number of private cars is increasing. All parts of the country are accessible by telephone, but only a small number of homes have a private line. About one-fourth of all households have televisions, but most have radios. Communication facilities are government-owned.

Education

Elementary schooling, lasting five years, is compulsory for all children beginning at age seven. Most (89 percent) complete the primary level. A sizable portion of these pupils (74 percent) go on to secondary schooling, which is divided into three sections. The first three years are called "guidance" and are of a general nature; the next three years are called "high school." Upon completion of high school, students are ready to begin a trade career. If they wish to go to college, they must complete a seventh year, called "preuniversity." Islamic studies are often stressed over secular training at most levels, but the sciences and math are popular. The literacy rate is 65 percent: approximately 75 percent for men and 55 percent for women. The University of Tehran, various provincial universities, and several smaller universities provide higher education.

Elementary schools often run on two shifts, with half of the students attending in the morning and half in the afternoon. This allows the growing population to receive an education despite a lack of buildings and teachers. Boys and girls attend separate classes, although not necessarily separate schools. Segregation of the sexes is a fundamental Islamic principle.

Health

Public health services are run by the government, but curative treatment services are divided between the government and private sector. Government facilities and private doctors accept the government health insurance that covers public employees and their families, but private hospitals demand a cash deposit upon admission. Infectious diseases like typhoid, measles, dysentery, and malaria are prevalent. More than 90 percent of all children are immunized against major childhood diseases. Water is safe in urban areas but not always in rural regions. The infant mortality rate is 55 per 1,000. Life expectancy averages 67 years.

FOR THE TRAVELER

The United States does not have diplomatic relations with Iran. To obtain a travel visa, one must contact Pakistan's embassy, which represents Iran in the United States. Visitors are expected to abide by Islamic law while in Iran. Vaccinations should be considered, depending on the length of stay and areas to be visited. A U.S. citizen must have special permission to visit the country. For information, contact the Iranian Interests Section, Embassy of Pakistan, 2315 Massachusetts Avenue NW, Washington, DC 20008.

A *Culturgram* is a product of native commentary and original, expert analysis. Statistics are estimates and information is presented as a matter of opinion. While the editors strive for accuracy and detail, this document should not be considered strictly factual. It is a general introduction to culture, an initial step in building bridges of understanding between peoples. It may not apply to all peoples of the nation. You should therefore consult other sources for more information.

State of
Israel

Boundary representations not necessarily authoritative.

BACKGROUND

Land and Climate

Covering 8,020 square miles (20,770 square kilometers), Israel is about the same size as New Jersey. This does not include the occupied territory (called the Administered Area) of the West Bank. Despite the country's size, the land and climate vary substantially by region. The terrain ranges from fertile valleys and flower-covered hills to unique deserts to the Dead Sea, which is the lowest point on earth (1,300 feet or 390 meters below sea level). The hot Negev Desert is home to the Mahktesh Crater, mountains, and oases. Eilat, a resort town, borders the Red Sea. On the west coastal plain, summers are humid and winters mild. The hills experience more comfortable summers but colder winters, and the Jordan Rift Valley has a relatively pleasant climate. The rainy season is from October to April. Some snow falls in the mountains, and Mount Hermon receives enough to support snow skiing. An efficient irrigation system makes agricultural land arable all year.

History

The Holy Land, from which the present state of Israel emerged, claims a long history of rule by different powers. A Hebrew kingdom was established from the 12 tribes of Israel that came out of Egypt with Moses. King David ruled this kingdom some three thousand years ago. After his son Solomon's reign, it split into two states—Israel and Judah—that were later destroyed by Assyria and Babylonia in the eighth and sixth centuries B.C. The populations were dispersed or taken captive, although many Israelites remained in the area.

After the Persian conquest of the Middle East, many Jews were allowed to return to the Holy Land to establish a nation and build a temple. The land later fell to the Greeks and then to the Romans. Heavily persecuted, the Jewish population declined sharply during the Byzantine era (A.D. 313–636). In the 600s, the area (named *Palestine* by the Romans) was conquered by Muslims who ruled for nearly one thousand years.

The Ottoman Turks controlled Palestine from the 16th century until World War I. In the 1890s, Theodor Herzl founded Zionism as an international movement to restore Palestine to the Jews. After World War I, the area came under British control. Various plans for partitioning the area were put forth but never actually implemented. When the Jewish people suffered so heavily from the Holocaust during World War II, they began to immigrate to Israel in large numbers. The British first tried to halt the process but were unable to stop Jews from seeking a new life in what they consider to be their land of inheritance. In 1947, the United Nations voted to divide the area into two states—one Arab and one Jewish. In May 1948, Israel proclaimed an independent state and the British withdrew. Neighboring Arab nations, opposed to an independent Jewish state, declared war and attacked. Subsequent wars were fought in 1956, 1967, and 1973. In 1979, Egypt and Israel signed a peace treaty; Egypt was the first Arab nation to recognize Israel's right to exist. Terrorism and border wars with Lebanon caused problems in following years, the major concern being the status of territories occupied by Israel in the 1967 war.

In 1987, after years of waging a terrorist campaign against Israel, the Palestine Liberation Organization (PLO) renounced terrorism but declared an independent Palestinian state in the occupied territories of the West Bank and Gaza. Israel rejected the declaration and persistent violence ensued, sometimes spilling over into Israel itself.

Plagued by the violence, pressed by the international community, and recognizing a greater opportunity for cooperation due to the Gulf War, Israel agreed in 1991 to discuss peace with its Arab neighbors.

Former war hero Yitzhak Rabin became prime minister in 1992 and gave vital support to fledgling negotiations. A 1993 breakthrough during secret talks in Norway eventually led Israel to grant the Palestinians limited autonomy in some occupied areas. By mid-1994, Gaza and one West Bank town (Jericho) had achieved autonomy. Also in 1994 was one of the greatest and most welcomed events: a peace treaty with Jordan that ended hostilities and opened the way for mutual cooperation on regional issues. Progress was limited on other issues, such as the status of the Golan Heights, occupied by Israel but once belonging to Syria. Still, Rabin and his PLO counterpart, Yasir Arafat, agreed in September 1995 to gradually extend self-rule to most of the West Bank (but not Jerusalem).

Opposition to this and other aspects of the peace plan intensified among both right-wing Israelis and militant Palestinians. The terrorist group *Hamas* sponsored violent attacks to undermine negotiations. Then, in an unthinkable act of Jew-against-Jew violence, a right wing Jewish student murdered Prime Minister Rabin after a peace rally in November 1995. Shimon Peres replaced Rabin in office and struggled against a wave of *Hamas* suicide bombings and continued right-wing opposition to implement signed peace agreements and forge ahead with other negotiations.

The peace process had become so divisive among Israelis that the 1996 election for prime minister was decided on fewer than 25,000 votes. Conservative (Likud Party) leader Benjamin Netanyahu defeated Peres to become the country's first directly elected prime minister (all others had been appointed on the basis of majority-party status in Parliament).

THE PEOPLE

Population

Israel's population of 5.4 million includes about 290,000 Israeli settlers in the West Bank, Gaza, the Golan Heights, and East Jerusalem. Israelis refer to the West Bank as Judea and Samaria, the biblical names for the region. Israelis do not consider East Jerusalem an occupied territory, but an integral part of Jerusalem. Nearly 90 percent of the people live in cities. The average population growth rate (1.4 percent) fluctuates with immigration. In 1992, it was 4 percent because 350,000 people emigrated from the former Soviet Union. Many also arrived from Ethiopia. Such immigration waves challenge Israel's ability to provide housing and jobs, but society is mostly able to absorb the newcomers. By law, all Jews in the world have the right to emigrate to Israel, as long as they can prove their identity (inherited through the mother) or are recognized converts.

Israel's Human Development Index (0.907) ranks it 21st out of 174 nations. This means most people have access to resources that allow them to pursue personal goals; they can gain a useful education, live in good health, and earn a decent wage.

Seventeen percent of Israel's citizens are Palestinian Arabs and members of the Druze and Circasean ethnic groups. The rest of the population (83 percent) is Jewish. The word *Jewish* does not describe an ethnic group or population—it is a religion, a culture, and a nation. There are three identities in Israel: religion, citizenship, and nationality. Someone could be Christian by religion, Israeli by citizenship, and Arab by nationality. A Jew is Jewish by religion and nationality, but Israeli by citizenship. Because Jews come from around the world, their ethnic makeup is mixed. However, they are usually divided into two ethnic heritages. Sephardic Jews come mainly from the Middle East and North Africa. Ashkenic Jews are from Europe. The Ashkenazim have generally dominated religion and politics, but the Sephardim are well represented in government and business. Despite intermarriage, equalizing incomes, and other factors, historical tensions between the two groups continue to divide Israelis.

Language

Hebrew is Israel's official language. Arabic has official status, is spoken by the Arab minority, and is taught from the fifth grade on in school. English, frequently used in commerce, is spoken by most Israelis and is also taught from the fifth grade on. Nearly all Israelis speak at least two languages, often because they or their parents emigrated from other countries after 1948. Today's immigrants attend government-sponsored *ulpan* classes to learn Hebrew. They also continue to speak their various languages amongst themselves.

Religion

The city of Jerusalem and surrounding areas have played an important role in the development of several of the world's major religions, including Judaism, Christianity, and Islam. Jerusalem therefore is holy to all three religions and is a source of conflict between them.

Judaism focuses on a unique relationship and responsibility between the Creator and the Jewish nation, as particularly outlined in the Bible's first five books of Moses. Once expressed primarily through temple rites, worship patterns now concentrate on personal action. Orthodox or observant Jews strictly adhere to certain behavioral imperatives, such as honoring the Jewish Sabbath from sundown Friday to sundown Saturday and following dietary codes. Most Jews are non-observant (secular) but are sensitive to and accepting of Jewish values. Two other traditions—reform and conservative Judaism—have small followings.

Political parties associated with the more orthodox Jews won a surprising number of seats in 1996 parliamentary elections, fulfilling their wish for more power to effect change in daily life—in areas such as Sabbath observance, the teaching of Jewish traditions in school, and continued rabbinical control over marriage, divorce, and other matters.

About 13 percent of the population is Muslim (mostly Sunni) and nearly 2 percent is Druze. The remaining 2 to 3 percent is Christian, about half of which is Greek Orthodox. Haifa is also the world center of the Baha'i faith, which emphasizes the unity of religion and the oneness of mankind.

General Attitudes

Israel is a land of informality, as evidenced in people's casual dress habits and custom to address each other by first name. Respect is shown in other ways—through courtesy and neighborly help, for instance. Israelis are civic-minded and involved in the community. In a large apartment complex, every family knows the others by name and knows at least a little about each family member. Israelis are inquisitive; they are avid readers and enjoy travel. They value determination, hard work, openness, frankness, and humor. The group, especially the family, is more important than each individual member, and Israelis enjoy sharing life with their family and friends. Most people want a home and comfortable life, but material possessions are less important than a strong family.

Israelis are devoted to their culture and state. Israel's very existence is greatly valued. Part of the people's pride for the nation comes with mandatory military service. Women serve two years and men serve three. Arab-Israeli men may volunteer for military service, but they are not drafted. Jewish immigration is encouraged as part of the Zionist movement, the ongoing effort to establish and maintain a Jewish homeland.

Personal Appearance

Most Israelis wear casual Western-style clothing. Men only wear suits and ties on formal occasions, otherwise preferring open-necked shirts and jeans. Women wear slacks and dresses. Orthodox Jews dress more conservatively (long sleeves for men, longer skirts for women). Men might cover their heads with an embroidered *kippah* cap or yarmulke. Youth like European and U.S. American fashions. Both men and women wear shorts and sandals in summer. Cotton fabric is preferred.

Among ultra Orthodox Jews, men wear black pants and jackets over white buttoned-up shirts with black hats; women do not wear pants and they cover their heads with a scarf. Muslims wear Western or traditional clothing.

CUSTOMS AND COURTESIES

Greetings

Informality governs most greetings. *Shalom* (Peace) is the usual greeting and parting phrase. It may be followed by *Ma Nishma?* (What's up?), *Ma Inyanim?* (What's happening?), or the more formal *Ma Shlomcha?* (How are you?). For women, this last phrase is *Ma Shlomech?*

Handshakes are common. Additional touching (hugging, kissing) depends largely on one's ethnic origin and the relationship between the greeters. People from Eastern cultures tend to touch more than Westerners. For instance, women might hug and kiss once or twice on the cheek. Close male friends may pat each other on the back or shoulder. Among the very religious, men and women do not touch in public.

People most often address others by first name once they have been introduced. This custom extends to most facets of life, including the military. Even school children call their teachers by first name.

Gestures

Hands are used often in conversation and make the discussion seem very lively. The most common gesture is to bring thumb and fingertips together, palm facing up, and move the hand up and down; this means "wait a minute" or "hold on." One expresses exasperation by shrugging the shoulders, sometimes also holding open palms up. Respect for elders is extremely important. For instance, one always gives up a bus seat to an older person.

Visiting

Israelis love to visit friends and relatives. They might drop by unannounced for a short visit or call ahead to arrange something. Invitations to dinner, especially on Friday evening or Saturday afternoon, are common. Invited guests usually take a gift such as flowers or chocolates.

Hosts always offer visitors refreshments. These include coffee, tea, or a cold drink, as well as cake, cookies, or snacks (nuts and sunflower seeds). In addition to visiting in the home, Israelis enjoy meeting at cafés for an evening of conversation.

Eating

On average, Israelis eat three meals a day. Breakfast is light. The main meal traditionally is in the early afternoon (except on Friday evening), and supper usually is light. Families are often too busy to eat all together, but they will at least gather for the Friday evening and Saturday afternoon meals. Conversation and a casual atmosphere accompany most meals. It is polite for guests to accept offers of additional food.

LIFESTYLE

Family

The family is central to Israeli life, and children are given a great deal of care and attention. Ties remain very strong, even as children become adults. Parents feel a deep responsibility to prepare and provide for a child's future. Married children expect to live near their parents or other relatives. They expect to care for their elderly parents. Families come together on holidays, especially Passover, and for big celebrations.

The father traditionally is the head of the family, but women have great influence in all decisions. Many women work outside the home; women comprise 35 percent of the labor force. Some families (7–8 percent) live in either a *kibbutz* or a *moshav*. In a *kibbutz,* families share the land, work, food, and dining hall equally. They concentrate on agriculture and technology. A *moshav* is a small village (less than one hundred families) where families live separately but cooperate in providing for the needs of the community and in marketing the village's products.

Dating and Marriage

Dating is common, and young people enjoy dancing, eating out, and going to movies. Among Muslims and Orthodox Jews, dating may be supervised or restricted. Weddings are a great social event in Israel, often including a large dinner party where singing and dancing last well into the night. Of course, traditions vary depending on cultural background. Parents are usually heavily involved in planning weddings and paying for the festivities.

There are no civil marriages in Israel. All weddings must be performed by a religious authority. Rabbis perform Jewish ceremonies and a *Khadi* handles Muslim weddings. Christians go to their clergymen. Divorce and other family issues are dealt with by religious courts. Each religion has the right to adjudicate family matters according to its own customs.

Diet

Israelis eat foods from a variety of cultures. Some of the more popular dishes include *falafel* (pita bread filled with balls of fried chickpea batter), *kebab* (meat and vegetables on a skewer), *tshulnt* (traditional bean stew), *burékas* (pastry filled with cheese and spinach), chicken soup, and Russian *borscht* (beet soup). *Gefilte* fish, a dish of baked or stewed ground fish brought to Israel by European Jews, is popular as a Sabbath dish because it can be cooked ahead of time and served cold. Vegetable salad, mixed with olive oil, lemon juice, and spices, is a staple and usually eaten every day. Salads usually do not contain lettuce. Chicken and fish are eaten more frequently than beef because they cost less. Fruits and vegetables are plentiful and fruit juices are often part of lunch or dinner. Milk products, such as yogurt and cottage cheese, are popular. Many people observe Jewish dietary laws that prohibit milk and meat being eaten together. However, a kosher diet is not important to the more secular Jews.

Recreation

Israelis like to go to movies and concerts. Musicians are highly regarded, as are poets. Hebrew poetry and folk music focus on the Jewish experience. Soccer and basketball are the favorite sports, followed by swimming, tennis, gymnastics, hiking, and camping. In their leisure time, people read, watch television, or visit friends. People like to take day trips to various places in Israel.

Holidays

Holidays are important in Israel; businesses close and public transportation stops. The Jewish calendar is based on the lunar standard. The month of *Tishrei* (September/October) begins with *Rosh Hashanah* (New Year), followed by *Yom Kippur* (Day of Atonement) on the tenth. The weeklong festival of *Succot* (Tabernacles) begins on the 15th. *Hanukkah* (Festival of Lights) is in December. *Pesach* (Passover) takes place six lunar months and two weeks after New Year's Day, and Holocaust Day is commemorated 13 days after that. Other important days include Memorial Day (20 days after Passover), Independence Day (21 days after Passover), and *Shavu'ot* or Pentecost (50 days after Passover). The Jewish day begins at sunset, not midnight. That is why *Shabbat* (Sabbath) begins at sundown on Friday and ends just after sundown on Saturday.

Commerce

State law requires that all workers have one day of rest each week, which is usually taken on Fridays by Muslims, Saturdays by Jews, and Sundays by Christians. Most workers belong to a labor union. General business hours extend from 8:00 A.M. to 1:00 P.M. and 4:00 to 7:00 P.M., Sunday through Thursday. Many shops are open all day. On Friday, businesses close around 2:00 P.M.

SOCIETY

Government

Israel does not have a written constitution. The president (Ezer Weizman) performs ceremonial duties, but the prime minister is head of government. All governments have been coalitions because no one party has been able to gain a majority of votes in the *Knesset* (Parliament). Its members (120 total) are elected at least every four years; voters cast ballots for parties, not for individual candidates. Likud and Labor are the two largest parties.

Economy

Israel's economy is well developed and modern despite a lack of natural resources. Agriculture employs 5 percent of the labor force and produces food for consumption and export. Chief products include citrus and other fruits, vegetables, beef, dairy, and poultry products. The strong industrial sector includes high technology, diamonds, and machinery. Tourism is another vital part of the economy. Growth (about 3 percent), unemployment (10 percent), and inflation (11 percent) fluctuate with immigration and the peace process, as well as global market trends. Taxes in Israel are very high. Real gross domestic product per capita is $14,700, which has tripled in the last generation. The currency is the new *shekel* (NIS).

Transportation and Communication

Bus, rail, and road systems are all well developed in Israel. *Sherut* taxis provide convenient transportation between cities; they carry up to seven passengers on fixed routes. In all cities except Haifa, buses and trains do not run on the Jewish Sabbath and holy days. Taxis and private cars are plentiful. Israel has a highly developed communications system with good domestic phone service. There are several radio and television stations and daily newspapers.

Education

The government provides both religious and secular school systems, and people are free to choose either. Citizens can also choose between schools taught in Hebrew or Arabic. School is free and compulsory through the tenth grade. Elementary school runs through sixth grade, junior high through ninth, and high school through twelfth. The high school diploma is necessary for college entrance and important for getting a job. Special private schools admit those who dropped out of school but later decided to finish a diploma. Most schools, including universities, hold classes six days a week. The Open University offers correspondence and radio courses to adults, and the *ulpanim* system offers immigrants the chance to learn Hebrew. Literacy among Jews is about 95 percent, while Arabs average somewhat lower.

Health

All Israelis are covered by a state-run health plan financed by salary deduction. It was introduced in 1995 to replace the system in which most care was provided at public facilities. The plan now dispenses payment for care provided by the private sector. Facilities are modern and the quality of care is high. The infant mortality rate is 9 per 1,000. Life expectancy ranges from 76 to 80 years.

FOR THE TRAVELER

U.S. tourists need a valid passport to enter Israel, but no visa is required for stays of up to three months. Certain occupied areas may require a permit. Travelers should drink plenty of liquids and wear hats in hotter areas. Visitors enjoy Israel's numerous archaeological, historical, and religious sites, as well as beautiful scenery. The Israeli Embassy is located at 3514 International Drive NW, Washington, DC 20008.

A *Culturgram* is a product of native commentary and original, expert analysis. Statistics are estimates and information is presented as a matter of opinion. While the editors strive for accuracy and detail, this document should not be considered strictly factual. It is a general introduction to culture, an initial step in building bridges of understanding between peoples. It may not apply to all peoples of the nation. You should therefore consult other sources for more information.

Japan

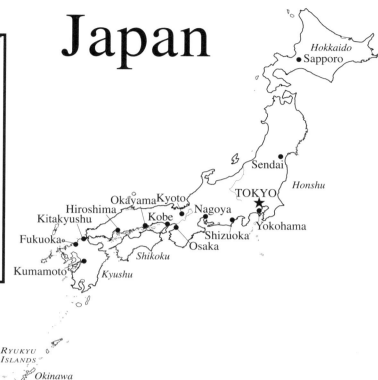

Boundary representations not necessarily authoritative.

BACKGROUND

Land and Climate

Japan consists of four main islands: Honshu, Hokkaido, Shikoku, and Kyushu. Covering 145,882 square miles (377,835 square kilometers), it is just smaller than Montana. Japan experiences all four seasons. On Hokkaido and in northern Honshu, winters can be bitterly cold. To the south, a more tropical climate prevails. Otherwise, the climate is temperate with warm, humid summers and mild winters. The western side of the islands is usually colder than the eastern side, which faces the Pacific Ocean. The islands are subject to typhoons in September. Japan also has many dormant and a few active volcanoes. Mild earthquakes are fairly common, and more destructive ones hit every few years. The January 1995 quake in and around Kobe killed more than five thousand people and was the worst of several quakes since a 1923 Tokyo quake that killed 140,000.

History

Japan is known historically as the "Land of the Rising Sun," as symbolized by its flag. Beginning more than two thousand years ago (with Emperor Jimmu in 600 B.C., according to legend), Japan has had a line of emperors that continues to the present. From the 12th century until the late 19th century, however, feudal lords or *Shoguns* held political control. These *Shoguns* expelled all foreigners in the 17th century on the suspicion they were spies for European armies. Not until 1853, when Matthew Perry (U.S. Navy) sailed into port, did the Japanese again have contact with the West. The *Shoguns* lost power in the 1860s and the emperor again took control. The current emperor, Akihito, took the throne in 1989. Akihito's father, Hirohito, was emperor from 1926 to 1989. Hirohito's reign was called *Showa*, which means "enlightened peace." The deceased Hirohito is now properly referred to as "Emperor Showa." Akihito's reign is called *Heisei*, meaning "achievement of universal peace."

Japan established itself as a regional power through military victories against China (1895) and Russia (1905). Involvement in World War I brought Japan enhanced global influence, and the Treaty of Versailles expanded its land holdings. The post-war years brought prosperity to the rapidly changing nation. It soon began to exercise considerable influence in Asia and subsequently invaded Manchuria and much of China. On 7 December 1941, Japan launched a successful air attack on U.S. naval forces at Pearl Harbor. Its military machine swiftly encircled most of Southeast Asia. But in 1943, the tide of the war turned against Japan. The United States dropped atomic bombs on Hiroshima and Nagasaki in the summer of 1945. Complete collapse of the empire and surrender ensued. A military occupation, chiefly by U.S. forces, lasted from 1945 to 1952. In 1947, Japan adopted a new constitution under American direction, renouncing war, granting basic human rights, and declaring

Japan a democracy. The United States and Japan have since maintained close political and military ties despite periodic trade tensions.

Japan's post-war focus was on economic development and the country experienced rapid change and modernization. The Liberal Democratic Party (LDP) generally controlled politics after World War II, but scandals in the 1980s and early 1990s led to high-level resignations, splinter parties, and a weaker LDP. In 1993, it lost its majority and served as a coalition partner to the rival Socialist Party under Prime Minister Tomiichi Murayama. Newly appointed LDP leader Ryutaro Hashimoto restored his party to power when Murayama resigned in January 1996. As a coalition partner, the LDP did not have to stand for early elections in order for Hashimoto to become prime minister and govern until general elections scheduled for 1997.

THE PEOPLE

Population

Japan's population of 125.5 million is growing at 0.3 percent annually. Although Japan's population is half that of the United States, it resides on less than 5 percent of the total territory of the United States. Japan is therefore one of the most densely populated countries in the world. Nearly 80 percent of all people live in urban areas. About 45 percent are concentrated in three major metropolitan areas: Tokyo, Osaka, and Nagoya. Tokyo is the world's most populous city. Japan is 99 percent ethnic Japanese, with a small number of Koreans (about 680,000) and Chinese. Native Ainu live mostly on Hokkaido. All non-Japanese must register annually with the police and do not have full citizenship rights.

Japan's Human Development Index (0.937) ranks it third out of 173 countries. The ranking reflects a high level of economic and social organization, but it does not take into account Japan's high cost of living and the stress inherent in an emphasis on work, a lack of affordable housing, and inflexible social institutions. Adjusted for women, the index (0.896) ranks Japan eighth out of 130 nations. This rank accurately reflects Japanese women's inferior social status and limited access to resources that allow them to pursue personal goals as freely as men.

Language

Japanese is the official language. Although spoken Japanese is not closely related to spoken Chinese, the written language (kanji) is related to Chinese ideographs (characters), which were adopted in ancient times. The Japanese also use two phonetic alphabets (hiragana and katakana) simplified from these characters. A third phonetic alphabet (romaji) uses Roman letters. English is taught in all secondary schools and is often used in business. The Japanese also place great worth on nonverbal language or communication. For example, much can be said with a proper bow. In fact, one is often expected to sense another person's feelings on a subject without verbal communication. Some Westerners misinterpret this as a desire to be vague or incomplete. The Japanese may consider a person's inability to interpret feelings as insensitivity.

Religion

Traditionally, most Japanese practiced a combination of Buddhism and Shinto. Shinto has no recognized founder or central scripture but is based on ancient mythology. It stresses man's relationship to nature and its many gods. All Japanese emperors are considered literal descendants of the sun goddess, Amaterasu. Shinto was important historically in ordering Japanese social values, as illustrated by the Code of the Warrior (Bushido), which stressed honor, courage, politeness, and reserve.

Shinto principles of ancestor veneration, ritual purity, and a respect for nature's beauty are all obvious in Japanese culture. Many households observe some ceremonies of both Shinto and Buddhism, such as Shinto marriages and Buddhist funerals, and most have small shrines in their homes. For most, however, this is done more out of respect for social tradition than out of religious conviction. About 1 percent of the population is Christian.

General Attitudes

Japanese society is group oriented. Loyalty to the group (business, club, etc.) and to one's superiors is essential and takes precedence over personal feelings. In business, loyalty, devotion, and cooperation are valued over aggressiveness. Companies traditionally provide lifetime employment to the "salaryman" (full-time male professional), and the salaryman devotes long hours of work to the company. This tradition was undermined by the recession of the early 1990s but is still a pillar of society. Devotion to the group reaches all ages; even members of a youth baseball team will place the team's interests over their own.

Politeness is extremely important; a direct "no" is seldom given, but a phrase like "I will think about it" can mean "no." Also out of politeness, a "yes" may be given quickly, even though it only means the person is listening or understands the speaker's request. The Japanese feel a deep obligation to return favors and gifts. They honor age and tradition. Losing face or being shamed in public is very undesirable. Gamam (enduring patience) is a respected trait that carries one through personal hardship, but it has also been used to dismiss the need for social change.

Nevertheless, even as many traditions remain strong, Japan's rising generation is beginning to revise society's view of economic security, family relations, politics, and male and female roles.

Personal Appearance

Conformity, even in appearance, is a characteristic of the Japanese. The general rule is to act similar to, or in harmony with, the crowd. Businessmen wear suits and ties in public. Proper dress is necessary for certain occasions. Conformity takes on a different meaning for the youth, however. They will wear the latest fashions (U.S. American and European) and colors, as long as these fashions are popular. Traditional clothing, called a kimono or wafuku, is a long robe with long sleeves, wrapped with a special sash (obi). The designs in the fabric can be simple or elaborate. The kimono is worn for social events or special occasions.

CUSTOMS AND COURTESIES

Greetings

A bow is the traditional greeting between Japanese. Persons wishing to show respect or humility bow lower than the other person. The Japanese shake hands with Westerners.

While some appreciate it when Westerners bow, others do not, especially when the two people are not acquainted. Therefore, a handshake is most appropriate for foreign visitors. The Japanese are formal, and titles are important in introductions. A family name is used with the suffix *san*. A Mr. Ogushi in North America is called *Ogushi-san* in Japan. The use of first names is reserved for family and friends. Between business representatives, the exchange of business cards (offered and accepted with both hands) most often accompanies a greeting.

Greetings used depend on the relationship. A worker might greet a superior with *Ohayogozaimasu* (Good morning), but he or she would greet a customer with *Irasshaimase* (Welcome). When business representatives meet for the first time, they may use *Hajimemashite* (Nice to meet you). *Konnichiwa* (Hello) is a standard greeting. *Ohayoh* (an informal "Good morning"), *Yahhoh* (Hey!), or *Genki?* (How are you?) are common casual greetings among the youth.

Gestures

Yawning in public is impolite. A person should sit up straight with both feet on the floor. Legs may be crossed at the knee or ankles, but placing an ankle over a knee is improper. One beckons by waving all fingers with the palm down. It is polite to point with the entire hand. Shaking one hand from side to side with the palm forward means "no." A person refers to himself by pointing the index finger at his nose. Laughter does not necessarily signify joy or amusement; it can also be a sign of embarrassment. One covers one's mouth when using a toothpick. Chewing gum in public is considered impolite. Young girls often walk hand in hand.

Visiting

Visits usually are arranged in advance; spontaneous visits between neighbors are uncommon in urban areas. The Japanese remove shoes before stepping into a home. There is usually a small hallway (*genkan*) between the door and living area where one stands to remove the shoes and place them together pointing toward the outdoors—or in a closet or on a shelf in the *genkan*. People take off their coats before stepping into the *genkan*. Slippers are often worn inside but not in rooms with straw-mat floors (*tatami*). Japanese traditionally emphasize modesty and reserve. Guests usually are offered the most comfortable seat. When offered a meal, they often express slight hesitation before accepting it. Light refreshments are accepted graciously. The Japanese deny compliments out of modesty. Guests avoid excessive compliments on items in the home because they would embarrass the hosts.

Guests customarily take a gift (usually fruit or cakes) to their hosts. People give and accept gifts with both hands and a slight bow. Some, especially the elderly, may consider it impolite to open the gift right away. Gift giving is extremely important, especially in business, because a gift says a great deal about the giver's relationship to, and respect for, the recipient. Food and drink are the most common gifts, as gifts for the house would quickly clutter small homes. Gift giving reaches its peak at the end of each year, when giving the right-priced present (the price is more important than the item) to all the right people (family, friends, officials, and business contacts) sets the tone for the coming year.

Eating

Although many young people eat while walking in public, it is generally considered bad manners for adults to do so. Therefore, snack foods sold at street stands are eaten at the stand. In a traditional meal, the Japanese typically eat from their bowl while holding it at chest level instead of bending down to the table. People eat most meals with chopsticks (*hashi*), but they generally use Western utensils when eating Western food. U.S. American fast-food is popular among the youth. The main meal is eaten in the evening. Because many men work late hours, they may eat dinner in office-building restaurants or on the way home.

LIFESTYLE

Family

The family is the foundation of Japanese society and is bound together by a strong sense of reputation, obligation, and responsibility. A person's actions reflect on the family. Affection, time together, and spousal compatibility are less important than in other cultures. While the father is the head of the home, the mother is responsible for household affairs and raising children. Traditionally, it was considered improper for a woman to have a job, but many women now work outside the home. Divorce and single parenthood are rare compared to other nations, due mostly to economic pressures and negative stigmas associated with both. Families generally have fewer than three children. In cities, families live in high-rise apartments or small homes. Larger homes are found in less-crowded areas.

Dating and Marriage

Youth in Japan are much like youth in the United States. They begin dating at around age 15 and enjoy dancing, going to movies, shopping, or eating out. They like Western music and fashion trends. The average marriage age is 27 for men and 26 for women. Weddings can be elaborate and expensive. Marriage ceremonies usually take place in hotels. The couple may wear traditional *kimonos* for the ceremony, Western wedding outfits for photographs and socializing, and different clothing for an evening party. Wedding guests bring gifts, often cash, and leave with gifts from the couple.

Diet

The Japanese diet consists largely of rice, fresh vegetables, seafood, fruit, and small portions of meat. Rice and tea are part of almost every meal. Western-style food is increasingly popular, especially among the youth. Popular Japanese foods include *miso* (bean paste) soup, noodles (*raman*, *udon*, and *soba*), curried rice, *sashimi* (uncooked fish), tofu, and pork. Sushi is usually a combination of fish (cooked or raw) and rice, with vinegar. Sometimes a vegetable, such as cucumber, is added to the dish or used instead of fish; then the dish is called *norimaki*. Sushi is expensive and reserved for special occasions.

Recreation

Baseball, soccer, volleyball, tennis, skiing, and jogging are all popular in Japan. The Japanese also enjoy traditional sports such as sumo wrestling (a popular spectator sport), judo, *kendo* (fencing with bamboo poles), and karate. Baseball, brought to Japan in the 1870s by an American, is the national sport. It is highly competitive at all levels. The entire country follows the annual national high school championships. Golf, while expensive, is popular among men. For leisure, people enjoy television and movies or nature outings. Older adults favor puppet theater (*bunraku*) and highly stylized drama (*noh* and *kabuki*). The Japanese also attend music concerts and theater.

Holidays

At the New Year, Japanese take an extended holiday from the last day or two in December to about the third of January. Businesses and government offices close while people visit shrines and relatives. Other important holidays include Adults' Day (15 January), when those who will turn 20 during the year are honored as coming of age; National Foundation Day (11 February); Vernal Equinox (in March); *Midori No hi* (Greenery Day, 29 April), a day to celebrate nature's beauty; Constitution Day (3 May); Children's Day (5 May); Bon Festival (15 August), a time when people take vacation and return to their ancestral homes to welcome visiting ancestral spirits with bonfires; Respect for the Aged Day (15 September); Autumnal Equinox (in September); Sports Day (10 October); Culture Day (3 November); Labor Thanksgiving Day (23 November); and Emperor Akihito's Birthday (23 December).

Commerce

Businesses are typically open from 8:00 A.M. to 5:00 P.M. or 9:00 A.M. to 6:00 P.M. Small shops and large urban shopping areas may stay open much later and do not close for lunch. Business dealings are conducted formally. Time is often required for decisions and agreements. The Japanese may be more interested in the person or company they are dealing with than the actual details of the deal. Many Japanese work late into the evening; overtime is a common necessity.

SOCIETY

Government

Japan is a constitutional monarchy. The emperor is head of state but has no governing power. The prime minister is head of government. He and his cabinet form the executive branch. Legislative power is vested in the *Diet*, consisting of the 511-seat House of Representatives (lower house) and the 252-seat House of Councillors (upper house). Japan has 47 prefectures (provinces), each administered by an elected governor. The voting age is 20. In addition to the LDP, major parties include the Social Democratic Party of Japan, Democratic Socialist Party, and New Frontier Party.

Economy

Japan is one of the most productive industrialized nations in the world. Inflation and unemployment are less than 3 percent, and gross domestic product (GDP) growth is more than 2 percent. Real GDP per capita is $20,520. Because Japan has few natural resources, it depends on imported raw materials for industrial success. Also, because more than 60 percent of the land is mountainous, only about 13 percent is suitable for cultivation. Japan must import nearly half of its food supply, including grains other than rice. Major crops include rice, sugar, vegetables, tea, and various fruits. Japan

is a leading producer of fish, accounting for 15 percent of the total world catch.

The economy is based on manufacturing. More than 95 percent of all exports are manufactured items, including automobiles, electronic equipment, televisions, and other items. Major industries include machinery, metals, engineering, electronics, textiles, and chemicals. The United States is Japan's biggest trading partner, but a trade imbalance and conflicts over market access are sources of friction between the two allies. Japan's *yen* (¥) is one of the world's strongest currencies.

Transportation and Communication

A highly developed, efficient mass-transit system of trains and buses is the principal mode of transportation in urban areas. "Bullet" trains (*Shinkansen*) provide rapid transportation between major cities. Subways are also available. Many people have private cars. Traffic is often heavy in Tokyo and other large cities. Japan has five international airports. Its communications system is highly modern and well developed. Newspapers and magazines are read by more than 65 million people.

Education

Japan has a high literacy rate (99 percent) and reading is popular. Education is generally free and compulsory from ages six to fifteen. Individuals must pay tuition for education thereafter. The curriculum stresses math and sciences. Students are in school Monday through Saturday, with one Saturday off a month. Many students attend private schools, provided they pass difficult entrance exams (even at the kindergarten level). Parents often enroll their children in *juku* (cram) schools to help them prepare for these tests. University entrance exams are rigorous, and competition among students is intense. Students study for years and cram for months to take them. Getting into the most prestigious schools is more important than one's ultimate performance. Graduation from the top universities usually guarantees students well-paying jobs. These universities are affiliated with specific high, middle, and elementary schools; hence, getting into the right elementary school can help guarantee one's future success.

Health

The Japanese enjoy one of the highest standards of health in the world. The infant mortality rate is only 4 per 1,000. Life expectancy is between 77 and 82 years. Companies are generally responsible for providing insurance benefits to employees, but the government also sponsors some social welfare programs. Medical facilities are very good. Pollution is a problem in Tokyo.

FOR THE TRAVELER

U.S. visitors need a valid passport but no visa for stays of fewer than 90 days. No immunizations are required. For detailed travel information, contact the Japan National Tourist Office, 1 Rockefeller Plaza, Suite 1250, New York, NY 10020; phone (212) 757–5640. You may also wish to contact the Embassy of Japan, 2520 Massachusetts Avenue NW, Washington, DC 20008.

Hashemite Kingdom of
Jordan

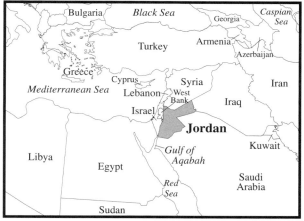

Boundary representations not necessarily authoritative.

BACKGROUND

Land and Climate

Covering 35,475 square miles (91,880 square kilometers), Jordan is about the size of Indiana. Most of it is desert. Cities are concentrated in the west. Jordan's only seaport is at Al Aqabah. Jordan shares the Dead Sea with the West Bank and Israel. It is the lowest point on earth at 1,286 feet (392 meters) below sea level. The Great Rift Valley (Jordan Valley), through which the Jordan River flows, forms a flood plain between the West Bank and Jordan. Jordanian territory is often called the "East Bank" because it lies east of the Jordan River. Olive, fig, and citrus trees grow in areas of adequate rainfall. Cattle, camels, sheep, donkeys, ostriches, snakes, and chickens are among the animals most plentiful in Jordan.

Winter (November–April) is cold and wet. Some snow falls in the mountains, and Amman's average temperature is 45°F (7°C). Spring and summer (May–October) are dry and pleasant in the west. On the desert, in the Jordan Valley, and near Al Aqabah, temperatures are much higher.

History

The region now occupied by Jordan has a rich history as part of the Fertile Crescent that was settled and conquered by many peoples. Amorites, Edomites, Moabites, and Ammonites were followed later by the Hittites, Egyptians, Israelites, Assyrians, Babylonians, Persians, Greeks, and Romans. The Arabs invaded in the seventh century and established the Umayyad Caliphate at Damascus (Syria). Christian crusaders ruled for a time, but the area has basically been Muslim since the Arab invasion.

The Ottoman Turks ruled from 1516 until the Great Arab Revolt (1916). The Arabs were aided by the British, who then created (1923) the Emirate of Transjordan as a semiautonomous region ruled by the Hashemite Prince Abdullah. Over the years, Britain gradually turned power over to local Arab officials, and in 1946 Transjordan became independent. In 1950, the country adopted its current name and included the territory now known as the West Bank.

King Abdullah was assassinated in 1951. His son, Talal, became king but was in poor health and was deposed. Shortly thereafter, Talal's 17-year-old son, Hussein, became the new Jordanian monarch. Hussein still rules today. In the 1967 War, Jordan lost control of the West Bank to Israel, and many Palestinian refugees fled to Jordan. This and other factors led to internal unrest and violence between the government and Palestinian resistance members (*fedayeen*) being protected by Jordan. They were expelled in the years following a 1970 assassination attempt against Hussein.

Even after 1967, Jordan claimed the West Bank and provided for Palestinian representatives in the Jordanian Parliament. In 1988, Hussein dropped all claims to the West Bank, eased tensions with the Palestinian Liberation Organization (PLO), and dissolved Parliament. Elections for the new Parliament in 1989 were only for Jordan. In 1991, Hussein restored multiparty democracy. This paved the way for full multiparty elections in 1993, when 534 candidates ran for 80 seats. A strong turnout brought a centrist-minded group of leaders to Parliament. This demonstrated support for King Hussein and his participation in the Middle East peace process.

That process eventually allowed Jordan and Israel to sign a historic peace treaty in October 1994. The borders were opened to tourism, trade, commercial flights, diplomacy, and mutual security. Not all Jordanians welcomed the treaty, and some were especially critical of King Hussein's positive relations with then Israeli Prime Minister Yitzhak Rabin. The treaty may become a key issue in November 1997 elections.

THE PEOPLE

Population

Jordan's population of 4.1 million is growing at 2.7 percent. The capital, Amman, has more than one million inhabitants. Only 30 percent of Jordanians live in rural areas. Except for small minorities of Circassians (1 percent) and Armenians (1 percent), all Jordanians are Arabs. While about one-fourth are of Bedouin descent, less than 5 percent are currently nomadic. Nomadic Bedouins move about (mostly in the south and east) to take advantage of seasonal changes and to graze their livestock. Bedouins live in tents; even semi-nomadic or permanent Bedouins often live in tents (complete with carpeting and nice furnishings).

Palestinians comprise about half of the Arab population. They either are refugees from the West Bank (having crossed into Jordan after the 1967 War) or were born in Jordan. A large number still live in refugee camps, even though they are Jordanian citizens. Palestinian and Jordanian Arabs enjoy mutual respect that comes from their common heritage, but Palestinians are keenly aware of their descent. Despite holding Jordanian citizenship, some Palestinians resent being called Jordanians. Most support establishing a Palestinian homeland.

Jordan's Human Development Index (0.758) ranks it 80th out of 174 countries. A growing number of people (mostly urban) have access to economic and educational opportunities that allow for personal progress.

Language

Arabic is the official language in Jordan. The Jordanian dialect (*Al-lahjah Al-Ordoniah*) spoken on a daily basis is considered the closest to classical Arabic. Slight dialect variations exist in different areas. Classical Arabic is used in schools and the media. Arabic has 28 letters. Although written in a distinct Arabic script, many of the letters have the same pronunciation as English letters. Arabic is not as different from English as, say, Chinese, but important differences do exist. For instance, adjectives follow nouns (e.g., car green), and different word structures are used when addressing men and women. And while English uses ancient Arabic numerals, Arabic uses ancient Indian numbers.

Circassians speak Circassian. Educated Jordanians often speak English or languages learned while studying abroad.

Religion

About 90 percent of the people are Sunni Muslims. Islamic values and laws are an integral part of society. Christianity is represented by a few different denominations in about 8 percent of the population. Each religious community has the right to regulate personal matters such as marriage, divorce, and inheritance according to religious traditions. Muslims believe that *Allah* (God) revealed his will and the *Qur'an* (Koran) to the Prophet Muhammad through the angel Gabriel.

Muhammad is considered the last and greatest prophet, but major biblical figures (Abraham, Moses, and others) are also accepted as messengers. Muslims demonstrate their faith and devotion to *Allah* by professing his name; praying five times daily; making at least one pilgrimage to Makkah, Saudi Arabia; donating money to the poor; and fasting each day during the month of *Ramadan*.

General Attitudes

Jordanians are good-natured, friendly, and hospitable. They place great worth on the family and traditions but are also very modern. Time schedules are less important than people. Patience is valuable. Jordanians are proud of their rich cultural heritage and their country's accomplishments.

Jordanians admire an educated, honest, and good-natured person more than a wealthy, uneducated one. Still, the wealthy are powerful and therefore command respect. Aggression is not admired, but bravery is. Because of the value placed on learning, parents will sacrifice much to provide a proper education for their children. Making a pilgrimmage to Makkah becomes increasingly important as one grows older.

Many Jordanians are suspicious of the peace treaty with Israel. Professional unions have banned their members from contact with Israel. Ordinary citizens fear domination by Israel's larger and more developed economy; some express concerns that secular attitudes from Israel will penetrate the more conservative values of Jordanian society. Many oppose any peace with Israel until a Palestinean homeland is established, and others are not willing to lay aside the years of animosity that has existed between the two peoples. At the same time, Jordanians try to remain optimistic about "normalization" and hope it will eventually bring prosperity to Jordan.

Personal Appearance

Most men wear Western-style clothing, often accompanied by the traditional white or red-checkered headdress. Some urban women also wear Western clothing, but most women wear traditional Islamic floor-length dresses and head scarves. In Western or traditional styles, clothing is always modest and never revealing. The youth enjoy European fashions. Adults and teenagers only wear shorts for sports. Jewelry (mostly high-quality gold) is an important part of a woman's wardrobe. It is a symbol of the woman's wealth and financial security.

CUSTOMS AND COURTESIES

Greetings

Jordanians warmly greet each other with a handshake. Close friends of the same gender often kiss on either cheek. Common verbal greetings include *Assalam Alaikum* (Peace be upon you), *Ahlan wa sahlan* (roughly, You are welcome in this place), *Sabah al khair* (Good morning), *Msa'a al khair* (Good evening), and the more casual *Marhaba* (Hello). After initial greetings, each person inquires about the other's welfare. When one joins or leaves a small gathering, it is customary to shake hands with each person.

Gender and age peers address one another by first name after an initial introduction. Other people are referred to by various titles, depending on their relationship to the speaker. For instance, adults are respectfully addressed as the mother

(*Um*) or father (*Abu*) of their eldest son. So, the parents of a boy named Ali would be *Abu Ali* and *Um Ali* to family friends and relatives. It is a sign of great respect to use *Al-haj* (for men) or *Al-hajjah* (for women) as nicknames for those who have completed a pilgrimmage to Makkah. Acquaintances may be addressed as "Brother" or "Sister" with the last name, by professional title, or by "Mr.," "Mrs.," or "Miss."

Gestures

Hand gestures are used for many purposes. When speaking of money, one rubs the thumb and index finger together. One might emphasize a point by punching a fist in the air or shaking the index finger at the person being spoken to. To show respect, one touches the fingers briefly to the forehead as the head bows slightly forward. Rubbing the back of the hand on the forehead shows great disrespect. Jordanians generally use the right hand or both hands to pass objects or eat. It is impolite to point the sole of one's foot or shoe at another person. Good posture is important, especially at social events.

Visiting

Visiting plays a fundamental role in Jordanian society. Close friends and relatives may visit without prior notice, but advance arrangements are otherwise expected. Men and women traditionally socialize in separate rooms. Westernized couples or close relatives might socialize in mixed company. No matter how short the visit, hosts nearly always offer their guests tea, coffee, Pepsi or Coke, or fruit drinks. During a longer visit, coffee is often served shortly before guests are expected to leave; one does not leave before this coffee is served. Guests not originally invited for a meal may be invited to stay if their visit extends into a mealtime. It is polite to initially decline—even up to three times—before accepting the offer. Jordanians entertain in the home more often than at restaurants because being invited to the home is a greater honor.

Guests might take gifts to hosts on special occasions or present hosts with sweets, flowers, or fruit if visiting after a long absence. The recipient does not immediately accept the gift, out of modesty. Visitors avoid excessive praise for the hosts' children, as this is considered bad luck for them.

Eating

After washing hands, the family gathers together for a meal either around a table (in many urban homes) or on the floor. No one eats until all are seated and a blessing is pronounced: *Bissm allah arrahman arrahim* (By the name of God, most gracious and most merciful). Some use the shorter *Bissm allah* (By the name of God). Many meals are eaten from a common platter. Pita bread is served with most meals. For some foods, utensils and separate plates are used. If guests are present, they are served first and the most, and a wider than usual assortment of food is prepared. Leaving a little food on the plate tells the host that the guest has eaten well and the host has been generous. At the end of a meal, diners say *Al hamdo lellah* (Thanks to God).

Coffee is important at all meals. *Qahwah Saadah* (Bedouin coffee) is bitter and drunk quickly from small cups. To indicate one is finished, one shakes the cup back and forth. Turkish coffee is sweeter; one drinks it slowly and does not stir it so as to keep the thick grains at the bottom of the cup.

LIFESTYLE

Family

The extended family is unquestionably the most important unit in Jordanian society. Members often live in the same city or housing area. Cousins are usually as close as brothers or sisters are in the West. Arabs love children and lavish time and attention on them. Likewise, the elderly are greatly respected and cared for by their children. Jordanians traditionally desire large families, but family sizes are declining due to economic pressures. To be able to help another member of the family is considered an honor and a duty. Parents often help or support their children even after marriage.

Gender roles follow mostly traditional lines. The mother cares for the children and household. Only about 10 percent of the workforce is comprised of women. The father is head of the family and expects to provide for it financially. Homes are constructed of stone and concrete, not wood. They vary in size, but nearly all have a special guest room where guests are received and where men can socialize in private.

Dating and Marriage

Dating does not occur in the Western sense. Young urban people often meet at universities or offices and persuade their parents to help them establish a courtship. Rural marriages are usually arranged. One-to-one dating is reserved for after the engagement party or after the marriage contract has been signed. The groom must give a bridal token to the bride's family. Women tend to marry in their early twenties, while men marry after they have means to support a family (usually by their early thirties).

Traditional wedding festivities are spread over three nights of dancing and singing. Men and women celebrate separately until the last night. The parties usually are at the respective parents' homes, although the final night might be spent in a hotel or large rented hall. Prior to *Lailat El-Dakhlah* (wedding night), the bride's hands are decorated with henna (a plant dye). On the wedding day, the groom is bathed by the men in his wedding party before they perform a native line dance in their finest suits. While they are singing and dancing, the bride is in another location sitting in a chair on top of a table. Her female wedding guests have sung and danced around her. When her father and brothers retrieve her from the chair, she cries as a symbol of sadness at leaving her home. She is then presented to her new husband, who is sitting alone on a chair on top of a table in his house. She joins him and they are married. A grand party with all guests ensues before the newlyweds are finally left alone.

Diet

Islamic law prohibits the consumption of pork and alcohol, and most Muslims obey these restrictions. Meals include meat and bread, along with vegetables and seasonal fruits (grapes, apples, oranges, apricots, watermelon, figs, etc.). Jordan's national dish is *mansaf*, a large tray of rice covered with chunks of stewed lamb (including the head) and *jameed* (yogurt sauce). Other popular dishes include *mahshi* (stuffed vegetables), *musakhan* (chicken with onions, olive oil, pine seeds, and seasonings), and *meshwi* (shish kebab). Lamb and chicken are the most common meats. Tomatoes, onions, eggplant, cabbage, and other produce are grown locally.

Recreation

Soccer is the most popular sport in Jordan, followed by volleyball, basketball, and the martial arts. Women do not partipate in public as men do, but they do play some sports in school and clubs. Watching television and movies or visiting others are common leisure activities. Cultural activities and festivals also provide recreation. Women enjoy visiting, shopping, and going to all-female parties. Jordanians enjoy traditional dancing, Arabic and Western music, and traditional crafts like wood carving, pottery, and weaving.

Holidays

National holidays include Labor Day (1 May), Independence Day (25 May), Arab Revolt and Army Day (10 June), King Hussein's Accession to the Throne (11 August), and King Hussein's Birthday (14 November). Christians celebrate Christmas and Easter, but these are not national holidays. Islamic religious holy days follow the lunar calendar, which is a few days shorter than the Western (Gregorian) calendar. *Eid al-Fitr* is a three-day feast at the end of *Ramadan*. During *Ramadan,* Muslims do not eat or drink from dawn to dusk; in the evenings, they eat with family and visit friends and relatives. *Eid al-Adha* is known as the Feast of Sacrifice and comes after the pilgrimage to Makkah. Jordan also marks the birth of the prophet Muhammad (*Moulid al-Nebi*).

Commerce

Government offices are open from 9:00 A.M. to 2:00 P.M., Saturday through Thursday. Businesses are open from 8:00 A.M. to about 2:00 P.M. and from 4:00 to 7:00 P.M. Most offices close on Friday, the Muslim day of worship. Christian businesses close on Sunday. Employers are responsible for employee benefits but also often give them gifts at holidays and have personal relationships with them. Jordanians prefer fresh food and, therefore, shop almost daily in open markets and small speciality shops.

SOCIETY

Government

The Hashemite Kingdom of Jordan is a constitutional monarchy, but King Hussein has wide-ranging powers. He appoints the prime minister, currently Abdul-Salam al-Majali, as head of government. The legislature has two houses: the elected House of Deputies and the appointed House of Notables. Citizens may vote at age 20. The elections in November 1993 were the first full multiparty elections since 1956. The conservative Islamic Action Group has the single largest voting block in the House of Deputies, but several other parties are also represented.

Economy

Unlike many other Middle East countries, Jordan is not an oil-producing nation. In fact, Jordan is dependent on oil-rich Arab states for aid and employment. When oil prices or supplies fluctuate, Jordan's economy suffers.

Jordan's few natural resources include phosphate, potash, and limestone. The most important exports are fruits and vegetables, phosphates, and fertilizers. Mining and manufacturing employ about 20 percent of the labor force. Agriculture employs 20 percent. Unemployment is more than 20 percent. The government is encouraging new industries and exports to stimulate the economy, which grew a healthy 5.5 percent in 1994. The currency is the Jordanian *dinar* (JD). Real gross domestic product per capita is estimated at $4,270. Poverty affects less than one-fifth of the total population.

Transportation and Communication

Jordan's roads are in good condition and connect all major cities. Camels are still used for travel in the desert, although modern vehicles are also common. In cities, taxis are available but expensive. Service taxis, which travel fixed routes and carry a small number of passengers, are less expensive and widely used. Buses are also common. Cars are too expensive for the average person. Communications systems are modern. Radio and television stations are owned by the government. The press is relatively free and very active.

Education

What Jordan lacks in natural resources it makes up for in human potential. Jordan has one of the most highly educated labor forces among Arab states. Adult literacy is about 84 percent (97 percent among the youth). Public education is free and compulsory for nine years and is available to qualified students through grade 12. The majority of all school-age children are enrolled. The school week is Sunday through Thursday. One must pass the *Tawjihi* exam to obtain schooling past the 12th grade. Jordan has four public and ten private universities in addition to many smaller institutes of higher education.

Health

While good medical care is available in Jordan, some people are still affected by cholera, hepatitis, typhoid, and other diseases. Still, life expectancy rates are relatively high, ranging from 70 to 74 years. The infant mortality rate is 32 per 1,000, which represents significant progress over the last few years. Government-sponsored immunization programs, as well as free health clinics, are improving health conditions. Nearly all Jordanians have access to these facilities.

FOR THE TRAVELER

A visa and valid passport are required for travel to Jordan. A visa can be obtained in advance or on arrival. No immunizations are required, but those for typhoid and cholera may be recommended if one is staying long. Boiled water must be used for brushing teeth, in ice cubes, and so forth. Do not take pictures of people praying; ask permission of other people before taking their picture. Non-Muslims should not enter a mosque. Do not discuss religion with Jordanians; it is a very sensitive subject. Expect to pay cash for most transactions.

Jordan offers a number of tourist attractions, including ancient monuments near Amman, Greek and Roman ruins, Byzantine art, Petra, the Dead Sea, and archaeological sites. For more detailed information, contact the Jordan Information Bureau, 2319 Wyoming Avenue NW, Washington, DC 20008. You may also wish to contact the Public Relations Office of the Embassy of Jordan, 3504 International Drive NW, Washington, DC 20008; phone (202) 966–2664.

CULTURGRAM '97

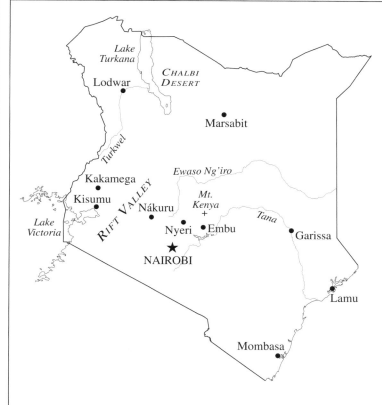

Republic of
Kenya

Boundary representations not necessarily authoritative.

BACKGROUND

Land and Climate

Covering 224,961 square miles (582,650 square kilometers), Kenya is about the size of Texas. It is located in East Africa on the equator. The northern plains are hot, arid, and semidesert. The population in that part of the country usually practices nomadic pastoralism, moving from one area to another, taking advantage of seasonal grazing patterns. In the southeast, near the coast, humidity is high and the climate is tropical. The western highlands are bisected by the fertile Rift Valley. The climate is moderate in the rich agricultural highlands. Lake Turkana (Lake Rudolf) lies near the Chalbi Desert in the north and Lake Victoria is on the southwest border. Mount Kenya rises in the center of the country to 17,058 feet (5,199 meters). From December to March, the Harmattan winds keep Kenya dry. There are two rainy seasons: the "long rains" from April to June and the "short rains" from October to November; the long rains are more reliable and heavier. Over the past several years, however, rain has been scarce in both seasons and a severe drought has brought hardship to people, particularly in the north. Kenya's unique topography and climate allow for abundant and diverse wildlife.

History

The first inhabitants of what is now Kenya were hunting groups (Dorobo or Bushmen) who lived on the vast plains of the area. They mixed with groups of the Bantu peoples from western Africa who had migrated east. It is estimated that by the 15th century the Bantu covered much of eastern Africa.

More than 50 percent of Kenya's current ethnic groups have Bantu origins. Other peoples from Arabia and North Africa also settled in this area and mixed with the original inhabitants. The Kiswahili language was developed by these mixed peoples.

In 1498, Portuguese explorers arrived and established trading posts, but they were driven out by the Arabs in 1729. After 1740, Arabs ruled the Kenyan coast from a capital on the island of Zanzibar. In 1887, the British East Africa Company leased the Kenyan coast from the sultan of Zanzibar. Kenya became a British protectorate in 1895 and was organized as a crown colony in 1920. Following a period of violent partisan uprisings (called the Mau-Mau Rebellion) in the 1950s, Great Britain granted Kenya its independence in 1963. It remained in the Commonwealth as a sovereign republic.

Jomo Kenyatta, leader of the independence struggle, served as the first president until his death in 1978. He formed a strong central government under one political party, the Kenya African National Union (KANU). He was followed by Daniel Teroitich arap Moi. In 1982, KANU was proclaimed the only legal political party. This was done to avoid having political parties based on tribes. Free elections were still held; all candidates simply had to register with KANU.

Economic difficulties, charges of human-rights violations, and political unrest brought calls for Moi to relinquish authoritarian rule and reopen the country to multiparty democracy. Democracy protests in July 1990 led to the arrest of several dissidents and a ban of publications that criticized the government. Moi denied all requests for multiparty elections.

Pressure from other countries eventually led Moi to change his position. First, in 1991, he rescinded the 1982 constitutional provision that gave KANU its dominance. Then, in January 1992, he allowed antigovernment protests. Dozens of political parties formed in anticipation of national elections, which were held in December 1992. Moi won the presidential election, but opposition parties made strong gains in Parliament.

Fighting between Kalenjin and Kikuyu ethnic groups in the western Rift Valley in 1993 left many people dead and more than 150,000 homeless. The government was accused of encouraging attacks as a way of discouraging multiparty democracy; Moi denied any role. Ethnic unrest, corruption, and political suppression spread and the crisis deepened in 1995. The violence threatens elections scheduled for 1997 and has been a setback for progress in a land where ethnic rivalries historically have not been a problem.

THE PEOPLE

Population

Kenya's population of 28.8 million is growing rapidly at 3 percent annually. Although 99 percent of the population is African, it is divided among at least 47 distinct ethnic groups that developed largely along linguistic lines. The largest of these groups include the Kikuyu (22 percent), Luhya (14), Luo (13), Kalenjin (12), Kamba (11), Kisii (6), and Meru (6). Smaller groups include the Embu, Maasai, Mijikenda, Samburu, Somali, Taita, Teso, Turkana, and others. About 1 percent of the population consists of Europeans, Asians, and Arabs. Nairobi, the capital, has a population of more than 1.5 million, but less than 25 percent of all Kenyans live in large urban areas. Most of the population is concentrated in the southern two-thirds of the country, with the majority residing in rural towns and villages. Kenya's Human Development Index (0.481) ranks it 130th out of 174 nations. Adjusted for women, the index (0.471) ranks Kenya 88th out of 130 nations. This indicates that, although Kenya has much to do in empowering its people to access opportunities for personal development, it is at least providing nearly as many choices to women as to men.

Language

English is an official language and is widely used, especially for business and official purposes. However, Kiswahili (also called Swahili) was proclaimed the national language after independence and is therefore also official. It was chosen over other languages because of its linguistic commonality with other Bantu-based languages in the country. It is promoted to encourage national unity. Each ethnic group speaks its own language as a mother tongue and communicates with other groups in Kiswahili.

Religion

The majority of Kenyans are Christians. About 40 percent belong to various Protestant churches and 30 percent are Roman Catholic. Approximately 6 percent are Muslim. Most Muslims live along the coast and in the northeast. About 10 percent of the people follow indigenous belief systems or nontraditional Christian beliefs.

General Attitudes

Kenyans are proud of their cultural heritage, their nation, and its accomplishments. Patriotism is evident in people's respect for the national flag. When and wherever it is raised or lowered, people stop to observe the short ceremony before moving on. The people are warm and friendly. Social systems are group oriented. The individual is expected to be willing to sacrifice personal interests for the interests of the group. The "group" is usually defined by family, which has the highest value in society. Failing to keep close ties with the extended family is considered rebellious behavior. Individuals are expected to share their wealth with poorer family members. For instance, a man with adequate finances may be expected to pay his less-fortunate brother's children's school fees. Wealthier individuals are also expected to help their community. After family (which may be of mixed tribal origin), Kenyans are loyal to tribal affiliations. Land ownership is valued as an indicator of social status.

Kenyans take pride in preserving African wildlife, an effort that has succeeded with considerable international cooperation. Since 1977, hunting has been banned and Kenya has led the fight to preserve the elephant population against poachers. Thirty percent of all Kenyan wildlife lives on several million acres of national reserves. Kenyan preservation values come from an ancient heritage that emphasized coexistence with animals. People believed the rains would stop if animals were unnecessarily killed. By 1995, the elephant population had made a strong comeback and other animal groups were thriving. But success has become a problem; wildlife are increasingly responsible for crop destruction, human deaths, and other damage. Parliament may consider limited hunting in the future.

Personal Appearance

Kenyans dress conservatively and modestly. Western-style clothing, with some African variations, is the norm. Imported second-hand clothing from Europe and North America is very popular and affordable; an entire commercial industry has developed around its trade.

Only children and tourists wear shorts. Women usually wear dresses, but many young urban women wear pants. Women often wear a *kanga* around their waist as a skirt, to cover their clothes, or shield themselves from rain and wind. A *kanga* is a long piece of colorful cotton fabric. Mothers use it to carry children on their backs. Rural and some urban women wear scarves. Sleeveless dresses or blouses are considered immodest. Light fabrics and short sleeves are common because of the warm climate. Small groups such as the Maasai, Samburu, and Turkana retain traditional dress.

CUSTOMS AND COURTESIES

Greetings

Greeting customs differ between ethnic groups. However, a handshake is common and important throughout the country. Supporting the right forearm with the left hand while shaking shows special respect for a leader or elder. In coastal areas, a traditional Swahili greeting is *Jambo!* (Greetings). *Habari gani?* (What is the news?) or just *Habari?* is common in non-coastal areas. The usual response is *Nzuri* (Good) or *Salama* (Peaceful). English greetings are also acceptable. Kenyans are friendly and greet others with warmth and politeness. They often ask about each other's family and welfare. Upon departing, Kenyans might say *Tutaonana* (We will see each other) or, if evening, *Lala salama* (Sleep peacefully).

Gestures

The right hand or both hands are used to pass and accept items. Using the left hand alone is improper. The verbal "tch-tch" or "tss-tss" sound expresses displeasure. Pointing at someone with the index finger is very rude. One beckons by waving all fingers of the hand. People often point with the lower lip. Approval may be shown with both thumbs extended up. It is improper to touch an elder. It is often considered improper to photograph another person without permission. Public displays of affection are not acceptable in most areas, although they are increasingly common in Nairobi. In all areas it is common for men to hold hands while walking in public, while a man and woman would not do so. Eye contact is important, as people are more willing to trust a person who will look them in the eye.

Visiting

Because of strong family ties and friendships, visiting is a common activity among Kenyans. Sunday is a popular day for making visits. Most visits are unannounced; people often drop by for conversation and a cup of tea. No rules exist about how long a visit lasts, but it is impolite for a host to ask guests to leave. Hosts endeavor to make guests comfortable. Invited guests might bring small gifts. Wine is common among Christians; flowers and tea leaves are popular for all groups. In rural areas, sugar, instant coffee, flour, and cornmeal are given.

Eating

When guests are invited to dinner, they usually have some time for conversation while final preparations are being made. After the meal, they stay for more socializing. Afternoon tea is a daily custom throughout the country. Depending on the type of food, and personal or family tradition, people may eat their meal with the right hand or use utensils. Using the right hand is more common in rural areas but is also practiced in cities. When utensils are used, a knife is held in the right hand and a spoon in the left. One washes the hands before and after eating, often in a bowl at the table. Among some traditional families, children eat separately from adults. Men are often served first. Among the Samburu, warriors avoid eating in the presence of women. European cuisine is prevalent in major cities. Indian restaurants are popular in Nairobi and Kisumu.

LIFESTYLE

Family

The family unit usually includes the extended family. There is much interaction between uncles, aunts, and cousins. In fact, children call their maternal aunts "mother" and their paternal uncles "father." The average Kenyan family is large. In urban areas, families are smaller and nuclear families are becoming more common. Aging parents are cared for by the family's youngest adult son. Because the family is a great source of pride, most Kenyans expect to marry and raise a family. A small number of educated women are choosing to avoid their traditional role as wives. Some have children but prefer life as a single parent. Women make up 40 percent of the labor force, one-third of college students, and up to half of all graduate students.

Dating and Marriage

Dating starts at about age 18 in cities but is still rather uncommon in villages. Men and women usually marry between the ages of 18 and 24. The dowry system, which involves a payment by the groom's family to the bride's family, is still in effect. However, money has been substituted for livestock as the medium of exchange for the dowry. Wedding details are largely handled by the families. Usually young people choose their partners, but some marriages are still arranged.

Diet

The most common meats in Kenya are goat, beef, lamb, chicken, and fish. Milk, *ugali* (a stiff dough made from cornmeal, millet, or sorghum), *uji* (porridge made from *ugali* ingredients), red bean stew, *kitumbua* (fried bread), *githeri* (corn and beans), and *chapati* (a flat bread) are staple foods. Popular fruits include pineapples, mangoes, oranges, bananas, and papaya. Also common are sweet potatoes and avocados.

Recreation

Soccer is the most popular team sport. Soccer leagues exist throughout the nation. Highly organized, although poorly equipped, leagues even operate in the poorest areas. They give urban youth a chance to develop discipline, teamwork, and physical skills. Track-and-field activities join soccer as the national sports. Kenya has produced some world-famous runners and other athletes. Many people enjoy wrestling, tug-of-war, and a traditional pebble or seed board game (sometimes called *bao* or *ajua).* Field hockey, cricket, and croquet are popular among urbanites. The Kenyan National Theater offers drama, concerts, and dance programs. Homemade drums and guitars commonly accompany dancing in rural areas. Storytelling, riddles, and proverbs are popular.

Holidays

Kenya celebrates New Year's Day; Easter (Friday–Monday); Labor Day (1 May); Madaraka Day (1 June), marking the birth of the republic; Kenyatta Day (20 October), celebrating Jomo Kenyatta's arrest in 1952 for opposing British authorities; *Jamhuri* or Independence Day (12 December); Christmas; and Boxing Day (26 December). Boxing Day comes from the British tradition of presenting small boxed gifts to service workers, tradesmen, and in the past, servants. It is now primarily a day for visiting family and friends. Special parades, meals, and church services often mark official holidays. For the Islamic population, the country also observes the three-day feast at the end of the month of *Ramadan* called *Idul-Fitr.* The first day is an official holiday for Muslims, but celebrations on the next two days occur after working hours. During *Ramadan,* Muslims do not eat or drink from sunrise to dusk. They eat meals after the sun goes down, and friends visit during the evening.

Commerce

Business and government hours are generally from 8:00 A.M. to noon or 1:00 P.M. and from 2:00 to 5:00 P.M., Monday through Friday. Some businesses are also open Saturday mornings. While prices are fixed in urban shopping areas, bartering is common in rural markets and at roadside stands. Each town has an open-air market twice a week, and roadside stands are open every day to sell fresh fruits and vegetables.

SOCIETY

Government

The Republic of Kenya has eight provinces. The president is head of government and chief of state. He selects a vice president from among members of the 188-seat National Assembly (*Bunge*). All citizens may vote at age 18. In addition to the governing KANU, major parties include the Democratic Party and two groups called Forum for the Restoration of Democracy (FORD-Kenya and FORD-Asili).

Economy

Kenya's usually stable economy suffered badly in the early 1990s from drought, political turmoil, market reforms, global recession, and other events. Growth was stagnant and inflation was 40 percent in 1994. Unemployment rose quickly and remains high. Because the population is expanding so fast, sustained economic growth is essential. Some market reforms have been scaled back, and for 1995 the government managed to keep inflation at 7 percent with tight fiscal policies. The economy grew by 5 percent.

Real gross domestic product per capita is estimated at $1,400, which has doubled in the last generation. While economic opportunities are increasing, about half of all people continue to live in poverty.

Although one-fourth of the labor force is employed in the public service and manufacturing sectors, the economy is based on agriculture, which provides nearly 65 percent of all export earnings and employs 75 percent of the workforce. The chief cash crops are coffee, tea, and horticultural products. Pyrethrum, a flower used to make insecticides, is especially important. Other agricultural products include livestock, corn, wheat, rice, cassava, and sugarcane. Kenya has traditionally been self-sufficient in food production, but it currently is not able to feed its population. Industries focus on small-scale manufactured items, oil refinement, and tourism. The vital tourist industry is well developed and concentrates on safaris and beach resorts. The currency is the Kenyan shilling (KSh).

Transportation and Communication

International and domestic air links are well developed. Trains and buses are also available for domestic travel, but they can be slow. Taxis are plentiful in Nairobi. Traffic moves on the left side of the road. Four-wheel-drive vehicles are used for safari trips and rural transport. Most rural roads are unpaved. Ports operate at Mombasa and Lamu. Kenya has one of Africa's best telecommunications systems. Most Kenyans listen to radio broadcasts in both Kiswahili and English. Relatively few people own televisions. The Kenya Broadcasting Corporation, once government owned, is now a private corporation indirectly controlled by the government. The newer Kenya Television Network (KTN) operates more freely and has more extensive programming. There are three daily national newspapers.

Education

Due partly to a rapidly increasing population and partly to government efforts, primary school enrollment increased in the 1980s but has since declined under economic pressures. Today about 58 percent of eligible pupils are enrolled in school, but the adult literacy rate is 74 percent and education continues to be important to Kenyans. All students pay fees, but public schools receive some government assistance (such as paid teachers). In many rural areas, children are taught in Swahili the first three years of school, after which instruction is in English. Urban schools usually begin instruction in English. Teacher training is free, but teachers are required to work for the government at least three years after graduation.

Complete education through the university level is available to competent students and to those who are able to pay tuition. There are both public and private schools. *Harambee* (self-help) schools are common in rural areas, depending more on private donations than on government funding. *Harambee* schools draw on the talents of educators from around the world, as well as parents, to offer hands-on agricultural training, academic subjects, and instruction on practical subjects like health and occupations.

Health

About three-fourths of all Kenyans have access to basic health care. Rural Kenyans continue to rely on traditional healing methods, but progress has been made in providing them with medical facilities, better sanitation, and other social services. Infant mortality rates have dropped and life expectancy has risen since the 1980s. The current infant mortality rate is 74 per 1,000; life expectancy averages 52 years. The internal refugee problem and ethnic violence threaten progress in these areas. Diseases are less prevalent in the highlands than in low-lying areas, where the climate is less temperate and services less available.

FOR THE TRAVELER

U.S. citizens must have a visa, a valid passport, and proof of onward passage to visit Kenya. Malarial suppressants are recommended for travel outside of Nairobi and yellow fever vaccinations are suggested. A $20 departure tax must be paid in hard currency.

Many foreign visitors travel to Kenya for its famous safari areas. Twenty-three national parks and 29 game reserves cover more than 7 percent of Kenya's total land area. Leading attractions are the populations of zebras, lions, elephants, leopards, cheetahs, giraffes, gazelles, monkeys, and many other animals. Do not purchase any items made from animals, as these have been outlawed. Hunting and poaching remain serious crimes. Do not travel alone; do not carry valuables in public. For more information, contact the Kenya Tourist Office, 424 Madison Avenue, New York, NY 10017; phone (212) 486–1300. You may also wish to contact the Embassy of Kenya, 2249 R Street NW, Washington, DC 20008; phone (202) 387–6101.

Republic of
Kiribati

Makin
Butaritari
Abaiang · Marakei
Tarawa
Maiana · Abemama
Kuria · Aranuka
Banaba · Nonouti
Tabiteuea · Beru
Onotoa · Nikunau
Tamana · Arorae

GILBERT ISLANDS

Abaroromga
(Canton)
Birnie · Enderbury
McKean · Rawaki (Phoenix)
Nikumororu · Manra (Sydney)
(Gardner)
Orona
(Hull)

PHOENIX ISLANDS

· Teraina (Washington)
· Tabuaeran (Fanning)

NORTHERN
LINE ISLANDS
Kiritimati
(Christmas Island)

Jarvis

Malden

Starbuck

SOUTHERN
LINE ISLANDS

Caroline

Vostock ·

Flint ·

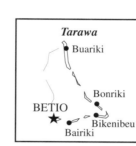

Marshall Islands
Hawaii
Micronesia
Kiribati
Solomon Islands
Tuvalu · Tokelau
Vanuatu · Samoa
Fiji · French Polynesia
Tonga
Australia
New Zealand

Boundary representations not necessarily authoritative.

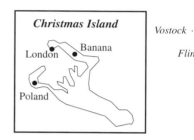

Tarawa
Buariki
Bonriki
BETIO · Bikenibeu
Bairiki

Christmas Island
London · Banana
Poland

BACKGROUND

Land and Climate

The small islands that form Kiribati (kee-re-BAHSS) stretch across hundreds of kilometers in the Central Pacific Ocean. Its 33 atolls form three principal groups: the Gilbert Islands, Phoenix Islands, and Line Islands. The Gilbert Islands lie south of the Marshall Islands and north of Tuvalu. To the east lies the Phoenix group (due north of Samoa) and then the Line Islands. Christmas Island is famous for sportfishing and its bird sanctuary.

Kiribati's climate is equatorial, with daytime temperatures usually above 82°F (28°C). The rainy season is from October to March. The dry season is from March to October, and droughts occur more frequently on the central and southern islands. There are no rivers, but most islands enclose a lagoon. The most populous island is Tarawa, which is shaped like a triangle; only the southern part is urbanized. North Tarawa and all other islands are without running water and electricity.

History

The first settlers of Kiribati probably came from Southeast Asia and Samoa in the 14th and 15th centuries. Europeans first visited in 1537 when Christmas Island was sighted by Spanish explorers. Commercial activity on the islands began in the early 19th century. The northern Gilberts were a favorite whaling ground, and deserting crews began to settle there around 1830. Hiram Bingham, a Protestant who established a mission on Abaiang in 1857, gave the Gilbertese a written form of their language.

During the latter 1800s, thousands of Gilbertese men were recruited to work overseas. They left because of drought and population problems, but they often found their employment conditions harsh. Many later returned to the islands.

In 1886, Britain and Germany signed the Treaty of the Unclaimed Pacific, each taking responsibility for islands in the Pacific that no other imperial power had claimed. Britain took the Gilbert and Ellice Islands. At the same time, U.S. and German labor companies were competing for labor recruits. German traders were worried the United States would colonize the islands and Germany would lose out on trade. They asked their government to annex the islands, but it refused because of the 1886 treaty. U.S. traders and Nabureimoa, King of Butaritari, asked the United States to annex the islands. Although Britain did not want another colony, it did not want to lose the islands to the United States, so it made the Gilbert and Ellice Islands a protectorate in 1892.

In 1916, both island groups were joined to form the Gilbert and Ellice Islands Colony. The Phoenix and Line Islands, which were never permanently inhabited, became part of the territory during colonial rule. Tarawa was the site of fierce fighting between Japanese and U.S. troops in World War II, as Japan had occupied the area in the early 1940s.

In 1974, the Ellice Islands held a referendum for independence and subsequently became Tuvalu. In 1977, internal self-government was established in the Gilberts and the islands became the independent Republic of Kiribati in 1979. It remains part of the Commonwealth.

OCEANIA

THE PEOPLE

Population

The population is about 79,400 and is growing annually at 1.95 percent. Nearly all inhabitants are Micronesian, and most live on the Gilbert Islands. A small number of Tuvaluans also live in Kiribati. One-third of the total population lives on Tarawa, the capital island.

Life is changing in the rapidly urbanizing South Tarawa area, where migrants from outer islands encounter the Western culture introduced by Christian missionaries and others.

Language

I-Kiribati (EE-kee-re-BAHSS) speak a Micronesian dialect called Gilbertese or Kiribati. The pronunciation of *Kiribati* is derived from the local pronunciation of the English word *Gilberts*. English is the official language but is rarely heard outside of urban South Tarawa. Speaking it in public is considered showing off and is mocked. Even on South Tarawa, people mix English and Gilbertese, using English mostly for words that do not exist in Gilbertese. Older people speak a more difficult and extensive version of Kiribati that younger generations have not retained.

The Kiribati alphabet has 13 letters. Some words are borrowed from English (and adapted to the Kiribati alphabet and pronunciation) because they were not indigenous to Kiribati, such as *te ka* (the car). Accents differ slightly by location.

Religion

Christianity was first introduced in the 1850s by American Protestant missionaries. The people have since become devout Christians. About 52 percent of people are Catholic, and 40 percent are Protestant (Congregational). Catholicism is more prominent in the north; it was introduced in 1880 by two Gilbertese who had become Catholic while working in Tahiti. Other Christian faiths with a strong presence include the Seventh-Day Adventists, the Church of God, and the Church of Jesus Christ of Latter-day Saints (Mormons). The Baha'i faith also has followers in Kiribati.

Before Christianity, *te maka* (power or magic) was prevalent as the people's belief system, which included the worship of Nareau (the Creator), the use of charms and spells, and the belief in spirits and ghosts. While no longer practiced on a large scale, it is still followed by some families.

General Attitudes

I-Kiribati laugh readily and easily. They are easygoing, practical, and spiritual. People generally accept life as it is; day-to-day concerns necessarily take priority over the future. Work must be done and food gathered, and since fish will still be in the sea and coconuts on the tree tomorrow, the future will take care of itself. I-Kiribati take great pride in their way of life, and many have no desire to adopt the lifestyles of other countries. Respect for *katei ni Kiribati* (the Gilbertese way) is strong. Status is maintained by acknowledging one's equality with others. To elevate oneself or fall behind the norm is considered bad.

People live modestly and are resourceful. For example, they use every part of the coconut tree: fronds for making mats, midribs to build houses, sap to make toddy, nuts to dry and sell as copra or use in cooking, and oil to make soap or refine for a body oil.

The group is more important than the individual. Obligations to extended family come before money, government, one's job, or personal gain. Families will go hungry to make sure their relatives have enough to eat.

Personal Appearance

Both men and women wear a *te bei* (lavalava), several yards of material worn around the waist to below the knee. Men usually wear T-shirts, unless working or fishing. Women wear a *tibutta*, a loose-fitting blouse gathered at the neck and a petticoat with hems that are often embroidered in colorful designs or the wearer's name.

Some secondary school students on South Tarawa wear knee-length shorts. Almost no women on outer islands wear shorts. Women do not wear long pants or sleeveless dresses.

When I-Kiribati gather in the *maneaba* (meeting house) for a feast, dance costumes include knee-length skirts made from coconut fronds or pandanus leaves. Male performers also wear woven mats wrapped and tied around their waists with belts of woven hair. These braided belts are made from female hair and are highly valued; they may be kept within a family for generations. Brightly colored bands crisscross the dancer's chest from shoulder to waist. Women wear belts of coin-size coconut shell disks or white seashells. Both women and men wear decorations on their fingers, wrists, and arms. They also wear a flower garland or colorful cloth wreath on the head.

CUSTOMS AND COURTESIES

Greetings

I-Kiribati greet each other with *Mauri* (Blessings). A more informal greeting, *Ko na era?* (Where are you going?), reflects people's inherent curiosity. It requires a response, even if vague, such as "To the store" or "To the north." Except at official gatherings, people usually do not shake hands when they greet. Instead, they nod their heads upward when saying *Mauri*. Handshakes are used to send someone off (such as to boarding school or work overseas) or between people who have not seen each other for some time.

To get someone's attention, I-Kiribati call out *Neiko* (Woman) or *Nao* (Man), even if the person's name is known. People address each other by given name in informal situations; even children address their parents by given name. A person's family name is often the given name of his or her father or grandfather. In more formal situations, one shows respect by using the titles *Nei* (Miss or Mrs.) and *Ten* (Mr.) before a person's given name.

Gestures

A raised eyebrow means "yes." People point with a wrinkled nose and nod rather than the fingers. Pulling at the lower eyelid with the index finger is a sign that one has seen a person showing off or making a mistake. A quick downward, inward wave of the hand means "come here."

It is improper to touch someone's head, which is considered the most sacred part of the body. If people are conversing, walking between them is rude. If it cannot be avoided, the passerby must crouch low or duck.

Members of the opposite sex do not display affection in public, but people of the same sex often hold hands or put their arms around the waist of a friend while walking or talking.

In a *maneaba,* people sit cross-legged, and on some islands it is considered rude to show the sole of the foot when doing so. Because modesty is important, people adjust their clothing upon sitting and standing to properly cover themselves.

Visiting

An integral part of socializing is visiting other people's homes. Most people entertain on their *buia,* a raised platform with a thatched roof but no walls. Guests may be invited to play cards or relax. To show respect, the host dusts off a place for the visitor to sit or puts down a clean mat. Guests are offered a drink and, if visiting near mealtime, something to eat. Guests show appreciation by accepting offered food. The group often shares a cigarette hand-rolled in pandanus leaves. A host might also call to a passerby to join the group. It is rude not to immediately accept, regardless of what one was planning. The length of stay depends on what the host has prepared. One could sit for a few minutes or stay for hours chatting over a pot of tea.

Arriving unannounced for a casual visit is common and part of daily life. On southern islands, custom requires one to call from a distance for the male of the household before approaching the doorway or the *buia.*

Other than casual talk or card playing, the home is not the place for formal entertaining. A *botaki* (feast) requires a written invitation delivered a few days in advance. It is usually held for a special occasion (first birthday, wedding, life's passages) or farewell and welcoming celebrations. *Botaki* are held in the *maneaba.* Every village has a *maneaba* and most churches have one as well. *Mane* means "to collect and/or bring together," and *aba* means "the land" or "people of the land." *Maneabas* are the center of community life, and strict traditions govern their construction, seating arrangements, member duties, and so forth. Some family groups have their own *maneabas.* When a person visits one for the first time, it is customary to bring a block of tobacco to be divided among the older men. For some occasions, a cash donation is required upon visiting.

Eating

To eat, I-Kiribati sit cross-legged on mats woven from pandanus leaves. The mats are either on the ground or on the *buia.* Diners pass bowls of food around; most use plates and spoons, although eating with the hands is perfectly acceptable and often the easiest way to eat fish. Traditionally, men eat first and women and children eat in a separate area after the men finish. One eats all of the food on one's plate. Eating more than a single helping compliments the cook. People converse freely during a family meal, but *maneaba* conversation takes place after dishes have been cleared and everyone is relaxing.

The morning meal is light and may include bread and a cup of tea or fresh toddy (coconut tree sap). Midday and evening meals are larger and include fish, rice, and coconut. Mealtimes may depend on the arrival of fresh fish: regardless of the hour, day or night, fresh fish necessitates a meal. However, on some islands eating fish for breakfast is believed to make one lazy. Fish is served in soup, fried in oil, coated with flour and fried, baked over a fire, or eaten raw.

LIFESTYLE
Family

The family occupies a central role in society. I-Kiribati live in extended families, and adoption among relatives is common. Adoption can be based on a verbal agreement or *bubuti,* a request that cannot be turned down; the word *bubuti* is never used lightly. If a couple cannot have children or desire more, they can *bubuti* one from a relative. Raising children is a serious responsibility in Kiribati culture, but being raised by biological parents with biological siblings is not necessarily the norm. The *bubuti* custom also provides social support for people, since one can request both items and services.

Upon marrying, a woman lives with her husband's family to learn from his relatives how to be a good wife. Large families are highly valued due in part to subsistence agriculture. Families need help fishing, collecting coconuts, and working in the *babai* pits. *Babai* is a taro-like, starchy root crop. Women are responsible for housework, cooking, and child care, but some also help men take care of the *babai* pits and collect coconuts. Women harvest shellfish and go net fishing, but usually only men fish from canoes and boats. The father heads the household, and the elderly receive great respect.

With land inheritance traditionally divided among a person's children, family plots are becoming increasingly small, and the government is encouraging people to have fewer children. In many families, children now share the land rather than divide it.

The average home has a thatched roof, stick walls, and a coral-rock floor. Woven coconut-frond mats cover the floor, while pandanus mats are used for sleeping. A home usually has a separate cookhouse.

Dating and Marriage

The youth interact through school and games; they do not go on dates. Some marriages are arranged in a traditional way, but most people choose their spouses. To make his intentions known, a young man sends a relative (usually an uncle) to tell the young woman's family he wants to propose. This gives her family time to prepare before his parents actually come with their request. The bride's family prefers a long engagement so they can weave sleeping mats for their new son-in-law and his family. The groom's family gives bolts of cloth to the bride's family in exchange for these mats.

A young woman's virginity is important and must be proven on the wedding night. To avoid potential disgrace, a couple sometimes chooses elopement, which is accepted as a common-law marriage. For a church wedding, the bride wears her best dress and the groom wears a borrowed suit, since he otherwise has no use for his own. If a man dies, it is common for an unwed brother to assume his place in the marriage. Divorce is handled by the family, not by the courts.

Diet

In addition to eating coconuts with fish, I-Kiribati grate them into tea. They also use coconut milk as a sweetener in breadfruit soup or as a marinade with curry for raw fish. Twice daily, young boys cut toddy, which is rich in vitamin C. Cutting toddy is a skill passed down through generations, and boys take pride in both their yield and quality of toddy. Boiled over a slow heat, toddy forms a thick, sweet molasses called *kamaimai.* This is used instead of sugar to sweeten drinks, or it can be made into a hard candy. Fermented toddy becomes an alcoholic drink known as *kakioki*.

I-Kiribati regularly eat fish, breadfruit, pandanus, papaya, and *babai*. They usually eat pork and chicken only at feasts. Imported rice and flour are daily staples. Imported canned food is becoming increasingly important to the urban population. Meals are cooked over an open fire and fried or baked. Without refrigeration, people use salt as a preservative and dry fish in the sun. Salt and sugar are the only two distinct seasonings, with curry used almost exclusively for raw fish.

Recreation

Nature is seen as a provider, so although children might play on the beach at low tide, people do not swim for pleasure or engage in water sports other than canoe racing. I-Kiribati outrigger canoes are some of the fastest in the world and require precision, balance, and skill to maneuver in changing winds. The most popular sports are soccer and volleyball.

A game unique to Kiribati is called *oreano*. A soccer-sized ball made of a heavy stone wrapped in coconut husk fiber is thrown between two teams of ten players. A team scores if the opposing side drops the ball. The first team to earn ten points wins. Bingo and card playing are favorite forms of entertainment, and videos are gaining popularity. Recreational dancing (called *twisting*) is popular, but it differs from traditional dance. Traditional storytelling dances are important and are reserved for special *maneaba* occasions. The costumes are as important as the performance itself. Dance techniques passed from one generation to another often are not shared outside the family.

Holidays

Public holidays include New Year's Day (1 January), Easter (Friday–Monday), Health Day (9 May), Independence Day (12–13 July), Youth Day (2 August), Human Rights and Peace Day (10 December), and Christmas (25–27 December). For Christmas, people attend a religious service and then a feast in the *maneaba*, where different families showcase local dances. I-Kiribati do not exchange gifts on holidays or celebrate birthdays, other than a family's first son's birthday.

Commerce

Businesses are open weekdays from 8:00 A.M. to 4:30 P.M. The one bank is open from 9:30 A.M. to 3:00 P.M. Stores, especially small family ones, are open as early as 7:00 A.M. and close as late at 6:00 P.M. Some are open on weekends but do not open until 1:00 P.M. on Sunday because of morning church services. Government offices close for lunch at 12:30 P.M.

Prices are fixed by the government, including those for fish sold on the side of the road. Business is a relatively new concept, so the atmosphere is informal. Most retailing is done through consumer cooperatives. Less than 10 percent of the population earns a cash income; on outer islands, teachers, nurses, and government employees are the only paid workers.

SOCIETY

Government

The Republic of Kiribati has a *beretitenti* (president) as head of state and government. Citizens elect the president from among a few candidates nominated by the 40-seat *Maneaba ni Maungatabu* (House of Assembly). The current president is Teburoro Tito. He has a vice president and cabinet, appointed from among the members of the assembly. The next elections are in 1999. All citizens may vote at age 18. Each inhabited island has a council, and the government is represented by an island clerk. Local authority is vested in the *maneaba* council of *unimane* (old men).

Economy

The economy is based on the export of copra (dried coconut), used to make coconut-oil soap and cosmetics. Copra accounts for up to 70 percent of the total cash income for the rural population. Most islanders live by fishing, growing their own food, and raising small livestock. Local industry is confined to small operations, handicrafts, fish salting, and small-boat building. Large foreign companies pay Kiribati for the right to fish its waters. A cash economy has only recently emerged on the outer islands, but it prevails on southern Tarawa. Inflation is low and economic growth keeps pace with population growth. The Australian dollar ($A) is used as the country's currency.

Transportation and Communication

Buses are available only on South Tarawa. Outer island travel is by foot, bicycle, or motor bike. Interisland air and boat links are available on irregular schedules. Telephones are available on Tarawa and increasingly on outer islands. There are no television stations, but one radio station broadcasts three times daily. A number of monthly newspapers sponsored by churches and a weekly newspaper (*Te Uekera*) are published.

Education

Schooling is compulsory for children between ages six and fifteen. The literacy rate is 80 percent, and most children receive a primary education. Because of fees and limited facilities, only about 15 percent of students attend secondary school. Kiribati participates in the University of the South Pacific (based in Fiji), and some students study in New Zealand and Australia. Tarawa has a Technical Training Institute, a Teacher's College, and a Marine Training School.

Health

The government maintains free medical services. Each island has a clinic with at least one nurse. Doctors at the Tungaru Central Hospital on Tarawa provide additional health care. They travel to outer islands to do dental or optometric work when necessary. The infant mortality rate is 62 per 1,000; life expectancy is 60 years.

FOR THE TRAVELER

U.S. citizens need both a passport and visa to enter Kiribati. Visitors should wear modest clothing. Drink only boiled water. There is little tourism in Kiribati because of its remoteness, but hotels and other facilities do exist. For more information, contact the Kiribati Visitors Bureau, PO Box 261, Bikenibeu, Tarawa, Kiribati, Central Pacific. You may also contact the Consulate of the Republic of Kiribati, 850 Richards Street, Suite 503, Honolulu, HI 96813; phone (808) 521–7703.

North Korea

(Democratic People's Republic of Korea)

Boundary representations not necessarily authoritative.

ASIA

BACKGROUND

Land and Climate

North Korea is bounded by the Yellow Sea to the west, the Sea of Japan (known in Korea as the East Sea) on the east, China and Russia to the north, and the Republic of Korea in the south. It occupies slightly more than half of the Korean Peninsula (55 percent) and covers some 47,250 square miles (120,540 square kilometers). It is just smaller than Mississippi and about 20 percent larger than South Korea. The landscape of North Korea is dominated by mountains and narrow valleys. As a result, the majority of the population resides on only about 20 percent of the land. The mountainous interior is isolated and sparsely populated. The climate is continental, with relatively long, cold winters and hot, humid summers interrupted by a two-week monsoon season. Spring and autumn are more temperate and pleasant. Summer rainfall accounts for more than half the total annual rainfall, which averages about 31 inches (79 centimeters).

History

North Korea was once a part of the kingdom called Koguryo, one of the three kingdoms on the peninsula that were finally united in A.D. 668. A new kingdom called Koryo ruled most of what is now North Korea until 1392, when Yi Song-gye took power and established the Choson (or Yi) Dynasty. The Choson Dynasty kings controlled the entire peninsula for the next five hundred years, until Korea was annexed by Japan in 1910. At the end of World War II, Korea was liberated from Japan. The United States and the Soviet Union decided to allow Soviet forces to accept the Japanese surrender in the northern part of Korea and U.S. forces to do so in the south. In the north, former anti-Japanese guerrilla Kim Il Sung, with the full support of the Soviet command, took power in 1948. He remained in firm control, carrying out several political purges to eliminate opposition figures, until his death in July 1994. His son, Kim Jong Il took his place as the nation's leader.

On 25 June 1950, the North Korean Army invaded South Korea, initiating a war that lasted three years and caused untold suffering to the Korean people. The United States and a military force from the United Nations (UN) supported the south, and China supported the north. In July 1953, a truce was established along the 38th parallel, the original prewar boundary. Near the town of Panmunjom, a demilitarized zone created as part of the truce separates the two Koreas today.

Technically, a peace treaty has never been signed and the two nations are still at war. There have been some minor border incidents and acts of terrorism, but no major fighting since 1953. Tunnels have been discovered that were dug from the North Korean side to South Korea and could have been used for a raid or invasion.

Kim Il Sung placed heavy emphasis on the reunification of the Korean Peninsula. In 1990, representatives from both countries held a series of historic meetings designed to promote better relations and encourage eventual unification. Talks continued through 1992, but little progress was made. Only minor treaties, statements, and agreements were signed. Each distrusts the other's military intentions and each wishes to determine the peninsula's future course.

In 1993, North Korea threatened to withdraw from the Nuclear Nonproliferation Treaty after international inspectors were refused permission to inspect the country's nuclear program. It was feared that North Korea had the capacity to manufacture nuclear weapons and already possessed a nuclear bomb. Relations with South Korea and other nations quickly soured. Only after various threats and months of intense negotiations with the United States did North Korea decide not to withdraw from the treaty. Some inspections from the International Atomic Energy Agency were granted in 1994, although UN demands were not fully met. Kim's death interrupted negotiations, but they continued under his son, and North Korea signed a nuclear accord. Hopes in both North and South Korea that contact might be allowed or that reunification would soon follow seemed dashed in 1995 when Kim Jong Il withdrew his country's commitment to the accord. Eventually, however, Kim agreed to accept the accord in exchange for help in developing alternate nuclear energy for domestic consumption.

Even as the nuclear issue took center stage, a more serious problem was becoming evident: economic disintegration. Food and fuel shortages were so acute by the end of 1995 that many people were defecting to South Korea or crossing the Chinese border (risking execution) in search of food. Massive flooding in 1995 also cut food supplies. North Korea finally asked for, and received, emergency aid from Western and other Asian nations—something unheard of for this isolated country. If North Korea does not soon receive (or, rather, accept) substantial outside help, it is feared the economy will collapse within a few years, possibly leading society into chaos.

THE PEOPLE

Population

North Korea's population of approximately 23.5 million is growing at 1.8 percent. Ethnic Koreans comprise almost the entire population. There are no significant numbers of other ethnic or cultural minorities in the country. About 60 percent of all people live in urban areas. North Korea's Human Development Index (0.733) ranks it 83d out of 174 nations, but this does not reflect the difficulties of the past two years. Basic social institutions exist but do not provide an opportunity for economic prosperity or personal advancement. Many people do not earn an income sufficient for their needs.

Language

The Korean language plays an important role in the identity of the Korean people. Korean is spoken in both North and South Korea and is written in a phonetic alphabet created and promulgated in the mid-15th century. The alphabet is called *Hangul* in South Korea but is known as *Chosongul* in North Korea. Although the Korean language is replete with words adapted from Chinese, North Koreans, unlike South Koreans, do not use Chinese characters with *Chosongul* in their newspapers and publications. They prefer to use only *Chosongul*, which is sufficient for most needs. There are also some differences in vocabulary between the North and the South, influenced somewhat by politics and by the contact each

country has had with other nations. Russian, Chinese, and English are taught as second languages in the schools.

Religion

The government of North Korea has constitutionally confirmed freedom of religion. In reality, however, the effectual state religion since the 1950s has been the veneration of Kim Il Sung, the "Great Leader." It is not known whether such veneration will extend to Kim Jong Il ("Dear Leader"). Kim Jong Il waits to assume his father's official political titles until the end or near the end of the mandatory three-year mourning period in 1997.

Despite the personality cult that existed under Kim Il Sung, the way of life and philosophy in North Korea echoes traditional patterns and is based fundamentally on Confucian thought. Roman Catholic and Protestant beliefs were introduced in the 18th and 19th centuries, respectively. *Ch'ondogyo* (also known as *Tonghak*) is an indigenous religion founded in 1860 as an eclectic combination of Buddhist, Confucian, and Christian beliefs. The present government points to this religion, which has organized a political party, as proof that religious freedom exists in North Korea. The government also permits Christians to meet in small groups under the direction of state-appointed ministers. Shamanism, a native belief in household and natural spirits, gods, and demons, may still have limited influence in rural areas, but it is mostly promoted by the government as an art form.

General Attitudes

The establishment of the Democratic People's Republic of Korea (North Korea's official name) brought about radical changes in the nature of traditional Korean society. The Confucian concept of filial piety and loyalty to one's lineage has largely been supplanted by an intense nationalism that is described as both fiercely proud and excessively paranoid. The interests of the state have taken priority over the interests of the family. Kim Il Sung, through extensive indoctrination, effectively united the North Korean people in the belief that their political system and way of life are superior. Although contemporary North Korean society is structurally and theoretically socialist, the most important and influential concept is Kim's idea of *chuch'e* (self-reliance). *Chuch'e* has a pervasive influence on the North Korean psyche. It colors every aspect of life, from popular music to political speeches and everyday conversation. *Chuch'e* gives people a reason to sacrifice, and it is what has convinced the people that they are better off than other nations.

CUSTOMS AND COURTESIES

Greetings

Confucianism has taught Koreans to behave with decorum and show respect for propriety. Greetings and introductions, therefore, tend to be rather formal. Handshakes are common among men, but a bow is still most common. A younger or lower-status person always bows until the other offers a handshake or returns the bow. When Korean men do shake hands, they extend the right hand, often supported at the wrist by the left hand to show deference, and slightly bow the head. When women meet, they usually extend both hands and grasp each other's hands. Children always bow to adults and wave or bow among themselves.

There are several phrases used in greeting, but the most common is *Anyonghaseyo?* (literally, "Are you in peace?"), which is used to ask "How are you?" The Korean language has different levels of formality, so this and any other greeting will differ depending on the people involved. For example, *Anyong?* is used with children, while *Anyonghashimnikka?* is used for superiors. The variations have the same meaning, but the different endings indicate levels of respect. When greeting a superior, one commonly asks about health and parents. When greeting a subordinate, the questions are about the spouse and children.

Gestures

It is not unusual to see men holding hands in public or a man walking down the street with an arm over a friend's shoulder. This is an expression of friendship. Touching between strangers or casual acquaintances, however, especially between opposite sexes, is considered inappropriate. In most situations, people maintain good posture to show respect for the host or speaker. Sitting in a relaxed manner is considered an insult. One takes care not to expose the bottom of the feet to another person while sitting. People give and receive gifts with both hands. Hands generally are not used much in conversation. Hats are removed in buildings, as well as in the presence of an elder or superior. One never looks a superior directly in the eye.

Visiting

North Koreans do not commonly visit one another unannounced, and arranged social visits are infrequent. Generally, people visit relatives for the Lunar New Year or Parents' Day but not often otherwise. Unless special business calls for it, a superior never visits a subordinate.

Invited guests are nearly always offered light refreshments, consisting of a drink, fruit, crackers, cookies, or coffee. It is considered polite and a sign of respect for guests to take a gift to the hosts. The value of the gift is far less important than the gesture of giving it. In most cases, a gift will be fruit, a beverage, or something from one's home region. Shoes and hats are removed indoors. In some cases, slippers are provided. Otherwise, people wear only socks in the home. Observing etiquette involves paying particular attention to the host and making sure his feelings are respected. Showing respect for the family and state are of utmost importance for most visits. Koreans are generous hosts. They view the care of a guest as basic good manners, so visitors are given the best the household has to offer. If there are many guests, then age or status determine who gets the best seat, the best cut of meat, the largest drink, and so forth.

Eating

Families rarely have time to eat daily meals together. Fathers often leave early in the morning and return late at night. They commonly eat their meals at workplace cafeterias. Koreans consider eating while walking on the street ill-mannered and offensive, something only a child is allowed to indulge in. Except during lengthy dinner parties, conversation during meals is quite limited. Eating with the fingers is considered impolite, but slurping soup and noodles is accepted; in fact, it is a practical way to eat hot food at the rapid pace Koreans are used to. Spoons for soup and chopsticks for all other foods are the most common utensils.

Restaurants in North Korea are difficult to get into and are very expensive. The average worker would almost never eat in a restaurant. Tipping is not allowed.

LIFESTYLE

Family

The family remains an important part of North Korean life. The population has been constantly exhorted by the government to "love your family, love your state," but obligations have been continually extended outward to embrace the larger society. Beginning in 1948, the government worked to break down the traditional extended family and clan system. Traditional Korean familial devotion was redirected toward the country's ruler, whom young children were taught to refer to as "Father Kim Il Sung." Through his "moral leadership and benevolent instruction" in all aspects of North Korean life, Kim was portrayed by the government-controlled media as a highly paternal figure and a near-god. His picture was everywhere and his will was obeyed before any other. His popularity weakened near the end of his life, as people realized that conditions were not improving.

For most families, the average monthly wage (about US$50) is enough to purchase daily necessities but not enough to pay for luxury or nonessential goods. Consumerism is discouraged in favor of austerity. However, workers can earn a variety of supplies, benefits, and gifts from either their employers or the government. Both parents usually work and their children go to day-care centers, often located at the workplace.

Dating and Marriage

Western-style dating is not allowed, and marriages are either arranged by the parents or carried out with their consent. The government has established minimum marriage ages (27 for men, 25 for women) to allow for the completion of military service and other obligations. Due to a shortage in the labor force, the government provides incentives for married couples to have large families.

Diet

Korean food generally is spicy. *Kimch'i* (a spicy pickled cabbage) and rice are the mainstays of the diet around which most other dishes revolve. Meals usually consist of a number of spicy vegetables, soup, fish, and *kimch'i*. Because of the lower economic level of North Korea, traditional Korean delicacies such as *pulkogi* (marinated beef) and *kalbi* (marinated short ribs) are not as common as in South Korea. A favorite food in North Korea is *naengmyon*, a cold noodle dish. The consumption of soybeans, corn, millet, and wheat is high. Two meals per day are standard during food shortages.

Recreation

Sports are popular; they are encouraged by the government, and sports facilities are plentiful. Soccer is the national sport. Many Koreans also play table tennis. Movies, plays, and operas, usually with strong political messages, are well attended. Family outings and picnics to North Korea's many parks and cultural and historical sites are common Sunday activities. Sunday is the worker's day of rest. Television is popular and widely available. North Koreans are accomplished in all traditional Korean art forms. Performances are highly polished and form is pursued over spontaneity or individuality.

Holidays

In addition to national holidays, many commemoration days can be declared holidays if local authorities are satisfied production will not be disrupted. The government has discontinued traditional Korean seasonal festivals. Official holidays include New Year's Day, the birthdays of Kim Il Sung (15 April) and Kim Jong Il (16 February), May Day (1 May), Liberation Day (15 August), Independence Day (9 September), Workers' Party Day (10 October), and Constitution Day (27 December).

Commerce

As with other key aspects of North Korean society, the government is closely involved in the mobilization of labor. Workers are expected to put in at least a 40-hour workweek in addition to attending various political and production meetings. Tightly controlled work teams laboring on farms and in factories are the norm. By 1958, all farms in North Korea were incorporated into more than three thousand cooperatives, each comprising about three hundred families on about one thousand acres. Once self-sufficient in agriculture, North Korea's emphasis has shifted toward mining and manufacturing. The North has about 80 to 90 percent of all known mineral resources on the peninsula, and the extraction of coal, iron ore, and other minerals fueled North Korea's past industrial growth. Without credits and trade with other former Communist nations, that growth has halted.

SOCIETY

Government

North Korea is a Communist state. The president is head of state and secretary of the ruling Korean Workers' Party. A premier is technically head of government. The 687-seat Supreme People's Assembly forms the legislature. The last legislative elections were in 1993. In all elections, only a single candidate is chosen to run for each office. The candidates are either from the Korean Workers' Party or a few minor, associated parties. Voters can only vote "yes" or "no" for each person, and they generally vote "yes." The voting age is 17.

Since assuming power, Kim Jong Il has retained his father's advisors in their posts, while at the same time increasing the de facto authority of younger men in preparation of their assuming formal control in the future. Most notable are a group of five military officers, who have most of the defense authority, and a few of Kim's relatives, who control economic and other aspects of North Korean society. Thus, a person with a high title, especially an elderly person, likely has little real power. It is not known whether the younger generation of leaders will be more open to the outside world.

Economy

Since the end of World War II, North Korea has changed from an agricultural to a semi-industrialized nation. The means of production are 90 percent socialized. Planning for economic development is centralized and set forth by the government in a series of seven-year plans. Major industries include mining, steel, textiles, chemicals, cement, glass, and ceramics. There is a shortage of light manufactured items (mostly consumer goods). Agricultural production is maintained through the heavy use of fertilizers and high-yield seeds. Without hard currency, the country cannot buy these and harvests are lower.

Although the North Korean economy developed at an impressive rate in the 1980s, it has shrunk every year since 1990 (declining 5 percent in 1995). This is due partly to the loss of the Soviet Union as a major trading partner but is also a function of poor planning, a U.S. trade embargo, and isolationism. North Korea is seeking ways to stimulate growth and production—even proposing free-trade zones and other market-oriented plans—but very little has come to fruition. The currency is the North Korean *won* (W).

Transportation and Communication

In North Korea, the rail system is the principal means of transportation. The Pyongyang subway is efficient and cheap. Few motor vehicles are available to the general population. The streets, roads, and avenues, at least in the major cities, are broad, tree lined, and well kept. Most Koreans usually walk or ride a bus to their destinations. Bicycles, once rare, are now a principal mode of transport. Ox carts are common in rural areas. Communications systems and the media are controlled by the government.

Education

North Korea has more than two hundred universities and colleges, more than four thousand high schools and specialized institutions, and nearly five thousand elementary schools and kindergartens. An 11-year education program is compulsory and free, and illiteracy has been all but eliminated. The estimated literacy rate is 99 percent. Competition is fierce for entry into the prestigious Kim Il Sung University and other institutions of higher learning. The socialist and nationalist focus of the North Korean educational system, while supplying the state with skilled and compliant workers, aims to produce uniformity in thought and action, with little room for individuality and diversity.

Health

Although quality is relatively poor, North Korea's socialist health-care system is extensive. Free health care is provided to the entire population. The average life expectancy ranges between 67 and 73 years. The infant mortality rate is 27 per 1,000. Malnutrition is spreading to many areas.

FOR THE TRAVELER

The United States does not maintain diplomatic relations with North Korea. To apply for a visa to travel to North Korea, an individual must apply directly to its government or through a country (such as Sweden) that has diplomatic relations with it. Vaccinations are not necessary. Foreign visitors are often assigned an escort who limits access to people and places. Although the U.S. government does not encourage travel to North Korea, it does not prohibit it. Still, groups traveling to North Korea must obtain a license from the Department of Treasury, Licensing Division, Office of Foreign Assets Control, 1500 Pennsylvania Avenue NW, Second Floor NX, Washington, DC 20220; phone (202) 622–2480.

South Korea

(Republic of Korea)

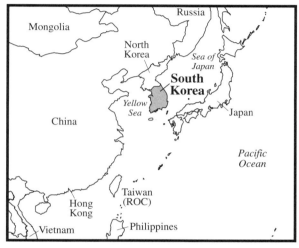

Boundary representations not necessarily authoritative.

BACKGROUND

Land and Climate

Covering 38,023 square miles (98,480 square kilometers), South Korea is slightly larger than Indiana. Its only border is shared with North Korea at the 38th parallel (called the "Truce Line"). Otherwise, as a peninsula, it is surrounded by water. At its closest point, it is 123 miles (196 kilometers) from Japan. Almost 70 percent of the land is forested; slightly more than 20 percent is suitable for cultivation. Hills and mountains dominate the east, while plains are found in the west and south. Korea's climate is temperate, but high humidity makes summers seem hotter and winters colder. Korea experiences all four seasons; spring and fall are the most pleasant times of the year. The monsoon season is from mid-July to mid-August. During this time, Korea receives half of its annual rainfall. Korea is traditionally known as the "Land of the Morning Calm."

History

Shilla kings united three warring kingdoms in A.D. 668 and began developing a rich Buddhist culture. By 935, the strong, new Koryo kingdom had become established on the peninsula. The name *Korea* comes from *Koryo*. During the Koryo era, the world's first movable metal-type printer was invented. Koryo fell to the Choson or Yi Dynasty in 1392. The Yi ruled for more than five hundred years. In the latter part of the Yi Dynasty, China and Japan sought control of Korea, a struggle that the Japanese eventually won. They annexed Korea in 1910.

At the end of World War II (1945), the Soviet Union entered Korea from the north and the United States entered the south by prearrangement to accept the surrender of Japanese troops. The peninsula was accordingly divided (at the 38th parallel) into two administrative zones. After attempts to hold nationwide elections failed, a pro-Western government was established in the south and Syngman Rhee became president. In June 1950, North Korean troops invaded South Korea, triggering a three-year war. The United States and United Nations sent troops to support South Korea. Concerned that war might spill into Chinese territory, China sent troops to aid North Korea. The war ravaged the peninsula and ended in a stalemate (a peace treaty has still not been signed), with the original border virtually unchanged. Violent border incidents have occurred over the years, and North Korean soldiers entered the demilitarized zone several times in 1996. South Koreans still conduct a monthly civil defense drill.

Rhee resigned in 1960 under charges of political corruption. Although elections were held the following year, General Park Chung Hee seized control and was elected president two years later. He was assassinated in 1979 by the head of the South Korean intelligence agency. A military coup followed and Chun Doo Hwan emerged as president. A 1987 constitution established direct presidential elections and protection of human rights. Roh Tae Woo was elected. Both Chun and Roh eventually faced criminal charges and were jailed in 1996.

The 1992 free elections were the first held without military involvement. Grassroots movements led authorities to accept elections in order to avoid possible future revolts. Kim Young Sam won the election and became the first civilian to occupy the Blue House (presidential mansion) in more than 30 years. Kim strove to reform government and continue economic progress but was plagued by three major man-made disasters that cost the lives of some two hundred citizens.

In 1990, North and South Korea had their first peace talks since the 1950s. Progress toward reducing peninsular tensions and even unifying the two Koreas was limited but promising. However, North Korea's nuclear program and U.S.-South Korean military relations led talks to falter in 1993. North Korea seemed to soften in 1994; families separated by the war hoped for reunion and plans were made to speed economic cooperation. However, North Korea withdrew its support for a nuclear accord in 1995 and negotiations stalled. In 1996, the United States and South Korea proposed four-nation peace talks with North Korea and China. Until such talks are accepted, letters, phone calls, visits, and all other communication between the two Koreas are officially impossible.

THE PEOPLE

Population

The Republic of Korea's population of 45.5 million is growing annually at 1 percent. Except for a small Chinese minority, the people are all ethnic Korean, making Korea one of the most homogeneous countries in the world. About 72 percent of the population lives in urban areas. South Korea's Human Development Index (0.882) ranks it 31st out of 174 nations. Adjusted for women, the index (0.780) ranks South Korea 37th out of 130 nations. These figures imply Koreans generally have very good access to resources that allow them to pursue personal goals but women are less likely to earn a decent wage or attend college. They are also underrepresented in government and business.

Language

The Korean language plays an important role in the identity of the Korean people. Korean is spoken in both North and South Korea and is written in *Hangul*, a phonetic alphabet created in 1446 because classical Chinese (the only written language available) was difficult to master. *Hangul* made it possible for the commoner to read and write. It has 24 letters (10 of them vowels), all of which are easy to learn. *Hangul* also instilled a national pride in Koreans that helped them preserve their culture during long periods of foreign occupation. Although not related to Chinese, Korean mixes numerous Chinese characters with the *Hangul* script in newspapers and government documents. English is taught in school and many people have a good understanding of it.

Religion

Confucianism permeates all aspects of Korean society. It encourages such practices as worshipping at shrines and ancestral tombs. In addition, Confucianism orders social behavior,

stressing righteousness and filial piety (family relationships), especially between father and son. More than one-quarter of the people follow the traditions of a folk religion called Shamanism. Important to Shamanism are geomancy, divination, avoiding bad luck or omens, warding off evil spirits, and honoring the dead. Nearly 30 percent of the population is Christian. Christianity is growing rapidly and many young people and government officials are Christian. Most Christians belong to a variety of Protestant churches. More than 15 percent of Koreans practice Buddhism.

General Attitudes

The Confucian ethic is evident in the general attitudes of Koreans. Many rituals of courtesy, behavioral formalities, and customs regulate social relations. Hard work and filial piety are valued. Koreans often use extreme modesty when speaking about themselves. They are reluctant to accept high honors and they graciously deny compliments. Success depends greatly on social contacts. Koreans are quick to make friends and they value their friendships highly. Friends expect to rely on each other for just about anything.

Giving gifts as a means of obtaining favors is common, especially in the workplace, and accepting a gift carries the responsibility of reciprocity. Open criticism and public disagreement are considered inappropriate because they can damage another person's reputation. Out of respect for the feelings of others, Koreans may withhold bad news or adverse opinions or express them in an indirect way. South Koreans are proud of their country's accomplishments, including the nation's modern economic success and the influence of its traditional culture.

Personal Appearance

Most Koreans, except for the elderly and some in rural areas, wear Western-style clothing. The youth wear modern fashions, and Korea has an active fashion industry. Clothing often depends on the event. In public, conservative dress is important. Bare feet are inappropriate. In the business world, Western-style suits and dresses are the norm. For special occasions or holidays, however, Koreans often wear traditional clothing. Women wear the *hanbok*, a two-piece, long dress that is often very colorful. Men wear trousers with a loose-fitting jacket or robe.

CUSTOMS AND COURTESIES

Greetings

Confucian principles, although less important in modern Korean society than in the past, are still an integral part of social interactions, including greetings. How one is greeted depends on one's age and social standing relative to the greeter. A bow is the traditional greeting, but it is usually accompanied by a handshake between men. As a sign of respect, the left hand may support or rest under the right forearm during the handshake. Women shake hands less often than men. Professionals meeting for the first time exchange business cards, presenting and accepting the cards with both hands after a handshake. A common greeting is *Annyong haseyo?* (Are you at peace?). Young children often greet each other with a simple *Annyong?* To show special respect, an honorific is added to the greeting: *Annyong hashimnikka?* Young children bow or nod in greeting adults.

Gestures

It is not uncommon for Korean men (usually younger) to hold hands or walk with a hand on a friend's shoulder. However, touching older people or members of the opposite sex is usually not appropriate. Feet are not placed on a desk or chair. One passes and receives objects with both hands (or the right hand, grasped at the wrist or forearm by the left). When yawning or using a toothpick, one should cover the mouth. Koreans beckon by waving the fingers together with the palm down. Beckoning with the index finger is rude. Facial expressions are often more important than body language in communicating unspoken things. When embarrassed, a person may respond by laughing. Eye contact is important in conversation among peers.

In general, people do not line up for things. In fact, because personal space is limited in Korea, pushing and crowding is common and generally not considered impolite.

Visiting

Guests invited to a home remove their shoes upon entering. While Western furniture is common, in traditional Korean homes guests are seated on cushions on floors that are heated from below (*ondol* floors). Men sit cross-legged and women tuck their legs to one side behind them. The guest receives the warmest or best position. When visiting relatives, men and women usually separate to socialize. For example, the women gather in the kitchen. Guests invited for a meal or party customarily bring a small gift in appreciation, often something that can be served at the gathering. Wrapped gifts are not opened in front of the giver. Refreshments are usually served and refusing them is impolite. A host accompanies a guest to the door or outside at the end of a visit.

Eating

At a dinner party, the meal will usually come before socializing. Koreans pass items and pour drinks with the right hand, supporting the forearm or wrist with the left hand. In restaurants, tipping is not expected, but the bill usually includes a service charge. Eating while walking on the street is not appropriate for adults. Chopsticks and spoons are the most commonly used utensils.

LIFESTYLE

Family

The family is the foundation of society and is bound by a strong sense of duty and obligation among its members. The father is the head of the family; he and the oldest son receive the greatest respect. The oldest son is given the best opportunities for education and success. Although women are active in Korean society (they comprise one-third of the labor force), their status is generally lower than men's, a cultural trait often reflected in the workplace and home. Women retain their maiden names when they marry. A Korean name consists of a one-syllable family name followed by a one- or two-syllable given name. Kim and Park *(Pak)* are the most common family names. In the extended family, the oldest members are paid the greatest honor. On a person's 60th birthday

(a milestone rarely reached in the past), extended family members gather for a grand celebration *(hwan'gap)*. Families may save money for years just to pay for the event.

Similar lavish attention is afforded to babies. After one hundred days of life, a small feast is held in honor of the child's survival to that point (also a date often not reached in the past). A much larger celebration *(tol)* is held at the first birthday. From the many gifts offered, what a child picks up first is thought to signal his or her fortunes in life. Although the nuclear family is now more common, especially in the cities, sons still expect to care for their aging parents. Because of the Confucian emphasis on family hierarchies, Koreans keep detailed genealogies. These records date back many centuries and include a person's birth, relations, achievements, and place of burial. In family clan gatherings, families that rank higher in the genealogy are treated with greater respect by the others.

Dating and Marriage

Dating usually occurs in groups. The youth enjoy going to movies, hiking, taking short trips, and socializing at bakeries and teahouses. While trends are changing, most Korean youth rarely have time for more serious dating before they enter college or the workforce. Young people often meet at parties organized for that purpose. In some cases, families still arrange marriages for couples who have met but not dated in the Western sense. Traditional wedding ceremonies were rather elaborate, but today they often take place in public wedding halls where couples wear Western-style clothing instead of traditional Korean wedding attire.

Diet

Korean food is generally spicy. Rice and *kimch'i* (a spicy pickled cabbage) are staples at almost every meal. Various soups are common. Rice is often combined with other ingredients, such as red beans or vegetables. *Pibibap* is rice mixed with bits of meat and seasoned vegetables. Chicken and beef are common meats. A favorite delicacy is *pulkogi*, strips of marinated and barbecued beef. Koreans also eat large amounts of fish and *dok* (pounded rice cake). Barley tea is served with most meals. *Soju* and *magulli* are common alcoholic drinks for socializing before meals. Fruit is popular as a dessert.

Recreation

Soccer is popular in Korea. South Korea's national soccer team competed in the 1994 World Cup. Koreans also participate in baseball, boxing, basketball, volleyball, tennis, and swimming. *Taekwondo*, the martial art, comes from and is popular in Korea. Unique to Korea is a form of wrestling called *ssirum*, where contestants are tied together during their match. Mountain climbing and hiking are favorite activities for weekends and vacations. Movies, art exhibits, and theaters also provide entertainment.

Holidays

The New Year is celebrated over three days (1–3 January). Families gather to exchange gifts, honor the dead, and enjoy large meals. Generally, everyone dresses in traditional clothing. After the memorial services, family members bow to each older person in a show of respect. Games are played and fortunes are told. Koreans celebrate the Lunar New Year (in the spring) by visiting hometowns or vacationing in winter resorts. The other important family holiday is *Ch'usok* (Harvest Moon Festival, held in the fall), when family members visit the ancestral tomb to offer food in honor of the dead. Larger family reunions are common at this time. Other holidays include Independence Movement Day (1 March), Children's Day (5 May), Buddha's Birthday (in May, observed according to the lunar calendar), Memorial Day (6 June), Constitution Day (17 July), Independence Day (15 August), National Foundation Day (3 October), and Christmas. Arbor Day (5 April), Armed Forces Day (1 October), and Korean Language Day (9 October) are marked by various celebrations but are not public holidays.

Commerce

Small, family-owned stores are usually open every day from early in the morning until 10:00 or 11:00 P.M. In many cases, the family lives above or near the store. Larger department stores close by 8:00 P.M. Other businesses are generally open from 9:00 A.M. to 6:00 P.M. Banks and government offices close earlier. The average workweek for a Korean is 50 hours, one of the longest in the world but shorter than it was in the 1980s.

SOCIETY

Government

The Republic of South Korea is divided into nine provinces (*do*) and six special cities (*jikhalsi*). The constitution provides for an elected president who serves a five-year term. The president appoints a prime minister who is technically, but not in practice, head of government. Members of the 299-seat National Assembly (*Kuk Hoe*) serve four-year terms. The majority party is the Democratic Liberal Party. The main opposition parties are the Democratic Party and the United People's Party. All citizens may vote at age 20. The next elections are in December 1997.

Economy

South Korea continues to experience rapid economic growth and development. The gross domestic product (GDP) grew at more than 6 percent annually in the late 1980s. A global recession and domestic difficulties caused slower growth in the early 1990s, but South Korea is still considered an Asian economic powerhouse. Growth for 1994 was about 8 percent. Since 1987, incomes have risen 50 percent and the middle class has grown to the point that most families identify themselves as part of it. Real GDP per capita is $9,250. South Korea's success is based on export-oriented industry.

The agricultural sector contributes about 11 percent of the GDP. Chief products include rice, barley, vegetables, and fish. About 16 percent of the labor force is employed in agriculture and lives in rural villages, cultivating small plots or collective farms. More than one-third of the labor force works in mining and manufacturing. The rest is involved in service occupations. Korea's industries include textiles and clothing, chemicals, steel, electronics, and automobiles. Shipbuilding is also important. Unemployment and inflation remain relatively low. The currency is the *won* (W).

Transportation and Communication

Air, rail, and bus connections provide a good transportation network between cities. Roads are paved and in good condition. Buses, private cars, and taxis handle public transportation in the cities. Seoul has an efficient subway and a quality express bus system, in addition to regular buses. Taxis are plentiful and inexpensive. Drivers will often stop for other passengers during busy hours. Driving habits are aggressive and accidents are common. There are numerous radio and television stations. Many daily newspapers are available. The postal and telephone systems are efficient and modern.

Education

Education is the most valued aspect of Korean culture, a virtue rooted in Confucianism. Education is considered the key to success, respect, and power. The government finances more than 75 percent of Korea's education expenses. Political demonstrations by college students usually occur every spring and are considered part of the students' duty to protect the people against social injustices. Although these activities have often been violent, they have been part of university life for much longer than Korea has been a republic. They decreased substantially after the 1992 elections but still occur when an appropriate cause arises. Schooling is compulsory between the ages of six and twelve, and nearly every child completes primary schooling. Eighty-eight percent of all children go on for secondary education. Secondary schools demand long hours and high performance. To enter a university, applicants must pass extremely competitive and rigorous entrance exams. They study intensively for months to pass them. Vocational training is also available. The adult literacy rate is 97 percent.

Health

All segments of the population have access to adequate health care. The best facilities are in Seoul. Most women receive prenatal care and medical attention during delivery. Nearly 80 percent of all infants are immunized. The infant mortality rate is 21 per 1,000. Adults can expect to live between 67 and 74 years.

FOR THE TRAVELER

A valid passport and visa are required of U.S. travelers visiting for more than 15 days. For shorter visits, only a passport is necessary. Water is generally not safe for drinking and should be boiled. No vaccinations are required. Korea has many historical sites and excellent mountain climbing opportunities. The tourist industry is well developed, and many people speak English. Although Western hotels are available, Korean-style accommodations (such as the *yogwan*) are inexpensive and provide a cultural experience. For more information, contact the Korea National Tourism Corporation, Two Executive Drive, Seventh Floor, Fort Lee, NJ 07024; phone (201) 585–0909. You may also wish to contact the Embassy of the Republic of Korea, 2320 Massachusetts Avenue NW, Washington, DC 20008; phone (202) 797–6343.

CULTURGRAM ™ '97

Kyrgyzstan

(Kyrgyz Republic)

Boundary representations not necessarily authoritative.

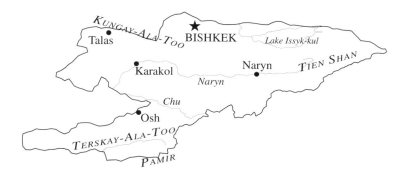

BACKGROUND

Land and Climate

Located in the heart of central Asia, the landlocked Kyrgyz Republic covers 84,400 square miles (198,500 square kilometers) and is similar in size to South Dakota. The terrain is mostly mountainous, with 40 percent of Kyrgyzstan being above 9,900 feet (3,000 meters). Of 28 lofty peaks, Victory (*Pobeda*) Peak is one of the world's highest mountains at 24,549 feet (7,439 meters). Glaciers are found in the snow-capped mountains; at 350 square miles, the largest is Inyl'chek on the Khan-Tengri Massif. Kyrgyzstan's picturesque rugged mountains and alpine meadows open to grassland steppes, then to broad-leafed and conifer forests and foothills, and to semiarid and arid deserts and river valleys, particularly the Ferghana and Chuiskaya Valleys at 1,600 feet above sea level. Kyrgyzstan has a wide variety of native flora and fauna: 4,500 plant species; 80 animal varieties, including rare snow leopards; 25 species of reptiles; and 385 species of birds.

Melting mountain ice and snow feed streams, rivers, mineral springs, and more than two thousand lakes. The largest lake, Issyk-kul, is the world's second largest alpine lake. Earthquakes are infrequent but strong. Kyrgyzstan has a dry continental climate with four seasons. Summers are hot and dry. On average, sunny weather can be expected 247 days per year. In the inhabited lowland valleys, average summer temperatures might rise to 86°F (30°C) but can reach 95°F (35°C) in western Kyrgyzstan. Winters are cold and snowy, with temperatures often below freezing.

History

Legends are integrated into the history of early Kyrgyz culture. For example, the origin of *Kyrgyz* is explained thus: Forty girls (*kyrk* is "forty"; *kyz* is "girls"), magically and simultaneously impregnated by one wandering man, became the mothers of 40 sons. Each son, in turn, founded one of the original 40 nomadic tribes.

Historically, national and territorial divisions of central Asian nomads were blurred by invasions and migration, as well as Turkic, Mongol, and Persian cultural influences. The Chinese recorded evidence of the Kyrgyz nation in 2000 B.C. Various records indicate establishment of Osh in 13 B.C. During this period, the first Kyrgyz language was developed.

The ancient Kyrgyz were reported to be one of the most powerful nomad tribes to persistently attack China, perhaps precipitating the building of the Great Wall of China. Sunni Islam was adopted under the Karakhanid *Kaganat* (Kingdom), which helped unify the various tribal and ethnic groups. In the tenth century, the Great Kyrgyz Kaganat developed and expanded because of its military prowess and ideal location on the Great Silk Road trade route.

At the beginning of the 13th century, however, the last Kyrgyz Kaganat fell to Ghengis Khan's Mongol invasions. With the state, the native written language was destroyed. Kyrgyz history was then transmitted via folk epics. Although there were many epics, *Manas* is the longest (more than one million lines long) and most significant. Manas was a major heroic figure said to represent the strength, independence, and unity of the Kyrgyz people.

By the 18th century, the Kyrgyz people were continuously being attacked by other khanates. Russian forces responded to Kyrgyz appeals for help by occupying northern Kyrgyzstan in 1876. At the same time, other ethnic groups began migrating to the area.

Russian protection soon became domination. The Kyrgyz language was reestablished (written in Cyrillic), roads were built, schools were opened, and new industries were organized, but the Kyrgyz were dissatisfied with Russian czarist rule. A 1916 revolt was quickly suppressed by Russian troops. Famine ensued and more than half a million Kyrgyz died; many others fled to China.

To placate the constantly rebelling Muslims, Russia declared the nation a Kara-Kyrgyz Autonomous Region in 1924 and eventually the Khirgizia Soviet Socialist Republic in 1936. But sporadic rebellions continued, as Stalin's forced collectivization and destruction of animal herds led to more starvation. Integrated into the Soviet system, the Kyrgyz people adopted or acquiesced to much of the Soviet culture, as evidenced in urban architecture and many social customs. But the nomadic spirit remained strong, and native traditions are being restored.

When the Soviet Union dissolved in 1991, Kyrgyzstan became an independent republic and elected Askar Akayev as president. Reelected in 1995, Akayev gained sweeping executive powers through a 1996 referendum to help him push market reforms through Parliament.

PEOPLE

Population

Kyrgyzstan's population of 4.7 million is growing at 1.5 percent. About one-third of all people live in cities. The mountains are largely uninhabited, but about 40,000 Kyrgyz are seasonal nomads. The capital, Bishkek, has 631,000 residents and Osh has 218,000. Ethnic Kyrgyz comprise 52 percent of the total population. Other groups include Russians (21 percent) in the north and Uzbeks (13 percent) in the south. Smaller groups of Armenians, Byelorussians, Chinese, Kazakhs, Tajiks, Ukrainians, and others also live in the country. Kyrgyzstan's Human Development Index (0.717) ranks it 89th out of 174 nations.

Language

The official language is Kyrgyz. Two major dialects, northern and southern, are joined by several small regional dialects. It is believed Kyrgyz is the base for all Turkic languages. Kyrgyz has been developed, extinguished, and reestablished many times. In 1924, it was based on the Arabic alphabet incorporating Kyrgyz vocalizations; in 1928, the Latin script was substituted; and in 1941, Cyrillic symbols were adopted by all Turkic-speaking republics in the Soviet Union. Kyrgyz can be transliterated with the Latin alphabet. It is being debated whether to drop Cyrillic and return to the Latin script or contribute to the development of an inter-Turkic alphabet.

Russian was the official language during the Soviet era and remains the primary language of urban and regional communication.

Religion

Although Islam is the official religion of Kyrgyzstan, and 70 percent of the population practices at least some Sunni Muslim traditions, many parts of Kyrgyzstan are fairly secular. Islam's influence is heavier in the south, but Muslim traditions have been modified by other religious and native influences. Other religions with followings include Russian Orthodox, various other Christian churches, and Judaism.

Ancient beliefs often are mixed with formal religion. For example, tradition holds that a horse carries the spirit of the dead from the Middle World to the Upper World. For this reason, a horse is sacrificed and served at the funeral gathering for a respected deceased elder. Totemism (tribal affiliation or kinship with a particular animal) is also widely observed. Worshiped totems include the reindeer, white camel, snake, eagle-owl, and bear. Celestial symbols (moon, stars, and heaven) are other important elements in Kyrgyz religious beliefs. Shamanism, black and white magic, and a belief in *arback* (living ancestral spirits) are strong even among secular families.

General Attitudes

Kyrgyz people are friendly, tolerant, soft-spoken, respectful of elders, and exceptionally hospitable. They are very proud of their nomadic heritage. Kyrgyz culture emphasizes the essential social component of business interactions, placing considerable value on casual, extended conversations with tea rituals or alcoholic toasts and with long dinners.

Social, political, and business networks are structured along extended family lines, with each family or clan providing support. This closed networking is sometimes referred to as "tribalism." However, the system is gradually changing to include "trustworthy" non-family members.

People are more important than schedules, and activities are more important than how quickly they can be accomplished. Hence, rigid time consciousness and punctuality are not part of traditional culture. Only the new generation of students, bankers, and merchants are becoming concerned about time and its relative value.

Personal Appearance

Kyrgyz women traditionally have waist-length hair and often wear it in a braid, but it is now common for less traditional women to cut their hair. Nearly all women in the urban north wear Western-style clothing. Some southern urban women wear colorful silk dresses and head scarves. Village women throughout Kyrgyzstan wear head scarves. Regardless of the style worn, clothing is modest; skirts cover the knees and sleeves cover the arms. Women do not wear slacks. Only younger urban women might wear jeans or mini-dresses. On cold winter days, women (but not as many youth) might wear a Russian *tumak* (fur hat). Women prefer silver jewelry to gold because silver is considered a color closer to white, and white brings good luck. Silver also protects against misfortune.

Traditional costumes are embroidered in nature motifs such as ram horns and floral patterns. White, ruffled, bell-sleeved blouses and long, full skirts are commonly covered by velvet aprons and close-fitting short or long vests. A special hat might be added for certain celebrations.

Although men wear Western-style clothing, they include the traditional white wool pointed hat (*kolpak*) for protection against the elements and as a sign of patriotism. An adult *kolpak* has a folded-up velvet black, white, or brown brim; a boy's brim is green or blue. The white surface is embroidered with nature motifs. Each *kolpak* has a tassel at its peak; the peak represents the mountains. Men do not buy a *kolpak* but receive it as a gift; the higher the peak, the more honored the recipient. In winter, older men might wear a *tumak*. A *tebetei* (fur hat decorated with a fox tail) was once worn by wealthy and honored men. Today this expensive style is becoming more popular.

CUSTOMS AND COURTESIES

Greetings

The standard Kyrgyz greeting is *Salamatsyzby* (Hello). Adult men might use the Islamic greeting S*alaam Aleikum* (Peace be upon you). Gentlemen often shake hands. Only women in business circles shake hands. Traditionally, a Kyrgyz woman bows to older men, especially if they are her husband's relatives. Older women greet children with kisses or a handshake. These customs are not as prevalent in cities as in villages.

When addressing an older person, a Kyrgyz might follow the Russian tradition of using the first name plus a patrynomic (father's first name with the suffix *-ovich* for a son or *-ovna* for a daughter). In villages, and increasingly in urban areas, Kyrgyz customs are replacing the Russian practice. In this case, a person is greeted by his or her father's first name, followed by *uulu* (son) or *kyzy* (daughter) and the person's own given name: *Kadyrbek uulu Ulan* (Kadyrbek's son, Ulan). In addition, Kyrgyz traditionally greet elders with special titles: *Ejay* (older sister) and *Agai* or *Baikay* (both mean older brother). The title comes at the end: *Salamatsyzby, Gulsara Ejay*. Young people address each other by first name.

Gestures

The Kyrgyz are modest in their gesturing. Pointing with the finger is impolite; one indicates direction with the entire hand. Public displays of affection, gum chewing, yelling, yawning, and blowing one's nose are considered impolite. At the end of a meal, Muslims might bring the hands together in a "prayer" position in front of the chest, raise them together to trace either side of an invisible circle, and return them to face level while saying *omen*.

Visiting

The Kyrgyz socialize at home or in the office but rarely at a restaurant. Homes are either modest-sized single-family dwellings or apartments. However, some Kyrgyz live in *bohz ooi* (yurtas, i.e., round tents) while tending their horses or sheep. Regardless of the home's structure, arriving guests remove their shoes before entering. They put on a visitor's pair of *tapochki* (slippers). It is impolite to visit before noon. Invited guests take a gift of candy, cake, flowers, or liquor. The most highly honored individual in a group is seated farthest from, but facing, the entrance.

Hosts serve several rounds of tea in *piallas* (bowls). To indicate one is finished, one covers the empty bowl with the hand. Bread or *borsak* (fried dough) is also usually served. It is impolite not to offer and not to accept at least a little bread. The hostess often does not drink tea or eat a meal with guests so she may properly care for them. When departing, one politely says *Kosh* (Good-bye) and *Rakhmat* (Thank you).

Eating

Kyrgyz families eat three meals a day together as schedules allow. Breakfast consists of black tea with sugar, honey or *varaynya* (preserves) and bread with butter. Lunch is a hot meal traditionally consisting of meat, rice or noodles, bread, and vegetables. Dinner is similar to lunch. Every meal begins and ends with several cups of tea (*chai*).

The typical home has no dining room; instead, a folded table is stored in the living room until needed. Everyone eats from a common plate in the center of the table. Each may have a small individual plate on which to place food. When guests are present, the hostess may place food on their plates. The host or special guest sits at the head of the table facing the door. The eldest guests sit closest to this position while the hostess sits nearest the kitchen. This seating pattern is retained even if the people eat seated on velvet floor mats, such as when guests are present. Women sit with legs tucked to the side or folded under, covered by a skirt. In villages, people often eat *pa kirghizi* (without utensils). Prior to the meal, the hostess pours warm water over guests' hands and into a bowl; they dry their hands on a provided towel. If a sheep is slaughtered for the meal, only the men eat the head (although children might receive the ears, a reminder to "listen" to their parents). Drinking and toasting (with the right hand only) are part of most meals.

LIFESTYLE

Family

Although families were once quite large, a nuclear family today customarily has two or three children. The youngest son is responsible for the welfare of his aging parents. When he marries, he and his wife move into his parents' home for at least six months. During this time, the new bride is instructed in cooking, cleaning, and hosting. Kyrgyz women are expected to raise children, maintain the house, and prepare for guests. More women are taking full-time jobs and assuming roles and habits traditionally reserved for men: driving, socializing in public, and so on. Although male and female roles slowly continue to change, a Kyrgyz man is to provide financially for his family. He is the undisputed head of the family and presides over social gatherings.

Dating and Marriage

Young people meet at schools, bars, concerts, and family parties. Another meeting point is Lake Issyk-kul. Dating prior to marriage is brief. Marriages were once arranged by the prospective parents. To solidify the agreement, the boy's parents would present earrings to the future bride and later give her parents a *kalym*, a large sum of money. A potential groom could kidnap an unwilling bride. She would be taken to the boy's home, and if his mother placed a scarf on her head, she was betrothed and had no voice in the decision. Today people choose their own spouses.

Wedding customs include *kalym*, *kiyit* (the exchange of clothes between the relatives of the bride and groom), *sepo* (a dowry for the bride), and *opko chaboo* (a sheep sacrificed for the meal). During the civil ceremony, the groom's mother places a white scarf on the bride's head. A common village ritual is *kyz kuumai* (chasing the bride). The bride is provided the fastest horse and must try to outrace the groom. If she outraces him, she can "choose" not to marry him.

Diet

Common Kyrgyz dishes include *plove* (rice with lamb, carrots, onions, and garlic), *manty* (steamed meat and onions sealed in dough patties), and *beshbarmak* (noodles and meat eaten with the fingers). The staple grain is rice. Also important are various breads, such as *byolko* (dark, long loaf) and *tahngdyr nahn* (flat bread). Desserts may be bread with *varaynya*, cakes, chocolate, or cookies.

Seasonal produce includes tomatoes, cucumbers, carrots, cabbage, apples, grapes, and melons. Nuts (especially walnuts) are readily available.

Islamic traditions forbid pork and alcohol; most families abstain from the forbidden meat but often not from the use of alcohol. Black tea (green in the south), the most popular drink, is called "red tea" (*kyzyl chai*), and is always drunk hot with heavy doses of sweeteners. *Kumiss* (fermented mare's milk) is sold at roadside stands in the spring and summer.

Recreation

Kyrgyz people enjoy outdoor activities. They recreate on Lake Issyk-kul, and hike, ski, or picnic in the mountains. Many families have *dachas* (mountain cottages) or go to health spas. Men fish and hunt. Older men play chess in parks. Soccer, wrestling, and basketball are popular sports. Traditional equestrian sports include *Aht Chabysh* (long-distance races), *Dzhorgosalysh* (pacers' races, popular for betting), *Oodarysh* (wrestling on horseback), *Tyin Enmei* (falconry on horseback), and *Kyz dzharysh* (girls' races).

Urban Kyrgyz gather to eat, drink, and talk. Especially in Bishkek, they enjoy ballet, drama, concerts, movies, the circus, art galleries, and historic museums. Most homes have televisions. Traditional music is played on the *komuz* (small guitar-like instrument) and *temir-komuz* or *oz-komuz* (mouth harp). On very special occasions, Kyrgyz gather in a yurta to listen to storytellers recite lengthy passages of the *Manas* epic.

Holidays

Kyrgyzstan's public holidays include New Year's Day (1 January), International Women's Day (8 March), International Workers' Day (1 May), Constitution Day (5 May), World War II Victory Day (9 May), and Independence Day (31 August). Christian holidays include Christmas (7 January) and Easter. Muslim holidays are *Nooruz* (New Year), *Orozo Ait* (*Ramadan* feast), and *Kurban Ait* (Day of Remembrance), all set by the lunar calendar.

Commerce

Businesses are open daily from 8:00 A.M. to 5:00 P.M. Food stores are open from 7:00 A.M. to 8:00 P.M. Bazaars open during the summer an hour earlier than food stores. Many women shop daily for some items like bread and milk. On weekends, they shop at bazaars for dry goods, meat and produce, clothing, hardware, housewares, and more. Retail prices vary between small shops, portable sidewalk stands, and the state department store (*Tsum*).

SOCIETY

Government

Kyrgyzstan is a democratic republic divided into six oblasts (political regions). The 1993 constitution guarantees basic human rights. President Akayev is head of state. Prime Minister Apas Djumagulov is the nominal head of government. The 150-member *Jogorku Kenesh* (Parliament) has two houses: the House of Deputies and the House of Representatives. More than two hundred political parties are active in Kyrgyzstan. Among the main registered parties are *Erkin Kyrgyzstan* (The Free Kyrgyzstan), Asaba, Party of National Renaissance, Party of Kyrgyz Communists, National Republican Party, *Ata-Meken* (Motherland), Agrarian Party, and Social Democrats of Kyrgyzstan. The voting age is 18.

Economy

Kyrgyzstan is making the difficult transition to a free-market economy. Restructuring has been slow and painful. Industrial output has declined sharply, and the economy depends largely on the export of cotton and tobacco. Industry (manufacturing, mining, and electricity) is centered in the north, while agriculture dominates in the south. Mined commodities include gold, antimony, mercury, uranium, coal, and natural gas. Despite its difficulties, Kyrgyzstan has been successful at controlling inflation and privatizing industries. As foreign investment increases and reforms succeed, the economy may reverse its negative growth in the next few years. Real gross domestic product per capita is $2,850. The monetary unit is the *som*.

Transportation and Communication

People prefer travel by private truck or car, but fuel is expensive. Public buses run in and between cities but are not always reliable or comfortable. North-south travel is difficult due to the terrain. Villagers continue to ride horses or use horse-drawn carts. Communications systems are improving, but many people only have access to public phones at post offices. There are several newspapers and radio stations in Kyrgyzstan. In addition to local television programming, broadcasts are received from neighboring countries.

Education

Education is highly valued. Children attend primary and secondary schools between ages six and seventeen. Kindergartens are also available. After secondary school, qualified students may attend college or a technical school for three or four years. The Education Law of 1992 encouraged the training of specialists to meet the needs of the new economy. By 1994, the number of higher education institutions had doubled to 24. Four of seven universities are in Bishkek, including the Kyrgyz State National University (with the Kyrgyz-American School of Business, Law, and the Humanities). The adult literacy rate is 97 percent.

Health

The free public health-care network is poorly equipped and staff are underpaid. Private hospitals and clinics provide better but expensive care. Popular alternative health care includes acupuncture, herbal medicines, and homeopathic treatments. Mineral waters, thermal springs, and sauna baths are common health preventatives. The infant mortality rate is 46 per 1,000. Life expectancy averages 68 years.

FOR THE TRAVELER

Although no immunizations are required, U.S. citizens need passports and visas to enter Kyrgyzstan. Upon arrival, travelers must register with the Passport Department of the region where they will be staying. Tourism opportunities are limited but improving. Water is not potable. For information, contact the Embassy of the Kyrgyz Republic, 1511 K Street NW, Suite 707, Washington, DC 20005; phone (202) 347–3732.

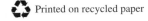 Printed on recycled paper

CULTURGRAM '97™

Laos

(Lao People's Democratic Republic)

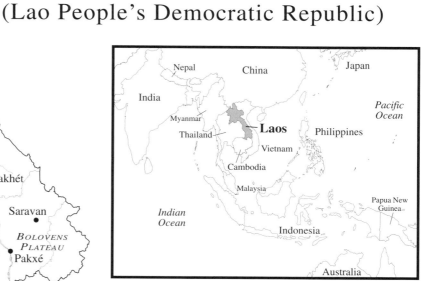

Boundary representations not necessarily authoritative.

BACKGROUND

Land and Climate

Laos covers 91,430 square miles (236,800 square kilometers), is slightly larger than Utah, and is one of the few landlocked countries of Southeast Asia. The Mekong River defines most of its western border and is important for transportation, although rapids make it impassable in some areas. It is also a source of fish and hydroelectric power. Steep mountains cover the north and northeast, which are only sparsely inhabited by ethnic minorities. Tropical forests are home to hardwoods (mahogany, teak, etc.) and lush foliage, as well as elephants, tigers, monkeys, and other animals. Most people live in areas such as the Plain of Jars, the Vientiane Plain, and the Bolovens Plateau. Laos has a tropical monsoon climate with a dry season from December to April and rain from May to November. It is always humid. Temperatures can get quite cold, but not freezing, in the northern mountains. In plateau areas, temperatures range from 57°F to 93°F (14–34°C), with January the coolest month and April the hottest.

History

People have lived and kingdoms flourished on Laotian territory for thousands of years, but written records are scarce for the era prior to the establishment of the first Laotian kingdom (Lan Xang) in 1353. Under Faaz Ngoum, it became a major regional trading center. Over the centuries, the kingdom struggled with neighbors for control of trade routes. Lan Xang lasted until 1713, when its three provinces split into separate principalities. These three small kingdoms eventually came under the influence of Siam (now Thailand). The French gained control of parts of Siam in the late 1800s, and the three Laotian principalities of Vientiane, Louang Prabang, and Champassak became a French protectorate in 1893.

The Japanese occupied Laos during World War II, but the French returned in 1946. Internal rule over a united Laos was granted to the King of Louang Prabang (King Sisavong Vong) in 1949, but Laos was still part of the French union. With the 1954 signing of the Geneva Convention, Laos became independent.

A northern leftist group, Pathet Lao, aided by North Vietnam, gained strength as a rival to the royalty during the 1950s and eventually took control of much of the country. Upon a cease-fire, the Pathet Lao became part of a 1962 coalition government, headed by Prince Souvanna Phouma. The Pathet Lao withdrew from that coalition in 1964. By then, Laos was becoming more and more involved in the war in Vietnam. After the Pathet Lao aligned with the Viet Minh (Communists), they fought against the government until a 1973 cease-fire. The Pathet Lao briefly participated in a new coalition but then took control of the country in 1975, sending the royalty into exile and declaring the Lao People's Democratic Republic. Kaysone Phomvihan, leader of the Pathet Lao, became president of the country.

The United States heavily bombed Laotian territory in the early 1970s in an effort to stop the flow of troops and supplies along the Ho Chi Minh Trail that ran from North Vietnam through Laos and into South Vietnam. This bombing left permanent craters in many villages. Since 1989, however, strained relations with the United States have improved.

When Phomvihan died in 1992, Nouhak Phoumsavan took the position of president and general secretary of the Communist Party. He tried to liberalize the economy to attract aid and investment. Personal freedoms and the political structure, however, were not liberalized. In 1996, the prime minister, General Khamtai Siphandon, consolidated his power and is now effectively in control of the government.

THE PEOPLE
Population
The population of Laos is 4.8 million and is growing at 2.8 percent annually. About 45 percent is younger than age 15. Less than one-fifth of the population resides in urban areas. The Lao government encourages population growth because it believes more people would help Laos meet future labor needs. Laos is an ethnically diverse country. Its 68 known ethnic groups are classified into a few major categories, which vary depending on who is defining the categories. Basically, the largest group is known collectively as the *Thaiz Lao* (including *Lao Lu* and *Lao Lum*). These are ethnic lowland Lao related to the Thais of Thailand. They comprise 50 percent of the population. The *Lao Tai* are distinguished from others in the country by their non-Buddhist beliefs; they make up perhaps 20 percent of the population. The *Phutheung* or *Lao Tchaen* are the various mountain peoples that generally are not related to other Laotians; some figures indicate they may comprise 15 percent of the total population. Percentages for other groups are difficult to assess. The *Lao Theung* (midland Lao) are Melanesians and considered descendants of the area's earliest settlers. The *Lao Soung* (highland Lao) include the ethnic groups of *Meo* and *Man*, and have their origins in southwestern China.

The country's Human Development Index (0.420) ranks Laos 138th out of 174 nations. Adjusted for women, the index (0.405) ranks Laos 96th out of 130 nations. Most people lack access to a useful education, economic opportunities, or quality health care that would provide a long, productive life.

Language
The official language is Lao, the native language of the *Lao Lum*, which is used in all official communications and taught in schools. Other main languages include Thai, Hmong, and Lao Thung. Some ethnic minority languages have never been codified in written form, but at least 30 languages have been documented. Lao tongues are tonal. Writing is phonetic and in a unique script. Transliteration into Latin letters differs widely and has not been standardized. Each letter makes either a neutral, high, or base tone. A small percentage of older people and those who attended high school prior to 1975 speak French, which has been the language of international commerce in the past. Some English is spoken.

Religion
Unlike other Communist lands, Laos did not suffer under a ban on religion. But the culture of communism did destroy much of the culture's Buddhist heritage. Theravada Buddhism is still the dominant cultural force in Laos, but a minority of people actually practice Buddhism in its purest form. The *Thaiz Lao* commonly worship at a pagoda, seek counsel from the *Bikkhu* (priest), or dress in Buddhist costumes for festivals. Many Laotians are not religious at all or consider Buddhism to be old-fashioned. Despite this, Buddhist (sometimes mixed with Hindu) rites and traditions are part of everyday life in Laos. Buddhism's four pillar virtues (*Brahma Vihara*) are *metta* (loving kindness and practice of goodwill), *karunna* (compassion), *mudhita* (sympathetic or altruistic joy), and *uppekkha* (equanimity). To cultivate these virtues, one must practice certain codes of conduct. Buddhism emphasizes the prevention of sin, not the cleansing of it.

Each ethnic Lao village has its own *wat* (temple), which is the focal point of village festivities and rituals. Several of the most famous *wats* in Vientiane have been turned into museums. It is common for villagers to take food to monks in a daily ritual where the monks do not look at the donors. Male donors remove their sandals. Women kneel as monks pass by in a procession to collect food offerings. Many boys spend some portion of their lives living as monks.

The *Phutheung* practice animism, which emphasizes a reverence for all living things. *Phu* means "spirits," and the *Phutheung* believe all objects are inhabited by spirits; they also venerate their ancestors. Each village has a *xemia* (medicine man) responsible for performing ritual sacrifices to the village spirits and for curing ailments.

General Attitudes
The Lao are a frank, open, and friendly people. They also have a strongly developed sense of courtesy and respect. It is considered very bad taste to publicly criticize a person since it results in a loss of face within the community. Necessary criticisms and suggestions should be made within a general context to avoid placing blame or shame on any individual. *Bo pen nyang* (Never mind) is a common expression that characterizes Laotians' feelings toward life. Life should be enjoyed at the moment; problems are not taken so seriously as to disrupt this enjoyment. Given the hardships people face in the country, this can be an invaluable attitude. Loyalty to family and friends is important. Showing anger or disappointment in public is inappropriate. Humility, modesty, and patience are the most admired characteristics.

Personal Appearance
Lao women wear Western-style blouses with colorful calf-length, sarong-style skirts (*phaaz silz*) made of locally handwoven materials in multicolor designs and fastened with a silver link belt. Urban women wear Western-style clothing. Some rural women wear short skirts with sleeveless blouses. Men wear trousers with casual, open-neck, short-sleeve shirts. Some rural men omit shirts when wearing a traditional sarong (*phaaz kham maaz*). Many men throughout the country wear T-shirts and shorts. Both men and women usually wear sandals. Formal clothing for men is a white, long-sleeve shirt with long pants. For women, it is a silk *phaaz silz* and special blouse. Traditional ethnic dress varies widely in each region, with color choices, headdress styles, and accessories differing the most.

CUSTOMS AND COURTESIES
Greetings
The formal greeting among Lao people is the *Pranobnom* or *Hveyz* (meaning "salute"), which involves placing one's hands together in a prayer position at chest level but not touching the body. The higher the hands, the greater the sign of

respect, although they should never be held above the level of the nose. At the same time, one might say *Sabaydi* (a shortened term for "May you have happy health"). The receiver can return the same word or *Hveyz Bra Theun* (Salute to the Lord Buddha). One might add a slight bow to show respect for persons of higher status or age. The gesture is not only an expression of greeting but also of thanks or regret. The *Hveyz* was technically abolished in 1947, so public officials do not use it, but it is appreciated especially by elders. Civil servants nod slightly; they shake hands with Westerners.

Informally, Lao may shake hands with members of the same sex or touch one another on the arm (never the shoulder) and greet with *Pey sey maa?* (Where are you coming from?) or *Kin khow leo bor?* (Have you eaten?). If the reply to the latter is *Bor* (Not yet), the greeter may go looking for something to feed the person. The Lao address each other by first name. Children address adults by first name, prefaced by *Loung* or *Yaa Loung* (Mr.), *Naaz* or *Yaa Naaz* (Mrs.). *Yaa* comes from *Ad Yaa* (Master). Variations of these titles are used depending on the person's relative age to the speaker or the speaker's mother or father, as the case may be. People nearly always use professional or official titles to address individuals who hold such titles, including doctors, teachers, police officers, commissioners, village presidents, and so on.

When parting, one uses the same gesture that was used upon greeting. To use a different gesture is an insult. That is, to greet with a *Hveyz* but leave with a handshake is rude.

Gestures

To beckon, one waves all fingers with the palm facing down. To indicate direction, one points with the forefinger or entire hand; for long distances, one points in the direction with the hand above the head. In some rural areas, distance can be measured by how long it takes to smoke a cigarette (e.g., that village is two cigarettes away). Rural time might be measured by the position of the sun relative to a bamboo or coconut tree.

As in many Asian cultures, the head is considered the most sacred part of the body; the bottoms of the feet are the least sacred. One never touches a person's head without expressed permission or uses the foot to point at a person or a sacred object (pagoda, Buddha statue, etc.). Men and women rarely show affection in public. It is forbidden for a woman to touch a Buddhist monk. When conversing with an elder or superior, one stands at a distance of a few feet. To pass in front of someone between two people, one asks permission and bows slightly until past. When conversing with a superior, one crosses the hands rather than keeping them by one's side.

Visiting

Lao people visit one another often. They usually make arrangements in advance. In rural areas, this means sending their children ahead to announce the visit. The most appropriate times to visit are after mealtimes or on weekends. It is customary to remove one's shoes or sandals when entering a Buddhist temple or a private home. At Lao homes that are raised off the ground, people leave shoes or sandals at the bottom of the stairs. In a traditional home, a person sits on low seats or cushions on the floor. Men may sit with legs crossed or folded to one side. Women sit with legs off to the side. Hosts may serve tea or fruit to guests; refusing such refreshments is impolite. It is not customary to bring a gift when visiting, although gifts from first-time visitors or on special occasions are acceptable.

Eating

Ideally, the family eats all meals together and works together. Urban families with wage earners are excused from the ideal. Mealtimes vary according to chief occupation and whether a farmer's wife works with him in the fields. The Lao eat with a fork in the left hand and a spoon in the right. However, they eat glutinous rice with the fingers. Lao food, which is very spicy, is served on a communal dish (or the banana leaf in which the food was cooked) with meat and vegetables cut into bite-size pieces. In a traditional home, the meal is served while diners sit on a mat on the floor. Conversation usually is reserved for after a meal. As a sign of respect to a guest, the host and his family will not raise their heads above the level of the guest's head. Therefore, they may bring the food in a squat position so as not to offend guests.

LIFESTYLE

Family

The Lao have large, close-knit families, often with three generations living together. The eldest man is the patriarch of the family and represents the household at village meetings. The Lao have great respect for their parents and elders. Women care for and nurture their children, teach them, and help their fathers work for a living. Lao men say Lao women are the real bosses at home. Lao men are responsible for providing for the family and doing any heavy labor. Children are taught to honor their parents. Extended families share resources, especially if they live in the same village. Among the northern *Hmong*, a widow becomes the wife of her late husband's brother. In some areas, men will marry younger sisters of deceased wives in order to maintain family alliances. It is an honor to have children (four are preferred) and a social disgrace to be without them. Some men have more than one wife, often marrying younger siblings of their first wife.

Dating and Marriage

Young people are relatively free to choose marriage partners. By tradition, which is still followed in some rural areas, a future groom must help the bride's family for three rice harvest seasons. This allows him to become well acquainted with the family before the wedding. Marriage might be established by elopement, living together, or a more elaborate wedding ritual. The groom gives a gift to the bride's parents as thanks for raising her properly. For the first few years of married life, the couple lives with the wife's family, until her first child is about one year old. The couple may then establish their own home or move in with the husband's family.

Diet

Sticky or glutinous rice is the staple of the Lao diet. *Lap* (sautéed buffalo innards mixed with onions, lemon grass, and spices, and served with a rice-flour sauce) is a typical Lao food. Rice is served with chili sauce or a spicy fermented fish sauce. *Ork paa* is a hot fish soup. *Mok paa* is fish cooked in banana leaf. *Pingz kayx* is grilled poultry, while *mok kayx* is poultry cooked in a banana leaf. Most foods are hot and spicy. Urban families eat more stir-fry and meat than villagers.

Beverages include coffee and tea. Cultivated foods are supplemented with wild fruits (papaya, mango, coconut, tamarind, banana) and vegetables from the forest as well as game, such as deer. Highlanders grow dry rice and depend on food from the forests.

Recreation

Popular sports for men are soccer, volleyball, and basketball. *Kartorz*, played by trying to keep a rattan ball in the air without using the hands, is the Lao national game. Women and girls do not play sports, being entirely too busy caring for the family. Whole families participate in dances at community celebrations. Traditional music is played on a *khene* (a type of bamboo flute). Villagers enjoy playing music, telling stories, and visiting each other. Urban Lao are more likely to dance at discos, watch videos, or listen to the radio.

Holidays

Official holidays include International New Year (1 January); Army Day (20 January); *Pi Mai*, the Lao New Year, governed by the lunar calendar; Labor Day (1 May); National Day (2 December); and *Bun That Luang*, a festival at a temple housing a relic of Buddha. Religious events are celebrated with a *basi* or *sukhwan*, a celebration involving offerings, food, and rice wine. In a string-tying ceremony, people wish good health and prosperity to friends by tying a string on the wrist.

Commerce

Urban office hours generally run from 9:00 A.M. to noon and from 2:00 to 5:00 P.M. Officially, government offices are also open Saturday mornings. Most shops are small, family-run businesses. They are open according to the wishes of the owners, typically until late afternoon. Villagers usually provide for their own basic needs, but they also sell crops and game for money to buy goods they cannot otherwise obtain.

SOCIETY

Government

The Lao People's Democratic Republic is a Communist state. The executive branch consists of a president as head of state and a prime minister (or chairman of the Council of Ministers) as head of government. In 1996, Siphandon added the office of vice president and named Sisavat Keobounphan to the post. The 85-seat Supreme People's Assembly is the nominally elected legislature, for which the next scheduled elections are in 1998. The body has no real legislative authority, as the Lao People's Revolutionary Party (LPRP) controls all government functions. All Laotians may vote at age 18.

Economy

Agriculture employs the majority of Laotians. The main crop is rice, but corn, vegetables, tobacco, coffee, and other foods are also grown. The government is attempting to expand industrial activities to tap the many resources of Laos, which include timber (58 percent of the land is covered with forests), gypsum, tin, and gold. Some private enterprise is also being encouraged. Laos exports electricity, wood products, coffee, and tin.

The economy depends heavily on foreign aid (mostly from Western nations) and must import manufactured goods, medicine, and machinery. Policies to attract foreign investment have largely benefited investors or the LPRP, and success has been limited. Real gross domestic product per capita is estimated at $1,760, but wealth is concentrated in urban areas. Subsistence farmers do not earn much of an income. Inflation is about 10 percent and unemployment is 20 percent. The currency is the new *kip* (NK).

Transportation and Communication

The transportation system is poorly developed. Most rural roads are unpaved; many are impassable in the rainy season. Public transportation is limited, and there is no rail service. Most people walk, but some have bicycles and motorbikes. Goods are transported over two land routes to seaports in Vietnam and Thailand. The Mekong River is navigable for two-thirds of its territory. Air travel is limited, with access dependent on weather conditions and confined to provincial capitals. Communications systems are also poorly developed, with limited electricity, few rural telephones, and few radio stations. Television is broadcast to Vientiane and Louang Prabang.

Education

The state provides free education for eleven years (ages six to seventeen), including five years of mandatory primary school and six years of secondary school. However, the system is inadequate. Many rural areas lack schools or paid teachers, and enrollment rates are low. Other children are kept on the farm to work. Some families distrust the government and do not send their children to school. Schools also lack materials and books. The adult literacy rate is 54 percent.

Health

Health standards are poor, as medical facilities in Laos are inadequate and almost nonexistent in rural areas. Life expectancy averages between 50 and 54 years, and the infant mortality rate is 99 per 1,000. Each province has a hospital, but these are poorly supplied and staffed. Malaria, trachoma, typhoid, hepatitis, tuberculosis, and dysentery are problematic in many areas. Water must be boiled before drinking.

FOR THE TRAVELER

Travelers need a passport and visa to enter Laos. Visas are granted only on proof of sufficient funds and onward passage. They should be applied for well in advance of one's trip. It is advisable to register with the police upon arrival. All items and services must be paid for with cash. Facilities outside the capital are underdeveloped. Travelers found distributing any type of religious material may be arrested and deported. Do not take photographs of military installations, property, or equipment; cameras will be confiscated.

For health advisories, call the U.S. Centers for Disease Control International Travelers' Hotline at (404) 332–4559. Although travel accommodations are often primitive, Laos offers unique experiences to travelers. The people are friendly and rural areas offer a wonderful glimpse at traditional Asian culture. For more information, contact the Embassy of the Lao People's Democratic Republic, 2222 S Street NW, Washington, DC 20008; phone (202) 332–6416.

Republic of
Lebanon

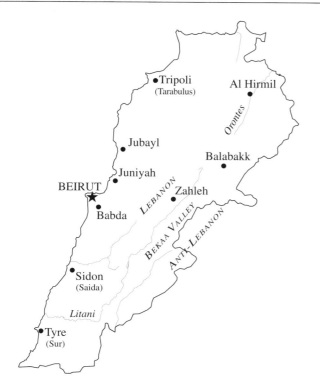

Boundary representations not necessarily authoritative.

BACKGROUND

Land and Climate

Covering 4,015 square miles (10,400 square kilometers), Lebanon is slightly smaller than Connecticut. A low coastal plain dominates the west but gives way to the Lebanon Mountains in the east. Nestled between the Lebanon Mountains and the Anti-Lebanon Mountains on the Syrian border is the fertile Bekaa Valley. Lebanon is home not only to its more famous cedar, pine, and cypress trees but also to olive, citrus, apple, and banana trees. The climate is influenced by the Mediterranean. Winters are mild, though wet, and summers are hot and dry. In Beirut, the average temperature in winter is 57°F (14°C) and in summer is 84°F (29°C). It is cooler in the mountains in the summer. Some winter snow falls at the higher elevations.

History

A small part of modern Lebanon, known as Mount Lebanon, was a Maronite enclave in the vast Ottoman Empire, which ruled much of the area from the 16th century to the beginning of the 20th century. Mount Lebanon and all of Syria became a French protectorate when the French and British drove the Ottomans out of the area during World War I. Lebanon became a republic in 1926, but French troops did not withdraw until 1946. Although Christians formed a slight majority of the population, other religions also had significant numbers. Therefore, the government was established to represent the major religious groups. The president was to be a Maronite Christian, the prime minister a Sunni Muslim, and the president of Parliament a *Shi'a* (Shiite) Muslim. All religious groups were to receive representation in the National Assembly according to their numbers.

The Christians refused to acknowledge any census after 1932, when they had a majority. This, along with social disparities between Christians and Muslims, led to internal tension and strife. A large number of Palestinian refugees from lands occupied by Israel settled in Lebanon in 1948 and 1967, further complicating internal problems. Civil war erupted in 1975. A 1976 cease-fire maintained a partial peace until 1982, when Israel invaded Lebanon and occupied the area south of Beirut. During a siege of Beirut, a multinational peacekeeping force (MNF) was sent to evacuate members of the Palestine Liberation Organization (PLO) from the city. Except for a brief period, the MNF remained until 1984.

Civil war erupted again in 1983. From 1987 to 1990, fighting was heavy and thousands died. The government could not operate normally or sponsor elections for Parliament, last elected in 1972. Amin Gamayel became president after Bashir Gamayel was assassinated in 1982. He served until 1988, when General Michel Aoun took control of the government. Aoun, a Maronite, ordered Parliament dissolved in 1989. However, Parliament did not recognize his authority and elected René Moawad president. He was assassinated a few days later by Aoun loyalists. Elias Hrawi was then elected president of Lebanon. Aoun was dismissed, but he continued to battle rival Christian forces.

Aoun finally surrendered in October 1990 and eventually received asylum in France. Under a peace accord, militias withdrew from Beirut and the Lebanese Army established control. A "Green Line" that had divided the city into East and West Beirut was removed and businesses began reopening, despite the devastation. By mid-1991, most militias throughout the country had disarmed and recognized the government's authority. Parliamentary elections were held in 1992. A treaty of mutual friendship was signed with Syria; it provides for joint institutions to govern economic, defense, and foreign policy issues. Syrian troops remain in Lebanon. With the 15-year civil war behind them, the people of Lebanon began the enormous task of reconstruction under the leadership of Prime Minister Rafik al-Hariri. In October 1995, President Hrawi's term was extended by three years, putting off elections until at least 1998.

THE PEOPLE

Population

Lebanon's population of 3.7 million is growing at 2.1 percent annually. Beirut, the capital, is the largest city and Tripoli is the next largest. About 85 percent of all people live in urban areas. The Bekaa Valley is filled with small, rural villages. About 95 percent of the people are Arabs and 4 percent are Armenians. Armenians immigrated early in the century to escape Ottoman persecution in their homeland. They live mostly in Beirut. Lebanon's Human Development Index (0.675) ranks it 101st out of 174 nations. People lack access to resources that allow them to pursue personal goals, but this will change as the economy improves.

Language

Arabic is the official language and is spoken by all. Lebanese Arabic, a dialect used in casual conversation, is similar to Syrian and Jordanian Arabic. Educated Lebanese often speak French and English. Members of the Armenian minority speak Armenian and some of them speak Turkish. It is common for people to speak more than one language, even three or four.

Religion

Lebanese society is based on religion. All citizens carry an identity card on which their religion is listed. While more than half the people were Christian two decades ago, Christians only account for 25 percent of the population today. The largest Christian church is the Maronite Church, an Eastern-rite religion that accepts the Roman Catholic pope. There are ten other legally recognized Christian churches, most of them Catholic- or Orthodox-related groups. Most of the rest of the population is Islamic. The largest groups are the Shiite Muslims and Sunni Muslims. The Druze, a group that broke away from Islam in the Middle Ages, is another significant faction. Unlike other religious groups, the Druze do not have an accessible body of scripture; traditions are passed by word of mouth. Consequently, little is known about the religion. There is a small Jewish minority.

General Attitudes

Lebanon has been deeply influenced by its long association with the West. At the same time, traditional values and attitudes continue to be important, creating a unique society. Compared to life in North America, life in Lebanon is fairly relaxed and lived at a slower pace. People tend to care more about personal relationships than time schedules. Also, while people are involved in local politics, personal relationships and family ties are often much more important than political ideologies in determining loyalties. Wealth, power, and prestige are highly admired.

On a personal level, the average Lebanese desires to have a family, own a home, and pursue economic prosperity. The Lebanese are very proud of their culture, heritage, and country. With an entrepreneurial spirit, a background in international finance, and a great desire to rebuild their nation, the Lebanese are confident in their ability to restore Lebanon to its former status as a modern and progressive Arab country.

Personal Appearance

Western-style clothing is the standard in Lebanese cities. Traditional rural Muslim women may wear a *chador* (long dress that covers the entire body) over their clothing. It is important to all people in Lebanon to be clean, neat, and stylish. Conservative suits and modest attire are most appropriate.

CUSTOMS AND COURTESIES

Greetings

Lebanese people take social amenities seriously. When one meets a stranger, acquaintance, or friend, it is important to exchange greetings, to inquire about the person's health and family, and in general to make polite small talk before getting down to any specific business. Handshakes are common for both men and women. Upon meeting or parting, close friends and relatives often kiss the air as they brush both cheeks. Urban residents use this custom with either gender, but in rural areas, only members of the same sex might greet in this manner—unless the two people are related. Personal space is somewhat limited and people may stand close in conversation.

Titles such as "Doctor" or "Professor" are used consistently where appropriate. In Arabic, these titles are commonly used with a person's first name, but Lebanese are also accustomed to hearing titles in English and French. Friends use each other's titles in meetings and act more formally than they would in other situations. The most common greeting is *Marhaba* (Hello), but urban dwellers might also use the French *Bonjour* (Good day), *Salut* (Hello), an English *Hi,* or the Arabic *Keef halik?* (How are you?) for women or *Keef halak?* for men.

Gestures

The Lebanese signify "yes" with one downward nod and "no" with an upward movement of the head or raised eyebrows, sometimes accompanied by clicking the tongue. One can also express "no" by shaking the index finger from side to side, palm facing out. Pointing or beckoning with the index finger is impolite. To beckon another person, one waves all fingers with the palm facing down. For many, it is offensive to pass or receive objects with the left hand. The right hand or both hands are preferred. People may cross the legs at the knee, but crossing an ankle over a knee risks offending any person toward whom the bottom of the foot points. One points the soles of the shoes or feet down toward the earth and not at another person. Eye contact is important. Men never curse in front of women. Public displays of affection, even between married couples, are not acceptable.

Visiting

Hospitality is a prized tradition in Lebanon. People feel honored to have guests in their homes, and they also enjoy visiting others. Relatives and close friends visit each other often and without prior arrangement. It is generally accepted that the formalities of calling ahead do not apply to people who are very close. Hosts usually serve tea or coffee to guests. Etiquette requires that such an offer be accepted. If invited to a meal, guests might bring flowers, a plant, a special dessert, or something for the home.

Guests invited for lunch generally do not leave until after 4:00 P.M., and dinner guests are expected to stay the entire evening. It is extremely impolite to leave immediately after eating. If a person has been visiting all evening and is about to leave, but another person comes to visit, it would be an insult to the newly arrived person for the first person to leave. Even if the new guest is visiting only the host, the previous guest stays to talk for a few minutes to show he is not leaving just because the new person arrived. Arguments about local and national politics are inappropriate, and the Lebanese do not ask about a person's religion. That would be considered an attempt to categorize or prejudge someone.

Eating

Whenever possible, the family eats meals (especially the main meal) together. Mealtime is an important time for family discussion. At the end of the meal, diners often praise the person's hands (usually the mother's) that prepared the food. Unspoken rules of hospitality require the host to make guests feel completely welcome. Offering food is one way to do this and Lebanese hosts are insistent that their guests eat—even if guests refuse the food initially. Because it is often customary to refuse an offer a few times before accepting it, the host assumes the offer will eventually be accepted.

Western eating utensils usually are used for eating European food or rice dishes. Lebanese tend to eat European foods part of the week and Middle Eastern foods the rest of the week. Except for rice, Middle Eastern foods are eaten either with the right hand, broken pieces of bread, or lettuce. Bread and lettuce serve as scoops. For example, *tabboule*—a popular salad made with parsley, minced onions, diced tomatoes, and other vegetables—is eaten with a lettuce scoop. Lettuce is not part of the salad. Meals served on formal occasions often consist of many courses and can last several hours.

LIFESTYLE

Family

Lebanese families tend to be strong and closely knit. Cousins and other relatives are expected to have close personal relationships. In fact, cousins generally are as close as brothers and sisters. Urban families usually are smaller than rural families. Discipline is strict, and children show respect for their parents and other elders. The father is head of the family. Mothers generally take care of the home and children. Many women who work outside the home do so out of necessity, not choice. Family loyalty is important. Unwritten class distinctions limit advancement opportunities for many people. The wealthy (traditionally Maronites, but now others as well) have access to fine education, good jobs, and luxuries, while the poor do not.

Urban residents often live in concrete apartment complexes, occupying units with between two and four bedrooms. More than one generation of a family may live in the same household. Rural people live in homes but also tend to share with other generations.

Dating and Marriage

Most urban Lebanese follow Western dating habits, although some conservative families may restrict dating to engaged couples. Rural Lebanese also continue to follow tradition, with families arranging some marriages. Because financial independence is customarily a prerequisite for marriage, men often wait to marry until their late twenties or early thirties. Women usually marry in their early twenties. Christian weddings are held in a church, while Muslims can be wed anywhere in the presence of a cleric and two witnesses. Among most Lebanese, wedding ceremonies are followed by dancing (bride and groom first), sometimes a belly dancing performance, and a dinner buffet. Before the buffet is opened to guests, the newlyweds cut the wedding cake and have a toast. Christians are generally opposed to divorce, although it is allowed by Islamic law for Muslims. Lebanese law provides for each religion to have a separate court system to handle matters of marriage, divorce, inheritance, and other such concerns, according to different customs.

Diet

The main meal of the day is eaten between noon and 3:00 P.M. This meal may last two or more hours. Specialties include various meat stews and some vegetarian dishes. A traditional meal for special occasions is the *meza*. It can be eaten at home or in a restaurant. A large group of people gather for this four- to five-hour event. Several dishes (maybe 20 or more) are all placed on the table; each person takes small portions from the dishes as often as desired. *Arak*, a traditional strong liquor, is served with Middle Eastern (not European) foods, except among devout Muslims. *Kibbeh* is a popular beef dish that can be baked, fried, or eaten raw.

Recreation

Soccer is the most popular Lebanese sport. People also enjoy swimming at the beaches in the summer. Movies are well attended. Skiing is a popular winter sport. One of the most common leisure activities is simply visiting friends and relatives. This is a common practice throughout the Arab world. Neglecting relationships by not visiting regularly constitutes improper social behavior. It is also an insult to the persons not being visited.

The Lebanese enjoy the cultural arts. Before the war, Beirut was a center for cosmopolitan Arabic culture. Music, literature, and other arts and entertainment are again part of the urban lifestyle. Night clubs and restaurants are popular evening destinations.

Holidays

National holidays include New Year's Day, Labor Day (1 May), and Independence Day (22 November). The end of the civil war is marked on 13 October. Christian holidays include Easter (Friday–Sunday), Assumption (15 August), and Christmas. Muslim holidays are set by the lunar calendar and include *Eid ul-Fitr,* the three-day feast at the end of the month of *Ramadan*. During *Ramadan*, Muslims go without food or water from sunrise to dusk and then eat in the evenings. The

Islamic New Year is followed later by *Eid ul-Adha* (Sacrifice Feast), held at the end of the pilgrimage to Makkah, Saudi Arabia. The prophet Muhammad's birthday is also celebrated.

Commerce

Most people work five days a week, but many work a partial day on Saturday. Business hours are generally from 8:00 A.M. to noon and 3:00 to 6:00 P.M., Monday through Friday. It is important to socialize before conducting business. When visiting someone's office, a person will likely be offered coffee or another drink (not alcohol), and the two will spend time getting to know each other or catching up on family news. Because Lebanon is a small country, many people know each other, so business is conducted on a personal basis. To establish business contacts, a person is far more successful if he is introduced by a mutual acquaintance. Lebanese business representatives often do not appreciate being approached by strangers.

SOCIETY

Government

Lebanon is a republic divided into five governorates. The Lebanese Parliament (a 128-seat National Assembly) has an equal number of seats reserved for Christians and Muslims. In addition, other major religious groups who fought in the war have representation in Parliament. By law, Lebanon's president must be a Maronite Christian, the prime minister must be a Sunni Muslim, and the parliamentary speaker must be a Shiite Muslim. This balance is necessary to promote harmony among the country's religions and was part of Lebanon's original constitution. The voting age is 21; all men, and women with an elementary education, are required to vote.

Economy

Post-war Lebanon is experiencing rapid economic growth and reconstruction. The growth rate in 1994 was 8 percent and in 1995 was 7 percent. Inflation has been lowered to less than 10 percent by aggressive fiscal policies. Lebanon has issued bonds and encouraged investment to finance reconstruction. Solidere is a company that is rebuilding central Beirut. The nationwide core development plan is called Horizon 2000. It focuses on rehabilitating Lebanon's physical infrastructure (including electricity, water, communications, and waste management) as well as rebuilding various structures and the Beirut International Airport. Horizon 2000, begun in 1995, is scheduled for completion in 2007.

Real gross domestic product per capita is estimated at $2,500. The lowest economic classes worry about being left behind in the reconstruction period, and it remains to be seen whether a strong middle class can emerge.

Foreign investment is essential for success, and it seems to be pouring into the main development projects. Financial and tourism industries seek to regain their former prominence. Agriculture is already regaining importance. Key crops include various fruits, grains, potatoes, tobacco, olives, and onions. The currency is the Lebanese pound (L£).

Transportation and Communication

Lebanon's transportation system is being reconstructed. New bridges and tunnels have been completed, as has a 15-kilometer highway in the south. A northern highway and a circular one around Beirut are being built, and a road between Beirut and Damascus, Syria, is planned. Passengers board buses from the back door and exit from either the middle or front doors. Taxis have red license plates. Many families own cars, and traffic can be heavy in urban areas.

The telephone network is being repaired, upgraded, and expanded. By the end of 1998, there should be one phone line for every three persons. Lebanon's media is active but somewhat controlled by a government ban on negative articles.

Education

Education is considered the key to a better life. The adult literacy rate is 90 percent. School reconstruction was one of the country's first priorities. To improve the current system, the government plans to implement mandatory attendance until age 14. Parents send their children to private schools whenever possible. These schools usually combine Lebanese and either French or U.S. American curricula to provide a stronger overall education. Children are strongly encouraged to prepare for college; those who go receive greater family respect than those who do not. Men are encouraged to study science and professional fields, leaving liberal arts more to women. Five major universities offer higher degrees, with several technical institutions offering training in carpentry, electronics, crafts, textiles, and so on. The American University of Beirut, founded in 1866, is the country's premier institution.

Health

Good medical care is generally available to all citizens, especially in urban areas. Public facilities exist, but people usually choose to pay more for higher quality care in private clinics and hospitals. Houses usually have two water systems: one for the kitchen that is chlorinated and safe to drink and one for the rest of the house that is not potable. The infant mortality rate is 38 per 1,000. Life expectancy averages between 67 and 73 years.

FOR THE TRAVELER

The U.S. State Department maintains a travel ban for Lebanon, citing the continued existence of terrorist groups that had previously held Western hostages. The ban is reconsidered every six months; for updates, call (202) 647–5225. Under the ban, no U.S. citizen may travel to Lebanon without permission. To apply for exemption from the ban, contact the Office of Passport Policy and Advisory Services, U.S. Department of State, 1111 19th Street NW, Suite 260, Washington, DC 20522–1705; phone (202) 955–0231. For additional information, you may also wish to contact the Embassy of Lebanon, 2560 28th Street NW, Washington, DC 20008; phone (202) 939–6300.

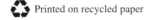 Printed on recycled paper

July 96

CULTURGRAM ’97

Kingdom of
Lesotho

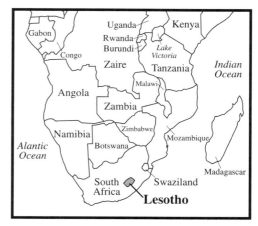

Boundary representations not necessarily authoritative.

BACKGROUND

Land and Climate

Lesotho (pronounced le-SUE-too) is a small, mountainous country slightly larger than Maryland and located in the east-central part of South Africa. Covering 11,718 square miles (30,350 square kilometers), it is completely surrounded by South Africa. Lesotho is divided into three basic geographic regions: the lowlands, which are about 5,000 feet (1,500 meters) above sea level; the foothills; and the highlands, which include peaks of 11,000 feet (3,300 meters). Most of Lesotho’s agricultural areas and the largest cities are located in the western lowlands.

Mountains dominate the east. The Drakensberg Mountains in southeastern Lesotho border South Africa and are divided from the Maluti Mountains by the Orange River. The Caledon River forms much of the western border. Because of its elevation, Lesotho does not have a tropical climate like other parts of southern Africa. Lesotho’s pleasant climate and sunny skies (averaging three hundred days a year) are increasingly inviting to tourists. Summer extends from November to January and winter is between May and July. Most rain falls from October to April. Temperatures average 90°F (32°C) in the summer and 40°F (4°C) in the winter. The highlands are cooler, and mountains receive snow in winter.

Lesotho’s waterways have potential for hydroelectric power and other economic development. A 30-year project (Lesotho Highlands Water Project) began in 1986. Six dams will be constructed to generate electricity, provide irrigation, improve highland access (with new roads), and store water for sale to South Africa.

History

The history of Lesotho, once called Basutoland, began when the Basotho nation was formed from the remnants of tribes scattered by Zulu and Matebele raids in the early 1800s. The people were united by Moshoeshoe (pronounced mo-SHWAY-shway) the Great, who ruled for almost 50 years (1823–70). During a series of wars with South Africa in the mid-1800s, Moshoeshoe lost considerable territory. After an appeal to Queen Victoria for protection against Boer (Dutch-origin farmers/settlers) advances, Britain annexed Basutoland as a territory in 1868.

Basutoland was temporarily annexed (1871) by the Cape Colony (one of the four colonies that later became South Africa), but the people revolted and became a British crown colony in 1884. Even when South Africa formed in 1909, Lesotho remained with the British. South Africa expected to someday annex the region but was never successful.

Internal self-rule was introduced in 1959 when a new constitution allowed for the first elected legislature. In October 1966, Basutoland was granted full independence from Great Britain as the Kingdom of Lesotho. When independence was granted, a constitutional monarchy was established, with Moshoeshoe II as head of state and Chief Leabua Jonathan as prime minister.

In 1970, Jonathan suspended the constitution and dissolved Parliament to keep his ruling party (Basutoland National Party or BNP) in power. Elections in 1985 were designed to favor the BNP and thus were boycotted by other parties. Jonathan's government was finally ousted by a bloodless coup in 1986. A six-man military council took over and technically vested power in the hands of the king. In reality, the king had little authority and the military junta ruled the country. After a power struggle, King Moshoeshoe II was forced into exile in 1990 and replaced by his son, King Letsie III, who was expected to be a puppet leader.

The junta promised to restore civilian rule by 1992, but it took another power struggle to bring about democratic elections in 1993. The BNP was heavily defeated by the Basotholand Congress Party (BCP). BCP leader Ntsu Mokhehle became prime minister.

Political stability remained elusive. Soldiers loyal to the BNP rioted in 1994. With military backing, King Letsie dissolved Parliament and the BCP government in August 1994. Intense pressure and domestic unrest forced him to reinstate Mokhehle's elected government a few weeks later. Letsie was able to have his father, who had returned to the country in 1993, reinstated as king in 1995. Peace was encouraged by South Africa and other countries in the region and a measure of stability was established. King Moshoehoe II died in a car accident in 1996. King Letsie returned to the throne under a pledge not to interfere with politics.

THE PEOPLE

Population

Lesotho's population of nearly two million is growing annually at 2.4 percent. The people of Lesotho are called Basotho (or Masotho for a single person). Their language is Sesotho. Between the 16th and 19th centuries, an influx of Sesotho-speaking peoples (refugees from tribal wars in surrounding areas) populated the region. This led to the development of the Basotho (or Sotho) ethnic group, giving Lesotho a fairly homogeneous population (nearly 80 percent Basotho). About 20 percent of the population is of Nguni origin (Xhosa and Baphuti tribes); some are San or Griqua. There are also small numbers of Europeans and Indians.

More than 40 percent of the people are younger than age 15. One-fifth of all people live in urban areas. The largest city, Maseru, has 110,000 inhabitants. Lesotho's Human Development Index (0.473) ranks it 131st out of 174 countries. This indicates that most people do not have adequate access to the resources necessary to pursue personal goals or enjoy a decent standard of living.

Language

Both English and Sesotho are official languages. Nearly all inhabitants speak Sesotho (also called "southern Sotho"), which is a Bantu language. English is used in business. It is also the language of school instruction after the fifth *standard* (grade). Therefore, most people are able to speak English. Zulu and Xhosa are also spoken by those who work in South Africa's mines or have contact with South Africa's Transkei region.

Religion

The Basotho are fairly religious; nearly 80 percent of the population is Christian. The three largest churches are the Roman Catholic Church, the Lesotho Evangelical Church, and the Anglican Church of Lesotho. Christian missions are scattered throughout the country. There is a small Muslim community in the north. About 20 percent of the population follows native belief systems. Some Christians continue to practice some native traditions or rites along with Christianity.

General Attitudes

The Basotho are a courteous, friendly people who are warm and hospitable to others. They laugh when embarrassed. Personal confrontation is avoided. Hence, Basotho often say what they think another person wants to hear or what would please the listener, even if reality or intentions might be otherwise. The Basotho treat the elderly with great respect. They are very proud of their families.

Lesotho's citizens are proud of their independent nation, even if it is surrounded by a larger, more powerful country. The Basotho are also proud of their native crafts, including weaving, pottery, and leather works. Individual shrewdness and independence are highly valued. Wealth is measured in cattle or sheep. People, especially in rural areas, tend to display a sort of passive optimism, believing that others will help them if they have trouble or that life will take care of itself. Except among the highly educated, one is considered to have reached one's potential upon fathering or bearing a child. The more children a man has, the more respected he is.

Personal Appearance

The Basotho dress in conservative, Western-style clothing but often cover it with a beautifully designed wool blanket, especially in rural areas. The blanket acts as a warm robe for cool evenings. Women tie it at the waist and men fold it on the shoulder when daytime temperatures warm up. Hats are common for men and women. People wear many types of hats, including U.S. American baseball caps. Most hats are woven from straw; the *Mokorotlo* or *Molianyeoe* is the traditional hat of Lesotho. It is conical in shape, much like the roof of a rural home, and has an intricately designed knob on top. Women generally do not wear slacks or shorts. The people are clean, neat, and concerned with an orderly appearance.

CUSTOMS AND COURTESIES

Greetings

Greetings tend to be somewhat formal in pattern. Upon shaking hands, two people greet by saying either *Lumela* (Hello) or *Khotso* (Peace be with you). This is followed by *U phela joang?* (How are you?). If acquainted, each makes polite inquiries about the other's family. They also typically ask *U tsoa kae?* (Where have you been?) and *U tsamaea kae?* (Where are you going?); an explanation is expected. The greeting process eventually evolves into a conversation. When two people pass on the street, or do not expect to engage in conversation, they use only the two basic greetings. Greeting habits vary somewhat, depending on whether men, women, young adults, or children are involved.

In farewells, the person leaving says *Sala hantle* (Stay well). The one staying says *Tsamaea hantle* (Go well). In very formal situations, one addresses others by title; otherwise one uses given names.

Gestures

Pointing with the index finger is impolite. One passes items with the right hand or both hands. It is common for friends of the same gender to walk down the street holding hands. Or if two people meet on the street and stop to shake hands and greet, they may hold the handshake throughout the conversation, regardless of their respective gender. Otherwise, members of the opposite sex do not touch or display affection in public. People use subtle movements of the head and eyes to convey positive or negative responses to something.

Visiting

The Basotho are hospitable hosts and enjoy having guests. Rural people usually visit without prior arrangement, as telephone and mail connections are not extensive. Upon arriving, a visitor knocks on the door and says *Ko ko* (knock knock). The hosts usually can recognize the voice and know a friendly visitor is at the door; they say *Kena* (Come in), and the visitor may then enter the home. It is extremely discourteous to enter without announcing one's presence in this manner, even if the door is open.

When visitors arrive, even if unexpected, it is polite for the hosts to invite them to stay for something to eat. If the visitor is far from home, the hosts offer them shelter for the night. Guests are nearly always served refreshments, such as tea and perhaps cookies or crackers. The Basotho customarily take tea in the afternoon. In rural areas, guests at tea are often served a full meal as well. Guests generally are not expected to bring gifts, but urban residents commonly will bring something to rural relatives.

Socializing among the Basotho not only takes place in the home but at public places such as the market or *moreneng* (chief compound) during a *pitso* (town meeting). The local chief usually calls a *pitso* to share important news or discuss something. If the news is good, an impromptu party may occur.

Eating

People in the capital city, Maseru, observe the continental style of eating, with the fork in the left hand and the knife remaining in the right. In villages, people often eat with their right hand or use a spoon, depending on the food. When families are not able to sit down together for a meal, food is left simmering on the stove around mealtime. When individual family members are ready to eat, they serve themselves and eat alone. When the family or group does eat together, the men and/or any important guests of either gender are served first and when they are satisfied, the women and children eat the remainder of the meal. Each person has a separate dish from which to eat. Finishing everything on one's plate is proper; men might have second helpings.

LIFESTYLE

Family

Lesotho has a strong patriarchal society centered on the family. However, because men often work outside the country during much of the year, women make many decisions and do most of the farm work. Women also work on the roads and in service occupations, comprising 44 percent of the labor force. While the nuclear family lives alone in large cities like Maseru, most rural extended families share a compound. It includes several buildings, a *kraal* (living space for animals), and a garden. The traditional *rondaval* or *ntlo* (home) is built of stone and sticks held together with cow dung, which

dries as hard as concrete and can be painted. Before it dries, people often draw intricate designs in it to beautify the home. Walls are thick, and the circular home is covered by a thatched roof. Windows are minimal to keep out cold. The diameter of the main home reflects the family's economic status. Its interior is not divided, so families usually have separate buildings for sleeping, cooking, storage, and so forth. Some homes are made of cement block.

Family members are expected to help one another. All those living in a compound contribute to its welfare by doing chores, cooking, minding the cattle, raising chickens, working for a wage and sharing part of it, and so forth. If one person in an extended family falls on hard times, other family members are expected to help if possible. But they are not expected to sacrifice their own needs to offer this help. When a man dies, his possessions are divided among his brothers and sons, who are expected to provide for his wife and any other women in his care.

Dating and Marriage

Young people meet through community activities, but Western dating is not common. Adult children usually remain with their parents until they marry, and often afterwards. Families are heavily involved in marriage/wedding negotiations. A groom's family is expected to pay a bride-price (in cattle or money) to the bride's family. When a woman marries, she moves to her husband's compound, which may be shared with his parents and others.

Diet

The Basotho diet consists of *mealie meal* (cornmeal), rice, potatoes, vegetables (cabbage, peas, etc.), and some fruits. When possible, people eat three meals a day. Modern cold cereals are becoming popular for breakfast, which is often eaten around 10:00 A.M. Lunch is the main meal and is eaten at midday. It traditionally consists of *Moroho* (cooked vegetables), *Nama* (meat), and *Papa* (corn mush). The evening meal is around 7:00 P.M. and contains the same foods eaten at lunch. *Nama ea Khomo* (beef), *Nama ea Khoho* (chicken), and *Nama ea Kolobe* (pork) are popular meats.

Holidays

Official holidays include New Year's Day, Army Day (20 January), and Moshoeshoe's Day (12 March). Tree Planting Day (21 March) is important because Lesotho is subject to severe soil erosion and has virtually no forests. The government sponsors tree-planting projects to provide future building and fuel supplies and to guard against further erosion. Other national holidays include Family Day (first Monday in July), Independence Day (5 October), and National Sports Day (first Monday in October). Easter (Friday–Monday) and Christmas are the most popular religious holidays. Boxing Day (26 December) comes from the British tradition of giving small boxed gifts to service personnel and tradesmen. It is now usually a day spent visiting friends and relatives.

Recreation

Soccer is the most important sport. Some urban residents play volleyball, netball (girls), and basketball. Visiting and holidays provide leisure and recreational opportunities. The Bosotho like to sing and can harmonize with ease. Most social gatherings involve some sort of singing.

Commerce

Businesses and government offices are open between 8:00 A.M. and 5:00 P.M., Monday through Friday. Some businesses open on Saturday until 1:00 P.M. More than 85 percent of the resident population is engaged in subsistence agriculture, so work schedules vary according to the season. As many as 250,000 men are gone at any one time to work in the mines or factories of South Africa. They may be in South Africa for several months each year or for several years. In Lesotho, the legal working age is 12.

SOCIETY

Government

Lesotho is a constitutional monarchy divided into ten districts. King Letsie III is head of state but has only ceremonial duties. Executive authority is vested in the prime minister. A new constitution went into effect with 1993 elections. Parliament's lower house has 65 elected members; the upper house consists of 22 principal chiefs and 10 appointed members. The voting age is 21. Local authority is vested in the village chief.

Economy

Lesotho lacks natural resources (except water) and relies largely on subsistence agriculture, which includes livestock raising. The economy also depends on wages earned by Basotho workers in South African mines. Their remittances account for between 50 and 75 percent of Lesotho's gross national product (GNP). These jobs are not permanent and unemployment can be as high as 50 percent at times. Real GNP per capita is $1,060 because of higher wages earned in South Africa. Poverty continues to affect about half of the population, and wealth is highly concentrated.

Grazing rights are communal, but arable land is allocated to individuals and families by local chiefs. Corn, wheat, sorghum, peas, beans, and potatoes are the main crops. Nearly all food is consumed domestically, but asparagus and beans are exported along with wool, mohair, cattle, and hides. Industries include textiles, clothing, and light engineering. Native crafts are also important to the economy. Tourism provides crucial foreign-exchange earnings.

Lesotho's geographic location and dependence on South Africa make the economy sensitive to political and economic changes in South Africa. The economy is growing by about 5 percent. Both the South African *rand* and the Basotho *loti* (plural is *maloti*) are acceptable currency in Lesotho. The *loti* (L) is backed by the *rand* (R).

Transportation and Communication

Maseru is a small city and it is easy to walk to its farthest points. A number of minibuses operate mostly along Maseru's main street and travel between cities in the lowlands. Other buses travel to eastern points. In keeping with British tradition, traffic moves on the left side of the road. Paved roads are generally in good condition, but most roads are not paved. Domestic air travel links Maseru with some mountain cities; a few flights go to other African countries. Some areas of the country are accessible only by horse or foot. The Basotho pony is famous in southern Africa for its surefootedness. It has been bred over the years specifically for mountain transport. Many people in remote areas have never traveled outside of their area.

The communications system is improving, but interior mountain locations are often accessible only by radio. Telephone service outside Maseru is sporadic. The government sponsors Radio Lesotho and two weekly newspapers. Several private newspapers also function. Television broadcasts are received from South Africa. For an hour each evening, Lesotho preempts the programming to show its own news and some entertainment. Most areas, except remote mountain locations, have access to television.

Education

The overall literacy rate in Lesotho is 68 percent, one of the highest in Africa. Unlike many countries, more girls are enrolled in school than boys. This is because boys must often tend flocks all day for months at a time when their fathers are working in South Africa. The educational system is largely administered by the three largest churches under the direction of the Ministry of Education. Influenced by the British colonial system, primary education consists of seven levels called *standards*. At their completion, an exam is administered. If students pass and their family can afford tuition and board, they begin secondary education. After completing another three years and passing an exam, students receive a Junior Certificate. Two more years in high school and completion of another exam enable students to attend the University of Lesotho at Roma. Vocational schools are also available. The Distance Teaching Centre provides basic education to those who do not or did not go to school.

Health

Because of Lesotho's elevation, many diseases common to Africa are not found within the country. Water is generally safe in the capital. Each district has a government hospital in addition to church-sponsored hospitals. The level of health care available varies with location. Services are better in urban areas and near the borders. Those living near the border can seek care in South Africa. Traditional medicine is practiced in remote areas. Life expectancy has risen over the last few years to a range of 61 to 64 years. The infant mortality rate has fallen to 67 per 1,000. Although this is still high, it is lower than in other parts of Africa.

FOR THE TRAVELER

U.S. visitors need a passport and visa to enter Lesotho. Anyone traveling to Lesotho through South Africa must also have a South African visa. No vaccinations are required. Lesotho promotes hiking, fossil hunting, pony trekking, birdwatching, and fishing. The tourism industry is developing to handle more visitors. For more information, contact the Lesotho Tourist Board, PO Box 52, Maseru 100, Lesotho. You may also wish to contact the Embassy of Lesotho, 2511 Massachusetts Avenue NW, Washington, DC 20008; phone (202) 797–5533.

Printed on recycled paper

Malaysia

Boundary representations not necessarily authoritative.

BACKGROUND

Land and Climate

Malaysia has two distinct land regions. Peninsular Malaysia is about the size of Alabama and is located south of Thailand and north of Singapore. Heavily forested mountains form the center of the peninsula and are flanked by coastal plains. Major rubber, palm oil, and other agricultural plantations are on the peninsula. East Malaysia is located on the island of Borneo and consists of two states, Sarawak and Sabah. The tiny country of Brunei lies on the coast near the juncture of these two states, which together are about the size of Louisiana. Malaysia's entire landmass covers 127,317 square miles (329,750 square kilometers). Sarawak is a broad coastal plain. Sabah's coastal plain gives way to mountainous jungle. Mount Kinabalu, the highest peak in Southeast Asia (13,455 feet or 4,101 meters), is in Sabah.

The climate is tropical. Humidity is high and temperatures range from 70° to 90°F (21–32°C). Monsoons are possible from June to September in the southwest and October to March in the northeast.

History

Many civilizations prospered on the peninsula long before European traders gained control, but recorded history begins in the 14th century. Local pirates were known to raid ships passing between China and India, and Asian traders established a thriving port and trade center at Melacca. An attack in 1509 on a Portuguese vessel prompted the Portuguese to capture Melacca in 1511. By the time the Dutch took control, in 1641 Melacca was no longer vital, so they did not pursue further development.

Britain acquired the island of Pulau Pinang (now Pinang) from the Sultan of Kedah in 1786. By the early 1900s, Britain controlled all the Malay states—including those on Borneo—as colonies or protectorates. The British brought in Chinese and Indian labor to work in the new rubber industry.

The Japanese invaded and occupied Malaysia during World War II. Under their occupation, Malaysian feelings for independence from foreign domination grew stronger. After the Japanese were defeated, the British created in 1946 the Malayan Union out of Melacca, Pulau Pinang, and the nine Malay states on the peninsula. In 1948, this union became the Federation of Malaya. That same year, Communist insurrections erupted and guerrilla terrorism spread throughout the countryside until it was quelled in 1959. Communist guerrilla warfare continued on a smaller scale against both the Malaysian and Thai governments until a 1989 cease-fire was signed.

In August 1957, Malaysia was granted independence from Great Britain. Six years later, the Federation of Malaya and the former British colonies of Singapore, Sarawak, and North Borneo (Sabah) united to become Malaysia in order to avoid a Communist takeover in Singapore. However, tension mounted between the Malay-dominated government in Malaya and the Chinese-dominated government in Singapore. The tension culminated in the creation of an independent Singapore in 1965.

In 1969, racial tension resulted in widespread rioting in Kuala Lumpur, the capital of Malaysia. Ethnic Malays were not satisfied with their share of the country's wealth, their access to business opportunities, and Chinese domination in some areas of society. The government changed the constitution in 1971 to give Malays more rights. A quota system established at the same time required Malay representation (at specified levels) in government, business, and education. Called the New Economic Policy (NEP), the system successfully improved the lives of many Malays. In 1991, the NEP was renewed as the New Development Policy (NDP) and altered to encourage help for poorer people of all races. Although the program has discouraged racial integration, it is credited with also discouraging violence between ethnic groups. And although some Chinese argue the NDP hampers economic growth, others feel it has provided greater equality and stable growth. Mahathir bin Mohamad, architect of the NEP/NDP, captured a fourth term as prime minister in 1995.

THE PEOPLE

Population

The 19.7 million people that live in Malaysia are racially and culturally diverse. Ties between people have developed through educational, social, sporting, and cultural organizations, but ethnic groups still remain essentially segregated. The largest group is the Malays. Together with other indigenous peoples, they make up 59 percent of the total population. Some of these other groups include the Sea Dayaks (*Ibans*), Land Dayaks (*Bidayuhs*), Kadazans, Kenyahs, Melanaus, and Muruts. They are mainly farmers, civil servants, or fishermen. The Chinese make up 32 percent of the population and live mostly on the peninsula in tin- and rubber-producing areas. Most large towns also have significant Chinese communities. The Indians (9 percent) are the third largest group. They also live on the peninsula. Malaysia's population is young, with 48 percent of the population younger than age 20. The population is growing at 2.2 percent annually. About 45 percent of Malaysians live in urban areas.

Malaysia's Human Development Index (0.822) ranks it 59th out of 174 nations. Adjusted for women, the index (0.768) ranks Malaysia 38th out of 130 nations. These figures reflect a society in which opportunities to advance and pursue personal goals are increasing, although women lag behind men in being literate or earning a decent salary.

Language

Malay (*Bahasa Melayu*) is the official language of Malaysia and is spoken in all areas of the country. It is closely related to ancient Sanskrit. The ethnic Chinese also speak one of various Chinese dialects (Cantonese, Hakka, Hokkien, Mandarin, or Min); the Indians speak Tamil. In Sabah and Sarawak, numerous indigenous languages are common, but the most prevalent are Iban, Dayak, and Khadazan.

Religion

Islam is the official religion of Malaysia, and ethnic Malays are nearly all Muslim. Non-Malays are free to choose other religions. The Chinese on the peninsula are chiefly Buddhist, with some Taoists and Confucianists. Some practice principles from all three. The Indians are generally Hindu or Sikh, but some are Christian. A number of Chinese families are also Christian.

In the states of Sabah and Sarawak, denomination percentages are different. In Sabah, about 38 percent are Muslim, 17 percent Christian, and the rest follow indigenous beliefs. In Sarawak, where there are more Chinese, 24 percent are Buddhist and Confucianist, 20 percent Muslim, and 16 percent Christian. The rest follow indigenous or other beliefs. Traditional beliefs and customs are often mixed with a person's formal religion.

General Attitudes

A person's ancestral background is often important to social status and future opportunities. Wealth is highly admired. Many Malaysians believe successes, failures, opportunities, and misfortunes result from fate or the will of God. But a growing number of those influenced by Western ideals believe they can succeed with a good education and hard work. Malaysians appreciate those with a connection to power, home ownership, and higher education. A car, considered a luxury item, is a status symbol.

Although people are proud of their country and generally loyal to Malaysia, they often identify first with their ethnic group, island, or region. Some ethnic tensions exist between the Malays (called *Bramiputras*) and Chinese over the quota system. The Chinese believe the policies make them second-class citizens, while the majority of Malays believe they provide the only avenue for *Bramiputras* to overcome traditional Chinese dominance in business.

Personal Appearance

Urban residents wear Western-style clothing more often than rural people do. However, both rural and urban people might mix traditional clothing with Western attire. Or they may change from Western clothing to traditional outfits for special purposes. For instance, Muslim men wear a *songkok* (black velvet cap) on Friday. When they attend mosque on Fridays, they also wear a long Arabic robe, loose jacket, and long *sarung* about their waists. Or they wear a traditional Malay outfit made of silk or cotton, with a gold brocade *sarung* folded around the waist.

In some areas, Muslim women with head covers, veils, and long dresses are as common as women wearing short skirts or pants. Some Indian women wear a *salwar khamis* (type of pantsuit with a long shirt). *Batik* fabric (traditionally hand colored with a hot-wax process) is popular for traditional dress.

CUSTOMS AND COURTESIES

Greetings

Men shake hands or greet with a slight bow or nod of the head. Women and elderly persons seldom shake hands but may offer verbal greetings. When greeting a close male friend, a man uses both hands to grasp the hand of the other. Business contacts exchange cards after an introduction.

Greeting phrases vary between ethnic groups and regions. Typical Malay greetings include *Salamat pagi* (Good morning) and *Apa Khabar?* (How are you?). A casual term is *Halo* (Hello). The Muslim phrase *Asaalam alaykum* (Peace be upon you) is used in more formal situations. The Chinese may greet with *Tze pau le ma?* (Have you eaten?) or *Ni hau ma?* (Are you feeling all right?).

How a person is addressed depends on his or her ethnic group, religion, age, and relation to the speaker. For example, professionals are addressed by title and surname (if they have one) or title and given name. Christians may adopt a Christian name. Malay men and women are properly called by their first name, e.g., Zahara binti Omar is *Puan* (Madam) Zahara. The other part of the name is formed from the father's given name. Hindus also form their names in this manner. The Chinese family name comes first, followed by a given name. So, Quah Yow Chun would be addressed by his full name or as Mr. *Quah*; his friends would call him *Yow Chun*. If his wife's name is Leong Ming Chu, she can be properly addressed as Mrs. *Quah* or Madam *Leong*, but her friends would call her *Ming Chu*. Chinese relatives usually do not address one another by name but by relation ("younger uncle," "second aunt," etc.). Indians call persons older than themselves "uncle" or "aunt."

Gestures

It is not polite to beckon adults, with the exception of close friends, or to point with the index finger. To beckon, one waves all fingers with the palm facing down. Giving and receiving gifts with both hands shows respect. One does not move objects with the feet or point the bottom of the foot at another person. Since the head is the most sacred point of the body, it is impolite to touch another person's, even a child's, head. One covers the mouth when yawning or using a toothpick. People bow slightly when leaving, entering, or passing by a group of people as a nonverbal "excuse me." Public displays of affection are inappropriate.

Visiting

Visiting is an important part of Malaysian life. People usually visit on weekends and after 8:00 P.M. In predominately Muslim states, the weekend is Thursday and Friday. Elsewhere, it is Saturday and Sunday. Urban residents are more likely to entertain in a restaurant, but rural people enjoy visits in the home. Close friends and family may drop by without prior arrangement, although urban dwellers call in advance. Guests invited to the home for a meal or socializing generally are not expected to arrive on time. Malaysians value people over schedules. One removes the shoes when entering a home. Hosts normally serve tea or coffee to guests and may offer cake, cookies, or biscuits. Drinks are offered and received with both hands. Guests are not expected to bring gifts, but something small (especially for the children) is usually appreciated.

Eating

Eating customs differ among ethnic groups. Most people eat three meals each day. Families try to eat together as often as schedules permit. Malays and Indians eat with their hands and with spoons. Chinese eat with chopsticks and spoons. A bowl of water is often available for washing before and after a meal. Except for some rural Muslims who eat on a floor mat, most people eat at a table, choosing foods from various serving dishes. Some groups refrain from eating certain foods. For example, devout Muslims do not eat pork or drink alcoholic beverages. Hindus and some Buddhists do not eat beef.

Guests are served first and begin eating first. It is impolite to leave food on the plate. In some families, one can place the chopsticks beside one's empty rice bowl to indicate one is finished. In others, dropping a few drops of one's drink on the plate could signal the end of one's meal. In restaurants,

Malaysians usually do not leave tips because service typically is included in the bill.

LIFESTYLE

Family

Family cooperation, loyalty, and unity are important in the Malaysian family. Even though nuclear families are more common in urban areas, young married couples live near their parents, and unmarried adults continue to live with their parents until they marry. Rural households are more likely to include more than one generation, usually parents, married sons and their families, and all unmarried children. Rural families are also larger than urban families, which tend to average two or three children.

Dating and Marriage

Although parents stress that dating should wait until after one's education is complete, dating usually begins around age 17 or 18 in urban areas. Young people enjoy shopping, going to movies, or eating fast-food. In rural areas, dating habits are more conservative and some marriages are arranged by families. However, the majority of couples make their own choices in consultation with family members. A marriage is seen as joining not only two persons but also two families. Customs and ceremonies vary by religion, but a celebration with relatives and friends usually accompanies the event.

Diet

Many cultures have influenced the Malaysian diet. Yet regardless of regional and ethnic differences, rice is a dietary staple for all. Malaysians eat it at least once a day. Fish is a primary source of protein, but protein is also derived from legumes, milk, soy, and other beans. Durians (large, oval-shaped fruits) are considered king among fruits. Other favorites include pineapples, bananas, and papayas. Common dishes include *Nasi Lemak* (buttered rice with dried anchovies and peanuts), *satay* (grilled meat on a stick), chicken or fish curry with coconut milk, *dim sum* (a traditional Chinese snack), and *bah kut teh* (Chinese pork soup). *Roti chanai* is bite-sized cooked wheat dipped in lentil curry.

Recreation

Soccer was introduced to Malaysia in the 19th century and is the country's most popular sport. Other sports include badminton, field hockey, cricket, rugby, and table tennis. There are also facilities for swimming, tennis, cycling, volleyball, and squash. Traditional activities include *sepaktakraw*, a competitive team sport played with a rattan ball; *main gasing*, spinning tops, which weigh several pounds, for long periods of time; and martial arts (particularly *silat*). Kite flying is popular on the peninsula. Local festivals, television, movies, and visiting friends also provide recreation.

Holidays

Among Malaysia's national holidays are International New Year's Day (1 January), Labor Day (1 May), National Day (31 August), and the Birthday of the *Yang di-Pertuan Agong* (first Wednesday in June). The Chinese New Year is a festival spanning several days in January or February.

The three chief Islamic holidays include *Hari Raya Puasa*, the three-day feast at the end of the month of *Ramadan*; *Hari Raya Haji*, the Feast of Sacrifice that comes at the end of the pilgrimage to Makkah, Saudi Arabia; and the birthday of the prophet Muhammad. During *Ramadan*, Muslims do not eat or drink from sunrise to sundown each day; they eat a meal and visit friends in the evening.

Wesak Day (in May) commemorates the birth of Buddha. *Deepavali,* a Hindu festival in October or November, celebrates the triumph of Lord Krishna over a demon king. Christmas is the main Christian holiday. The Dayaks also celebrate the harvest, venerate the dead, and honor heroes. The Kadazan Festivals in May also celebrate the harvest.

Commerce

Wage earners usually work a five-and-one-half-day week. Businesses generally are open between 8:30 A.M. and 5:00 P.M., Monday through Friday. Some are open Saturday mornings. In many cases, businesses are closed for one hour at lunch. Rural people may shop daily for basic supplies; urban dwellers usually shop weekly.

SOCIETY

Government

Malaysia, a constitutional monarchy, has 13 states. Sarawak and Sabah are considered self-governing states with foreign policy and other powers delegated from the federal government. In 9 of the 11 peninsular states, rulers are hereditary and compose a Council of Rulers. These rulers alternate as king of the country for five-year terms. The king is referred to as the Supreme Head of State (*Yang di-Pertuan Agong*). The current king, Tuanku Ja'afar Ibni Almarhum Tuanku Abdul Rehman, took office in April 1994 and will serve through 1998. He has some executive powers, but the real governing power rests with the prime minister and Parliament. Parliament has two houses: the *Dewan Negara* (Senate) and the *Dewan Rakyat* (House of Representatives). Sarawak and Sabah have 27 and 20 seats, respectively, in the 192-seat House of Representatives. The Senate has 58 members, 32 of whom are appointed by the king, with 16 elected by state legislatures. Prime Minister Mahathir's governing party is the National Front. The main opposition parties include the All-Malaysia Islamic Party, Democratic Action Party, and Malay Party Spirit of '46. The voting age is 21.

Economy

Malaysia has a strong and dynamic economy that averages 8 percent annual growth. Exports from the growing manufacturing sector increase every year, and tourism is developing rapidly. Electronics and automobile manufacturing have played important roles in the boom, with the help of foreign investment. The Malaysians produce a car known as the Proton Saga. Timber, oil, and palm oil have joined tin and rubber as Malaysia's top exports. Malaysia is the world's largest exporter of natural rubber and palm oil. About 30 percent of the workforce is engaged in agriculture. Besides the major export crops, Malaysians cultivate rice, coconuts, cocoa, fruits, coffee, tea, and pepper. Fishing is also important.

Real gross domestic product per capita is $7,790, which has tripled in the last generation. Prosperity is rising, while absolute poverty now affects fewer than one-fourth of all people. The international drug trade has a strong presence in Malaysia, causing the government to take aim at drug traffickers. Anyone (Malaysian or non-Malaysian) arrested for possessing illegal drugs is subject to the death penalty. The monetary currency is the *ringgit* ($).

Transportation and Communication

Bicycles, motorcycles, and cars are the principal means of transportation; buses, trains, and airplanes are used for longer trips. Following the British tradition, traffic moves on the left side of the road. The majority of roads are paved and the national highway system is well developed. Taxis are plentiful in the cities. A light-rail system functions in Kuala Lumpur. Both domestic and international communications systems are good. There are several television and radio stations. More than 60 newspapers are available in the country's major languages.

Education

Education is considered the key to social status and success. Six years of primary and three years of secondary education are compulsory. Students then take an examination to determine whether they may continue school for two more years in a secondary school or in a trade school, both of which require a modest tuition. Most students are instructed in Malay and are required to learn English. Chinese and Indian students, however, may attend special schools where instruction is in their native language. These students generally spend an extra year in school because they must also learn Malay.

Secondary school graduates may take an exam to enter two years of preuniversity education. Malaysia has seven universities and more than thirty other institutions of higher learning. Degrees from British, Australian, and U.S. American universities abroad are valued. The government sponsors adult correspondence courses. The literacy rate averages 82 percent. This represents about 85 percent for the peninsula and 65 percent for Sarawak and Sabah.

Health

Medical care is subsidized, with both central and state governments operating hospitals and clinics. Nearly all Malaysians have access to health care. Fees are low, and the quality of care does not depend on one's income. The government has sponsored national immunization, fluoridation, and hygiene campaigns. The infant mortality rate has dropped from more than 25 to only 14 per 1,000; life expectancy ranges from 68 to 71 years. Problems still exist, of course. Rural care is not as good as in cities, and high costs are leading the government to privatize 12 general hospitals in the next ten years.

FOR THE TRAVELER

A passport is necessary for U.S. travelers to enter Malaysia, but a visa is not needed for stays of up to three months. A yellow fever vaccination is recommended but is only required of those coming from an infected area. Cholera vaccinations should be considered. Malaria suppressants are recommended. For travel information, contact the Malaysia Tourist Information Center, 818 West Seventh Street, Suite 804, Los Angeles, CA 90017; phone (213) 689–9702. You may also contact the Embassy of Malaysia, 2401 Massachusetts Avenue NW, Washington, DC 20008; phone (202) 328–2700.

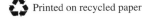 Printed on recycled paper

July 96

CULTURGRAM '97

Republic of
Mali

Boundary representations not necessarily authoritative.

BACKGROUND

Land and Climate

The seventh largest country in Africa, Mali is about twice the size of Texas. It covers 478,764 square miles (1,240,000 square kilometers). Situated in the middle of West Africa, Mali's north is in the southern Sahara Desert. Further south is the semiarid Sahel with limited vegetation, mostly in the form of bushes and a few trees. Together, desert or semidesert regions cover 70 percent of Mali. Only in the deep south can one find forests and some jungles. The fertile Niger River area is home to most of Mali's economic activity. The river's northern delta is annually submerged. Mali's three seasons are the rainy season, stretching from May to October in the south but including only about a month of irregular rainfall in the north; the fresh or cold season (cool and dry), from November to February; and the hot season, from March to May or June.

History

From the seventh to the nineteenth centuries, parts of Mali were ruled by the kings of the Ghana, Malinke, Songhai, Bambara, and Toucouleur Empires. The Songhai Empire in the 15th and 16th centuries covered twice the territory of modern Mali. In the 14th century, Mali was one of the most important centers of commerce in Africa. Tombouctou (Timbuktu) was a center of Islamic learning. Malians are proud of their history, retaining it through tale and song.

The French began ruling at the turn of the 20th century, and Mali was a French colony (Western Sudan) until 1960, when it gained independence under a socialist government led by Modibo Keita. In 1968, a group of military officers staged a successful coup and renounced socialism. A military government ruled until 1979 with Moussa Traoré as president. In 1979, civilians were added to the cabinet and a political party was formed called the Democratic Union of the People of Mali (UDPM). Traoré continued as the country's president and general secretary of the UDPM. When popular demonstrations in 1991 were met with Traoré's orders to shoot civilians, key army officers rebelled and staged a coup. Traoré was arrested and put on trial in 1992 and the UDPM was disbanded. Traoré was convicted of ordering the deaths of those who died in the 1991 riots. His death sentence has not yet been carried out.

Since that time, significant steps toward democracy have been taken. A new constitution was drafted and a National Assembly elected. Also elected was President Alpha Oumar Konare. Unfortunately, 1993 student riots forced Konare's prime minister to resign. Rioters set fire to the president's home and the National Assembly building. Konare responded by meeting with student leaders and committing to change the educational system. He also made some changes within his cabinet. Konare worked early in his tenure to negotiate with Tuareg rebels, who have long struggled to gain independence for their light-skinned ethnic group. The Tuaregs live in Mali, Niger, and Burkina Faso and have fought all three governments. Fighting in Mali decreased significantly after government negotiations began. It is clear that, while many challenges face this fledgling democracy, Malian leaders are ready to address them peacefully.

THE PEOPLE

Population

Mali's population is about 9.37 million, with an annual growth rate of 2.9 percent. Nearly 90 percent of Malians reside in the more fertile southern third of the country, while 10 percent (mostly nomadic people) live in the arid north that comprises two-thirds of Mali. Seventy-five percent of all people live in rural areas. Mali's Human Development Index (0.222) ranks it 172d out of 174 nations; adjusted for women, the index (0.195) ranks Mali 128th out of 130 nations. The rating indicates Malians' lack of access to resources that allow for personal development and progress.

Of the country's 20 major ethnic groups, several comprise less than one percent of the population. The Bambara make up the largest group (approximately one-third of the population) and generally populate the central and southern regions. The second largest group is the Malinke of the southwest and west. The Sarakole live in the northwest near Mauritania. The Peulh (or Peul), seminomadic herders who traditionally inhabit the northern desert, comprise some 17 percent of the population. Many Peulh have migrated south and settled in the Mopti region due to deteriorating living conditions in the north. The Songhai live in the northeast along the Niger River, as do the Bozo, who earn their living from fishing in the Niger Delta. The Dogons live on and around the Bandiagara escarpment (also called the Dogon Cliffs) in the eastern center. The Menianka and Senufo inhabit the southwest, along the Burkina Faso border. The Tuaregs live in the east.

Language

Mali's large number of languages and dialects reflects the ethnic diversity of the country. The official language, French, is spoken by government administrators and in urban areas and is the primary language of instruction in school. However, the most widely spoken tongue is Bambara. Many Malians speak three or four languages. As is common in Africa, language is mainly oral. Books are published in at least four Malian languages, but history is transmitted by narration from generation to generation, from master to scholar, and from parent to child. A special caste, the Griot, has the responsibility to recount and sing the great past.

Religion

Ninety percent of all Malians are Muslim. Most of the rest, especially in the south and along the Dogon Cliffs, adhere to traditional religions, which usually emphasize animism. About 1 percent are Christian. The Peulh, Sarakole, Moor, Songhai, and Tamashek have been Muslim for a long time. More recent converts to Islam still practice some aspects of their traditional faiths concurrently, such as using masks or totem animals and wearing *grigri* charms (amulets used to protect a person from harm or illness). Most Malians are tolerant of other religions, since they mix practices from different belief systems.

General Attitudes

Malians are usually polite and friendly. This helps ensure mutual respect among friends and strangers. If they feel slighted, Malians may use a host of unexpected, teasing comments. These are usually humorous and are regarded as attempts to be nice and not offend. Malians often make jokes with other groups about family names or castes. These "joking cousin" remarks help maintain friendly ties and avoid harshness between the many different groups. Malians are rarely confrontational. They adapt to nature rather than try to dominate it. Time is oriented more toward tradition and convenience than innovation or urgency. Among Muslims, the "will of *Allah*" is seen as affecting all events.

Even though many villages are composed of only one ethnic group, traditional social position and caste membership are often more important than ethnic origin. Between similar ethnic groups, caste membership determines one's relative position. However, between dissimilar groups, such as the light-skinned peoples versus the dark-skinned sub-Saharan Malians, ethnicity is still the main distinguishing factor and cause of long-standing tensions. Traditional roles are often more important than assumed roles. A driver born as a "noble," for instance, may be more respected than a government official from a blacksmith family.

Traditional moral codes remain prevalent. For example, robbery may be a reason to beat a criminal, while embezzlement of public funds (a relatively modern crime) may be pardonable. One must care for one's family and clan, but general civic loyalties are shallow. At the same time, students can be a vocal and powerful force in society.

Personal Appearance

Western clothing is common in urban areas, although women tend to wear traditional clothing more often than men. Men wear trousers, not shorts, and a shirt. Rural Muslim women wear wraparound skirts, blouses, and sandals; animist women may omit blouses and shoes. Among some ethnic groups, animist boys first wear pants after circumcision (5–12 years old). Neatness and modesty are valued throughout the country.

CUSTOMS AND COURTESIES

Greetings

Men and women either shake right hands when meeting or (sometimes when greeting a member of the opposite sex) clasp their own hands and bow slightly. A man of power (such as a village chief) will always initiate a handshake. Otherwise, a person joining a group or entering a room initiates a handshake with each adult in the room or area, beginning with the eldest or most senior.

Verbal greetings vary between ethnic groups. If a person's language is not known, one can greet that person in a more commonly spoken language and the other will respond in his or her own language. For example, if one person uses the French *Bonjour* (Good day), the other might respond with the Bambara equivalent, *Nse*. It is impolite not to greet someone when passing them on a path or street. Greetings among friends are usually followed by inquiries about one's family members and their health. Greetings that precede conversation can often last several minutes.

A family name provides information about a person's ethnic, caste, and geographic origins. Depending on how much trust exists between greeters, Malians may or may not announce their family name to strangers. Rather, they will introduce themselves by their first name. Often, it is only when people are acquainted that one learns the family name of another. Friends generally address one another by given names.

Gestures

Because the left hand is considered unclean, it is disrespectful and unhygienic to take a Malian's left hand, offer the left for a handshake, offer food or money with it, or accept anything with it. The only exception is when a close family member or friend leaves on a long trip, in which case the left hand is used in a handshake as a special gesture to indicate the two people will see each other again. One may show special respect during a regular handshake by touching one's own right elbow with the fingertips of the left hand while shaking right hands. Respect may also be shown by touching the forehead with the right hand after a gentle handshake or by touching the chest over the heart with the right hand after shaking. It is impolite to point or gesture with the index finger; one should use the entire hand.

Visiting

Visiting plays an integral part of Malian society, as it is a way to maintain kinship bonds and friendships. Not visiting someone for an extended period of time reflects on the value of the relationship. Visits between rural friends and relatives occur often and usually unannounced, as making prior arrangements is difficult without telephones.

Guests remove their shoes before entering a room or stepping on a mat. Visitors are offered water when entering a compound and may be given the best seating. In villages, guests bring small gifts to their hosts, often including tea, sugar, or kola nuts. Compliments are usually appreciated but are denied for modesty's sake. If visitors arrive while hosts are eating, the guests will usually be invited to share the food, but unexpected guests may politely decline the meal. Guests are usually offered refreshments, which they offer to share with the hosts, as it is very impolite to eat in front of others.

If visiting a *dugutigi* (village chief), one takes special care to show respect. In a village meeting, visitors who do not speak the local language (such as government officials or foreigners) will not talk directly to the chief but to one or more persons who pass the communication to the chief and vice versa.

Eating

Urban families usually use a spoon and often other utensils when eating their meals, but eating food with the right hand is traditional. Rural people continue to follow this tradition. Family members eat from communal bowls. The male head of the family determines which groups eat from one of several communal bowls. For example, men and boys may share one bowl, with small children and/or women sharing another. Being married or unmarried is also a distinction, as is one's relative age. Adult men and women seldom eat from the same bowl. Each person eats from the portion of the bowl that is directly in front of him or her.

LIFESTYLE

Family

Traditionally, Malians favor large families, although urban families are becoming smaller. The infant mortality rate is still high, and some parents believe they must produce children as "life insurance" to provide a posterity and sufficient hands for agricultural labor. The family or clan chief's authority is incontestable. Babies receive a lot of affection, but children receive family responsibilties as early as age five. Older children care for younger ones. The elderly enjoy great respect. The extended family is cohesive, and members who can are obligated to help family members in need, no matter how distant the relationship. The average wage earner cares for ten people. Saving money is almost impossible.

For most, life functions at the subsistence level. Crops depend on sufficient rain and surpluses are rare. Houses are made of mud, rocks, and sometimes cement. Few households have electricity or running water. Even for city dwellers, these services are frequently interrupted.

Dating and Marriage

Dating norms vary with the locale. In urban areas, dating begins at about age 15 and promiscuity is widespread. In rural areas, rules differ according to the ethnic or social group. Individuals usually accept the judgment of their families in the choice of a marital partner. Marriage rules are strongly influenced by Islam, but the position of the woman is less dependent than in other Muslim countries since she can, under certain conditions, divorce her husband and rejoin her family. Polygamy is still practiced (as allowed and controlled by Islamic law), but it has been increasingly seen as an economic burden. A Muslim man who wishes to take another wife usually seeks the approval of his first wife and then must provide for all wives (up to four) equally. In urban areas, many women no longer accept the status of second, third, or fourth spouse. But some rural women appreciate the extra help that multiple wives can represent.

Diet

The dietary staple is millet. Prepared as a dough-like substance (*To*) or like porridge, it is often dipped in a leaf or vegetable sauce and occasionally a meat sauce (goat, sheep, or chicken). In the north, milk, dates, and wheat are important foods. Urban residents eat rice when possible. Restaurants that serve Western dishes are found in Bamako and in regional capital cities. Malnutrition is widespread in Mali.

Recreation

The most popular sport in Mali is soccer. It is inexpensive and, as a spectator sport, provides people with an opportunity to sit together and talk while watching the game. Also, informal peer groups, known as *groupe de "grain,"* often meet together to drink tea and socialize. In Bamako and other urban areas, wealthier people spend considerable time watching television and videos.

Holidays

National holidays include New Year's Day, Army Day (20 January), Labor Day (1 May), and Independence Day (22 September). The most important religious holidays are the feast at the end of *Ramadan* (the Islamic month of fasting, when Muslims go without food and drink during the day and eat in the evenings) and, 40 days later, *Tabaski* (feast of mutton). The dates for these feasts change each year because Islam uses the lunar calendar, which has 28-day months. Christmas and Easter Monday are observed in cities as days off from work. In animist areas, festivals associated with the seasons are celebrated with mask dancing.

Commerce

Most Malians work in agriculture and are not normal wage earners. Wage earners are usually government employees who work 40-hour weeks. The largest such group is Mali's teachers. Because wages are in arrears, many must also work in agriculture to support their families. In urban areas, the number of unemployed people probably exceeds 50 percent. Many of these survive as street vendors. Government offices and larger stores are open from 7:30 A.M. to 2:30 P.M., Monday through Saturday, except Fridays, when they are open from 7:30 A.M. to 12:30 P.M. and from 4:00 to 7:00 P.M. Markets and street vendors are open until late into the evening and on Sundays. Open-air markets are open each week and provide opportunities not only to buy basic goods but also to socialize.

SOCIETY

Government

Mali is a multiparty democracy. President Konare is head of state; he cannot legally seek reelection in 1997. A prime minister (Ibrahima Boubaca Keita) is head of government. Malians directly elect the 116 members of the National Assembly to five-year terms. The voting age is 21. Konare's Association for Democracy (Adema) is the dominant party, but small opposition parties also hold seats in the assembly.

Economy

Mali's few natural resources are limited to small deposits of gold, limestone, uranium, and other minerals. Eighty percent of the labor force is employed in agriculture. Harvests are often poor due to drought or grasshoppers. There is little industry and the government controls most enterprises. Mali's main exports include cotton, cattle, gold, and peanuts. Small enterprises are growing in urban areas, but the purchasing power of the domestic market is limited. Tourism is not significant because Mali lacks the necessary infrastructure (hotels, transport, services, etc.).

Real gross domestic product per capita is $550, which has hardly improved since before independence. Although a small urban middle class has some access to economic opportunities, most people are poor. The country depends on aid and development projects from industrialized countries. The currency is the *Communauté Financière Africaine franc* (CFAF).

Transportation and Communication

Mali is served by international airlines and is linked to Senegal by train. Travel by road is difficult, since most roads are unpaved and only intermittently passable. However, a recent major effort has extended paved roads from central Bamako to the city's outlying districts. In addition, paved roads link most major cities. From August to December, the Niger River is usually navigable by larger ships. Canoes and small craft can use the river year-round. The availability of public transportation is increasing. Buses link major cities, but outlying areas are usually only accessible by pickup trucks or vans that carry passengers and their cargo.

Radio and television are operated by the government. Television broadcasts can be received in most regions, but access to a television and power source is limited in rural areas.

Programs are mostly in French. Radio broadcasts are in local languages. Until just before the 1991 coup, there was only one (government) newspaper. An opposition paper was instrumental in the pre-coup demonstrations. It and numerous other dailies now prosper as part of a free press. Telephone connections are generally good, but they are not extensive. Most people must go to a post office to make or receive a call. Mail is delivered to postal and government offices, not to homes. Rural people often pass mail from hand to hand in the letter's intended direction.

Education

A low literacy rate (27 percent) stems from a primary school enrollment rate of 15 percent and the use of French as the language of instruction. Nearly 40 thousand adults read and write in local languages (mostly Bambara). Rural schools are sparse, as villagers must pay for expensive construction materials themselves. Professional training is still relatively rare. Public schools, as well as Catholic, American, and French schools, serve urban areas. Rural Catholic or Protestant missions usually include a school. Many people send their children (mostly boys) to Islamic (Koranic) schools and leave them in the care of the teacher. Several colleges offer a bachelor's degree, but Mali's first university is only now being built in Bamako. When completed, the existing colleges will join as departments of the single university.

Health

Medical facilities and services are inadequate or nonexistent in much of the country. On average, there is only one doctor for every seventeen thousand people and one sickbed per two thousand people. Clinics are often without staff or supplies. Hospitals in the regional capitals have inadequate equipment. The infant mortality rate is 104 per 1,000. Life expectancy is between 44 and 47 years. Widespread epidemics of malaria cause several thousand deaths each year. Influenza, dysentery, venereal disease, guinea worm, and German measles cause frequent sickness. Yellow fever, cholera, bilharzia, and rabies are also present. Public hygiene is poor in urban areas where sewage collects in open gutters.

FOR THE TRAVELER

A visa and valid passport are required for U.S. citizens to enter Mali. Yellow fever vaccinations are also required if one is coming from an infected area. Other vaccination recommendations depend on the purpose and length of stay. Water is not potable and should be treated or boiled. In areas where the guinea worm is endemic, water must be strained through cotton cloth. Eat only thoroughly cooked and hot foods; wash and peel fruits and vegetables. Many travel agencies offer programs and interesting travel options. Famous sites are Mopti, Djénné, and the Dogon Cliffs. Overland travel to some areas is not secure. Likewise, crossing the Sahara is unsafe. Check with the U.S. embassy in Mali or call (202) 647–5225 for current travel advisories. You may wish to contact the Ministry of Tourism, B.P. 191, Bamako, Mali; phone 223–22–56–73. The Embassy of Mali is located at 2130 R Street NW, Washington, DC 20008; phone (202) 332–2249.

A *Culturgram* is a product of native commentary and original, expert analysis. Statistics are estimates and information is presented as a matter of opinion. While the editors strive for accuracy and detail, this document should not be considered strictly factual. It is a general introduction to culture, an initial step in building bridges of understanding between peoples. It may not apply to all peoples of the nation. You should therefore consult other sources for more information.

Republic of the

Marshall Islands

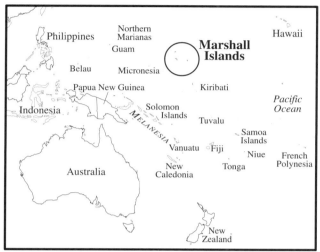

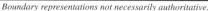

Boundary representations not necessarily authoritative.

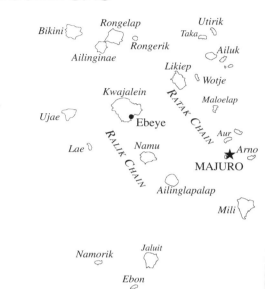

BACKGROUND

Land and Climate

The Republic of the Marshall Islands (RMI), located in the north Pacific Ocean, is in the easternmost part of Micronesia. It sits between Hawaii and Papua New Guinea and is north of Fiji. Though difficult to measure, the Marshall Islands include some 700,000 square miles (1.8 million square kilometers) of the Pacific Ocean. The total land area, however, is only 70 square miles (181 square kilometers), which is a bit larger than Washington, D.C. There are two chains of atolls about 130 miles (200 kilometers) apart. The Ratak (eastern or sunrise) chain is made up of 15 atolls while the Ralik (western or sunset) chain has 16 atolls. There are 1,152 islands in these two atoll chains. Atoll islands are coral based and have sandy soil. They are flat and usually narrow.

The climate is hot and humid throughout the year on most islands. The average temperature is 84°F (29°C); the difference between day and night temperatures is about 10°F (5°C). There is more rainfall in the southern atolls. Trade winds blow from December to March, and the typhoon season is from August to November.

History

The original Marshallese are believed to have sailed in large canoes from Indonesia and the Philippines through Melanesia. They lived by fishing and cultivating root trees and crops. Neither money nor alcohol were present in the culture. The Marshallese were renowned for their seamanship and for developing an elaborate system of navigation (*meto*) using wave and current patterns represented in stick charts. Unlike Western navigation, these maps emphasize patterns over specific landmarks.

The first Europeans to encounter the islands were Spanish explorers in the early 1500s. However, explorers were fearful of the dangerous reefs that surrounded the Marshalls, so few dared to visit until British Captains Gilbert and Marshall arrived in 1788. Forty years later, Otto von Kotzebue, a Russian explorer, named the islands after the British captain. Soon, whalers began to frequent the islands. Missionaries and traders followed.

The colonial era started as a number of governments realized the value of the islands for trade and military purposes. The Germans established a coaling station on one atoll in 1878 and later started coconut plantations to produce copra (dried coconut meat), from which coconut oil is extracted. With the end of World War I, the Japanese took control of the undefended Marshall Islands. Under a League of Nations mandate, they became the official ruling power. They too realized the value of the islands and launched several attacks from them in World War II. The Japanese lost control of the islands when U.S. forces moved across the Pacific. The United States, under a mandate from the United Nations, administered the islands after the war as a Trust Territory (including the Marshalls, Marianas, Micronesia, and Belau). The Marshall Islands separated from the Trust Territory in 1979

OCEANIA

and established its own unique relationship with the United States. A constitution was ratified by voters on 1 May 1979.

The United States currently maintains a missile range on Kwajalein Atoll as part of the Strategic Defense Initiative. The United States also conducted 66 atomic tests from 1946 to 1958 on Bikini and Eniwetok Atolls. There is still much controversy over the tests. Some Marshallese receive and continue to press for financial compensation for damages suffered during the testing.

In 1986, the republic entered into a Compact of Free Association with the United States. Under the compact, the RMI has complete responsibility for its national affairs except in the area of defense. The United States takes responsibility for all security and defense matters relating to the RMI and provides it with substantial financial subsidies. The compact is subject to renewal after fifteen years. In 1991, the RMI became a member of the United Nations.

THE PEOPLE

Population

Approximately 60,000 people inhabit the Marshall Islands. While there is primarily only one ethnic group (the Marshallese), immigrants from neighboring islands, Germans, Japanese, and U.S. Americans have all influenced the ethnic mix. Recently, many Filipino workers have come to the islands to help meet labor needs.

More than half of the people live in the urban centers of Majuro and Ebeye, while the remainder live on outer islands. The population growth rate is extraordinary. At 3.8 percent, it is one of the highest in the world. Reduced infant mortality, infrequent family planning, and improved health care have contributed to rapid growth. More than half of the population is younger than age 15. On outer islands, the population of each atoll usually can be traced to one or two family lines.

Language

While English is the official government language and is taught in all schools, few people speak it fluently. Marshallese is the language spoken on a daily basis. It belongs to the Malayo-Polynesian language family and is related to the languages of neighboring countries. The two dialects of Marshallese, Ratak and Ralik, are connected to the geography of the two atoll chains. There are also minor dialectic differences from atoll to atoll.

Religion

Most Marshallese are Christians, with a majority practicing Protestant faiths. Roman Catholic, Church of Jesus Christ of Latter-day Saints (Mormon), Seventh-Day Adventist, Assembly of God, and Baha'i faiths also have active congregations in the country. First introduced by Spanish missionaries in the 1500s, and later reintroduced by New England Congregationalists in the 1850s, Christianity plays an important role in community life. The Marshallese have adapted Christianity to their own culture by making unique feasts, festivals, dancing, and singing part of religious life. Most people honor the Christian Sabbath and are also religious in their homes. Christmas is a time of great celebration. Groups practice dancing and singing months before the holiday.

Indigenous religion has all but disappeared, although many still believe in and practice traditional medicine.

General Attitudes

Mantin-Majel, the Marshallese way or manner, is important. It generally means a casual or carefree way of life. For example, *babu* is a favorite activity (see Visiting). Interactions are particularly nonconfrontational and people are generally reserved in public. Marshallese will often say what listeners expect to hear. They rarely display rudeness. Time is not as important as interpersonal relations. *Awa in Majel* (Marshallese time) means that meetings and appointments begin when they start and not always at a specific hour. It is more important to wait for all to arrive than to start on time. The family is very important; the group is always more important than the individual. People show respect to the elderly, especially to a woman or an *irooj* (land-owning chief). Sharing and borrowing are more common concepts than owning or having. Privacy on the small islands barely exists. People often sit together to be supportive of each other, without ever exchanging words.

Personal Appearance

Most men and women wear Western-style clothing. Modesty is important. Men on less traditional islands often wear shorts without shirts, although formal occasions dictate they wear jackets, shirts with ties, and long pants. On some islands, men nearly always wear shirts. Women wear muumuu-type dresses that cover their legs and shoulders. Traditionally, women never wear pants or shorts. However, the younger generation, influenced by Western media and dress, is starting to change its fashion sense, much to the distress of the elders. T-shirts, jeans, skirts and makeup are making their way via the media to the capital (Majuro) and the outer islands. Women with long hair usually wear it tied in a bun.

CUSTOMS AND COURTESIES

Greetings

Iokwe (pronounced YAH-quay) is the all-purpose greeting appropriate in almost any situation. Like *Aloha* in Hawaiian, it has many meanings based on inflection. It might mean "hello," "good-bye," "love," or "like," and in certain situations it can be an expression of frustration or remorse. Handshaking is not universal, but when people do shake hands they might continue shaking for a prolonged period, even for an entire conversation. The common greeting *Itok im mona* (Come and eat) is used both literally and as a general greeting. It is typical for people, particularly on outer islands, to invite passersby in for conversation and a drink of *ni* (coconut water), *jakaro* (coconut sap), coffee, or whatever is on hand. People usually do not address one another by name. Instead, a more general reference such as *motta* (friend) might follow *Iokwe*.

Gestures

In Marshallese culture, pointing at or touching another person's head is improper because the head is considered the most sacred part of the body. One calls someone to come over by waving all fingers with the palm facing down. A person might subtly raise their eyebrows to acknowledge another's presence, to agree, or to indicate "yes." A quick hissing sound might be used to get one's attention. It is impolite to walk between two people in conversation. If one absolutely must pass between them, custom dictates lowering one's head (below the level of conversation, if possible) and saying *Jolok bod* (Excuse me). Prolonged eye contact is not common in conversation. Respect is best shown by looking down rather than into someone's eyes.

Visiting

Visiting is an important aspect of Marshallese society. If people do not visit or accept visitors, others may wonder if something is wrong. From short walks to longer boat trips, the practice of wandering around to visit and chat is a national pastime and is referred to as *jambo*. Individuals and/or families *jambo* at all hours on any given day. Hosts often share drinks and food with their guests. Refreshments range from native fruits or fish to imported rice, canned meats, and drinks. Visitors are seated on mats (*jaki*) woven from pandanus leaves. New *jaki* are used as sleeping mats, while old ones are used to sit on. It is customary to remove one's sandals before sitting down.

Men sit cross-legged and women tuck their legs to the side. Out of modesty, women are particularly careful to cover their thighs. Many people also lie down (*babu*) to converse, propping their heads with a large stone, coconut, or window sill. Windows in homes are often at ground level to allow the breeze to cool sleepers at night. Pointing one's foot at anyone else is impolite, and one is careful not to step over seated persons but to walk around them. Visits can last from a couple of minutes to a long time. Visitors and hosts often sit without speaking, simply enjoying each other's presence.

Eating

Most Marshallese foods are eaten with the fingers. If a visitor is presented with food but is not hungry, custom dictates that he or she eat a small amount to show appreciation to the host. The more guests eat, the greater their appreciation. Hosts are disappointed or confused when a guest refuses an offer of food because they enjoy the opportunity to be hospitable. It is better for guests to wrap up offered food and take it with them than to give it back. A common expression, *Kan dikdik kan in iokwe* (Little food with lots of love), speaks to the sharing of food even when there is not enough left for the family. When there is an abundance of food, people may eat many meals or small snacks in a day. Young children usually are fed first. If family members catch a big fish and cook it, they are obligated to share part of it with neighbors and members of the extended family. They might, therefore, take a full plate of tuna to a friend or relative. A couple of days later, the recipient would return the plate full of bananas or another food.

LIFESTYLE
Family

The family is the center of Marshallese life. It is the basis of interpersonal and hierarchical relations and land ownership. It is generally much larger than a nuclear family, with many relatives living together as part of an extended family household. Informal adoption is common, and children are often cared for by members of their extended family. This arrangement is flexible and can extend beyond blood relations. Grandparents often care for their grandchildren. Older people are also highly respected and taken care of. The society is matrilineal in that land is passed down through women, yet men often act as representatives and wield a great deal of day-to-day power. Women are responsible for child rearing and cooking. They also work outside the home, contributing to copra production, food gathering, and traditional weaving.

Dating and Marriage

Dating starts during adolescence. Because any display of affection between genders is considered socially inappropriate, meeting at night (locally called *nightcrawling*) is the typical method of courtship. Boys approach girls' houses at night, crawling and throwing pebbles to get the attention of their dates. After dating, the next step is to *koba*, equivalent to living in a common-law marriage. A couple makes a commitment to each other, starts living together, and might start raising children. Many people later formalize their relationship and marry in a church.

Diet

Agricultural products in the Marshall Islands include coconuts, bananas, breadfruit, limes, taro, pumpkins, and papayas. Fish, chicken, and pork are also part of the Marshallese diet, especially during feasts (*kemem*). Imported foods include rice, flour, sugar, coffee, tea, and canned meats. They compose an increasingly greater proportion of the diet. There are few customs regarding which foods are appropriate at which times. However, dinner, which usually includes fish, is the main meal of the day. *Kwanjin*, breadfruit baked on coals and scraped, is popular. So are *jaajmi* (raw fish) and *taituuj* (fried banana pancakes). On outer islands, people often cook over open fires or in ground ovens.

Recreation

Sports, including volleyball, basketball, baseball, swimming, and canoe racing, are popular. Most schools and towns host local field days. The Marshall Islands send a team to the Micronesian Olympics. Marshallese also enjoy storytelling.

Holidays

Christian holidays, such as Christmas and Easter, are celebrated. Christmas is a time for singing, dancing, worshipping, and eating. Months of preparation are involved. Constitution Day, the national holiday, is observed 1 May. Many atolls celebrate Liberation Day (various dates) to mark when the Americans liberated them from the Japanese during World War II. Compact Day, celebrating the 1986 agreement with the United States, is 21 October. On New Year's Day, people carol in return for gifts. Other public holidays include Memorial Day (1 March), Fisherman's Day (first Friday in September), Labor Day (last Friday in September), President's Day (17 November), and *Kamoolal* or Thanksgiving Day (first Friday in December).

Commerce

Urban business hours are from 9:00 A.M. to 5:00 P.M. On outer islands, the hours are more informal, as businesses often operate out of people's homes. Most stores are closed on Sunday.

SOCIETY

Government

The Marshall Islands has a constitutional government in free association with the United States. The government is divided into three branches. The legislative branch includes 12 traditional chiefs in the council of *Irooj* (upper house), as well as 33 members elected to the *Nitijela* (lower house). President Amata Kabua heads the executive branch and was elected by the *Nitijela*. He is a traditional chief and has been in office since 1979. The judicial branch consists of a Supreme Court, a High Court, and a Traditional Court that handles land disputes. The country attempts to balance both Western and traditional systems by incorporating into the formal government the influence of the land-based social system of *irooj* (land-owning chiefs), *alaps* (lords), and *rijerbal* (workers). While eroding in the cities, the power of the *irooj* and *alaps* and the respect granted by the *rijerbal* remain strong on outer islands. This blend has both positive and negative aspects, with the traditional system sometimes undermining democracy but also providing strong leadership support. The voting age is 18. The last parliamentary elections were in November 1995. All legislators are independents; there are no formal political parties.

Economy

There are two economies in the Marshall Islands, the traditional or subsistence economy and the modern or money-centered economy. The currency is the U.S. dollar ($). The subsistence economy revolves around fishing and farming. It was sustainable for generations because people took only as much as they needed. However, the dramatic increase in population has put pressure on both the land and the sea. The traditional economy is also undermined by the lure of modernity. The modern economy revolves around copra, or the production of coconut oil, which accounts for 90 percent of all exports. Also driving the modern economy are outside funding, including government and military spending; the service industry, particularly in urban centers; and the production of handicrafts, especially by women on outer islands. Commercial fishing has become an important revenue source. National product per capita is about $1,500.

Balancing the two economies is difficult. The modern economy affords many alternatives but also brings the complications of dependence and rapid, if not unchecked, modernization. While the traditional economy at its best is sustainable, it is inadequate for the growing needs of the Marshallese, as the population expands and skills are lost or forgotten. Agriculture, fishing, and tourism are the development priorities for coming years.

Transportation and Communication

Ships and planes serve the transportation needs of the Marshall Islands. The urban centers have the only major roads suitable for vehicular traffic. Outer islands have cleared paths suitable for bicycles and push carts, and there is usually a major path that can be traveled by pickup truck. The majority of islanders walk. A fleet of ships delivers supplies and passengers to outer islands and collects copra. There is limited domestic air service to each atoll, but the country is connected to international carriers through the Majuro airport. Urban centers have phone service and newspapers, while outer islands communicate through high-frequency, solar-powered radios. There are a couple of television stations in urban centers. On some outer islands, people watch videos on televisions connected to generators. There is one public radio station.

Education

Universal public schooling is available through grade eight. A competitive national exam determines admission to the nation's two public high schools. As a result, fewer than half of eligible students attend school beyond the eighth grade. Marshallese is the language of school instruction; however, elementary schools use a bilingual curriculum and greater emphasis is placed on English at the secondary level. The College of the Marshall Islands is in Majuro. Students also pursue post-secondary education in the United States or at off-island schools in the region. The adult literacy rate is 93 percent.

Health

Hospital facilities and medical care are available in urban areas. The outer islands have trained health assistants who handle less serious cases and preventive care. The health status of the Marshallese is good compared to those in other developing nations, but there are concerns about diabetes, diarrhea and intestinal diseases, nutritional deficiencies, and influenza and pneumonia. The high infant mortality rate (48 per 1,000) is related to water quality, nutrition, and a lack of medical resources. The average life expectancy is 62 to 65 years.

FOR THE TRAVELER

A passport is recommended for travel to the Marshall Islands. U.S. citizens do not need visas but must have a round-trip ticket with a departure date shown within one month of arrival. Travelers pay a departure tax of $15. Outer island travel is planned most easily from Majuro. A rental car is unnecessary for touring Majuro as there are many taxis and a bus service. Plans frequently change and delays are to be expected. Drinking water often comes from rain catchments; while generally safe, it should be boiled or treated. For cultural information, a visit to the Alele Museum is recommended. Further information can be obtained through the Embassy of the Republic of the Marshall Islands, 2433 Massachusetts Avenue NW, Washington, DC 20008; phone (202) 234–5414.

Boundary representations not necessarily authoritative.

Islamic Republic of

Mauritania

A F R I C A

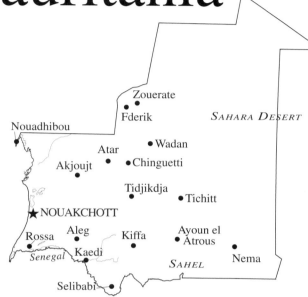

BACKGROUND

Land and Climate

The Islamic Republic of Mauritania covers 397,953 square miles (1,030,700 square kilometers) and is about the size of Texas, Oklahoma, and Kansas combined. Of the three main geographical regions (Sahara, Sahel, and Riverine), the Sahara takes up the northern two-thirds; it is characterized by shifting sand dunes, large rock outcroppings, little or no rain, and very limited vegetation. The semiarid Sahel to the south supports savanna grasslands suitable for nomadic cattle and goat herds. The fertile soil of the Riverine region along the Senegal River supports rice, tropical vegetation, and crops for the country. Fishing grounds along the coast are among the richest in the world and, along with iron ore mined in the north, are one of the country's main natural resources.

Mauritania is hot and dry, although winter temperatures do cool somewhat. During the hottest time of the year (which peaks in May), daytime temperatures reach well over 100°F (38°C), and dusty harmattan winds blow from the northeast. Desertification has intensified in the last 30 years, and the expanding desert threatens the south's farmland.

History

Moors from the north of Africa began migrating to the area in the third and fourth centuries. Their use of camels allowed for extensive trade by caravan. Traders carried West African gold, slaves, and ivory north to present-day Morocco and Algeria to exchange them for salt, copper, and cloth. Important trade towns were established in Chinguetti, Wadan,

Walata, and Tichitt. Islam later spread through this network. In the tenth century, the great Ghanaian Empire controlled much of the south; its capital was near Walata. Arabs gained control in the 16th century. Islam flourished, the Arabic language spread, and the region became a center for *marabouts* (Islamic scholars) and learning.

With territories already in Algeria and Senegal, France established a protectorate over present-day Mauritania in 1903. In 1920, France declared it a colony but gained control only in 1934. French interest in Mauritania was minimal, and this influenced their level of investment in the country. France granted independence in 1960, and the nation elected Moktar Ould Daddah as president. Daddah held office for 18 years, during which time he nationalized the iron mines, took Mauritania out of the *franc* zone, and created Mauritania's own currency, the *ouguiya*.

Daddah also acquired the southern third of Western Sahara (Morocco claimed the northern two-thirds) in 1975, after Spain withdrew from the territory. The Polisario Front, a guerrilla force favoring independence for Western Sahara, soon began attacking Nouakchott and the railroad. In 1979, Mauritania signed a peace treaty with the Front and relinquished its claim to the Western Sahara.

Prior to that, costs associated with the war, combined with severe droughts and lower global demand for iron ore, undermined Daddah's popularity. He was overthrown and imprisoned until 1979, when he left the country. Another coup in 1984 brought Maayouia Ould Sid'Ahmed Taya to power.

Taya's initial actions proved popular: he normalized relations with Morocco, became neutral in the ongoing Western Sahara conflict, and held elections for municipal councils. In 1989, he was challenged by rising ethnic tensions along the Senegal River. Moors clashed with minority Black Africans over land, cattle, and other issues. As part of the overall dispute, Arab Mauritanians attacked Black African Mauritanian merchants in Senegal, prompting Senegal to expel the Arabs. Although this was primarily a racial dispute, Taya's regime cast it more as a political fight with Senegal and began killing Black Africans in the Riverine region. Because many of these Mauritanians belong to ethnic groups that also inhabit Senegal, the government began expelling tens of thousands of them (as if they were Senegalese) from their homeland.

By 1991, Western governments were threatening to cut off aid, and Taya moved to ease tensions. Although racial harassment continued on a smaller scale, Taya began repatriating some of those who had been expelled. Taya sponsored democratic reforms and stood for elections in 1992, but his victory was disputed by opposition parties. Local elections in 1996 were considered free and fair, perhaps signalling greater democracy in the future.

PEOPLE

Population

Mauritania's population of 2.2 million is growing at 3.1 percent per year. Most people live in the coastal and Senegal River regions. About half a million reside in the capital, Nouakchott. The majority population of Moors is divided between White Moors (30 percent) and Black Moors (40 percent). The term *Moor* was coined by the Romans to describe certain North Africans. In their own language, Moors call themselves *Bidhane* (Bedouin) or *Bidhany* in the singular. The French term is *Maure*; the English is *Moor*, sometimes also written as *Maur*.

Black Moors descend from the sub-Saharan African slaves of the White Moors. Slavery has a long history in the Sahara, and Mauritania was the last country to formally abolish it in 1980. Today, vestiges of this system still exist in the form of house servants and chattel slaves. While slaves were indeed property to be bought and sold, they were taken into a family and treated as members of that family. Nevertheless, they were consigned to lives of heavy or menial labor without hope for freedom. Today, White and Black Moors share the same language, culture, and values, but they still are not well integrated. Black Moors tend to live in poorer circumstances than Whites. They are, however, represented in government and are working for greater equality.

Mauritania's Black African population (30 percent) includes the Pulaar, Soninke, and Wolof. The Pulaar and a related group, *Halpular* (or Toucouleur), form the largest minority. The Pulaar are traditionally cattle herders and dairymen, but the Halpular are farmers. The Wolof inhabit the coastal areas and are reputable fishermen. The Soninke are farmers and traders; they live primarily near the Mauritania-Senegal-Mali border. Relations between the Moors and Black Africans are tenuous at best. They are divided by history, language, and culture. For instance, Moors speak Arabic but Black Africans speak their own tongue and usually French.

Language

The national language is Hassaniya, an Arabic dialect. It is spoken by nearly 80 percent of the population. French is the primary language of business and higher education. The Pulaar speak Pulaar (also called Fulani); the Halpular speak Fulfulde, a dialect of the same language. The Wolof speak Wolof and the Soninke speak Soninke. Most of these indigenous languages have incorporated some French and Hassaniya terms.

Religion

Essentially all Mauritanians are Sunni Muslims. Islam's seventh holy city is Chinguetti. *Islam* means "submission" and *Muslim* means "one who has submitted." Muslims surrender to the will of God (*Allah*) and keep the five pillars (or guiding principles) as defined by the *Qur'an* (Koran): professing one's faith; praying daily; fasting during *Ramadan*; giving alms; and making a pilgrimage to Makkah, Saudi Arabia. The faithful are called to prayer five times each day with *Allah akbar* (God is great).

During the holy month of *Ramadan*, Muslims fast between dawn and dusk every day. This observance commemorates the revelation of the *Qur'an* to the prophet Muhammad and is a time of purification and self-discipline. Friday is the day for men to go to mosque and pray.

Islam in Mauritania reflects the influence of indigenous African beliefs about the existence of ghosts, spirits, and supernatural powers. Some *marabouts* make charms (*gris gris*) to ward off evil, curse someone, grant fertility, and so on.

General Attitudes

Moors tend to be stoic and reserved, while Black Africans are more animated and gregarious. All Mauritanians place high value on friendship, family ties, honesty, politeness, modesty, and respect for elders. Social rank is more important than material wealth. Rank is determined largely by family history and name.

The Moors are ordered by a caste system, with *marabout* families having the highest rank and slaves the lowest. In between are various other castes, including warriors, herders, artisans, hunters and fishers, and so on. More modern Moors do not emphasize the caste system, especially if they belong to a less desirable caste.

A strong sense of loyalty to one's ethnic group is paramount. The needs of an individual are less important than those of the community. Poverty is a relative term, as the low standard of living is offset by sharing. Muslims accept life as being controlled by *Allah*, often saying *Inshallah* (God willing) to acknowledge that circumstances are beyond their control. This allows many to feel no need to change their lives. Many people associate modernization with Westernization, which they see as a threat to traditional Islamic values.

Personal Appearance

Men typically wear a *boubou* (or *dara'a*), a long, draping robe in white or blue. They also wear turbans wrapped in various ways about the head and/or face to protect against the sun and blowing sand. A *boubou* may be decorated with intricate embroidery. Black Africans are more likely to wear brightly colored clothing or even Western attire.

Moor women wear a *moulafa*, a large piece of colored cloth that is wrapped around the body and draped over the head. A skirt and possibly a shirt are worn beneath the wrap but not seen in public. Black African women usually wear a *pagne* (wraparound skirt) along with a colorful *boubou* and headwrap. All women value and wear jewelry, especially gold. As a status symbol, many decorate their skin with henna dye.

CUSTOMS AND COURTESIES

Greetings

Mauritanian men shake hands with men but offer verbal greetings to women. Greetings can be lengthy, and men might hold hands while talking. After an initial handshake with an elder, one often touches one's right hand to the heart. The most common initial greeting is *Salaam Alaykum* (Peace be with you), to which people reply *Wa Alaykum Salaam* (And peace be with you). Moors might also say *Iyak labass* (On you no evil), to which one responds *Labass* (No evil). In Soninke, this phrase is *An moho*; the response is *Jam*. For the Wolof, it is *Nanga def*, with the response being *Jam rekk*. And among Pulaar speakers, one says *M'bda* and is responded to with *Jam tan*. Throughout Mauritania, *Il humdu li'llah* (Praise be to God) is a standard response to good news.

In greeting an elder or social superior, a Moor may place the elder's right hand on his head as an act of respect and submission, while the elder will gently try to withdraw his hand from the person's head before leaving it.

Gestures

Mauritanians use the right hand for making all gestures, eating, touching others, and passing objects. It is considered impolite to establish eye contact with an elder. A person makes a clicking sound with the tongue to show he or she is listening to or agrees with the speaker. To disagree, one sucks air through the teeth with the lips pursed. Public displays of affection are unacceptable, but friends of the same gender may hold hands. Married couples do not walk together in public; the husband leads out and the wife follows behind.

Visiting

Paying frequent visits to friends and relatives is an imperative social obligation. Guests may drop by at any time and stay up to three days. Mauritanians are generous to guests and may even slaughter a goat for special visitors. People returning to a rural village are expected to bring back gifts, especially if they received a parting gift before taking their journey. Otherwise, visitors are only expected to bring news of their family and village.

When entering a house or tent, Mauritanians remove their shoes. Hosts offer guests something to drink, such as water, juice from a baobab tree, or *zrig* (milk, water, and sugar whipped together with a whisk). Later, mint tea is prepared. Guests arriving at mealtime are expected to stay and eat. After the midday meal, everyone usually takes a nap. Men lounge together on palm mats. Women more likely lounge with other women. They never lie on their backs or stomachs, as this is considered provocative; instead, they lounge on their sides. Much visiting occurs outdoors because it is too hot inside.

Served among Moors in small glasses and sipped quickly, tea is offered to guests in three ceremonial rounds. With each round, more sugar and mint are added to symbolize three aspects of life: bitter like life, sweet like marriage, and sweetest like having children.

Eating

Meals usually are served at midday and in the evening. People may snack in the morning. Mauritanians eat with their right hand from a communal platter or bowl placed on the ground. Prior to eating, they wash their hands in a water basin. Men and women eat from separate platters and may even eat in separate rooms. Diners eat the portion of food directly in front of them but take meat from the center of the plate. One forms balls of food in the hand before placing them in one's mouth. Hosts often encourage guests to eat more. After the meal, people lick their fingers clean and then wash again in the water basin.

LIFESTYLE

Family

Extended families are very close and often live within the same compound surrounded by a high wall. Anyone with an income is expected to share earnings with the extended family. It is not uncommon for one person to support an entire family in a remote village, including distant relatives. Northern homes may be built of rock with a clay roof, but most homes are made of mud bricks and thatched roofs. Urban homes make greater use of concrete. Nomadic families live in large tents that are elaborately decorated on the inside and may be well appointed.

The father is the head of the family, followed by the eldest son. The father provides money, clothing, and other necessities. In rural families, he often works away from the home village and his family sees him only occasionally. Parents strive to have as many children as possible, as this brings them respect in the community and helps ensure they will be cared for in their later years. Young children help with chores, including caring for animals or tending a garden; urban children might sell candy or other small items.

Dating and Marriage

Dating in the Western sense does not exist. If young people do meet, it is kept secret from the parents. Otherwise, families often choose brides for their sons. It is not uncommon for a couple to meet for the first time at their wedding. Celebrations can take up to three days and involve feasting and dancing. The groom is expected to pay the bride's family a cash dowry according to his family's social rank and wealth. The bride's family gives the couple furnishings. Men may have up to four wives, but most Moor men have only one. Many Black Africans have two or more.

Diet

Moors eat rice and/or *couscous* on a daily basis. *Couscous* is made from sorghum flour carefully sifted and rolled into small balls and then steamed. Vegetables (carrots, lettuce, potatoes, and onions) are added in season. *Idhin* is a kind of butter often poured on *couscous*. The only fruit available in northern areas is dates, which grow in oases. Bread is eaten in the morning or for snacks. The southern diet includes fish, rice, millet, corn, and vegetables. People may eat porridge or bread and butter in the morning, rice with dried fish or a peanut or tomato sauce in the afternoon, and steamed millet flour with beans or milk in the evening. Along the Senegal River, mangoes are abundant in season; guavas, limes, and other citrus fruits are also seasonally available.

Recreation

Men and boys play soccer, and men enjoy camel racing. Women do not play sports but do enjoy afternoon card games together. They also get together to do embroidery and have tea. Children often make their own toys, drum on pans and washtubs, sing, and dance. Mauritanians love to dance, particularly on special occasions. Families often come together in a circle to sing and dance. People may also gather together to listen to a visiting *marabout*.

Holidays

Islamic holidays are set by the lunar calendar. The most important include *El Fitr*, *Tabasky*, and Muhammad's birthday. *El Fitr* is the feast at the end of *Ramadan*. Some 40 days later, *Tabasky* honors Abraham for his willingness to sacrifice his son. For this day, Mauritanians dress in their finest and feast on mutton.

National holidays include New Year's Day (1 January), International Women's Day (8 March), Labor Day (1 May), Islamic New Year, and Independence Day (28 November). In the north, some people celebrate *Getna* when the dates are ripe. Families camp among the date palms and feast on dates.

Commerce

Business hours are from 8:00 A.M. to 6:00 P.M. with a three-hour afternoon break from the heat. Many people participate in commerce, whether it be running small stores or selling goods at open markets in larger villages and cities. The government sets prices for bread, tea, and sugar. In villages where cash and/or markets are not common, some people use payment-in-kind to obtain items they do not produce themselves.

SOCIETY

Government

Mauritania is a republic with a strong executive president. President Taya's party, the Social and Democratic Republican Party (PDRS), dominates the national scene, but opposition parties have been legal since 1991, including the Union for Free Democratic Forces (UFD) and Union for Democracy and Progress (UDP). The legislature is divided between the 56-seat Senate (*Majlis al-Shuyukh*) and the 79-seat National Assembly (*Majlis al-Watani*). Senate members are chosen by local municipal councils, while National Assembly members are directly elected by citizens older than age 18.

Economy

Despite Mauritania's rich fishing grounds and iron ore deposits, the country remains one of the poorest in the world. Real gross domestic product per capita is $1,650. The country's Human Development Index (0.359) ranks it 150th out of 174 nations, reflecting a lack of opportunities for personal progress. The majority relies on subsistence agriculture and animal husbandry for a living. Recent droughts have killed many livestock, the major measure of wealth in Mauritania. The government is trying to overcome problems with currency devaluation, foreign debt, and the inefficiency of state-run enterprises. Some industries are being privatized. Mauritanians often work in other African nations as traders. With caravan trade part of their heritage, many Moors buy goods from distant villages or countries and return to sell them in Mauritania's markets. Traders are esteemed over laborers, the latter being associated with lower castes and even slavery. This has created a glut of underemployed traders and a lack of skilled or motivated labor. Women often form cooperatives to make mats, grow gardens, and produce artisan goods.

Transportation and Communication

Mauritania has two paved roads connecting the capital with Rosso and Nema. Dirt roads are impassable in the rainy season. Although transportation is difficult, one can get most places by *bush taxi*, a network of crowded minibuses that travel on set routes without schedules. The railroad transports iron ore from Zouerate to Nouadhibou when sand is not covering the tracks.

Phones do not exist in many villages, so traditional forms of communication are essential. Travelers are used as couriers to take news or tape-recorded messages to friends and relatives. Most people also listen to nightly radio transmissions for such news. Larger cities have phones, a postal system, and newspapers.

Education

Mauritania's education system is based on the French model, which requires that students pass exams to move from one level to another. Most young children (younger than eight) learn some math and Arabic by attending Koranic schools. After that, most attend at least the first year of primary school. However, schooling is not mandatory, and some children stay home to help the family work or because their parents distrust formal education. The language of instruction is either French or Arabic, depending on the decision of the individual village. The few students who complete the primary level by age 13 may attend high school for another six years. It is split into junior and senior levels. The university in Nouakchott takes high school graduates who pass difficult entrance exams. The adult literacy rate is about 36 percent.

Health

Hospitals and clinics exist in larger cities such as the 12 regional capitals, but they often lack supplies, electricity, water, and medicine. Clinics with foreign doctors are available only to the wealthy. Most outlying areas have no access to medical care. Children suffer from the lack of fruits and vegetables in their diets. People along the Senegal River are at risk for malaria and guinea worm. Intestinal parasites are common throughout the country. Water usually is not potable. The infant mortality rate is 84 per 1,000, and life expectancy averages 48 years.

FOR THE TRAVELER

U.S. citizens need a valid passport and tourist visa to enter Mauritania. To obtain a visa, one must have a letter of invitation from someone in Mauritania, proof of yellow fever vaccination, proof of onward passage, and sufficient funds. Travelers should speak French or Arabic, dress conservatively, treat water, and take all necessary personal items. For information, contact the Mauritanian Embassy, 2129 Leroy Place NW, Washington, DC 20008.

CULTURGRAM '97

Republic of
Mauritius

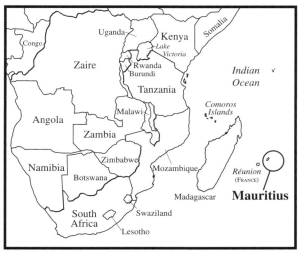

Boundary representations not necessarily authoritative.

BACKGROUND

Land and Climate

Mauritius is a 718-square-mile (1,860 square kilometers) volcanic island in the Indian Ocean, 690 miles (1,113 kilometers) east of Madagascar. The country includes the islands of Mauritius, Rodrigues, and several smaller, uninhabited islands. Lush vegetation covers the island throughout the year. The landscape is marked by impressive mountains that rim a central plateau, deep extinct volcanic craters, rivers, streams, and waterfalls. Surrounded almost entirely by coral reefs, Mauritius has a continuous belt of beaches with lagoons and crystal-clear waters. These waters are always warm (70–80°F or 21–27°C), making swimming possible year-round. About 54 percent of the land is arable. Forests are found in the southwest. The climate is tropical. Winter (May–November) is warm and relatively dry, while summer (November–May) is hot, wet, and humid. Typhoons are possible during much of the summer.

Mauritius is known for its many species of rare birds and plants, some of which exist nowhere else in the world. Three of the world's rarest birds that live on Mauritius are the Mauritian kestrel, the echo parakeet, and the pink pigeon. All are nearly extinct, and scientists and bird-watchers come from all over the world to try to see the birds. Mauritius is also known for being the home of the now-extinct (for more than three hundred years) dodo bird, a member of the pigeon family. The dodo is a popular theme for tourist souvenirs today.

History

Malay and Arab sailors are thought to have visited the island in the 16th century. It appeared on a map as early as 1502. The Portuguese were the first Europeans to set foot on Mauritius. As a tribute to explorer Pedro Mascarenhas, the islands of Mauritius, Rodrigues, and French-owned Réunion are known as the Mascarene Archipelago. In September 1598, Dutch Admiral van Warwyck arrived on the uninhabited island and named it Mauritius in honor of Prince Maurice of Nassau. The Dutch were the first to settle the island in 1638, but they abandoned it in 1710 when sugarcane cultivation proved a failure. The Dutch are credited with introducing sugar (now a productive industry) and deer to the island, but they are also charged with causing the extinction of the dodo bird.

Guillaume Dufresne d'Arsel claimed Mauritius for France in September 1715 and named it *Isle de France*. From 1735 to 1746, Mauritius flourished and developed under the direction of François Mahé de Labourdonnais. The British won Mauritius from France in 1810.

After the abolition of slavery in 1834, indentured laborers from India were brought to work in the sugarcane fields. While the British officially ruled Mauritius, they allowed French culture, language, and a Napoleonic law code to be maintained by the Franco-Mauritians, who remained the largest European ethnic group on the island. Mauritius gained independence in March 1968 through the leadership of Sir Seewoosager Ramgoolam, who became the nation's first prime minister. Mauritius remained part of the Commonwealth, recognizing Great Britain's Queen Elizabeth II as nominal head of state.

The 1980s and early 1990s were dominated by the leadership of the Militant Socialist Movement (MSM) and its coalition partners. MSM leader Aneerood Jugnauth was elected prime minister in 1982 and reelected in 1991. His term was to have expired in 1996, but an attempt to change the constitution so Jugnauth could override a Supreme Court ruling led the country's president to dissolve Parliament in November 1995 and hold early elections in December. Opposition candidate Navin Ramgoolam won a landslide victory. His Mauritian Labor Party captured 60 of 70 parliamentary seats to open a new chapter in Mauritian politics. In 1996, Prime Minister Ramgoolam announced intentions to strengthen democratic institutions by introducing equal opportunity, antidiscrimination, and antitrust legislation and possibly creating a senate with appointed members.

THE PEOPLE

Population

There are 1.12 million people on Mauritius, a population that is growing annually by 0.9 percent. The country's Human Development Index (0.821) ranks it 60th out of 174 nations. Adjusted for women, the index (0.722) ranks Mauritius 49th out of 130 ranked nations. These figures suggest that society provides choices and opportunities for personal development to men but not as many to women. Political reform may address that discrepancy.

About 68 percent of the people are Indo-Mauritians, descendants of laborers brought from India to work for the British on sugar plantations. Another 27 percent are Creoles, descendants of Black Africans (from West and East Africa) brought by the French to the island as slaves. Sino-Mauritians (of Chinese origin) account for 3 percent of the population and Franco-Mauritians (of French origin) make up 2 percent. The mixture of these very different ethnic groups has given Mauritius a cosmopolitan and diverse culture. Approximately 40 percent of the population inhabits the urban area that stretches from Port Louis, the capital, to Curepipe.

Language

English is the official language of Mauritius but is not spoken much in day-to-day communication. French and English are used in government and business activities. Road signs are in English, and most newspapers and media communications are in French. But Creole, Hindi, Urdu, Hakka (a Chinese dialect), and Bojpoori are the main spoken languages. Creole (spoken by 90 percent of the population) was developed in the 18th century by early slaves who used a pidgin language to communicate with each other and with

their French masters, who did not understand the various African languages. The pidgin evolved with later generations to become a useful, casual language. Bojpoori (also written "Bhojpuri") on Mauritius is an amalgamation of that Indian dialect and several other Indian dialects originally spoken by early Indian settlers. Most Mauritians are at least bilingual.

Religion

All of the world's major religions—Christianity, Islam, Hinduism, and Buddhism—are represented on the small island. Slightly more than half the population is Hindu, although there are two main sects. While the two generally share common beliefs, Sanathan Hindus accept the existence of three primary gods and various secondary gods. Arya Samajists only recognize the existence of one god. Important to all Hindus are the principles of reincarnation, *karma* (doing good deeds), and the illusionary state of mortal life. Seventeen percent of Mauritius's population is Muslim, accepting only *Allah* as God. Many of the Chinese are Buddhists. Thirty percent of the people are Christians, belonging to the Roman Catholic Church, the Anglican Church, or various other denominations.

General Attitudes

The Mauritian people are family oriented and religious. They are also optimistic, outgoing, intelligent, generous, and industrious, with a generally relaxed attitude toward life. This is evident in their casual approach to time schedules. People are more important than schedules and being late for an appointment is not inappropriate. Mauritians have an ability to synthesize and adopt new ideas and cultures, combining orthodox Eastern philosophical values with a Western sense of rationalism, innovation, and achievement.

Personal Appearance

Most urban people wear Western-style clothing and only wear traditional attire on special occasions or holidays. However, in rural areas, many men still wear a *langouti* (wraparound cotton garment that extends to the feet and is tied at the waist) on a daily basis. Women also often wear traditional clothing, such as the *saree* (a wraparound skirt, with one end draped over the shoulder). The *saree* is usually worn with a *choli* (tight blouse). Muslim women may wear the *bhajoo* (broad pants that narrow at the ankle and are worn with a long shirt that extends to the knees). Many married Indo-Mauritian women wear a red *tika* on their forehead to signify their husbands are alive. A *tika* is made chiefly from vermilion powder. Casual dress tends to be conservative. Modesty is important.

CUSTOMS AND COURTESIES

Greetings

Mauritians usually shake hands when they meet. The French greeting *Bonjour* (Good day) is a commonly used term. Among the Hindu Indians, the *Namaste* is the traditional greeting, especially in rural areas. A person places the palms together (fingers up) in front of the chest or chin and says *Namaste*, sometimes bowing slightly. English greetings are also acceptable. Among friends and relatives, kissing on both cheeks and hugging is common.

Gestures

It is not proper to pass or receive items with the left hand. Instead, one uses the right hand or both hands. The bottom of one's foot or shoe should not point at another person. People beckon by waving all fingers together with the palm down.

Visiting

It is not customary to call before visiting. Guests are always welcome. Tea with sugar and milk is served, often with savories, biscuits, or sweets. The host usually will insist that the guest accept food and drink. It is considered polite for the guest to accept and sample everything served. Guests are not expected to bring gifts, but they may give flowers to the hostess of a formal lunch or dinner.

Eating

Mauritians generally eat with a spoon, fork, and knife, but Indian families often eat with the fingers of the right hand. A guest usually is given the option of using silverware or eating with the hand. An unexpected guest at dinnertime will be invited to share the meal. Hindus do not eat beef. Muslims do not eat pork or drink alcoholic beverages. During the ninth lunar month, or *Ramadan*, Muslims do not eat or drink from sunrise to sundown; they eat meals only in the evening or before sunrise.

LIFESTYLE

Family

Mauritian society places strong emphasis on family solidarity. It is common for extended families—aunts, uncles, and other relatives—to live together. People have great respect for the elderly; it is the duty of their children to take care of them. Traditionally, families have been large. However, the trend now is to have fewer children (perhaps two or three). The government encourages this trend through family-planning programs.

Dating and Marriage

Western-style dating is not common but is increasing among the urban population. Chastity is important, especially among Indo-Mauritian women. Marriage is a strong tradition. Many Indo-Mauritian families arrange marriages for their children, generally with the consent of the bride and groom. Sometimes, grooms in Muslim families follow the practice of giving a dowry to the bride's parents. Divorce is not well accepted and is relatively rare. A wedding is one of the biggest events for all Mauritian families, regardless of the ethnic group or religion. It tends to be a lavish and expensive affair. Wedding ceremonies are conducted along religious lines and vary accordingly. Among Hindus, for example, a bride and groom perform a ritual of walking around a fire during the *Vivaha* (marriage ceremony). As part of a Muslim ceremony, the bride and groom drink from a common cup to signify the

beginning of their lives together. Women typically marry in their early 20s, while men marry a few years later.

Diet

Rice is the main staple. *Roti* (Indian flat bread) is also a staple for many. French breads are immensely popular, especially at breakfast. Vegetarian cooking is common because of the religion-based food preferences of Hindus and Muslims. Indian cuisine is most common, but Creole, Chinese, and spicy variations of all three are also available. Fresh seafood is popular. Some dishes include *faratas* (similar to pancakes), *briani* (rice and vegetables with a mixture of meat, chicken, or fish, and a number of spices), *vanneyen* (chopped fish meatballs in a fish broth), *dohl pouri* (thin bread with meat and curry sauce inside), chicken curry, pickled vegetables, and seasoned squid. Most Mauritians drink tea with milk and sugar after meals. Fruits, Indian sweets, French pastries, and peanuts are popular snacks during the day and especially during afternoon tea.

Recreation

Soccer is the national sport. Horse racing is a popular spectator activity. Movies are the primary entertainment, along with informal social gatherings among friends and family. Listening to music and watching television are also common recreational activities. Playing cards and dancing the *sega* (a Mauritian dance) are especially popular in rural areas. Bar cafés, where men gather to talk and drink, are found in both rural and urban areas. People enjoy swimming and water sports. Wealthier Mauritians increasingly go to discos, casinos, and restaurants.

Holidays

In addition to religious holidays for all major religions, there are a few national holidays. They include New Year's Day, Independence Day (12 March), and Labor Day (1 May). With a large population of Christians, the nation celebrates Christmas and Easter. The Spring Festival (in January or February, also called the Chinese New Year) and *Ching Ming* (when the dead are honored) are the two most important holidays for the Chinese. Two holidays significant to the Muslims are *Eid-ul-Fitr*, a three-day feast that commemorates the end of *Ramadan*, and *Eid-ul-Adha*, a feast marking the end of the pilgrimage to Makkah, Saudi Arabia.

Hindu festivals usually celebrate the victory of a god or principle. For example, *Divali* (Festival of Lights) focuses on the triumph of *dharma* over *adharma*, or light over darkness. The *Cavadee* celebrates the feat of Idoumban, who carried two mountain peaks on his shoulders. *Holi* is a time when people sprinkle each other with colored water in celebration of Prince Bhakta Pralad's defeat of the wicked Holika. During *Maha Shivaratree*, it is popular to dress in white and pour sacred water on a representation of Shiva, one of the three primary Hindu gods. The water is drawn from the Grand Bassin, a high-altitude lake that is located in a volcano crater. Special ceremonies take place at the lake on the Great Night of Shiva, which is during the summer festival.

Commerce

Businesses generally are open from 9:00 A.M. to 4:00 P.M., Monday through Friday. Some are open Saturday mornings. Most towns have an open-air market that might be open most days (as in the case of Port Louis) or one day each week. Prices in these markets are negotiable.

SOCIETY

Government

Mauritius is a parliamentary democracy. Queen Elizabeth is represented by a governor general, currently Sir Veerasamy Ringadoo. President Cassam Uteem is chief of state. Prime Minister Ramgoolam is head of government. His coalition partner, Paul Berenger, is deputy prime minister. The MSM is now the official opposition party in the 70-seat Legislative Assembly. A few smaller parties also have representation. Elections are held at least every five years; the voting age is 18. Mauritius is divided into nine districts and three dependencies. Local councils govern in urban areas. The country has practically no army and has been politically stable since independence.

Economy

The Mauritian economy has been dominated by the sugarcane crop since the 19th century. The sugar industry accounts for 40 percent of all export earnings and employs more than 20 percent of the labor force. Grown on plantations and small farms, sugarcane covers 90 percent of the arable land. However, it has become less important in recent years due to an increase in earnings from textile exports (44 percent of export earnings) and tourism. Tea, grown in the highlands, is the second most important crop. All but a few staple foods are imported.

Manufacturing industries include textiles, electronics, gemstone cutting, knitted wear, and others. The number of tourists visiting the island has increased dramatically over the last decade, helping Mauritius attain almost full employment. Mauritius has been successful in attracting foreign investment and diversifying its economy to ensure continued growth. Real gross domestic product per capita is $11,700, which has more than tripled since 1960 and is still rising. This figure reflects the economy's success and generally indicates a bright future for the country. A large budget deficit for 1995 may strain growth in 1996 and 1997. Both inflation and unemployment are low. The currency is the Mauritian *rupee* (Re).

Transportation and Communication

All areas of the island are accessible by roads. Buses provide the main form of public transportation. Although crowded, they are reliable and fairly inexpensive. Taxis are available in most areas. Fares are negotiable and usually agreed upon in advance. Following the British tradition, traffic moves on the left side of the road. Mauritius has its own airline, Air Mauritius. Several international airlines fly weekly to Mauritius. The telephone system services most of the island and is quite reliable. Although the telecommunications system is small, it provides good service. There are two radio stations and four television stations, one of which receives broadcasts from neighboring Réunion. The island also has several daily newspapers and other periodicals.

Education

The government has placed great emphasis on education over the last several years. Primary and secondary schooling are free and available to all. Families that can afford the fees send their children to private schools. The literacy rate is 81 percent. Nearly all children are enrolled in primary school and more than half advance to secondary school. The University of Mauritius provides opportunities for higher education, emphasizing agricultural sciences and technology. Many Mauritians attend universities abroad, mainly in France, the United Kingdom, and India.

Health

The public health-care system provides basic services to all citizens free of charge. There are many qualified doctors, both employed by the government and engaged in private practice. Private clinics provide more comprehensive medical care for those who can afford it. Health conditions are steadily improving, as all people have access to safe water, good sanitation facilities, and prenatal care for women. Nearly all infants receive their immunizations. The infant mortality rate is 17 per 1,000. Life expectancy ranges from 66 to 74 years.

FOR THE TRAVELER

Although a visa is not necessary for U.S. visitors staying less than three months, a valid passport and proof of return ticket or onward passage are required. No vaccinations are required, unless one is coming from an area infected with yellow fever. Some vaccinations may be advisable, however, depending on the nature and length of the trip. Consult a physician for more details. Mauritius promotes itself as a scuba diving, snorkeling, swimming, sunbathing, fishing, and exploring paradise. Warm, clear waters and relative isolation from large development draw a growing number of tourists. For details regarding travel opportunities, contact the Mauritius Tourist Information Office, 8 Haven Avenue, Suite 227, Port Washington, NY 11050; phone (516) 944–3763. You may also wish to contact the Embassy of Mauritius, 4301 Connecticut Avenue NW, Suite 441, Washington, DC 20008; phone (202) 244–1491.

Mongolia

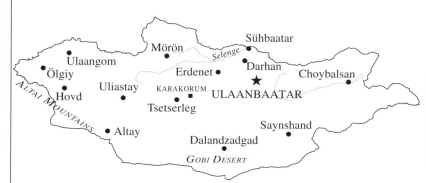

Boundary representations not necessarily authoritative.

BACKGROUND

Land and Climate

Mongolia is about the same size as Alaska. Covering 604,247 square miles (1,565,000 square kilometers), this land-locked country is sandwiched between Russia and China. Mongolia has three mountain ranges; the highest is the Altai Mountains, located in the far west. Much of southern and eastern Mongolia is occupied by a vast plain. The Gobi region (Mongolia's semidesert), lies in the south. It can go years without rain but also has high mountains, oases, and forests. Rivers are mainly in the north. The important Selenge River drains into Lake Baikal, Russia.

Mongolia has an extreme continental climate with long, cold winters and short summers. Little snow falls and annual precipitation usually is less than 15 inches (37 centimeters) per year in the wettest areas. Mongolia is called the "Land of Blue Sky" because it averages 257 cloudless days a year. Winters are very cold (usually below freezing). When bliz-zards send enough snow to cover the grass, livestock cannot graze and therefore die. This type of weather is called *zud*. Summer (June–August) can be warm, with temperatures reaching above 70°F (21°C). Spring is the rainy season. Less than 1 percent of the land is arable, 8 to 10 percent is for-ested, and the rest is pasture or desert.

History

Chinggis (Genghis) Khan consolidated the Mongol nation, created the first unified Mongol state, and adopted Buddhism in the 13th century. He and his descendants built an empire that stretched from Korea to Hungary, the largest continuous land empire ever known. His grandson, Khubilai Khan, founded the Yuan Dynasty in China in 1279. The Mongol Empire began to fragment in the 1300s and Mongols retreated to their homeland. Returning forces clashed, however, with the Oirad Mongolian tribe and civil war ensued. Dayan Kahn's imperial forces defeated the Oirads around 1500. During the reign of Dayan Khan's grandsons, Buddhism was reintroduced (it had waned with the fall of the empire) and spread rapidly.

Civil war between the loosely confederated Mongolian nobles in the 1600s led the Khalka Mongols to ally them-selves with the Manchus of China. The Manchus, who estab-lished the Ch'ing Dynasty in China, eventually dominated all of Mongolia. During the Ch'ing Dynasty, southern Mon-golia became Inner Mongolia (now part of China) and present-day Mongolia was Outer Mongolia. The Manchus preserved the nobility and the church and dominated the nation through these institutions. Local fiefs (called *banners*) had a fair amount of autonomy.

By 1911, when the Ch'ing Dynasty collapsed, the Mongol-Manchu alliance had already dissolved and the Mongols de-clared their independence. Because the Eighth Living Bud-dha (head of Buddhism in Mongolia) was the only unifying political and religious figure in the country, a theocratic mon-archy was established under his leadership. It ended in 1919 when the Chinese invaded. They were driven from the capital by the White Russian Army in 1921, but the Red (Bolshevik) Army allied with Mongolian national hero Sukebaatar to lib-erate the country in July 1921. When the Living Buddha died in 1924, Mongolia was declared a Communist people's re-public. The Communists destroyed the nobility and Buddhist monasteries; thousands died in fighting the changes. A one-party state and a centrally planned economy were established.

With communism's collapse, Mongolia was able to break its economic and political dependence on the Soviet Union. In 1990 elections, Mongolians elected their first president and a new Parliament. With a new constitution in 1992, Mongolia's name was changed from the Mongolian People's Republic to Mongolia. Elections in 1992 established a democratic-style government but not a full democracy, since the ruling (former Communist) party—People's Revolutionary Party—held on to privileges that kept the opposition weak. Dramatic change occurred with 1996 parliamentary elections, when the opposition Democratic Union Coalition (representing several parties) earned 49 of 75 seats to topple the Communists.

THE PEOPLE

Population

Mongolia's population of 2.5 million is growing annually at 2.6 percent. One-fourth of the people live in the capital, Ulaanbaatar, and another fourth live in other cities. The rest are spread throughout rural Mongolia. The country's Human Development Index (0.604) ranks it 110th out of 174 countries. Access to resources that allow people to achieve personal goals is limited but improving.

Mongolia's population is quite homogeneous. More than 90 percent is made up of subgroups of the Mongol nationality, the largest being the Khalkha (79 percent of the total). They are mostly concentrated in the central and eastern areas of the country. Distinctions between the Khalkhas and other Mongols (including Buryads, Dorwods, Oolds, Bayads, Dzakhchins, Uriyankhais, Uzemchins, and Bargas) are minor. They may be expressed through dialects, certain traditions, and folk costumes. The largest non-Mongol ethnic group is the Kazakhs (5.9 percent). They are a pastoral, Turkic-speaking, Muslim people who live in extreme western Mongolia.

Language

Mongol belongs to the Altaic language family. The majority of people speak the Khalkha Mongol dialect. It is also used in schools and for official business. Other Mongol dialects are used by their respective groups. Mongolia's traditional script was replaced under communism with a Cyrillic alphabet similar to that used for Russian. In 1991, Parliament voted to revive the old script. It will eventually be used in all official business and is slowly being introduced in schools. The process is slow due to the lack of printed materials and the fact that few adults can read it. The Mongol alphabet has 26 letters; text is written vertically and individual characters are written differently depending on where they appear in a word. Vowels and consonants are not written separately (as with printed English) but are connected together.

Kazakhs use their own language with a Cyrillic alphabet in schools and local government. Better educated Mongols speak Russian, and many Russian words have been incorporated into the Mongolian language. The use of English is spreading rapidly, and many official signs are written only in the traditional script and English.

Religion

Traditionally, Mongols practiced a combination of Tibetan Buddhism (also called Vajrayana Buddhism) and Shamanism. Tibetan Buddhism shares the common Buddhist goals of individual release from suffering and reincarnation. Tibet's Dalai Lama, who lives in India, is the religion's spiritual leader and is highly respected in Mongolia. As part of their shamanistic heritage, the people practice ritualistic magic, nature worship, exorcism, meditation, and natural healing.

At the beginning of the 20th century, Mongolia had hundreds of monasteries and about 50 percent of all men were monks. The Communist antireligion campaign in the 1930s destroyed the extensive monastic system. Atheism was promoted and monasteries were closed (shamanistic practices survived). From 1945 to 1990, only one monastery (Gandan in Ulaanbaatar) was in operation.

Reform has allowed freedom of religion, and well more than one hundred monasteries have reopened. Many young people are receiving an education through these traditional centers of learning, and people are once again able to practice cherished traditions. Boys are increasingly applying to become monks, and Buddhism is rapidly regaining its popularity. Kazakh Muslims are free to practice Islam.

General Attitudes

Mongols are proud of their history, especially the era when their empire stretched across much of Asia and Europe. As pastoral nomads, Mongols have always regarded themselves as freer than settled nations. This way of life has given them a love for the environment and wildlife. Cows and sometimes elk wander freely on city streets. Mongols appreciate wide-open spaces and feel a oneness with nature. They also value their families. A fast-running horse is prized everywhere. Storytelling is a traditional art. Voting is so important that rural residents will ride for hours on a horse just to reach a polling station.

Now that Mongolia is emerging from decades of Communist rule, society is in a state of flux. Because conformity was fostered under communism, people are not used to personal initiative, entrepreneurship, and risk taking. Mongolian egalitarianism emphasizes shared values and common goals. The nation is searching for ways to help people understand that talent, different opinions, and personal performance are important factors in establishing a democratic society.

Personal Appearance

Western-style clothing is common in urban areas. The youth wear jeans and Western-style jackets. In rural areas, the *deel* (a traditional Mongol gown or tunic) is more popular. A woman's *deel* is made of bright colors and has silk ornaments and fancy buttons. A man's *deel* is less intricate. Both have a sash, embroidered cuffs, and designs. Urban women often have a silk *deel* for special occasions. A winter *deel* commonly is lined with sheepskin or fur. In the coldest weather, urban people wear heavy coats, fur hats, and leather boots. Kazakhs have their own traditional dress.

CUSTOMS AND COURTESIES

Greetings

A handshake is the most common greeting in urban areas. A standard greeting in formal situations or among strangers is *Ta sain baina uu?* (How do you do?). Acquaintances prefer more casual greetings like *Sain uu* (Hello) or *Sonin yutai ve?* (What's new?). In rural areas, people exchange their pipes or snuff as a greeting and ask questions about how fat the livestock are, how favorable the particular season is, and so forth.

Mongolian names consist of a patronymic and a given name. All people are called by their given names. The patronymic is rarely used in ordinary speech and never alone. Its purpose is to distinguish between people who might have the same name. It is the possessive form of the person's father's name. For example, a person named Hashbatyn Hulan is called Hulan and the father is known as Hashbat. A title often follows the given name. It is used to recognize a person's rank, seniority (in age or status), or profession. For example, a respected teacher might be addressed as Batbayar *bagsh*, or an honored elder as Sumiya *guai* (Mr.). *Guai* is also used for women. Sometimes a person with a close relationship to an older person will call that person *Uncle* or *Aunt*, even though they are not related.

Gestures

The right hand is preferred for making gestures. Passing items with the left hand is impolite. Rather, people use both hands or the right hand (supported under the elbow with the left hand). Mongols use their open hand to point. Pointing with the index finger is seen as threatening. To beckon, one waves all fingers with the palm facing down. Crossing the legs, yawning, or making eye contact are avoided in the presence of an elder. Women often cover their mouths when they laugh. Mongols do not like to be touched by people they do not know. Unavoidable contact, such as in line or on a crowded bus, is not offensive. However, kicking another person's foot, even accidentally, is offensive if the two people do not immediately shake hands to rectify the insult.

Mongols use gestures to show appreciation, and gestures often take the place of a verbal "thank you." Some use a respectful gesture (*zolgah*) when first meeting after the new year: the younger person gently holds the elbows of the older person, whose forearms rest on the younger person's forearms; the older person lightly touches his lips to the younger person's forehead.

Visiting

Mongols enjoy having guests in their homes and are known for their hospitality. Unplanned visits are common among Mongols, but international visitors wait for an invitation. The host and family members usually greet guests at the door in modern apartment buildings or outside a *ger* (a circular, domed, tent-like home) in rural areas. The door of a *ger* always faces south. When entering a *ger*, people customarily move around to the left. During formal visits, the host sits opposite the entrance; women sit to the left and men to the right.

Hosts serve tea with milk to guests. *Airag* (fermented mare's milk) might be served instead of tea during summer, and vodka may be served at any time. Guests often give the hosts a small gift. For holidays or birthdays, more valuable gifts are given. On very important occasions, a younger person presents *khadag* (a blue silk band) and a silver bowl filled with *airag* to an elder or a person of higher social rank as a sign of deep respect and well-wishing.

Eating

Breakfast in rural areas might include dairy products and tea. In cities, people add bread and sometimes meat. Midday meals in cities are becoming more Westernized, while rural people generally eat dairy products. Dinner is the main meal of the day throughout the country. The whole family sits together for dinner in the evening. Western utensils are common for all meals, but some people use chopsticks. Most urban dwellers use a knife to cut meat and a spoon to eat rice or vegetables. In urban apartment blocks, people have dining tables and chairs. In rural areas, people sit on the floor or on small stools to eat from a low table. In the evening, soup is served in separate bowls. If the main dish is boiled meat, diners eat it from a communal bowl.

At restaurants, meals are served European style. Toasts are commonly made to all seated at the table. A host often insists on paying for the meal. Tipping is not practiced.

LIFESTYLE

Family

Most Mongols live in nuclear families. Elderly parents live with the family of their youngest son (or daughter if they have no sons). That son inherits the family home and what is left of the herd (after older sons have received equal shares). Grandparents are treated with great respect for their wisdom and life experience, which they use to help raise their grandchildren. The father is head of the family, but the mother is responsible for household affairs. In urban areas, both spouses generally work outside the home. Due to a housing shortage, three generations often share a small apartment, with parents sleeping in the living room and children and grandparents in the bedrooms. Urban families have one or two children.

In rural areas, husbands take care of herding and slaughtering, while wives handle milking and food preparation. Older children care for younger siblings. In urban areas, families live either in high-rise apartments or in a *ger*, with its surrounding fence and storage shed. Most rural families live in a *ger*. A *ger* is a tent with a four- or five-piece wooden lattice, a roof frame, and a door. Its average size is 18 feet (5.5 meters) in diameter. The *ger* is covered with one or more layers of sheep-wool felt and a white cloth. It is easy to erect or dismantle and is warm in cold seasons. A *ger* in or near a city will have electricity but not heat or water. Nomadic extended families often live in a camp of several *gers*.

Dating and Marriage

Traditionally, marriages were arranged between families. Today, individuals make their own decisions. Dating between schoolmates and coworkers commonly leads to marriage. People usually marry between the ages of 18 and 25. Wedding ceremonies take place in "wedding palaces." Afterwards, many couples now go to a Buddhist monk to have their future predicted. A large feast treats as many relatives and friends as the new couple's families can afford to feed. In rural areas, the couple then moves into a *ger* provided by the husband's family. In urban areas, they often struggle to find housing. Mongolian families traditionally exchange gifts in conjunction with the wedding. The groom's family usually gives livestock, while the bride's family offers jewelry and clothing.

Diet

The Mongolian diet consists largely of dairy products, meat, millet, barley, and wheat. People usually eat mutton or beef at least once a day. Rice is common in urban areas. The variety and availability of vegetables and fruits are limited by the climate. Potatoes, cabbage, carrots, onions, and garlic are generally available. Wild berries and, in a few areas, apples grow in Mongolia. In the summer, people eat milk products (dried milk curds, butter, *airag*, and yogurt) instead of large quantities of meat. A common dinner meal is *guriltai shul* (mutton and noodle soup). Boiled mutton is popular. A favorite meal is *buuz*. It is a steamed dumpling stuffed with diced meat, onion, cabbage, garlic, salt, and pepper. A boiled version of the dumpling is called *bansh*. Salt is widely used as a seasoning.

Recreation

Mongol wrestling, horse racing, and archery are the most popular sports. The entire country gets involved in the annual wrestling championships. People also enjoy boxing, soccer, volleyball, basketball, and table tennis. Watching television, going to movies, or going on nature outings are popular leisure activities. Visiting friends and family members is also important. In summer, people spend as much time as possible in the countryside. Small cabins in the hills around the capital are popular summer homes for those who own them. Others visit rural relatives. Sunday is a favorite day for picnics. Mongolians enjoy singing. Traditional songs are often sung at weddings or family gatherings. Traditional dance and music performances at a theater in Ulaanbaatar are popular. The youth enjoy rock concerts.

Holidays

Official holidays include New Year's Day (1 January), the Lunar New Year, Children and Women's Day (1 June), and Mongolian People's Revolution or *Naadam* (11–13 July). *Naadam* is celebrated with horse races, wrestling, and many other events. The Lunar New Year is called *Tsagaan Sar* (White Month). A major holiday marked by family gatherings, *Tsagaan Sar* is preceded by days of house cleaning. Between 1969 and 1994, Women's Day was held 8 March, but this day was merged with Children's Day in 1995 to cut back on the number of holidays and thereby curb male drinking.

Commerce

Weekday urban office hours are generally from 9:00 A.M. to 1:00 P.M. and 2:00 to 6:00 P.M. Shops are open from 8:00 A.M. to 8:00 P.M. Offices may open for a half day on Saturday, but shops keep normal hours. Grocery stores have the same hours as shops but often are open on Sunday. A large open market featuring consumer goods, rural crafts, and assorted items operates several days a week on the capital's outskirts.

SOCIETY

Government

Punsalmaagiin Ochirbat is president and head of state. He faces elections in 1997. A prime minister is head of government. Mongolia's 76-seat Parliament is called the Great Hural. All citizens may vote at age 18. The country is divided into 18 provinces and three autonomous cities (Ulaanbaatar, Darhan, and Erdenet).

Economy

Animal husbandry is a key economic pursuit for nearly half of the people. They raise horses, cattle, bactrian camels, sheep, goats, and yaks. Farming is not widespread. A small light-industrial base produces animal-skin clothing and building materials. Mongolian goats produce cashmere wool, which has become a valuable export. Mongolia is rich in copper, gold, zinc, tungsten, and silver. In 1994, copper accounted for more than half of all export earnings. In creating a free market, Mongolia must overcome several challenges. For example, while citizens may now own property, people are not sure how to grant land ownership in a traditionally nomadic society. And while foreign investment is welcomed, many state enterprises continue to operate as if in a socialist market. Still, progress since 1990 has been promising. Inflation has fallen as steadily as the economy has expanded. Unemployment remains a serious problem. Poverty affects one-fourth of all people, and prosperity is still available only to a few. Real gross domestic product per capita is $2,389. The currency is the Mongolian *tugrik* (Tug).

Transportation and Communication

Paved roads are common in cities, but only about 15 percent of all roads are paved. Cities have buses and trolleys. Cars and trucks are important outside urban areas. Private ownership of cars is limited but increasing. Nearly all international trade and some passenger travel is conducted on the Trans-Mongolian Railway, which connects Ulaanbaatar with Naushki, Russia, and Erenhot, China. The Mongolian airline provides domestic travel and links to Beijing and Moscow.

Telephones are not common. Mail moves slowly. Radio and television stations are government owned, but there are dozens of private newspapers.

Education

The public school system provides free and compulsory education for eight years, beginning at age seven. Students spend two additional years in either general education or vocational training. Mongolia has a literacy rate of more than 90 percent because the government takes education to even remote areas. Higher education was once carefully regulated, but it is now being reformed and liberalized.

Health

Free medical care is administered throughout the country by the government. However, doctors tend to concentrate in the capital and other cities. There is a shortage of imported medicines, and health-care facilities are poorly equipped, especially in rural areas. Maternity and child care are the highest priorities for now. Alcoholism is a serious problem among men. Private insurance and higher-quality private clinics (especially dental) are being integrated into the system. The infant mortality rate is 42 per 1,000. Life expectancy averages 64 to 68 years.

FOR THE TRAVELER

U.S. citizens need a valid passport, as well an an entry and exit visa, to travel in Mongolia. They must also register with police at the Citizens' Information and Registration Center. A packaged tour, or hired guide or translator, is recommended. Mongolia has many cultural and historical sites of interest, including the "dinosaur graveyard" in the Great Gobi Reserve, the ancient city of Karakorum, the medieval Erdene-Dzuu monastery, and the summer palaces of the Eighth Living Buddha. Drinking water should be boiled. Travelers often pay higher than normal prices. U.S. dollars are often accepted, but no change is given. Traveler's checks are becoming more acceptable. Personal toiletries and sunscreen may not be available. For more information, contact the Mongolia Society, 322 Goodbody Hall, Indiana University, Bloomington, IN 47405; or the Embassy of Mongolia, 2833 M Street NW, Washington, DC 20007.

Boundary representations not necessarily authoritative.

Kingdom of
Morocco

BACKGROUND

Land and Climate

Morocco is about the size of California. It covers 172,413 square miles (446,550 square kilometers). The Western Sahara, which Morocco claims and administers, has 102,703 square miles (266,000 square kilometers). Spain controls two coastal enclaves (Ceuta and Melilla) in the north. Morocco lies on the northwest corner of Africa and is across the Strait of Gibraltar from Spain. Traversing the middle of the country from north to southwest are two snow-capped mountain chains: the Middle Atlas and High Atlas. South of the High Atlas lie the Anti-Atlas Mountains, and to the north, along the Mediterranean Sea, runs the Rif Massif range. Most of the country's agriculture is between the mountainous interior and the Atlantic coastal lowlands, into which flow the Oum er Rbia and Tensift Rivers. To the south and east of the Atlas chains, the land becomes increasingly arid the closer it gets to the Sahara. The climate varies with the geographic zone and elevation. The coastal north and west have mild winters and pleasant summers, while interior cities experience more extreme temperatures in both seasons. Winters in the mountains are colder and wetter, but summers are cool and nice. Towns closer to the Sahara can be hot in the summer and cool in winter.

History

The earliest known settlers of Morocco were Imazighen (often referred to as Berbers), believed to have come from southwestern Asia. Because of its strategic location, Morocco's history is replete with foreign invasion and rule, beginning with the Phoenicians and continuing with the Romans, Vandals, Visigoths, and Greeks. The Arabs invaded in the seventh century and introduced Islam to Morocco. The Imazighen fought off direct Arab rule and established an independent kingdom in the eighth century. Two powerful Amazigh dynasties prospered until the 13th century, even expanding for a time into other regions. Following other invasions, the Alaouite Dynasty, which claims descent from the prophet Muhammed, took control in the 17th century. In 1787, Morocco signed a peace and friendship treaty with the United States as one of the first independent nations to recognize the United States as a sovereign nation; the treaty is still in force.

European nations became involved in Morocco in the 19th century, and France made the country a protectorate in 1912. The French ruled until Morocco's independence in 1956, when a constitutional monarchy was established. French and, secondarily, U.S. American influence are still strong in Morocco. The current king (in power since 1961) is Hassan II. He is a direct descendant of kings in the Alaouite Dynasty that began in 1660.

In 1975, Morocco occupied the Western Sahara following threats of invasion that forced Spain to cede control of their former colony. Morocco began developing the region but was opposed by its neighbors, particularly Algeria. Some objecting nations supported a rebel group called the Polisario Front. The United States supported Morocco. The ensuing conflict was very expensive and cost many lives. Determined to retain the Western Sahara, Morocco devoted many resources to providing schools, hospitals, roads, and housing to the people of the Sahara.

Negotiations between King Hassan's government and the Polisario guerrillas began in 1989 as part of a United Nations effort to solve the problem. In 1991, the United Nations agreed to help administer a referendum in the Western Sahara, giving the people a chance to choose annexation by Morocco or independence. A cease-fire went into effect in September 1991, ending 15 years of fighting. The referendum was scheduled for 1992 but was then postponed indefinitely until it could be determined who would be allowed to vote. Negotiators failed to break an impasse between Polisario leaders and Morocco over voter registration lists, so the United Nations suspended its activities in 1996. Regional leaders urged the United Nations to reconsider in order to avoid a resumption of violence.

THE PEOPLE

Population

The current population is about 29.2 million and is growing annually at 2.1 percent. Morocco's population is composed of three main ethnic groups, the largest being the Imazighen (Berbers) and Arabs. Living throughout the south are the Haratin, descendants of slaves brought up from West Africa. Among the Imazighen are a number of regional groups that call themselves by different names. For instance, people of the Rif refer to themselves as Irifin and people of the High Atlas refer to themselves as Ashilhayn. About half of all people live in urban areas, and urban migration is swelling city populations. Casablanca and the metropolitan area of Rabat and Salé account for about 35 percent of Morocco's urban population. More than half the people are younger than age 20. The Western Sahara has an official population of about 217,000, most of whom are ethnic Sahrawi. These are nomadic peoples who live by animal husbandry and subsistence agriculture. Morocco includes them in their official statistics, trade calculations, budgets, and so forth.

Morocco's Human Development Index (0.554) ranks it 117th out of 174 countries. Adjusted for women, the index is only 0.450, reflecting a disparity in female education and earning power. Overall, many people still lack access to resources that would help them pursue personal goals.

Language

The main official language is Arabic, although French also has official status. French is used widely in business, government, and higher education. Moroccan Arabic, called *Derija* (which literally means "dialect"), is the most widely spoken tongue. *Derija* is quite different from the classical Arabic of the *Qur'an* (Koran), the scriptural text of Islam. Imazighen peoples, or some 60 percent of the population, speak Amazigh dialects in addition to Arabic. Prominent dialects include Tashilhayt (spoken in the High Atlas and Souss Valley), Tarifit (spoken in the Rif region), and Tamazight (spoken in the Middle Atlas). Hasaniya, an Arabic dialect, is spoken around Goulmime and south, including in Western Sahara. Spanish can still be heard in the north, which was formerly under Spanish control. English is gaining popularity.

Religion

Islam is the official religion. The king is both the political and spiritual leader of his people. All ethnic Moroccans are Muslim. Conversion to another religion is not recognized by the state. Popular religion mixes aspects of various folk beliefs with traditional Islamic practices. Some Christians and Jews live in Morocco. Jews are mostly native to Morocco, while Christians have European roots. Friday is the Muslim day of worship, when a sermon is spoken at the mosque during the noon prayer. Women are not barred from this activity, but they usually worship at home. Muslims believe in a monotheistic God (*Allah*) and a day of judgment. They accept most Biblical prophets but consider Muhammad to be the last and greatest prophet. Muslims believe he received *Allah's* revelations through the angel Gabriel and recorded them in the *Qur'an*. Religion is a matter of daily practice. The five pillars of Islam that Muslims strive to accomplish are to pray five times daily, profess *Allah* as God and Muhammad as his prophet, give of their income to help the poor, fast each day during the month of *Ramadan*, and make at least one pilgrimage to Makkah, Saudi Arabia.

General Attitudes

Moroccan culture is deeply rooted in Islam. When fortunes turn, people tend to attribute the cause to *Allah*, and the phrase *Insha'allah* (If God wills) is frequently heard. This belief is strongest in rural areas. Urban Moroccans, especially the more educated, do not adhere to it as much. Moroccans value family, honor, dignity, generosity, hospitality, and self-control (particularly of one's temper). A calm attitude gains respect. Women are traditionally restricted to domestic roles, but in urban areas they receive more education and may work outside the home.

Personal Appearance

The national garment is the *djelleba*, a hooded caftan worn by men and urban women. Although Western-style clothing is common throughout Morocco, many people still wear the *djelleba*—particularly for special occasions. Western attire is modest. Moroccans believe it is important to be neat, well-groomed, and appropriately dressed so one will be treated with respect. Women may cover their heads with scarves, but some do not. When entering a mosque, Moroccans wear clothing that covers the entire body (except the head and hands); they remove the shoes. One does not wear short pants and other recreational attire in public; shorts are reserved for the beach.

CUSTOMS AND COURTESIES

Greetings

Moroccans generally shake hands when greeting each other. One might touch the heart after the handshake to express pleasure at seeing the other person or to show personal warmth. Rural children conventionally kiss the right hand of their parents or elders to show respect when greeting. Westernized people might greet close friends or relatives by brushing or kissing cheeks.

Assalam Oualaikoum (Peace be upon you) is commonly used as "hello." People also use *Sbah al Kheir* (Good morning) and *Msa al Kheir* (Good evening). More formally, one might say *Ahlan Wasahlan* (Pleased to see you). Friends may exchange the phrase *Labess*, which means both "How are you?" and "Fine." Greetings between friends also include inquiries about each other's well-being and that of their families. Repeated enthusiastic phrases of welcome are often extended to guests. Less fervent greetings might be considered rude. It is polite to greet an acquaintance when passing on an urban street, but people do not greet strangers. In rural areas, most people know one another, so men greet men and women greet women when passing on the street.

People always use titles in formal situations and to address acquaintances. Friends address each other by first name. Elders might be referred to by a title such as *hadj* (an honorable title reserved for those who have completed a pilgrimage to Makkah) or the equivalent of "aunt" or "uncle."

Gestures

Moroccans pass items with the right hand or with both hands, not with the left. It is impolite to point at people and improper to let the bottom of the foot point toward a person. Moroccans generally consider it improper to cross their legs. Those who do might cross their legs at the knees but would not place an ankle over a knee. One hails a taxi by raising a hand.

Visiting

Frequently visiting friends and relatives is considered necessary to maintain relationships. Visiting is most popular on holidays but may occur at any time. Between family members, it is acceptable to visit unannounced. Whenever possible, friends make arrangements in advance. This is less common in rural areas, where telephones are not always available for calling ahead.

Moroccans are warm and gracious hosts. Social visits can last several hours. Guests invited for dinner in urban areas are not expected to take gifts. However, hosts will appreciate a gift of candy or a small toy for their children. If urban residents visit a relative or friend in a rural area, they are expected to take a gift (staple foods, clothing, household items). Guests invited to a wedding or special event may take gifts for the newlywed couple or person being honored.

Guests generally are offered refreshments. Refusing them is impolite, although guests sometimes give a token refusal before accepting the offered item. Milk and dates are served as a sign of hospitality. Mint tea is often offered to guests, business associates, or anyone with whom one might spend a few minutes during the day. It is considered a friendly, informal gesture that is affordable and easily prepared.

Guests please their hosts by complimenting them on their home. Men and women do not always socialize together. Rural couples more often socialize separately, while urban couples will socialize in mixed company. Men often associate in public coffeehouses, especially on weekends, holidays, or *Ramadan* evenings. At the end of *Ramadan*, heads of households give gifts of money or goods to the poor.

Eating

In most homes, the family eats the main meal of the day together. Before and after eating, each person washes the hands. In rural areas, a basin of water is provided; urban residents wash in the sink. Moroccans eat with their fingers from a large communal dish, using the right hand only. Diners eat from the section of the dish directly in front of them.

Hosts serve the guests' plates and encourage them to eat as much as they like. If the hosts think guests have not eaten enough, they urge them to eat more. In traditional homes, it is impolite for guests to finish eating before the hosts, as this can imply the food did not taste good. Mealtime is an important time for conversation; guests who do not join the discussion embarrass the hosts. In restaurants, service is typically included in the bill, which is usually paid by the host.

LIFESTYLE

Family

Moroccan social life centers on the extended family. One's family is a source of reputation and honor as well as financial and psychological support. It is one's duty to provide financial support to other members of the extended family when it is necessary or requested. The tie between mother and son is the most important relationship. Children are indulged but are also expected to contribute to the family by attaining a respectable position in society. Adult children expect to care for their aging parents when it becomes necessary. Parents generally do not interfere with the domestic or private affairs of their children's families. Polygamy is legal but not frequently practiced. A man may have up to four wives, but he must have permission from any wives he already has and must provide for each equally. Divorce, although frowned upon, is not uncommon.

Dating and Marriage

Dating in the Western sense does not occur in Morocco. In rural areas, young men and women often do not meet their mates until they are to be married. Urban couples meet in various situations, ask permission of their parents to marry, and have time to get acquainted before they get married. When a couple is to be married, the man pays the woman's father or eldest brother a sum of money to meet her wedding expenses. This payment sometimes inhibits a man from marrying because he cannot afford it. Women usually bring a dowry into the marriage. A woman is expected to be a virgin before marriage. Most women marry by their early twenties.

Weddings signify a new union between families and are celebrated as lavishly as possible. A wedding usually lasts two days. The first day is for the bride's female relatives and friends to come together and sing and dance. They decorate the bride's arms and legs with henna dye. On the second day, the groom's family and bride's family celebrate the wedding together to show they are one family.

Diet

Mutton, beef, and chicken are the principal meats in the Moroccan diet. Popular dishes include *kefta*, ground beef or mutton, seasoned and cooked over charcoal; *tajine*, a meat and vegetable stew; and *harira*, a tomato-based soup with beef or mutton, chickpeas, and lentils. Couscous (steamed semolina) is usually eaten on Fridays. Coastal Moroccans cook fish in a variety of ways. Mint tea is the national drink. Islam prohibits the consumption of pork and alcohol, and although some men drink alcohol, it is not socially acceptable.

Recreation

Soccer is by far the most popular sport. Morocco's national soccer team competed in the 1994 World Cup. Many Moroccans also enjoy basketball. Nonathletic forms of recreation include visiting friends, visiting coffeehouses (men only), and going to the beach. Beach volleyball is gaining popularity. Attire on Morocco's many fine beaches ranges from *djellebas* to bikinis.

Holidays

Each year, Muslims observe *Ramadan*, a month of fasting and prayer. During this observance, no eating, drinking, or smoking is permitted from dawn to sunset. In the evenings, families eat together and then visit relatives or friends. Business is slower than usual during this month. Children, pregnant women, travelers, foreign visitors, and the ill are exempt from the fast.

Significant holidays include *Aid al Saghir* (the three-day feast at the end of *Ramadan*), *Aid al Kebir* (the feast at the end of the pilgrimage to Makkah), and *Mouloud* (celebrating the birth of Muhammad). Because Muslims use a lunar calendar (28-day months), the dates of these holidays constantly change in relation to the Gregorian calendar. In addition, numerous *Moussems* (religious festivals) are held throughout the year. Official public holidays include International New Year (1 January), Throne Day (3 March), Youth Day (9 July), Green March Day (6 November), and Independence Day (18 November).

Commerce

A weekly *souk* (market) is held in nearly every town. It is often the only source of basic foods, clothing, crafts, household items, and personal services such as hair cutting for rural people. Urban residents have access to many shops and stores and can shop on a daily basis if necessary.

SOCIETY

Government

Morocco is a constitutional monarchy, but King Hassan II has broad powers as head of state. The king names a prime minister and other ministers to run the government, but he retains ultimate executive authority. Members of the *Majlis Nawab* (Chamber of Representatives) are elected partly by direct elections (for 222 seats) and partly by indirect special interest elections (for 111 seats). The special interest groups include political parties, labor unions, and community organizations. There are several parties with relatively equal strength in the legislature. The voting age is 21.

Economy

Agriculture is the backbone of the economy, employing half the labor force. Most agricultural production is carried out by subsistence farmers, but a small modern sector produces enough food to account for 30 percent of all export earnings. Morocco has the world's third largest deposit of phosphate, which accounts for 17 percent of export earnings.

Tourism is growing in importance to the economy. About 15 percent of the labor force works abroad, primarily in western European countries such as Belgium and France. The money these workers send back to Morocco helps offset the country's foreign debt. A small manufacturing sector is growing and bringing export revenues to the country. The currency is the Moroccan *dirham* (dh).

To stimulate sluggish economic growth, the government is selling more than one hundred state-owned enterprises and encouraging other economic reforms. Unemployment is high, and low wages prompted strikes and labor unrest in 1995.

Real gross domestic product per capita is $3,370, which has tripled in the last generation. About 37 percent of the population lives in poverty. Urban residents can often earn a decent income, but conditions are not as good in rural areas. The upper class holds most of the wealth.

Transportation and Communication

Paved roads connect all major cities and provide excellent access to the rest of the country. Public buses and interurban taxis are available throughout the country. Rural people walk, ride bicycles or motorcycles, or use mules when carrying loads. Urban dwellers use the public transit system. Seven airports offer national service. A rail system connects the major cities of the north. The government provides basic telegraph, telephone, and postal services throughout the country. Service is considerably better in urban areas than in rural regions. There are two televisions stations; the government-owned station broadcasts nationwide, while the private station serves major urban areas. Two national radio stations and eight regional stations serve the country as well.

Education

Since the 1980s, the government has devoted considerable resources to improving Morocco's education system. The adult literacy rate—50 percent—is 15 percent higher than in 1985. Literacy among the youth (ages 15–19) is even higher, reflecting the government's efforts to build schools and train teachers. Still, fewer than two-thirds of all eligible children actually attend school. Girls and rural children are less likely than boys and urban residents to attend school. Of those who begin primary school, about 60 percent go on to secondary school. Preschool offers religious and patriotic instruction. The primary (six years) and secondary (seven years) levels are patterned after the French system; instruction is in Arabic. Students who complete secondary education may seek further education; there are 13 universities and a number of other institutions.

Health

Morocco lacks a comprehensive national health-care system, but the Ministry of Health is trying to provide services to every region of the country. Each province has at least one hospital and some clinics, but these generally do not meet the needs of the entire population. Facilities are severely limited in rural areas. While water in urban areas is usually potable, rural water supplies are not as clean. The infant mortality rate is 46 per 1,000; life expectancy is between 67 and 71 years.

FOR THE TRAVELER

A valid passport is required, but a visa is not necessary for U.S. travelers staying up to 90 days. No vaccinations are required. Only thoroughly washed and peeled fruits and vegetables should be eaten. Beaches, historical sites, and desert castles are the main attractions in Morocco. For more detailed information on travel opportunities, contact the Moroccan National Tourist Office, 20 East 46th Street, Suite 1201, New York, NY 10017; phone (212) 557–2520. You may also wish to contact the Embassy of Morocco, 1601 21st Street NW, Washington, DC 20009; phone (202) 462–7979.

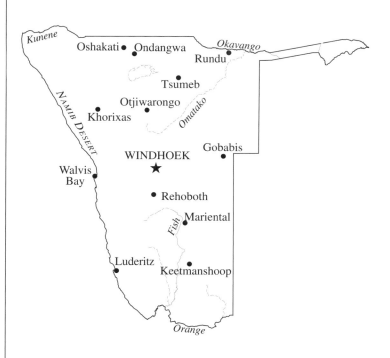

Republic of
Namibia

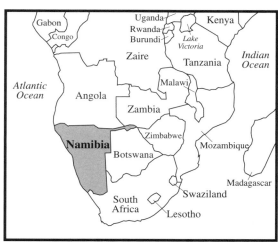

Boundary representations not necessarily authoritative.

BACKGROUND

Land and Climate

Namibia, covering 317,816 square miles (823,144 square kilometers), is the driest country in sub-Saharan Africa. Its central plateau is flanked by two deserts: the Kalahari to the east and the Namib to the west. The coast is usually foggy and cool because of the Benguela current. The plateau covers about half of Namibia, rising abruptly from the desert to an elevation of over 3,300 feet (1,000 meters). High mountains are in the Kunene region. The Fish River Canyon is the second largest in the world. In the north, *iishana* (Oshiwambo word for temporary water holes caused by flooding in the rainy season; singular, *oshana*) support subsistence agriculture, livestock, and wildlife. Etosha Pan National Park is built around the largest *oshana*, which covers some 1,900 square miles (5,000 square kilometers). *Omurambas* (dry river beds) are also a distinctive part of the Namibian landscape. A short rainy season from mid-October to November is followed by a longer one from January to April. Rains are sporadic and unpredictable. The rest of the year is extremely dry, with daytime temperatures around 104°F (40°C). Winter temperatures can get cold in central and southern regions but not below freezing. Temperatures in the north rarely reach below 50°F (10°C) and then only at night.

History

At least 11 ethnic groups inhabited present-day Namibia before German colonization in the late 1800s. It is believed the San people were the first to migrate to the area, as evidenced by ancient rock paintings found in the southern and central areas. The San today may also be called Bushmen.

They comprise at least four tribal groups, and what the entire group should be called is a matter of some debate. Other ethnic groups followed the San into the area, including Owambo, Herero, Nama, Namib, and Rehoboth Basters.

Namibia became a German protectorate called South West Africa in 1884. After its defeat in World War I, Germany lost authority over Namibia in 1920. The League of Nations gave Britain a mandate to prepare South West Africa for independence. The British turned administration over to South Africa. By 1946, South Africa claimed to annex the region and ignored United Nations (UN) protests. South Africa instituted apartheid (segregation) and confined each tribal group to a homeland or to "townships" on the outskirts of urban centers.

By 1957, the South West Africa's People's Organization (SWAPO) had emerged as a leading multiracial force to oppose South Africa's occupation. SWAPO guerrillas began with violent attacks in 1967, and fighting eventually (in the 1980s) became a large-scale war against South Africa's Defense Forces. Under pressure and upon losing key battles, South Africa agreed to withdraw in the late 1980s. It retained Walvis Bay, a deep-sea port, until March 1994.

Homelands and townships were abolished, and elections in 1989 gave SWAPO a majority stake in the new government. Independence was formally recognized on 21 March 1990 under UN Resolution 435. Sam Nujoma became president and was reelected in 1994. SWAPO's power is based among the Owambos, the majority ethnic group, but it favors a multicultural society and encourages constructive diversity.

PEOPLE

Population

Namibia's population of 1.7 million grows by 3 percent per year. Under apartheid, Namibia's many tribal and ethnic groups were classed into 11 ethnic groups. However, these classifications are broad, and the different groups in each class do not necessarily consider themselves part of the "assigned" group. Namibia is a nation in progress, or a people whose sense of national identity is yet in its infancy. Hence, ethnic divisions described here may change as the nation evolves.

Bantu-speaking peoples are the Owambo, Herero, Kavango, Caprivian, and Himba. The San (Bushmen), Namas, and Damaras are classified as Khoisan people. The Coloureds, including Rehoboth Basters, descend from intermarriage between European settlers and the Khoisan people. White Namibians are mostly Afrikaners but also include small pockets of German and British descendants of original colonists. The Owambo form the majority of people (51 percent). The Nama/Damara group is second largest at 13 percent. About 70 percent of the population is concentrated in the far north.

Namibia's Human Development Index (0.611) ranks it 108th out of 174 countries. Many people still lack access to economic prosperity and the chance for personal advancement, but gains are being made with democracy.

Language

To help unify Namibians, the government has chosen English as the official language, while at the same time guaranteeing all people the right to speak their own language. Ten "national languages" are spoken by the major ethnic groups. Most Namibians speak one or two indigenous tongues as well as English or Afrikaans, the official language before independence. The Owambo speak any of eight or more dialects of Oshiwambo. The Herero and Ovahimba speak Otjiherero. The Nama speak Nama and the Damara speak Damara, but these two are so closely related, they are usually listed as Nama/Damara or Damara/Nama. Most Kavango speak RuuKwangali, but a significant minority speak other tongues. The majority of Caprivian speak SiLozi, and the largest San groups speak Ju/'hoasi. Nama/Damara and Ju/'hoasi are Khoisan languages. The Coloureds and Rehoboth Basters speak Afrikaans. A small number of people speak German.

Religion

Namibia is a predominantly Christian country. Christianity was introduced by German missionaries in the 1800s. Catholic and Lutheran churches have the largest indigenous followings. Most Afrikaans speakers belong to the Dutch Reformed Church. All Namibians take care to dress well on Sunday. Older women cover their heads before entering a church. People who call themselves prophets have begun to form rural churches based on Christianity but using traditional worship practices. About 10 percent of rural people continue to follow indigenous beliefs exclusively. Regardless of their individual faiths, Namibians are highly religious. Ceremonies and important meetings are opened and closed with prayer. Schools begin the day with prayer and hymn singing.

General Attitudes

Because Namibia is a young and evolving nation, and because its citizens are of widely diverse ethnic and cultural backgrounds, it is difficult to describe general attitudes or shared attributes. Nevertheless, some common ground exists in important areas, which contributes to Namibia's nation-building. Namibians value family, education, and hard work. Individual success—in higher education, government, business, etc.—brings honor to the entire family. All Namibians respect high status, as defined by old age, wealth (often measured in livestock), political power, advanced educational degrees, and great service to one's people. People do not try to make themselves look better than their peers or family, nor do they praise themselves or volunteer for highly regarded positions. One's peers must nominate one; colleagues or family members praise each other.

Namibians also have a strong capacity to forgive, as evidenced by a national reconciliation campaign to heal the wounds of war. People once on opposite sides of the war for independence live peacefully together in their communities. Namibians are more interested in forging a new and peaceful future than on gaining revenge for past wrongs. Despite this and other promises of independence, Namibia faces challenges related to rapid urbanization, modernization, increased crime, income gaps, and changing lifestyles.

Personal Appearance

Namibians wear Western-style clothing, although pan-African styles are becoming popular among the educated elite. Urban women wear skirts, trousers, and shorts, but in rural areas long skirts are more acceptable. In both rural and urban areas, men usually wear trousers and dress shirts. It is important to have a clean and neat appearance. Clothes are ironed, with creased collars and pleats. Shirts are tucked in. Children wear school uniforms.

Herero women often wear Victorian-style dresses made with 11 yards of fabric that form a large bell-like skirt. They also wear a shawl and a large matching hat. Some older Damara women wear a similar dress as their traditional dress. The Victorian dresses were introduced by German missionaries in the 1800s to replace more revealing native attire.

CUSTOMS AND COURTESIES

Greetings

Namibians greet formally but enthusiastically. Men usually greet with a strong handshake. One always shakes with the right hand, and the left hand is placed on one's right elbow. Eye contact among equals shows sincerity. Women greet men and women by shaking hands, but they may kiss or hug close female friends.

There are as many different greetings as there are languages and situations. In one major Oshiwambo dialect, one says *Walelepo Nawa* (Good morning) and *Ngepi Nawa* (Good afternoon). *Moro* (Good morning) is the Herero version of the Afrikaans greeting *More*. The Nama/Damara say *Mire* (How are you?). Using titles shows respect. Elders with high titles can be called *Sir* or *Madame*. Older Owambo are called *Meme* (for women) or *Tate* (for men). High government officials are addressed by their titles.

Gestures

Namibians use many hand movements in general communication. Hand motions can indicate direction or show the placement of the sun to represent time. Forming a "V" with the middle and index fingers shows support for the Democratic Turnhalle Alliance (DTA), a political party. Holding a right fist up in the air is the symbol for SWAPO.

A passing car flashes its headlights to say "hello." A hitchhiker waves his or her arms to stop a ride. If a possible ride is full, the driver might pound a fist on the other hand or place a flat hand over a fist. Twirling a finger in a circle means the driver in not traveling far.

Public displays of romantic affection are improper, but family members or friends of the same gender may hold hands. Overall, Namibians expect to show their best side when in public.

Visiting

Visiting among family and friends is an integral part of life. Frequent visits maintain friendship and assure reciprocated visits. It is rarely necessary to prearrange visits. Hosts serve guests coffee, tea, or *cooldrink* (any soft drink or juice). Guests stay at least an hour. A rural visit often occurs outdoors, usually in the shade of a tree. If hosts offer food, it is impolite for a guest to refuse it. Whole families participate in visiting, but children are sent away to play after they have greeted the adults. Sunday is the most important visiting day. Friends may visit after church, and relatives often gather for a hearty midday meal. Bad luck is expected to come to a family that is not sufficiently visited after the birth of a new baby or after a move to a new home.

Eating

Although urban residents eat with Western utensils, rural people more often eat with the right hand. This is especially true of children. Urban Namibians usually eat three meals. Businesses and schools often close for the lunch hour so people can eat at home.

In rural areas, people may eat only two meals. Breakfast usually is no more than bread and tea or coffee. Prayers typically are said before midday and evening meals. Plates are prepared ahead of time in the kitchen and served all at once. Hosts give their guests the best treatment possible.

There are many fine restaurants in Windhoek, but they are expensive. *Take-away* food is reasonably priced and found in every city.

LIFESTYLE

Family

Rural Namibians live in extended family groups in one village. Ties are strong, even though migration to urban areas has separated many families. All members must contribute to the betterment of the family through wealth, good behavior, and even by having a baby. Adult family members work hard and give everything they can to the children for a good start in life. In turn, grown children are expected to support their elders. Families function as a group, even among urban residents who tend to have nuclear households. Rural Namibians often visit urban relatives and may stay for long periods of time. It is common for a niece, nephew, or younger sibling to stay with an urban relative to attend a better school, look for work, or help care for small children. Urban families likewise try to visit their rural home often. As more people migrate to cities and stay with relatives, the tradition of wealth-sharing is coming under heavy pressure to change.

Still, oldest sons are expected to help support their families once they begin to work. Both urban men and women work. Children live with their parents until married. Many children are raised partially by their grandparents, as more women enter the workforce. Children born out of wedlock usually are raised completely by grandparents. Most rural women maintain traditional roles and are encouraged by their husbands and families to stay home to raise their children. However, rural women inherited broad responsibilities when men migrated over the years to work in cities.

Dating and Marriage

Traditionally, a young man asked a girl's parents permission to date her, but urban young people now openly congregate in groups, and boys and girls meet at dance clubs or school functions. In northern rural areas, girls and boys meet secretly. Here, if a young couple is seen in public, they are assumed to be having a serious relationship and are expected to marry. Rural women often get married between the ages of 15 and 18. In urban areas, marrying between 18 and 25 years is more common.

Marriage customs are changing with modernization, but traditions remain strong. A man brings his parents to the home of his girlfriend, where his parents then ask permission for the two to marry. Both sets of parents ritually agree to the marriage and to be called on to resolve future marital problems. In many Namibian cultures, the groom must pay *lobola* (bride-price) in the form of cattle or money to the bride's parents before the marriage can take place. The wedding is in the church, and the reception is held at the bride's home or in a reception hall. At the reception, traditional music and dancing add life to a huge feast.

Diet

Rural families grow their own staple crops like maize and *mahangu* (sorghum), but urban dwellers buy what they eat. Rice is popular in urban areas among those who can afford it. Most processed foods are imported from South Africa and are expensive. Maize and *mahangu* are pounded into fine flour and cooked into porridge. Grain is accompanied by beef, chicken, or mutton. People buy goats or sheep and slaughter them at home. *Braais* (barbecues) and *potjiekos* (pot food) are popular traditional ways of cooking. *Potjiekos* is any meal cooked in a three-legged cast-iron pot over a fire. Fish is available when the *iishana* flood, and boys use slingshots to bring down small birds. Tea and coffee are served throughout the day, especially when guests come, and with every meal.

Recreation

The most popular sport for men is soccer, followed for some by rugby. Women play *netball*, which is similar to basketball, except the ball does not touch the ground. Visiting others is the most common leisure activity.

Dance clubs can be found in all towns, cities, and in some rural areas. *Lang Arm* (waltz) music was introduced by the Germans and has become entwined in the traditions of the south. Northern music is more rhythmic in nature and involves African drums and three-part harmony singing. Children learn to sing early, and music plays a part in most aspects of life. Music from other parts of Africa, such as *Kwasa Kwasa* from Zaire, is gaining popularity.

Holidays

Holidays, like national identity, are evolving and not necessarily the same for all Namibians. For example, on Heroes' Day (26 August) the Ovambo mark the beginning of the armed resistance to South Africa, while the Herero honor ancestors killed by German colonizers. Independence Day (21 March) is important to SWAPO supporters but not necessarily to others. The main celebration at Oshakati, where the fight for independence began, includes dance competitions, fireworks, and concerts. Other holidays are New Year's Day (1 January), Easter, Workers' Day (1 May), Cassinga Day (4 May, marking a massacre of eight hundred refugees during the war and honoring all SWAPO war dead), Africa Day (25 May), Ascension, Human Rights Day (10 December), Christmas (25 December), and Family Day (26 December). The Day of the African Child (16 June) is not a public holiday but honors the 1976 slaying deaths of Soweto children.

Commerce

Government office hours are weekdays from 8:00 A.M. to 5:00 P.M., with a lunch break. Private business hours vary. Banks usually are open from 9:00 A.M. to 4:00 P.M. Urban Namibians buy goods from modern shops, but rural inhabitants have access only to basic goods, and prices are high. Minibuses often transport scarce or expensive items to rural northern areas.

SOCIETY

Government

Namibia is a parliamentary democracy with a president, prime minister, and 72-seat Parliament. The prime minister is Hage Geingob. The first elections for Namibia's 13 regions took place in 1992. The voting age is 18. Tribal chiefs are highly respected and their advice or permission is often sought. While final decisions are left to elected officials, they usually follow the advice of a chief.

Economy

The government is the largest employer of wage earners, but most Namibians are subsistence farmers or are employed in agriculture and fishing. Namibia exports cattle and smaller livestock, fish, and *karakul* pelts (sheep skin). Mining is the most important industry, producing diamonds, uranium, and copper for export. Tourism is a major growth industry with significant potential. Many people are engaged in the informal economy, and some 30 percent are officially unemployed. Real domestic product per capita is $4,020. Namibia relies heavily on South Africa's economy, and the Namibian dollar (N$) is tied to the South African *rand*. Namibia has an open market, but nearly all goods are imported from South Africa.

Transportation and Communication

Most Namibians do not own cars. Buses and taxis are available in Windhoek. The Intercape bus offers service from Windhoek to larger towns and cities on the main North-South highway. Trains also connect major cities. People otherwise walk or bike short distances and "hike" greater distances. "Hiking" refers to travel by minibuses. They operate on fixed routes but without schedules. Overcrowded and slow because of frequent stops, minibuses are nevertheless safe and inexpensive. Hitchhiking with private vehicles is legal and common.

Fewer than 10 percent of all homes have telephones, but the ratio climbs to half for urban areas. Every post office has pay phones that accept a prepaid phone card purchased at the post office. Rural access to phones is increasing. Radio broadcasts reach virtually all areas of Namibia and are therefore more important than the one national television station. Broadcasts are made in all major languages, and radio is the major source of news, sports, announcements, and traditional music. The *New Era*, a government newspaper, features news in English and Oshiwambo. There are three other major papers.

Education

Namibian children attend school year-round, with vacations in May, September, and December through January. Most schools are boarding schools. The students stay in hostels and are given all meals at school. Fees can be expensive and therefore can prohibit attendance by the poor. Still, about 70 percent of all eligible children are enrolled, and the adult literacy rate is 76 percent. To receive a high school diploma, students must pass difficult exams in grades ten and twelve. The University of Namibia is the only university, but three colleges of education offer teaching diplomas and three agricultural colleges offer two-year diplomas. Many of Namibia's professionals in the new cultural elite were educated abroad during the struggle for independence.

Health

Under apartheid, private hospitals served white people, and less-advanced public hospitals served all others. Although all races may now use any health-care facility, private hospitals are too expensive for the majority. Government hospitals are understaffed and overcrowded. Clinics are found in most towns, although villages often share a clinic a few miles away. They serve all citizens for a low flat rate, and the unemployed receive free services. Clinics provide prenatal care, immunizations, checkups, and the diagnosis and treatment of disease. Rural clinics are staffed by trained nurses; doctors are available in urban areas. In small towns, doctors may visit weekly to see patients with serious problems.

The infant mortality rate is 62 per 1,000, and the life expectancy rate averages 62 years. Tuberculosis is endemic in part of Namibia, and malaria is widespread in the north. Other diseases (river blindness, schistosomiasis, ring worm) are present in various regions.

FOR THE TRAVELER

U.S. citizens do not need a visa to travel in Namibia, but a passport is necessary. No immunizations are required if traveling directly from the United States, but a yellow fever vaccination is required if one passes through an infected country. The Etosha National Park offers wildlife viewing; the desert environment allows one to see animals from great distances. Prehistoric rock paintings, Fish River Canyon, and the Namib Desert are among Namibia's many treasures. For information, contact the Embassy of the Republic of Namibia, 1605 New Hampshire Avenue NW, Washington, DC 20009.

 Printed on recycled paper

Kingdom of
Nepal

Boundary representations not necessarily authoritative.

BACKGROUND

Land and Climate

Nepal, a predominantly mountainous country, is about the same size as Wisconsin. It covers 54,362 square miles (140,800 square kilometers). The Himalayas in the north contain some of the world's highest peaks; six are higher than 26,000 feet (7,900 meters), including *Sagarmatha* (Mount Everest). The middle hills comprise the native lands of the famous Gurkha foot soldiers and the site of the capital, Kathmandu. To the south lies the Terai, the cultivated fields and subtropical jungles that form the northern rim of the Gangetic Plain. Elevation primarily determines Nepal's climate. While temperatures are fairly moderate around 5,000 feet (1,500 meters), they reach extremes of hot and cold at lower and higher elevations, respectively. Soils and vegetation are also diverse and may vary within a short distance. The cool summers and harsh winters of the north contrast with the subtropical climate of the south. Monsoons from the Indian Ocean bring abundant rainfall to the sub-Himalayan regions between June and September.

History

Various legends surround the ancient history of Nepal. In the sixth century B.C., the Kirati (of the Rai and Limbu tribes) ruled the land. During their reign, Buddha was born in the plains of Nepal. The rule of the Mallas (10th–18th centuries A.D.) in the fertile Kathmandu Valley is known as Nepal's Golden Age of Arts. In 1769, the King of Gorkha, Prithvinarayan Shah, defeated the Malla rulers and other principalities to unite the country. An invasion attempt by the British East India Trading Company failed to conquer the infant country in the early 1800s. The British were so impressed with the courage and tenacity of the Gurkha soldiers that they accepted Nepal as a sovereign nation; Nepal never became a British colony. In 1846, the first Rana took control of the government and became prime minister. The Ranas ruled with an iron hand by taking advantage of the young kings.

The Shah monarchs received their sovereignty again when supporters of King Tribhuwan overthrew the Ranas in 1951 and brought him to power. Soon after, Nepal opened to the outside world for the first time. For introducing democratic principles, Tribhuwan is known as the "Father of the Nation." After several unsuccessful experiments with coalition governments and parliaments, King Mahendra inaugurated in 1960 the *Panchayat Raj* multitiered system of government. This allowed the king to control the government through a partyless system of ministers and a national assembly *(Rastriya Panchayat)*.

Demonstrations for democracy in 1990 led King Birendra, the son of King Mahendra and Nepal's ruler since 1973, to cancel the ban on political parties. He dissolved the *Panchayat* government and allowed an interim one to be formed by representatives of the Congress and Communist Parties, along with some nonparty human-rights activists. A new constitution was drafted and free elections were held in 1991. The Nepali Congress Party (NCP) gained a parliamentary majority, but the government soon found it difficult to meet high voter expectations. Economic difficulties led to strikes and other unrest in 1993. Elections in 1994 brought the Communists to the helm, with Man Mohan Adhikary as prime minister. The NCP built a coalition with two smaller parties to create a parliamentary majority in 1995 and force Adhikary from office. NCP leader Sher Bahadur Deuba became prime minister. By early 1996, Adhikary and his supporters were demanding the NCP step down, reflecting a tenuous and combative political atmosphere.

THE PEOPLE

Population

Nepal's population of 21.5 million is growing annually at 2.4 percent. To slow the rapid growth, the government encourages family planning through the mass media. Nepal's Human Development Index (0.343) ranks it 151st out of 174 countries. This reflects not only poverty but a general lack of social institutions that provide Nepalese with opportunities for personal advancement. The Kathmandu Valley is densely populated. Most people live in rural settlements near water sources; few towns have more than ten thousand inhabitants. Many groups seasonally shift from one elevation to another to take advantage of climatic conditions favorable to cultivation and pasturage. Others, especially in mountainous districts, periodically go to India for temporary employment, to purchase supplies, and to trade goods.

Nepal is ethnically diverse, but caste and religion separate the people more fully than race does. About 50 percent of the people are Indo-Aryans. These include the two highest Hindu castes, the *Brahmins* (traditional priests) and *Chetris* (which includes both the ruling Shah Dynasty and the untouchable occupational classes). The majority of the Indo-Aryans are of various Tibeto-Burmese groups that have migrated over millennia from the north or east into Nepal; these include the Gurung, Magar, Rai, Limbu, Thakali, and Sherpa, among others. Some other major groups, such as the Newar and Tharu are probably of mixed origin. Indians and Tibetans also live in Nepal.

Language

As many as 20 major languages are spoken with many different dialects. Nepali, an Indo-Aryan tongue related to Hindi, is the official language. Most people speak Nepali to some degree, but they more readily use their native tongue. A growing number of urban residents have some fluency in English. Because many private schools and colleges use English as the medium of instruction, especially at the post-secondary level, the ability to speak English is associated with better education and higher social status.

Religion

Nepal is the only official Hindu state in the world; about 88 percent of the population is Hindu. Except those in the upper castes, Hindus and Buddhists (8 percent of the population) often share the same customs and worship at each other's shrines. Many local animist traditions have also been adopted by the Hindus. Although Muslims (3 percent) do not mix their worship with others, they respect the other religions and are respected by them. There are a few Christians. Proselyting is officially forbidden. Although the Hindu caste system has officially been abolished, it is widely practiced, especially in rural areas.

General Attitudes

Nepalese are religious, family oriented, and modest. Physical purity, spiritual refinement, and humility are highly valued.

Acceptance of incidents as the will of fate or *karma* (consequences of past deeds) is widespread. A majority of people believe to some extent that *bhoot* (ghosts), *pret* (evil spirits), *bokshi* (witches), and *graha dasha* (a bad position of the planets) can cause disease in people and livestock, as well as crop failures or accidents. Incense, flowers, and foods are offered to pacify the spirits and planets. A rooster or male goat may also be sacrificed. Class consciousness is expressed in the language used to address other persons; class distinctions affect many social relations.

In general, Nepalese believe Westerners are honest, punctual, rational, pragmatic, and fair. At the same time, they have great pride in their own traditions. Westerners are valued as friends because they are good sources of information about the outside world. Until the 1960s, most things from the outside world were called *belayti* (British). After the arrival of U.S. aid programs, however, Westerners and improved crops and livestock generally became known as *amerikane* (American).

Personal Appearance

Western-style clothing is most often worn by men, but traditional attire is still common for women. Many wear the *sari* (a long, colorful, wraparound dress) and a *cholo* (blouse). Women of Tibetan background wear a wraparound jumper *(bhaku)* and a colorful apron if married. Women in the south and unmarried girls often wear *Punjabi* clothing (colorful pants, tight from the calves down, with a matching tunic that reaches to the knees). Married Hindu women wear a red *tika* (made from vermilion powder) on their foreheads and vermilion powder in the part of their hair to signify that their husbands are alive. Widows do not wear the *tika*, powder, jewelry, or colorful clothing. Wearing proper clothing for a formal situation is important.

CUSTOMS AND COURTESIES

Greetings

Namaste is the traditional greeting. A person places the palms together (fingers up) in front of the chest or chin and says *Namaste* (or *Namaskar* for superiors). Adults do not *namaste* children. In informal situations, one might raise the right hand in a *salaam* (salute-like) gesture for both greetings and farewells. At formal social gatherings, a guest may be adorned with a *mala* (flower necklace) when greeted. In certain Buddhist communities, a *khada* (white cotton scarf) may be offered instead of a *mala*. The Nepalese generally do not shake hands, although educated men may shake hands with Westerners or each other. In greetings, it is polite to use titles ("Professor," "Doctor," "Director") or the suffix *-jee* (or *-jye*) with the last name. The Nepalese usually ask permission before taking leave of others.

Gestures

It is rude to touch another person's head or shoulders. Men do not touch women in public. Even physical affection between married couples is reserved for the privacy of the home. However, members of the same sex express friendship by walking arm in arm or hand in hand. One never points the bottom of the foot at another person or uses it to move objects. If one's foot touches another person, immediate apologies are necessary. A person beckons by waving all fingers with the palm down. Other finger gestures, including pointing, are impolite. Parents make a chopping motion with their hand to express anger at their children. If foods or flowers displayed at bazaars are touched, they become impure. A person does not whistle inside a home or at night. Winking at a person of the opposite sex is vulgar. Cows are sacred; one may not point a foot at them or touch them. When passing a temple, a *stupa* (Buddhist shrine), or a banyan tree, a person will walk around it (if necessary) to keep it on the right. A person's right side keeps evil spirits at bay and shows veneration for the temple, *stupa,* or tree.

Visiting

Visiting others is an important social custom, and relatives and friends get together as often as possible. Hosts are patient with late-arriving guests because people are more important than schedules. Even if a Nepalese wears a watch, which is common, time is thought of more as a series of events or tied to seasons than as a matter of minutes and hours. Visitors are made welcome in Nepalese homes, even if uninvited or unannounced. Nepalese are warm and hospitable. Some people may be shy about inviting strangers (Nepalese or Westerners) into their homes if the strangers are considered better off than they are. Still, because Hindus believe being kind to strangers can enhance their status in the next life, they will not turn away someone in need.

Hosts usually offer tea with sugar and milk to guests; it is polite to initially refuse the refreshments before taking them. When entering a home, a Hindu temple, or a Muslim mosque, one always removes the shoes. Guests invited to a meal may bring small presents for the children, especially during holidays and special occasions. Gifts from guests without a regular income may include food or drinks. In general, one uses the right hand for eating and for giving or receiving objects. Gifts are not opened at the time they are received. In the southern region, a person stays with his or her gender group at social gatherings. This is not as prevalent in the north.

Eating

In most homes, men and/or any guests are served first, followed by children; women eat last. People usually eat food with the hand and sometimes a spoon. Because of the Hindu principle of *jutho* (ritual impurity), food is not shared from the same plate or utensils. When one drinks water from a communal container, one's lips do not touch the container. Higher-caste Hindus are careful that their food is not touched by people outside their caste or religion. Indeed, water cooked or food prepared by any caste lower than one's own is considered *jutho*, or impure, and cannot be eaten. At social gatherings involving more than one caste, *Brahmins* cook the food because everyone else is of a lower caste and can eat the meal. Only *roti* (flat bread) can be prepared by a lower-caste person. *Jutho* is less important among northern Buddhists. When eating out, the person with the higher income insists on paying.

LIFESTYLE

Family

The family takes precedence over the individual. The elderly are respected and cared for by their families. In many traditional families, aunts, uncles, and other relatives with their respective families live together and share the same kitchen.

Among the educated, sons are increasingly setting up separate households after marriage rather than living with the extended family. Land is inherited and divided equally between the sons of a family. Women are gaining some property rights, but they generally have few rights or privileges in society. They are responsible for the household and farming (except plowing) and do not socialize in public as much as men. Many women, mostly those living in urban areas, work outside the home. Rural women are often married before they are 18. They join their husband's extended family at that time and are expected to care for his parents. Some rural men have more than one wife.

Most rural families live in modest houses made of stone and mud, with a few small windows. An upper level may be used to store food. Houses in the cities are built from bricks, stone, or reinforced concrete. Urban apartment buildings cannot be taller than five stories. Those who live in apartments often share water and bathroom facilities with others.

Dating and Marriage

Customs related to marriage vary among the different castes. Traditional marriages are arranged by parents, although sometimes with the consent of the marriage partners. Marriage is sacred, divine, and considered to endure beyond death. Conventional dating and divorce are rare. For the Nepalese, *sat* (chastity) is the most important virtue a woman can bring to a marriage. Sherpas might live together before getting married. Weddings are times of great celebration and feasting. They are expensive and may last up to three days. In the Terai region, a dowry is common.

Diet

Diet varies according to region. Rice with lentil soup and vegetable curry are the main dishes in urban areas or for the rural upper class. Many high-caste people are vegetarian or eat only goat meat. Muslims do not eat pork. The middle castes eat goat or chicken when they are available; some eat water buffalo. Hindus do not eat beef; it is a crime to kill a cow. Meat usually is not consumed more than a few times a month, and then in small quantities. People eat larger quantities only at festivals. Sherpas and Tibetans eat more meat than other groups. Fruits and vegetables are used in season; fruits are considered a snack or dessert.

Millet and corn are staples for most Nepalese, although rice is a staple in the Terai. *Roti* may be prepared with different grains. Wheat is preferred, but a *Brahmin* will also eat a corn *roti*. Poorer people more often eat millet and buckwheat. Hill people eat mush (*dedo*) made of cornmeal, millet, or buckwheat.

Recreation

Several movie theaters in Kathmandu show films from India. U.S. American movies are not allowed in theaters. Many upper- and middle-class families have televisions and VCRs. Video theaters created by families in large cities and small towns show up to three movies a day to local people. In rural areas, people most often provide their own entertainment. Nepal is a country of many festivals and celebrations. People sing and dance on such occasions, and men play cards. The youth fly kites. Popular sports include soccer, volleyball, and badminton. Many adults consider games and sports only for children.

Holidays

Nepal has its own calendar (*Bikram Samvat*), with the new year in mid-April. But dates for religious holidays and festivals are based on the phases of the moon. *Dashain* (two weeks in September–October) celebrates the inevitable triumph of virtue over the forces of evil; it is a time of gift giving, family gatherings, feasts, and rituals performed for the Goddess of Victory. During *Tihar* (three days in October–November), rows of lights are displayed on every building in worship of the Goddess of Wealth. *Tihar* provides married women a time to go home to their parents, receive special treatment, ritually purify themselves, and pray for sons. Sons are special because they stay near the mother (and are not married off into another household, as are women) and can care for her in her old age. *Holi* (February–March) is a lively social event during which people drink heavily, dance in the streets, and throw colorful powders on each other. *Bhoto Jatra* (April–May) is a great festival attended by the king and queen. The birthdays of the king (28 December) and queen (8 November) are also celebrated. Christmas (25 December) is an official holiday. On the full moon of the month *Baisakh* (April–May), the day Buddha was born, the day he was enlightened, and the day he passed into nirvana are commemorated.

Commerce

Business hours are generally from 10:00 A.M. to 5:00 P.M., Sunday through Friday. Open-air markets have different hours and may operate on varying days throughout the country.

SOCIETY

Government

Nepal is a constitutional monarchy. King Birendra is chief of state, but the prime minister runs the government. Parliament is comprised of a 60-member upper house (National Council) and 205-seat lower house (House of Representatives); only members of the House are elected by the people. The House appoints 50 members of the Council, and the king appoints 10. The voting age is 18.

Economy

Agriculture is the mainstay of the economy. It provides employment for 93 percent of the labor force. Including forestry, agriculture accounts for a major portion of Nepal's export earnings. Jute and rice are the major export crops. Most farmers have virtually no cash income. Due to lack of capital and technology, most urban people are economically dependent on agrarian enterprises. Existing industrial activity usually focuses on processing agricultural goods. Tourism is the second most important industry.

The incomes of more than four million Nepalese working in India, including the Gurkha soldiers, are a major support to the economy. Private trade across the Indian border helps bring needed goods into Nepal. While unemployment is relatively low, underemployment (meaning workers work below their skill level or do not work full-time) may be as high as 40 percent. Inflation is around 30 percent.

One of the poorest countries in the world, Nepal's real gross domestic product per capita is $1,170. Sixty percent of all people live in poverty, and income distribution is skewed toward higher castes. The eastern and central regions are more developed and affluent than western regions. The currency is the Nepalese *rupee* (NR).

Transportation and Communication

All major transportation facilities are owned by the state. Roads are better and more numerous in the south. Most people travel by foot or bicycle. Buses are becoming more popular. Animals are often used to pull carts. Few people own cars. There is a state domestic airline, as well as a few smaller private airlines. Traffic travels on the left side of the road. Telephone use is increasing. Radio Nepal serves most of the country and Nepal Television broadcasts to most of the population. The official newspaper, *The Rising Nepal*, is available in Nepali and English.

Education

Primary school education is free. The government pays teacher salaries at this level but only subsidizes wages (50–75 percent) at higher levels of education. Even though education is a major concern for the country (more than 85 percent of children are enrolled in primary school), facilities are often inadequate. In rural areas, girls generally leave school by age 12 to care for younger siblings or help the family farm its land. Secondary school students must pay fees that are often too expensive for villagers. These schools, located only in larger towns, are also less accessible to villagers. The literacy rate is 26 percent; for women it is only 13 percent. The government is seeking to reform the system to provide better instruction and better access. Tribhuwan University in Kathmandu is the main university; branch campuses operate in other urban centers. Mahendra Sanskrit University is the other major university.

Health

Despite a high infant mortality rate (81 per 1,000) and a relatively low life expectancy (53 years), health conditions have improved in Nepal in recent years. Health services are slowly expanding. Still, water is not potable and diseases such as meningitis, typhoid, and hepatitis are widespread. Hospitals are not well equipped, and many people turn to traditional healers rather than go to a hospital.

FOR THE TRAVELER

U.S. citizens need a visa and valid passport to travel to Nepal. A tourist visa is only good for travel in certain areas and permission must be obtained for more extensive travel, especially for mountain climbing. Hiking is a common way to tour Nepal, but the U.S. State Department recommends visitors register with the U.S. Embassy in Kathmandu before embarking. Travelers may wish to call (202) 647–5225 for travel advisories. Immunizations are recommended for the diseases mentioned above. For more information, call the U.S. Centers for Disease Control and Prevention International Travel Hotline at (404) 332–4559. For information regarding travel, send a self-addressed, stamped envelope to the Royal Nepalese Embassy, 2131 Leroy Place NW, Washington, DC 20008.

New Zealand

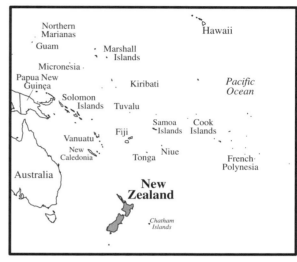

Boundary representations not necessarily authoritative.

BACKGROUND

Land and Climate

New Zealand covers 103,737 square miles (268,680 square kilometers) and is about the same size as Colorado. The indigenous name for New Zealand is *Aotearoa* (land of the long, white cloud). This mountainous island nation lies in the South Pacific about 1,000 miles (1,600 kilometers) southeast of Australia. The two principal land forms are North Island and South Island. Stewart Island is south of South Island and Chatham Islands are far to the east. Numerous other small islands are mostly uninhabited. The more populous North Island has fertile agricultural land, the largest man-made forest in the southern hemisphere, and a few isolated snowcapped volcanoes. It also boasts hot springs, mud pools, and geysers in its thermal region.

On South Island, the Southern Alps provide magnificent scenery and opportunities for sports such as snow skiing. There are many glaciers, lakes, and rivers. Southwest coastal fjords rival those of Norway. Coastal lowlands are used for agriculture. Both islands have many sandy beaches. The climate is temperate, with plenty of sunshine, adequate rainfall, and few extremes in weather. In the winter, however, particularly in the south, high humidity makes it seem rather cold, even though average winter temperatures rarely go below 40°F (4°C). Summer highs average about 73°F (23°C). The seasons are opposite those in the northern hemisphere. January is in the middle of summer and July is in the middle of winter.

History

The first discovery of the islands is attributed to Kupe, the Polynesian explorer. Maori migrations from Polynesian islands probably began before A.D. 900. These early Maori were warlike but highly organized and skilled in many crafts. In 1642, Dutch explorer Abel Tasman sighted the islands and named them *Staten Landt*. He did not go ashore because of an unfriendly Maori reception, and the islands remained largely uncolonized until the early 1800s. Dutch geographers changed the islands' name to *Nieuw Zeeland*—after the Dutch province of Zeeland—but the Dutch never had any direct influence on the islands. Instead, England's Captain James Cook, who first visited the Maori in 1769, opened the door to European (chiefly British) settlement.

In 1840, the Maori and Great Britain signed the Treaty of Waitangi, allowing *kawanatanga* (governance) by the British monarch but granting the Maori legal protection and rights to perpetual ownership of their lands and resources. Only the Crown was entitled to buy land from the Maori, but individual settlers did not always abide by the law. Colonization and European settlement proceeded rapidly after 1840, even as the Maori population declined due to disease and the use of modern weapons in tribal disputes. In 1852, Britain granted New Zealand internal self-government, and by 1907 the nation

OCEANIA

became an independent dominion within the British Empire (later, Commonwealth). In the 20th century, the Maori population rebounded and the Maori people integrated with residents of European descent. However, the Maori maintain many distinct aspects of their cultural heritage.

New Zealand contributed heavily in terms of human resources to both world wars. After World War II, New Zealand turned its focus from European ties to Pacific ties, developing trade links with growing Asian economies. By the 1990s, with Europe integrating on its continent, people in New Zealand began to question the value of remaining within the Commonwealth. Some government officials and public leaders argued that retaining the British queen as nominal head of state hindered New Zealand from becoming a fully independent republic. Prime Minister Jim Bolger, elected in 1990 and reelected in 1993, went so far as to suggest in 1994 that New Zealand should elect its own head of state in the next few years. This would effectively take New Zealand out of the Commonwealth. Many New Zealanders favor such a move in the future, but not before the year 2000.

THE PEOPLE

Population

New Zealand's population of 3.6 million is growing annually at 1.8 percent. The majority (80 percent) of New Zealanders are *Pakeha* (mostly of European descent), and about 10 percent are Maori. Many *Pakeha* (4–6 percent) are part-Maori. The Maori are Polynesians and live mainly on North Island. Other Polynesians (Tongans, Samoans, Cook Islanders) comprise close to 5 percent of the population. Most of these people migrated to New Zealand after 1946. Immigration from Pacific islands continues but is being overshadowed by immigration from Asia. Chinese and Indians now comprise some 2 percent of the total population. Many Chinese have come from Hong Kong in search of a home before China takes control of Hong Kong in 1997.

New Zealand's main metropolitan areas are Auckland, Christchurch, and Wellington (the capital). Auckland and its suburbs hold one-fourth of the nation's people and constitute New Zealand's commercial and industrial center. New Zealand's Human Development Index (0.919) ranks it 17th out of 174 nations. Adjusted for women, the index (0.868) ranks New Zealand 12th out of 130 nations. The disparity is due to differences in incomes earned by men and women. Overall, most people have excellent access to the resources necessary for them to pursue personal goals.

Language

English and Maori are both official languages. Maori is used for Maori ceremonies or other special occasions. Maori people also speak English, and about 10 percent of *Pakeha* speak Maori. Many Maori words (*Pakeha*, *kiwi*, etc.) have been adopted into English. Some New Zealand English words or phrases differ from American English. For example, a car's trunk is a *boot* and the hood is a *bonnet*. Others include *come around* (come over), *over the road* (across the street), *pop downtown* (go downtown), and *go to the loo* (go to the bathroom). A *bathroom* is a place to take a bath, *lift* is an elevator, and *petrol* is gasoline. A *bit of a dag* is a humorous character.

Religion

Most New Zealanders (81 percent) are Christians, including Anglicans, Presbyterians, Roman Catholics, and Methodists, among others. Only about 11 percent attend church on a regular basis. Attendance is higher on religious holidays. About 1 percent of New Zealanders are Hindu or Buddhist. Most of the rest of the population either does not affiliate with a religion or has not specified a particular belief.

General Attitudes

New Zealanders are open, friendly, and hospitable. Their lifestyle is more relaxed and informal than in the United States. For example, while a U.S. citizen might discuss occupations, incomes, and career objectives with colleagues, a New Zealander is more apt to discuss leisure activities and family interests. New Zealanders are, on the whole, self-reliant, practical people. They enjoy working around their homes and gardens. They believe their society should be a caring one, helping people through useful public programs. New Zealanders admire those who are community oriented and nonaggressive. They value home ownership, a good education, and friendship.

New Zealanders have a bicultural society in which *Pakeha* and Maori share many values and customs. The Maori heritage emphasizes family, truth, and a strong sense of community. Despite the general harmony between *Pakeha* and Maori, relations were strained in 1995 and 1996 over a land settlement dispute. Some Maori demand the return of or compensation for lands they lost in the late 1800s. Some even seek greater autonomy on their lands. The government has been willing to negotiate on some issues but contends that compensation must be limited and some lands cannot be restored.

Personal Appearance

Western-style clothing is the standard. People wear casual clothing in public, although it is usually neat and clean. Adults generally reserve shorts for recreational activities. European fashions are popular, but New Zealand also has its own fashion industry. Maori wear traditional costumes for ceremonies and cultural events.

CUSTOMS AND COURTESIES

Greetings

New Zealanders greet with a handshake. In formal situations, men often wait for women to offer their hand before shaking. *Pakeha* greet formally with, "Hello, how are you?" More informal greetings include "Hello" or "Hi." But most common would be *Gidday* (Good day), *Yeah, Gidday*, or *Gidday, How's it going?* After an initial introduction, most people switch from addressing each other by title and surname to using first names.

Maori may greet with a hug or a traditional *hongi*—pressing noses together with eyes closed. The *hongi* is used with non-Maori on a *marae*, the sacred space in front of a Maori *wharenui* (great house). Some Maori greeting phrases include *Naumai* (Welcome to one person), *Tenakoutou* (Welcome to many), *Haere mai* (Come hither), *Kia ora* (Hello), *Tena koe* (Hello to one person), and *Tena korua* (Hello to two people). Upon parting, Maori may say *Haere ra* (Farewell) and reply *E noho ra* (Stay well).

Gestures

New Zealanders often supplement their conversation with hand gestures. Waving at a friend is a sign of recognition, but younger people like to raise both eyebrows in the direction of their friend. Traditional social courtesy is valued but not necessarily practiced by all segments of the population. So, people may no longer give up bus seats to an elderly person or open a door for a woman; however, it is considered polite to avoid chewing gum or using a toothpick in public and to cover yawns with the hand. Personal space usually is important during conversation; standing too close is uncomfortable for many people.

Visiting

New Zealanders entertain often in the home. They like to have friends over for dinner. Garden barbecues are especially popular on weekends. Guests are expected to feel at home. They might remove their shoes unless told otherwise by the hosts. Dinner guests do not arrive empty-handed, but almost always take a gift. Good wine is appropriate if the hosts enjoy it, but flowers, a potted plant, or a box of nice chocolates are also acceptable gifts. House guests always leave a gift with their host family. When welcomed on a *marae*, one leaves a *koha* (gift of money). The *koha* is a donation toward the cost of hospitality; the larger the gift, the more important the giver.

Dropping by a friend's home unannounced is quite common, although such visits after 8:00 P.M. are not appropriate. Inviting people for afternoon *tea* (around 3:00 P.M.) is also popular. Hosts take out the best tablecloth, cups, and saucers and serve fairly substantial refreshments—enough to be considered a meal by some.

Even when not invited for tea or a meal, guests are nearly always offered refreshments. It is rude not to at least offer something to drink. Indeed, even a repairman who is staying more than a few minutes would be offered—and would probably accept—a drink. Common refreshments include coffee, tea, soft drinks, finger sandwiches, cakes, biscuits, and cookies.

Eating

New Zealanders eat a light breakfast before work or school (or by 8:00 A.M.). Lunch is in the early afternoon, and dinner (many call it *tea*) is around 6:00 P.M. The family generally eats dinner, the main meal, together. Dessert is often included, and coffee is nearly always served at the end, especially in restaurants. People eat in the continental style, with the fork in the left hand and the knife remaining in the right. Hands are kept above the table. When finished with a meal, a person places the utensils parallel on the plate. If they are not parallel, the person is not considered finished.

When people eat out, dinner is closer to 8:00 P.M. In a fine restaurant, the staff consider it their job to let diners take their time. They do not hurry unless requested. At restaurants, people generally are quiet and do not speak too loudly. Ice is not served with drinks, and water is only served on request. New Zealanders usually do not practice tipping because wages are considered the duty of the employer, not the customers.

LIFESTYLE

Family

A traditional *Pakeha* family has two parents and two children. Women account for at least 40 percent of all workers, so it is common for both parents to work. The number of single parents is increasing. Family ties are looser than they once were, but people still believe in supporting one another. Parents often give financial help to their adult children until they finish their education.

Most families own their homes. Many people have vegetable and flower gardens. Among Polynesians, extended family connections are important. In some cases, several generations live together in one house. For Maori, the *marae* is important in binding families together. Ceremonies (*hui*), important meetings, and recreational activities take place on the *marae* and in the *wharenui*.

Dating and Marriage

Although most New Zealand parents restrict one-to-one dating until their children are 15 or 16, group social activities usually begin around age 12. The youth enjoy going to movies, dancing, and having parties. Older teens may go with a group of friends to the local pub for dancing and drinking. People usually marry when they are in their mid-twenties. Many choose to live together before or instead of marrying. Weddings can be lavish, with a home or garden ceremony followed by a large party, which may include a sit-down meal and a dance.

Diet

Once mostly influenced by traditional British cuisine, the New Zealand diet has become lighter and more diverse in recent years. *Kaimoana* (seafood) and fresh vegetables play a greater role than in the past. Red meat is eaten less often and portions are smaller. Beef, pork, and roast lamb are still common, as is fish, but poultry is gaining in popularity. Fruits are plentiful. Meat pies and sausage rolls (sausage wrapped in pastry) were popular, but people now more often prefer hamburgers, pizza, and fish and chips. *Vegemite* (yeast extract) is used as a bread spread, but peanut butter, honey, and jam are also popular. Fruits are abundant, including apples, bananas, apricots, peaches, nectarines, plums, cherries, strawberries, and tomatoes. New Zealanders believe their cheeses and ice cream are among the best in the world.

A ceremonial Maori meal is the *hangi*, a combination of meat, seafood, potatoes, *kumara* (sweet potatoes), carrots, and other vegetables all cooked in wire racks lined with cabbage leaves. The dish is steamed for hours in an *umu* (earth oven).

Recreation

Many New Zealanders love sports. Rugby is a popular sport in winter, as is soccer. Cricket is a favorite sport in the summer. Girls and women often play *netball*, a half-court game similar to basketball. Tennis, lawn bowling, and *athletics* (track-and-field) are also enjoyed in the summer. Since no area is far from the mountains, sea, or rivers, there are many opportunities for mountaineering, *tramping* (hiking), fishing (both deep-sea and freshwater), hunting (on a limited basis), swimming, walking, jogging, and sailing. New Zealanders work hard, but they also enjoy their leisure time. They spend considerable time outdoors, playing sports, gardening, or fixing up their homes. Gardening is one of the most popular leisure activities, and people take pride in growing produce to share at a weekend barbecue.

Holidays

Official public holidays include New Year's (1–2 January—an extra day to finish off or continue a summer vacation), Waitangi Day (6 February, for the 1840 treaty), Easter (including Friday), Anzac (25 April, to honor the armed forces and war dead), Queen Elizabeth II's Birthday (first Monday in June), Labour Day (fourth Monday in October), Christmas, and Boxing Day (26 December). Boxing Day comes from the old British tradition of giving small boxed gifts to service workers or the poor on the day after Christmas. It is now a day to visit and relax. Each region celebrates an Anniversary Day.

Commerce

Normal shopping and business hours are from 8:30 A.M. to 5:30 P.M., Monday through Thursday, and from 8:30 A.M. to 8:30 P.M. on Friday. Many shops are open on Saturday and increasingly on Sunday, and corner *dairies* (convenience stores) stay open late seven days a week. Government offices are open from 9:00 A.M. to 5:00 P.M., and banks are open until 5:00 P.M. on weekdays.

SOCIETY

Government

New Zealand is a parliamentary democracy within the Commonwealth. As such, it recognizes Queen Elizabeth II as head of state. She is represented in the country by a governor general (Sir Michael Hardie-Boys). The head of government is the prime minister, who is also leader of the majority party or coalition in Parliament. Parliament is called the House of Representatives. Its 99 seats expanded to 120 in 1996 to accommodate a new proportional representation system (MMP or mixed member proportional). New Zealand is divided into 16 regions, 57 districts, and 16 towns. The main political parties include the National Party, New Zealand First Party (a new, conservative group), New Zealand Labour Party, and Alliance Party. The voting age is 18.

Economy

New Zealand has a modern industrialized economy. But while only 5 percent of the population is employed in agriculture, New Zealand's international trade depends heavily on the sector. The most important exports include wool, lamb, mutton, beef, fruit, fish, and cheese. New Zealand is the world's largest exporter of wool. Exports to Asia are increasing. Important industries include food processing, textiles, machinery, and wood and paper products. Tourism is another vital economic sector.

Real gross domestic product per capita is $14,990, which has doubled in the last generation—a reflection of growing prosperity and a strong middle class. Unemployment is relatively low but higher among Maori. A successful free-trade agreement with Australia, called Closer Economic Relations (CER), took effect in 1990 and has boosted trade. Economic growth since 1990 has averaged 4 percent; for 1995 it was estimated at nearly 8 percent. The currency is the New Zealand dollar (NZ$).

Transportation and Communication

A private car is the preferred mode of transportation, although many urban residents ride a bus to work. All major cities have good bus systems. Trains and a domestic airline also operate between cities and industrial centers. Many people use bicycles for short-distance transportation. Ferries regularly carry passengers and cars between the two main islands. An excellent communications system provides efficient domestic and international service. Numerous radio and television stations and other media operate throughout New Zealand.

Education

Education is free and compulsory between ages six and sixteen. Many enter school at age five, but preschools are also available. Secondary education begins at age 13. Secondary school students wear uniforms. Some high schools are segregated by sex. More than half of all students continue two years after the compulsory requirements to finish high school (also called *college*). A rigorous state exam given in the fifth year of secondary school is required for university admission. The government administers seven universities. A recent policy to charge tuition is restricting access for some students. An excellent system of technical education is available to those who do not pursue a university degree. Continuing and vocational education opportunities are also available. The adult literacy rate is 99 percent.

Health

A comprehensive social security program covers the aged, disabled, sick, and unemployed. The public health-care system maintained by taxes has been reorganized in the past few years; some elements of care are being privatized or simply left to an emerging private sector. The changes are a matter of some contention and debate. Public hospitals still serve the poor and needy, while income earners are expected to carry private insurance. Private hospitals receive some government subsidies. Medical facilities are generally good and readily available. The infant mortality rate is 7 per 1,000. Life expectancy ranges between 73 and 80 years.

FOR THE TRAVELER

U.S. citizens do not need a visa for stays of up to three months, but a valid passport and proof of sufficient funds are required. Proof of a return ticket is also necessary. Water is safe to drink. Remember to drive on the left side of the road. New Zealand offers beautiful scenery and a variety of vacation ideas. For travel information, contact the New Zealand Tourism Board, 501 Santa Monica Boulevard, Suite 300, Santa Monica, CA 90401; phone (800) 388–5494. You may also wish to contact the Embassy of New Zealand, 37 Observatory Circle NW, Washington, DC 20008; phone (202) 328–4800. Consulates are also located in several major U.S. cities.

CULTURGRAM ™ '97

Republic of
Niger

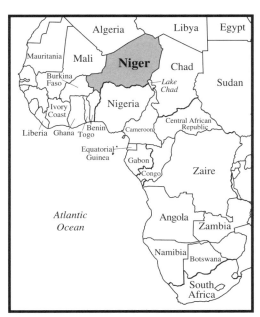

Boundary representations not necessarily authoritative.

BACKGROUND

Land and Climate

Niger (nee–ZHARE), a landlocked country three times larger than California, covers 489,189 square miles (1,267,000 square kilometers). Four-fifths of it is part of the Sahara Desert. Desertification and the growing Sahara are causing severe problems in Niger; droughts occur more frequently and last longer than in the past.

Southern Niger is part of Africa's semiarid region called the Sahel, which receives rain and supports scrub brush and baobab trees. All of Niger's farming is done in the Sahel or near desert oases. The Niger River flows near Niamey, making the southwest the most fertile region. Niger is one of the hottest countries in the world, with average daily temperatures above 90°F (32°C) during the hottest months. There are two hot seasons, one before and one after the rainy season (June–September). From November to February, harmattan winds blow sand off the desert and moderate temperatures.

History

Nomads traversed the area of Niger more than five thousand years ago, but little is known of their history. Tuaregs entered Niger from the north in the 11th century and established a sultanate in Agadez by the 15th century. Niger served as an important trading crossroads for mighty African empires, including the Songhai Empire of Gao in the 16th century. Even today, Tuareg caravans continue to carry salt across the desert. In the 17th century, Djermas settled as farmers near present-day Niamey. Hausaland (southern Niger and northern Nigeria) became the site of a jihad (Muslim holy war) by the Fulanis in the early 19th century, which helped ensure Islam's presence in Niger.

Despite strong resistance by local ethnic groups (especially the Tuaregs) to French military incursions after 1890, Niger became a French colony in 1922. The French moved the capital from Zinder to Niamey in 1926, and that small fishing village grew rapidly to hold nearly a half million people today. In the late 1950s, a fierce political struggle ensued among Nigeriens over independence from France, which was finally granted in 1960. Niger was led by President Hamani Diori until a coup on 15 April 1974, when General Seyni Kountche assumed power as head of the Supreme Military Council. Kountche is generally credited with leading a regime marked by political stability and lack of corruption. A 1984 drought forced Kountche to negotiate for massive food aid after years of near self-sufficiency.

After Kountche's death in 1987, the Supreme Military Council continued to govern with General Ali Saibou at its head. Presidential elections were held in 1989, but only Saibou and members of his party were on the ballot. Ethnic and student unrest, as well as general discontent throughout the country, led to increased tension between the government and citizens. In 1991, a national conference appointed an interim prime minister, leaving Saibou with only token powers. A High Council of the Republic governed until 1993 elections restored civilian rule under a new constitution.

The first democratically elected civilian government, headed by President Mahamane Ousmane, proved unstable. A deteriorating economy, ethnic rebellions, and political rivalries weighed heavily on the young democracy. Elections in January 1995 forced Ousmane to appoint his rival, Hama Amadou, as prime minister. Their rivalry soon paralyzed the government, leading to numerous strikes and unrest. In

January 1996, military leaders deposed both Ousmane and Amadou and installed a civilian transitional government under Boukary Adji. Elections were promised by the end of 1996 after universal condemnation by other West African nations and the broader international community.

THE PEOPLE

Population

Niger's population of 9.28 million is growing at 3.4 percent annually. More than 80 percent of people live in rural areas. About 56 percent of the population is Hausa. Other major groups include the Djerma (22 percent), Fulani (9), Tuareg (8), Kanouri (4), Toubou, and Gourmantche. Djermas live mostly in the southwest around Niamey, the capital and largest city. The Hausa population centers around Zinder (88,000 people), although Hausaland stretches east nearly to Lake Chad and west nearly to Dosso. The Tuareg and Fulani tend to be seminomadic, though many Tuaregs can be found near Agadez and throughout the north. For years, the light-skinned Tuaregs waged a violent rebellion against several African states, claiming repression from black African rule. Although the Tuareg goal of an independent state has not been realized, a peace accord was signed with Niger in April 1995 and all combatants were granted amnesty. Niger's Human Development Index (0.207) ranks it last of 174 countries for its poverty, lack of education, and poor health conditions.

Language

French is the official language, but only about 10 percent of Nigeriens speak it. Most can speak Hausa, which is used for communication and trade between ethnic groups. Ten languages have official recognition in Niger: Arabic, Boudouma, Djerma, Fulfulde, Gourmantchema, Hausa, Kanouri, Tamachek, Tasawak, and Toubou. Many people are multilingual.

Religion

More than 90 percent of Nigeriens are Muslim. They accept major Biblical prophets but believe Muhammad was the last and greatest prophet. The *Qur'an* (Koran) or scripture of Islam, is composed of revelations from *Allah* (God) to Muhammad. Muslims show devotion by praying five times daily while facing Makkah, giving money to the poor, fasting during daylight hours for the month of *Ramadan* (*Azumi* in Hausa), professing there is no God but *Allah*, and trying to make a once-in-a-lifetime pilgrimage (*hajj*) to Makkah. Men visit the mosque on Friday afternoon to pray and worship. Women who go to mosque pray in a different area, but most pray at home or in the fields. Children memorize Arabic verses written with charcoal on wooden boards at local Qur'anic schools. Animist practices exist, primarily in villages, and are often mixed with Islamic rites. A few larger cities have Christian churches.

General Attitudes

Nigeriens patiently accept life as it comes. They often end sentences with *Inshallah* (Arabic for "God willing") to indicate things are out of their control. This allows them to be stoic in the face of frequent hardships. But they laugh often and rarely display real anger in public, especially when it involves personal matters. Time is flexible; waiting is a fact of life. Events and appointments do not necessarily begin on time. People tend to identify with their family, village, ethnic group, and religion before any political party or the nation.

Gender roles are rigidly defined. Women do all the work of the home, such as making flour, collecting firewood, going to the market, drawing each day's water from the well, and caring for the children. Both men and women work in the fields.

Personal Appearance

It is impossible to describe a "typical" Nigerien because of the diverse ethnic and social groups. While an urban professional may wear a suit and carry a briefcase, a village male might wear a long robe and carry a sword. Urban men also wear *boubous* (long robes) or a shirt-and-pant "suit" of matching material. Most men wear hats. Tuareg men wear large green or indigo turbans that cover the entire head except the eyes, while Tuareg women reveal the whole face. Fulanis often wear long black robes and plastic shoes. Formal dress for men usually includes *boubous* with extensive embroidery. Men and women of many ethnic groups have distinct facial scars or tattoos; these are often applied to newborns and then discolored over time to make them stand out.

Women often wear a *pagne*, a colorful cloth wrapped as a skirt or made into a blouse. Married women drape an extra *pagne* around their shoulders, and may use it to carry children on their backs. Most women wear some makeup (especially eyeliner), earrings, other jewelry, and head scarves. Women elaborately braid their hair, while men usually keep their hair short. Adults dress as neat, clean, and modest as possible.

CUSTOMS AND COURTESIES

Greetings

Before any conversation, it is important to exchange greetings, which usually include inquiries about a person's health, family, work, and the weather. The greeting depends on the season and time of day. For example, in Hausa, *Ina kwana* (How did you sleep?) is appropriate in the morning, but in the afternoon *Ina oni* (How did you pass the day?) is used. A response to either is *Lahiya lau* (In health). Responses are always positive; only after the greeting is over is it appropriate to admit to illness or bad times.

Nigerien men shake hands upon meeting and saying goodbye. The handshaking may continue for several minutes, until all greetings are exchanged. To show special respect, one might touch the upper chest with one's right hand and return to the handshake. It is polite to shake the hand of every adult at a small gathering. For large groups, one raises the hands to chest level, palms out, and gives a verbal greeting. Traditional Muslim men do not shake hands with women. Some urban Nigeriens may greet with a kiss to each cheek. In the east, Kanouris greet by shaking a closed fist at head level and calling *Wooshay! Wooshay!* (Hello! Hello!).

People are generally addressed by title, which is often job related. For example, a taxi driver would be called *mai mota* (person with the car). It is respectful to address the elderly as *tsohoua* (old woman) or *tsohou* (old man). Any Muslim who makes a pilgrimage to Makkah, Saudi Arabia, earns the title of *el hadj* for men or *hadjera* for women.

Gestures

It is impolite to use the left hand alone for gestures or eating because it is reserved for personal hygiene. One uses both hands together to pass or receive an object. Flicking the five fingers out in an open-handed gesture is insulting. To indicate "five," one brings all the fingertips of the hand together. To beckon, one waves the fingers of the right hand, palm facing down. One can also get a person's attention by snapping the fingers or hissing. Students snap rather than raise their hands to signal the teacher. A loud snap can be produced by shaking the hand so the index finger snaps against the middle finger. One can point by puckering the lips in the indicated direction.

It is improper for men and women to hold hands in public or otherwise display their affection. However, it is common for male friends to hold hands. To indicate approval or agreement, Nigeriens make a clicking sound deep in the throat. Traditionally, only people of equal social standing make extended eye contact. Younger people look down to show respect.

Visiting

Visiting someone's home is a sign of respect. Invitations are rarely issued; people are expected to drop in. Guests are offered the best seat and then something to drink. A large bowl of water for everyone to drink from may be presented. Guests remove shoes when entering a home or sitting on a mat. Gifts are necessary if the visitor stays the night. *Goro* (kola nuts), peanuts, onions, fruit, or soap are common gifts.

Tea is an important visiting custom for Tuaregs, Fulanis, and others. There are at least three rounds of tea. Sugar and mint are added each time to make the strong tea progressively sweeter. To describe the three rounds, Nigeriens use the phrase "Strong like life, subtle like friendship, sweet like love." Made in small, blue teapots over coals, the tea is served in very small cups. Leaving before all rounds are finished is impolite. After a visit, it is polite for the host to accompany guests to the door of the house or compound or even to walk them home.

Eating

Meals are generally served in a communal bowl and eaten with the right hand or a spoon. Nigeriens generally drink after, not during, the meal. The main meal, which may be in the afternoon or evening, often consists of millet paste and a spicy sauce. Rural men and women eat separately, sitting on woven mats. Urban men and women eat together at a table. An urban breakfast may consist of bread and coffee, but a rural breakfast is generally leftovers from the day before. Snacks eaten throughout the day include peanuts, sugarcane, dates, fruit, or candy. People also chew kola nuts.

Restaurants vary from a table on a street corner to expensive outdoor restaurants in large cities. Women usually prepare food sold on the street, but only men eat in public. Men selling cooked meat walk through the cities, balancing a tray on their heads. They also sell bread and coffee on street corners in the morning. Women sit by open fires making *kosai*, a deep-fried bean cake, or doughnut-like *beignets*.

LIFESTYLE

Family

The family structure dominates Nigerien culture. Children must respect their parents. Older people are highly honored and must be obeyed by younger ones. It is common for the elderly to live with their adult children. Children are seen as belonging to the entire community and they may be disciplined by neighbors or friends. Wealthier persons are expected to share with and help the extended family.

The husband is the head of the family. Muslim men may have up to four wives, and animists can take more. Each wife has her own section within a walled family compound. The husband has his own section and spends time with each wife in rotation. Wives take turns cooking for all. The more wives a man has, the more important he is considered to be. Young men are moving away from this tradition, however, because of the financial responsibility and other challenges. Polygamy is less common among the urban educated. Homes are thatched or made of mud bricks. Common family activities often take place under a thatched roof in a corner of the compound.

Dating and Marriage

It is not proper for boys and girls to date without chaperones. Young men and women in cities may meet at arranged social events such as dances or weddings, where the seating is always male-female-male-female. Marriages are typically arranged by the family. The groom's parents pay an elaborate dowry to the bride's parents as part of the agreement. Village girls often marry in their teens (around 15) and boys between 18 and 25, while urban people marry later. It is not proper for a woman to be unmarried. The traditional marriage ceremony lasts three days, with a big feast for friends. In some parts of Niger, the bride must identify (in the spirit of fun) one of two hooded men as her husband. She is given hints if necessary.

Diet

Millet, sorghum, rice, beans, and macaroni are the staple foods. They are eaten with sauces often made from okra, baobab leaves, peanuts, and tomatoes. Goat is the most commonly eaten meat. Yams, potatoes, lettuce, carrots, and tomatoes are available in the cold season (November–February). Fruits like mangoes come in the hot season. Popular foods include *kilshi* (spiced beef jerky), *hura* (fermented milk with millet and hot pepper), and *brochette* (like a shish kebab). *Tuwo,* pounded millet with a tomato or okra sauce, is common in most villages.

Recreation

Traditional dancing, known as *tam-tam*, is popular in the villages where hired drummers play so young women can dance. Audience members place coins on the foreheads of the dancers they prefer. The money drops to the ground and is swept up by the drummers' apprentice for their pay.

Women and men do not often spend leisure time together. For all Nigeriens, visiting is the most popular form of recreation. Women socialize when pounding millet, braiding hair, or (on special occasions) painting intricate designs on their hands and feet with henna. Soccer is the favorite sport of boys. Traditional wrestling is popular with men and there is a national competition each year. Men might go to outdoor movie theaters in large cities; karate and Indian romance films are popular. The Tuaregs enjoy camel racing.

Holidays

New Year's Day is 1 January. Reconciliation Day is 24 April. Independence Day is 3 August; people plant trees to combat increasing desertification. The Proclamation of the Republic (before actual independence) is celebrated 18 December. School holidays are at Christmas and Easter.

The Islamic calendar is based on the lunar month, so dates for religious holidays vary from year to year. They include Muhammad's birthday (*Mouloud*), which is the only day married women celebrate outside their family compounds; a feast, called *Karamin sallah* or "little feast," at the end of *Ramadan*, a month in which people do not eat or drink during daylight hours; and *Tabaski* (40 days after the *Ramadan* feast), which commemorates Abraham's willingness to sacrifice his son. On *Tabaski*, also called *Babban sallah* or "big feast," a sheep is slaughtered and shared with friends.

Commerce

Business hours are from 8:00 A.M. to 6:00 P.M., but government and private stores close from noon to 3:00 P.M. for *sièste*, a break to escape the afternoon heat. Markets remain open during *sièste* and are themselves a social event; people dress up, meet friends, and chat at the market. Roadside tables offer everything from batteries to cookies in the evening. Store prices are fixed, but it is considered an insult not to bargain in the markets. Water is purchased daily from men who pass in the streets balancing large buckets on a pole across their backs. Post offices provide banking services.

SOCIETY

Government

Niger has seven *départements* divided into thirty-eight *arrondissements*, each of which is led by a *préfet*. Work of the 83-member National Assembly was suspended by the 1996 coup. Most large cities, including Zinder, Tahoua, and Agadez, still have sultans who hold office based on lineage. Villages often have a chief, a man chosen based on birth and ability. The central government ultimately makes most decisions, but on the local level the word of a sultan or chief carries great weight.

Although the judicial system is based on French civil law, most disputes are solved by traditional methods, such as going to a respected elder or chief. The legal voting age is 18. Men and women stand in separate lines to vote, and a husband may cast his wife's vote if she wishes.

Economy

Niger is one of the world's poorest countries. For several years, it benefitted from uranium exports. But demand for uranium is now very low and the economy is suffering. Uranium still accounts for 60 percent of all exports, but the earnings are minimal. Most people (90 percent) are engaged in subsistence agriculture and herding. Most wage earners work for the government, but the private sector is slowly growing. For many months each year, young village men work for wages in neighboring countries and then return in the rainy season.

Real gross domestic product per capita is $820, which has hardly changed for a generation. Most people either have no income or their income is insufficient for their needs. Social institutions are currently unable to provide the rising generation with access to better economic conditions. Niger receives international aid and imports many of its consumer items.

The currency is the *Communauté Financière Africaine franc* (CFAF).

Transportation and Communication

Only major highways and city roads are paved. Highways connect Niamey to N'guigmi in the east and Agadez in the north. The road between Zinder and Agadez is not yet fully paved. Only wealthy Nigeriens own cars. People often walk long distances to visit relatives and friends or to gather firewood and haul water. They may also use a motorcycle, moped, or bicycle, or ride a donkey or camel. A national bus line travels major routes, but most people take *bush taxis* (*taxis de brousse*). *Bush taxi* cars carry 8–10 passengers (vans hold 17–25); they leave when full, so no schedules are definite. Every city has an *auto-gare*, a central gathering point for *bush taxis*, usually near the market. Villagers take *bush taxis* to the weekly market, and the cars or vans often become loaded with livestock, grains, and other goods. During the taxis' frequent stops, vendors sell goods and snacks to passengers through the windows. Taxis also stop for prayer times.

Few people have telephones, but post offices usually have a public phone. The government broadcasts on both radio and television. Television is often watched outdoors, where it is cooler, and is powered by car batteries in villages without electricity. Niger's first (1990) independent newspaper, *Haske* (light), competes with a government paper, *Le Sahel*, and other smaller papers.

Education

The school system is modeled on France's, which requires one to pass difficult exams to advance from primary school to junior high and then high school. French is the language of instruction, which makes learning difficult for primary school children who have never spoken it before. Enrollment in primary school is mandatory, but only about one-fourth of students actually go. More boys have the opportunity to attend school than girls. The average literacy rate is 12 percent. For many families, Qur'anic schools are a more vital part of education. There is a university in Niamey.

Health

Malnutrition, malaria, and measles are all serious problems. Even "minor" problems like diarrhea may be deadly due to lack of proper medical care. The infant mortality rate is 109 per 1,000. Life expectancy averages 45 years. Only the largest cities have hospitals and there is a shortage of trained health-care workers. Larger villages may have a clinic. There is no charge to be seen by a clinic nurse, but patients must buy their own medicines. Traditional herbal medicine is important in rural areas.

FOR THE TRAVELER

U.S. citizens need a valid passport and visa to enter Niger. Yellow fever and cholera immunizations are required, as are malaria prophylactics. Drink only treated or boiled water. Tourism is not well developed, but there is a lot to experience, from Agadez's 16th-century mosque to Niamey's giant market. For more information, contact the Embassy of the Republic of Niger, 2204 R Street NW, Washington, DC 20008.

A *Culturgram* is a product of native commentary and original, expert analysis. Statistics are estimates and information is presented as a matter of opinion. While the editors strive for accuracy and detail, this document should not be considered strictly factual. It is a general introduction to culture, an initial step in building bridges of understanding between peoples. It may not apply to all peoples of the nation. You should therefore consult other sources for more information.

Federal Republic of
Nigeria

Boundary representations not necessarily authoritative.

BACKGROUND

Land and Climate

Covering 356,668 square miles (923,770 square kilometers), Nigeria is about the same size as California, Nevada, and Utah combined. Its geography is as diverse as its people and culture. About 31 percent of the land is suitable for cultivation; 15 percent is covered by forests or woodlands. Desert areas are found in the far north. The country also features the grassy plains of the Jos Plateau in the north-central region, sandy beaches and mangrove swamps along the coast, and tropical rain forests and parklands in the central region. Nigeria is divided into three areas by the Niger and Benue Rivers, which meet and flow together to the Gulf of Guinea. These three regions (north, southeast, southwest) correspond roughly to the boundaries of the three largest ethnic groups. The climate in the north is dry; the rainy season is from April to October. In the south, it is hot and humid year-round.

History

Nigeria, with its many ethnic groups, has a rich and diverse history that stretches back to at least 500 B.C., when the Nok people inhabited the area. Various empires flourished in different regions for centuries. The Hausa, who live in the north, converted to Islam in the 13th century and established a feudal system that was solidified over time. The Fulani built a great empire in the 1800s. In the southwest, the Yoruba established the Kingdom of Oyo and extended its influence as far as modern Togo. The Ibo, located in the southeast, remained isolated. At the end of the 15th century, European explorers and traders made contact with the Yoruba and Benin peoples and began a lucrative slave trade. The British joined the trade in the 1600s but abolished it in 1807. Coastal cities served as trading bases; most slaves taken from this region were shipped to North and South America as opposed to Europe. Although no European power had as yet colonized the area, British influence increased until 1861, when Britain declared the area around the city of Lagos a crown colony. By 1914, the entire area had become the Colony and Protectorate of Nigeria.

When Nigeria became independent in 1960 (a republic in 1963), tensions began to rise among the various ethnic groups. After two coups and much unrest, the Ibo-dominated eastern region attempted to secede and establish the Republic of Biafra. Two and one-half years of civil war (1967–70) followed, and the Ibo were forced back into the republic after more than one million people died.

In 1979, national elections held under a new constitution established a representative civilian government. This government, however, lasted only until late 1983, when a military coup left General Mohammed Buhari in control. He banned political parties. In the summer of 1985, Major General Ibrahim Babangida led a coup to become the nation's new military leader.

Nigeria established an electoral commission in 1986 to organize the transition to civilian rule by 1992, but elections scheduled for 1989 were not held. Timetables were altered and state elections between two officially approved parties occurred in 1991. In preparation for democracy, the capital was moved from Lagos to Abuja in December 1991. The move was to be completed after the new government took power. Many new buildings and modern infrastructures were built to receive the government. The city only began resembling a capital in 1995 and has yet to see a full transfer of institutions.

National elections set for 1992 were held in June 1993. However, once it was apparent that Moshood Abiola (a Yoruba) would win, Babangida refused to accept the results. He annulled the election and announced the military would hold a new vote with new candidates. Rioting broke out in many cities. After a power struggle, Babangida resigned and was soon replaced by rival general Sani Abacha in November 1993.

Abacha dissolved democratic institutions and declared himself ruler of Nigeria. Human-rights abuses, corruption, and oppression became Abacha's hallmarks. Strikes and unrest failed to force him from power. International pressure even failed to stop the execution of nine Ogoni activists in 1995. The Commonwealth later suspended Nigeria's membership. Abacha promised a return to democracy by 1998, beginning with legalizing political parties in late 1996. World leaders are doubtful the elections will materialize or be fair, pointing to the 1996 murder of Abiola's wife by unknown assailants as evidence of the government's continued abuse of power.

THE PEOPLE
Population
Nigeria's population of 101 million is growing rapidly at 3.1 percent. The country is home to more than 250 ethnic groups, the largest of which include the Hausa (21 percent of the population) and Fulani (9 percent) in the north, the Yoruba (20 percent) in the southwest, and the Ibo (17 percent) in the southeast. Other smaller groups like the Ogoni make up 9 percent of the population. Each ethnic group has a distinct cultural heritage.

Nigeria's Human Development Index (0.406) ranks it 141st out of 174 countries. Adjusted for women, the index (0.383) ranks Nigeria 100th out of 130 nations. The average person lacks access to resources and social institutions that would allow for personal advancement and economic prosperity.

Language
More than 250 languages are spoken in Nigeria. English is the official language, although less than half the population can actually speak it. Many consider English a foreign language. Pidgin English is often used in casual conversation. Each ethnic group also has its own distinct language. Hausa, Yoruba, Ibo, and Fulani are widely spoken. Educated Nigerians are often fluent in several languages.

Religion
Nigeria primarily is divided between Muslims and Christians. The north is mostly Muslim, and the southeast is primarily Christian. About half the people in the southwest are Muslim; half are Christian. In all, about 40 percent of all Nigerians are Christian and 50 percent are Muslim. Nigerians who follow traditional African belief systems (10 percent) are spread throughout the country. Many Christians and Muslims also incorporate traditional African worship practices and beliefs into their daily lives.

General Attitudes
Individual Nigerians tend to identify first with their ethnicity, next their religion, and then their nationality. This helps explain the difficulty in uniting them or in solving disputes. Educated Nigerians avoid using the word "tribe," preferring "ethnic group"; however, the average person is not insulted by the word "tribe" when discussing ethnicity. People take great pride in their heritage. Tensions exist between various groups due to their traditional spheres of influence, as well as past conflicts. For instance, the Ibo control land where the oil reserves are, and they are still bitter about the Biafra war. Yorubas tend to control the press and financial sector; prodemocracy groups are primarily Yoruba. The Hausa have held political and military control since independence.

Northerners tend to be quiet, reserved, and conservative in dealing with others. To them, raising the voice indicates anger. Southerners are more likely to be open and outgoing. They enjoy public debate and arguing. They may often shout to make a point or attract attention; shouting does not necessarily indicate anger. Daily life in Nigeria moves at a relaxed pace. Schedules are not as important as the needs of an individual.

Nigerians are dismayed that plans for democracy have been unfulfilled. They continue to hope for a more peaceful and democratic future, despite the current situation. Nigerians are sensitive about their past status as a colony and have been striving to create a modern industrial society that is uniquely African and not a "carbon copy" of Western society.

Personal Appearance
Dress varies according to the area and culture, but dressing well is important for all Nigerians. Northern Muslims dress conservatively. Attire is more casual and more Western among the Ibo. Most people prefer traditional African fashions to Western clothing, although T-shirts and pants are worn in urban areas. Traditional men's dress is loose and comfortable, with a shirt extending to the knees. Women and young girls usually wear a long, wraparound skirt, a short-sleeved top, and a scarf. Nigerian fabrics are known for their bright colors and unique patterns. Nigerian fashions are popular in other African countries.

CUSTOMS AND COURTESIES
Greetings
In Nigeria, greetings are highly valued among the different ethnic groups. Neglecting to greet another or rushing through a greeting is a sign of disrespect. Therefore, people are courteous and cheerful when exchanging greetings. Because of the diversity of customs, cultures, and dialects in Nigeria, English greetings are widely used throughout the country. People use *Hello* but perhaps not as often as *Good morning*, *Good afternoon*, and *Good evening*. Nigerians treat

others with respect and expect to be treated likewise. After the initial greeting, people usually inquire about one's well-being, work, or family. The appropriate response is usually *Fine*, but one listens to this response before proceeding with the conversation. Personal space between members of the same sex is limited, and Nigerians may stand or sit very close when conversing.

Gestures

Nigeria is a multicultural nation and gestures differ from one ethnic group to another. Pushing the palm of the hand forward with the fingers spread is vulgar and should be avoided. Nigerians do not point the sole of the foot or shoe at another person. They pass objects with the right hand or both hands but usually not the left hand alone. Nigerians often wink at their children if they want them to leave the room when guests are visiting.

Visiting

Visiting plays an important part in maintaining family and friendship ties. It is common for people to visit their relatives frequently. Unannounced guests are welcome, as planning ahead is not possible in many areas where telephones are not widely available. Hosts endeavor to make guests feel comfortable and usually offer them some refreshments. Invited guests are not expected to bring gifts, but small gifts are appreciated. For social engagements or other planned activities, a starting time may be indicated, but guests are not expected to be on time. Late guests are anticipated and they do not disrupt the event.

Eating

Eating habits vary between different ethnic groups. Some eat with the hand (right hand only), while others use utensils. Hands generally are kept above the table. Families try to eat at least the main meal together.

Eating while walking is considered rude. Tipping is common in restaurants and for most personal services.

LIFESTYLE

Family

Although specific details of the family structure vary from one ethnic group to another, Nigerian families are generally male dominated. The practice of polygamy (having more than one wife) is not uncommon. By Islamic law, a Muslim male can have up to four wives with the consent of the other(s), provided he can care for each wife equally. Many other Nigerians also practice polygamy. While the sheltered status of Muslim women in Nigeria is similar to other Islamic countries, most other Nigerian women enjoy a great degree of freedom, both in influencing family decisions and in openly trading at the marketplace. About one-fifth of the labor force is female. Large families traditionally share the work load at home. Nigerians have deep respect for their elders. Children are trained to be quiet, respectful, and unassertive in their relations with adults.

Dating and Marriage

Marriage customs vary, but the payment of a bridal token or dowry is common throughout the country. The groom is expected to give money, property, or service to the family of the bride. Western-style dating is not common in rural areas, but it is practiced by some youth in urban areas. Women usually marry by the time they are twenty and men marry in their mid-twenties. Living together without a formal marriage ceremony is common and socially acceptable. Many couples simply find a wedding to be too expensive.

Diet

The mainstays of the Nigerian diet are yams, cassava (a starchy root), and rice. Nigerians are fond of hot, spicy food. Their meals normally are accompanied by a pepper sauce made with fish, meat, or chicken. Climatic conditions also provide for a wide selection of fruits and vegetables to supplement the diet. Because of the tsetse fly, dairy cattle are scarce in coastal regions, but canned margarine, cheese, and powdered milk are used as dairy-product substitutes. The Fulani who herd cattle have dairy products, and they eat yogurt (and sell it mixed with millet and sugar).

Recreation

Nigerians primarily enjoy soccer, although the wealthy also like wrestling, polo, cricket, and swimming. Nigerians are extremely proud of their national soccer team, which represented the country in the 1994 World Cup. People do not have access to working movie theaters, but they watch videos and television. U.S. American productions are most popular. Live theater and art exhibits are well attended by the educated elite.

Holidays

National holidays include New Year's Day, Labor Day (1 May), and National Day (1 October). In addition, Christian and Muslim holy days are celebrated by the entire country. Muslim holidays vary according to the lunar calendar and include *Maulid an-Nabi* (Muhammad's birthday, usually in the fall), *Idul Fitr* (a three-day feast at the end of the month of *Ramadan*), and *Idul Adha* (the Feast of Sacrifice, usually in the summer). During the month of *Ramadan*, Muslims go without food and drink from dawn to dusk. In the evenings of that month, families eat together and visit friends. Christian holidays include Easter (Friday–Monday), Christmas, and Boxing Day (26 December). Boxing Day is a day for visiting. It comes from an old British tradition of giving small boxed gifts to service workers the day after Christmas.

Commerce

Most businesses are open from 8:00 A.M. to 1:00 P.M. and from 2:00 to 4:00 P.M., Monday through Saturday. Shops in the Muslim north close at 1:00 P.M. on Friday, the Muslim day of worship. Government offices usually close by 3:00 P.M. each day. Business is rarely discussed on the phone, and appointments are scheduled in advance.

SOCIETY

Government

Nigeria is a military dictatorship. Before the 1993 elections were canceled, the government was to have been modeled after that in the United States, with a president, a two-chamber legislature, and an independent Supreme Court. That would still presumably be the system if democracy is established, but General Abacha has also advocated a rotating federal presidency. For the present time, Abacha rules as head of the Provisional Ruling Council. He is also defense minister in a cabinet with 31 other ministers. The military controls many aspects of the government. There are currently no legal political parties, but prodemocracy pressure groups are as active as possible. Political parties are supposed to be legalized by 1997 in preparation for 1998 elections. The voting age is 21.

Economy

Nigeria's economy is one of the largest in Africa. It has great potential for high productivity, diversity, and vitality. Unfortunately, political turmoil, fluctuations in the world oil prices, corruption, and poor central planning have left the economy near collapse. This rich oil nation has a very poor population. Real gross domestic product per capita is estimated at $1,560. Many people have no income or do not earn enough to meet their needs. Unemployment and inflation are high, and poverty levels have risen to more than 40 percent. Attempts to diversify the economy have met with some success. The recent export of roses and fresh produce to Europe produced substantial earnings in a short period of time. Nevertheless, the economy's true potential remains untapped.

Agriculture employs about 54 percent of the population. Nigeria is a major producer of peanuts. Other key crops include cotton, cocoa, yams, cassava, sorghum, corn, and rice. Rubber and cocoa are important exports. When petroleum deposits were discovered, oil became the largest export earner for the economy. It now accounts for 90 percent of all export earnings. In addition to oil-related and agriculture-processing industries, Nigeria has textile, cement, steel, chemical, and other industries. The currency is the *naira* (N).

Transportation and Communication

Nigerian cities are linked by roads, railroads, and air routes, but traffic is heavy on the roads, about half of which are not paved. Many people travel by bus in and between cities because few own cars. Fuel is expensive. Taxis are plentiful in the cities. Nigeria has a modern telephone system, but it is often poorly maintained. The government is expanding the system. The once active press is now restricted by the government. Most newspapers are printed in English. There are several radio and television stations.

Education

Each of Nigeria's 30 states provides primary and secondary education and some offer higher education. About 70 percent of primary-school-age children are enrolled overall. While 85 percent of all pupils complete the primary level, only about 20 percent enroll in secondary school. School instruction is in English, but a new Education Ministry program promotes the use of an area's dominant native tongue in primary schools. The ministry notes that children are being required to grapple with a new language before they can even learn the skills they should acquire. By the time they are 12, most students perform poorly in both English and standard skills. The new program, being tested in a few districts, is designed to give students basic skills first and introduce English later. Critics claim it will only add to ethnic tensions because not all of Nigeria's languages will be used in schools. The military government may yet choose to suspend the program.

The government supports almost all higher educational institutions. Although education for rural people is limited, previous government programs have doubled enrollment in some areas. Educational emphasis is on applied science and technology, with a goal to introduce more Nigerians into the skilled workforce to replace foreign labor. A considerable number of Nigerians attend universities around the world, often on scholarships from the Nigerian government. Nigeria is known for a well-educated workforce, even though the adult literacy rate in only 53 percent (42 for women).

Health

Less than 70 percent of the population has access to health care, and public hospitals are understaffed and poorly supplied. The best care is available at medical colleges. Private clinics are too expensive for most people. Facilities and care are inadequate in rural areas, and infant mortality remains relatively high at 73 per 1,000. Twenty percent of all children die before they reach age five. Only two-thirds of all one-year-olds are immunized. Life expectancy is about 56 years. Tropical diseases present serious challenges for the people.

FOR THE TRAVELER

A visa and valid passport are necessary for U.S. citizens to enter Nigeria. Proof of sufficient funds may also be required. Travelers should carry passports at all times. Due to violence, the harrassment of foreigners, and poor airport security, the U.S. State Department has warned that travel to Nigeria is dangerous. For recorded updates, call (202) 647–5225. Nigeria is also a center for serious business and charity scams, many of which target U.S. citizens. Before conducting any business with anyone in Nigeria, U.S. citizens are urged to contact the U.S. Department of Commerce.

Water is not potable. Fruits and vegetables should be washed with treated water and peeled or cooked before being eaten. Vaccinations for yellow fever, cholera, and typhoid are recommended. Travel to any country after Nigeria will require proof of yellow fever vaccination. Malaria suppressants (mefloquine) are essential. Foreign visitors may be charged higher than normal rates for taxis; agree on a fare before departure. Do not expect to use credit cards or traveler's checks. More information is available from the Federal Ministry of Information and Culture, 15 Awolowo Ikoyi Road, Lagos, Nigeria. Or contact Nigerian Tours, 368 Broadway Room 307, New York, NY 10013; phone (212) 791–0777. You may also wish to contact the Embassy of Nigeria, 2201 M Street NW, Washington, DC 20037; phone (202) 822–1500.

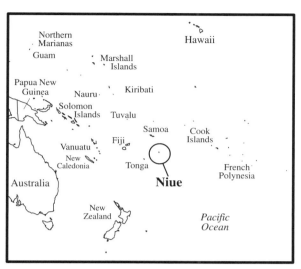

Niue

Antiope Reef

ALOFI ★

Hakupu

Niue

Beveridge Reef

Boundary representations not necessarily authoritative.

BACKGROUND

Land and Climate

The island of Niue is one of the world's smallest self-governing states, covering just 100 square miles (260 square kilometers), which is a bit larger than Washington, D.C. Niue is one of the largest coral islands on earth, formed after volcanic eruption through gradual geological uplift. It now stands about 200 feet (60 meters) above sea level. Niue is rimmed by cliffs and surrounded by coral reefs. Only small vessels can approach the wharf at Alofi, Niue's capital. The perimeter is marked by caverns, chasms, and rugged moonscapes caused by centuries of weathering and shifting. Niue's interior is flat and has a thin soil over the limestone bedrock. There are no lakes or rivers; water is obtained from several deep boreholes that reach the island's underground water table.

The climate is tropical, with summer (December–March) daytime temperatures averaging around 82°F (28°C); in winter (June–September) the average drops to about 72°F (24°C). Droughts are common, and a destructive cyclone reaches the island about once every decade. A prevailing trade wind from the southeast makes the seas on the east coast much rougher than on the west.

History

From the people's language it is clear that both Tongan and Samoan immigrants populated the island some 1,000 to 1,500 years ago, although oral history names five original settlers. Also accounted for in oral histories is the introduction of the coconut, intervillage rivalries, and contacts with other islands. The first *patuiki* (head chief) appeared about four hundred years ago.

Captain James Cook visited Niue in 1774, but the hostile reception he received led him to name the island "Savage Island." Although whalers and missionaries called at Niue several times, it was not until 1846 that a man named Peniamina introduced Christianity on Niue. In 1849, he was joined by a Samoan named Paulo, who spread Christianity to all parts of the island, brought peace among the villages, and prepared the people to accept foreigners.

The British missionary George Lawes arrived in 1861, ushering in the island's transformation by introducing European clothing and goods, writing, and a money economy. Young Niueans gained contact with the outside world by contracting or being indentured to work abroad. Still, society's governing structure remained largely intact, even when Niue asked for protection from the British Crown. In 1901, the first New Zealand colonial administrator arrived.

Change in the form of medical care, radio broadcasting, harbor facilities, and so forth came gradually over the next 50 years. Then, in 1959 and 1960, two destructive cyclones led to an era of rapid change. The reconstruction effort required what was for Niue an enormous influx of materials, vehicles, and organizational support. At about the same time, global efforts to end colonialism led New Zealand to propose a timetable for Niuean independence. Self-government was instituted in 1974. Sir Robert Rex became the premier and served until his death in 1992. He helped form Pacific regional organizations and came to personify his nation in the region. Frank Lui became acting premier in 1992; he was elected to the post in 1993.

PEOPLE

Population

Niue's population of some 1,800 people is declining each year. At its peak, the population reached six thousand, but the

OCEANIA

relative lack of economic opportunity and resulting emigration decreased the number to present levels. In fact, Niue is underpopulated. Certain villages seem almost deserted and there are many vacant houses. Nearly everyone has close ties to someone overseas, and overseas visits are common. More than 12,000 Niueans live in New Zealand.

Niueans are Polynesians. Noticeable differences once existed between the *motu* (islanders) in the north and the *tafiti* (foreigners—traders who settled on the island a century ago) in the south. However, this distinction has essentially disappeared due to intermarriage. A small number of Samoans, Tongans, and Europeans live on the island.

Language

The Niuean language can be traced to Samoan and Tongan roots. Dialects, like the people, once differed between north and south, but they have largely disappeared. Most adults speak both Niuean and English fluently.

Niueans value their language and, given the small population and the strength of foreign influence, have done a remarkable job of maintaining its use. Niuean is spoken in the home and at most social events. It is the language of school instruction for five- to eight-year-olds and is then mixed in decreasing amounts with English until high school, where all courses except Niuean culture are taught in English. Business and government affairs are conducted mostly in English.

Religion

Only a few vestiges of pre-Christian beliefs remain, such as a *tapu* (taboo) area in Hakupu that is still respected. Almost all Niueans belong to one of five denominations. The largest is *Ekalesia Niue*, the local offspring of the London Missionary Society that is most closely related to Congregationalism and counts 75 percent of the population as members. Ten percent belongs to the Church of Jesus Christ of Latter-day Saints (Mormon). Smaller numbers belong to the Seventh-Day Adventist, Roman Catholic, and Jehovah's Witness faiths. Due to its history and prominence in society, *Ekalesia Niue* has considerable influence in the political arena. Members of the main denominations mix freely in daily life, but they tend to socialize or work more closely with people of their own faith.

General Attitudes

Since Niue's first contact with Western culture, two main forces have influenced Niuean attitudes: missionary Christianity and the island's relationship with New Zealand. Yet, underlying these factors is the uniqueness of the Niuean culture. The influence of *Ekalesia Niue* is best exemplified by the fact that boating, fishing, swimming, dancing, sports, business, and broadcasting are either frowned upon or prohibited on Sunday. Also, a good deal of social life is organized by and around churches.

New Zealand's influence is evident in clothing styles, food and drink, housing, business practices, and Niue's form of government. The majority of Niueans have personal contacts in New Zealand.

From traditional culture, today's society has retained staple food choices, means of subsistence, and, most importantly, the place of the individual within the *magafaoa* (extended family). Political life also still shows traces of the pre-Western era. Unlike other Polynesian societies on islands where food was more abundant and surpluses allowed a hierarchy to be supported, Niuean villages had a loose structure and authority was widely dispersed. Village councils made most decisions; there were no hereditary ranks or aristocracy. These tendencies persist today.

Niuean life seems to have a weekly rhythm. Religion prevails on Sunday; on weekdays during business hours, Western culture prevails; and the rest of the time is most typically Niuean.

Personal Appearance

With a few exceptions, Western-style clothing is most common. Men often wear a *pareu* (wraparound cloth) for reef activities such as evening fishing, and women wear a *pareu* at home. On special occasions, both sexes of all ages wear leis of fragrant maile leaves or of frangipani flowers (in season). People also wear traditional dress for cultural events.

On weekdays in public, men wear shirts and slacks and women wear modest blouses and skirts. Women do not wear sleeveless tops and often even wear a T-shirt or *pareu* over a bathing suit when swimming. School children wear uniforms through high school. In casual (weekend) settings, most people feel comfortable in shorts, T-shirts, and sandals or bare feet.

CUSTOMS AND COURTESIES

Greetings

Niueans greet each other at work with normal English greetings or in Niuean with *Fakaalofa atu!* (Love be with you!) or the informal *Mafola?* (OK?). Niuean greetings dominate at home or in the village, although people who have spent time overseas might also use English. Men usually shake hands. Women friends meeting after a long absence kiss the cheek.

Niueans might address one another by first names, but nicknames are more common. In fact, most people have more than one nickname that may be used by different people or on different occasions. Nicknames are typically the abbreviation of the Niuean and English versions of one's given name.

When parting, people say *Koe kia!* (Good-bye). For two people, the phrase is *Mua kia!*, and for three or more it is *Mutolu kia!* Informal English phrases are also common. If an individual is leaving for a long time, it is most appropriate to say *Monuina [e fenoga]!* (Blessings [on the voyage]!).

Gestures

Niueans, though much inclined to speaking, are more reticent with hand gestures. However, facial gestures are quite important. For example, raising the eyebrows indicates agreement. One can give directions by motioning with the head or eyebrows rather than pointing. A double shrug of the shoulders conveys negative feelings. Whistling is not common; anciently, it was associated with the sound that approaching spirits made and so was avoided.

Visiting

Informal visits can occur anytime, although Sundays are the favorite time to visit friends and extended family. For casual visits, a flexible and relaxed atmosphere prevails. Customs are more important on special occasions, particularly weddings, funerals, haircuttings, and ear piercings.

These last two events are peculiar to Niue and have become common in this century (although they are in gradual decline). Boys usually do not have their hair cut until they are at least seven years old. At some point after that, but before a boy leaves adolescence, he will have a haircutting ceremony. All the families who in the past have invited the host family to haircuttings are in turn invited to the event. Guests are expected to make a cash contribution in advance; these are opened and tallied.

Before the haircutting day, a temporary shelter (*fale*) from the sun or rain is constructed with coconut leaves. This area, adjoining the host family's home, is then lavishly decorated. Food in large quantities is gathered, including taro, large fish, chickens, pigs, and canned food. Important guests take a turn cutting off a lock of the youth's hair, often making speeches for the occasion. Meanwhile, the food is divided and set aside for guests according to how much they contributed to the event. When the affair is over, the food is distributed and guests take it home with them. Typically, the receipts of the hosts (which can be thousands of dollars) exceed their expenses.

Ear piercing is the corresponding custom for girls, and the event is likewise celebrated with speeches, financial contributions, and food.

After a respected person dies, the family receives visitors for several days. Except for close friends, these visitors arrange to come in groups (such as a family or social organization). They sit while one or a few spokespersons give a brief speech of condolences. The bereaved may pass around refreshments. Each visitor hugs the bereaved person(s) upon leaving.

Eating

Most people eat breakfast and dinner (called *tea*). Wage earners might eat a light lunch at work. Some families use the traditional *umu* (earth oven) for cooking, but many have electric or gas ranges. At special or traditional events, large leaves serve as plates; Western-style dishware is used on a daily basis. Western utensils are common, but so is eating with the fingers of the right hand.

Families gather at a table for all regular meals. Foods may be more traditional staples, such as taro and pork cooked in an *umu*, or they may more closely resemble those eaten in New Zealand, such as bread, potatoes, oven-roasted meat, and so on.

For social events like weddings, eating is a primary activity. Long tables are piled high with taro, roast pig, and other traditional foods; guests help themselves and eat picnic-style. Most Niueans lament the common practice of packing up extra portions to eat at home, but there is usually too much food for those present to finish, so the practice continues.

LIFESTYLE

Family

The *magafaoa* is the center of Niuean life. Children might be raised by an aunt, uncle, or grandparent due to family circumstances. In fact, the term for parent, *matua*, is used not only for a biological mother or father but for the guardian of a child. It is also sometimes used to address elderly family members.

Land is owned by the *magafaoa*, not by an individual, and land courts must keep genealogical records dating several generations back in order to settle ownership disputes. Oral genealogies in various forms extend back to the first settling of the island. *Magafaoa* membership is patrilineal, and the head of the family is usually a man. Traditional roles are well understood. Men hunt and fish; women cook, care for children, and keep the household. Still, roles are flexible and allow for overlap; paid work is open to both sexes.

Most *magafaoa* land is used for subsistence farming. Bush gardens of taro and other vegetables are owned and worked by the entire family. Similarly, fishing and *uga* (coconut crab) hunting are shared activities; family obligations govern the distribution of the goods. Economic enterprises (ranging from shopkeeping to beekeeping to pig raising) that occur outside the *magafaoa* area can be individually owned. Most adults have some source of income outside the family, but the *magafaoa* does cooperate in caring for the elderly or unemployed.

Not only do *magafaoa* members share work and food, they also contribute time and efforts to preparing for special events such as haircutting and ear piercing ceremonies. For certain occasions, friends, business associates, and others are also obligated to help.

Within the *magafaoa*, nuclear units are generally able to set up their own household, usually (but not always) on land belonging to the *magafaoa*. Plenty of housing is available, but a few families have a home custom-built on leased land. Land cannot be sold, but it can be leased for periods of up to 60 years.

Dating and Marriage

Young people meet and date in many ways: through school, sports, church, social groups, and dances. Openly affectionate behavior in public is rare, but Niueans are quite tolerant of intimacy between unmarried young men and women. Most young people face the problem that there are few eligible partners to whom they are not related.

Weddings usually are prepared by the bride's extended family. They put up the *fale* for the reception, invite a large number of guests, and provide a feast. This is held after the church ceremony. Most families serve alcoholic beverages, especially beer. As part of the wedding celebration, members of different families or groups of friends perform songs and dances, wearing traditional costumes. In some families, relatives give various outfits to the couple and expect the bride and groom to change clothes several times during the event in order to show off as many elegant outfits as possible. At some point, guests toss small amounts of money at the couple and make wishes (often humorous) for their future.

After the wedding, the couple most often takes up residence with or near the husband's family. They become part of his extended family for all practical purposes, although the bride never entirely loses her obligations to her original family. In some cases, especially when a girl marries a foreigner, the couple might join the wife's extended family.

Diet

While Niueans consume plenty of imported food, their staples are grown locally. Taro is the primary food, but cassava, yams, bananas, breadfruits, coconuts, and papaws are also common. Some families raise pigs and most have chickens (although they tend to eat frozen imported chicken). Since all villages are fairly close to the sea, most families engage in fishing and reef gathering of crustaceans and shellfish.

In addition to chicken, Niueans import beef, canned corned beef, sliced bread, nontropical fruits and vegetables, beer, juices, and soft drinks. Imports arrive only every six weeks and so cannot be relied upon as staples.

A favorite local dish is *faikai*, chunks of fish marinated in coconut cream; another is *takihi*, slices of taro and papaw wrapped in leaves and baked (ideally in an *umu*). Small bakeries produce several varieties of bread, including coconut bread.

Recreation

Cricket (in summer) and rugby (in winter) are the most popular sports. People also enjoy volleyball, soccer, tennis, table tennis, *netball*, and track events. Alofi has a nine-hole golf course. Cultural events, sometimes competitive, are occasions for traditional song, music, and dance. Some churches have accomplished choirs that devote a good deal of time to their art. Young people can be found at weekend dances in several halls around the island, and there is usually at least one *fiafia* (party) in progress each weekend.

In their leisure time, men like to fish (for food or for sportfish—marlin, wahoo, or tuna), hunt (usually for birds), and do woodwork. Some are skilled at making the *vaka* (outrigger canoe), commonly used for fishing. Women make baskets, hats, and other handicrafts. They make many household items from treated pandanus fiber and coconut fronds. Embroidery is also popular, and tie-dyeing has lately come into fashion. Show days, such as one at Hakupu each June, are occasion for athletics and for displaying handicrafts.

Holidays

National holidays include New Year's Day, Commission Day (2 January), Easter (Good Friday–Easter Monday), Anzac Day (25 April), Queen Elizabeth II's Birthday (first Monday in June), Constitution Day (19 October), Peniamina's Day (a Monday in late October), Christmas, and Boxing Day (26 December). Overseas Niueans often return to the island from around Christmas to early January.

Commerce

Offices and shops are open only on weekdays until 4:00 P.M. Alofi has an open-air market on Friday mornings. Niue has three general stores; all other retail trade is handled by small, family-owned operations. Other businesses, from construction to hospitality, also operate on a small scale.

Until the early 1990s, most available employment was with the government. Today, the balance is shifting toward private employment (helped by the fact that the government has privatized some state-owned enterprises). Entrepreneurship and the profit motive are recently introduced concepts that contrast with traditional culture.

SOCIETY

Government

Niue is a self-governing territory in free association with New Zealand, which is about 1,000 nautical miles from Niue. This means New Zealand handles external affairs and defense for Niue. Like New Zealand, Niue recognizes Britain's Queen Elizabeth II as head of state. The legislative body is called the Assembly, which has 20 members (one from each village and six elected at large). The premier is head of government, elected from and by the Assembly after each general election. The voting age is 18.

Economy

Niue relies heavily on aid from New Zealand, Australia, and the United Nations. It also earns income from tourism, the sale of stamps, access fees to fishing waters, remittances from Niueans working overseas, and small amounts of exports to New Zealand. Principal exports include honey, papaws, and handicrafts. The working currency is the New Zealand dollar (NZ$). Niue coinage is sold to coin collectors.

Transportation and Communication

Niue has one perimeter and three cross-island roads. Motor vehicles are common. There is no public transit system, but government workers are provided with transportation to work. Niueans drive on the left side of the road. Links to other countries are limited. A supply ship calls every six weeks, but other vessels stop infrequently at Alofi, the only accessible harbor. Flights to and from Hanan International Airport vary in schedule. Airmail service is routed through Auckland, New Zealand, and depends on flight schedules.

A government-run radio and television station broadcasts six days a week for a few hours each day. Most residents have access to a telephone. There is one weekly newspaper.

Education

Schooling is free and compulsory for ages five to fourteen and conforms to New Zealand standards. Pupils from all villages commute to the one primary school and to Niue High School in Alofi. Most students finish primary school (gaining a Fifth Form Certificate), but few finish high school. College courses can be taken through the local branch of the University of the South Pacific (based in Fiji), but students must go abroad for full university study.

Health

The government provides most medical and dental services free of charge. New Zealand-trained and expatriate doctors do island rounds, and maternal and child-care support are provided at the basic level. Alofi has a hospital that can handle most needs, but patients requiring advanced treatment are evacuated to New Zealand. Infant mortality is low and most tropical diseases are absent. Dengue fever epidemics arise at times, but the illness is rarely fatal. Water usually is safe to drink.

FOR THE TRAVELER

U.S. citizens need a valid passport and proof of onward passage to enter Niue for up to 30 days. Visas are required for longer stays. Niue is a healthful destination with a pleasant climate, a welcoming people, comfortable if simple accommodations, and many scenic wonders. Crime is so rare that for years the prison was closed for lack of prisoners. For more information, contact the Embassy of New Zealand, 37 Observatory Circle NW, Washington, DC 20008; phone (202) 328–4800.

CULTURGRAM '97

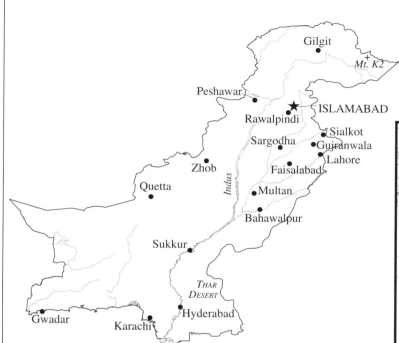

Islamic Republic of
Pakistan

Boundary representations not necessarily authoritative.

BACKGROUND

Land and Climate

Covering 310,401 square miles (803,940 square kilometers), Pakistan is about the same size as Texas and Oklahoma combined. Northern Pakistan has some of the world's highest and most spectacular mountains, including K2 in the Karakoram range. South of Islamabad, the country is mostly flat. Most people live in the fertile Indus River Valley, which runs through the center of the country. The Thar Desert lies to the southeast. There are four provinces (Punjab, Sind, Baluchistan, and the North-West Frontier), the Northern Areas, and Federally Administered Tribal Areas (FATA). Pakistan controls a portion of Jammu and Kashmir, known as Azad Kashmir; India controls the other part. Earthquakes are common in Pakistan, and flooding can occur during the rainy season (July–August) along the Indus River. Except in the highlands, the climate is usually hot. In the winter, temperatures average about 50°F (10°C).

History

Pakistan's modern history began with the arrival of Arab traders in the eighth century. The Arabs introduced Islam to the Indian subcontinent. Muslim warriors conquered most of the area in the 900s. By the 16th century, Muslim power reached its peak under the Moghul Dynasty. Although many inhabitants converted to Islam, the majority of the population (including India) remained Hindu. By the 1800s, the British East India Trading Company had become the dominant power in the area, and the last Moghul emperor was deposed in 1858. After World War I, British control of the subcontinent (basically India, Pakistan, and present-day Bangladesh) was contested by various independence movements that united for a time under Mahatma Gandhi. Mohammed Ali Jinnah was leader of the Muslim League and began advocating separate Muslim and Hindu nations in 1940.

In 1947, Britain granted independence to the entire area. Muslim leaders feared Hindus would control the new country and pressed for independence. A choice was given to each region ruled by a native prince to join either India or Pakistan. The areas that chose Pakistan became East and West Pakistan, separated by 1,000 miles of India. The people of Kashmir (northern India) chose Pakistan, but their Hindu prince chose India, so the area remains in dispute and violence continues today.

East Pakistan (inhabited by Bengalis) declared independence in 1971, which prompted civil war. Indian troops defeated Pakistani troops sent to quell the movement, and the Bengalis formed Bangladesh. In the power vacuum created by the army's defeat, Zulfikar Ali Bhutto was elected leader of Pakistan. During a period of civil unrest in 1977, General Mohammed Zia ul-Haq seized control of the government and jailed Bhutto, who was hanged in 1979. Zia postponed elections indefinitely, suspended civil rights, and established *Shari'a* (Islamic law) as the basis of all civil law. In 1988, Zia was killed in a plane crash. Free elections were held and

Bhutto's daughter, Benazir Bhutto, was elected prime minister. She became the first female leader of an Islamic country. Although Bhutto restored civil rights and attempted reforms, poverty remained widespread. She was ousted by the opposition in 1990. Elections in October 1990 brought Nawaz Sharif to power. He began to liberalize the economy and reform the bureaucracy. An attempt by the president to dismiss Sharif in 1993 was overruled by the Supreme Court, and he remained in office. Benazir Bhutto returned to the office of prime minister through elections in 1993. On the basis of her party's parliamentary majority and regained political strength, her choice for president, Farooq Leghari, was elected by both houses of Parliament and four provincial legislatures.

THE PEOPLE

Population

Pakistan's population of 131.5 million, growing annually at 1.3 percent, is one of the world's largest. More than 40 percent of the people are younger than age 15. The majority (67 percent) live in rural areas. The two largest cities are Karachi (eight million) and Lahore (four million). The capital is Islamabad.

Pakistan has five major ethnic groups. The Punjabi is the largest, comprising about 65 percent. The other four groups are the Sindhi, Baluchi, Pashtuns (also called Pakhtuns), and Muhajir (immigrants from India and their descendants). Pakistan is also home to more than three million Afghan refugees, who live in camps on the border.

Pakistan's Human Development Index (0.483) ranks it 128th out of 174 nations. Adjusted for women, the index is only 0.360. This reflects a wide gap between women and men in income and literacy levels. Only a minority of people have access to opportunities for personal advancement.

Language

Many languages are spoken in Pakistan due to the diversity of ethnic groups and the great difference between dialects in a single language. English is an official language and is used by the government and educated elite. It is also taught in school. But the other official language, Urdu, is being encouraged as a replacement for English in these cases; it is also the nation's unifying language. While only 7 percent of the people speak Urdu as a native tongue, most speak it in addition to their own language. Each province is free to use its own regional languages and dialects. Major languages correlate with the ethnic groups: Punjabi, Sindhi, Baluchi, Pashtu, and so forth.

Religion

The force uniting the diverse peoples of Pakistan is Islam. About 97 percent of the people are Muslims. Most of these (77 percent) are Sunni Muslims, while the remainder are *Shi'a* (Shiite) Muslims. Islam pervades every facet of a Pakistani's life from birth to death, and people believe their destiny is subject to the will of *Allah* (God). Muslims accept major Biblical prophets from Adam to Jesus, but they hold Muhammad as the last and greatest of *Allah's* prophets. Muslims believe in a resurrection and a final judgment, but do not accept Jesus as the son of *Allah*. The *Qur'an* (Koran), comprising revelations made to Muhammad, is the chief scripture of Islam. The remainder of the people are either Christian or Hindu, or belong to other religions. Freedom of worship is guaranteed.

General Attitudes

Most Pakistanis are devout Muslims and live according to the philosophy that the will of *Allah* is evident in all things. *Inshallah* (God willing) is a term commonly employed to express hope for success on a project, for one's family, or for a positive outcome to events.

Pakistan is a nation of diversity, and people often identify first with their group before identifying with the country. Differences are evident between ethnic groups, with Pashtuns and Baluchis being more conservative and traditional than the other major groups. Differences also exist between urban and rural populations, the latter being more conservative.

Today's Pakistan faces important questions about its future, including how much influence *shari'a* should have on society. Most people support the current moderate approach in which *shari'a* is used when practical, but Western legal and business practices also exist. This allows for certain personal freedoms, but some Pakistanis oppose the mixed system because they believe it undermines Islamic values.

Personal Appearance

Although Western-style clothing is worn in Pakistan, the national dress, the *shalwar-qameez*, is more common in both rural and urban areas. Made of cotton, the *shalwar-qameez* differs for men and women. Men wear solid, plain colors and add a vest or coat for formal occasions. For women, the colors are brighter and patterns bolder, with more tailoring common. Women wear a *dupatta* (scarf) around their heads and sometimes another long scarf around their shoulders. Men usually wear some kind of headdress, and it is often possible to determine a man's ethnic group from his hat. Some wear turbans, others pillbox-type hats, and others *karakuli* (fez-type) hats. There are many variations. It is important to dress conservatively. Despite the heat, Pakistanis cover their legs, arms, and heads in public. Men only wear shorts for athletic events and women never do.

CUSTOMS AND COURTESIES

Greetings

A handshake is the most common greeting, although close friends may embrace if meeting after a long time. Women might greet each other with a handshake or hug. It is not appropriate for a man to shake hands with a woman or to touch her in public, but he may greet a man's wife verbally without looking directly at her. Verbal greetings often include lengthy inquiries about one's health and family; when conversing with each other, men might place the right hand over the heart during this part of the greeting. In Pakistan, the most common greeting is *Assalaam alaikum* (May peace be upon you). The reply is *Waalaikum assalaam* (And peace also upon you). Good-bye is *Khodha haafis*. In more formal situations, people address others by title and last name. They use first names for friends and relatives.

Gestures

It is not proper for the bottom of one's foot or shoe to point at another person. Therefore, people may sit with both feet on the ground or squat. If sitting on the floor, or if crossing the legs, one positions the feet so as not to point them directly at others. Items are preferably passed with the right hand or both hands. To beckon, one waves all fingers of the hand, with the palm facing down. Using individual fingers to make gestures is impolite. Male friends may walk hand in hand or with their arms over each other's shoulders, but it is inappropriate for members of the opposite sex to touch in public.

Visiting

As throughout the Islamic world, visiting between friends and relatives is an important social custom and occurs as often as possible. Hospitality is important and guests are made to feel welcome. In small groups, each person is greeted individually. Personal rapport is important. Visitors are often treated to coffee, tea, or soft drinks and may be invited to eat a meal. Visitors should accept this hospitality, although refusing politely with good reason is appropriate. Guests often bring gifts if well acquainted with the hosts or if the occasion calls for a present. Gifts might include something for the children, a decoration for the home, fruit, or sweets. Above all, gifts should not be too expensive because that could embarrass the hosts. It is customary to socialize before a meal and then to leave soon after the meal is finished. In traditional homes, men and women do not socialize together. Rather, men receive their male guests in a special room to enjoy conversation and refreshments.

Eating

In urban areas, many people have dining tables, in which case they may eat with utensils or the hand. In rural areas, people sit on the floor or ground to eat. Whenever possible, the whole family eats together, usually sharing the same platter, with each member eating from the portion directly in front of him or her. *Chapati* (bread) is used to scoop up the food. Often fathers feed young children and mothers feed infants. In large groups, men and women eat in separate areas. Extended families often gather for large meals. During the month of *Ramadan*, Muslims do not eat or drink from sunrise to sundown each day. They eat together in the evenings, which are also occasions to visit or offer prayers. During *Ramadan*, it is polite for non-Muslims to not eat or drink in front of Muslims during daylight hours.

LIFESTYLE

Family

The family is the center of social life and support. Although increased modernization has brought many women into public life, men continue to act as head of their homes. It is common for the extended family—a father and mother, their sons, and the sons' families—to live together in the same household. The presiding male of the family has significant influence over the lives of all family members, although women are increasingly taking on active decision-making roles. Islamic law permits a man to have up to four wives if he can care for each equally, but very few actually have more than one. The elderly are highly respected.

Nuclear families are generally large, with the average woman bearing six children in her lifetime. The government stresses family planning to help curb population growth. In the past, large and powerful feudal families had significant power over politics and the economy. As wealthy landowners, they still have considerable influence, although the military

and bureaucracy have played equally powerful roles since independence. Today, the people often turn to these feudal families when government bureaucracy fails. The average family works hard for a basic living, which does not often include the luxury of modern conveniences.

Dating and Marriage

Boys and girls have little contact with each other; they attend separate schools and are not allowed to date (except among Westernized urban Pakistanis). Individual choice of marriage partners has traditionally played a small role in the marriage process. Arranged marriages are still the norm. Formal engagements may last from a few months to many years, depending on the age of the couple when the arrangements are made. In many cases, the bride and groom meet for the first time on their wedding day. Pakistanis view marriage as a union of two families as much as a union of two people. Both families participate in the wedding preparations. A Muslim holy man, usually called a *Qazi* in Pakistan, completes the marriage contract between the two families. Wedding rituals are elaborate, and men and women celebrate separately. Pakistan has a low divorce rate.

Diet

The mainstay of the Pakistani diet is *chapati* or *roti*, an unleavened bread similar to pita bread. Pakistani food is generally hot and spicy, with curry being one of the most popular spices. Islamic law forbids the consumption of pork and alcohol and there are strict civil laws regarding the sale and consumption of alcoholic beverages. A type of yogurt is a common ingredient in meals. Rice is part of most meals and desserts. *Pillau* (lightly fried rice with vegetables) and *biryani* (rice with meat and spices) are two customary dishes. *Kheer* is a type of rice pudding.

The most common meats are lamb, beef, chicken, and fish. Only more affluent families are able to eat these regularly; the poor eat them on special occasions. For marriage feasts, chicken curry is common. There are significant regional differences in cuisine. For example, while curries and heavy spices prevail in the south, barbecuing is more common in the north. The *kebab,* strips or chunks of meat barbecued over an open grill on a skewer, is cooked with or without spices and is prepared in various ways. Pakistanis enjoy a number of vegetables and fruits. Tea is the most popular drink.

Recreation

Introduced during the British colonial period, cricket, field hockey, and squash are among the most popular national sports. Sports developed in Pakistan include a type of team wrestling, called *kabaddi*, and polo, which was adopted by the British and exported to England. Pakistanis also enjoy soccer and tennis. Going to movies, watching television (or videos), having picnics, listening to native music, and visiting friends and family members are other forms of recreation.

Holidays

Secular holidays include Pakistan Day (23 March); Labor Day (1 May); Independence Day (14 August); Defense of Pakistan Day (6 September); Anniversary of the Death of Quaid-e-Azam, or Mohammad Ali Jinnah, the nation's founder (11 September); *Allama Iqbal* Day (9 November); and the Birth of Quaid-e-Azam (25 December). Bank holidays are in December and July.

Islamic holidays are regulated by the lunar calendar and fall on different days each year. The most important include *Eid-ul-Fitr*, the three-day feast at the end of *Ramadan*; *Eid-ul-Azha* (Feast of the Sacrifice), which commemorates Abraham's willingness to sacrifice his son, as well as the *haj* (pilgrimage) to Makkah, Saudi Arabia; and *Eid-i-Milad-un-Nabi*, the birth of the prophet Muhammad. *Eid-ul-Fitr* is the most important holiday because it ends *Ramadan*. During *Ramadan* evenings, many towns sponsor fairs and other celebrations.

Commerce

Since approximately half of the population is engaged in agriculture, most work schedules are determined by the seasons and crops. In urban areas, business hours extend from 8:00 A.M. to 4:00 P.M., Sunday through Thursday. In the summer, this schedule is extended by 30 to 40 minutes. Open-air markets and street-side vendors are common; large towns have major bazaars, divided into many tiny shops that are grouped by the product they sell.

SOCIETY

Government

Pakistan is a republic. Its president is head of state and has more constitutional authority than the prime minister, who is head of government. President Leghari supports Prime Minister Bhutto's plans for limiting presidential powers because such constitutional changes would result in fewer conflicts between the two offices. Parliament has two houses: an 87-seat Senate and a 217-seat National Assembly. The prime minister is the leader of Parliament's majority party (currently the Pakistan People's Party), and the president is elected by that body and the four provincial legislatures. The main opposition party, the Pakistan Muslim League, is split into at least three different factions, with the Nawaz Sharif faction being the strongest. Numerous small parties hold seats in Parliament. The next elections are scheduled for 1997. The voting age is 21.

Economy

Pakistan is primarily an agricultural country; more than half of the people are employed in agricultural pursuits. Pakistan emphasizes high-yield grains to keep pace with a growing population. Agriculture accounts for about 70 percent of all export earnings. Chief products include rice, cotton, wheat, sugarcane, fruits, and vegetables. Clothing and textiles are also important exports. At the time of independence, Pakistan had very little industry. Over the past several years, however, industrialization has grown substantially. Remittances from Pakistani workers in other countries are an important source of revenue. Sharif's economic liberalization program encouraged foreign investment and greater production, and Bhutto's current privatization plan seeks to make industry more efficient. Despite progress, inflation (11 percent), a high debt, and other matters hinder development. Certain resources, natural gas being the most important, could play a role in future development. Real gross domestic product per capita is $2,890, which has more than doubled in the last generation. Still, it is difficult for many families to meet basic needs. Short-term borrowing from landlords and others is not uncommon. While income distribution is becoming more equal, poverty continues to affect 30 percent of the population. The currency is the Pakistani *rupee* (Re).

Transportation and Communication

Local transportation consists of donkeys and horse-drawn carts in rural areas. In cities, buses, minibuses, and motorized rickshaws are available. Although 40 percent of the roads are paved, many are in poor condition. Roads in rural areas are not paved and many areas are not accessible by car. The Grand Trunk Road is a paved highway that begins in India and runs from Lahore to Islamabad to Peshawar. Following the British tradition, traffic moves on the left side of the road. There is a domestic airline and a railway. Most people do not own telephones; phones are available in hotels, shops, and restaurants. There are several radio stations and newspapers and one television station.

Education

Characteristic of most developing countries, Pakistan's rate of illiteracy is high, especially among women. Children either cannot attend school or drop out after only a few years to help the family. Only 36 percent of the people are literate. Still, government efforts have increased the number of primary schools available in rural areas. Primary schooling is free. At secondary levels, efforts are directed at training technicians to aid in expanding the nation's industrial base. Educational facilities, however, are not equipped to meet the needs of the people.

Health

Medical services in Pakistan are limited. Fully equipped hospitals are located in urban areas but generally are understaffed. Outside the cities, medical care is scarce. The government is trying to increase the number of doctors available in the rural areas, but many seek more lucrative employment abroad. Water is not safe for drinking in most areas, and malaria is widespread. The infant mortality rate is 100 per 1,000. Life expectancy averages 58 years.

FOR THE TRAVELER

A visa and a valid passport are required of U.S. citizens going to Pakistan. Nondiplomatic travelers staying more than 30 days must register with the police. Visitors with a U.S. passport must pay a $20 fee. Permission must be obtained to visit certain areas that are considered hazardous. A traveler may wish to check with the U.S. Embassy in Islamabad upon arrival for any travel warnings. For recorded advisories, call the U.S. Department of State at (202) 647–5225. Information regarding travel opportunities may be obtained from Pakistan International Airlines, 521 Fifth Avenue, New York, NY 10175; phone (212) 370–9158. You may also wish to contact the Embassy of Pakistan, 2315 Massachusetts Avenue NW, Washington, DC 20008; phone (202) 939–6264.

CULTURGRAM™ '97

Independent State of
Papua New Guinea

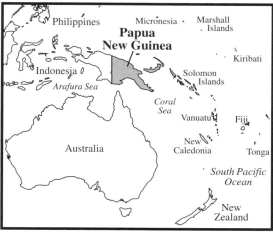

Boundary representations not necessarily authoritative.

BACKGROUND

Land and Climate

Papua New Guinea occupies the eastern half of New Guinea, the second largest island in the world. The country lies just south of the equator and north of Australia. Covering 178,259 square miles (461,690 square kilometers), Papua New Guinea is slightly larger than California and includes a number of smaller islands to the east and north. With rain forests, innumerable waterfalls, winding and powerful rivers, palm trees, white sand beaches, and coral reefs, Papua New Guinea is a rugged and magnificent country. The highest peak, Mount Wilhelm, stands at 14,793 feet (4,509 meters) in a range that forms a formidable barrier to north-south ground transportation. The Sepik and Fly Rivers are the country's two most famous waterways. Tropical forest covers about 80 percent of Papua New Guinea and swamps cover much of the coastal land. The pristine forests are under severe threat of decimation from foreign loggers who clear-cut pine, mahogany, and walnut trees for huge profits. Plants, animals, and tribal peoples will lose their habitat within 20 years if clear-cutting is not replaced by sustainable logging enterprises.

The basically tropical climate varies with altitude. The northern wet season lasts from December to March and the dry season from May to October. The south and east are subject to different weather patterns, and their wet season is March to August. Temperatures average around 80°F (27°C) for the lowlands and the high 60s for the Highlands. Some outlying islands get much hotter.

History

Several waves of migration from Asia and the South Pacific islands have taken place for centuries. It is believed the Highlanders were among the first farmers in the world, settling the Highlands thousands of years ago. The early Papua New Guineans worked and hunted with wood, stone, or bone tools and weapons. Indirect European contact brought the sweet potato to the island via Asia, radically changing the local diet and culture.

While European explorers visited the island as early as 1512, it was not until the 1800s that serious claims were laid to New Guinea and Europeans started to colonize it. Because of territorial disputes, what is now Papua New Guinea was divided into a German territory in the north and a British territory in the south. Even with colonization, New Guinea remained largely unexplored until the 1930s and virtually uninfluenced by the outside world until after World War II.

Australia governed the British area beginning in 1906 and took control of the German area after World War I. The Japanese briefly held the island in World War II but were driven out by Allied forces. Following a 1949 trusteeship agreement, a legislative council composed mostly of Australians was formed in 1951 as the first step toward independent home rule. A House of Assembly, which had more indigenous representation, was convened in 1964, but internal self-government did not come until 1973. Independence was granted in 1975. Elections, have been held on a regular basis since independence; the latest was in 1992.

OCEANIA

THE PEOPLE

Population

The population of Papua New Guinea is about 4.3 million and is growing at 2.3 percent. The majority (86 percent) lives in rural areas. About 98 percent of the people are Melanesian (mostly Papuan). Within this group, there is a wide range of physical types from shorter, muscular people of the Highlands to lighter-skinned people of the coast and very dark-skinned people of Bougainville. Rebels on Bougainville have fought a war of secession since 1988. A peace treaty expected in 1994 did not materialize because rebel leaders refused to attend the document signing. Other groups include those of Polynesian, Micronesian, Chinese, and European descent. Politically, the country is sometimes divided into four groups: Papuans (in the southern Gulf of Papua region), Highlanders (in the central, mountainous region), New Guineans (in the northern Sepik and Ramu River valleys), and Islanders (on outlying islands). The capital, Port Moresby, is the largest city with 193,000 inhabitants.

Papua New Guinea's Human Development Index (0.508) ranks it 126th out of 174 nations. Adjusted for women, the index (0.487) ranks the country 86th out of 130 countries. Only a minority of people have access to resources that help them pursue personal goals.

Language

Linguists have catalogued 836 distinct languages in Papua New Guinea, most of which fall within two basic language stocks: Melanesian and Papuan. The country's rugged terrain accounts for much of the diversity; for centuries, most tribes lived in isolation from one another.

English is the official language and is taught in public schools. The language used at home, however, is almost always that of one's language group. Melanesian Pidgin (*Tok Pisin*) is the most widely used language, allowing different groups within Papua New Guinea to communicate with one another. It was developed by early colonialists and their indigenous laborers. It has roots in English, German, and the local languages of the island of New Britain. *Tok Pisin* contains fewer than 1,800 words, which makes it easy to learn. Motu is the most common indigenous language, used primarily in the Papuan region. In isolated rural areas, many women and older people know only their local language.

Religion

A majority of Papuan New Guineans are Christian, primarily Catholic and Lutheran. The country has been heavily influenced by Western missionaries for the last century, and the result has been a major conversion from animism to Christianity. Strong beliefs in witchcraft and ancestor worship remain and coexist with Christianity. People in remote areas often follow traditional theologies.

General Attitudes

Papua New Guinea is beginning to feel national pride and cohesiveness. The people are proud of their diversity and land, which they know is rich in natural resources. Most individuals have a strong sense of belonging to a tribe or language group. They are proud of their families, their ancestors, and the land their families possess. Tribes, not the government, own the land they live on. People value their gardens and their own physical abilities, endurance, and strength.

People feel a desire for material things and a sense of inadequacy in not being able to obtain them. This is not due to the lack of resources but because people do not save money for personal needs. Family and clan loyalty is strong and members have an obligation to share their income and possessions. So, while wealth is desired, it is often not possible to accumulate. Reciprocation for sharing is always expected.

People are event oriented. Meetings or gatherings may not take place on time. Events more often begin when everyone arrives rather than according to the clock.

Personal Appearance

Western-style clothing is most common, with traditional attire limited to extremely remote areas. Men wear shorts or pants, but shirts are optional when men are hot or doing physical labor. Women wear skirts in almost all areas, but pants are sometimes acceptable in urban areas. Both men and women often wear a *laplap* (wraparound sarong). Women usually wear Western tops and brightly colored *meri* blouses. Rural women may go without a top when hot, working, or nursing babies. Rural people seldom own shoes and often have tattered clothing. Traditional wear for special ceremonies might include loincloths, feathered headdresses, facial paint, beads, and shells. Most people use *bilums* (woven string bags). Women hang them from their heads and support them with their backs to carry heavier loads. Men do not carry heavy loads in a *bilum*; they hang it from the shoulder to carry personal items such as tobacco or betel nut.

CUSTOMS AND COURTESIES

Greetings

Papua New Guineans greet by shaking hands. The common question *Yu orait?* (How are you?) is often responded to with *Mi orait. Na yu?* (I'm fine. And you?). Both terms are Melanesian Pidgin. Other greetings vary depending on the area and language group. While Pidgin is used between ethnic groups, people greet members of their own language group in their local language. This is referred to as the *tok ples* (talk place). Using one's *tok ples* is considered rude if members of other ethnic groups are present.

When one passes a stranger, a nod of the head and a smile are adequate gestures. When passing acquaintances, the gestures are accompanied by a short greeting such as *Moning* (Good morning), *Apinun* (Good afternoon), or *Gutnait* (Good evening). When addressing an important official, one uses the appropriate title with a full name. In most other cases, people address one another by first name. It is common to call an older man *papa* and an older woman *mama*.

Gestures

Head, eye, and eyebrow gestures are important to communication. For example, one might answer the question "Where are you going?" by slightly lifting the head, raising the eyebrows, and moving the eyes in the direction planned. Simply raising the eyebrows can show agreement or acknowledgment. A short hiss and sideways motion of the head indicates disgust or derision. A "tsk-tsk" noise (made by the tongue on the roof of the mouth), accompanied by shaking the head from side to side, can mean surprise, awe, or sympathy. The "thumbs-up" sign is considered offensive to some. Staring at a person of the opposite sex is very offensive. To flag down a public motor vehicle (PMV), one points to the pavement or waves a hand down and toward the road. Men often hold hands in public as a sign of friendship, as do women, but this is not acceptable for members of the opposite sex.

Visiting

Papua New Guineans may spend a large portion of each day visiting, often stopping in at the home of a relative or friend to share some food, smoke tobacco, or chew betel nut and discuss the day's news. Visits are welcomed, whether impromptu or planned; they are usually informal and often lengthy. Visitors often bring gifts of food, but such gifts are not required. Hosts who receive food as a gift also give a gift when they visit. During an unscheduled visit, hosts do not always stop what they are doing. Visits from relatives can last days or weeks, with the host family providing food and shelter for as long as the guests stay. Hosting long-term guests is becoming especially difficult for urban families because of the high cost of living.

Eating

In general, people eat two large meals and snack throughout the day. Breakfast is called *moning kaikai* (morning food) and dinner is *apinun kaikai*. Some people also eat lunch (*belo*). The most common utensil is the spoon. Hands are used otherwise. Tin plates, bowls, and cups are common throughout the country, but large leaves are still used for plates in rural areas. An important person—a village elder, guest, or parent—carefully divides the food. Guests are not expected to eat everything, but it is important to eat some food and then either take the rest home or give it to others at the gathering. There are rarely second helpings, and asking for them can imply the host has not provided adequately. Most people sit on the ground or floor when eating, although tables might be used in urban areas.

LIFESTYLE

Family

The extended family is the basis of support for most people. While a household is usually occupied by the nuclear family, a child often refers to having more than one mother or father and numerous siblings who, in Western society, would be called aunts, uncles, and cousins. The nuclear family is usually large, with parents raising an average of six children. Couples who are infertile or who have recently lost a child are often given an infant or child by relatives. A great deal of obligation and duty is associated with family. Extended family members share food, wealth, and work. A family clearing a garden area expects help from relatives and will feed those who provide assistance. Extended families live near one another and often form small village hamlets. The most able family members take care of aging parents.

A majority of family structures are patriarchal, although there are some matriarchal societies in Papua New Guinea. Men usually handle construction activities, such as house or boat building or clearing land. They also wage relatively frequent tribal fights with bows and arrows and, increasingly, homemade shotguns and other modern weapons. Women usually cook and prepare food and take care of small children, animals, and the garden. Rural dwellings typically are made of a thatched roof and locally available materials. Urban housing is usually modern and expensive. In cities, both men and women may work outside the home.

Dating and Marriage

Dating traditions and marriage ceremonies vary greatly among the many cultures of Papua New Guinea. A marriage ceremony may take place over a period of days or weeks and involves a great deal of feasting, all-night singing, and exchanging gifts and food. A woman is officially purchased and her family compensated for its loss through a negotiated bride-price, which is exchanged in a ceremony before the wedding. A typical price might include several pigs, money, and food. The groom's extended family contributes to the bride-price and the bride's extended family shares it.

Diet

The staple food in the Highlands is *kaukau* (sweet potato), while on the coast and in the lowlands *saksak* (a starchy extract from the sago palm) is the main source of calories. Taro is a staple of both regions, as are a myriad of fruits and vegetables from bananas to yams. Along the coast, seafood and coconuts are important. Throughout the country, pigs are raised and butchered for feasts. Small marsupials, wild pigs, birds, and eggs are supplemental sources of protein. Bats, eels, and tree kangaroos are eaten in some areas. Store-bought items, such as rice and tinned fish, are staples in money-rich areas, but they are luxuries elsewhere. Beer is popular as a status drink among men.

The common method of cooking for a family is in a pot or hollow piece of bamboo over an open fire. A *mumu* is traditional for large groups. One type of *mumu* is made by heating rocks over a fire and lining a hole in the ground with them. Food is placed on leaves in the hole and covered with a mound of mud or leaves. Water is poured in to steam cook the food.

Recreation

The national pastime is to sit and talk (*stori*). Men (and occasionally women) enjoy playing cards. The organized sport of choice is rugby, but basketball, volleyball, and soccer (taught in school) are also popular when a ball and field are available. Community tournaments are sometimes held, often in connection with a celebration or political campaign. People also spend leisure time fashioning useful items such as *bilum* bags or weapons. Boys and men hunt birds and wild game with slingshots and bows and arrows. Traditional musical instruments include the *kundu* (hourglass-shaped drum covered with lizard skin) and the *garamut* (log with a small, hollowed-out portion where a stick is rhythmically beaten).

Holidays

National holidays include New Year's Day (1 January), Independence Day (16 September), Christmas, and Boxing Day (26 December). Boxing Day is named for the British tradition of giving small boxed gifts to servants and tradesmen the day after Christmas. It is now a day to visit friends and family. Each province also has its own holiday. Some of the local festivals include the Port Moresby Show, featuring traditional and modern events (mid-June); the Yam Harvest Festival of the Trobriand Islands (June–August); the Mount Hagen (July) and Goroka (early September in even-numbered years) cultural shows; the North Solomons Festival of the Arts (1 September); and the Tolai Warwagira two-week festival in Rabaul (November).

Commerce

Businesses are open from 8:00 A.M. to 5:00 P.M. on weekdays and 8:00 A.M. to noon on Saturday. Markets and small shops may have extended or irregular hours and are often open on Sunday. Most prices are fixed and bartering is not common, except for crafts or artifacts sold by individuals. Banks are open from 9:00 A.M. to 2:00 P.M., Monday through Thursday, and until 5:00 P.M. on Friday. Post offices are open from 9:00 A.M. to 5:00 P.M., weekdays, and 9:00 to 11:00 A.M. on Saturday. Only a small percentage of Papua New Guineans earn a regular wage.

SOCIETY

Government

Papua New Guinea is a parliamentary democracy within the Commonwealth, and Britain's Queen Elizabeth II is the ceremonial head of state. She is represented in the country by a governor general, Wiwa Korowi. The prime minister, Paias Wingti, is head of government and is chosen by the majority party in Parliament. There are 109 members in the elected national Parliament. Each of Papua New Guinea's 20 provinces has a provincial assembly, which elects a premier. At the village level, elected council and committee members settle local disputes. National and provincial elections are preceded by intense and sometimes violent campaigns. The next national elections are in 1997; the voting age is 18.

Economy

Most people (about 86 percent) are subsistence farmers, growing their own food and usually a small cash crop such as coffee. Copra, coffee, palm oil, cocoa, tea, and coconuts are the principal agricultural products. Chief industrial products include coconut oil, plywood, gold, copper, and silver. The Panguna copper mine on Bougainville was a main income source before 1990, when the rebellion shut it down. Several other mines were attacked or shut down by angry landholders wanting a larger share of profits, a situation which led to a crisis of confidence in mining investment. Because of this, the economy suffered negative growth in 1991. The overall crisis passed by 1993, and growth surged in 1994 by more than 6 percent. A new gold mine was opened, adding to the advances. Australia is the main trading partner. Papua New Guinea imports most of its manufactured goods. The currency is the *kina* (K).

Real gross domestic product per capita is $2,410, which has improved in the last generation. And while most (73 percent) people live in poverty, economic growth is expected to improve conditions. This will occur if revenues are used to reform social institutions and create or expand economic opportunities. Without reform, the rising generation has little expectation of a better life.

Transportation and Communication

Because of Papua New Guinea's ruggedness, travel between cities is often by air. Except for the Highland Highway, which links the Highland region to the coast at Lae, the road system is limited and often not suitable for travel. Highways and city roads usually are paved, but rural roads are not. Public travel is inexpensive because of the system of PMVs—privately owned buses and trucks. Cars are driven on the left side of the road. Travel by boat and ship between coastal and island towns is common. Foot travel on trails and roads is particularly common in rural areas. Most people do not have telephones, except in metropolitan areas. Communication in remote areas is made possible by two-way radios operated by government health centers, by one-way radio, and by word of mouth. Television, newspapers, and postal service are generally confined to major towns.

Education

For Papua New Guineans, schooling is a privilege. The cost of sending a child to a public school is relatively high for many families. This and other factors keep many children from going to school. Students who do attend begin at age seven. About half finish the six grades of primary education, and perhaps one-third pass on to high school (grades 7–10) after taking a comprehensive scholastic test. Unfortunately, going to high school is expensive because of tuition and living costs, so even qualified students often do not enroll. High school graduates are encouraged through government scholarships to attend the university in the capital or technical and teacher colleges throughout the country. Literacy is about 52 percent.

Health

Papua New Guineans are covered under a national healthcare system that usually requires only a small fee for services and medicine. Hospitals are located in provincial government centers but often are not well equipped. Health aid posts administer vaccinations, perform minor surgery, and dispense medicine in remote areas. Many people must walk for hours to reach such a post. Traditional herbal medication is still common. The infant mortality rate is 62 per 1,000, although it is much higher in remote areas where prenatal care is limited. Typhoid and other water-borne diseases and infections are common, along with hepatitis and respiratory and sexually transmitted diseases. Malaria is common on the coast, in the lowlands, and on islands. Life expectancy is about 57 years.

FOR THE TRAVELER

A visa and valid passport are required of U.S. citizens. A 30-day tourist visa can be obtained on arrival in Port Moresby. Travelers staying longer than 30 days must obtain a visa in advance. Vaccinations are recommended for cholera, tetanus, typhoid, and hepatitis. A malarial prophylactic should be taken. In remote areas, drink rainwater or water that has been treated or boiled. Avoid eating undercooked meat; peel fruits and vegetables before eating. Credit cards generally are not accepted outside resort areas. Some cities, especially Port Moresby, have a *raskol* (thief) or crime problem. Do not go out alone after dark, and keep a careful watch on your belongings. For more information or travel brochures, contact the Embassy of Papua New Guinea, 1615 New Hampshire Avenue NW, Suite 300, Washington, DC 20009; phone (202) 745–3680.

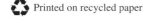 Printed on recycled paper

CULTURGRAM ™ '97

Republic of the
Philippines

Boundary representations not necessarily authoritative.

BACKGROUND

Land and Climate

Of the Philippines's 7,107 islands, only about 25 have towns. Most of the population lives on eleven main islands, of which Luzon and Mindanao are the largest. Covering 115,830 square miles (300,000 square kilometers), the Philippines is about the size of Arizona, but the islands are spread over a much larger territory. Many islands are mountainous, and there is a potential for volcanic and earthquake activity throughout the country: a 1990 quake caused death and damage; the 1991 eruption of Mount Pinatubo buried entire villages and affected global weather patterns through 1993.

The climate is generally tropical and humid. The Luzon highlands, near Baguio, have a very mild climate and low humidity. Philippine soil is very fertile; 26 percent is suitable for cultivation. About one-fourth of the land is covered with forests (down from 40 percent a decade ago). The rainy season extends from June to October. Typhoons are likely from June to November, but they may occur during any season because the Philippines is in the typhoon belt.

History

Malay peoples migrating from Borneo in the 13th century first inhabited Panay Island. Already living on other islands were the Negritos and the Indons (Ifugao and Igorot). Malay fiefdoms spread throughout the islands, including Luzon, and were often at war with one another. Muslim missionaries gained a presence in the 14th and 15th centuries among Malays who had spread south to Mindanao.

When Magellan made the first Western contact in the Philippines in 1521, he found the warring fiefdoms of the north and the Islamic society of the south. He claimed the entire area for Spain. China, Japan, and other countries tried to conquer the Philippines, but Spain maintained control for nearly four hundred years. José Rizal, writer and patriot, helped inspire a revolt against Spain in 1896. Spain lost a war to the United States and turned the Philippines (not a part of the original conflict) over to U.S. control in 1899. Preferring self-rule, the Filipinos, led by Emilio Aguinaldo, tried to repulse U.S. troops. Internal strife continued until 1901, when U.S. control formally began. Japan invaded the Philippines in 1941 and remained until U.S. forces returned near the end of World War II.

On 4 July 1946, the Philippines became an independent republic, but the United States maintained a military presence. Through the 1960s, unrest over inequality between landowners and tenant farmers threatened government stability and inspired revolutionary movements that are still active. In 1972, President Ferdinand Marcos declared martial law and ruled by decree, effectively controlling all opposition until 1986. During his regime, graft and corruption increased and the standard of living for the peasants did not improve.

When Marcos refused to accept defeat in 1986 elections, it took a peaceful "People's Power Revolution" to drive him from office. After Marcos fled the country, election winner Corazon Aquino took office. Marcos died in Hawaii in 1989.

Aquino survived seven coup attempts as she tried to reform the government and economy, but was not able to reach many of her goals. She chose not to run for reelection in 1992, but elections were peaceful and democratic. Aquino's successor, Fidel V. Ramos, inherited a weak and inefficient system and was plagued by natural disasters. Ramos successfully met many challenges, allowing legislative candidates loyal to him to win majorities in both houses of Congress in 1995.

The long official relationship between the United States and the Philippines ended at the latter's request in 1992. Accordingly, the United States pulled out all troops and returned Subic Naval Base and Clark Air Force Base to Philippine control. While many local jobs were initially lost, the government converted the two bases into special economic zones. Domestic and foreign investment quickly filled the gap and created many new private-sector jobs.

THE PEOPLE

Population

The Philippines's population, 73.2 million, is growing at 2.2 percent per year. About 40 percent is under age 15. The country's Human Development Index (0.677) ranks it 100th of 174 nations. Adjusted for women, the index (0.625) ranks the Philippines 64th of 130 countries. These figures indicate that many Filipinos do not yet have real opportunities to improve their socioeconomic status. More than nine million people live in metropolitan Manila. The people are predominantly of Malay descent: 91.5 percent are Christian Malay and 4 percent are Muslim Malay (Moros). About 1.5 percent are Chinese. The remainder includes a number of indigenous descendants of pre-Malay peoples. Negritos still inhabit the uplands of islands around the Sulu Sea, while the Aetas live around Mount Pinatubo. The Igorot and Ifugao of the Cordillera mountains in northern Luzon are best known for their stunning two-thousand-year-old rice terraces in Banaue.

Language

English and Pilipino are official languages. English is the main language of business, government, and higher education; it is also the language of instruction for some schools and for math and science in all schools. Filipinos refer to Pilipino as Tagalog, a dialect from Luzon. Many ethnic groups that speak one of more than 80 other languages or dialects were hesitant to adopt Pilipino when it was introduced in the 1960s because it was based on Tagalog. But it is now a primary language for daily communication between speakers of different dialects. In Luzon, even spoken English is heavily laced with Tagalog words in informal conversation. Speaking in a dialect that someone present might not understand is considered rude. However, some groups speak only their own dialect; this is particularly true in the Visayan region where Cebuano dominates.

Religion

The Philippines is the only predominantly Christian nation in Asia. Approximately 83 percent of the population belongs to the Roman Catholic Church. Six percent belongs to the Philippine Independent (or *Aglipayan*) Church, and 3 percent belongs to various other Christian churches. Muslim *Moros* live mainly on southern islands, particularly Mindanao. They have tried to secede from the Philippines, engaging in guerrilla warfare over the past several years. Violent clashes between Christians and Muslims occur even as official negotiations continue. In remote areas, people are still heavily influenced by traditional folk beliefs, worshipping a variety of gods. A number of Buddhists also live in the Philippines.

General Attitudes

Filipinos have been influenced by the Chinese, Malayan, Spanish, and U.S. cultures. Consequently, many aspects of these different cultures are evident in Filipino society. Individualism is less important than the family. Bringing shame to individuals reflects on their family and is avoided at all costs. Interdependence is more important than independence. Although casual and fun loving, Filipinos are sensitive people and consider making social relationships run smooth to be more important than expressing personal views or delivering bad/unwanted news. To avoid hurting or displeasing others, Filipinos may use a third party to deliver bad news or might say "maybe" when they mean "no." "Yes" can mean "maybe." Confrontation is avoided. Frankness can be a sign of a lack of culture. In general, Filipinos have a relaxed view of time and may not always begin meetings or appointments promptly.

Accepting a favor obliges a Filipino to repay with a greater favor, although never with money. Innovation, change, and even competition are sometimes considered gambles that could bring shame if a person fails. Changing social or religious habits may be regarded as ingratitude to parents. Fatalism is a common attitude, characterized by the expression *Bahala na*, which means, roughly, "Accept what comes and bear it with hope and patience." Success may also be attributed to fate rather than ability or effort. The Latin concept of *machismo* is evident in the Philippines; the ideal man is a macho man. Men often make comments about women passing by on the street, but such comments are ignored.

Personal Appearance

Manual workers wear shorts and a T-shirt. Others wear denim jeans or Western suits. Farmers wear long shirts and long pants to protect themselves from the sun. Office workers wear long pants and a shirt. Some men, mostly professionals, may wear the traditional *barong*, a white or pastel-colored embroidered shirt that hangs over the pants. Women generally wear Western-style dresses or skirts with blouses; they may also wear jeans and T-shirts. Government employees wear uniforms, although not necessarily every day; the style identifies the agency. Teachers even have a different uniform for each day of the workweek. Rubber sandals are common footwear for casual situations. An active clothing industry produces for export and domestic consumption. A fair complexion is considered the sign of someone who does not have to labor in the fields and is, therefore, considered more beautiful or desirable than a darker complexion.

Traditional clothing is worn by some ethnic minorities in highland villages and on outlying islands. Filipino formal clothing includes an elaborately embroidered *barong* for men, made of finer fabric than the everyday variety. Women wear a *terno*, a full-length dress with a scoop neckline and butterfly sleeves.

CUSTOMS AND COURTESIES

Greetings

Initial greetings are friendly and informal. Handshakes are typical, but verbal greetings are acceptable alone. To show additional respect or enthusiasm, one places the free hand on top of a handshake or uses it to pat the other person's shoulder. Common informal greetings include *Saan ka pupunta?* (Where are you going?) and *Saan ka galing?* (Where have you been?). A typical response is *Diyan lang* (There, only.). *Kumusta ka na?* (How are you doing?) is more formal. *Anong balita?* (What's new?) and *Ayos ba tayo 'dyan?* (Is everything alright?) are used among friends. Just as common are the English "Hi!" and "Good morning." Young people show respect to adults by addressing them with a proper title. If a professional title (Doctor, Manager, Chief) is not appropriate, then *Sir*, *Ma'am*, or a familial title based on the age difference and relationship of the speakers is used. It is common for young adults to address older adult strangers as *Tita* (Auntie) or *Tito* (Uncle). The elderly might be called *Lola* (Grandmother) or *Lolo* (Grandfather). Numerous other such titles exist in most dialects. Those equal in age and status address each other by first name or nickname. If one has a professional title, however, even peers may address one by that title to acknowledge the individual's achievement or status.

Gestures

Hand movement is not excessive in conversation, but Filipinos do use various hand and body gestures to communicate. Raising the eyebrows can mean "hello" or "yes." To beckon, one waves all fingers with the palm facing down. A quick head nod can mean "I don't know." Pointing is often done by puckering the lips. A shoulder shrug with open palms facing up means *Bahala na.* A widely opened mouth means "I don't understand." Men offer bus seats to women. Younger people kiss the hand of older relatives or place that hand on their forehead to show respect. Women commonly walk arm in arm or hand in hand, and men may put their arms around each other's shoulder, but displays of affection between men and women are considered inappropriate. Public kissing is for children (who kiss parents or relatives).

Visiting

Filipinos enjoy visiting as often as possible, especially in the *barrios* (small villages or suburbs). Rural visits are often unannounced, but urban ones are less frequent and more planned. Social visits last longer than those with a specific purpose. Guests do not typically take gifts, since the visit itself is considered a gift. However, a guest who has been away for a long time is expected to bring a small, inexpensive gift (*Pasalubong*) to the family. Guests are treated with great hospitality and are always offered something to drink. Men prefer beer or sugarcane gin, while women may have soft drinks or coffee. Food is also typically served, except for very short visits. Guests can decline refreshments, but hosts insist until the guests decline three times. The woman of the house is referred to as *Maybahay* or *Mrs.*, but never *hostess*. If she is unmarried, then *Aling* is used as a prefix to her given name.

Although socializing in the home is most popular, people also enjoy public areas. Drinking is a primary activity. Urban neighborhoods often have a central park where people can socialize. Villages nearly always have a plaza where political events, dances, meetings, and socializing occur and basketball can be played nearby.

Eating

Filipinos usually eat three meals a day, with at least two snack periods (*merienda*) between meals. Rural families usually eat all meals together, while urban families eat breakfast and dinner together on weekdays and all meals on weekends. The spoon and fork are the most common utensils. Typically, one pushes food onto the spoon with the back of the fork. Hands may be used in large rural gatherings when utensils are in short supply. Guests are seated nearest the head of the home and are always served first. No one eats until after the guest has had a bite or two. Guests show their appreciation by eating heartily. Refusing any offers is impolite, except for health reasons. In restaurants, leaving a 15 percent tip is customary, unless the bill includes a service charge, in which case one should still leave a small tip.

LIFESTYLE

Family

The extended family is the basic social unit, and more than one generation often lives together in the same household. The average rural family has four children; urban families are smaller. Family ties are very strong; adult children who can do so must support their parents and any needy siblings. Many Filipinos work overseas to earn money for the extended family at home. Recipients of such aid are expected to return help when possible or necessary. Individual family members may sacrifice much to help provide others (especially children) a better life. Or they may work to help find employment or opportunities for relatives within the country.

Filipino women generally enjoy equality with men, holding government, business, and industry positions. Rural women work alongside men in the rice fields. Women also manage the household and family finances and care for the children. A mother's advice to her child is taken very seriously.

Homes built from cement and hardwood are preferred, although bamboo huts are often used by the poor. Most homes have one or two bedrooms, a kitchen, and a *comfort room* (bathroom). Rural families may rely on outhouses and outdoor kitchens, but they usually have electricity and a water supply.

Dating and Marriage

In urban areas, dating begins in the early teens. Dancing is popular, as is moviegoing. In rural areas, habits vary according to religion and tradition. Singing karaoke is popular. Most people marry before they are 30 years old. The groom and his family pay for the wedding ceremony and reception. The bride often does not see her bridal gown until the day she is married. Grooms often wear a *barong* made of pineapple fiber. Common-law marriages may be acceptable if the family cannot afford a wedding.

Diet

Rice, the main staple food, is prepared in a variety of ways and is often included in desserts. Fish, the primary source of protein, is accompanied by vegetables and tropical fruits. A typical meal might consist of boiled rice, fried fish, a vegetable, and fruit for dessert. Fruit is also often eaten for breakfast. Pork, beef, chicken, goat, and (in rural areas) dog are favorite meats. Garlic is a common spice. *Adobo* is a stew of chicken and pork in garlic, soy sauce, and vinegar. Meats are often roasted and served on skewers. *Kare-kare* is a stew of meats and vegetables served in a peanut sauce. Street vendors sell *balot*, a fertilized duck egg with an embryo. A favorite snack is the *halo-halo*, a drink made from sweetened beans, milk, and fruits served in colorful layers with crushed ice. Seafood is common at restaurants and resorts. For large celebrations, the *lechon*, a stuffed pig roasted over a charcoal fire, is very popular.

Recreation

People spend leisure time socializing or going to movies; the Philippines is a major producer of films. North American films are also available. Video machines and rental stores are found everywhere. Families enjoy picnics at the beach. Sports are generally played on Sunday. Boys favor basketball. Girls play sports mostly in school. Volleyball and track are popular. Other recreational activities include gambling, attending horse races or cockfights, and playing *mahjong*, a Chinese table game played with tiles.

Holidays

Filipinos celebrate several national holidays and dozens of local *fiestas*. The latter provide entertainment and recreation but also encourage former residents to visit family. National holidays include New Year's Day, Easter (Thursday–Sunday), Bataan Day (9 April), Labor Day (1 May), National Heroes Day (6 May), Independence Day (12 June), All Saints' Day (1 November), Bonifacio Day (30 November), Christmas, and Rizal Day (30 December). Christmas is the most celebrated holiday, with decorating beginning as early as September. Children in many areas go door to door singing carols and receiving money and sweets. On Christmas Eve, urban families gather to exchange gifts and enjoy a large feast of special dishes. In rural areas, people also enjoy a large meal, but exchanging gifts is less common. The Christmas season extends through 6 January (Three Kings Day) and is a time of family reunions and great merriment.

Commerce

General business hours extend from 8:00 A.M. to noon or 1:00 P.M. and from 2:00 to 5:00 P.M., Monday through Friday. However, in metro Manila, stores are often open much later and do not close during the day. Hours vary in rural areas. Urban residents shop at modern malls and markets, as well as traditional stores. Rural people rely on their gardens and shop at small markets. *Sari-saris*, small convenience stores run out of a home, dot the country. They stock canned items, household supplies, drinks, candy, and other sundry items.

SOCIETY

Government

The Republic of the Philippines has 72 provinces, which are divided into municipalities made of *barangays* (barrios). The central government is led by a president. Congress consists of a 200-seat House of Representatives and a 24-seat Senate. Most government offices are in Quezon City, the former capital named for Manuel Quezon, the first president of the country when it became a U.S. Commonwealth in 1935. The voting age is 15 for local elections and 18 for national elections.

Economy

The Philippines's economy is based on agriculture, which employs 45 percent of the labor force and accounts for about one-third of all exports. The most important crops include rice, corn, coconut, sugarcane, abaca, and tobacco. In addition to agricultural products, the country exports electronics, clothing, minerals, and chemicals. Real gross domestic product per capita is $2,550. Income distribution is fairly unequal and poverty affects more than half of the total population. Despite problems, the economy began to show strong growth by 1994. Tax and business reforms are attracting investment. The currency is the Philippine *peso* (P).

Transportation and Communication

Many middle-class Filipinos own cars, but others rely on public transportation. Metro Manila has numerous buses, taxis, and jeepneys. A *jeepney* is a highly decorated type of minibus built on the frame of old U.S. military jeeps. They travel on relatively fixed routes and stop when waved at from the sidewalk. They carry 10–20 passengers for a low fare; passengers tap or pound on the roof when they want to stop. Traffic is heavy and driving habits aggressive. Rural transportation systems are less developed and often rely on a motorcycle version of the jeepney. Travel by foot, bicycle, motorcycle, and on animals is also common. In addition to a domestic airline, ferries and *banca* boats provide interisland transportation. Although the communications system is generally good, service is not extensive in rural regions and between islands. Middle-class homes have phones if service is available in the area.

Education

Education is highly valued in the Philippines. Young children can attend kindergarten at age five and preschool before that. Nearly all children begin six years (June–March) of elementary school at age six or seven. A few schools have a seventh year of elementary education. Four years of high school follow for 70 percent of all children. One year of military training is included in the high school curriculum. Graduation is at age 16 or 17. Many go on to college or vocational training. The literacy rate is 94 percent.

Health

Medical service in Manila is generally good. Rural areas usually have a health unit, but it may lack supplies. In 1995, a new law established universal health insurance, paid for mostly on the basis of taxation and other government funds. Before, insurance was difficult to afford and unemployed persons had no insurance. The government sponsors free vaccinations for children. Poor sanitation and poverty are the main reasons for a relatively high infant mortality rate of 50 per 1,000. Life expectancy ranges from 63 to 68 years. Pollution, especially in Manila, is a serious health hazard.

FOR THE TRAVELER

For stays of up to 21 days, U.S. travelers need a valid passport and proof of onward passage but not a visa. The country is fairly safe, but guerrilla violence can flare up. Recorded advisories are available from the U.S. Department of State at (202) 647–5225. For travel information, contact the Philippine Tourist Office, 556 Fifth Avenue, New York, NY 10036. The Embassy of the Philippines is located at 1600 Massachusetts Avenue NW, Washington, DC 20036; phone (202) 467–9300.

Russia
(Russian Federation)

Boundary representations not necessarily authoritative.

**E
U
R
A
S
I
A**

BACKGROUND

Land and Climate

Russia is the largest country in the world. At 6,592,734 square miles (17,075,200 square kilometers), it is nearly twice the size of the United States. Russia is bounded by the Arctic Ocean in the north, by the Pacific Ocean in the east, and in the south and west by many countries. Four of the world's largest rivers (Lena, Ob, Volga, and Yenisey) and the world's deepest freshwater lake (Baikal) are in Russia. Most of the country's territory consists of great plains, but there is a large tundra in the extreme north and much of western Russia is covered by forests. Parts of eastern Russia are desert. The low Ural Mountains divide Russia in two parts: the smaller European and the larger Asian regions. The climate is generally dry and continental, with long, subzero winters and short, temperate summers.

History

Slavic peoples settled in eastern Europe during the early Christian era. In 988, they were converted to Christianity by Prince Vladimir. At the beginning of the 13th century, the area was conquered by the Mongols, who dominated the Slavs for 240 years. The Slavs defeated the Mongols in 1480 and regained their sovereignty. In 1547, Ivan the Terrible (1533–84) was the first Russian ruler crowned Czar of Russia. He expanded Russia's territory, as did Peter the Great (1682–1724) and Catherine the Great (1762–96). The empire reached from Warsaw in the west to Vladivostok in the east. In 1812, Russian troops defeated France's Napoleon, and Russia took its place as one of the most powerful states on earth.

When Czar Nicholas II abdicated because of popular unrest during World War I, Vladimir Lenin, head of the Bolshevik Party, led the 1917 revolt that brought down the provisional government and put the Communists in power. Lenin disbanded the legislature and banned all other political parties. A civil war between Lenin's Red Army and the White Army lasted until 1921, with Lenin victorious.

In 1922, the Bolsheviks formed the Union of Soviet Socialist Republics (USSR) and forcibly incorporated Armenia, Azerbaijan, Georgia, Ukraine, and Belarus into the union. During Lenin's rule, which ended with his death in 1924, many died as a result of his radical restructuring of society. Lenin was followed by Joseph Stalin, a dictator who forced industrialization and collective agriculture on the people. Millions died in labor camps and from starvation. Germany invaded the Soviet Union in 1941, and World War II (the "Great Patriotic War") eventually took more than 25 million Soviet lives.

Nikita Khrushchev, who took over after Stalin's death in 1953, declared he would build real communism within 20 years, but his reforms and policy of détente with the West were opposed by hard-liners and he was replaced by Leonid Brezhnev in 1964. Until his 1982 death, Brezhnev orchestrated the expansion of Soviet influence in the developing world, and he ordered the invasion of Afghanistan.

In 1986, soon after Mikhail Gorbachev came to power, he started *perestroika* and attempted to reform government by introducing *glasnost* (openness) and freedom of speech. Many of his reforms failed, exposing in the process inherent weaknesses in the Soviet system. The union quickly unraveled in

1991 after many republics declared independence. Russia's Boris Yeltsin moved to introduce his own reforms.

In 1993, after months of political battles with legislators, Yeltsin dissolved Parliament and called for elections. Parliament instead voted to impeach Yeltsin and his opponents seized the White House (parliament building) in an effort to overthrow the government. Following street riots, the showdown turned violent and militants were forced from the building by tank fire. Even with Yeltsin victorious in that crisis, an anti-Yeltsin ultranationalist party emerged far stronger than expected in new parliamentary elections. On the other hand, voters approved a new constitution supported by Yeltsin. At the same time, a violent civil war with separatists in the Chechnya region tarnished Yeltsin's image and caused international concern. Despite alternate efforts at peace and at crushing the rebellion, Russia remains unable to solve the Chechnya problem. The war continued well into 1996. In March 1996, Russia and Belarus formed a political union, closely linking their societies but stopping short of an actual merger.

Questions about Yeltsin's leadership, health, and economic policies allowed Communists and other factions to present a strong challenge to him in the 1996 national elections. By allying with former enemies after the first round of balloting, Yeltsin was able to claim a substantial victory in 1996 to become Russia's first freely elected president. Communists had a strong showing and will therefore have a voice in Yeltsin's government.

THE PEOPLE

Population

The population of Russia is about 149.6 million and is growing annually at only 0.2 percent. There are some 120 different ethnic groups, but most are small. Ethnic Russians form 82 percent of the entire population. Other groups include Tartars (4 percent), Ukrainians (3 percent), Chuvashes (1 percent), Belarusians (less than 1 percent), Udmurts, Kazakhs, and others. The capital and largest city is Moscow, with a population of more than 10 million. Other large cities (one to three million residents each) include St. Petersburg, Novosibirsk, Nizhniy Novgorod, Yekaterinburg, Saratov, and Samara. Most Russians still live in rural areas, but young people are moving to the cities. Russia's Human Development Index (0.849) ranks it 52d out of 174 countries. Social institutions exist that could provide people with opportunities for personal success, but they do not yet function well enough for many people to take advantage of them. Gaps between rich and poor, skilled and unskilled, and healthy and ill are widening and threatening Russia's development.

Language

Russian is the official language, and it was also the main language of the Soviet Union. Russian uses the Cyrillic alphabet, which consists of 33 letters, many of them unlike any letter in the Roman (Latin) alphabet. Non-Russians also speak their own languages. For example, Tartars speak Tartar, Chuvashes speak Chuvash, and Udmurts speak Udmurt. These individual languages are only taught at schools in the republic (state) of Russia where the ethnic group is prominent. Non-Russians speak Russian in addition to their native language.

They often consider Russian a second language and do not speak it on a daily basis. For their part, ethnic Russians are not required to study other local languages. Foreign language courses are growing in popularity, with English, French, German, and Spanish being the most common.

Religion

The Russian Orthodox Church is the dominant religion. After the October Revolution (1917), the Communists separated the church from the state (which were previously tightly bonded) and discouraged all religious worship. Many churches were forced to close under Lenin and Stalin. Mikhail Gorbachev was the first Soviet leader to change official policy and tolerate—even support—religion. Yeltsin also embraced the church, which is regaining its influence. Churches other than the Russian Orthodox are scarce in rural areas, but nearly every major religion and many Christian churches have members in cities. Islam is practiced in some southern regions.

General Attitudes

In Russia's long history of totalitarianism, its inhabitants have had few opportunities to make their own decisions, whether ruled by a Czar or the Communist Party. Personal initiative, personal responsibility, and the desire to work independently were suppressed by the state, and one was expected to conform to official opinion and behavior.

In the current climate, Russians are searching for new social values. The resulting confusion and chaos have led some to wonder whether the old ways weren't better—as evidenced in the Communists' strength during 1996 elections. Many Russians are not happy with their rapidly changing society, characterized by high prices, increasingly violent and rampant crime, unemployment, and a reduced quality of life. Some feel unprepared to pay such a high price for future economic benefits. Others, especially the younger generations, are eagerly taking advantage of the open environment. Indeed, Russians are learning the value of discussion and compromise, personal creativity, and risk-taking. This long-term process carries hard lessons such as financial loss, political polarization, economic instability, and social disruption.

Friendship is extremely important in Russia. Russians are warm and open to, as well as trusting of, their friends. They rely on their network of friends in hard times and will go to great lengths to help friends whenever possible.

Although intensely proud of "Mother Russia" and its achievements, Russians are basically pessimistic and usually do not express much hope for a better life in the future (except among the youth). Even generally happy and optimistic Russians might not show their true feelings in public but rather express frustration with everyday life. A general feeling in Russia is that the "soul" of Russia is different from that of other countries, that development cannot take the same course as it has in Europe, for example. Russians often believe they must find a different path that takes into account their unique historical heritage and social structure. In general, Russians desire to be remembered not for the negative aspects of the Soviet period and its aftermath but for Russian contributions to world literature, art, science, technology, and medicine.

Personal Appearance

Russian clothing styles are the same as in Europe but not as sophisticated. Jeans are popular among most age groups, except older women. In winter, people wear *chapkas* or *ushanki* (fur hats). Shorts are becoming popular among the younger generation; young women like short skirts. The older generation dresses conservatively.

CUSTOMS AND COURTESIES

Greetings

When meeting, Russians shake hands firmly and might say *Zdravstvuyte* (pronounced sdrav-STVUH-teh, it means "Hello"), *Dobry dien* (Good day), or *Privet* (a casual "Hello"). Some women prefer not to shake hands, but it is impolite for a man not to offer his hand. Friends and family may kiss on the cheek. The question *Kak dela?* (How are you?) is taken literally; Russians answer in detail and at length. Asking the question without waiting for a full response is rude. *Kak dela?* is not used as a formal greeting. Titles such as *Gospodin* (Mr.) and *Gospozha* (Mrs.) were not used under the Communists, but they are being revived. In addressing an older or respected person, one uses the given name and a patronymic (the possessive of the father's first name), but surnames are preferred in formal greetings. It is considered inappropriate for a younger person or subordinate to address an elder or superior in a casual manner.

Gestures

Pointing with the index finger is improper but commonly practiced. It is impolite to talk (especially to an older person) with one's hands in the pockets or arms folded across the chest. To count, a Russian bends (closes) the fingers rather than opens them.

Visiting

Russians like to visit and have guests. Sitting around the kitchen table and talking for hours is a favorite pastime. One usually removes shoes when entering a home. Hosts generally offer refreshments, but guests may decline them. Friends and family may visit anytime without prior arrangement. They make themselves at home and usually can expect to be welcomed for any length of time. Visits with new acquaintances are more formal and require prior notice.

Giving gifts is a strong tradition in Russia, and almost every event (birthdays, weddings, holidays, etc.) is accompanied by presents. For casual visits, it is common (but not required) for guests to bring a simple gift (flowers, food, or vodka) to their hosts. The object given is less important than the friendship expressed by the act. Flowers are given in odd numbers; even numbers are for funerals. If a bottle of vodka (which means "little water") is opened, custom dictates it be emptied by those present.

Eating

Eating with the fork in the left hand and the knife in the right is standard, but many people use only a fork. People keep the hands above the table and not in the lap. Most Russians like to eat a large breakfast whenever possible. Soup is common for lunch or dinner. Traditionally, a popular feature of any meal is *zakuski* (appetizers). There are many different kinds of *zakuski*; eating too many may spoil an appetite. Russians put more food than they can eat on the table and leave some on the plate to indicate there is abundance (whether true or not) in the house. Guests who leave food on the plate indicate they have eaten well.

Russians generally do not go to lunch in cafés or restaurants because the few that exist are fairly expensive. Instead, people eat at workplace cafeterias or bring food from home.

LIFESTYLE

Family

The family is the basic social unit in Russia, and most people expect to marry and have children. The average urban couple has one child, but rural families are larger. Because housing is difficult to obtain, young couples often live with their parents for some time. It is the normal practice to support children financially until they reach adulthood. The father is considered the head of the family. Both husband and wife usually work, but women are also responsible for housekeeping. Men rarely share in household duties. Child care is available, but few families can afford it. When the elderly live with their children, they often provide child care and do the shopping.

Urban apartments are small and it is common for a family of three or more to live in one room. A typical apartment has one room, a kitchen, and a bathroom. Rural homes are small but larger than apartments. While they have more room, they often lack running water.

Dating and Marriage

When young people date, they usually go to movies or for a walk in a city park. Sometimes they go to bars or cafés, but this is presently too expensive for many people. Instead, the youth like to have parties in their apartments when their parents are not home. Many couples live together before or instead of marrying. There is a new trend to be married in a church first and then to have an official civil ceremony in a "wedding palace," the only place people could get married before 1991.

Diet

Although food is plentiful, many products are expensive or available only in hard-currency markets. For the common person, this means fruits and vegetables are difficult to come by. Hence, menus consist mainly of bread, meat, dairy products, and potatoes. To improve the diet, a growing number of people in urban areas are growing vegetable gardens on plots near the city. People on fixed and limited incomes (mainly the elderly) eat more bread than anything else. Common Russian foods include *borsch* (cabbage soup with beets), *pirozhki* (a stuffed roll), *golubzi* (stuffed cabbage leaves baked with tomato sauce and eaten with sour cream), and *shi* (soup with sour cabbage). *Borsch* is still one of the most popular foods in the country. Its ingredients (potatoes, cabbages, carrots, beets, and onions) almost complete the list of vegetables used in everyday life. Pork, sausage, chicken, and cheeses are popular, but they are often very expensive. Russians prefer tea to coffee. Mineral water, juice, and soda are readily available at high prices. Russians drink far more vodka than wine.

Recreation

Russians have little leisure time because of the hours they devote to getting food, working extra jobs, or taking care of their households. Urban Russians spend their spare time at their *dachas* (country cottages), if they have them, relaxing and growing fruits and vegetables for the winter. There are relatively few nightclubs, and entertainment usually ends by

11:00 P.M. Even Moscow is essentially dark and quiet after that hour.

The country's favorite sport is soccer. Russia's national soccer team competed in the 1994 World Cup. Winter sports such as ice skating, hockey, and cross-country skiing, are particularly popular in Russia. Watching television is the most common way to spend extra time. Gathering mushrooms is a favorite summer activity. Russia has a grand and abiding heritage in cultural arts. The people highly appreciate theaters and movies, but these are available only in big cities. Rural people can watch movies at *dvorets kultury* (palaces of culture), which serve as community recreation centers.

Holidays

New Year's Day is the most popular holiday in Russia. Almost everyone decorates fir trees and has parties to celebrate the new year. Grandfather Frost leaves presents for children to find on New Year's Day. Christmas is on 7 January, according to the Julian calendar used by the Russian Orthodox Church. Women's Day is 8 March. Solidarity Day (1 May, also known as May Day) is a day for parades. Before 1991, people were required to attend; now they attend voluntarily and the nature of the celebrations has changed dramatically. Victory Day (9 May) commemorates the end of World War II and is deeply important to the older generation. Easter and Christmas observances, long interrupted by communism, regained their prominence in 1990.

Commerce

The business week is 40 hours, with Saturdays and Sundays off. Offices generally are open from 9:00 A.M. to 6:00 P.M. They close at lunchtime (1:00 P.M.). Prices in state stores are not negotiable, but prices are flexible on the streets, where an increasing number of items are sold. Capitalism is booming in Russia and a new generation of entrepreneurs is beginning to thrive. Numerous small businesses and joint ventures with foreign firms are finding success, and employees are buying state-run factories and working to make them profitable.

Under communism, there were no incentives for bureaucrats to perform well or even be nice to clients, so the usual answer to any question was "No." This practice is still found in society, but "no" is no longer final. One must simply bargain and be persistent to get what one wants. Russians prefer having social interaction before discussing business. Trying to do business on the phone without seeing the prospective business partner is ineffective. One often spends a lot of time in meetings before even a small deal can succeed.

SOCIETY

Government

Russia is a federation of 21 autonomous republics. The 1993 constitution provides for a president (Boris Yeltsin) as head of state and a prime minister (Viktor Chernomyrdin) as head of government. The president is strong and has power to dissolve Parliament, set foreign policy, and appoint the prime minister. The Federal Assembly has two houses, a 176-seat Federation Council and the 450-seat State Duma. The Constitutional Court is Russia's highest. The voting age is

18. An array of political parties are represented in the *Duma*. The actual party names are less important than their alliances. Communists form the largest block, but not a majority, and nationalists and liberals form other substantial voting blocks.

Economy

Russia's natural resources give it great potential for economic growth and development. Natural gas, coal, gold, oil, diamonds, copper, silver, and lead are all abundant. Heavy industry dominates the economy, although the agricultural sector is potentially strong. Russia's economy is weak and unstable. Liberal reforms designed to attract foreign investment and privatize the economy led to higher unemployment, high inflation (about 100 percent), and lower production. Organized crime and corruption weigh heavily on the economy's ability to perform well. Real gross domestic product per capita is $6,140 and falling, as poverty increases as fast as wealth. The currency is the *ruble* (R).

Transportation and Communication

Most people use public transportation. Major cities have subways, trolleys, and buses. Taxis are expensive and hard to find, but unofficial taxis are increasingly common. Domestic air travel is not always reliable. Railroads are extensive, but service is poor. The telephone system is old and inadequate. The press is free, active, and constantly changing.

Education

Education is free and compulsory between ages six and seventeen. In 1994, new curriculum guidelines were introduced to encourage choice and innovation over previous approaches to teaching, but many public schools are unable or unwilling to implement the reforms due to lack of money and clear local leadership. Students attend primary, middle, and high school. They specialize in their last two years, and several electives are available. Private schools provide high-quality education to children of the wealthy and influential. Education is highly valued, and Russia's literacy rate is 99 percent. More than five hundred universities, medical schools, and technical academies are found throughout the country.

Health

Medical care is free, but the quality of service is poor. Doctors are highly trained and qualified but lack modern equipment and medicine to adequately treat their patients. Private clinics provide better care but are expensive. The infant mortality rate is 26 per 1,000. Life expectancy ranges from 64 to 74 years. Common major diseases are alcoholism, cancer, diabetes, and heart ailments. Diptheria, dysentery, and other intestinal maladies are spreading.

FOR THE TRAVELER

U.S. travelers are required to have a valid visa and passport to enter Russia. Vaccinations are not required, but some may be recommended. While drinking water is generally safe, bottled water is recommended. There are many opportunities to experience the Russian culture through travel; contact your travel professional for more information. You may also wish to contact the Consular Section of the Russian Embassy, 1825 Phelps Place NW, Washington, DC 20008.

A Culturgram is a product of native commentary and original, expert analysis. Statistics are estimates and information is presented as a matter of opinion. While the editors strive for accuracy and detail, this document should not be considered strictly factual. It is a general introduction to culture, an initial step in building bridges of understanding between peoples. It may not apply to all peoples of the nation. You should therefore consult other sources for more information.

Printed on recycled paper

Samoa

(Western Samoa and American Samoa)

WESTERN SAMOA

Asau
Aopo
Sala'ilua Satupaitea Tuasivi
Taga
Savai'i
APIA
Faleolo
Upolu Salani

Boundary representations not necessarily authoritative.

PAGO PAGO
Tutuila

AMERICAN SAMOA

Olosega
Ofu *Ta'u*
Luma
MANU'A ISLANDS

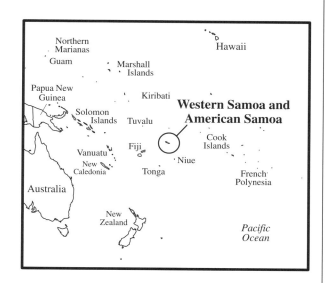

Northern
Marianas
Guam Marshall
Islands Hawaii
Papua New
Guinea Kiribati
**Western Samoa and
American Samoa**
Solomon
Islands Tuvalu
Cook
Islands
Vanuatu Fiji
New Niue
Caledonia Tonga French
Polynesia
Australia
New
Zealand *Pacific
Ocean*

BACKGROUND

Land and Climate

The Samoan Islands are located in the South Pacific Ocean, north of New Zealand and near Fiji and Tonga. Independent Western Samoa, with Apia as its capital, is comprised of two large islands (Savai'i and Upolu) and a few smaller islands. Covering 1,100 square miles (2,850 square kilometers), it is roughly the same size as Rhode Island. About half of the islands are covered with forests. The narrow coastal plains rise to a rugged mountain interior. The islands are still subject to volcanic action.

American Samoa is much smaller than Western Samoa. At 77 square miles (199 square kilometers), it is only a little larger than Washington, D.C. Pago Pago is the capital, located on the island of Tutuila. Ta'u, Ofu, and Olosega form the Manu'a Islands. There are a total of seven islands. The climate is tropical and humid, but southeast trade winds often make temperatures pleasantly mild. Temperatures change little, seldom rising above 85°F (29°C) or falling below 75°F (24°C). Most rainfall occurs from December to March. Even during the rainy season, it is sunny for much of each day.

History

What little is known about Samoa's early history comes from oral history. It is generally accepted that Polynesians migrated to Samoa around 600 B.C., coming from the west. Samoa's closest contact was with Fiji and Tonga. In 1772, the Dutch became the first Europeans to visit the islands. Few written records were kept until the 1800s. Colonization did not begin until the 1830s. Missionaries from the London Missionary Society brought Christianity to the people, who quickly accepted it. The Samoan Islands were ruled by chieftains until the 1860s, when they came under control of the British, Americans, and Germans. Eastern Samoa was later annexed by the United States and Western Samoa by Germany.

After Germany's defeat in World War I, Western Samoa was given to New Zealand as a United Nations trusteeship. It finally achieved independence in 1962 as the Independent State of Western Samoa. It maintains a special treaty relationship with New Zealand. Western Samoa became a member of the Commonwealth in 1970 and joined the United Nations in 1976.

American Samoa became important to the United States during World War II, when Pago Pago was a key naval base.

OCEANIA

Although annexation occurred in 1904, the U.S. Congress did not accept the islands until 1929. Because of the base at Pago Pago, American Samoa was administered by the U.S. Navy. In 1951, that authority was transferred to the U.S. Department of the Interior. A new constitution was drafted in 1960 and the first elections for governor took place in 1977, when Peter T. Coleman was elected. Coleman was reelected several times after that and served until he was defeated in November 1992 elections. He remains head of the local Republican Party.

THE PEOPLE

Population

The population of Western Samoa is about 209,000 and is growing at 2.4 percent annually. Most people are ethnic Samoans of Polynesian descent. About 7 percent are Euronesians, or persons of mixed European and Polynesian heritage. They descend from interracial marriages that occurred during the colonial years. Europeans comprise 0.4 percent of the population.

The population of American Samoa is much smaller, with about 57,000 people living there. American Samoa's population is growing at 3.8 percent annually, despite emigration. Eighty-nine percent of the population is Samoan, 2 percent Caucasian, 4 percent Tongan, and 5 percent comes from other groups or is of mixed heritage.

Western Samoa's Human Development Index (0.651) ranks it 102d out of 174 nations. This indicates many people can earn an income to support basic needs, but opportunities for personal advancement are limited. No Human Development Index is available for American Samoa, but it would be slightly higher than Western Samoa's.

Language

Both nations of Samoa speak Samoan, a language related to Hawaiian and other Polynesian tongues. In American Samoa, English is the second official language. English is also spoken by many people in Western Samoa. The Samoans are proud of their language and prefer to speak it over English in daily interaction.

Religion

Almost all Samoans are Christian, and the people are religious. About half are associated with the London Missionary Society, which introduced Christianity to the people in 1831, and belong to the Christian Congregationalist Church. Many other Christian churches are also represented, the largest of which include the Roman Catholic, Methodist, Church of Jesus Christ of Latter-day Saints (Mormon), and Seventh-Day Adventist faiths. In general, people honor the Christian sabbath and are also religious in their homes. Many families hold evening prayer services (lasting 10–15 minutes).

Visitors arriving during this service wait until it is over before entering the home.

General Attitudes

Samoans have a strong sense of what is called *fa'a Samoa*, or the "Samoan Way." This generally means a casual way of life that is also careful to preserve tradition. *Fa'a Samoa* allows Samoans to be flexible toward some changes, in understanding the ways of foreigners, and with time schedules. However, it also reminds the people of their heritage and customs. Part of that heritage is a leadership system known as *matai*. In the extended family or kinship group (*aiga),* a *matai* (head) holds authority. The *matai* is selected by members of the group. From birth, Samoans learn and function within this hierarchical order, which forms the basis of the Samoan political system, family life, economic livelihood, and social life. Respect for superiors and adults is important.

Samoans have a speech-centered culture. There are many unique ways of communicating a thought, an expectation, a wish, or a command. Expressed in a certain way, a "yes" may really mean "no." Samoans will often say what they think the listener expects to hear. It is usually considered far worse to disagree with someone in authority or not to give the anticipated reply, than not to do what has been agreed on. In Samoa, the individual is not as important as the family or group. Sharing and using are more common concepts than owning or having. One is expected to help others within the family, regardless of the cost.

Personal Appearance

Although some men and women wear Western-style clothing, most Samoans wear traditional Samoan attire. Men wear a *lava lava* (a straight, wraparound skirt) with a shirt. Samoan custom forbids women to wear pants, except when participating in athletic events. They usually wear a *puletasi* (a long dress). On Sunday, almost all people wear white. Samoans also feel that a smile is an important part of their personal appearance.

CUSTOMS AND COURTESIES

Greetings

Samoans prize eloquent speech. For this reason, they offer a formal greeting such as *Susu mai* or *Afio mai* (meaning "Listen" or "Come") before beginning a conversation. Use of these terms in greetings indicates special respect. While English greetings are acceptable in American Samoa, Samoan terms are used more often.

Gestures

One beckons by waving all fingers with the palm facing down. Pointing with the index finger is impolite. Swaying from side to side indicates contempt or anger. A person passing a house where village chiefs are gathered must lower an umbrella or other items being carried to at least hip level. Cars do not drive past such gatherings, but people may walk past. These gestures demonstrate respect for the chiefs.

Visiting

Visitors are not invited to enter a Samoan home until the host has laid out floor mats for the visitors to sit on. In more modern homes, chairs are used instead of mats. The head of the home then welcomes the guests. It is customary to leave one's shoes outside and sit cross-legged on mats. The legs may also be tucked behind a person but never stretched out in front. One does not prop up the legs when sitting in a chair. When a guest enters a home, the host delivers speeches of welcome and the guest makes an appropriately formal response. Visitors are expected to sit where the host indicates. It is impolite to speak to someone in a home while standing. Social customs compel the host to make a guest feel as welcome as possible. Samoans believe that anything a person has is at the disposal of others. The attitude of sharing is manifested by the importance of gift giving. After receiving a gift, a person expresses appreciation and often presents a gift in return.

Eating

Most Samoan foods are eaten with the fingers. During a meal, a bowl of water often will be provided for washing hands. A guest may request one before the meal if it is not offered, because hands should be clean before eating. If hosts present food to a visitor who is not hungry, he or she takes a small amount to show appreciation. Hosts will be disappointed if a guest refuses all offers of food or other hospitality; it is improper to make hosts believe their hospitality has failed.

If offered *kava* (a bitter drink made from the roots of the *yaqona* plant), the guest holds the cup out in front, spills a few drops on the floor mat, and says *Manuia* (Good luck) as a sign of respect for the host family. It is impolite to eat while walking on the street.

LIFESTYLE

Family

A typical Samoan village is made up of a series of families. A family member is anyone who is related to the *matai* by birth, marriage, or adoption. The *matai* of a village form the *fono* (council), which governs the affairs of the village. Each *matai* is responsible for the labor, activities, well-being, and housing of his family. Family members are strongly obligated to share their sustenance with the extended family and, to some extent, the entire village. Land is held in trusteeship in the name of the *matai*. Extended families normally have between 20 and 30 members. Young children are taught not to bother adults and are usually under the supervision of older children. Any adult may freely scold or discipline children when necessary. Discipline within the home is generally strict, and children are taught to respect authority.

Diet

The basic agricultural products in Samoa are bananas, breadfruit, pineapples, papayas, coconuts, copra, yams, and taro (a starchy root). Pork, chicken, and fish are often part of Samoan meals, especially during feasts (*fiafias*). Between 15 and 20 percent of all food is imported.

Recreation

Samoans have their own version of cricket, which they enjoy playing. They also enjoy dancing. In fact, dancing and singing are an important part of life, especially during *fiafias*. Boating events, volleyball, rugby, and basketball are also popular.

Holidays

Christian holidays, such as Christmas and Easter, are celebrated in both parts of Samoa. In Western Samoa, the national holiday is 1 June. In American Samoa, the national holiday is Flag Day (17 April). The Swarm of the *Palolo* is celebrated each year (usually in late October) when the *palolos* (coral worms) come out to propagate their species. The Samoans consider the worm a delicacy and gather them during this time. White Sunday (second Sunday in October) is a day for children.

Commerce

Business hours generally extend from 8:00 A.M. to noon and from 1:00 to 4:30 P.M., Monday through Friday. The business atmosphere is informal.

SOCIETY

Government

The Independent State of Western Samoa is a constitutional monarchy under a native chief. Chief Susuga Malietoa Tanumafili II has been head of state since 1963. The prime minister (Tofilau Eti Alesana) is head of government. Only those with *matai* titles may become members of the 47-seat Legislative Assembly. All adults older than age 21 may vote. The last legislative elections were in 1994. The country's two political parties are Tofilau's Human Rights Protection Party (HRPP) and the Samoan National Development Party (SNDP).

The Territory of American Samoa is an unincorporated U.S. territory administered by the U.S. Department of the Interior. The U.S. president is chief of state. The governor is head of government. Governor A. P. Lutali was elected in 1992 but faces elections in November 1996. The American Samoan legislature is called the *Fono*. Its 21-seat House of Representatives is an elected body whose members serve two-year terms (one seat is reserved for a nonvoting Swains Island delegate). Its next elections are in November 1996. The voting age is 18, and the Democratic and Republican Parties are the only active political parties.

Members of the 18-seat Senate are chosen by senate districts, according to the *matai* tradition.

Although the people of American Samoa are considered U.S. nationals, they are not U.S. citizens and are not subject to federal taxation. They have one nonvoting representative in the U.S. House of Representatives.

Economy

Agriculture and fishing are the mainstays of both economies. More than half of the population in Western Samoa is employed in agriculture, which is responsible for 90 percent of the country's export earnings. Western Samoa exports coconut oil and cream, taro, cocoa, copra, and timber. Tourism is becoming increasingly important as a source of income. The currency is the *tala* (WS$).

In American Samoa, the government is the largest employer, followed by the tuna canning industry. Tuna is the main export, although raw tuna must be imported to be canned. Pet food is also an important export. Tourism is not as important as in Western Samoa, but it is developing. American Samoa conducts 90 percent of its trade with the United States. The currency is the U.S. dollar ($). The standard of living is generally higher in American Samoa than in Western Samoa, due mostly to aid from the United States. Real gross domestic product per capita for Western Samoa is $1,869. American Samoa's gross national product per capita is $2,600.

Transportation and Communication

Public transportation is fairly widespread throughout Samoa. Most people do not own cars and many have no need for them. Interisland boat transportation is available. Telephones are common in most of American Samoa and in Apia, the capital of Western Samoa, although other areas of Western Samoa lack full service. In Western Samoa, telegrams are the most reliable form of international communication. Television and radio are popular. Local newspapers are available. In American Samoa, the government produces a free daily newsletter. A variety of weekly publications are also available.

Education

In Western Samoa, education is essentially free and compulsory between the ages of seven and fifteen. Inadequate finances and facilities limit educational opportunities for some members of society. The adult literacy rate is about 95 percent. Many students travel to New Zealand and other countries for higher education. In American Samoa, education is also free and compulsory. It is based on the U.S. system. There is a two-year community college, and many students travel abroad for higher education. The literacy rate is nearly 99 percent.

Health

Hospital facilities and medical care are generally available and of good quality. The quality is somewhat better in American Samoa than in Western Samoa. In Western Samoa, the infant mortality rate is 36 per 1,000, and life expectancy is between 66 and 71 years. In American Samoa, the infant mortality rate is 19 per 1,000, and life expectancy ranges from 71 to 75 years. Water generally is safe and tropical diseases are not a threat.

FOR THE TRAVELER

In both Samoan nations, no visa is required for stays of up to 30 days. A passport is necessary for Western Samoa and proof of citizenship (if a U.S. citizen) is required in American Samoa. Water is safe and no vaccinations are required. The tourism industry is in its infancy, but the islands offer a pleasant climate, many beautiful beaches, and other sites.

For information about Western Samoa, contact the Western Samoa Visitors Bureau, Private Bag, Apia, Western Samoa. Western Samoa does not maintain an embassy in the United States, but the Western Samoan Mission to the United Nations may have more information on the country: 820 Second Avenue, Suite 800D, New York, NY 10017, phone (212) 599–6196. You may also contact the Royal Western Somoa Consulate, 94–531 Waipahu Street, Waipahu, HI 96797; phone (808) 677–7197.

For American Samoa, contact the Office of Tourism, American Samoa Government, PO Box 1147, Pago Pago, American Samoa 96799; phone (684) 633–1091. The Pago Pago address is in the U.S. postal system, but postage for international delivery is required for Western Samoa. For additional information on American Samoa, contact the American Samoa Liaison Office, 401 Waiakamilo Road, Suite 201, Honolulu, HI 96817; phone (808) 847–1998.

CULTURGRAM '97™

Kingdom of
Saudi Arabia

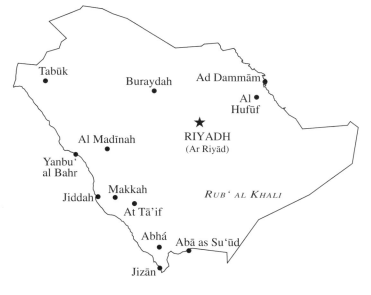

ASIA

BACKGROUND

Land and Climate

Saudi Arabia is the dominant country on the Arabian Peninsula. Covering 750,965 square miles (1,945,000 square kilometers), it is about one-fourth the size of the United States and is the world's 12th largest country. The Red Sea borders the west and the Persian Gulf (known as the Arabian Gulf in Saudi Arabia) lies to the east. Most of the country is a vast, arid plain of sand and rock, with rugged mountains to the southwest. There are no major rivers or lakes. Deserts dominate much of the east and south. The largest sand desert in the world is the Rub' al Khali. Some cultivated fields and green oases can be found, and irrigation is making more agriculture possible, but most of the country is dry and barren. Saudi Arabia's greatest natural resource is crude oil, followed by natural gas, iron ore, gold, and copper. The desert climate is subject to extremes in temperatures, sandstorms, and heat.

History

Arabia has a rich and colorful history that extends for several thousand years. Notable history begins in the seventh century when the prophet Muhammad began proclaiming the message of Islam from the centers of Makkah and Al Madīnah. Islam soon spread from the peninsula to parts of Asia and northern Africa, as well as other regions of the world. The Arabs had a very advanced society. They invented algebra and excelled in many of today's modern sciences. After several centuries of advancement and power, the Arab Empire began to decline after the 13th century.

The peninsula was inhabited by dozens of nomadic tribes, many of which were often at war with one another. In 1902, Abdul Aziz Al-Saud recaptured his ancestral home in Riyadh. After 30 years of fighting, he united the major factions and declared himself king of Saudi Arabia. Four of the king's sons succeeded him in the monarchy: Saud, Faisal, Khalid, and now King Fahd bin Abdul Aziz. Another son, Abdullah, is the crown prince.

King Fahd has been a positive influence on peace and stability in the Middle East. When Iraq invaded Kuwait in 1990 and threatened Saudi Arabia, the Saudis hosted the international coalition that liberated Kuwait and protected Saudi Arabia. During and after the 1991 Gulf War, questions of political and social liberalization were raised. While Saudi Arabia determined it would retain its conservative customs, some political changes were announced in 1992. King Fahd suffered a stroke in November 1995, and his recovery has been difficult. His ability to stay on the throne has been doubted by some, but he continued to hold meetings in 1996. Should Fahd abdicate, Crown Prince Abdullah is next in line to rule. Abdullah already performs many duties as regent.

THE PEOPLE

Population

The rapidly growing (3.6 percent annually) population of Saudi Arabia is about 18.7 million. This figure includes foreign workers (about 4.6 million) who are not citizens. Most foreign workers are from other Islamic countries, but a sizable U.S. American community also exists and is associated with the oil industry. Saudi nationals comprise 75 percent of the total population. Of that number, 90 percent are Arabs and about 10 percent are of Afro-Asian heritage, descendants of settlers from throughout the Islamic world. The Arabs are descendants of many nomadic tribes, some of which, like the Bedouins, still exist.

Saudi Arabia's Human Development Index (0.762) ranks it 76th out of 174 nations. Adjusted for women, the index (0.514) ranks Saudi Arabia 81st out of 130 nations. These figures reflect the fact that women earn less than 10 percent of the nation's income and have fewer opportunities to pursue personal goals than do men. Overall, Saudi society does not provide resources that allow the average individual to share in the country's prosperity, but progress is being made toward that goal.

Language

Arabic is the official language of the kingdom. It is also the language of the *Qur'an* (Koran), the scripture of Islam. English is used in business and educated circles.

Religion

Islam is the only legally and officially recognized religion of Saudi Arabia. Arabia is the birthplace of the revered prophet Muhammad and Saudi Arabia is the home of Islam's two most sacred cities: Makkah and Al Madìnah. Non-Muslims are not permitted to enter these cities. The Arabian peninsula is the center of the Islamic religion, which has spread throughout the world. Each year, hundreds of thousands of Muslims complete a pilgrimage (*Hajj*) to Makkah as part of their religious duties. During the *Hajj*, male pilgrims are expected to wear a white, two-piece, towel-like garment called the *Ihram*. Women can wear traditional clothing but cannot wear a veil. Part of the *Hajj* includes a walk (seven times) around the *Ka'abah* (House of God) at the large Sacred Mosque. All Muslims in the world face toward this *Ka'abah* when they say their daily prayers to *Allah* (God).

Islam accepts all Biblical prophets through Jesus, but Muhammad is the last and greatest of all prophets. Although Muslims believe in a life after death, they do not accept Jesus Christ as God's son. The *Qur'an* (Koran) contains *Allah*'s revelations to Muhammad. Religion is a matter of daily practice and a way of life for Muslims; it is not just a matter of belief and acceptance. In addition to a once-in-a-lifetime pilgrimage and five daily prayers, Muslims also practice their faith through *Shahada* (professing *Allah* as the only god and Muhammad as his messenger), *Zakat* (giving of one's income to help the poor), and fasting during the month of *Ramadan*. Together, these practices are referred to as the "Five Pillars of Islam."

The laws of Saudi Arabia are based on *Shari'a* (Islamic law). All Saudi citizens are Muslims and are restricted from joining any other religion. Foreigners are allowed to practice religion in the home as they wish.

General Attitudes

Life in Saudi Arabia is more relaxed than in fast-paced Western nations. Saudi Arabians prefer to establish trust and confidence before proceeding with business. Saudis are conscious of personal and family honor and can easily be offended by any perceived insult to that honor. The people are generous and hospitable. Privacy is important.

Saudis generally prefer to maintain cultural tradition in the face of modernization. While some may desire more liberal social and political practices, these people are in the minority. Most Saudis are proud that their conservative culture has escaped many of the social problems facing Western nations. While Saudi society may seem closed or repressive, Saudis remind Westerners of the country's strong families, low crime rate, and lack of drug problems.

The people are very religious. Islamic customs therefore play a key role in determining cultural practices. Saudi Arabians are proud of the strength of their modern country and are very patriotic; at the same time, their chief devotions are to family and religion.

Personal Appearance

Saudi Arabian men and women continue to wear traditional Arab dress. Men wear a *ghutra* (headdress) and *thobe* (ankle-length shirt, usually white, that covers long pants). A cloak (*mishlah*) is often worn over the *thobe*. The *ghutra* is not removed in public. Some men have adopted Western dress for certain occasions, but the majority retain the customary clothing. A *ghutra* is usually either red checkered or completely white. It is held in place by an *igal* (braided black cord). The white *ghutra* is usually made of lighter fabric and may be seen more often in the summer. Depending on the location, women in public have veiled faces (veiling is not practiced in some areas) and wear an *abaaya* (black robe that covers the entire body). The *abaaya* is often worn over beautifully tailored dresses. Modesty is of utmost importance, even in the heat of the Saudi summers. Visitors are expected to dress conservatively. Tight-fitting or revealing clothing is unacceptable.

CUSTOMS AND COURTESIES

Greetings

Saudi Arabians use several forms of greeting. The most common is a handshake with the right hand and the phrase *As-Salaamu 'Alaykum* (Peace be upon you). Frequently, males will follow up by extending the left hand to each other's right shoulder and kissing the right and left cheeks. The greeting used depends on the individuals' relationship to each other and their status in society. When accompanied by a woman wearing a veil, a man normally will not introduce her, and one does not expect to shake hands with her. The term for "Good morning" is *Sabah al-Khair,* and for "Good evening" it is *Mesah al-Khair.* A casual hello is *Marhaba.*

Gestures

It is impolite to point with the finger or signal to another person with the hand. One also avoids using the left hand for gesturing. All objects are passed with the right hand or both hands, never with the left alone. It is an insult to point the bottom of one's foot at another person. It is also impolite to cross an ankle over the knee, although crossing one's legs at the knees is acceptable and common.

Visiting

Invitations to a Saudi Arabian home are often given to a man alone. If his wife is invited, she may be sent to eat with the other women in a separate room or quarters. It is inappropriate for a first-time guest to take a gift to the woman of the house. Otherwise, gift giving is common. Dinner guests usually present flowers, sweets, or other small items to the hosts as appreciation for their hospitality.

The Saudis take great care in providing for their visitors. Tea or coffee is served. When a person has had enough to drink, he will cover the cup with the hand or shake it gently from side to side several times and say *bes* (enough). Otherwise, an empty cup is quickly refilled. Alcoholic beverages are never offered in the home and are not presented as gifts. Islamic law prohibits the consumption of alcohol. Coffee is served at the end of a gathering just before it is time for the guests to leave. Toward the end of a business meeting, Saudis may lose interest and direct the conversation to nonbusiness matters.

Eating

Western dining etiquette is only observed in more Westernized circles. In general, Saudis eat food with the fingers of the right hand only. Bread may be torn with the left hand but is eaten with the right. The Saudis delight in preparing an abundance of food for their guests. Hosts encourage guests to take second helpings and are pleased when they do, but a person can also politely decline further helpings. In restaurants, a service charge is usually included in the bill. The main meal of the day is in the mid-afternoon (usually after 2:00 P.M.), when children are home from school and parents from work. This custom has changed for those whose offices remain open in the afternoon. The main meal for these families is in the evening. Conversation is often minimal during the main course of a meal; people prefer to talk before and especially after the meal—while they drink tea or coffee.

LIFESTYLE

Family

Although the Saudi Arabian family is traditionally a strong, male-dominated unit, women exercise considerable influence in the home. Most families live as extended families, but nuclear families are common in urban areas. Even so, sons and their families usually live in a neighborhood close to their father's home. The family is the key to Saudi Arabian society. Infidelity is a crime.

The separation of male and female is a way of life in Saudi Arabia. Rules governing the actions of women are based on Saudi Arabian law and custom and are designed to respect and protect a woman's modesty and honor. A woman's behavior reflects on her family's reputation. Men and women have separate workplaces. Female doctors treat women and children; if they treat men, they are veiled. Women cannot socialize in public with men and are usually accompanied by a male relative in public. Women are not allowed to interact with men outside their family and are forbidden to drive a car or ride a bicycle. Many of these laws also apply to foreigners. Despite the restrictions on public life, men and women can associate freely in the privacy of the home.

Dating and Marriage

Marriages are usually arranged, but a growing minority of young men and women in urban areas are being allowed to choose their mates. Because of the separation of sexes, dating is not practiced. A traditional Saudi Arabian wedding is an Islamic ceremony followed by separate parties for the men and women. Traditionally, men pay a dowry for their brides. Although Islamic law allows a man to have up to four wives, most Saudi men have only one wife. To have more than one, a man must receive the consent of his wife or wives and must provide equally for each. Chastity is the most important thing a woman can bring to marriage.

Diet

Saudi dishes are composed mainly of rice with lamb or chicken and are mildly spicy. *Kabsah* (rice and lamb) is a favorite dish throughout the country. Rice is also often served with vegetables and a green salad. Desserts are commonly fruits, eaten with Saudi coffee (brewed with cardamom). Seafood, including a variety of fish, is popular on the coasts. Coffee or tea is served before all meals. Buttermilk and camel's milk are also popular beverages. Muslims do not eat pork or drink alcohol.

Recreation

Soccer is the national sport, but only men are allowed to play or watch at the stadium. Saudi Arabia's national soccer team competed in the 1994 World Cup. Sporting clubs exist throughout the country. Saudi men also enjoy horse and camel races (no betting is allowed, but winners receive prizes), as well as hunting and hawking (falconry). Hawking involves hunting for small game with falcons and requires great skill in training the birds. Young men enjoy volleyball, basketball, swimming, wrestling, and roller skating. Women are generally not involved in sports and do not participate in most other leisure activities, but girls play volleyball and other sports at school. Women enjoy visiting other women; going on family outings to museums, playgrounds, and amusement parks; or doing volunteer work. Videos are popular among all, but there are no movie theaters.

Holidays

The Islamic calendar is based on the lunar month, which makes a year up to 11 days shorter than a Western calendar year. Therefore, holidays vary from year to year, with the exception of National Day, which is celebrated 23 September. Islam does not use Christ's birth as a reference point for counting years; rather the calendar begins at the year of the *Hegira*, the migration of Muhammad from Makkah to Al Madìnah in the seventh century. The year 1995 roughly corresponds to the Islamic year 1415. The most important Islamic holidays celebrated in Saudi Arabia include the three-day feast (*Eid al Fitr*) at the end of *Ramadan* and the Feast of the Sacrifice (*Eid al Adha*), which commemorates the willingness of Abraham to sacrifice his son and celebrates the annual *Hajj*, during which it occurs. The birth of the prophet Muhammad and the Islamic New Year are also celebrated.

During the Islamic month of *Ramadan*, Muslims do not eat, drink, or smoke from sunrise to sunset each day. Meals are in the evening. No eating is permitted in public (even by foreigners) during the daytime throughout this month. During *Eid al Fitr*, extended families gather for a big feast, people visit senior relatives, and children receive gifts and wear new clothes.

Commerce

The workweek runs from Saturday to Wednesday, with Thursday and Friday comprising the weekend. Friday is the Muslim day of worship, when people go to the mosque to pray and hear recitations from the *Qur'an*. Women often stay home to pray. Those who go to the mosque may pray in designated areas, separate from the men. Government offices are open weekdays from 7:30 A.M. to 2:30 P.M. Private business offices are open from around 8:00 A.M. until noon and between 3:00 and 6:00 P.M. General banking hours are from 8:00 A.M. to noon and from 5:00 to 8:00 P.M. Markets, shops, and *souks* (outdoor markets) are open from 9:00 A.M. to noon and from 3:00 to 9:00 P.M. Government offices and banks are closed on Friday, but retail businesses are open in the afternoon and evening. During *Ramadan*, office hours are in the evening and extend past midnight. An increasing number of women work in professional fields and business.

SOCIETY

Government

The kingdom is divided into 14 regions called governorates, each of which is headed by a governor, or *Emir*, who answers directly to the king. The king is chief of state and head of government; he rules with the Council of Ministers. Before 1992, the king, crown prince, and Council of Ministers established all laws. In March 1992, however, the king issued a new "system of governance" (the first written body of law the kingdom has had) that changed the country's political structure and guaranteed citizens a number of basic rights. The *Qur'an* remains the country's official "constitution." The new system provides for a Consultative Council (*Majlis Ashura*), comprised of 60 appointed members, that advises the king and Council of Ministers. The Consultative Council can express its opinion on any matters, review and initiate laws, and overrule cabinet decisions if the king agrees. Each governor also has a ten-member Consultative Council, and governorates now have greater autonomy to make certain decisions.

The governance system states that all kings after the current crown prince will be elected by all the princes (there are more than five hundred) and that new crown princes will be appointed and can be dismissed by the king. This change effectively eliminates the hereditary line of rule. The new body of laws does not provide for elections or a representative legislature, but its attention to human rights and public dialogue on policy matters represents a major change for Saudi Arabia.

Economy

Saudi Arabia has a strong economy. It is growing at about 3 percent annually. Real gross domestic product per capita is $9,880, a high level for a developing country. The country's oil wealth has allowed for a significant improvement in living conditions over the past generation.

Saudi Arabia enjoys low unemployment and low inflation. Indeed, many workers from other countries form the bulk of the labor force. In the late 1930s, huge oil reserves were discovered. Petroleum and petroleum products form the base of Saudi Arabia's economy, accounting for nearly 90 percent of all export earnings. The Saudi Arabian Oil Company is the world's largest oil company. Because of the harsh climate and terrain, the country imports many foods, but dates, grains, and livestock are produced locally. The country is self-sufficient in wheat and nearly so in poultry and dairy products. The unit of currency is the Saudi *riyal* (R).

Transportation and Communication

The kingdom is continually expanding its infrastructure. Most families own a car. The most convenient way to travel between cities, however, is by airplane. A high-speed train goes from Dammàm to Riyadh. Taxis and buses are common in the cities. In desert areas, the camel is still used for transportation (especially among the Bedouin), but automobiles are also common. Saudi Arabia's telecommunications system is modern and extensive.

Education

Kindergarten lasts for two years and is for children ages four through six. Both boys and girls are in classes together. At age six, however, when compulsory education begins, boys and girls go to separate schools. Boys attend six years of primary schooling (*ibtida'i),* followed by three years of intermediate schooling (*mutawassit*) and three years of secondary education (*thanawi*). After one year of secondary school, a student follows either a science or a literary track. All schooling, including university, is funded by the government. Education for girls did not really begin until the 1960s, when the first effort to provide schools for girls began. By the 1980s, the same basic system of education that is available to boys became available to girls. Many women study at universities for their degrees. The literacy rate has increased considerably in the past few years; it is currently 62 percent. The government is committed to improving the quality of education and increasing accessibility to it.

Health

Although health standards are not equal to those in the West, they are improving rapidly. Free medical treatment is available to all citizens of the kingdom and to pilgrims that come each year to Makkah. There are now several modern hospitals in the major cities, and rural clinics continue to improve care. The infant mortality rate is 49 per 1,000. Life expectancy is between 67 and 70 years.

FOR THE TRAVELER

Saudi Arabia does not issue tourist visas. Only business (or work) and religious visas are available and a person must be sponsored by a Saudi organization to get one. Foreigners who travel to Saudi Arabia are expected to abide by its social laws and customs, including conservative dress standards and laws regarding the role of women in society. For more information, contact the Royal Embassy of Saudi Arabia, 601 New Hampshire Avenue NW, Washington, DC 20037.

Republic of
Senegal

Boundary representations not necessarily authoritative.

BACKGROUND

Land and Climate

Senegal lies in the most western part of Africa. The Gambia (a separate country) almost divides Senegal into two parts. Covering 75,749 square miles (196,180 square kilometers), Senegal is about the size of South Dakota. Most of the country north of The Gambia is flat, with rolling plains and few trees. Part of the north, which lies in Africa's semiarid Sahel region, is subject to desertification. The southeast has plateaus more than 1,600 feet (487 meters) high and the southwest consists of wetlands and forests. Four major rivers flow through the country from east to west. Dakar, the capital, is an important port for West Africa. Senegal has two distinct seasons: the sunny, dry season (November–June), with moderate temperatures; and the hot, humid rainy season (July–October), with temperatures often above 90°F (32°C). Rains fall a bit earlier below The Gambia. Dakar and other coastal areas are generally cooler than the rest of the country.

History

Black Africans have historically lived in the area now called Senegal. Great empires and independent kingdoms existed in the area from A.D. 300 to the 19th century. Islamic merchants from North Africa introduced Islam to the animistic peoples of the area in the 10th century. Portuguese sailors first traded with the people in the mid-1400s but were replaced by the French, English, and Dutch in the 1500s. The slave trade was established, and peanuts were introduced as a new crop to supply European demand. Several million West Africans were shipped to the Americas as slaves between the 16th and 19th centuries. Many were sold at an auction house that still stands on Goree Island (near Dakar).

By the 1800s, France began to dominate the area, conquering various kingdoms and establishing Senegal as one of several colonies in its federation of French West Africa. Slavery was abolished in 1848, but French economic, educational, political, and judicial systems remained intact at the administrative level. After World War II, many began to demand independence. On 4 April 1960, the colony gained independence as a sovereign nation, beginning as a member of the Mali Federation. France and Senegal still maintain close political, economic, and social ties. Senegal is also an active member of the United Nations.

After halting a destabilizing coup attempt in neighboring Gambia, Senegal moved to create a loose federation (known as Senegambia) with Gambia. The two nations retained full sovereignty but shared military and economic systems. The alliance was dissolved in 1989. In 1981, Senegal's constitution was amended to eliminate restrictions on various political parties. Abdou Diouf was elected president and his party, the Socialist Party, came to dominate Parliament. Diouf was reelected in 1988 and 1993.

Senegal generally has enjoyed good relations with other West African nations. In 1989, however, hundreds died when violence broke out between Moors of Mauritania and Black Africans of Senegal over a land and grazing dispute. The border between the two countries was closed, but calm was restored through negotiations. Senegal has otherwise participated in regional and international peacekeeping missions.

THE PEOPLE

Population

Senegal's population of approximately nine million people is growing at 3.1 percent annually. More than 40 percent of the people are younger than age 15. Dakar has more than 1.5 million inhabitants, but the majority (62 percent) live in rural areas. Most of the people are Black African, including the Wolof (36 percent), Fulani or Peul (17), Serer (17), Toucouleur (9), Diola (9), and Mandingo (9). About 1 percent are European and Lebanese and there are other smaller groups. The Lebanese have been in Senegal for many generations and form an influential merchant class.

Senegal's Human Development Index (0.340) ranks it 152d out of 174 nations. Adjusted for women, the index (0.316) ranks Senegal 111th out of 130 nations. Only a minority of people have access to resources that allow them to pursue goals for personal development.

Language

Although French is the official language of instruction, business, and government, six major local languages are spoken in Senegal. These include Wolof, Serer, Alpuular, Mandingo, Diola, and Bassari. Wolof, the native language of the dominant ethnic group, is most widely used. In fact, non-Wolofs north of The Gambia are bilingual in Wolof and their own ethnic language. Educated Senegalese also speak French. Some speak English, although it is not widely understood throughout the country. Senegalese languages are oral tongues. Although a few attempts have been made to make these tongues written languages, most rural people conduct their lives in their oral languages, for which reading and writing do not exist. Many Muslims use the Arabic alphabet to write in Wolof or one of the other oral languages.

Religion

About 90 percent of the population is Muslim, and about 6 percent is Christian (mostly Catholic). The constitution guarantees freedom of religion and separation of church and state. Both Muslim and Catholic holy days are national holidays. In practice, however, Islam dominates social and political activities. The *marabouts* (Muslim religious leaders) influence voting patterns and economic practices. Their power has a strong impact on the country's development. The *marabouts* became powerful during the drive for independence. They were the movement's most vocal and supportive leaders and drew many animists to Islam because of their popularity.

Many Senegalese, especially in the south, combine their formal religion (Islam or Christianity) with indigenous animist practices and ceremonies. For instance, villagers believe in zombees, spirits, and *geniis*. They often wear a *grigri* (charm) around their arms, stomach, or neck. The *marabout* writes the charm in Arabic on paper and encases it in leather to be strong on a string.

General Attitudes

Senegal has many diverse ethnic groups within its borders, each with its own history, language, and culture. Interactions between these groups and with non-African cultures have produced a multicultural people proud of their origins. Typically, a person's allegiances extend toward the family first, and then, in descending order, to an ethnic group, to a religion, to Senegal, to French West Africa, and finally, to Africa. Personal relations, including doing favors and returning them, are extremely important in daily life.

Concepts of time and distance are defined by a person's background. For example, a Senegalese farmer, whose way of life may not include motor vehicles, will consider a five-hour walk to another village a short trip. But an urban professional might drive rather than walk a short distance. Most other aspects of life are widely different between urban and rural classes. For instance, while wealthy and educated women may hold public office and be employed in important business positions, rural women rarely have such opportunities. Throughout the country, women are responsible for the daily functions of the household. The Senegalese, urban and rural, are interested in domestic and world politics and appreciate exchanging ideas with foreign visitors.

Personal Appearance

Senegalese place great emphasis on their appearance and personal hygiene. Most bathe more than once a day, and perfumes or colognes are popular. Dressing well is important. Men do not go out in public without a shirt, and few women (only urban youths) wear pants or shorts. Only beggars might be barefoot in public. Revealing clothing is not appreciated. People wear beachwear only on the beach; shorts are for athletics.

Villagers and most adult urbanites wear traditional clothing. Young urban dwellers wear Western fashions until they get older. Traditional clothing for men includes loose-fitting cotton robes (*boubous*) worn over bouffant pants and a loose shirt. The amount of embroidery indicates one's level of wealth. Women wear a long robe over a long, wraparound skirt (*sarong*). Muslim women do not wear veils. Muslim women who have made a pilgrimage to Makkah, Saudi Arabia, wear a white scarf, while men wear a white headdress; these people are treated with great respect.

CUSTOMS AND COURTESIES

Greetings

Courtesy is extremely important, so greetings should never be neglected. Senegalese greetings vary depending on the circumstances and how well people know each other. Shaking hands and kissing alternate cheeks three times (a French tradition) is common in urban areas. Rural Senegalese only shake hands, and social rules determine who may shake with whom. A minority of Muslim men do not shake hands with women. When joining or leaving a small group, one must greet each individual separately. Whatever greeting was used between two people is also used when parting. Upon parting, most Senegalese ask each other to extend best wishes to their families and mutual friends.

Gestures

Senegalese receive and give objects with their right hand or with both hands. Use of the left hand is considered unclean. Scratching in public is impolite, as are public displays of affection, although some urban youth hold hands. It is inappropriate to eat while on the street. Senegalese tell street vendors they are not interested in their goods by motioning with a pushing back gesture and avoiding eye contact. They hail taxis by raising one arm. In traditional families, children and women curtsy to their elders to show respect. People avoid eye contact with a member of the opposite sex or a person considered to be a superior (in age or status). Men and women keep their distance in public and are expected to be dignified and reserved around members of the opposite sex. More relaxed behavior is acceptable with members of the same gender, age, or status. Between men, sharing a kola nut (which contains a mild caffeine stimulant) is a gesture of friendship.

Visiting

Senegalese enjoy visiting one another often in the home. Because most do not own telephones, dropping in uninvited is acceptable and appreciated. Still, uninvited guests try to visit before mealtimes, either in the late morning or early evening. Work, health, family matters, and mutual friends are briefly discussed before a visitor addresses the purpose of the visit. Guests may be treated to three rounds of tea, with more sugar added in each round.

Senegalese are hospitable and can make a guest feel comfortable without expecting anything in return. However, friends will often bring gifts such as fruit or some cookies for the children. Hosts will offer a drink (usually nonalcoholic), but foreign visitors do not drink water unless it is bottled. To decline a drink, it is polite to say one has just finished drinking. It is impolite to refuse other refreshments. Although smoking is widespread among males, visitors to traditional Muslim homes avoid cigarette smoking until they leave. It is considered bad manners for women to smoke. Asking personal questions is impolite; it is considered bad luck to ask specific questions about children, such as when a baby is due, how many children one has, or what their ages are.

Eating

Generally, breakfast is between 6:00 and 9:00 A.M., lunch from noon to 1:30 P.M., and dinner from 8:00 to 9:30 P.M. In traditional homes, the sexes and different age groups eat separately. The main dish usually is served in large bowls placed on mats on the floor or ground, or on coffee tables. Several people eat from the same bowl using the fingers or a spoon, depending on personal habit, the occasion, and the dish. Proper etiquette for eating is stressed to children at an early age. It is important for diners to have clean hands, eat only from the portion of the communal dish directly in front of them, and avoid eye contact with persons still eating. One uses only the right hand to eat. The left can assist the right when one eats difficult foods, such as fruit or meat with bones. Occasionally, particularly when hosting Western visitors, some urban Senegalese follow French customs, eating at tables from individual plates with utensils.

LIFESTYLE

Family

In general, the family is a source of strength and pride for Senegalese. In most rural areas and among traditional urban families, extended families live together in compounds (with a separate dwelling for each nuclear family). But there is an urban trend for nuclear families to live in single households, often with relatives in the neighborhood. Baptisms, circumcisions, marriages, funerals, and other important ceremonies are cause for elaborate celebration. Most families live at subsistence levels as agricultural workers, although there is a growing middle class and a small, wealthy elite. The elderly receive great respect and are cared for by their families.

Dating and Marriage

Western-style dating, where relative strangers go out with one another, is uncommon in Senegal. People tend to go out in groups or in couples with a person they and their families know. In fact, a couple's families tend to be heavily involved in courtship. Traditional families arrange marriages, but more urban residents are marrying according to their choice. Couples are often encouraged to marry young. However, it is acceptable for college students to wait until after they finish school. Many Muslims practice polygamy. Islamic law permits a man to have up to four wives, but he must have the consent of the other wife (or wives), and, according to the Qur'an (Koran), he must divide his resources and time equally among each wife's household.

Diet

Food preparation and presentation are skills that Senegalese females learn at an early age. Each ethnic group has its own traditional dishes, and some urban women also cook French meals. Many believe wealth is measured by body size, because the wealthier the family, the more oil and rice can be used in preparing dishes. Meals usually consist of one main dish of rice, millet, or corn, over which is served a sauce composed of vegetables, meat (traditional Muslims do not eat pork), poultry, fish, beans, or milk and sugar. A dessert of fruit and/or yogurt might be served. One popular dish is yassa: rice and chicken covered with a sauce made of sliced onions and spices. Another is thiebou dien, a meal of fish and rice that is typically eaten for lunch. A traditional Wolof dish is mbaxal-u-Saloum: a sauce of ground peanuts, dried fish, meat, tomatoes, and spices served with rice.

Recreation

Traditional wrestling is the national sport. However, soccer is the most popular sport. Senegalese avidly follow international competitions. Other favorites include basketball, track-and-field, and jogging. Many people in urban areas enjoy movies and books. Concerts, discos, and videos are popular in areas with electricity. After the harvest, rural families visit relatives in urban areas. They also enjoy dancing. Family and village celebrations provide the main form of recreation for most rural people.

Holidays

Senegal celebrates Islamic, Catholic, and national holidays. They include New Year's Day, Mawloud (celebrating the prophet Muhammad's birth), Easter, Independence Day (4 April), Labor Day (1 May), Ascension, and Whitmonday. On Tabaski, the head of each household sacrifices a lamb in honor of Abraham's willingness to sacrifice his son. Korite marks the end of Ramadan, the month of fasting when Muslims go without food or drink from sunrise to sundown each day of the month. Tamkharit, the Islamic New Year, is also the day on which Allah determines people's destinies. Islamic holidays follow the lunar calendar and thus fall on different dates each year. All Saints' Day (1 November) and Christmas are also celebrated.

Commerce

Muslims do not schedule business meetings during prayer times, which take place five times each day. If a meeting runs into prayer time, it might be stopped so the people can pray, depending on the individuals involved and whether the area is traditional or Westernized. Meetings are formal in most cases, and participants do not remove jackets or roll up sleeves. Government offices are open Monday through Friday, 7:30 A.M. to 4:00 P.M., with a short lunch break. Urban businesses follow the same general schedule, Monday through Saturday, but some stay open until 6:00 P.M.

SOCIETY

Government

Senegal, a multiparty democracy since 1981, is divided into ten regions. The elected president serves as chief of state, and the prime minister is head of government. Habib Thiam became prime minister in 1991. The *Assemblée Nationale* (National Assembly) has 120 seats. The main opposition party is the Senegal Democratic Party. Other parties exist but do not have much power in Parliament. All citizens may vote at age 18.

At the rural level, a system of local chiefs and religious leaders provides local leadership and judicial services. Local authority is often more important to the average person than departments of the central government.

Economy

Senegal has an agriculture-based market economy, and 75 percent of the population works in agriculture. Since introduced by colonial powers, peanuts have remained the country's main cash crop and occupy about 40 percent of all cropland. Other agricultural products include millet, cassava, cotton, rice, poultry, and vegetables. Farmers depend on rain for their crops, but a few projects are experimenting with irrigation.

After the Ivory Coast, Senegal has the most developed manufacturing sector in French West Africa. The most important industries include peanut oil extraction, tourism, phosphates, and food processing (which accounts for 27 percent of all exports). Fish processing is the key component in Senegal's food processing industry.

Real gross domestic product per capita is $1,750, higher than some other African countries. This reflects a higher level of economic development, but its benefits are enjoyed by a minority of (mostly urban) people. Inflation and debt hinder progress on many fronts. France's 1994 devaluation of West Africa's currency, the *CFA franc*, has also severely hurt the local economy.

Transportation and Communication

Major cities are linked by paved roads, while inland villages are connected by unpaved paths and waterways. An airline services the northern and southern coasts. A railroad system extends from Dakar to the north and to Mali in the east. Most people do not own cars; they travel by public transport (buses, taxis, or a minivan system for longer distances), horse and buggy, bicycle, motorcycle, or on foot. The government sponsors a daily newspaper, other political parties sponsor weekly papers, and an independent daily is also available. While most urban residents have access to information through print, radio, or television, villages are often isolated because they lack electricity and postal services. Most rural people travel to nearby towns for postal services. They usually have access to a daily radio news broadcast. Radio stations broadcast in local languages, while oral or written messages passed from person to person are the most effective means of communication among villagers.

Education

Senegal's educational system is based on the French model. Classes are taught in French, which is considered the nation's unifying language. About 31 percent of the population has learned to read and write in French, but because French typically is not spoken in the home, most children do not speak it when they begin school. Also, textbooks are from France and do not teach from a local perspective. Therefore, many see school as being irrelevant to their daily activities, so they drop out of school early. Still, officials hesitate to drop French as the language of instruction because they fear most ethnic groups would resist an educational system based on a single ethnic language. In addition, they believe dropping French would isolate Senegal from the rest of the world. School attendance is also affected by the need for children to work in the fields, by a distrust of secular (versus religious) education, and other factors. About half of all students enter and complete a primary education, and about one-third of those go on to a secondary school. Children often attend Koranic schools where they learn some Arabic and about Islam.

Health

Although health conditions are improving, diseases and infections continue to affect many Senegalese, particularly those in rural areas who cannot afford or do not have access to medical treatment. There is one doctor for every 16,000 persons, but 70 percent of all physicians practice in Dakar. While Dakar doctors have access to modern facilities, rural health-care facilities often lack equipment and medical supplies. The infant mortality rate, currently at 49 per 1,000, has been decreasing for several years. Life expectancy ranges from 67 to 70 years.

FOR THE TRAVELER

U.S. travelers need a valid passport to enter Senegal, but a visa is not required for stays as long as 90 days. Proof of onward passage is required. Water is not potable, but bottled water is safe to drink. Malaria suppressants, as well as hepatitis, tetanus, polio, and typhoid immunizations are recommended. Beware of pickpockets and con men, especially in Dakar and at the airport. Serious crime is rare, but travel south of the Casamance River is dangerous for foreigners. Tourism is increasingly important to Senegal's economy and many travel opportunities are available. For more information, contact the Senegal Tourist Office, 310 Madison Avenue, Suite 724, New York, NY 10017; phone (212) 286–0977. You may also wish to contact the Embassy of the Republic of Senegal, 2112 Wyoming Avenue NW, Washington, DC 20008; phone (202) 234–0540.

 Printed on recycled paper

Republic of
Sierra Leone

Boundary representations not necessarily authoritative.

BACKGROUND

Land and Climate

A country of diverse landscape, Sierra Leone covers 27,699 square miles (71,740 square kilometers) on the coast of West Africa; it is about the size of South Carolina. Near Freetown, beaches rise into 3,000-foot (915-meter) mountains; elsewhere, coasts are flat. The north is mostly forest-savanna; the south is cleared forest used for planting. Pockets of rain forest are scattered throughout the eastern Loma Mountains. The rainy season lasts from May to November. Freetown, the capital, receives up to two hundred inches of rain a year. Humidity and temperatures are high year-round. Daytime temperatures are often above 90°F (32°C). During the harmattan, there is a brief respite from the heat and humidity. In this one-month period that begins in late December, the country is swept by cool, dry, dusty winds out of the northeast.

History

Because Sierra Leone was outside the realms of sub-Saharan West African empires, little is known of its history before the 15th century. After that, the lives of the indigenous people were influenced by two major events: the arrival of European explorers, merchants, and slave traders; and the repatriation of slaves from abroad. In 1462, Portuguese explorers encountered the coast and named the region "Lion Range" (*Serra Lyoa*) because of the thunderous roars heard coming from the steep peninsular mountains.

Great Britain became involved in Sierra Leone because of the lucrative slave trade and its desire to compete with the growing French colonization of West Africa. Britain repatriated some slaves when slavery was declared illegal and maintained a presence so missionaries could "civilize" the Africans. The British traded commodities such as timber, palm kernels, ginger, arrow root, gum, ivory, hides, palm oil, and rubber. After diamonds and gold were discovered, Britain proclaimed a protectorate over Sierra Leone in 1896. During colonial rule, the combined influences of trade and missionary education permanently altered traditional tribal society.

Independence was granted in 1961 and the first prime minister was Sir Milton Margai. After Margai's death, his half brother, Albert Margai, became prime minister. When Albert lost the 1967 elections, the military sponsored a coup to keep him in power. After two more coups, the elected prime minister, Siaka Stevens, was able to take office in 1968. Stevens's party, the All People's Congress (APC), gained complete control of Parliament by 1973, and Stevens ruled a one-party state until he retired in 1985. He was succeeded by Joseph Momoh. By 1990, opposition to APC rule was high and Momoh promised a return to multiparty democracy. When it became clear he was stalling, Momoh was forced from power in 1992. The leader of that coup, Captain Valentine Strasser, took power as chairman of the National Provisional Ruling Council (NPRC).

Strasser scheduled and later canceled elections, but he promised a return to civilian rule by the end of 1995. The date was later set for February 1996. Strasser organized a commission to help prepare election materials and register voters. The program suffered from numerous delays, including an intensification of a 1991 rebellion by the Revolutionary United Front (RUF), a group associated with factions in war-torn Liberia. Strasser invited Nigerian troops to Sierra Leone in 1995 to help fight the rebels but was unsuccessful in defeating them. The war had devastated the economy, killed more than ten thousand people, and left thousands of others homeless and starving.

With no end in sight, Strasser's deputy, Brigadier Julius Maada Bio, staged a palace coup in January 1996. He immediately scheduled peace talks with RUF while at the same time proceeding with election plans. Fair and multiparty elections were held on schedule, with 13 parties contesting 68 legislative seats and the office of president.

Ahmad Tejan Kabbah of the Sierra Leone People's Party (the country's oldest party, founded in 1951) was elected president. He met with RUF leader Foday Sankoh and set a June 1996 deadline for peace. With the return to democracy, Sierra Leoneans are quickly working to resume economic and social progress.

THE PEOPLE

Population

Sierra Leone's population, about 4.7 million, usually grows 2.6 percent annually. Due to emigration and war, however, it did not grow in the early 1990s. The country's Human Development Index (0.221) ranks it 173d out of 174 nations, reflecting the lack of opportunity most people have to determine the level of their participation in society or to direct the course of their lives.

Eighteen ethnic groups (referred to as "tribes") make up the population. The Mende (31 percent) and Temne (30 percent) are the two largest groups; the Limba is a distant third (8 percent), and other groups follow. The Krios, descendants of returned slaves, live mostly in Freetown. A majority of the people (66 percent) live in rural areas, although cities are densely populated. Nearly all Sierra Leoneans are Black Africans, but a small number are Lebanese. The Lebanese make up an important segment of the merchant class. Although they have been in Sierra Leone for several generations, the Lebanese are not considered to be Sierra Leonean.

Language

English is the official language and is used in government, but only the educated speak it. Krio, a mixture of primarily English, Yoruba, and African languages, is the common language. Most people speak their tribal language and Krio, although in remote villages only the tribal language is spoken. Mende dominates in the south and Temne in the north. French is taught in secondary schools because of the country's many francophone neighbors.

Religion

Both Christianity and Islam are practiced in Sierra Leone, but neither claims a majority of people. Religious affiliation crosses ethnic and family lines. People of different faiths live in harmony because of their willingness to accept various beliefs as part of their eclectic (rather than exclusive) approach to religion. Most people believe in a Supreme Being, lesser deities, and a spirit world. Those who convert to a formal religion usually retain traditional animist beliefs as well, especially because animism is tied to daily life. Participation in secret societies, where socioreligious activities take place, is high, even among Christians and Muslims. Christianity was brought to Sierra Leone by returned slaves and gained converts through missionary schools. Islam is the fastest growing religion. Most Sierra Leonean Muslims are Sunnis. Lebanese Muslims are Shiites.

General Attitudes

Sierra Leoneans consider themselves first members of their ethnic group and secondly Sierra Leoneans. Concerns are more provincial than national. People tend to be realistic and practical about their circumstances, which enables them to bear difficult situations. Two common Krio expressions are *Na so God say* (It is God's will) and *Ow fo do?* (What can you do?), to which the response is *Na fo biah* (You must bear it). Education is valued as the key to a better way of life. People strive for material wealth because it is a sign of security; young men often flaunt their possessions. There is no strict social hierarchy, but members of the chief's family are treated with great respect, as are the educated or wealthy. Sierra Leoneans are traditionally nonmilitant and peaceful, although a recent rise in militarism and violence indicates this may be changing for young men.

Personal Appearance

Western-style clothing is nearly universal for men and boys. Women wear *lappas*, two yards of ankle-length cloth tied about the waist and topped with an African or Western blouse. Women's heads are often covered, wrapped with fabric that usually matches the *lappa*. *Lappas* are commonly made of brightly colored cotton cloth imported from Europe and Asia. Trousers are almost unheard of for women, as are shorts for anyone but young boys. Maintaining a good appearance, regardless of the weather or one's wealth, is a priority. People wear traditional clothing on special occasions. For example, over a *lappa*, women wear matching long gowns made from *gara*, locally died cotton brocade. Men wear *gara* shirts with matching trousers. Around the shirt collar and pant cuffs is *planting*, fancy embroidery in a contrasting color.

CUSTOMS AND COURTESIES

Greetings

It is imperative that one exchange greetings with a Sierra Leonean before beginning the topic of converstion. Greetings vary depending on the ethnic group. In Krio, "Hello" is *Kushe*. In Mende it is *Bua*, and in Temne it is *Seke*. Men and women shake with the right hand. If meeting a person of high rank, one customarily supports one's right arm with the left arm—implying that the other's hand is of great weight. The Mende may shake another's hand and then touch the same hand to their heart. When greeting, it is polite to ask *Ow di bodi?* (How are you?) in Krio. In any language, the response is typically the Krio phrase *A tel God tanki* (I give thanks to God). Good-bye might be said with *A de go* (I'm going) or *Nain dat* (That's all).

People often address by the title *Mr.* or *Miss* followed by their first name. Other terms vary according to age relationship. For example, when one addresses someone of the same age, *brother* or *sister* is acceptable. One may use *auntie, uncle, ma*, or *pa* to address older people. To call a stranger *padi* (friend) is common.

Gestures

It is impolite to put one's feet on a chair that is used for sitting. Pointing the soles of one's feet toward another is a sign of disrespect. It is also improper for a woman to whistle. Sierra Leoneans frequently hiss to get someone's attention and use the phrase *Ah sey!* (I say). To express displeasure in a rude way, Sierra Leoneans may "suck teeth" (make a sound by pulling air between pursed lips). People use only the right hand for passing items. Members of the same sex often hold hands or maintain close body contact while talking, but this is rare between members of the opposite sex.

Visiting

Friends visit or *keep time* with one another frequently. Men enjoy sitting in the evenings and drinking fresh palm wine. Women socialize at the cooking house of the family compound. It is common upon meeting a Sierra Leonean to be told to expect a visit, but it is rare to receive an invitation. Unannounced guests are always welcome. It is not necessary to bring a gift when visiting another's home, but it is important to accept what the host offers—usually water or food. Honored guests often are given food upon departure. Although an event may have a designated starting time, guests might not arrive until up to two hours later. When guests leave, they are escorted at least to the edge of the host's property.

Eating

The traditional meal usually is served on a large platter with a bed of rice and a smaller amount of sauce in the center. The sauce is not mixed with the rice. Bones are left in the food; soft ones are eaten and harder ones are put aside. Eating practices vary according to locale and situation. In many homes, the husband may be served separately while the wife and children eat together. When visitors are present, adults eat from the common platter; children may be given spoonfuls of rice in their hands or a separate bowl. In villages, people eat with the right hand while squatting on the ground. In towns, spoons and chairs are more common. People do not drink during a meal; at the end of the meal a cup of water is passed around to drink from and to wash the face and hands.

Restaurants are uncommon, but urban people can buy a plate of rice at a "*kukri* house." Snacks (*street food*) such as bread and margarine, fried potatoes, fried plantains, fruit, roasted groundnuts, homemade candies, and cookies are available in towns.

LIFESTYLE

Family

Extended families are important in the lives of Sierra Leoneans. This is manifested by the fact that aunts may be addressed as *mother* and cousins as *brother* or *sister*. Three to five generations may live within a family compound. This allows for care of both the young and old while the able-bodied work in the fields. Where there is more than one wife in the compound, the wives share daily tasks and child rearing. This may not be the case for a paramount chief's wives, who may retain separate residences. Women generally take care of the compound, work in the garden and the market, and raise children, while men hunt, clear land, and do farm work. Men may also help with the upbringing of the children but to a lesser extent than women. Most women give birth to nine children throughout their life. On average, six survive to maturity. *Fostering* is the custom of loaning a child to a childless woman to raise as one who will care for her in her old age; a child might also be lent to a wealthy person or relative who will educate and provide for him or her.

Dating and Marriage

Due to the coeducational system, relationships form early between boys and girls. Although parents try to discourage it, pregnancy among young girls is common. Dating without intending to marry is accepted in urban areas but not in villages. A date may be just a walk through the town or a chat on the veranda. Marriage customs differ according to the locale. In villages, a marriage may be arranged at any age, but it does not formally take place until the girl reaches puberty. The prospective husband agrees to pay the bride's parents a marriage payment after a great deal of negotiating and, sometimes, input from the whole village. It is the preparation for marriage, not the wedding itself, that is the event. After marriage, the woman lives in the husband's family's household. Polygamy is common. Western-oriented Sierra Leoneans choose their spouses.

Diet

Locally grown crops are supplemented by imported items, such as tea, sugar, salt, and canned goods. The staple food is rice, eaten with a *plassas* (sauce), the most common one being made from pounded cassava leaves, palm oil, and chili peppers. The diet also consists of groundnuts, sweet potatoes, beans, fish, chicken, goat, small bush animals such as *ground pigs* (large rodents), *freetambos* (miniature deer), and an abundance of seasonal tropical fruit (bananas, plantains, pineapples, star fruits, breadfruits, papayas, oranges, grapefruits, mangoes, and coconuts). The Fulas herd cattle that are occasionally slaughtered and sold in the market. Meals tend to be unbalanced when the price of fish, beans, or groundnuts is high; then the diet consists mainly of rice and leaf sauces. Malnutrition is widespread among children because they receive the smallest portions of protein-rich foods (eggs and meat). Typically, a midday snack is followed by a large meal in the late afternoon; leftovers are put aside for the following morning's breakfast.

Recreation

Soccer is a popular sport and matches are usually well attended. Lack of resources and leisure time make other organized sports uncommon. However, schoolchildren compete in a variety of events (mostly track-and-field) during Sports Week. One event is the *paw paw* race, in which students run while carrying smaller students on their backs. Urban movie theaters usually show Indian, karate, and action-filled U.S. American films. Reggae music is widely popular. Disco dances that last until dawn accompany special events, even in towns without electricity, where a generator and sound system are rented for the occasion. Traditional music, dance, and theater play important, symbolic roles in the lives of people, especially those living *up-country* (outside of the capital). Strangers are not permitted to attend certain events where traditional performances take place. Photography is often prohibited, even in public shows.

Holidays

Sierra Leone's national days are Independence Day (27 April) and Revolution Day (29 April). Western and Christian holidays such as New Year's, Easter, and Christmas are universally celebrated, as is Pray Day, the last day of the Muslim month of *Ramadan*. The tradition surrounding New Year's and Easter is to have a party, sometimes with a sound system, at a nearby river or beach. In towns with high hills, like Kabala, the New Year's tradition is to climb the mountain, taking along livestock to be slaughtered for a celebratory feast. Masquerades are a popular part of big celebrations: masked "devils," which are often associated with specific secret societies, entertain the people. On any holiday, children often go door-to-door asking for (and sometimes dancing and singing for) money.

Commerce

Government offices and retailers are primarily open from 9:00 A.M. to 5:00 P.M. Open-air markets are active during daylight hours. Evenings bring out a different selection of goods: freshly cooked food and items such as cigarettes, soap, *mosquito coils*, and aspirin. Towns have a designated "market day" that is an expansion of the everyday market, with merchants from nearby villages selling more varied goods. Prices are fixed only in stores; bargaining is expected in markets.

SOCIETY

Government

Sierra Leone is a multiparty democracy. The president is chief of state. The unicameral House of Representatives has 68 seats for elected members. Twelve seats are reserved for traditional chiefs. The Sierra Leone People's Party is joined by the People's Democratic Party and the United National People's Party as the country's strongest parties. The voting age is 18. The 1996 elections were the first since 1967.

Economy

Despite such natural resources as diamonds, gold, bauxite, and rutile (a derivative of titanium), Sierra Leone remains a poor country with 75 percent of its people engaged in subsistence agriculture. The civil war has burdened economic institutions, forcing people to flee their farms and shutting down mining interests. Prior to 1992, government corruption had facilitated the smuggling of diamonds and crops out of the country, hampering the economy. Mining operations are expected to begin again in 1997, but reconstruction will take some time. Sierra Leone relies on food subsidies from abroad and imports most manufactured goods. Export crops include palm kernels, coffee, cocoa, ginger, kola nuts, and piassava. Freetown benefits from a small amount of tourism. The currency is the *leone* (Le), which is sometimes referred to as the *pound*. One *pound* equals two *leones*.

Real gross domestic product per capita is $880, a figure that rose somewhat in the last generation but then dropped to nearly equal the level for 1960. The vast majority of people are very poor, earning far less than they need. Two-thirds of all people live in absolute poverty, and only a small wealthy class enjoys the benefits of economic opportunity.

Transportation and Communication

Two paved roads link northern and eastern Sierra Leone with the capital. Most roads are unpaved, but the government plans to improve road conditions throughout the country. Common forms of transportation are *poda-podas* (lorries), taxis, mopeds, and bicycles. *Poda-podas* are small pickups fitted with seats and a roof; they carry people, goods, and animals. In rural areas, people generally walk, except when traveling extremely long distances or when transporting a large load (such as to or from the market). Freetown has a large natural harbor. Postal service is fairly reliable, but rural delivery is unpredictable. Telephones are most common in Freetown but also operate in surrounding areas and larger *up-country* cities. The capital has several daily newspapers. The national radio broadcast can be picked up throughout much of the country, but television is limited mostly to the Freetown area.

Education

Formal education is based on the British model. Schools are often run by missions. Classes are taught in English, although in rural primary schools instruction in local languages is common. Children may begin school at age five. The dropout rate is high because of parents' inability to pay fees and other difficulties. About one-fifth of school-aged children attend secondary schools. The curriculum often does not address the needs of rural people. The adult literacy rate is 29 percent (only 15 percent for women). Indigenous education, bush schools, or secret societies teach children skills and customs perceived as necessary by village elders. Such training prepares children to join society as adults. Sierra Leone has several teacher-training colleges and one university.

Health

Government-provided health care is inadequate. Most services, such as vaccinations, are provided by the World Health Organization and mission hospitals. People generally rely on a combination of traditional and Western medicines. Limited knowledge of nutrition and preventive care results in chronic illnesses such as malaria, anemia, and gastrointestinal diseases. Also prevalent are tuberculosis, schistosomiasis, leprosy, and various skin lesions (attributable to nutritional deficiencies) that are slow to heal because of the climate. Water is not potable. Goiter is endemic in the northeastern highlands, where the iodine content of the water is low. The infant mortality rate is 139 per 1,000. Adults expect to live an average of 47 years.

FOR THE TRAVELER

A passport, visa, and proof of yellow fever and cholera vaccinations are required of U.S. visitors. Malarial suppressants are essential and other vaccinations recommended. Drink only bottled soda, bottled water, or undiluted palm wine. Peel fruits and vegetables before eating. Avoid swimming in fresh water. Beware of pickpockets and petty theft. A 1995 U.S. Department of State travel warning remained in effect for much of 1996. For updates, call (202) 647–5225. For travel information, contact the Embassy of Sierra Leone, 1701 19th Street NW, Washington, DC 20009; phone (202) 939–9261.

Republic of
Singapore

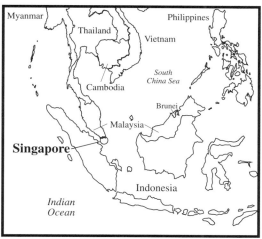

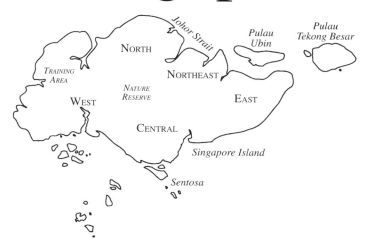

BACKGROUND

Land and Climate

Singapore is an island about the same size as the city of Chicago (244 square miles or 633 square kilometers) and is located off the southern tip of the Malaysian Peninsula. Several smaller islands also belong to the republic. Part of Singapore occupies land that was reclaimed from the sea through landfill operations. Singapore is actually a city-state; there are essentially no rural areas and no other cities.

Nature preserves on the central plateau (534 feet or 163 meters) are home to some 139 species of birds, various small forest animals, trees, and more than 700 plant species. Bukit Timah, the largest reserve, was established in 1883. Singapore's climate is pleasant and virtually unchanging. Temperatures range between 78°F (25°C) and 82°F (28°C) all year. It is humid and rainy throughout the year. Cool night breezes are common.

History

Before a Buddhist prince named the island Singa Pura and established a thriving port in the 14th century, only a tiny fishing village called Temasek existed on the island. For many years, the island was a source of conflict between various mainland interests. In the 19th century, the British were attracted to Singapore's strategic location and natural deepwater ports. In 1819, Sir Stamford Raffles established a British trading post on the island and obtained it as a possession in 1824. The trade city, created out of a mangrove wetland, soon began to thrive.

Singapore became a British crown colony in 1948. Internal self-rule was granted in 1959. The activities of several radical political organizations (most notably the Communists) caused leaders to accept a merger with the Federation of Malaya in 1963. Singapore's inclusion in Malaysia caused domestic political problems, and Singapore declared its independence in 1965. Lee Kuan Yew, first named prime minister in 1959, led Singapore for 31 years. He is credited for shaping Singapore into a solid economic power and for stressing practicality over ideology.

Lee resigned in 1990 in favor of a younger man, Goh Chok Tong. Lee remains leader of the People's Action Party (PAP). Goh has continued Lee's policies, citing the need to encourage strong social values through legislation. In 1996, Goh released funds to finance projects that further the country's five shared values: nation before community and society above self; family as the basic unit of society; community support and respect for the individual; consensus, not conflict; and racial and religious harmony.

THE PEOPLE

Population

Singapore's population of 2.9 million is growing at 1 percent annually. The population density is more than 11,400 persons per square mile (4,400 per square kilometer), making Singapore one of the most densely populated countries in the world. The entire population lives in urban areas. Three major Asian cultures are represented in Singapore. Slightly more than 76 percent of the population is Chinese, 15 percent is Malay, and about 6 percent is Indian. Various other groups are also represented, including Caucasians (Europeans, North Americans, Australians) and Japanese.

Chinese, Malay, and Indian Singaporeans enjoy good relations with one another. If individuals share the same religion,

A
S
I
A

their ethnicity does not inhibit intermarriage. Malay associate somewhat less often with the other two groups because their Muslim dietary codes make it difficult to enjoy Chinese festivals. Devout Muslims do not eat pork and require other meats to be prepared in a certain way; since Chinese do not abide by these practices, it is difficult to include their Malay friends in these events. In all, religion plays a greater role in determining social relations than does race, but there are no serious conflicts between religions or races.

Singapore's Human Development Index (0.878) ranks it 35th out of 174 nations. Most people have access to economic prosperity and opportunities for personal advancement. Malay have lagged in economic statistics in the past and so receive government assistance (exemption from school fees, for example) to help improve the balance.

Language

Malay, Chinese, Tamil, and English are all official languages. Malay is the national language; Lee Kuan Yew declared this in 1959 as a gesture to neighboring Malay states. Malays were also the island's original inhabitants. English is the language of administration and is used most widely in science, technology, commerce, and tourism. The government encourages the use of all the languages in order to maintain traditional cultures and values. The Chinese speak a number of different Chinese dialects (Hokkein, Chaozhou, and Cantonese, among others), but *Putonghua* (Mandarin) is gradually replacing other dialects to become Standard Chinese. Most Singaporeans are at least bilingual.

Religion

Singaporeans enjoy constitutionally guaranteed freedom of worship. Buddhism, Taoism, Confucianism, Islam, Christianity, Hinduism, and Judaism, as well as a number of smaller religions, are all practiced in Singapore. About half of the people, most of whom are Chinese, are either Buddhist or Taoist. Many practice a combination of Buddhism, Taoism, and Confucianism. Nearly all Malays are Muslim. Ten percent of the population is Christian, and about 5 percent (mostly Indian) is Hindu. A significant minority, many of them Chinese, are either atheists or agnostics (called "free-thinkers"). Christians generally are either Chinese or Caucasian. These religions all operate in harmony, with Buddhist and Hindu temples next to Muslim mosques and Christian churches. Singapore has two Jewish synagogues. Singaporeans discuss religion freely and openly. In some cases, such as marriages or family matters, religions are allowed to establish government-recognized laws for their members.

General Attitudes

Singaporeans consider their nation to be unique among modern societies because they hold to traditional Asian values (the "shared values"). The work ethic is strongly advocated and Singaporeans have a reputation as one of the world's best workforces. Likewise, high moral and ethical values are stressed in government and business.

The nation's attention to a well-ordered society has allowed it, as Singaporeans believe, to build a highly prosperous modern economy without suffering the social drawbacks inherent in liberal democracy. Cultural ideals and traditions are enforced by laws and programs. For example, a single and never-married mother cannot purchase low-cost housing from the government or get public health benefits for her children. Also, financial incentives are given to young people who buy apartments near their parents so they can care for them in their old age.

Singaporeans value discipline, self-control, education, honesty, and humility. Shaming another person in public, or causing him or her to "lose face," also shames the offending individual and is a breach of social courtesy. Likewise, conformity is stressed because "antisocial" acts shame one's entire family.

Members of the rising generation, having benefited from their parents' success with establishing racial harmony and economic stability, look to the "Five C's" as lifelong goals: career, condominium, car, cash, and credit card. Career is defined by getting the proper educational qualifications that will allow for career advancement. Condominiums are desired because they are nicer than the more ubiquitous government-built flats (apartments). Cars are very expensive due to the lack of space on the island. Cash is defined by the ability to afford material possessions, and credit cards are only available to those with a certain minimum salary.

Personal Appearance

Most people wear Western-style clothing. Lightweight fabrics are the norm, and the youth enjoy the latest fashions. However, traditional attire is also still worn, including the Indian *sari* (wraparound skirt worn by women), *salawar kameez* (Punjabi pajama-like outfit), *cheongsam* (Chinese dress), and *kebaya* (Malay dress), among others. Modesty in public is important.

CUSTOMS AND COURTESIES

Greetings

Greeting customs vary according to age, ethnicity, and situation. Chinese people shake hands, perhaps adding a slight bow for older people. Malays greet with the *salaam*: two people bring right palms together, as if to shake hands, then slide them apart; each person then touches the palm to his or her heart. Traditional Indians join their palms together in prayer position at chest level, raise them in front of their face, bow slightly, and say *Vanakkam* (Tamil for "Hello"). Typical Chinese greetings include *Ni hao ma?* (How are you?), *Whei* (Hello), or the Cantonese *Neih sihk-jo faan meih a?* (Have you eaten yet?). Malays greet with *Selamat pagi* (Good morning), *Selamat petang* (Good afternoon), or *Selamat malam* (Good evening). More formal Malay terms include *Selamat sejahtera ke atas anda* (I wish you peace and tranquility) or the Muslim phrase *Assalam alaikum* (Peace be upon you).

English greetings are employed between different ethnic groups. Upon being introduced, business representatives and other officials often exchange business cards.

Friends and relatives address each other by given (or personal) name, but titles and family name are used in formal or business settings. Chinese names begin with the family name followed by a two-character given name. So, a single woman named Lee Hwi Chern is properly addressed by her full name or as Miss Lee. Many Chinese (especially Christians) adopt Western names, which come first. So Catherine Tan Leng Yan is Miss Tan, but Catherine to her friends. Some Chinese do not use their full names in business: Richard Lee Peng Liang becomes Richard Lee. Malays have no surnames, but a given name followed by the father's given name. These are separated by *bin* (son of) or *binti* (daughter of): Daud bin Hakim (addressed as Mr. Daud) or Salmah binte Jufri (Miss Salmah). Indians may have the same basic name structure as Malays, or their given name may be followed by a family clan name: Prabu Naidu is addressed as Mr. Naidu.

Gestures

Touching another person's head is impolite. Singaporeans cross legs at the knee; they do not rest an ankle on the knee. It is impolite for the bottom of the foot to point at a person. Also, feet are not used to move objects. Hitting the fist into the cupped hand is inappropriate. One beckons by waving all fingers of the right hand with the palm facing down. Finger gestures, such as pointing or forming the rounded "OK" sign, are considered rude. A slight bow when joining, leaving, or passing a group of people shows courtesy. Malays and Indians do not touch members of the opposite sex in public. For all groups, public displays of affection are inappropriate.

Visiting

Visiting relatives is important in maintaining family relations. Married children regularly visit their parents and join them for a weekend meal (Saturday for one set, Sunday for the other set of parents). Friends also enjoy getting together. Calling in advance is usually necessary. Invited guests are expected to be punctual. Hosts nearly always offer their guests something to drink; it is impolite not to. Chinese typically serve tea or juice; Malays, juice or coffee; Indians, tea or coffee. On special holidays, hosts arrange a number of sweet-meats and other refreshments on the coffee-table for all guests to enjoy.

If a host or guest gives a gift, the recipient opens it later, not in the giver's presence. Most families require that shoes be removed before one enters the home. Singaporeans also remove shoes when entering temples, shrines, or mosques.

Eating

The family tries to eat dinner together each day, but work schedules often interfere. At the very least, they eat lunch together on Saturday. Most families sit around a table to eat, but Malays and Indians may sit on a floor mat (for traditional meals or festive occasions). Diners wash and dry their hands before the meal. In Indian and Malay homes, men eat first followed by women and children.

Diners typically have individual bowls (or plates, or even a banana leaf) of rice. Each person can also take small portions of meats and vegetables from the serving dishes placed in the center of the table or mat. One does not put a full meal in the bowl at the beginning but takes small amounts from the various dishes throughout the meal. Chinese use chopsticks for rice. Malays and Indians eat with the fingers of the right hand. All groups use spoons and forks for some types of food. When guests are present, hosts offer second and third helpings. It is polite to accept the second helping but to leave a little food behind (on the serving dishes, not in one's own bowl) to show one has been well fed. If all the food is eaten, the hosts feel they have not adequately provided for the guests, or the guests are considered greedy.

Singaporeans eat out often, especially if both spouses are employed. In restaurants, a service charge is included in the bill and tipping is uncommon. Muslims do not eat pork and require that all other meat be *halal*, cooked according to specific customs with separate utensils. Many restaurants and other food-service establishments have instruments reserved for this purpose. Hindus and Buddhists do not eat beef.

LIFESTYLE

Family

Cooperation, loyalty, respect for elders, and unity are deeply valued in all Singaporean families. Children (an average of two or three) are expected to obey their parents and care for them (financially and otherwise) in their old age. Elderly parents sometimes live with their married children but may also live alone nearby. Since both spouses often work outside the home, grandparents might provide child care. For some families, the father remains the primary provider and the mother cares for the children at home. Women have equal political, employment, and educational rights. Men are encouraged to share household responsibilities, but the burden usually rests on women. However, an increasing number of families now have domestic maids to care for the children and household.

Dating and Marriage

Parents often discourage dating until children have completed their education because dating interferes with their studies. Still, at around age 17, young people begin going to movies, taking walks, dancing, and enjoying other activities together. Most Singaporeans marry in their latter twenties. Wedding traditions vary according to religion and personal choice. A non-Muslim marrying a Muslim must first convert to Islam. The ceremony takes place in a community hall. Guests enjoy traditional food and music and give the newlyweds money. Two-hour Hindu ceremonies in temples are followed by a vegetarian meal. Some Indians also have their weddings in community halls. Among the Chinese, the groom might visit the bride's parents for tea on the wedding day to ask for permission to take away their daughter. Then, after taking wedding photos, they hold an evening celebration at a restaurant. Guests give the bride or groom (depending on who invited them) an *ang pow* (red envelope with money) as a gift. All marriages must first be registered with the Registry of Marriages before any traditional ceremony takes place.

Diet

Rice is eaten on a daily basis. With it, people enjoy fish, seafood, and chicken cooked in a wide variety of ways. Chinese noodles are popular for lunch. *Roti prata*, an Indian dough-bread, is enjoyed for breakfast by all groups. *Dim sum* (Chinese dumplings) are favorite snacks. *Poh piah* are spring rolls filled with shredded turnip, bamboo shoots, bean curd, prawns, and pork. Fish-head curry (in a sauce with tomatoes, pineapple, and green onions) is a favorite dish. Spicy Malay foods are dipped in peanut sauce. Pineapple, papayas, bananas, durians, and mangoes are among the most common fruits.

Recreation

Singaporeans enjoy soccer, badminton, basketball, tennis, and golf. Water sports of all kinds are popular. Young people like to learn such martial arts as *tae kwon do*. Older people prefer Chinese exercise *(taijiquan)* and *petanque* (French lawn bowling). People have access to a wide variety of cultural arts, as well as movies and television programs.

Holidays

Public holidays include International New Year (1 January), Chinese New Year (set by Chinese lunar calendar), Easter (including Friday), Vesak Day (celebrating the birth, enlightenment, and nirvana of Buddha and held during the fifth lunar month), Labor Day (1 May), and Singapore National Day (9 August). Other Chinese celebrations are held throughout the year.

Some non-Chinese holidays include *Hari Raya Puasa*, which is a feast at the end of the Islamic month of *Ramadan*. During *Ramadan,* Muslims go without food or drink each day from sunrise to sundown. Other religions are welcome to join in *Hari Raya Puasa* as an expression of tolerance and renewal. *Hari Raya Haji*, another Muslim festival, celebrates the pilgrimage to Makkah, Saudi Arabia. *Deepavali* (Festival of Lights) for Hindus and Sikhs celebrates the triumph of light over darkness. Thousands of lights decorate stores and homes during this time of national goodwill. Christmas is also celebrated.

Commerce

While shops are usually open seven days a week for as many as ten hours a day, most businesses are generally open from 8:30 A.M. to 5:30 P.M., Monday through Friday, and until 1:00 P.M. on Saturday. If a business is open on Sunday, it is required by law to close on another day. Shops are not under this restriction. People shop at open-air markets, neighborhood "provision shops," supermarkets, and shopping centers.

SOCIETY

Government

Singapore is a democratic republic. The president, Ong Teng Cheong, is head of state, but the prime minister (Goh Chok Tong) exercises executive authority and heads the government with his cabinet. The 81-seat Parliament is dominated by the ruling PAP. The voting age is 21; all citizens are required to vote in national elections (the last one was in 1996). Small opposition parties exist but have little power. Singaporean democracy is not well understood by outsiders. Freedoms are restrained to prevent extremism and to maintain social harmony. Stability has only been the norm since the 1960s, and most people appreciate the PAP for its success in creating a prosperous, efficient, and unified nation. Government leaders try to provide reasonable avenues for dissent and expression and are seeking to balance the desire for greater personal liberties with society's overall needs.

Economy

Although Singapore is the smallest country in Southeast Asia, its entrepreneurial economy is the most prosperous. Economic growth has averaged more than 8 percent since the 1980s; for 1995, it was nearly 9 percent. In addition, inflation is low and unemployment is less than 3 percent. Real gross domestic product per capita is $18,330.

Much of Singapore's trade consists of receiving exports from other countries and then reexporting them. Petroleum refining is the largest industrial activity of Singapore, but the republic has also become an important world financial center and manufacturer. Tourism is actively promoted throughout the world. Most of the country's food is imported. The United States and Malaysia are two of Singapore's largest trading partners. The currency is the Singapore dollar (S$).

Transportation and Communication

Singapore is served by international airlines and is linked to Thailand and Malaysia by road and rail. All roads are paved and well maintained. The Mass Rapid Transit (MRT) subway serves most areas. The communications system is fully modern and extensive. Radio and television facilities are operated by the government. Newspapers are privately owned but must be licensed.

Education

Schooling is compulsory for children ages six to sixteen. Six years of primary education are followed by at least four years of secondary education. Nearly all children complete primary schooling, and 70 percent finish secondary school. After ten years of schooling, many continue in vocational schools or preuniversity programs. Children study their mother tongue in school as well as English. English is the language of instruction. The National University of Singapore was established in 1980, and there are various other technical schools of higher learning. In addition, many students travel abroad for higher degrees. The adult literacy rate is 90 percent, but among 15- to 19-year-olds it approaches 100 percent.

Health

All health facilities and services are excellent, but the government does not pay for them. Employees contribute 20 percent of their wages to a Central Provident Fund (CPF), matched by an equal amount from employers. One's account can be used to pay for medical services, housing, and even investments. A high standard of health is attributed to good housing, modern sanitation, and a general concern for sound hygienic practices. Singapore is often referred to as the cleanest city in Asia. The infant mortality rate is 4 per 1,000. Life expectancy ranges from 74 to 79 years.

FOR THE TRAVELER

No visa is necessary for U.S. travelers staying up to 30 days, but a passport is required. Travelers coming from a yellow fever infected area need a vaccination certificate. Water is safe to drink. Laws regarding littering, jaywalking, or drug possession are strictly enforced. It is wise to carry prescriptions for all medications to avoid any difficulties with authorities. Singapore is a favorite tourist destination for many reasons. Even transit visitors with more than five hours to spare can take a free city tour. For information, contact the Singapore Tourist Promotion Board, 590 Fifth Avenue, 12th Floor, New York, NY 10036; phone (212) 302–4861. The West Coast address is 8484 Wilshire Boulevard, Suite 510, Beverly Hills, CA 90211; phone (213) 852–1901. You may also wish to contact the Embassy of Singapore, 3501 International Place NW, Washington, DC 20008; phone (202) 537–3100.

A *Culturgram* is a product of native commentary and original, expert analysis. Statistics are estimates and information is presented as a matter of opinion. While the editors strive for accuracy and detail, this document should not be considered strictly factual. It is a general introduction to culture, an initial step in building bridges of understanding between peoples. It may not apply to all peoples of the nation. You should therefore consult other sources for more information.

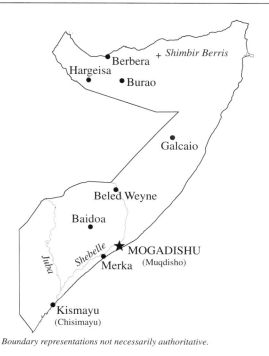

Boundary representations not necessarily authoritative.

Republic of
Somalia

BACKGROUND

Land and Climate

Somalia, situated on the Horn of Africa, covers 246,300 square miles (638,000 square kilometers). Somalia's northern Guban, a semiarid plain parallel to the Gulf of Aden, gives way to the Ogo Highlands, where Shimbir Berris, the highest peak, reaches 7,900 feet (2,400 meters). Grazing rangeland south of the mountains and west of the Indian Ocean covers most of the country. Pasture quality depends on the amount of rain received from April to June and September to October. The most fertile land lies between the Juba and Shebelle Rivers, where crops are grown commercially. Lower Juba (south of the Juba River) is covered by thick bush but still supports some farming and livestock production. Much of Somalia has been damaged by drought and overgrazing. Drought between 1994 and 1996 is the cause of malnutrition and starvation for settlements on the Juba River.

Somalia is a hot, semiarid country, although Mogadishu is humid. Some cities have average annual temperatures above 88°F (31°C). The Guban is often 100°F (38°C). The cooler mountains experience all four seasons.

History

Somalis have inhabited the Horn of Africa for centuries, occupying an area from near the Gulf of Aden, south to the Tana River in Kenya, and west to Harar in Ethiopia. Somali ivory, ostrich feathers, leopard skins, frankincense, and myrrh were carried as far away as China along early long-distance trade routes. While Somalis remained inland, the coast hosted visitors and settlers from India, Persia, Arabia, and Portugal. Their influence on architecture, clothing, language, and customs is evident today.

Islam was introduced to Somalia in the ninth century by Arab sheiks who married into Somali families. Arabs controlled the southern coast between the ninth and nineteenth centuries, with the Sultan of Oman ruling as far south as Zanzibar until European exploration began in the 1800s. The French, British, and Italians all competed for territory. In the 1880s, British Somaliland was established in the north, Italian Somaliland in the south, and French Somaliland around present-day Djibouti. The British ceded lands it held west of the Juba River to Italy in 1925.

Somalis opposed colonialism and still have bitter feelings about the era. A rebellion launched in 1900 against Britain lasted until 1920; it failed but it intensified Somali nationalism and led to independence. In 1960, British and Italian Somalilands were united to form the Somali Republic.

Undermined by clan rivalries and corruption, the new parliamentary government never stabilized. Military leaders staged a successful 1969 coup. General Mohammed Siad Barre became president and suspended the constitution. He sought to reorder society and end tribal institutions by declaring Somalia a socialist state. The regime received significant military aid, especially from the Soviet Union.

With many ethnic Somalis living in neighboring countries, clashes over borders were common for many years. During the Cold War, both the Soviets and U.S. Americans supplied arms to the various conflicts. The abundant weapons, controversial resettlement of refugees, official corruption, and political repression all combined to spark a 1981 civil war between government forces and insurrectionists. The northern Isaak-led Somali National Movement (SNM) joined forces with the United Somali Congress (USC), composed mostly of Hawiye subclans, to fight the Darod-led government. In 1991, the Siad government collapsed and Somalia's political disintegration followed. The northern groups broke with the USC and declared an independent Somaliland, proclaiming the 1960 union illegal. This northern republic has not been internationally recognized but maintains its sovereignty claim.

Meanwhile, southern alliances dissolved and Mogadishu was split between rival Hawiye subclans. The city plunged into anarchy and the entire country was left without a central government. By 1992, famine, disease, and war threatened much of the population. A U.S.-led United Nations effort was launched to stop the dying. While the initial goal was largely met, rebuilding a viable government proved elusive, and Somalis began to resent international involvement in their political affairs. Anarchy returned and foreign troops were gone by March 1995. Soon after, Somalia split into regions ruled by rival warlords who continue to fight for territory and influence. The fighting inhibited efforts in 1996 to relieve food shortages along the Juba River. If drought causes the harvest to fail as expected, a full famine may once again engulf southern Somalia.

PEOPLE

Population

About 7.3 million people live in Somalia. Related to the Afar, Oromo, and other Cushitic peoples living on the Horn of Africa, Somalis constitute 95 percent of the population. Minority groups include the Somali-speaking Hamari in Mogadishu and a related Arabic-speaking people living in other coastal cities; the Bajun, farmers and fishermen of Swahili origin; the Barawani, who speak a language related to Swahili; and other Bantu-speaking farmers living mostly along the Shebelle River. Before 1991, urbanization was increasing and about one million people lived in Mogadishu.

Somali society is organized into large extended clan families, ranging in size from 100,000 to as many as two million. There are six very large clans (Darod, Isaak, Hawiye, Dir, Digil, and Rahanwayn) and a number of medium-to-small groups. Each of the larger families is further divided into lineage units that may range from 10,000 to 100,000 individuals. Additional divisions are made in these groups based on kinship alliances of smaller extended families. Once two people know each other's name and clan membership, it is possible for them to know exactly where they fit into society and what their responsibilities are to each other. In rural areas, one can ask about another's lineage directly, but in an urban area it is more polite to identify it through indirect questions (about the person's home region, for example).

Language

Somali belongs to the Cushitic language family. It has three main dialects, each of which is difficult for speakers of the other two to understand. The dialects include *Af-Maymay,* spoken between the Shebelle and Juba Rivers; *Af-Benaadir*, spoken on the coast from Mogadishu south; and standard Somali spoken everywhere else. English, Italian, and Arabic are spoken by various educated Somalis.

Until recently, Somali was an unwritten language; songs and poetry played a significant role in oral communication. In the 20th century, unique local scripts emerged and Latin alphabets were introduced by Westerners. By the late 1960s, more than ten local scripts were being used in Somalia. Each script's usage depended on the clan to which its author belonged, its usefulness, and other factors. In 1972, the government adopted a Latin-based script and began to introduce it in schools and government documents. Literacy increased dramatically, due partly to a campaign to teach reading and writing in rural areas. The script has yet to be fully standardized and uniformly adopted.

Religion

Nearly all Somalis are Sunni Muslims. A small number are Christians. All towns have mosques; many on the coast are hundreds of years old, and some Mogadishu mosques are up to one thousand years old. Muslims believe in a single God (*Allah*) and that Muhammad was his last and greatest prophet. Islamic scripture, the *Qur'an*, is believed to be the word of *Allah* as revealed to Muhammad. Muslims are taught to practice their religion through praying five times daily; giving alms to the poor; making a pilgrimage to Makkah, Saudi Arabia; abstaining from alcohol and pork; and attending to other duties.

General Attitudes

Most Somalis in the interior have had little exposure to anything outside of Somalia; even during the colonial era, European culture did not extend much beyond coastal cities. In the countryside, colonial powers were distrusted and disliked, and today's Somalis view foreign assistance as having political motives. They may accept and be grateful for short-term assistance, but they sense paternalism quickly and may react violently to what they view as the belittling of their culture or character. In addition, each person considers himself or herself to be equal among Somalis, even though larger clans claim higher status. Somalis consider themselves subservient to no one but *Allah*. Unlike in some Muslim countries, women own property and manage businesses, even as they occupy a vital position in the extended family.

Somalis cherish self-reliance, autonomy, and tradition. They value friendship based on mutual respect. Verbal thanks is not often expressed, since giving obligates the receiver to reciprocate—unless the gift is charity, which is seen as an offering to *Allah* and requires no thanks.

Personal Appearance

Somalis are generally tall and slender with narrow features. Urban men wear Western pants or a flowing plaid *ma'awiis* (kilt), Western shirts, and shawls. On their heads they may wrap a colorful turban or wear a *koofiyad* (embroidered cap). Rural men wear two five-yard lengths of cloth—one wrapped around the waist to hang below the knees and the other wrapped around the upper body, or carried on the shoulder. For women, the most fashionable northern dress is the *direh*, a long, billowing dress worn over petticoats. The southern favorite is the *guntino*, a four-yard cloth tied over one shoulder and wrapped around the waist. Rural women wear sturdier varieties of the same clothing. All women wear shawls and head scarves. With the exception of a minority near the southern coast, women usually do not veil their faces. Women like sparkling, colorful touches in their everyday clothing. During religious holidays, children customarily receive new clothes if the family can afford it.

Somalis bathe and wash often. They clean their teeth with sticks from a particular tree and polish them with powdered charcoal. Children wash their feet before going to bed. Women burn incense to perfume their bodies and homes. Henna gives women's hair and skin a glowing reddish tone.

CUSTOMS AND COURTESIES

Greetings

Somalis greet each other by name or, in the case of relatives, by a word that shows their relationship (uncle, cousin, etc.). General greetings vary according to region and situation, but *Nabad* (Peace) is accepted nearly everywhere. The common southern variation is *Nabad miya?* (Is there peace?). Its equivalent in the north is *Ma nabad baa?* The Islamic greeting *Asalaamu aleikum* (Peace be upon you) is a common formal greeting, to which the response is *Aleikum ma salaam* (And peace be upon you). Such phrases are followed by inquiries about the general health and welfare of the individual and an exchange of information. *Iska warran?* (What's the news?) and *Maha la shegay?* (What are people saying?) are used as a "How are you?" in some parts of the country.

Men firmly shake hands with each other three times before putting that hand to their hearts. In some southern areas, women shake hands with each other and then kiss the hand they have shaken. Somalis of the opposite sex who are not related usually do not touch when meeting.

Gestures

Somalis use sweeping hand and arm gestures to dramatize speech. The eyes follow the direction of the hands, and the fingers may flutter. Many ideas are expressed through specific hand gestures. For example, placing both index fingers parallel to one another indicates "the same." A swift twist of the open hand and wrist means "nothing" or "no." A thumb under the chin indicates fullness. Snapping fingers may mean "long ago" or "and so on."

Visiting

Somali women socialize at home or at the market. Visitors need not take gifts or food to their hosts. Before entering a family compound, visitors announce their presence and wait a while in order not to surprise the family. Urban hosts serve guests sweet, spicy tea with milk and perhaps other refreshments. In rural areas, hosts offer tea or milk. A favorite time for urban visiting is late afternoon, when most work is done and it is not too hot. In rural areas, night is better, as farm chores are completed and animals have settled down. When families socialize, men and women usually interact separately.

Tea shops, which often have tables outside, are centers for men to socialize and discuss current affairs. After lunch, men chew *khat*, a leafy green branch from a tree grown in the Ethiopian highlands and elsewhere. Women usually do not chew *khat*. After many hours of chewing, a mild high results; sustained use can lead to addiction.

Eating

When more than the immediate family is eating, men and women usually eat separately. In rural restaurants, women might choose to eat in rooms or areas separate from men. For the family meal, men are usually served first and the women and children eat later. Diners wash their hands in a bowl of water before and after the meal. On festive occasions, hands are also perfumed after the meal. When eating, people gather around a large common platter set on a table or on a mat on the ground. Diners eat with the right hand from the portion directly in front of them; guests are usually given larger servings. Young children are fed from the hand of the mother or a relative. The left hand usually does not have direct contact with food, as it is reserved for personal hygiene and prayer purification. Overeating is considered unacceptable.

LIFESTYLE

Family

Children assume their father's surname and clan affiliation. A mother's family may be from another clan, but warm relationships exist among cousins who knew each other as children. The mother retains her maiden name and position in her clan. Family loyalty is important and families help one another in times of need. It is assumed that help will be reciprocated if needed in the future. Any good deeds bring honor to the family, clan, and society. The most fortunate members of a family feel especially obligated to help the others. Because resources are scarce, the hierarchy of who should be aided is clear. For instance, the extended family of the father's relatives has first priority. Aid can include such things as food, money, or shelter. Urban families might take in children of rural relatives and put them through school. War and repeated droughts have severely strained this system of mutual aid, and social cohesion has suffered—especially in urban areas.

Dating and Marriage

Dating in the Western sense does not exist in Somalia, although it is common for young men and women to participate jointly in traditional dances. Virginity is valued in women prior to marriage. Divorce is legal and does occur. Arranged marriages are common; brides in these cases are often much younger than the grooms. Marriage to a cousin from the mother's side of the family (that is, of different lineage) has traditionally been favored as a way to strengthen family alliances, but this practice has been disrupted somewhat. Since 1991, Somalis have tended to trust only members of their own clan for marriage. Weddings are celebrated by both families. Special foods, like *muqmad* (dried beef in clarified butter) and dates are served. In some areas, the couple is sequestered for a seven-day honeymoon.

Diet

Urban staple foods consist of locally produced meats and imported rice. In farming areas, sorghum, millet, corn, and sesame are common staples. Among nomads, milk from camels and goats is the main food available, supplemented with grains bought with money from the sale of animals. The milk is made into several varieties of yogurt.

Most people eat pancakes made from flour or millet for breakfast, rice or millet served with milk and *ghee* (butter) for lunch and/or supper, and a small snack of milk or a bean dish in the evening. Nomads typically do not eat lunch when they are herding animals away from their homes. Vegetables gradually are being added to the diet, but they are still a novelty. Bananas, papayas, and mangoes are seasonal and plentiful. In some places limes are always available, and grapefruit abound in season. Italian pasta has become popular in the cities as an alternative to rice. Fish is a staple in coastal towns.

Recreation

The youth enjoy soccer. Videos are popular in towns. Organized sports have basically been destroyed by war. Cultural arts, however, remain vital leisure and social activities. Poetry is one of those arts and Somalia is viewed as a nation of poets. Today, poems and songs, part of the oral culture that still flourishes, are recorded on cassettes and sent wherever Somalis live. Many poems are about love, but others contain political commentary. This political poetry is called *gabay*. Common poetic metaphors known throughout society help unify Somali culture. People also perform plays and music. Accompanied by songs, stringed musical instruments (in the south), and drums, Somali dancers perform in two parallel lines of men and women, or in circles.

Holidays

Observed Islamic holy days include *'Eid al Fitr* (three-day feast at the end of *Ramadan*), *'Eid al Adha* (Feast of Sacrifice, honoring Abraham's willingness to sacrifice his son), and *Mawliid*, the prophet Muhammad's birthday. Muslims fast from dawn until dusk each day of the holy month of *Ramadan*. Prior to the current crisis, independence from Britain in the north was celebrated on 26 June and from Italy in the south on 1 July. The ancient Persian New Year (*Dab Shiid*, or "Starting Fire") is celebrated in many parts of Somalia.

Commerce

Organized commerce has been greatly disrupted. Open markets form the basis of daily commercial activity.

SOCIETY

Government

Southern Somalia has no central authority, although a Western-style government does control the self-declared Republic of Somaliland. Traditional political structures based on clan affiliation and *shari'a* (Islamic law) govern local affairs. For example, a Somali man in certain clans is customarily part of a *shir*, an open deliberation forum of extended families or clan groups. *Shir* decisions are made by consensus; through elected chiefs, a *shir* can declare war or peace, make policy for participating clans, and even dissolve itself if the alliance breaks down. Disputes within and between families are often solved through informal arbitration panels set up by a *shir*, through dialogue, or by war. Since alliances change, a *shir* is not a source of permanent authority.

Economy

Animal products accounted for the bulk of Somalia's exports before the civil war. Meat, in the form of live animals, was shipped to Saudi Arabia and other markets; hides and skins were also exported. Somali sheep are especially prized in the Middle East. Agricultural products such as bananas were exported from the south. Nomads herd camels, cattle, sheep, and goats. Northern economic activity is resuming with some exports to the Middle East.

Political instability, lack of a skilled labor force, poor land utilization, and other factors have inhibited economic growth in the past. However, Somalia could access marine resources and possible oil fields. Agriculture and minerals are also areas of significant future potential. Somalia's Human Development Index (0.246) ranks it 166th out of 174 countries. Real gross domestic product per capita is estimated at $1,001. The currency is the Somali shilling (SoSh).

Transportation and Communication

The system of roads in Somalia consists mostly of dirt tracks. It does extend between major cities, however, and large trucks once traveled the routes with passengers and goods. A system of minivans transports passengers between towns in times of peace. An international airport at Mogadishu, smaller airports in other towns, and dirt landing fields all exist in Somalia. The Mogadishu airport has been closed to regular international traffic since 1990, but it allows some chartered flights. Northern cities receive regular flights.

Somalia's telephone system no longer works, but a satellite hookup links Mogadishu to other cities. The postal system has also collapsed. The Hargeisa radio station and Radio Mogadishu have been destroyed. Somalis stay informed about international and some local events by listening to the British Broadcasting Corporation (BBC). Oral communication continues to spread news within Somalia.

Education

Somalia's formal education system, from primary levels through university, has been essentially destroyed by war. Somalis, however, value education and many people have established private schools for the interim. Reestablishing public schools will be a challenge for future governments.

The educational system that existed before the war began in the 1940s. Until 1972, the language of instruction was Arabic, English, or Italian. Traditional schools, where students learned the *Qur'an* in Arabic, served as kindergartens. The introduction of the written Somali script allowed the language to be used in school and in adult literacy programs. By 1975, 47 percent of all Somalis older than age ten could read and write in Somali and/or Arabic. However, initial gains did not last; by the 1980s, only one in ten children was able to attend school. The current literacy rate is about 27 percent.

Health

Somalia's health-care system has largely been destroyed; there are no modern hospitals. Primary-care clinics are run by or rely on international organizations. Violence has forced many of them to discontinue services. Malaria, tuberculosis, and other infectious diseases are prevalent. Children, women of childbearing age, and the elderly have suffered because of unsafe water, poor nutrition, and a lack of medical services. Some 300,000 people died in the famine of the early 1990s. Life expectancy averages 36 to 46 years; the infant mortality rate is 120 per 1,000.

FOR THE TRAVELER

Visas are not available for travel to Somalia; few people other than relief workers are visiting. Travel is not impossible, but it is a challenge that requires one to carry rations and take health and safety precautions. Travelers in the south must hire armed guards. The Somali Mission to the United Nations is at 425 East 61st Street, Suite 702, New York, NY 10021.

CULTURGRAM '97

Republic of
South Africa

Boundary representations not necessarily authoritative.

BACKGROUND

Land and Climate

Covering 471,445 square miles (1,221,043 square kilometers), South Africa is slightly larger than Texas, New Mexico, and Oklahoma combined. The country's large interior plateau averages about 5,000 feet (1,500 meters) above sea level. Primarily savanna and semidesert, the plateau is rimmed by a narrow coastal belt, which is subtropical along the east coast and has a Mediterranean climate along the southwestern cape. The three most important rivers are the Orange, Vaal, and Limpopo. Snow is confined to the Drakensberg and Maluti Mountains in the east. The seasons are opposite those in the northern hemisphere. Generally there is little humidity, except in the KwaZulu/Natal Province along the east coast. The country of Lesotho is completely surrounded by South Africa and sits on a high plateau in the east. Swaziland (near Mozambique) is nearly engulfed by South Africa. South Africa is noted for its long beaches, green forests, rugged mountains, and great canyons. Diversity among plants and wildlife adds to its scenic beauty.

History

The Khoikhoi, San, and other Africans lived in southern Africa for thousands of years, although little is known of their history. In 1652, the Dutch established a provisions station at Cape Town. It supplied ships with fresh foods as they sailed around the tip of the continent. French Huguenot refugees joined the Dutch colony in 1688 and Germans came later. The colonists became known as *Boers* (farmers). They clashed at times with indigenous groups but stayed mainly in coastal areas. Britain gained formal possession of the Cape Colony in 1814 as a result of the Napoleonic Wars. Dissatisfaction with British rule led many Boers to migrate to the interior between 1835 and 1848. Their migration, which they call the Great Trek, led to war with the indigenous Zulus, Xhosas, and other Black African tribes. The Boers won most of the battles and gained control of large tracts of land.

After the discovery of gold and diamonds in these Boer territories in the late 19th century, Britain annexed parts of the area. Tension erupted into the Boer War (1899–1902), in which the Boers were defeated. Britain combined its colonies, Cape and Natal, with the Boer republics of Orange Free State and Transvaal to create the Union of South Africa in 1910.

Following its election to power in 1948, South Africa's National Party (NP) devised the apartheid system that separated the country's population into racial groups: blacks, Coloureds, Indians, and whites. In 1961, the country gained independence from Great Britain and subsequently withdrew from the British Commonwealth over criticism of its racial policies. For the next three decades, South Africa was the scene of turmoil and violence. The African National Congress (ANC), formed in 1912 to fight for black rights, was banned in 1960. It then launched, with other groups, a guerrilla campaign against the government. Many ANC leaders, including Nelson Mandela, were jailed. In the 1970s and 1980s, international sanctions and boycotts damaged the economy and isolated the government.

Frederik Willem (F. W.) de Klerk took office in 1989 and began to move the country toward true democracy. De Klerk freed political prisoners such as Mandela, desegregated hospitals and other public facilities, and gave the ANC legal status. Mandela later suspended the ANC's guerrilla war. Violent clashes continued, however, between rival black political groups—especially between Zulu supporters of the Inkhatha Freedom Party, led by Mangosuthu Buthelezi, and the mostly

Xhosa ANC. The two groups had long been at odds over the course of South Africa's future and other issues.

Most apartheid provisions were abolished in 1991, and the international community began lifting trade sanctions against South Africa. In 1992, de Klerk sponsored a popular referendum to determine white voters' support for his reforms. Voters gave him a clear victory and the necessary support to conduct constitutional talks. Mandela and de Klerk won the Nobel Peace Prize in 1993 for their efforts to build democracy.

Despite sporadic violence (sometimes by white extremists) and predictions of disaster, multiracial, multiparty elections were peacefully held in April 1994. Mandela was elected president, and de Klerk became one of two vice presidents. The country and the world were amazed at how a nation could make such a transition without sending former rulers into exile or without sparking a civil war.

For the next several months, Mandela implemented his *Masakhane* (Nguni for "Let us build each other") campaign. Two national anthems (one Boer, one black nationalist), a new flag, new names for old apartheid-era places, free school lunches for all, new housing projects, better health care, and the promotion of both white and black values all became part of the campaign and South Africa's transformation. Blacks and whites both expressed relief and positive feelings about their new future together. The transition to democracy was completed in May 1996 with the approval of a new constitution. Citing the document's lack of attention to certain economic and moral issues, de Klerk withdrew his party from the government three years early. He resigned his post in June 1996 and the NP became the opposition party in Parliament. The challenges facing South Africa are formidable, but leaders are addressing them. Even the NP vows to help the government make progress by being a responsible opposition party.

THE PEOPLE

Population

South Africa's population of 45.1 million grows annually at 2.6 percent. The majority of the population (75.2 percent) is comprised of Black Africans, mostly from nine ethnic groups. The Zulus are the largest (18 percent), followed by the Xhosas, North Sothos, South Sothos, Tswanas, Shangaan-Tsongas, Swazis, South Ndebeles, and Vendas. Each has its own cultural heritage, language, and national identity. Before migration patterns led groups to mix with one another, most lived in distinct areas of southern Africa. This inspired the apartheid concept of "homelands," in which blacks were assigned to live in marginal territories covering just 15 percent of the country. Homelands were abolished in 1992 and the government is working to restore confiscated lands where possible.

Whites (13.6 percent) include English-speaking descendants of English, Irish, and Scottish settlers and Afrikaans-speaking descendants of Dutch, German, and French colonials. Afrikaners traditionally had large families, but their population growth has slowed in recent years. Coloureds (8.6 percent) are people of mixed race—most often descendants of early white settlers, native Khoikhoi, and slaves imported from the Dutch East Indies during South Africa's colonial period. Indians (2.6 percent) are generally descendants of indentured laborers brought from India during the 19th century or of Indian immigrants who came between 1860 and 1911.

Language

The languages spoken in South Africa are as diverse as its ethnic groups. Afrikaans (a Dutch derivation) is the native tongue of about two-thirds of all whites and most Coloureds, and English is the original language of most other whites and the Indians. English is commonly used in business circles and between some ethnic groups. Many blacks speak Afrikaans and/or English in addition to native languages.

The blacks' native tongues include a variety of Bantu languages, which are roughly divided into four language families: Nguni, Sotho, Tsonga or Shangana, and Venda. Most blacks speak a Nguni language, with Zulu and Xhosa being most prominent. They are joined in the Nguni group by Transvaal Ndebele, Swazi, and Mbayi. Sotho languages (South Sotho, North Sotho, and SeTswana) dominate central South Africa. In addition to the major Bantu languages, a few mixed languages have developed to facilitate communication between various black ethnic groups. Typical is a mixture of Zulu and Xhosa or of a Sotho tongue mixed with Zulu. The mixed languages are used only between ethnic groups, since people prefer to speak their original languages at home or within their own groups. With the advent of majority rule, many white South Africans are learning one of the major native languages. This is helping them become more aware of their diverse culture and is encouraging greater social integration.

Religion

About 60 percent of blacks and most whites and mixed-race people are Christians. Afrikaans-speakers belong primarily to the Dutch Reformed Church. English-speaking whites generally belong to other denominations, including Anglican, Lutheran, Presbyterian, Roman Catholic, and Methodist. Blacks typically belong to African Independent Churches, such as the Zion Christian Church, that combine Christian and traditional African beliefs in their worship patterns. From 10 to 20 percent of blacks adhere solely to indigenous belief systems. Most Indians are Hindus, although about 20 percent are Muslims and 10 percent are Christians. South Africa's Jewish community is small compared to other religions, but it has had a significant impact on the country's development.

General Attitudes

Today's South Africa and the attitudes of its people are changing rapidly. Fear among whites of black majority rule has given way to confidence that a government in which power is shared between competing interests can maintain stability and rights for all. Whites are now moving on with life and trying to learn more about their black countrymen. At the same time, they continue to value their European heritage. Afrikaners consider themselves sturdy and independent.

Feelings among blacks are also changing from anger toward whites to anticipation at being more fully involved in a prosperous economy and equal political system. They are encouraged by the fact that they have a black president, that whites are genuinely interested in them, and that they have equality under the law. They are generally aware that their economic situation will not immediately improve and are willing to accept their newly acquired measure of respect, equality, and dignity that was denied them before 1994. Blacks do not want to marginalize whites or take away their wealth; instead, they wish to share in the opportunities that create wealth and prosperity. Blacks generally value education as the key to a better life. They express optimism about the future and are anxious to exercise their rights and obligations in the new system. At the same time, they express frustration with the pace of some reforms and have clearly indicated they will not be patient for too many years without visible improvements in their standard of living.

Mixed-race South Africans also benefit from the multiracial system, as their representation in Parliament before 1994 was not significant. What seems to unite all peoples is their common claim to South Africa as home, their willingness to look more to the future instead of the past, and a growing desire to build a nonracial and fully democratic society.

Personal Appearance

Urban South Africans wear Western-style clothing, usually made from lightweight cotton. People tend to be well dressed in public. Men wear suits or shirts and trousers; some wear shorts and kneesocks. Women generally wear comfortable dresses or modest pants. Indian women often wear a *sari*, a wraparound-type dress. Some rural blacks retain traditional clothing habits for special purposes or everyday attire. This may include a variety of headdresses and colorful outfits. They also wear Western-style clothing on a daily basis, but women include a scarf or other headdress and wear either a dress or a blouse and skirt.

CUSTOMS AND COURTESIES

Greetings

Because of ethnic diversity, various greetings are used in South Africa. English-speakers use *Hello* and *Good morning*, phrases understood by most South Africans. Young English speakers say *Howzit* (slang for "How are you?") to friends. Afrikaans speakers say *Goeie more* (Good morning). The Zulu and Swazis greet each other with *Sawubona* (literally, "I see you," meaning hello) or *Kunjani* (How are you?). An acceptable response to either is *Yebo* (Yes). The Xhosa greeting, *Molo*, and the Sotho-language-group phrase *Dumela* have similar meanings. All South Africans shake hands when they greet, but handshakes differ between groups. Some use firmer, others lighter, shakes with one hand; many rural people use both hands. Sometimes black friends greet with an intricate triple handshake that involves interlocking the smallest fingers, clasping fists, and interlocking fingers again. In all groups, close friends and relatives may hug.

Using first names with strangers or older people is generally impolite. Professional titles or the equivalents to "Mr.," "Mrs.," and "Miss" are preferred. It is polite to call an older black man "father" (*Tata* in Xhosa, *Ntate* in SeSotho, or *Baba* in Zulu) or older woman "mother" (*Mama* in Xhosa and Zulu or *Mme* in SeSotho). Friends use first names and nicknames.

Gestures

South Africans frequently use hand gestures in conversation. It is impolite to point at someone with the index finger or to talk with one's hands in the pockets. The right hand is more often used for handshakes, to pass objects, or to gesture. Receiving an object with cupped hands is polite. Indicating "peace" or "two" by forming a "V" with the index and middle fingers is rude if the palm faces inward. Some people shake a hand with index and little fingers extended (the others folded) to express "Hello" or "Good-bye."

Visiting

Visiting is an important social activity for most groups. When possible, visits are arranged in advance, but unannounced visits among good friends or relatives are common, especially in areas where telephones are not accessible. South Africans are hospitable. They enjoy conversation and socializing. Gender and age groups tend to socialize amongst themselves; association between such groups is more formal.

Guests usually are served refreshments. In Indian homes, it is impolite to refuse these, and it is polite to accept second helpings if eating a meal. Among most people, dinner guests are not expected to bring a gift but will often bring something to drink (juice, wine, etc.). Etiquette varies between different ethnic groups. When guests leave, they usually are accompanied by their host to the gate, car, or street.

Eating

Urban South Africans generally observe the continental style of eating, with the fork in the left hand and the knife remaining in the right. In rural areas, people often eat with spoons or their fingers. It generally is not appropriate for adults to eat on the street unless they are eating ice cream or standing at a vendor's stand. In restaurants, tipping is discretionary.

LIFESTYLE

Family

White families are small, live as a nuclear unit, are generally close-knit, and enjoy a good standard of living. Blacks have strong extended family ties, even if nuclear units are not always complete. Children are taught to respect their elders and obey their parents. Relatives play an important role in caring for children and providing aid to those in need. This has been necessary due to years of apartheid when fathers had to work far from home; resettlement in the future may help strengthen black nuclear units.

Diet

One's diet is often determined by economic status. Beef, mutton, a variety of curries, green vegetables, pumpkins, and other foods are eaten. Staples include potatoes and rice. Wine, tea, coffee, beer, and soft drinks are common beverages. Rural South Africans and others eat *mealie meal* (cornmeal porridge, sometimes cooked with vegetables and meat). Dinner, usually eaten after 6:00 P.M., is the main meal. The *braaivleis* (barbecue) is a popular weekend event and usually features *boerewors* (beef and pork sausage). Fresh fruit and vegetables are abundant and often sold by farmers from roadside stalls. *Biltong* is a popular jerky-like snack made from various types of meat.

Recreation

Soccer, rugby, boxing, swimming, sailing, and boating are popular. All ethnic groups value competitive sports. Those who can afford equipment or club memberships participate in cricket, squash, lawn bowling, golf, field hockey, and tennis. Horse and car racing draw crowds. South Africans appreciate their many beaches and recreational facilities, including swimming pools, parks, libraries, and movie theaters.

Dancing, playing music, attending festivals, and enjoying cultural events are popular throughout the year.

Holidays

The official holidays in South Africa include New Year's Day, Easter (including Good Friday and Family Day on Monday), Human Rights Day (21 March), Freedom Day (27 April), Workers' Day (1 May), Youth Day (16 June), National Women's Day (9 August), Inheritance Day (24 September), Reconciliation Day (16 December), Christmas, and Day of Goodwill (26 December). Each religion also observes other important holidays.

Commerce

In general, businesses and shops are open from 8:30 A.M. to 5:00 P.M., Monday through Friday, and until 1:00 P.M. on Saturday. Shopping centers and supermarkets stay open into the evenings and on weekends. Banks and government offices are open from 9:00 A.M. to 3:30 P.M., Monday through Friday, and until 11:00 A.M. on Saturday. Few businesses and shops are open on Sunday. Pavement (sidewalk) vendors offer sundry items, and small retail businesses (*Spaza* shops) run from black suburban homes sell a variety of items to neighborhood residents.

SOCIETY

Government

South Africa's president, chosen by an elected Parliament on the basis of the majority party's recommendation, is chief of state and head of government. President Mandela had two vice presidents but is now only joined by Thabo Mbeki of the ANC. Any party with at least 5 percent of the seats in Parliament has the right to a post in the president's cabinet. This and other provisions will change when 1999 elections institute simple majority rule. For now, only the three main parties (ANC, NP, and the Inkatha Freedom Party) met this requirement and hold cabinet posts. The Inkatha leader, Chief Buthelezi, is home minister.

Parliament has two houses: a 90-member Senate and a 400-seat National Assembly. The latter body is elected directly by the people, while Senate members are elected by the country's nine provinces (ten members each). All citizens are eligible to vote at age 18. The 1994 national elections represented the first time blacks could vote and participate as full citizens of their country. Municipal elections were held in 1995.

Economy

South Africa is the richest country in Africa, and whites generally enjoy a high standard of living. The country's Human Development Index (0.705) ranks it 95th out of 174 nations. Real gross domestic product (GDP) per capita is $3,799. These figures reflect a wide gap between whites and blacks in terms of income, because whites earn far more than the per capita GDP and blacks usually earn far less. Manufacturing is the most important sector of the economy, followed by mining. The most important exports include gold, other minerals and metals, food, and chemicals. Nearly two-thirds of all export earnings traditionally come from mining (gold, diamonds, chrome, and coal). South Africa has a relatively large industrial base and diversified economy, and new investment is allowing for strong and steady growth. Wine is now a fast growing export. Tourism is important and also growing. Unemployment is highest among black workers. The currency is the *rand* (R).

Transportation and Communication

Railroads carry freight and passengers throughout the country. South African Airways serves all major cities of the republic and some overseas destinations. The road system is good and extensive. Many urban commuters take minibus *taxis* to work. An advanced telecommunications system is the best on the continent. Television is available throughout the country, with four channels broadcasting in English, Afrikaans, and the Nguni and Sotho language groups. One cable channel offers a mix of U.S. and British programming. Several radio stations broadcast in all of South Africa's languages. Radio and television services are provided by the government-regulated South African Broadcasting Corporation, but there is a move toward decentralization.

Education

Apartheid segregated educational systems by race. Schooling was free and compulsory for white children between the ages of seven and sixteen. Where accommodations permitted, attendance was compulsory for Coloureds and Indians between seven and fourteen. For blacks, a separate government agency oversaw education, which was only compulsory for the first four years. As in other areas of South African life, segregation in education has been dismantled. It will, however, take some time before all children receive the same opportunities within a uniform system. Blacks receive instruction in their native language to the seventh grade and choose between English and Afrikaans after that. There are 19 universities in South Africa. Literacy rates vary between the different ethnic groups and are estimated to be whites, 99 percent; Indians, 85; Coloureds, 60; and blacks, 50.

Health

Medical services are socialized, but some private sector participation is also incorporated. Until 1990, many medical facilities were segregated and blacks had inadequate facilities. Public hospitals and clinics are now open to all races. Free care is given to all pregnant women and to children younger than age six. Disease and malnutrition remain more common among blacks than whites. The infant mortality rate is 46 per 1,000. Life expectancy ranges from 63 to 68 years. Whites enjoy better rates than other groups.

FOR THE TRAVELER

U.S. visitors need a valid passport to enter South Africa, but visas are not required for tourist stays. Vaccinations are not necessary, but proof of yellow fever vaccination is required of travelers coming from a yellow fever endemic zone. South Africa's tourism industry is well developed and awaits a flood of post-apartheid visitors to showcase the country's beauty, diversity, and culture. For more information, contact the Embassy of South Africa, 3051 Massachusetts Avenue NW, Washington, DC 20008; phone (202) 232–4400.

A *Culturgram* is a product of native commentary and original, expert analysis. Statistics are estimates and information is presented as a matter of opinion. While the editors strive for accuracy and detail, this document should not be considered strictly factual. It is a general introduction to culture, an initial step in building bridges of understanding between peoples. It may not apply to all peoples of the nation. You should therefore consult other sources for more information.

Democratic Socialist Republic of
Sri Lanka

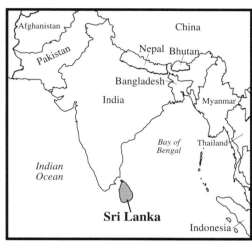

Boundary representations not necessarily authoritative.

BACKGROUND

Land and Climate

Shaped like a teardrop, the island nation of Sri Lanka sits less than 20 miles off the coast of India. Covering 25,332 square miles (65,610 square kilometers), it is slightly larger than West Virginia. About 25 percent of the land is forested (down from 40 percent due to deforestation). The north and east are flat and require irrigation to cultivate rice. Ancient hydro-engineering techniques are still in use and are admired even by the modern engineers expanding the irrigation system. Sri Lanka's south-central region is mountainous. Two peaks (Mount Pidurutagala and World's End Peak) are located near the center of the island. Tea, rubber, and coconut plantations dominate the central mountains, although terraced rice paddies are not uncommon. Sri Lanka has a tropical climate, with temperatures averaging 80°F (27°C) year-round. Highland areas are cooler but also receive more rain than lowland regions. Seasonal monsoons affect the island.

History

The first inhabitants of Sri Lanka, the Veddahs, have largely been assimilated into society; little is known of their past. Around 500 B.C., an Indo-Aryan group led by Prince Vijaya migrated to Sri Lanka and formed a small kingdom. The present-day Sinhalese descended from this group. In 307 B.C., the Indian Prince Mahinda, son of the great Buddhist King Asoka, introduced Buddhism to the Sinhalese. While Buddhism later floundered in India, it remained strong in Sri Lanka. Hindu Tamils also came to the island at an early date and have kept some cultural and religious ties with the state of Tamil Nadu in India. A second migration of Tamils occurred in the 19th century when the British brought them from India to work on tea plantations.

Sri Lanka was well-known to other nations throughout history, including the Romans and early Arabs (who called the island "Serendip"). Various European powers came to dominate coastal areas, but inland areas remained autonomous until the 19th century. The Portuguese (16th century) were followed by the Dutch (17th century), who were replaced by the British in 1796. In 1815, the British defeated the last native ruler, King of Kandy, and established the island as the Crown Colony of Ceylon.

In 1948, the island peacefully obtained freedom from British rule. The nation has held successive free elections since that time and has never experienced a dictatorship. In 1971, a Maoist group led an uprising of unemployed, educated young people and caused the government to declare a state of emergency to forcibly quell the violence. In 1972, partly in response to the unrest, a new constitution changed the name of the country from Ceylon to Sri Lanka (meaning "resplendent island") and introduced limited socialist measures such as nationalization of some industries.

Yet another new constitution in 1978 declared the country a democratic socialist republic and created a strong presidency. About the same time, Tamil factions seeking an independent Tamil state (called Tamil Eelam) in northern Sri Lanka became violent and began leading insurgent campaigns against the government. In the 1980s, Tamils clashed with Sinhalese in several confrontations that led to thousands of deaths. At the same time, Sinhalese Maoists again attempted to overthrow the government at the cost of some 60,000 lives.

Violence peaked in 1987. The government granted the Tamil language official status, implemented other reforms, and accepted India's offer to send troops into the Tamil areas to establish peace. Although the separatists had originally agreed to turn their arms over to the Indian forces in exchange for autonomy, they backed out and began fighting the Indian troops. By 1988, the Sinhalese were violently protesting the presence of the Indians and a new government came into office promising to send the Indians home. President Ranasinghe Premadasa negotiated the end of Indian involvement, and the last troops were gone by March 1990.

Premadasa's actions won the short-term cooperation of Tamil guerrillas, who halted militant activities to participate in elections. Moderates gained several seats in the national Parliament. However, fighting broke out again, with entire villages being massacred by opposing ethnic groups. By the end of 1991, the Liberation Tigers of Tamil Eelam (LTTE) had taken control of many areas north of Vauvuniya, including Jaffna. In May 1993, Tiger terrorists killed Premadasa at a political rally. Premadasa's prime minister, Dingiri Banda Wijetunge, became interim president until elections in 1994.

In those elections, Premadasa's United National Party, which had governed for 17 years, lost to a leftist coalition called the People's Alliance. Chandrika Bandaranaike Kumaratunga of the Sri Lanka Freedom Party was elected president on a platform of bringing peace to the country. A widow of a politician killed during the 1980s, she immediately opened talks with the LTTE. Hopes for peace were high until May 1995, when talks collapsed and fighting erupted once more. In a massive offensive, the government recaptured Jaffna in December 1995. The president offered a peace proposal to grant limited autonomy to Tamils and revise the constitution, but no agreement could be reached. By June 1996, when several villagers were killed in a rebel attack, it was clear the violent conflict may be far from over.

THE PEOPLE
Population
Sri Lanka's population of 18.3 million is growing annually at 1.1 percent. The Sinhalese constitute 74 percent of the population and are concentrated in the southwest. The Tamils are divided into two groups: the Ceylon Tamils (12 percent), whose ancestors lived on the island for centuries, and the Indian Tamils (6 percent), whose ancestors were imported during the British colonial era. About 400,000 Tamils live outside of Sri Lanka, either in India or the west. Tamils live in the north, east, and south-central areas. Moors (locally called Muslims) comprise 7 percent of the population. Malays, Burghers, and Veddahs make up the other 1 percent. Burghers are descendants of Dutch colonists and Veddahs are a remnant of the island's original inhabitants. Colombo, the capital, is the largest city with 1.5 million people.

Sri Lanka's Human Development Index (0.704) ranks it 97th out of 174 countries. Many people lack access to resources that would allow them to pursue personal goals.

Language
Both Sinhala and Tamil are official languages in Sri Lanka, but Sinhala is considered to be primary. It is an Indo-European language with roots in Sanskrit and Pali. Its written form is more formal than the spoken version. Tamil belongs to the Dravidian group of languages. English is the primary language of business, and about 10 percent of the population speaks it.

Religion
Since the introduction of Buddhism by the Indian Prince Mahinda, Sri Lanka has been a stronghold of Theravada Buddhism, the more conservative branch of the religion. It is practiced by nearly 70 percent of the population, primarily among the Sinhalese. Although freedom of worship is guaranteed by the constitution, the government has given special status to Buddhism. About 15 percent of the people (mostly Tamils) practice Hinduism. Many Buddhists also honor various Hindu deities. Tamil worship centers on the Hindu god Shiva. But many gods exist in the hierarchy, each having a specific purpose. For instance, women pray to Paththini for health and fertility; businessmen seek the blessings of Kataragama (or Skanda); and students can receive help with learning from Ganesh or Saraswathi. The Moors are mostly Muslims, while 8 percent of the population is Christian.

General Attitudes
Sri Lankans are friendly and have relatively open attitudes. They value loyalty to one's group, respect for others, and their ethnic and religious identity. Ethnic divisions run deep, and few people socialize outside of their respective groups. The two greatest values in society are the family and education. Family members help one another and are very close-knit. Parents will sacrifice or work all their lives to provide their children with as much education as possible. Nearly all young people desire a good education. Teachers and persons with a university degree are highly respected in society. Material wealth is also desired, and people are willing to work hard to obtain it. The wealthy, especially those who have become successful in private business, are respected but in a different way than educated people are. In other words, family and education are still more important than money.

The traditional caste system that once dominated society is fading in public life. Most people do not discuss it, and being from a lower caste usually does not limit one's economic or political mobility. However, since one's surname gives indication of caste, everyone is aware of his or her place within the system, and that awareness does play a role in social interaction. That is, people still marry and associate with others of the same caste. For religious ceremonies, certain castes perform certain functions.

Personal Appearance
Although the youth and people in cities wear Western-style clothing, traditional forms of dress remain popular. Women may wear a *saree* (a wraparound dress that reaches to the ankles) with a tight blouse. The *saree*, made from a very long piece of fabric, is draped over the shoulder and wrapped at the waist in a way that creates tailoring without being sewn. Women also wear a *redda* (a wraparound skirt that is tucked at the waist) with a blouse (*hatte*) that leaves the midriff bare. Traditional attire for men may include loose-fitting trousers

combined with a long shirt that reaches to mid-thigh. The shirt has long, loose sleeves and buttons to the neck. Men might also wear a *sarong* (a piece of cloth wrapped around the waist, sometimes held by a belt or *lunghi*) that reaches to the ankles with a *banian* (a sleeveless shirt that looks like a tank top) and a handkerchief draped over the right shoulder.

CUSTOMS AND COURTESIES

Greetings

Forms of greeting vary between ethnic groups. The traditional greeting of placing one's palms together in front of the chest and bowing the head slightly is widely practiced. This is accompanied by the Sinhalese phrase *Ayubowan* (ah-you-byu-one) or the Tamil *Vannakkam* (one-eh-come). Both terms mean "May you be blessed with the gift of a long life." Men often shake hands with men while greeting, but they do not touch women in public. Titles are important to Sri Lankans, even among close friends. Acquaintances and strangers use the more formal equivalents of "Mr.," "Mrs.," and "Miss." If one is speaking English, the title precedes the surname; otherwise, it follows the name. Colleagues might use the title with a given name. Among close friends and relatives, familial titles replace formal ones. For example, in Sinhala one addresses an older male friend as *aiya* (older brother), a younger female cousin as *nangi* (younger sister), and so on.

Gestures

Sri Lankans use the right hand for passing objects and eating. They use both hands when giving and receiving gifts; a gift presented with only one hand is not given wholeheartedly. To express sincere or gracious giving of any object, one can touch the right forearm with the left hand while giving with the right. Men often hold hands in public, but it is improper for members of the opposite sex to do so. Women are forbidden to touch a Buddhist monk.

The head is considered the most sacred part of the body; the bottom of the feet is the least sacred. People do not touch another's head, nor do they use a foot to point at anything. Pointing with the index finger is likewise impolite. One beckons with the hand held at head level, palm facing out, and all fingers waving together. It is improper to pass between two people in conversation; if it is unavoidable, the passer ducks slightly and apologizes before passing. People remove shoes before entering Buddhist temples or Hindu shrines.

Wagging or tilting the head from side to side indicates agreement. Shaking it gently during conversation means one is listening. But shaking it firmly with the mouth closed can mean "no."

Visiting

Visiting is a favorite pastime. Sri Lankans are very hospitable and strive to make all guests comfortable. Friends often drop by unannounced and are warmly received. Sri Lankans also enjoy inviting relatives and friends to their homes. In such a case, guests may bring a small gift of food or other item. Depending on the hosts, guests might remove shoes before entering the home. Once seated, guests are offered tea, usually sweetened with milk and sugar. It is impolite to refuse such an offer, although one can ask for a substitute (such as water). Hosts usually offer simple snacks, and guests are obliged to eat a little bit. While most visiting occurs in the home, Sri Lankans also enjoy meeting at parks or restaurants and they often take short sight-seeing excursions together.

Eating

Lunch is the largest of three daily meals. The family eats together and all members eat with their right hand. The mother serves men and any guests before other members of the household. After the meal, most people drink water and wash their hands in a bowl of water.

Sri Lankans of all religions seek to avoid those things that would cause spiritual pollution. Because food enters the body, it is considered a prime source of potential pollution. Those who adhere strictly to Buddhist doctrines do not eat flesh of any kind. Some Buddhists, however, include fish or eggs in their diet. Hindus do not eat beef or pork, and Muslims do not eat pork.

LIFESTYLE

Family

The extended family is important in society. Even if a nuclear family has its own household, it will often live very close to relatives. The husband dominates the family, but the wife manages the the household and has influence in all family matters. Women have economic and political opportunities outside the home but are expected to maintain all household responsibilities as well. Women do not go out alone after dark. Parents expect to provide their children with all basic needs, even into adulthood. The elderly receive deep respect and younger family members often yield to their advice and counsel. Children expect to care for their elderly parents if necessary.

Dating and Marriage

Dating in the Western sense is not common in Sri Lanka. Boys and girls get to know each other mostly through school, but getting together (even in groups) generally is not done. If a young couple desires to have a boyfriend/girlfriend relationship, they are expected to eventually marry. Such couples do go out to parks and so forth, but not always with the knowledge of their parents. More and more people are choosing their own mates, especially in urban areas, but arranged marriages are still very common. Sexual purity is an essential part of the marriage contract on the part of the woman. Marriage between members of different ethnic groups is socially unacceptable.

The timing of various wedding events—when the parties arrive, have the ceremony, sign papers, leave, arrive at their new home—is governed by astrology. Each event is calculated to the minute so as to give the marriage the best possible start. Weddings are a time for family, friends, and food.

Diet

Rice and curry are staples in Sri Lanka. Each ethnic group has contributed dishes to the overall cuisine. A variety of curries (from the Sinhalese) are very popular. Sri Lankans typically consume little meat, but they do eat large amounts of legumes (from the Tamils) and nuts. A main meal usually begins with rice or bread, followed by a curry or *dahl* (lentils) and a vegetable (cabbage, carrots). One popular food is *Pol Sambol*, scraped and spiced coconut. *Katta Sambol* is a very spicy mixture of fried onions and chilies. The Burghers are known for their cakes and sweetmeats.

Recreation

Cricket is the most popular sport, followed by soccer, table tennis, volleyball, and netball (for girls). Most sports are played by men, although girls do play them in school. Attending Western and Sri Lankan movies are favorite pastimes. Sri Lanka has a long tradition in the dramatic arts and people enjoy both live and puppet theater. During New Year festivities, Sri Lankans participate in a number of activities, from indoor games just for women to outdoor sports such as elephant racing or wrestling. Traditional music played on small drums and sitars is popular throughout the country; the urban youth like electric keyboards and guitars. Sri Lankans cherish their many traditional dances.

Holidays

Every full moon (*Poya* Day) is a holiday. *Wesak Poya* in May is celebrated as Buddha's day of birth, enlightenment, and death. Each major religion has at least one national holiday. For example, the country marks *Idul Fitr* (a feast at the end of *Ramadan*, the Islamic month of fasting) and *Idul Adha* (Feast of the Sacrifice) for Muslims. Christians celebrate Easter (including Good Friday) and Christmas. *Deepawali* (Festival of Lights) is a Hindu holiday celebrating the triumph of light over darkness. Thousands of lights decorate stores and homes at this time of goodwill. Many other religious holidays honor Buddha or Hindu deities. The Tamil *Thai-Pongal* Day marks the "return" of the sun after a month of evil days; the sun brings a new period of goodwill. The Sinhala and Tamil New Year is usually celebrated in April with great fanfare and rejoicing. Political holidays include National Day (4 February), May Day (1 May), and National Heroes' Day (22 May).

Commerce

Business and government offices are generally open weekdays from 8:30 A.M. to 12:30 P.M. and from 1:00 to 4:30 P.M. Larger towns have a daily open market; small towns have a weekly *Polla* (market) day. Rural residents must travel to the nearest town on *Polla* day to buy basic goods.

SOCIETY

Government

Sri Lanka's central government is headed by a president and a prime minister. Each of the eight provinces has substantial control over local affairs. Parliament has 225 members. The voting age is 18. Rural villages often have a chief or headman.

Economy

Despite an educated workforce and growth potential, the economy is somewhat hampered by continued fighting. Its 1994 growth rate of 5 percent would be considerably higher if peace were firmly established. Foreign investment and tourism seem somewhat immune to the war, but some potentials cannot be realized without greater stability. Agriculture employs half of the labor force but does not contribute as much to export earnings as industry, which is dominated by apparel manufacturing. Tea, rubber, and coconuts account for most agricultural exports. Unemployment is high, but the number of private-sector jobs is steadily increasing. Sri Lanka benefits from foreign assistance and remittances from the nearly one million Sri Lankans who work abroad (mostly in the Middle East).

Real gross domestic product per capita is $2,850. Many people earn enough to meet basic needs, but income distribution is somewhat unequal and poverty affects 40 percent of the population. The currency is the Sri Lankan *rupee* (SLRe).

Transportation and Communication

Buses and taxis are plentiful in urban areas. Major cities are linked by paved roads and rail service. Other roads are not paved and may be difficult to travel in some areas. Rural residents travel on foot, by bicycle, or by bus. Traffic moves on the left side of the road. Few Sri Lankans own cars. Many newspapers, printed in Sinhala, Tamil, and English, can generally print what they please. Radio and television broadcasts are available in the major languages. Private homes generally lack telephones, but public phones are in post offices.

Education

Schooling, which begins at age five, is free and compulsory at the primary and secondary levels. The adult literacy rate is one of the highest in Asia (89 percent). For young people, the rate is 96 percent. Nearly all children (97 percent) complete primary schooling and 86 percent go on to complete the secondary level. The average adult has completed seven years of school, a high achievement for the region. The government stresses the development of vocational skills, but traditional values also help maintain a strong liberal arts track. Young people generally aspire to higher education. Entrance to universities is based on "A-level" exams (patterned after the British model). The competition for slots is so intense that students often pay to take after-school "private tuition classes" that help prepare them for the exams. Even if students do not get into college, a good "A-level" score will help them get a better job.

Health

Sri Lanka has both public and private health-care facilities, with private hospitals and clinics providing higher quality (but expensive) care. In rural areas, *ayurvedic* medicine is widely practiced; it stresses the use of herbs and natural cures. The infant mortality rate is 21 per 1,000. Life expectancy is between 70 and 75 years.

FOR THE TRAVELER

U.S. citizens need a valid passport to enter Sri Lanka, but no visa is required for stays of fewer than 90 days. Vaccinations may be recommended depending on one's itinerary. Malarial suppressants are advisable outside Colombo. Food should be hot and well cooked; fruits and vegetables should be peeled or cooked, and water should be treated. Avoid ice and dairy products. From ancient cities to national parks to southern beaches, there is much to experience in Sri Lanka, which was once called the "Pearl of the Indian Ocean." For more information, contact the Embassy of the Democratic Socialist Republic of Sri Lanka, 2148 Wyoming Avenue NW, Washington, DC 20008; phone (202) 483–4025.

Republic of the
Sudan

Boundary representations not necessarily authoritative.

BACKGROUND

Land and Climate

At 967,494 square miles (2,505,810 square kilometers), Sudan is the largest country in Africa and is almost one-third the size of the continental United States. Most of Sudan is a large plain. The White and Blue Nile Rivers flow north, eventually converging to form the Nile River, which empties into the Mediterranean Sea. A swampy area (*as Sudd*) dominates a large region in the far south. The Nubian Desert in the north is separated from the Red Sea by low coastal hills. Hills and mountains also run along the border with Chad. The climate varies according to region and altitude, from tropical forests in the south to deserts in the north. In Khartoum, temperatures remain high throughout the year; rain is rare, and dust and sandstorms are common. In the south, however, the rainy season may last up to nine months. Or it may not come at all. The drought of 1991 was Sudan's third drought in six years and its effects were widespread. In 1993, Sudan had a good crop year. The good harvest continued into 1995.

History

Sudan has a long and interesting history. Contacts between Egypt and Nubia, Sudan's northern area, date to several millennia B.C. In Biblical times, the area was known as Cush, named for the Nubian Kingdom that ruled northern Sudan between the eleventh and fourth centuries B.C. Cush also briefly ruled Egypt (713–671 B.C.). During the early years of the Christian era, Sudan was part of the Christian Kingdom of Aksum, centered in Ethiopia. When the Arabs successfully invaded Egypt in the seventh century, a treaty with Nubia forbade Nubian settlement in Egypt and Muslim settlement in Sudan.

The area remained Christian until the 15th century, when it fell to Egyptian domination. Still, Sudan continued to be semiautonomous for a number of years. Egypt began a complete conquest of Sudan in 1821, a process it completed in 1874. Between 1881 and 1885, Muhammad Ahmad Abdullah led a successful revolt against Egypt. But in 1898, Egypt regained control of the region with the help of the British, who became corulers of the region. Two years after Egypt claimed sole ownership of Sudan, an agreement was reached (in 1953) with Britain to grant Sudan self-rule. The Sudanese people had also voted for an independent state, which was proclaimed in 1956. Unfortunately, democracy did not last long.

Since 1958, when a military coup toppled the civilian government, control of Sudan has alternated between civilian and military governments. As each civilian government was unable to solve Sudan's many problems, including a civil war with the south, the military would take power. One such coup in 1969 brought Gaafar Nimeiry to power. In the 1970s, he recognized special autonomy for the south and ended the civil war. He also implemented policies to stimulate the economy. However, his program of Islamization in the 1980s, which sought to impose Islamic law (*shari'a*) on the whole country, rekindled the civil war and eventually led to a coup in 1985. The officers involved sponsored free elections in 1986, but the new government under Sadiq Mahdi was unable to end the civil war and improve economic conditions. In 1988, because of the fighting, relief supplies destined for people affected by drought were not delivered. At least 250,000 people died. Mahdi was overthrown in 1989 by Omar Hassan al-Bashir.

Al-Bashir suspended the constitution and dissolved Parliament and all political parties. Much of his attention was directed toward the war with the Sudan People's Liberation Movement (SPLM). The SPLM's original goal was the establishment of a secular, democratic state, free from control by Islamic law. After years of fighting, however, rival factions formed (chiefly between the Dinkas and Nuers) within the SPLM, and southern militias began fighting each other for territory and power. They committed atrocities equal to those committed by government forces. These acts included wholesale destruction of southern villages and their inhabitants.

With economic conditions at a standstill and drought affecting much of the country, people throughout Sudan faced starvation again in 1992, but relief efforts had to be suspended due to fierce fighting. By 1993, southern forces had weakened significantly and Sudan allowed some relief efforts to proceed. However, they were halted again in early 1994 when the government launched a massive offensive against rebels in the far south, and refugees began to flee towards Uganda. Some shipments were able to get through in 1995.

General al-Bashir declared a unilateral cease-fire in July 1994 and opened negotiations with SPLM representatives. He announced his willingness to create a federal system that would give the southern non-Muslims more control over certain aspects of their lives. Talks collapsed in September, with the SPLM rejecting the proposals as not going far enough. Fighting resumed by November, more refugees were forced to flee, SPLM factions intensified their internal battles, and the southern war continued into 1996. The SPLM continued to break up, however, as some factions signed peace treaties with the government in 1996.

Such minor events could not overshadow the government's plummeting popularity, poor economic conditions, and Sudan's isolation from other nations that accuse it of sponsoring terrorism. In June 1996, prominent members of society denounced the government and demanded that a transitional one take its place until democratic elections could be held. While no action is likely to be taken, the demands reflect a rising level of discontent among traditional government supporters and could signal future change.

THE PEOPLE

Population

Sudan's population of 30.1 million is growing annually at 2.3 percent. Nearly 40 percent of the population is Arabic. Up to 20 percent (from other ethnic groups, such as the Fur, a Black African group) follows Arabic customs and lives in the north or central regions. The Nubian minority (about 8 percent) is concentrated around the Nile in northern Sudan. The Dinka, Funj, Nuer, Shilluk, and other Black African peoples of southern Sudan constitute half of the total population. Between 20 and 25 percent of all people live in urban areas. Khartoum, the capital, has a population of almost two million. Forty-five percent of the population is younger than age 15.

There is a sharp cultural distinction between the people of northern and central Sudan and those in southern Sudan. The cultural information in this *Culturgram* focuses on the Arabic- and Nubian-speaking peoples of the north and center. Historical and statistical information, however, necessarily cover the entire country. The lack of cultural information regarding the southern Sudanese does not reflect a bias against them. Rather, it reflects a lack of reliable information.

Sudan's Human Development Index (0.379) ranks it 144th out of 174 nations. Adjusted for women, the index (0.332) reflects the fact that women are less likely to earn a decent income or gain an education. Overall, most Sudanese lack access to resources that would help them improve their lives.

Language

While Arabic is the official language of the entire country, it is the primary language only in northern and central regions. More than one hundred other languages are spoken, including Nubian, Nilo-Saharan languages (Dinka, Nuer, Bari, Lotuko, etc.), Zande, and others. Until 1956, English was an official language in the south and is still spoken by some.

Religion

The majority of the Sudanese are Sunni Muslim (70 percent). They live in the north and central areas and dominate politically. The Christian population (5 percent) lives chiefly in the south. The rest of the people follow indigenous beliefs. Religious loyalties play an important role in Sudanese politics. For example, the powerful Ummah Party is associated with the Mahdist movement that began in the late 19th century. Mahdists, who are Sunni Muslims, believe the Muslim teacher Muhammad Ahmad Abdullah was a guide (*al-Mahdi*) sent to establish God's will on earth. His son created the Ummah Party. Abdullah's great-grandson, Sadiq Mahdi, was a prime minister in the late 1980s.

General Attitudes

For all the outward formalities of life, northern Sudanese are surprisingly vocal and expressive. They are an individualistic people given to expressing their opinions openly, although almost always in a polite and considerate manner. They also believe strongly in putting up with the surprises of everyday life. They view whatever happens as the will of God, which should be accepted. To Westerners, Sudanese may also appear to be generally disinterested in a given matter. But this habit of quietly appraising a situation does not imply a lack of concern, nor does it rule out future action.

Sudanese society is highly stratified. In addition to an underprivileged lower class, there is also a middle class (in cities) and a small upper class. Government positions are usually filled by members of the upper class. The Islamic institution of *zakat* (tithing to help support the needy) offsets major economic disabilities (in the north) to a surprising extent. Some significant differences—social as well as economic—are apparent between various segments of the population. The vast cultural differences that exist between the Arabic speakers of the north and non-Arabic speakers of the south are a significant social challenge, and a great deal remains to be done before the southern Sudanese are socially and economically equal with their northern counterparts.

Personal Appearance

In Khartoum, many men wear Western-style clothing. However, such clothing is less prevalent in rural areas, where flowing robes and turbans are common. Women rarely wear Western dress. In fact, they are required to follow the Islamic dress code; women must be covered from head to ankle in public. The nomadic people of the desert wear heavy robes to protect them from the heat and blowing sand. In all cases, conservative clothing is the standard. Attire that is not modest is unacceptable in public.

CUSTOMS AND COURTESIES

Greetings

Hospitality is a Sudanese trait shared with the rest of the Arabic world. The northern Sudanese are formal and traditional, yet cordial, when greeting friends as well as strangers. A firm but gentle handshake with a member of the same sex is always in order, and friends frequently embrace. A man will not touch a woman in public, but he may shake hands with her if she extends her hand first. The usual verbal greeting is *Salaam'alaykum* (Peace be upon you) or *Ahlan wasahlan* (Welcome), followed by *Kayf Haalak?* (How are you?).

Gestures

As in other North African countries, use of the left hand is generally improper. A person will pass or accept items only with the right hand or both hands, never with the left alone. Pointing the finger is considered rude. It is offensive to allow the bottom of one's feet (or shoes) to point toward another person.

Visiting

The Sudanese home is the owner's private domain, and one usually does not visit without an explicit invitation. Such an invitation is a distinct honor, and visitors may take a small gift (but never alcohol) as a token of appreciation. Hosts usually offer guests coffee, tea, or juice, perhaps with some kind of food. Guests should not refuse refreshments, since expressing hospitality is important to the Sudanese. Conversation is kept on a social level, even if one is involved in business dealings with the host. One does not ask about the women of the household or discuss personal topics. However, one may ask generally about a person's health, the well-being of his family, and work.

Eating

Sudanese families normally sit on the floor during a meal. They eat food with the fingers of the right hand only, never with the left. Most Sudanese have one large meal a day. Western-style restaurants are available in Khartoum.

LIFESTYLE

Family

The Sudanese family is a strongly male-oriented, patriarchal, extended organization. Three generations of males and their spouses and children usually live in the same household. This pattern is the norm throughout Sudan but is less dominant in Khartoum, where smaller, nuclear families are found. The trend toward nuclear families is also visible in other large cities. The home is a cohesive, private place, to which one can always return for support. Although it is male dominated, the home is managed by the women of the family. Women's roles are quite different from those of men, but women are not necessarily considered subservient.

Dating and Marriage

Western-style dating does not occur in Sudan. Marriages represent the joining of two families, and consequently their arrangement is a matter of concern to all members of both families. However, such arrangements are rarely made without approval from potential mates. Marriages tend to endure well.

Diet

Sudanese foods are typically Near Eastern. Lamb, goat, and fowl are the usual meats. Pasta-like dishes are also popular. Other common foods include pancake-like breads made of sorghum or millet flour and spicy soups with meat or eggs. Regional dishes, often highly spiced, are typical in the south.

Drought, civil war, and a poor economy have combined to bring malnourishment and famine to hundreds of thousands of people. More than one million people have no regular access to food and water. Crops have failed. For many, nutrition comes only from relief organizations, and those groups cannot serve the areas where fighting is the worst or where government or rebel forces restrict relief efforts. Malnutrition nationwide among children is more than 25 percent and increasing.

Holidays

While the official calendar is the Western (Gregorian) calendar, daily life is regulated by the Islamic lunar calendar. Muslim holy days (the Prophet Muhammad's Birthday, Islamic New Year, etc.) are important, particularly the feast at the end of *Ramadan*. During the Islamic month of *Ramadan*, Muslims go without food or water from dawn to dusk. In the evenings, families eat together and visit friends and relatives. National holidays include Independence Day (1 January), Unity Day (3 March), Labor Day (1 May), and others determined by the government.

Commerce

The Sudanese government is the country's largest employer. A strong business class controls the commercial sector. Business hours are generally from 8:30 A.M. to 2:00 P.M., Saturday through Thursday. Friday is the main day of worship for Muslims. Business hours may vary slightly in the winter and from region to region.

SOCIETY

Government

Sudan is an Islamic state. Because the military suspended the civilian government in 1989, there is no legislature or democratically elected leaders. In March 1996, the government did sponsor limited multiparty elections, but few people knew anything about them; General al-Bashir was elected president. In reality, a 13-member Revolutionary Command Council (RCC) runs the country and is chaired by al-Bashir. A 22-member cabinet advises the RCC. Hassan al-Turabi, an Islamic cleric, is said to be the de facto leader of the country, even though he is not a member of the RCC. Al-Turabi seeks to spread Islamic fundamentalism and to increase the influence of *shari'a* on all aspects of Sudanese life.

Economy

Sudan's economy is based on agriculture, which employs 80 percent of the labor force. Grains (millet, sorghum, wheat, barley), cotton, peanuts, beans, and sesame are the main crops. Cotton is the main export, accounting for 44 percent of total export earnings. Sesame, peanuts, and gum arabic are also exported. Sudan is the world's principal supplier of gum arabic. Industrial activities usually center on processing agricultural items. The development of other industries is hindered by high foreign debt, inadequate transportation systems, and the civil war. Drought has also damaged the economy, but when the country has a successful crop (i.e., rain) year it has the potential to increase economic growth by more than 5 percent. Inflation is more than 100 percent annually. Reforms implemented in 1992 showed some promise of improving long-term economic conditions, but the government canceled most in 1993 to calm public anger over short-term sacrifices. Austerity measures were introduced again in 1996.

Real gross domestic product per capita is $1,620, a figure that has risen slightly since 1960. Eighty-five percent of all rural people live in absolute poverty as subsistence farmers. The currency is the Sudanese pound (£Sd).

Transportation and Communication

More than half of Sudan's roadways are unpaved and often in disrepair. This makes transportation difficult. However, the government currently is investing in infrastructure, including the national railroad and other transportation networks, in hopes of improving the economy. Relatively few people own private cars. Taxis and buses are available in Khartoum. The communications system is large but poorly maintained and barely adequate. There are five radio and two television stations.

Communications and other systems that rely on electricity suffered in 1995 from frequent and long power outages. At times, parts of Khartoum received power only 12 of every 24 hours. Since most electricity is generated by hydroelectric dams, the level of available power depends on water levels in rivers (principally the Blue Nile).

Education

Nine years of education is compulsory, but this requirement is often not enforced. Facilities are generally inadequate, especially in rural areas. The official adult literacy rate is 43 percent (31 percent for women and 55 for men). About half of school-age children in northern and central regions are enrolled at the primary level. Three-fourths complete primary schooling, but only about one-fifth go on to the secondary level. The University of Khartoum is a four-year and graduate university.

Health

Parasitic diseases are endemic, particularly in the central and southern parts of the country. Yellow fever, cholera, and malaria are active throughout the country. The health-care system is inadequate; there are not enough clinics and doctors to serve the needs of the people. Malnutrition also strains the nation's facilities. The infant mortality rate is 78 per 1,000. Life expectancy averages 55 years.

FOR THE TRAVELER

A visa and valid passport are necessary for entry to Sudan. Visas are issued for visits of seven to ten days. Proof of sufficient funds or a letter from one's employer is also required. The U.S. government suggests travel is not safe because of the civil war and unstable political conditions. Before departure, call the U.S. Department of State for recorded travel advisories: (202) 647–5225. The United States withdrew embassy personnel in January 1996 and, therefore, cannot help U.S. American travelers in the country.

Water is not potable, and dairy products should be avoided. Visitors should be sure all food is well cooked and served hot. Fruits and vegetables should be washed and peeled. Vaccinations for yellow fever, cholera, typhoid, and possibly other diseases are recommended for those traveling to Sudan. Malarial suppressants are also recommended. For more information, contact the Embassy of Sudan, 2210 Massachusetts Avenue NW, Washington, DC 20008; phone (202) 338–8565.

Kingdom of
Swaziland

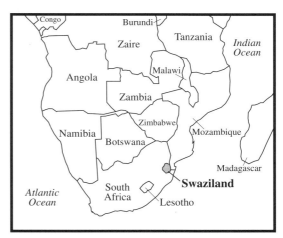

Boundary representations not necessarily authoritative.

BACKGROUND

Land and Climate

Swaziland is the smallest nation in the southern hemisphere. With an area of approximately 6,704 square miles (17,363 square kilometers), this landlocked country is about the same size as Massachusetts. Despite its size, Swaziland has four well-defined geographic regions that parallel each other and extend the length of the nation from north to south.

The eastern Lubombo region (a 600-meter plateau and escarpment) is adjacent to the Lubombo Mountains and the border with Mozambique. Because of its difficult terrain, it is used mainly for cattle grazing. To the west, the Lowveld's fertile soil supports agriculture and some game farms. Irrigated farms support sugarcane, citrus, cotton, and corn. The remainder of the Lowveld is open savanna or dense African bush. The Midveld also supports considerable agriculture, including pineapples. Its hilly region gives way to the Hiveld in the far west, where cattle grazing and commercial forestry are the principal economic pursuits. Most people live in the Midveld and Hiveld regions.

Swaziland experiences four seasons. Frequent rains in the hot summer (October–February) are followed by a cooler fall (March–April) and a cold, dry winter (April–August). Warmer temperatures return in the dry spring (August–October). Swaziland's forests are all man-made; original woods were lost to logging and replaced by managed timberlands.

History

In the mid-18th century, groups of Nguni tribesmen arrived in southern Swaziland from Mozambique by way of central Africa. They were peaceful herdsmen, searching for fertile grazing lands for their cattle and protection from warring tribes. Some of these early tribes successfully defended the area of present-day Swaziland from the Shaka Zulu and encroaching white immigrant farmers.

Around 1810, Sobhuza I was proclaimed king and began to unify the many Swazi clans. But it was not until the 1840s in the reign of King Mswati II, who succeeded Sobhuza, that Swaziland became a nation. It was also about this time that the first white traders settled near present-day Manzini.

To stabilize the nation after Mswati's death, a provisional government was formed among the Swazis, South Africans, and British. This brought British influence and settlement to Swaziland at the end of the 1890s. The kingdom soon became part of the British Empire. In 1921, King Sobhuza II was crowned *Ngwenyama* (Lion) of the nation. He is credited with buying land back from settlers and returning it (up to half of today's territory) to traditional local chiefdoms. His rule lasted until his death in August 1982, which made him the longest-reigning monarch in modern Africa. The British granted independence on 6 September 1968 under a Westminster-type constitution. After trying unsuccessfully to adapt to this style of government, Sobhuza dissolved Parliament and assumed all powers for the throne in 1973. Citing the now-defunct constitution as incompatible with traditional Swazi customs and beliefs, Sobhuza governed the rest of his life under a technical state of emergency.

Upon the death of Sobhuza II, the Queen Mother held the throne as regent until Sobhuza's son (Mswati III) turned 18. For these years, a council of elders (*liqoqo*) governed by decree. King Mswati III was crowned in 1986. He governed under the state of emergency until 1993, when he sponsored free parliamentary elections.

PEOPLE

Population

The Swazi people (called emaSwati or people of Mswati) are a mixture of several Bantu groups (Nguni, Sotho, Thonga, and so forth). The assimilation of the migrating tribes that entered the region in the mid-1700s with those already present (emaKhandzambili) resulted in a population of 970,000, which is growing at 3.2 percent. A few clans of the emaSwati claim kinship to the ancient indigenous peoples that inhabited the region in prehistoric times. There are few other ethnic groups except a sizable Zulu enclave in the south. Some African and non-African expatriates also live and work in Swaziland. Most people (77 percent) live in rural areas. Manzini (75,000) and Mbabane (52,000) are the two largest urban centers.

Swaziland's Human Development Index (0.522) ranks it 124th out of 174 countries. Many people still lack access to resources that would allow them to pursue personal goals.

Language

SiSwati and English are the official languages of the kingdom. SiSwati is closely related to siZulu; both are Nguni derivatives of ur-Bantu, which preceded many Bantu tongues. So closely related are siSwati and siZulu that when the British created an English name for the kingdom, they inadvertently used the siZulu pronunciation of *t* (sounds like *z*) in King Mswati II's name and devised the name *Swaziland* instead of the more accurate *Swatiland*.

English is the official language of government and education. People often mix siSwati and English in informal conversation. SiSwati spelling is not yet uniform, but it uses the same basic alphabet as English. SiSwati also employs the click, a sound made by sucking the tongue back from the upper front teeth (like a "tsk-tsk" sound in English) or from the clenched side teeth (as if urging on a horse in English). There are several clicks, represented most often by the letter *c* but also by *q* and *x* and by combinations like *ch*, *nq*, *ngc*, and others.

Religion

Swazis are primarily Christians, but they freely mix indigenous beliefs and practices with formal Christianity. Many Western churches have congregations in Swaziland, the largest of which are Roman Catholic, Anglican, and Methodist. One of the country's largest churches, with more African than Western roots, is the Zionist Christian Church. Found throughout southern Africa, Zionists are known for holding festive worship services and wearing white, green, and blue robes to church. The country's few Muslims are mostly Indians or Pakistanis.

Of the many traditional practices mixed with Christianity, consulting a *sangoma* is quite popular. A *sangoma* heals by faith or with traditional medicines, can be paid to place or remove a curse (*muti*) on someone, and is a fortune-teller.

General Attitudes

Swazis are warm and trusting. Traditionally, elders are highly respected. This continues to be a characteristic of Swazis today, except among younger urban dwellers. Although many parents cannot afford to send their children to school, education is highly valued. Many bright and capable youngsters find patrons to pay their school fees or obtain scholarships in order to continue their schooling.

Personal space is very small; people stand close when conversing or lining up. Personal privacy is not considered very important. Swazis are group oriented and gregarious. Wanting to be alone or not discussing one's personal activities with neighbors is considered antisocial.

Personal Appearance

In general, Swazis dress in contemporary Western clothing for business, recreation, and socializing. Schoolchildren wear uniforms, with specific colors for each school. It is rare and considered inappropriate for a Swazi woman to wear pants, although some urban non-Swazi women may do so. Traditionally, married women cover their heads in public, frequently with a brightly colored scarf. Swazis take pride in dressing well for shopping and social visits, and they are always neat and clean. Cleanliness extends to the home and possessions, too.

Although traditional dress is always worn for ceremonial occasions, it might also be seen in casual, business, or formal settings. The *lihiya*, a single length of printed cloth, forms the basis of Swazi traditional dress for both men and women. *Emahiya* (the plural of *lihiya*) are tied around the waist and over the upper body, across one shoulder. Men add a *lijobo*, an animal skin worn at the waist, and a traditional stick weapon known as a *knobkerrie*. Men and unmarried women decorate their hair with feathers, while married women wear distinctive domed headpieces shaped like early Swazi beehive huts. Both sexes wear beaded necklaces.

CUSTOMS AND COURTESIES

Greetings

Swazis shake hands and exchange greetings when meeting friends, acquaintances, or strangers. The most acceptable greetings are *Sawubona* when addressing one person and *Sanibonani* when addressing more than one. Both literally mean "I see you." Friends may say *Kunjani?* (How are you?). To show respect, one adds a professional title or a social title like *make* (MAH-gay) for an adult woman, *babe* (BAH-bay) for an adult man, *sisi* for a girl, and *bhuti* for a boy. *Nkhosi*, the praise name for royalty, may be used when one is unsure of a person's title. Handshakes are always with the right hand. One's left hand briefly supports one's own right forearm. When the left drops away, the speakers may continue to grasp right hands for a while. Friends make polite inquiries about health and family to begin a conversation.

Gestures

Hand gestures have great significance to Swazis. Hands add emphasis and description to spoken words. Gestures alone may also be used, such as softly touching the mouth to indicate that the speaker should talk more loudly or placing an index finger against one's mouth to indicate a request for silence. Swazis always use the right hand to offer and receive a gift, to eat, and to greet another person. Using the left hand is extremely rude, as it is traditionally reserved for cleaning after one goes to the bathroom. SiSwati has no words for "right" or "left." So, in giving directions to go left, one refers to "the side of the hand with which you do not eat."

It is improper to point one's finger at another person, especially an elderly person. When indicating a person or a grave, one uses the fist as a sign of respect. A bent finger may sometimes be acceptable. To show respect during conversation, a Swazi will speak softly and/or avoid eye contact by looking down. Public displays of affection, even between spouses, are frowned upon. Swazis use a verbal click to express exasperation.

Visiting

Swazis generally welcome both spontaneous and planned visits by family and friends on weekends, holidays, and during family celebrations. Family members are expected to stay in close touch through frequent visits, although that is changing as young urban Swazis find it expensive and time-consuming to travel often to their rural homesteads. Most visits of a few hours or even a day are spontaneous, while stays of a week or more usually are planned so that the host family can set aside housing and food and inform other family members who might wish to see the visitor.

The host family makes visitors as comfortable as possible, even setting aside an extra portion of each meal in the event that a guest may arrive. If no guest comes to eat the extra food, it is served at the following meal. Overnight visitors usually are offered accommodation in *indle Gogo* (grandmother's hut), the best and most highly respected place on the homestead. Guests generally do not bring gifts.

Eating

Traditionally there are two meals a day (morning and afternoon). Both consist of meat, vegetables, and a stiff porridge (*liphalishi*) made from maize. In a rural homestead, males eat their meals in an enclosure near the entrance to the cattle *kraal* (corral), while females eat in the kitchen. The Swazi custom is for all men to eat from a common bowl using wooden spoons, unless meat is served. Meat is eaten with the hands. Men receive the choicest cut of meat and the head. Women also share a bowl, as do boys and girls, but they are unlikely to have spoons. In more modern rural and most urban families, each individual has a separate bowl and both sexes eat under one roof.

LIFESTYLE

Family

Led by the oldest male, usually the grandfather, the Swazi family is extended and closely knit. A homestead generally includes unmarried adult children and sometimes married sons and their families. Families have an average of six children. Important family decisions, such as the marriage or burial of a family member or the purchase of an expensive item, are made by consulting several relatives. In contemporary families with younger members living away from the homestead, family consultation can be complicated, but it continues to be the basis for decision making. Women do not become as involved in these decisions until they are older or widowed.

Mothers primarily care for children, although older girls take care of younger siblings and do household chores. Fathers own all family assets, which pass to the eldest son on the death of the father. During the widow's two-year mourning period, she wears special attire and is unable to remarry. By tradition, a widow may then be taken as an additional wife by her late husband's brother. These customs are changing with modernization and greater female education.

Children take on chores at an early age. Boys usually herd the family's livestock. Cattle is an important status symbol for a family. Children are taught to respect all adults, not just their parents, but urban children may not always obey. Children often make their own toys, although a boy's favorite is any ball with which he can play soccer. When rural boys turn 18, they may build their own hut on the homestead.

A typical urban home is of masonry construction with a tile roof, an internal water system, and two to six bedrooms. A rural homestead consists of a *kraal* and three to eight single-room round or rectangular huts with thatched roofs. One hut serves as the kitchen. Water is carried from a well or river.

Dating and Marriage

Dating habits are mostly Westernized, with couples attending movies and musical events. Young women usually marry before age 25 and men before 30. Arranged marriages now are rare and are resented by most Swazis. Polygamy is legal for those families who marry according to traditional law. Swazi men wed under a more Western civil law cannot practice polygamy. Urban women prefer the Western marriage.

The common factor in all marriages, Western or traditional, is the payment of *lobola* (a dowry) by the husband's family to the bride's parents as a sign of respect and gratitude for rearing the woman who will join their family. Most families today find it impossible to pay the expected price of several head of cattle. The first two head of cattle must be the family's two best cows—one to be given to the grandmother and the other to the bride's father. It is possible to pay the two cows and then owe the rest after getting married. It may take a lifetime to pay *lobola*. One might also pay two cows plus a cash "equivalent" (in reality, lower than the value of the cattle) for the rest. Another option is to promise that any *lobola* received by the new couple's first daughter belongs to that girl's maternal grandmother; this is sometimes wrongly interpreted as the girl belonging to her grandparents. Many couples simply live together and raise a family as if married until *lobola* can be paid.

A traditional wedding is a two-day event. The bride's family brings her to the groom's home to begin the festivities. There is dancing and two beasts are slaughtered. The following day is for eating, drinking, and giving gifts to the groom's family.

Diet

In addition to maize, basic foodstuffs include fruits (oranges, bananas, and peaches) and vegetables (cabbage, spinach, and lettuce). Meat is an important part of a Swazi meal, although poorer rural families may go weeks without eating any. Modern urban dwellers may eat traditional foods but are likely to replace the porridge with rice or mashed potatoes. Their meals may also contain fruits and beans, as well as some Western foods.

Recreation

Urban Swazis play soccer, tennis, squash, volleyball, and golf. Rural Swazis perform traditional dances and play soccer. Men and women perform traditional dances separately; such dancing usually accompanies most Swazi celebrations. Schoolchildren compete in track-and-field events, *netball* (similar to basketball, for girls), and soccer (for boys). Movie theaters and nightclubs are found only in urban areas, although even small communities frequently have a *take-away* restaurant and bar for socializing. Musical events featuring performers from South Africa sometimes last all night. Swazis spend most vacations visiting family members at the traditional homestead.

Holidays

There are three major traditional Swazi events: *Lusekwane*, *Incwala*, and *Umhlanga* (Reed Dance). For *Lusekwane* in late December, young men bring branches of the *lusekwane* tree to the royal residence to build a cattle byre. *Incwala*, a few days later, is highlighted by the king tasting the new harvest's fruits. Lasting several days, it includes feasting, singing, dancing, and the slaying of a bull. *Umhlanga* takes place in late August or early September. The nation's young maidens bring bundles of reeds to the royal residence to build windbreaks. The event includes dancing and is a traditional display of marriageable girls.

New Year's Day, Easter, Ascension, Christmas, and Boxing Day (26 December) are all observed. Swaziland also marks Independence Day (6 September) and National Flag Day (25 April). Swazis celebrate the birthdays of King Mswati III (19 April) and King Sobhuza II (22 July).

Commerce

General business hours are from 8:00 A.M. to 1:00 P.M. and 2:00 P.M. to 5:00 P.M., Monday through Friday. Most businesses are also open on Saturday morning. Government offices are closed on Saturday. The government regulates certain dress standards for teachers and other civil servants.

SOCIETY

Government

Swaziland is an absolute monarchy with no written constitution. However, Parliament does act as an advisory body. In 1993, Swaziland held its first direct parliamentary elections. Fifty-five members of the 65-seat House of Assembly are now elected representatives of each *inkhundla* (constituency or district). The king appoints the other ten members, as well as all members (mostly chiefs) of the 20-seat Senate. There are no formal political parties. The appointed prime minister is Prince Jameson Mbilini Dlamini. King Mswati III is held in high regard by his people. The judicial system balances traditional Swazi laws and customs with a version of Roman-Dutch law. If a discrepancy arises between the two systems, the nontraditional courts hold precedence.

Economy

Swaziland is often referred to as the middle class of sub-Saharan Africa because it ranks among the more prosperous of the continent's developing countries. This is due to the government's stability and its support of a free-enterprise system. Swaziland actively recruits foreign investment, protects against expropriation and industry nationalization, and allows the free holding of industrial lands.

Gross domestic product per capita is $1,700. Most people are farmers. Even wage earners grow some staple crops like maize. An increasing number of women are becoming wage earners—mostly in the informal economy or in self-employed agricultural and handicraft enterprises. Expatriates once filled the bulk of skilled and managerial positions, but the emphasis has shifted toward filling these spots with local labor. This is especially important because of high unemployment.

The sugar industry is most important to Swaziland's economy. Sugarcane is produced and refined before being exported. The country also produces citrus fruits, canned fruits, cotton, vegetables, meat products, and timber. Asbestos, diamonds, and coal are mined. The currency is the *lilangeni* (E).

Transportation and Communication.

Most people travel by foot for short distances and sometimes longer ones. Buses provide public transportation both within communities and between major population centers. Traffic moves on the left side of the road. About one-fourth of all roads are paved, but secondary gravel roads are kept in good repair. The railway transports imports and exports but not passengers.

Radio and television broadcasts reach most of the country. Programs are broadcast in both siSwati and English. In some areas, South African stations are also available. Daily newspapers are in both siSwati and English. The postal system is slow but reliable. The telephone system is efficient, although many homes do not have telephones.

Education

Primary and secondary education are neither compulsory nor entirely free. Primary classes generally are taught in siSwati, but English is used exclusively from the secondary level on. For higher education, which is free for qualified students, there are two campuses of the University of Swaziland, three teacher-training colleges, two nursing colleges, various vocational institutions, and the Swaziland College of Technology. The government provides adult education to improve the literacy rate (74 percent).

Health

Six full-service hospitals are linked in a network with numerous clinics, public health centers, and health outreach facilities, assuring that 80 percent of all Swazis live within an hour's walk of health care. Government programs combat infectious diseases, promote family planning, and provide immunizations to children. Along with these programs, midwifery, faith healing, and traditional healing are common. The infant mortality rate is 91 per 1,000, and life expectancy ranges from 53 to 61 years.

FOR THE TRAVELER

U.S. citizens do not need a visa to enter Swaziland, although a valid passport is required. Tourism is a major industry; hiking and game viewing are popular. Water may not be potable outside of resorts. Although Swaziland has a warm climate all year, winter nights are cool and a jacket or sweater is needed. For more information, contact the Embassy of the Kingdom of Swaziland, 3400 International Drive, Suite 3M, Washington, DC 20004.

A *Culturgram* is a product of native commentary and original, expert analysis. Statistics are estimates and information is presented as a matter of opinion. While the editors strive for accuracy and detail, this document should not be considered strictly factual. It is a general introduction to culture, an initial step in building bridges of understanding between peoples. It may not apply to all peoples of the nation. You should therefore consult other sources for more information.

CULTURGRAM '97™

Syria

(Syrian Arab Republic)

Boundary representations not necessarily authoritative.

A S I A

BACKGROUND

Land and Climate

Syria covers 71,498 square miles (185,180 square kilometers) of territory in the Middle East. It is about the same size as Indiana and Illinois combined. The coastal region includes the coast on the Mediterranean Sea as well as the narrow range of Anti-Lebanon Mountains to the south. This western edge of Syria receives adequate rainfall. The much larger eastern region is dominated by a desert that extends from Damascus to the Euphrates River. Northeastern Syria contains fertile agricultural land. Few forests are found in the country. The disputed Golan Heights near the Israeli border are currently occupied by Israel. Summers are hot and dry. Coastal winters (December–February) are mild and rainy. The north is colder and receives some snow.

History

Syria is an ancient land with a rich cultural heritage. Aleppo is one of the world's oldest continuously inhabited cities and Damascus is one of the oldest continuously inhabited capitals. In its early history, the area was controlled by various people, including the Akkadians (2300 B.C.), Amorites (2000 B.C.), Hittites (1500 B.C.), and Assyrians (700s B.C.). For centuries, the area was a vital part of a wide commercial and political network. It was conquered by Alexander the Great in 333 B.C., ruled by his successors (the Seleucids), and then brought into the Roman Empire in 64 B.C.

Christianity was strong in Syria until the Muslim conquest in A.D. 634. The first Muslim empire, the Umayyad, ruled the expanding Islamic lands until 750. Egypt controlled the region at times until the Ottoman Empire conquered it in 1516.

Syrian territory continued to be a vital trade and political center. France governed the area under mandate after World War I. An independence movement emerged in the 1920s, but full sovereignty was not realized until 1945. Elections were held in 1947, but economic and political pressures in the new state led to unrest and a series of military coups. In 1970, Hafez al-Assad took power.

Assad rules Syria with strict control. His government maintains the martial law declared in 1963 to combat domestic dissent. In 1982, thousands died as the military crushed a fundamentalist rebellion. Running unopposed in the 1991 elections, Assad received 99 percent of the vote to gain his fourth seven-year term as president. In the past several years, President Assad has attempted to shake the country's image as a terrorist state by expelling terrorists, helping solve the hostage crisis in Lebanon, and cooperating with international forces in the Gulf War (1990–91).

Syria fought wars with Israel in 1948, 1967, and 1973. Tensions between the two nations remain over their respective military involvement in Lebanon and Israel's occupation of the Golan Heights. However, both nations are participating in the Middle East peace effort. Syria insists on the return of the Golan in exchange for peace, a very sensitive issue in Israel because of Jewish settlers in the occupied area. Other issues, including Lebanon, are also difficult to resolve; but negotiations continued in 1996 despite various setbacks. Most Syrians believe the Golan must and will be returned to Syria.

PEOPLE

Population

Syria's population of about 15.4 million is growing at 3.7 percent per year, one of the world's highest growth rates. Most Syrians (90 percent) are Arabs. The largest minorities are Kurds and Armenians. Smaller groups of Turks, Circassians, Assyrians, and some Palestinian refugees also inhabit the country. About half of all Syrians live in urban areas. Damascus has more than 1.5 million residents. Aleppo, the focal point of northern trade routes, has 1.2 million. Almost half of the population is younger than age 15.

Syria's Human Development Index (0.761) ranks it 78th out of 174 countries. Adjusted for women, the index (0.560) is much lower. These figures reflect the poverty that continues to afflict the general population, especially in rural areas. While a growing number of people have resources that allow them to pursue personal opportunities, many continue to lack access to a decent income. This is especially true of women.

Language

Arabic is Syria's official language and the native tongue of Syrian Arabs. Minorities speak Arabic as a second language. At home, they speak their native tongues of Kurdish, Armenian, Aramaic (by Assyrians), and Circassian. The educated elite often speak French, which is taught in school.

Religion

While Syria is officially a secular state, the nation's political leaders try to keep policies in line with Islamic principles. Islam is even more important in people's daily lives. About 74 percent are Sunni Muslims. Other Islamic groups (16 percent) include the Alawites, of which President Assad is a member; the Druze; and the Shiites. The Alawites are a secretive branch of Shi'a; their rites and doctrines are not well-known. Friday is the Muslim day of worship.

Christians account for 10 percent of the population; they enjoy equal political rights in Syria. Christian denominations include Greek Orthodox, Armenian Orthodox, Syrian Orthodox, Syrian Catholic, Maronites, and other smaller groups. A few thousand Jews live in Damascus and Aleppo.

General Attitudes

Syrians are dignified and proud of their heritage. Urban residents tend to be better educated, more cosmopolitan, and more liberal in their thinking. Conservative values are more prevalent in rural areas but are also preserved by many urban families. In general, Syrians admire people with higher education, fame, power, and/or wealth acquired through hard work and overtime. They appreciate someone who is nice but assertive and who has good moral values. Hypocrisy is widely disliked. Syrians have as general goals attaining a good education, buying a home (there is no financing; purchases are in cash), and having an adequate income to provide for a family. Owning a car is also an important goal. The younger generation is more influenced by Western attitudes and the desire to obtain money and luxury as quickly as possible.

Syrians are somewhat divided in their political opinions. Some want the country to become an Islamic republic; others favor more political freedom and some form of democracy.

They are very interested in the prospects for Middle East peace and generally favor a settlement over more conflict. Syrians often disagree with U.S. policy but admire U.S. Americans for their lifestyle and educational opportunities.

Personal Appearance

Syrians have traditionally dressed very conservatively, avoiding revealing attire of any kind. This attitude still dominates in rural areas, where both Muslim and Christian women cover their hair. One can often tell a woman's home region by her clothing and hair covering. Rural men might wear Western or traditional Arabic clothing. Bedouin women wear long dresses and the men wear *jalabas* (long robes) and a *keffiyah* (head covering).

Urban Syrians favor Western clothing. Men wear suits and ties, or shirts and slacks. More conservative women will wear a coat or heavy dress, dark stockings, and a head scarf over their clothing while in public. Some also wear a veil. More liberal women wear Western dresses without covering. Still, tight pants, blouses that expose the upper arm, and short skirts are considered too revealing.

CUSTOMS AND COURTESIES

Greetings

Syrians shake hands when they greet each other, although very religious individuals will not shake hands with members of the opposite sex. Men may embrace, depending on the closeness of their relationship. They might also kiss on each cheek, as do women. Men only kiss women on the cheek if they are close relatives. Children may kiss the back of their parents' or grandparents' hands as a greeting to show respect.

Greetings are very warm. Common phrases include the traditional Islamic wish *Asalaam alaykum* (Peace be upon you) and the reply *Wa alaykum Asalaam* (And peace upon you), as well as the less formal *Marhaba* (Hi). Hosts might welcome arriving guests with *Ahlan wa sahlan*. One might inquire *Keef haalak?* (How are you?) to begin a conversation.

Adults are addressed by a title and last name. If a person does not have a professional title, his or her last name is preceded by *Sayedy* (Mr.), *Sayedaty* (Mrs.), or *Anesaty* (Miss). Using a person's first name is very impolite, unless he or she is a close friend or an acquaintance who is close in age. One might appropriately refer to someone as the mother or father of their oldest son. Some educated families use the oldest daughter's name if the parents have no sons. It is also acceptable to call an older man *Aam* (uncle) or an older woman *Khaleh* (aunt), even if the speaker is not related to him or her.

Gestures

Syrians pass items with the right hand or both hands, but not the left alone. They avoid pointing at other people or using fingers to indicate direction; the entire hand is preferred. It is inappropriate to do anything with the feet that would cause them to point at another person. Hence, men cross their legs at the knee but would not rest the ankle of one leg on the knee of the other. Women do not usually cross legs in public; they sit with knees close together and covered. It is unacceptable for women to sit with knees apart unless they are wearing very loose, long skirts. In Syria, one might gesture with one's eyes to get a person's attention or even to relate information. Syrians believe eyes have a language all their own.

Visiting

Visiting family and friends is an essential aspect of Syrian society. If adult children live near their parents, they usually visit them at least weekly. Other close relatives receive a visit at least biweekly. If one lives far away or has business or professional obligations that prevent frequent visits, telephone calls are acceptable.

Visitors are warmly welcomed; even unexpected visitors are never turned away. If a phone is available to both parties, however, it is polite to call ahead. Syrians enjoy having guests and try hard to make them comfortable. They offer refreshments (usually a fruit-based juice or lemonade) or coffee and sit down to social conversation. If a visit is especially pleasant, it may extend into mealtime and the guest is invited to join the family for a meal.

Business usually is not discussed in the home; it is also inappropriate to take bad news to a family at their home. Business associates are more often entertained at restaurants. Some urban families may also receive friends at a restaurant or private club if they feel their apartments or schedules cannot accommodate entertaining at home. The host pays the entire bill at a restaurant.

Eating

The family meal is important to Syrians. Children wait for their father to come home before they all sit down to eat. Lunch (2:00–3:00 P.M.) is the main meal of the day for most families. If a non-related male is eating with a rural or very conservative urban family, the children and mother will eat separate from the men. Some foods are eaten with the hands, and others with utensils. A spoon is the most frequently used utensil.

When guests are present, hosts urge them to eat more than one helping. Guests usually decline the offer twice out of politeness before accepting the third offer. Hosts typically accept a polite decline on the third offer. Finishing one's food shows how one cares for the hosts.

During the Islamic month of *Ramadan*, Muslims do not eat or drink from sunrise to sundown each day. In the evening, meals are served and friends visit one another. During *Ramadan*, people pay special attention to the needs of the poor; business hours are also shorter.

LIFESTYLE

Family

The family is the center of an individual's life. Any individual achievements advance the entire family's reputation. Many social events are organized by and for the family. Children look to their parents as role models. They give special respect to their father who sets discipline and is the primary provider. The mother devotes herself to the children and helps them in all aspects of life. Syrians consider staying close to one's parents and showing them respect to be important. Most Syrians will not show respect to someone who treats his or her parents poorly. Because of the care they receive from their parents, children expect to provide care for them when they are elderly.

The extended family is very close and, although nuclear family households are most common in urban areas, some homes still hold more than one generation.

Dating and Marriage

While dating is becoming common in more Westernized circles, it still occurs mostly among young adults of college age and is restricted to cousins and close friends of the family. Even Westernized adults who can choose their own mates are careful to choose someone the family approves of. Among more traditional people, dating is not common and families play a dominant role in selecting marital partners for their children.

The Muslim engagement is a sign that the couple has permission to be in public together and to go on dates before getting married. It begins with dating and is formalized later by a ceremony that indicates the couple has made the final decision to marry.

Wedding customs depend on the family. Westernized families have a traditional ceremony followed by a reception in mixed company. Conservative families hold separate parties for men and women. The men have a religious ceremony, while the women enjoy music and dancing. The bride receives presents at this party, where she also changes into several party dresses before donning the white wedding dress.

Diet

Wheat is Syria's staple grain; lamb is the most popular meat. Favorite fruits include oranges, apples, grapes, figs, peaches, apricots, cherries, and plums. Breakfast often consists of Turkish coffee, cheese, yogurt, olives, eggs, bread, and tea. On Fridays or holidays, most families serve fava bean salad (with tomatoes, garlic, lemon juice and olive oil) for brunch. Cheese is made from lamb or goat milk. *Tabouk* is a popular parsley salad with cracked wheat, green onions, and tomatoes. *Kebbeh* is spiced meatballs. A *Mezza* is a table full of appetizers often served at restaurants and clubs. It includes pastes made from chick-peas and eggplant; meat (raw or grilled) dishes mixed with spices and wheat; pickles; olives; and breads. Devout Muslims do not eat pork or drink alcohol.

Recreation

Soccer is the most important sport in Syria and has an avid following. Basketball has gained popularity, especially among schoolboys. Water sports are popular in coastal cities. Women play sports (basketball, volleyball) but not competitively. Young women dance; older women enjoy exchanging recipes and doing crafts together. Visiting friends and relatives or socializing with them in a coffee shop or restaurant is a common leisure activity. Young Westernized people may go to a movie, but the older generation prefers to watch television or a video. Families enjoy outdoor activities.

Holidays

Syria's secular holidays include New Year's Day, Revolution Day (8 March), Labor Day (1 May), Martyr's Day (6 May), Egyptian Revolution Day (23 July), and Libyan Revolution Day (1 September).

Islamic holidays are set according to the lunar calendar. *Eid al-Fitr* is a three-day celebration at the end of *Ramadan*. Early-morning prayers are followed by visits to all family members, beginning with the grandparents. Children receive money and gifts, everyone gets new clothing, and people give to the poor. The four days of *Eid al-Adha* also include prayers and visiting, but Syrians slaughter a sheep to commemorate Abraham's willingness to sacrifice his son. The meat is divided three ways for the poor, the extended family, and the nuclear family. At the end, people congratulate pilgrims to Makkah, Saudi Arabia. The Birth of the Prophet Muhammad and *Ashura* (the Shiite Day of Atonement) are two other important holidays.

Christians celebrate Easter, although observances are distinctly separate between Eastern Orthodox and Western-rite faiths. Armenian Orthodox Christians celebrate Christmas on 6 January, while other Christians celebrate it on 25 December.

Commerce

Banking and government office hours are from 8:00 A.M. to 2:30 P.M., Saturday through Thursday. Businesses and stores generally open at 9:00 A.M. and close at 2:00 P.M., opening again around 4:00 P.M. for three hours. Prices are set by the government.

SOCIETY

Government

Syria is a republic comprised of 14 provinces. President Assad is chief of state and has strong executive powers. He has three vice presidents. A prime minister (Mahmud Zu'bi) is head of government. He heads a Council of Ministers (cabinet). The 250-seat legislature is called the People's Council (*Majlis al-Chaab*). Laws are generally based on Islamic law (*shari'a*). Since the 1960s, when the ruling Ba'ath Party (Arab Socialist Resurrectionist Party) came to power with an ideology of liberty, unity, and socialism, few other political elements have been able to gain much influence in Syria. Other parties exist, but Ba'ath dominates political life. The voting age is 18.

Economy

Syria has traditionally been an agricultural nation. Industrial output now accounts for most of the country's export income, but agriculture still employs about one-third of the labor force. In addition to petroleum and textiles, Syria exports cotton, fruits and vegetables, wheat, and chickens. Except for small businesses, most industries are controlled and owned by the state. These include oil refineries, utilities, the railway, and various manufacturing plants. However, the government is now allowing the private sector to share ownership of some firms. This is expected to improve production and efficiency over time.

Syria's economy experienced strong growth after the Gulf War due to international aid and investment, but the rate of growth for 1994 was only 4 percent. Inflation is more than 15 percent. Skilled labor is in short supply, which hampers industrial growth. Real gross domestic product per capita is $4,960. Many families require two or three jobs to meet basic expenses, and a significant portion of the population does not have access to the benefits of economic prosperity.

Transportation and Communication

Syria's location has long made it a crossroads for the region. It has two major ports, Tartùs and Latakia, and two international airports (at Damascus and Aleppo). An adequate system of roads and railways serves the country, but public transportation (mainly buses) is inefficient. Urban families often have cars. Service taxis and microbuses are available in larger cities; they run along set routes and pick up passengers until full. They also travel between cities. In rural areas, agricultural products are transported by donkey.

Most urban homes have telephones and televisions. The government owns the one television and radio station in Syria, but people have access to international broadcasts through satellite dishes, especially in Damascus.

Education

The bulk of all students are enrolled in public schools, but private religious and private secular schools also operate in Syria. Children attend six years of primary school, three years of middle school, and three years of high school. Until recently, up to one-fourth of all students dropped out after only a few years. This is now illegal and most children complete at least the required nine years prior to high school. The adult literacy rate is 68 percent. For women it is only 51 percent, reflecting a traditional bias against sending girls to school. The literacy rate is higher among the current generation of pupils. Parents who can afford it often pay for private tutors to supplement their children's public education.

Students often enroll in vocational training or work in a family business after their formal schooling. Others prepare for higher education. Syria has four universities located in Damascus, Aleppo, and Latakia. The Institute of Petroleum and Chemical Engineering in Hims also offers professional training.

Health

Syria's government provides free health care to its citizens, but private care is of higher quality and is preferred by those who can afford it. Government facilities often lack modern equipment and adequate supplies, especially in rural areas. Sanitation is often poor. Poverty, ignorance about free immunizations provided by the government, and malnutrition contribute to the country's high infant mortality rate of 41 per 1,000. The life expectancy rate averages 67 years.

FOR THE TRAVELER

U.S. citizens must have a valid passport and visa to visit Syria. A transit visa is available upon arrival for those staying up to three days, but visas must be obtained in advance for longer visits. Water is not potable and should be boiled or treated for all purposes, including brushing the teeth. Meat should be well cooked and hot, and it is best to cook all vegetables and peel all fruits. For recommended health precautions or immunizations, call the Centers for Disease Control international travelers' hotline: (404) 332–4559. Tipping at hotels or restaurants will improve service; a tip may initially be refused but will be accepted on the second or third offer.

Syria is a contrast of ancient mosques and castles, museums, and modern nightlife. The *Souk Al Hamedica* in Damascus is one of the world's oldest markets. For tourist information, contact the Embassy of the Syrian Arab Republic, 2215 Wyoming Avenue NW, Washington, DC 20008; phone (202) 232–6313. Or write to the Ministry of Tourism, Furat Street, Damascus, Syria.

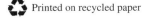 Printed on recycled paper

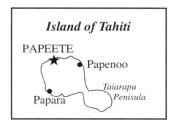

Island of Tahiti

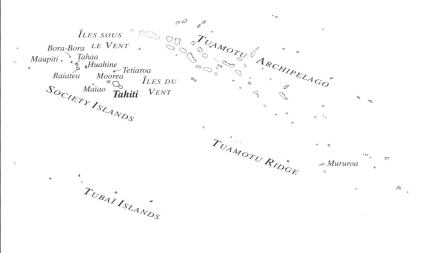

Tahiti

(French Polynesia)

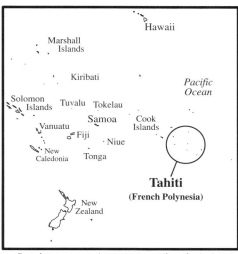

Boundary representations not necessarily authoritative.

BACKGROUND

Land and Climate

Tahiti is part of the Society Islands, which are part of French Polynesia, a self-governing territory of France. The Society Islands include the groups of *Îles sous le Vent* (Leeward Islands) and *Îles du Vent* (Windward Islands). Tahiti is part of the latter group and is the main inhabited island in the Society Islands. Tahiti is the anchor of the islands, which are also collectively referred to as "Tahiti and her islands." French Polynesia actually stretches across a wide area of the Pacific Ocean about halfway between California and Australia. The territory includes five archipelagos: the two groups of the Society Islands, the Marquesas Islands, the Tuamotu Archipelago, and the Tubuaï Islands. This *Culturgram* focuses culturally on Tahitian society, but much of the information is applicable to neighboring islands. Statistical information concerns French Polynesia as a whole.

French Polynesia's 130 islands extend over an area as large as Europe, but their combined land area is only slightly larger than Rhode Island (1,413 square miles or 3,660 square kilometers). The Society Islands are a blend of volcanic peaks and lush tropical forests. White, sandy beaches surround each island. Coral reefs provide quiet lagoons of crystal-clear waters in all the groups except the Marquesas. The other Society Islands include Bora-Bora (famous for its lagoons and two volcanic peaks), Huahine, Maïao, Maupiti, Moorea, Raiatea, Tahaa, and Tetiaroa (owned by Marlon Brando). Tahiti's climate is subtropical, tempered by trade winds throughout the year. January and February are the hottest months, with temperatures between 85°F and 90°F (29–32°C). Otherwise, temperatures average between 70°F and 80°F (21–27°C).

History

Tahiti and most of French Polynesia was initially inhabited by Polynesians, although their exact origin is not certain. They began to settle on Pacific islands between 2000 and 1000 B.C. The first Polynesians probably reached the Society Islands in the third century A.D. Before European colonization, the islands were ruled by local chiefs. Englishman Samuel Wallis charted and claimed the islands for Britain in 1767. In 1768, they were claimed by the French, but it was some time before Europeans actually began to settle on Tahiti. In 1769, England's Captain James Cook came to the island. The crew of the *Bounty* mutinied against their commander, Captain William Bligh, and escaped to the islands in 1788.

OCEANIA

The Pomare Dynasty reigned on Tahiti until Queen Pomare IV signed a treaty with France (1843), making Tahiti a French protectorate in exchange for help in bringing neighboring islands under her control. Her son (Pomare V) abdicated in 1880 and the islands became a colony of France. Territorial status was granted in 1957; internal self-rule was obtained in 1977.

Tahiti was known more for tourism than anything else for the next several years. In September 1995, the usually tranquil streets of the capital, Papeete, were rocked with riots sparked by France's resumption of it nuclear testing program. France eventually exploded six bombs underwater at the Mururoa atoll, a practice that provoked international condemnation and created considerable unease in Tahiti. Pro-independence groups gained some strength by the event. In June 1996, the leading pro-independence party Tavini Huiraatira was banned from staging a protest for fear another riot might erupt. All of the unrest, not to mention substantial damage done during the September riots, harmed the tourist industry and threatened economic stability.

THE PEOPLE

Population

Approximately 220,000 people live in French Polynesia. More than half (about 127,000) live on Tahiti. Papeete, the capital of French Polynesia, is the largest city, with more than 80,000 residents in and around it. The population grows at 2.2 percent annually. Polynesians account for most of the population: 78 percent. However, many Polynesians have a mixed heritage that includes either Chinese or European ancestry. About 12 percent of the people are Chinese, forming primarily a merchant class. They are descendants of laborers imported in the 19th century to work in a new cotton industry. The venture failed, but the laborers settled down. Locally born French citizens account for 6 percent of the population, and native French or other Europeans comprise 4 percent.

Language

French is the official language in the territory. It is used exclusively in the schools and is spoken widely on Tahiti. Tahitian, however, is an official regional language for the Society Islands. It remains the language used by the majority of the people and is spoken in the home, especially on the other Society Islands. The Tahitian alphabet has 13 letters. All syllables end with a vowel. The Chinese community speaks the Hakka variety of Chinese or French or Tahitian. One's proficiency in the French language affects one's economic status. English is not widely spoken, although it is understood in tourist areas. Each of the different island groups in French Polynesia has its own language. Some are similar to Tahitian and others are very different.

Religion

Tahitians no longer worship the many gods of nature they once did, but they are still influenced by traditional beliefs. Missionaries from the London Missionary Society arrived just before the end of the 18th century and other Christian missionaries soon followed. The people embraced Christianity and are deeply religious today. Currently, 55 percent of the population is Protestant (converts to the Evangelical Church represented by the London Missionary Society). About 30 percent is Roman Catholic; 6 percent belongs to the Church of Jesus Christ of Latter-day Saints (Mormons); and 2 percent is Seventh-Day Adventist. White is the most common color worn for Sunday services. A variety of other Christian religions, as well as Judaism and Buddhism, are represented on the island.

General Attitudes

Tahitians value personal relations and are warm and receptive, although they may seem shy to strangers before they become better acquainted. They enjoy life and try to live as simply and happily as possible. Time is more flexible in Tahiti than in most industrialized nations—people are more important than schedules and life is lived at a more casual pace. Still, the West has influenced society and the pace of life is quicker than it once was, especially in Papeete.

Personal Appearance

Lightweight, informal clothing is worn throughout the year. Clothing is always neat and clean. Footwear for both men and women is usually a pair of thongs or sandals without stockings or hose. Dresses of *pareu* cloth are worn at home and at the beach. Women usually wear dresses instead of shorts. Although Tahitians are at home in Western-style clothing, they continue to wear more traditional clothing made from simple cloth wrapped around the waist.

Many visitors know the Tahitians for their traditional dance costumes, which they wear for special occasions or performances. There are many types of these costumes, but some include skirts made of grass *(more)* or cotton fabrics. Local plants and grasses are used for headdresses, belts, and necklaces. Dyes are extracted from hibiscus flowers and other plants. *Puroutu* (missionary dresses) more fully clothe a woman and are worn by those performing slow hula dances.

CUSTOMS AND COURTESIES

Greetings

Tahitians shake hands when they meet and use French greetings such as *Bonjour* (Good day) in formal situations. If one's hand is dirty, one offers a wrist, elbow, or even a shoulder instead. It is impolite not to shake hands with every person in a small gathering (fewer than 30 people). Women might kiss each other on the cheeks when greeting, especially after a long separation. A traditional Tahitian phrase of welcome is *Ia ora!*

Gestures

People beckon by waving all fingers with the palm down. Pointing with the index finger may be considered rude. The most commonly understood gesture in Tahiti is a smile.

Visiting

Tahitians (and French Polynesians in general) emphasize *joie de vivre*, or "joy of life." They are relaxed, natural, and invariably try to make their guests comfortable. A favorite maxim is, "If you act like old friends when you first meet, you will soon feel that you are," and Tahitians try to make that maxim a practice. Guests are free to compliment their hosts on their home or family, but they should avoid singling out any one object or item of decor. Otherwise, the host may be embarrassed. It is customary to remove one's shoes before entering the home.

Eating

Tahiti enjoys a great variety of culinary choices, with excellent French and Chinese cuisine in addition to traditional native foods. Western dishes are also readily available. Etiquette varies greatly depending on the food and the family. Traditional Tahitian foods are eaten with the fingers, while Chinese food is eaten with chopsticks. Utensils are supplied on request and are used in the continental fashion—with the fork in the left hand and the knife remaining in the right.

It is impolite for guests to refuse food or make excuses for not eating. However, politeness does not require a person to eat everything on the plate. Leaving a little extra will ensure that a second (or third) helping is not served and will satisfy the host that the guest has been well fed. Sometimes, guests are offered a meal and the host family will not join in eating. Guests are expected to accept the invitation and not mind if the family watches. In restaurants, tipping is not customary and is discouraged because it violates the tradition of Tahitian hospitality.

LIFESTYLE

Family

Traditionally, Tahitian families were large, usually with many children and several generations living under the same roof. It is still common for couples to live with the husband's or wife's parents for a time after marriage, but increased contact with Western culture is leading to more nuclear families. Still, family ties are strong. In Polynesian culture, children are precious and their upbringing is often shared by grandparents or other sets of adoptive parents *(faamu)*. This system of informal adoption remains active today, making family relations somewhat complex.

Dating and Marriage

In most Polynesian cultures, girls are more closely supervised than boys. Dating, as practiced in Western societies, is generally not found in French Polynesia, except among the French youth and perhaps in Papeete. Tahitians usually get together in groups to dance, sing, talk, or participate in sports. Marriages traditionally are influenced by the families, who used to make decisions based partially on social class. However, classes no longer exist and youth have greater freedom in choosing spouses. Marriages are a festive time for feasting and merrymaking.

Diet

Tahitians eat three meals a day. A light breakfast consists of bread and a hot drink. Supper in the evening is also a light meal (except at restaurants and parties). The main meal is at midday. The Tahitian diet consists of fish and other seafood, chicken, pork, sweet potatoes, breadfruit, rice, and local fruits and vegetables. *Poisson cru* is uncooked fish marinated in lime juice, often served as part of salads. Fruits include papayas, mangoes, pineapples, and bananas. A type of spinach *(fafa)* is also common. Banana or papaya purées *(poe')* are popular as desserts. They are baked, covered with sugar and coconut milk, and served hot. Coconut milk also covers a popular chicken and pork casserole that includes *fafa*. Fish is often marinated before being baked or grilled. *Tamaaraa* is a Tahitian feast common at parties and in resort areas.

Recreation

Recreation is of prime importance in the life of a French Polynesian. Sports, television, movies, and dances are popular ways to spend leisure time. Soccer is the national sport. Boxing, volleyball, basketball, and cycling are enjoyed. Canoeing, wind surfing, swimming, fishing, and diving top a long list of popular water sports. Because Tahiti is a tourist location, recreation can be a way of life for many who work in the travel industry.

Holidays

National holidays include New Year's Day, Easter Monday, Labor Day (1 May), Ascension, Pentecost Monday, National Bastille Day (14 July), Assumption of Virgin Mary (15 August), *Toussaint* (All Saints' Day on 1 November), Veterans' Day (11 November), and Christmas. Bastille Day, the French national holiday, is celebrated during the middle two weeks of July and is known as the *Tiurai* (meaning July). It is considered the most spectacular celebration of the year. Celebrations include parades, athletic competitions, dancing, pageantry, and cultural events. The festivities do not necessarily honor the French but commemorate Polynesian warriors and Tahitian culture. Dance and song competitions are popular, especially during *Heiva Taupiti*, a season of celebrations that begins in May and culminates with *Tiurai*.

Commerce

Government offices are open from 7:30 A.M. to 3:30 P.M. Most stores open from 7:30 to 11:30 A.M. and from 2:00 to 5:30 P.M. Chinese shops are often open from 5:30 A.M. to 10:00 P.M., seven days a week. Other stores are generally closed on Sunday, although Sunday morning is the most important day at the Papeete market, where local merchants sell food, crafts, and flowers.

SOCIETY

Government

French Polynesia is a territory of France and is governed by French authorities. The chief of state is France's president, Jacques Chirac. He is represented in French Polynesia by a French high commissioner. The territory has two representatives in France's National Assembly and one in France's Senate. Locally, a Territorial Assembly with 41 elected members chooses a president to be head of government. Gaston Flosse was elected in 1991 as president of the territorial government.

Two main political parties, the People's Rally for the Republic and the Polynesian Union Party, are joined by a number of smaller parties in the Territorial Assembly. Pro-independence parties have made some gains in the past few years, but they are still weak compared to the major parties. Flosse is a member of the People's Rally for the Republic Party, which is a pro-French organization. The voting age is 18.

Economy

French Polynesia's economy is strongly linked to tourism and the *Centre Experimental du Pacifique* (CEP), France's nuclear testing program. The CEP is coordinated by the French military, which employs a large portion of the labor force. Agriculture is important, producing copra and coconut oil (80 percent of all export earnings), mother-of-pearl (14 percent of exports), vanilla, and various foods for domestic consumption. Tourism is a crucial source of foreign-exchange earnings and much of the labor force is employed by the tourist industry. As a result, tourist facilities are nearly always being improved or built. The economy, once reliant on subsistence agriculture, now provides most people with a decent standard of living. The estimated gross national product per capita is $7,000. The currency is the *Comptoirs Français du Pacifique franc* or *CFP franc*.

Transportation and Communication

Tahiti is linked to other countries by a number of airlines, and small commuter airlines provide efficient domestic service. Motorbikes and cars are the most common form of private, local transportation. Buses are numerous and keep fairly regular schedules. *Le truck* is a popular form of local transportation that carries passengers to various locations on Tahiti. In keeping with the people's tradition of hospitality, tipping taxi drivers or other service personnel is not acceptable. Ferry services operate between some islands. Telecommunication systems are adequate for interisland and international communication.

Education

The French government has established primary, secondary, and vocational schools on the islands that comply with French educational standards. School is compulsory and free from ages six to fourteen. Primary education lasts until age 11 and secondary to age 18. At age 14, students enter various tracks depending on their aptitude and choice. Private schools are heavily subsidized by the government and follow a public school curriculum. Adult education programs are popular and free. Many students travel to France or other countries for higher education. Nearly all (98 percent) of Tahiti's young people can read and write.

Health

Medical services are subsidized by the government and are adequate for most needs. Two major hospitals and several private clinics are located on Tahiti, but facilities are limited on other islands. Still, throughout the territory, health conditions are generally good and improving. The infant mortality rate is 15 per 1,000. Life expectancy ranges from 68 to 73 years.

FOR THE TRAVELER

A passport is necessary for U.S. citizens to visit the islands; visas are not required for stays of up to one month. No vaccinations are necessary for Tahiti, which is generally free of tropical diseases, but health certificates may be required of those entering from yellow fever endemic zones. Tahiti has an excellent tourist industry. The islands offer beauty, warmth, and relaxation. For detailed information, contact the Tahiti Tourist Promotion Board, 300 North Continental Boulevard, Suite 180, El Segundo, CA 90245; phone (310) 414–8484. You may also wish to contact the Embassy of France, which is responsible for the diplomatic affairs of French Polynesia: 4101 Reservoir Road NW, Washington, DC 20007–2186; phone (202) 944–6200.

Taiwan
(Republic of China)

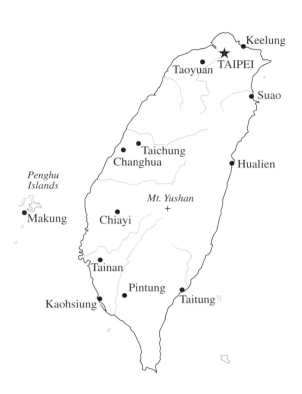

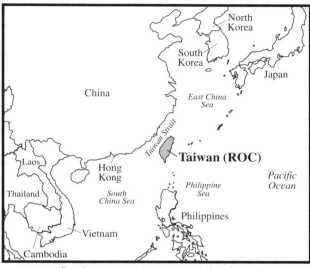

Boundary representations not necessarily authoritative.

ASIA

BACKGROUND

Land and Climate

Covering 13,892 square miles (35,980 square kilometers), Taiwan is about the size of Massachusetts and Connecticut combined. It is located about 100 miles (160 kilometers) east of mainland China. The government on Taiwan also controls the Penghu Islands and other islands near China's coast (Chinmen, Matsu, and Wuchiu). A north-south mountain range forms the backbone of Taiwan. The highest peak, Yushan, rises 13,110 feet (3,996 meters) above sea level. The western half of Taiwan contains the greater population and most of the agricultural activity. Taiwan's climate is subtropical. In the north, the warm, humid summer lasts from May to October. January and February can be cold and rainy; some snow falls at higher elevations. Southern Taiwan is warmer, with rain mostly in the summer. Taiwan experiences numerous small earthquakes each year. Typhoons are possible from June to October. The average temperature is 75°F (24°C).

History

Chinese immigration to Taiwan began as early as the T'ang Dynasty (A.D. 618–907). In 1628, the Dutch took control of the island. In 1683, the Manchus of mainland China conquered the island and made it a province of China. The island was ceded to Japan following the Sino-Japanese War (1895) and remained under Japanese control until 1945. During that period, forces on mainland China battled for control of the government. A successful revolution inspired by Sun Yat-sen founded the Republic of China (ROC), but the new government was overshadowed by a period of contending warlords. Sun's *Kuomingtang* (KMT) political movement was led by Chiang Kai-shek after Sun died (1925). Chiang battled the Communist forces of Mao Zedong, and they both fought against a Japanese invasion. After Japan was defeated, civil war continued and Chiang's forces fled from Mao's army, establishing the ROC government on Taiwan.

Chiang's KMT-led government declared itself the legitimate government of all of China and established a policy to eventually reunite with the mainland. Plans by the People's Republic of China (PRC) to invade the island were blocked in 1950 by the United States. In 1954, the United States signed an agreement to protect Taiwan in case of attack from the mainland. The United States and much of the world recognized the ROC claim to legitimacy.

In 1971, however, the PRC was admitted to the United Nations in Taiwan's place. In 1979, the United States also normalized diplomatic relations with the PRC and broke them with the ROC. Relations between the United States and Taiwan continue on an unofficial basis. In fact, many countries have only informal political ties to Taiwan, while they enjoy relatively strong economic relations.

The KMT ruled Taiwan as a one-party state under martial law. Its National Assembly members took office in 1946 on the mainland and held power until the late 1980s when political reforms led to most lifetime legislators' retirement. After

Chiang Kai-shek died in 1975, his son Chiang Ching-kuo replaced him as president. Taiwan directed its greatest efforts at modernization and developed a thriving economy. Martial law was lifted in 1987 and various reforms allowed a multiparty democracy to begin emerging in 1989. Lee Teng-hui was elected president by the National Assembly in 1990. He is the first native Taiwanese to lead the country. Multiparty legislative elections were held for the first time in December 1991. Lien Chan became premier.

The ROC remains in a technical state of war with the PRC, and two years of military service is required of all young men. For many years, the ROC refused all contact with the PRC, but this began to change after 1987 when trade and communication restrictions were eased. Political debate prior to the country's first direct presidential elections in 1986 centered on the ROC's future relationship with the PRC. The PRC opposes calls on Taiwan for independence, but most people in the ROC also oppose reunification with the PRC. Tensions increased in the weeks leading to the election, and the PRC even sponsored provocative war games in the Taiwan Strait to intimidate ROC voters and leaders. In the end, peaceful elections returned President Lee to office and the PRC concluded its games without a major incident. Both nations called for dialogue and some form of cooperation. The 1996 elections marked the first time in all of China's history that the people were allowed to directly elect a president.

THE PEOPLE

Population

The population of Taiwan is 21.5 million. It is growing annually at slightly less than 1 percent. The original inhabitants of Taiwan make up only 2 percent of the population. They are divided among several ethnic groups, some of which maintain their languages and traditions. The rest of the people are ethnic Chinese. They include Taiwanese (84 percent) and mainland Chinese (14 percent). The latter group migrated to the island after World War II. The Taiwanese are descendants of migrants who left China between the 17th and 19th centuries. As the mainland Chinese who came after 1947 pass away, their children (with no memory of the mainland) feel that Taiwan is their real home.

Language

The official language is Mandarin Chinese. However, the majority of the people also speak Taiwanese, the language of the first Chinese immigrants. Hakka, another Chinese dialect, is also spoken. Some older people speak Japanese and the aborigines speak their own native languages. English is a popular second or third language for students and is widely understood in urban areas. Although the official language of Taiwan and mainland China is the same (Mandarin), vocabulary and idiomatic differences exist. In Taiwan, school children use a simplified character system that helps them "sound out" a word—something impossible to do with standard characters, which must be memorized.

Various systems of romanization (representing Chinese characters and words in Roman letters) have been developed by Westerners and adopted by the government to help Westerners who cannot read Chinese characters sound out names, read signs, and follow maps. The average Chinese would not understand or use romanization. Romanizations differ; for example, the character for "please" can be written *Quing* or *Ching*, depending on the romanization.

Chinese is a tonal language. Each written character can have up to five different meanings, depending on the tone with which it is spoken. For instance, *Ma* can mean "horse" or "mother," and can even function as a question mark, all depending on the specific tone (voice inflection) used.

Religion

Ninety-three percent of the people practice a combination of Buddhism, Confucianism, and Taoism. Confucianism, while emphasizing ancestor veneration, does not proclaim loyalty to any specific deity. It orders social patterns and relationships, forming the Chinese value system. Worship rituals and beliefs come mainly from Buddhism. About 5 percent of the people follow Christianity, in various forms. Some important Chinese figures, such as Sun Yat-sen, have been Christians. Freedom of religion is guaranteed in Taiwan.

General Attitudes

People in Taiwan are generally reserved, quiet, refined, and friendly. Frankness or abruptness, especially in offering criticism of any kind, is avoided. Causing public embarrassment or bringing shame to anyone (a "loss of face") is unacceptable. Loud, tacky, or boisterous behavior is usually regarded as being in poor taste. The Confucian ethic of proper social and family relationships form the foundation of Chinese society. Schools and government foster the tradition of respect for, and obedience to, parents. Moral standards are generally high. Traditionally, men and women do not show affection in public, although this is changing in the larger urban areas. An individual's actions reflect on the entire family, and people act with this in mind.

Taiwan is a changing society; new social patterns are developing. This causes tension with traditional ideas, but people are adjusting to new concepts. In Taiwan, Westerners are treated with special courtesy and respect; those who return that courtesy are appreciated.

Personal Appearance

Western-style clothing is the norm in Taiwan. The youth, especially in large urban areas, enjoy the latest fashions. Most adults appreciate conservative clothing. Western suits and ties are most common for businessmen. Women wear dresses more often than do women in the United States. Cleanliness and neatness are the most important factors in appearance.

CUSTOMS AND COURTESIES

Greetings

Asking others if they have eaten *(Chr bau le meiyou?)* is a common Chinese greeting. The greeting stems from the tradition to never let anyone go hungry; it was always polite to ask if others had eaten and offer them a meal. Today it is used simply as a "How are you?" Other common greetings are *Ni hau ma?* (Are you at peace?), *Hai hau ma?* (Is everything okay?), and *Ching dzwo* (Please sit), which is spoken to visitors to the home. After initial greetings, polite questions may follow. Adults often ask young people about their schoolwork; the elderly appreciate inquiries about their health.

A nod of one's head and a smile are considered appropriate when meeting someone for the first time, but for acquaintances and close friends, a handshake is most common. A slight bow shows respect. Chinese names are arranged with the family name first, consisting of one or two syllables. A one- or two-syllable given name follows. People generally address others by their full name. Only in rare cases are given names used alone. If speaking to someone in English, one uses a title with the surname, such as "Dr. Yu" or "Mr. Lee."

Gestures

One uses the open hand to point; using the index finger is rude. Beckoning is done by waving all fingers with the palm down. People commonly "write" a character in the air when explaining it. It is common for young female friends to hold hands in public. Putting one's arm around the shoulder of another is often inappropriate. Shaking one hand from side to side with the palm forward means "no." People do not use their feet to move objects such as chairs or doors. While sitting, one places the hands in the lap. Winking is impolite. One hands an object to another person, especially an older person, with both hands. In conversation, a person referring to himself points to his nose.

Visiting

People usually remove their shoes before entering a home, and they wear slippers inside. Guests recognize and greet the elderly first. Visitors are likely to receive tea, candy, fruit, or a soft drink. Dinner conversation often centers on the meal—how it was prepared, what ingredients were used, and where they were obtained. When guests leave, the host often escorts them some distance from the home. To this, the guests offer some token resistance and thank the host graciously for the hospitality.

When one visits a home for the first time, presenting a small gift, such as fruit, is appropriate. Gifts are also given to hosts during New Year's celebrations. People use both hands when exchanging gifts or other items. Gifts are not opened in the presence of the giver. Hosts and guests appreciate sincere compliments but will politely deny them out of modesty. Visitors should not admire an object too much, as the host may feel obligated to present it as a gift. It is polite to stand when a guest, a superior, or an elderly person enters a room.

Eating

Chopsticks and a soup spoon are the common eating utensils in Taiwan. Food is placed in the center of the table. Each person at the table is given a personal bowl of rice. They are served or serve themselves from the dish(es) at the center of the table, placing small amounts of food in the rice bowl. They hold the bowl near the mouth and eat the food and rice with chopsticks. Diners take from the main dish as often as necessary to complement the rice. Bones and seeds are placed on the table or on a provided plate but never in the bowl of rice or on a plate of food. When the rice bowl is empty, it is refilled. Leaving rice in the bowl is impolite. Children are taught to finish all of their food out of respect for farmers and parents. When finished, a person places the chopsticks side by side on the table.

At a restaurant, a host expects to pay. Guests may offer politely to help but should not insist. If using a toothpick, one covers the mouth with the other hand. It is not proper for adults to eat while walking on the street.

LIFESTYLE

Family

Families in Taiwan have traditionally been large, but a government family-planning program encourages families to have only two children. An education campaign has reduced population growth and the size of today's nuclear family. It is not uncommon for elderly parents to live with their children. In rural areas, larger extended families often share the same home. Although family members do not openly display affection in the Western manner, families have a deep-rooted unity and sense of obligation to each other. Family members will agree rather than cause disunity in the family. The family as a unit also maintains control over the individual. Children generally yield to the counsel of their parents or to the advice of the oldest member of the extended family.

Dating and Marriage

Except perhaps in urban areas, Western-style dating is not common in Taiwan. Students concentrate on their education and associate with peers but seldom date as couples. Dating generally begins once they are working or pursuing higher education. Those who do date enjoy going to movies or dining at restaurants. People usually date only one person at a time. Men generally marry between the ages of 27 and 30, and women about three years earlier.

Diet

Rice is eaten with nearly every meal. Soup, seafood, pork, chicken, vegetables, and fruit are common foods, as are noodles and breads. Sauces are an important part of each meal. Most foods, including vegetables, are stir-fried. Tea is often served with the meal. Mealtime is important in the family and is seldom missed.

Recreation

The most popular forms of recreation are watching movies, going on picnics, listening to music, and hiking. People also enjoy basketball, ping pong, volleyball, baseball, badminton, tennis, and soccer. Baseball is extremely popular among the youth, and Taiwan's Little League champions consistently do well in the Little League World Series. Taiwan has a professional baseball league. The elderly enjoy shadowboxing as a form of exercise and relaxation.

Holidays

Different calendars are used in Taiwan for different reasons. The Western (Gregorian) monthly calendar is used for official purposes, and political holidays are scheduled accordingly. However, the year in Taiwan does not correspond to the year in the West. Rather than beginning from the birth of Christ (the A.D. system), the Chinese traditionally begin a new year system for each dynasty or republic. The current republic officially began in China under Sun Yat-sen in 1912. Therefore, 1997 is the year 86 in Taiwan. Official holidays include the ROC's Founding Day (1 January), Youth Day (29 March), Chiang Kai-shek's death (5 April), the Birth of Confucius and Teacher's Day (28 September), Double Ten National Day (10 October), Sun Yat-sen's Birthday (12 November), and Constitution Day (25 December).

The Chinese lunar calendar determines Buddhist holidays and the most important celebration of the year, the New Year. It usually falls in February and is celebrated with fireworks, feasts, and worship at various temples. Ancestors are venerated and children receive money in special red envelopes from their elders. The summer Dragon Boat Festival is also popular.

Commerce

A five- or six-day, 44-hour workweek is common for wage earners. The traditional break from noon to 1:00 P.M. is being discouraged. Many families own small retail or service shops and have their homes above or near the store. These stores may open as early as 7:00 A.M. and remain open until 10:00 or 11:00 P.M. Family members take turns working in the store. People can purchase food and other supplies at these stores, but they are more likely to shop at larger grocery and department stores. Night markets are popular in some areas. Held outdoors, they feature prepared foods, entertainment, and consumer goods.

SOCIETY

Government

Taiwan is a multiparty democracy. It is administered through sixteen counties (*hsien*), five municipalities (*shih*), and two special municipalities (*chuan-shih*): Taipei and Kaohsiung. The president is chief of state and the premier is head of government. The legislature is composed of a Legislative *Yuan* and a National Assembly. The first National Assembly seated in 1946 included "representatives" of provinces in China. This was part of the Nationalist leadership's claim to authority over China. The current National Assembly is comprised of representatives for Taiwan only. The three largest political parties include the Nationalist Party (KMT), the Democratic Progressive Party (DPP), and the New Party (NP). Elections for the Legislative Yuan are held at different intervals than for the National Assembly. The voting age is 20.

Economy

Taiwan has maintained dynamic growth for three decades, averaging more than 5 percent every year. Incomes have grown steadily to the point that a strong middle class enjoys a relatively high standard of living. Taiwan is in the top 20 percent of trading nations and is a major exporter of textiles, electronics, machinery, metals, timber products, and high-technology items. It is also a major international investor, especially in Asia. Taiwan's early growth was fueled by a very efficient agricultural sector and then by adaptable cottage industries. The system created a broad base that could easily adapt to global economic trends, allowing Taiwan to avoid the negative impact of world economic fluctuations. Taiwan's economy remains strong; its foreign reserves are among the largest in the world. Unemployment and inflation are both low, and the average annual gross national product per capita is estimated to be more than $12,000.

Taiwan's wealth allowed it to announce, in 1991, a six-year, $300-billion modernization program that has been significantly improving everything from schools to sewer systems to roads. Many foreign companies have major contracts to help complete these projects. The currency is the New Taiwan dollar (NT$).

Transportation and Communication

In the early 1980s, only the wealthy owned cars, especially given the 100 percent import tax. Most people traveled by motorcycle, motorized bicycles, bicycles, and public transportation. Buses and trains were heavily used. Today, many more people own cars (the import tax was reduced and incomes are higher), and traffic jams are much more prevalent. A rapid transit system is being developed to alleviate congestion. Taxis are readily available and reasonably priced. In rural areas, walking and riding bicycles are still important. Most people in cities have a telephone, while rural inhabitants have access to public phones. Past restrictions on the press were eliminated by 1994, and private radio, television, and newspaper concerns are free to operate.

Education

Education is very important in Taiwan. Schooling is free and compulsory for nine years (to age 15), but plans are being implemented to extend the requirement to twelve years. Most people welcome this change because they believe it will further Taiwan's economic development. Entrance to universities is determined by examinations given each July. Students work hard to prepare for these exams, sometimes studying sixteen hours a day, seven days a week, for an entire year. While many students travel abroad for higher education, university and other higher education facilities in Taiwan are good and more students are remaining in Taiwan. The adult literacy rate is 86 percent (92 percent for men). Taiwan's education system has produced a highly skilled labor force.

Health

Taiwan has a modern health-care system. Private insurance programs cover the needs of most, and the government provides care for those who cannot afford it. A new regionalization system, designed to create public health facilities and offer basic care to all people, is being established. The infant mortality rate is 6 per 1,000. Life expectancy ranges from 72 to 78 years.

FOR THE TRAVELER

A visa and valid passport are required for U.S. travelers staying more than two weeks. A transit visa is issued on arrival for those staying less than two weeks. AIDS test are mandatory for those staying more than three months. No vaccinations are necessary. Boiled or bottled water is recommended. Many national treasures that likely would have been destroyed during China's Cultural Revolution, had they remained in the PRC, are displayed at the National Palace Museum. The ROC has not only preserved much of the Chinese culture, but it has also developed a culture of its own. Do not take photographs inside Buddhist temples without permission. For more information, contact the Taiwan Visitors' Association, 166 Geary Street, Suite 1605, San Francisco, CA 94108; phone (415) 989–8677. You may also contact the Taipei Economic and Cultural Representative Office (TECRO), 4201 Wisconsin Avenue NW, Washington, DC 20016–2137; phone (202) 895–1800. TECRO also has offices in several major U.S. cities.

The Republic of

Tajikistan

Boundary representations not necessarily authoritative.

ASIA

BACKGROUND

Land and Climate

The Republic of Tajikistan (*Tojikiston*) covers 55,251 square miles (143,100 square kilometers) and is slightly smaller than Wisconsin. However, most of the land is mountainous and crossed by jagged peaks, the highest of which is Peak Communism at 25,548 feet (7,787 meters). The most abundant natural resources, minerals and hydroelectric power, are found in the Tien-Shan and Pamir Mountains, the highest ranges in central Asia. Animals in the Pamirs must grow large to counter the cold; among those found in this desolate land are the world's largest bears, cattle (the yak), and sheep (the Marco Polo).

Tajikistan's climate varies considerably according to altitude. In northern lowlands, the average temperature in January is 30°F (-1°C) and in July is 81°F (27°C). Temperature variation in southern lowlands is more extreme, with summers as hot as 122°F (50°C). Mountain winter temperatures are often as low as -51°F (-46°C). Rainfall is moderate in the valleys. Heavy snow closes mountain passes five months of the year.

History

Ancestors of the Tajiks had developed an advanced civilization in central Asia as early as 2100 B.C. More recent ancestors include the east Iranian peoples who inhabited the Persian Empire's tributary states of Bactria and Sogdiana in the sixth and seventh centuries B.C. In 329 B.C., Alexander the Great founded Alexander-the-farthest, the present-day city of Khojand. Arab invaders later followed Alexander. During the ensuing centuries, this area was part of a much larger territory later referred to as Turkestan, an affluent center of world trade. Caravans loaded with silk and spices from China and India followed the Silk Road on their way to Asia Minor and Europe. The trade route brought with it many conquerers, including Ghengis Khan.

Over the centuries, the Tajiks developed an impressive culture, often adopting the knowledge of invaders. The magnificent ruins at Bukhara and Samarklad (in Uzbekistan) are products of Tajik culture, and Tajiks have made important contributions to Persian literature for more than nine hundred years. Artificial irrigation was introduced in very early times, the Chinese taught the Tajiks to dig wells and how to use iron, and the Romans introduced glassmaking. Also, many domesticated plants, such as the pea and wheat, have their origin in the area of Tajikistan.

In the 15th century, feuding tribes, economic decay, and the discovery of a seaway trade route led to a collapse of trade along the Silk Road. Tajiks were dominated by neighboring Afghans from the mid-1700s until the 1860s, when Russia gained control. The entire region became subject to the Great Game between expanding British and Russian Empires. After years of conflict, the two divided the area, with Russia retaining lands inhabited by Tajiks. The Russians further attempted to absorb the Tajik region after the 1917 Bolshevik Revolution; a resistance war raged between 1918 and 1926. But the rebellion never had a chance against Russian troops, and the area of Tajikistan became a Soviet republic in 1929. The Soviets proceeded to collectivize agriculture and accelerate industrialization to link the economy to other republics. Contact with other nations was severely restricted.

Anti-Soviet sentiment was never far from the surface, and in the late 1980s, Tajik protests became more vocal and even violent. After the dissolution of the Soviet Union in 1991, Tajikistan declared independence and became a founding member of the Commonwealth of Independent States (CIS).

In 1992, a clan-based power struggle erupted into civil war. Tens of thousands died and about one million people were displaced by two years of fierce fighting between factions of the Soviet-era power elite and an opposing coalition of Islamists and liberals. Government forces defeated the opposition but failed to gain control of all rebel-held territory before the cease-fire brokered by the United Nations took effect in 1994. Rebels soon regained some territory and began fighting anew for greater representation in government. The crisis worsened in 1996, and fighting almost threatened the capital of Dushanbe. Tavildara, 125 miles east of Dushanbe, is a rebel stronghold. Fighting continued into the summer of 1996 with little hope for a resolution.

PEOPLE

Population

In 1990, some six million people inhabited Tajikistan. About 62 percent were Tajiks, 23 percent were Uzbeks, and 8 percent were Russians. The remainder included Ukrainians, Byelorussions, Tatars, Kazakhs, Kyrgyz, Turkmen, Germans, Koreans, and members of at least 90 other nationalities. There has been no census since 1992, and many Russians and other minorities have left. The 1996 population is estimated to be 5.7 million. Only 28 percent of the people live in urban areas. Although ethnic groups are widely distributed throughout the country, Uzbeks are more commonly found in the southwest and west, while Russians live in larger towns and Dushanbe (population 600,000).

More ethnic Tajiks live outside of the country than in; 4.2 million are in Afghanistan, one million in Uzbekistan, and others in Kyrgyzstan, Kazakhstan, Iran, China, and Pakistan. Some are refugees who may return to Tajikistan later.

Ethnic Pamiris live on the world's highest inhabited plateau, a 14,000-foot table in the Pamir Mountains characterized by barren peaks, deep valleys, and a lack of vegetation. The Pamiris are divided into smaller groups according to their spoken dialects, including the Shugnani, Wakhi, Darwazi, and Yazgulami.

Language

In 1989, Tajik (*Tojiki*) replaced Russian as the official language, and its everyday use is becoming more prevalent. Tajik belongs to the southwest Iranian group of languages and is closely related to Farsi or Persian. Each region has its own dialect and accent. Although there are variations in sounds and vocabulary, these dialects are mutually intelligible among Tajiks. In the eastern Badakhshoni Kuhi Autonomous Region, people speak Pamiri, which belongs to the eastern Iranian language group. Uzbek, too, is spoken by many people.

Traditionally, these languages were written in Arabic script, but Cyrillic script has been used since 1940. Although some Tajiks would like to see a return to the Arabic script, it remains too costly for the young country to change its textbooks. Russian is still taught in many schools, especially at the university level, and many urban dwellers are more comfortable with it than with Tajik. Russian is the primary language of communication between ethnic groups.

Religion

Most Tajiks and ethnic Uzbeks are Sunni Muslims. The Pamiris, on the other hand, are mostly of the Isma'ili (Shiite) sect, although their practice of Islam is more moderate than in other parts of the world. Their leader is the Aga Khan, who has also helped provide food to the region. Russian Orthodox and other Christian churches are also represented, and there is a small Jewish community.

Islam in Tajikistan features elements of Sufi mysticism and shamanism. Because Tajikistan was a stronghold of Islamic resistance to Communist rule, the Soviets isolated Tajiks from extensive contact with Iran and Afghanistan. In more recent years, many Tajiks have again joined Islamic opposition movements, not so much out of religious devotion as out of a need for a base from which to encourage political reform.

The flow of community life, especially in rural areas, centers on the village mosque. Daily prayers, local celebrations, festivals, and feasts involve the mosque. The *mullo* (cleric) is a leader in the village and is supported by villagers. Much pride is taken in having a nice mosque. Since independence, more emphasis has been placed on the study of the *Qur'an* (Koran) and Persian, celebration of religious holidays, and use of the Arabic script. The use of alcohol and *ozodii zanon* (freedom for women) campaigns have left their marks, as alcohol is still consumed and women are not required to comply with certain restrictions found in other Muslim countries.

General Attitudes

Tajiks have a well-deserved reputation for hospitality. To their friends they are kind, gentle, and unfailingly generous. Tajiks feel a kinship with extended family and others from the same town or region and often fear or despise those from other areas. Leadership is maintained by the strongest warlords around whom cults of personality develop. Accordingly, a Tajik is an enemy to fear but a friend to cherish.

Characteristics much admired in Tajikistan include being willing to share, helping others, and caring for those who are alone. Although Tajiks are reserved, they are always ready for a social gathering or party, especially for weddings and birthdays. Aspirations differ, from wanting to get a good education abroad to wanting one's own plot of farmland.

Personal Appearance

Most urban men wear Western-style clothing to work. Some still wear a four-cornered or a round hat called a *toqi* or *tupi*, which are regionally distinctive in color and design. Women more commonly wear colorful traditional Tajik dresses (*curta*) with long, contrasting-colored pants (*aezor* or *pajomah*) underneath; many wear scarves on their heads. Quite typically, women wear earrings and necklaces. Rural women dress more conservatively, wearing a *faranji* on their heads and sometimes using it to veil their faces when a man approaches. Village men, especially elders, wear a long coat (*joma* or *chapan*) kept closed with a bandana-type tie (*meeyonband* or *chorsi*) around the waist. They may also wear a man's *curta*.

Traditionally, adults do not wear shorts. Scanty dress is considered offensive. Schoolchildren wear uniforms.

CUSTOMS AND COURTESIES

Greetings

Men commonly greet each other by shaking hands, whereas women either embrace or shake hands. Tajiks may also place the right hand over the heart before, during, or after a handshake. Friends (men or women) who have not seen each other for some time may embrace and kiss each other three times on opposite cheeks. Urban men and women may greet each other with a handshake, but rural men usually do not touch women in public, greeting verbally instead. The standard verbal greeting is the Arabic *Assalaam alaikum!* (Peace be upon you!); the reply is *Waalaikum assalaam* (And peace also with you). Close friends might simply exchange *Salom* (Tajik for "Peace"). A common Tajik greeting is *Chee khel shoomo?* (How are you?) and the Uzbek equivalent is *Yakhshi me seez?* Russian speakers often say *Kak dela?* (How are things?). Upon parting, Tajiks say *Khair!* (Good-bye) or *To didana!* (See you later!)

When addressing elders and those in high positions, one uses titles and given names or surnames. Friends use nicknames and given names. Very important persons visiting a rural village may receive a formal greeting that includes the offering of bread and salt followed by speeches from both sides.

Gestures

In rural homes, people usually sit cross-legged on the floor. It is improper to point the bottom of one's shoe or foot at another person. Pointing directly at someone or beckoning with one finger is considered rude; one uses the entire hand instead. Respect is shown by looking down while speaking to someone. People usually pass items with the right hand, with the left hand placed on the heart or supporting the right arm.

Visiting

Socializing in the home or at a large hall for weddings, memorials, or birthdays is an important aspect of Tajik society. Meals for these occasions can last for hours and involve several courses; dancing often follows.

The traditional house includes a special room set aside for entertaining; on some occasions only men gather here, while for others men and women socialize together. It is customary to remove shoes before entering and to sit on thick cushions (*kurpacha*) spread on the floor. Men sit cross-legged. Women sit with both legs tucked under and to the side. Hosts usually offer tea to their guests, as well as fruit and nuts. Whether it is mealtime or not, food is cooked for visitors. The most common days for visiting are Saturday and Sunday, although anytime will do. Friends do visit, but relatives visit one another more often; daughters frequently visit their mothers.

Eating

Most Tajiks eat with their fingers at traditional meals and in rural areas, although utensils are more common in cities. Three meals are customary in the cities, while some rural people eat only breakfast and supper. Breakfast (*nonishta*) usually includes a cup of tea (*choi*). Families eat together on the floor, with food placed on a low table or a cloth. At traditional meals, food is served in communal dishes shared by those sitting close by. At some special occasions, food is served on platters and guests prepare their own plates. Unleavened bread (*non*) or regular bread is served at all meals. Guests are expected to eat at least a little; it is best to eat as much as possible. Although Tajiks are mostly Muslim, alcohol (usually vodka) is served for special occasions. It is common for

everyone around the table to take turns making toasts. Many Tajiks observe the month-long Muslim fast during *Ramazon*. They break the daily dawn-to-dusk fast with an evening meal. After all meals, one holds the hands cupped at chest level while grace is said. Upon conclusion of the prayer, one runs the hands down the sides of the face and wipes them together.

LIFESTYLE

Family

The extended family (*oilai kalon*) is the center of Tajik society. Tajiks know the general kin ties of everyone else in a rural villages and use this information as a behavioral guide. Because one shares character and reputation with one's relatives, one is also bound to share material goods. Rural households usually contain several generations. The elderly receive respect and care from their children and often help care for their grandchildren and teach them how to behave in culturally required ways. These large families live in mud-brick structures of several rooms, surrounded by high mud walls that provide security and keep animals and/or gardens inside. Within such compounds (*havli*), it is common to find three or four houses led by the senior male. Work is divided by gender and age. Women and girls cook, wash, garden, care for children, help work in the fields, produce cheese and other milk products, and process foods to store for winter. Men and boys work in the fields and take care of the family livestock. Urban families are smaller, often live in apartments, and have more evenly divided chores.

All family decisions are finalized by the elders. Mothers are the main disciplinarians, although fathers take action in the case of severe punishment. As men grow older, they spend more time involved in community discussions in mosques and teahouses.

Dating and Marriage

It is not normal for members of the opposite sex to show affection in public, and in rural areas there is no opportunity for dating. Urban teenagers do attend movies and other events in mixed groups but not as couples.

Some weddings are quietly arranged several years in advance by the families involved. Families often compete to provide the best and most food for as large a wedding celebration as possible. The extravagant events often deplete the family's resources. The wedding takes place over three days, capped by a blessing (*nikoh*) from a religious leader.

Since the war has killed many men, young teenage girls now might agree to become a second or third wife. Allowed by Islam, but illegal under secular law, such marriages are tolerated because they relieve economic strain on the girls' families.

Diet

The Tajik diet is comprised of vegetables (potatoes, tomatoes, cucumbers, carrots, peppers, squash), fruits (especially grapes, melons, and apples) and meats (beef, mutton, chicken) together with *non*. Rice mixed with meat and carrots (*palav*) is a favorite dish. Pasta filled with various meats or squash (*mantu*) is popular, as is skewered meat (*shashlik*). Many people eat yogurt and other dairy products. Puddings and pies are common urban desserts. A traditional Tajik sweet dish is *halvo* (paste of sugar and oil). Nuts and dried fruits (raisins, apricots) are served as snacks. Meals are followed by black or green tea. Urban residents enjoy a more varied diet than their rural counterparts.

Recreation

Popular sports include soccer, basketball, tennis, and volleyball. Men play *buzkashi* to celebrate the birth or circumcision of a son. In this rough polo-type game, teams of horsemen try to carry a goat from one spot through a set of poles and back again. Players not in possession of the animal do anything to get it away from the man who is hanging on to it; great horsemanship is required. Opera and concerts are performed in Dushanbe. Many people watch television or go to movies. Radio broadcasts are popular in rural areas.

Tajiks love dancing; special occasions always include either a live band or music from tapes to which men dance with women or men, or women dance with women. Popular summer activities include swimming in rivers and artificial lakes or having picnics around Dushanbe.

Holidays

Public holidays include New Year's Day, *Id-i-Ramazon* (feast at the end of *Ramazon*), International Women's Day (8 March), *Id-i-Navruz* (Islamic New Year), Victory Day (9 May, for World War II), *Id-i-Qurbon* (Feast of Sacrifice honoring Abraham's willingness to sacrifice his son), Independence Day (9 September), and Constitution Day (6 November).

Commerce

Weekday office hours are 9:00 A.M. to 5:00 P.M., with an hour break for lunch. Most people buy food at open-air markets (*bazaars*). Nearby, street vendors and small shops sell everything from imported clothes to cooked food. Prices may be set for small items, but one must bargain extensively for large purchases. Government stores that once stocked goods from all over the Soviet Union are now basically empty.

SOCIETY

Government

When Tajikistan became independent, it had a presidential system of government. That system was abolished in the wake of the 1992 civil war but was restored under a new constitution in 1994. Imomali Rahmonov was elected president. As head of state, he holds most executive authority. A prime minister, currently Yakhio Azimov, is head of government; he is primarily responsible for the economy and infrastructure. Legislative power is vested in the 181-member Parliament (*Majlisi Oli*). The voting age is 18.

Tajikistan is divided into three regions, the largest of which (containing half the territory but less than 3 percent of the population) is the Autonomous Region of Badakhshoni Kuhi. This region is governed almost independently by rebels.

Economy

Poorest of the former Soviet republics, Tajikistan is also one of the most rural; half the people work in agriculture. Minerals (gold, iron, lead, mercury, bauxite, tin) and hydroelectric power from the mountains, together with cotton, silk, fruits, and vegetables, form the foundation of the economy.

Unfortunately, the economy is hampered by the loss of Soviet-era trade and supply links and the war. The standard of living has deteriorated sharply, with many facing food shortages. Russia remains the main trading partner, but efforts are underway to increase business with other countries. Tajikistan's Human Development Index (0.643) ranks it 103d out of 174 nations. Most people lack access to resources that would allow them to pursue personal goals. Real gross domestic product per capita is $1,740. The currency is the Tajik *rubl*.

Transportation and Communication

Rural transportation needs are met primarily by tractors, horses, donkeys, and by walking. Only a very small number of trucks and private cars travel the deteriorating roads in isolated areas. Buses run between major towns, and some areas are connected by train. Urban residents use electric trolleys and buses, and sometimes taxis and minibuses. A small goverment airline flies to otherwise inaccessible areas.

Most large urban areas have extensive phone networks, but service is unreliable. Rural areas lack proper phone access. Most people have televisions and radios. Programs are broadcast in Russian, Tajik, and Uzbek. Newspapers also print in these languages.

Education

Under the Soviets, the adult literacy rate rose to 96 percent. The civil war and collapsing economy have brought disarray to all levels of education. Primary school enrollment is down, as fees have been introduced and schools are no longer heated in the winter. Textbooks in rural areas are scarce, and many teachers fled during the war. The number of students in secondary schools has remained steady, with a slight increase in schools conducted in Tajik (as opposed to Russian). Several universities and institutes, as well as various technical and vocational schools, provide postsecondary education.

Health

Dispensaries staffed by paramedics and midwives are located in almost all rural villages, and there are hospitals/clinics in each district capital. The overall health situation in Tajikistan is deterioriating. Together with a high population growth rate and the emigration of medical specialists, the country is experiencing an increase in infant and maternal mortality rates. Generally, the emphasis is on treatment and hospitalization rather than prevention. Hospitals are poorly supplied. The infant mortality rate is 60 per 1,000. Life expectancy averages 69 years.

FOR THE TRAVELER

U.S. travelers must have a valid passport and obtain a visa in advance through the Russian Embassy. Travel is not recommended. For recorded advisories, call the U.S. State Department at (202) 647–5225. There are few hotels. Water should be boiled or treated. Avoid walking alone at night or in remote places. Bring a supply of film, a first-aid kit, and personal toiletries. Tajikistan has a variety of interesting archaeological and historical sites. For more information, contact the Embassy of Russia, 2650 Wisconsin Avenue NW, Washington, DC 20007; phone (202) 298–5700.

CULTURGRAM '97

United Republic of
Tanzania

Boundary representations not necessarily authoritative.

BACKGROUND

Land and Climate

The United Republic of Tanzania covers 364,899 square miles (945,090 square kilometers). It consists of mainland Tanganyika and three low coral islands that lie off the coast in the Indian Ocean: Mafia, Pemba, and Zanzibar. The combined size of these humid islands is about equal to that of Rhode Island. Tanganyika (about the size of Texas) is a land of great variation. It either shares or borders on three of Africa's greatest lakes (Victoria, Nyasa, and Tanganyika). Most of the country is either low-lying coastal plain, upland plain (the Serengeti), or highland plateau. Mount Kilimanjaro, the highest point in Africa, rises to 19,340 feet (5,895 meters). Africa's lowest point is the floor of Lake Tanganyika at 1,174 feet (358 meters) below sea level.

Tanzania's equatorial climate—hot, humid, and 90°F (32°C) on the coast—is tempered by inland elevations where temperatures are mild. Rains fall primarily from March to May and October to December, with seasonal variations from north to south. The tsetse fly infests nearly two-thirds of the mainland, making widespread livestock production nearly impossible.

History

Various peoples inhabited the area now known as Tanzania for thousands of years before traders from southern Arabian began arriving in the eighth century. The Arabs founded the city of Kilwa as they began settling the coast. Over many generations, Arabs mixed with the local Bantu populations to produce both the Swahili language and the modern peoples of the coastal regions. The Portuguese arrived in the 15th century. The Portuguese and Arabic overlords from Oman and Muscat developed a series of populous and powerful trading cities and sultanates—particularly on the islands of Zanzibar and Pemba. The Sultanate of Zanzibar firmly controlled both the islands and the mainland coast until the mid-1800s. In 1886, Tanganyika became a German protectorate. Zanzibar retained its independence but lost control over Kenya to the British. In 1920, Tanganyika fell under British rule as well.

In 1961, Tanganyika was granted independence, followed in 1963 by a fully independent Zanzibar. In 1964, the two nations merged to form Tanzania. For the most part, this union has been very successful, although the Arab majority on Zanzibar would like more control over the economy and politics of the island than they presently hold. The country became a socialist republic under Julius Nyerere. His Party for the Revolution (CCM—*Chama Cha Mapinduzi*) worked to unite and develop a country of many ethnic groups.

Nyerere stepped down as president after constitutional reform in 1985 and chose Ali Hassan Mwinyi to succeed him. Mwinyi was reelected without opposition in 1990, as the ruling CCM was the only legal political party, but promised to step down after the next democratic elections. Multiparty district and regional elections were held between 1992 and 1995, and full national multiparty elections were in October 1995. Polling was chaotic and opposition groups charged fraud, but the independent judiciary ruled the election results would stand. CCM candidate Benjamin Mkapa was elected president and the CCM maintained a majority in Parliament.

THE PEOPLE
Population

Tanzania's population of 28.7 million is growing at 2.5 percent annually. About one-third of the population lives in urban areas. The largest city is Dar es Salaam, with more than 1.5 million people. Dodoma, which replaced Dar es Salaam as Tanzania's capital, is expected to grow when the transition is complete at the end of the century. More than half of all Tanzanians are younger than age 20. Tanzania's Human Development Index (0.364) ranks it 147th out of 174 nations. Most people lack access to opportunities for pursuing personal goals or enjoying economic prosperity.

Ninety-nine percent of the population is African, coming from some 130 different ethnic groups. Thirty of these are Bantu-speaking groups. The Nyamwezi-Sukuma (12.6 percent of the population) is the only group with more than one million members. There are three Nilotic ethnic groups, two Khoisan, and two Afro-Asiatic. The merchant/trader class is dominated by people of Lebanese, Palestinian, and Indian origin. Arabs are most numerous on Zanzibar.

Language

Swahili (*Kiswahili*), the primary official language, developed along the coasts of Kenya and Tanzania as a trade language between Africans and Arabs. It is a mixture of various Bantu languages and Arabic. Tanzanian Swahili follows a more traditional form than the Swahili spoken in Kenya. Zanzibar is considered to have the purest Swahili. English is Tanzania's second official language. It is used in business, government, and higher education.

More than one hundred languages are spoken in Tanzania. Most people speak the language associated with their ethnic group, but they generally also speak Swahili. Nyerere made Swahili official at the time of independence to foster pride in the people's African identity. To help spread use of the language, he urged people to buy radios and Radio Tanzania began broadcasting in Swahili. The language is still taught on the radio, and it is still evolving.

Religion

On the mainland, more than one-third of the population is Christian. Another third is Muslim. On Zanzibar, nearly all inhabitants are Muslim. About one-third of the population follows indigenous beliefs, although many of these people have also accepted some Christian or Islamic beliefs. Muslims believe *Allah* (God) chose the Prophet Muhammad and revealed the words of the *Qur'an* (Koran) to him through the angel Gabriel. As part of the practice of Islam, Muslims profess the name of *Allah* and proclaim Muhammad's calling. They pray five times daily and expect to make a pilgrimage to Makkah, Saudi Arabia, sometime in their life.

It is not unusual for professed Christians to mix their beliefs with local traditions. Thus, a local priest and a traditional healer might carry equal respect in a "Christian" village. The two belief systems are not considered contradictory because each has a place in the people's daily lives. The government is neutral when it comes to religion and has actively tried to promote religious tolerance throughout the country.

General Attitudes

Tanzanian social systems are group oriented, regardless of ethnic affiliation. Individuals are expected to put themselves second to group welfare. Consequently, Tanzanians are extremely polite and generous people, particularly in public. It is considered impolite to pass a person (unless in a large crowd) without showing a sign of recognition, even if only to smile. Tanzanians do not use obscene language of any kind, even mildly. Any kind of verbal abuse or criticism, especially in public, is a major offense reflecting on the person's upbringing and background. Nevertheless, foreigners often perceive Tanzanians (and East Africans in general) as being abrupt and occasionally impolite. This is partly because the word "please" is not native to the Bantu languages spoken by East Africans. The Swahili equivalent, *tafadhali*, has actually been borrowed from Arabic but is still not integral to the culture. As a result, people often make requests without a "please," which is not impolite but simply a cultural habit. *Asante* (Thank you) is also an adopted term, but it seems to be used widely in the culture today. Whether spoken or not, thanks is usually shown with a returned favor or kindness. A deed is considered greater than verbal gratitude.

Personal Appearance

Urban Tanzanians usually wear Western-style clothing, but they dress conservatively. Shorts and other revealing attire are not proper, except in clearly defined work or recreational situations. In rural villages, many people wear traditional clothing associated with their specific ethnic group. Many also wear readily available secondhand clothing from the United States or Europe and imported clothing from China and India. Muslim men might wear a *kanzu* (long, embroidered cotton gown) with a matching skullcap or they may simply prefer Western-style clothing, with or without a skullcap. Some wear a *kanzu* only when going to the mosque. Muslim women might cover their hair but almost never their faces. They often wear *kangas* or *kitenge* (several pieces of colorful, cotton wraparound fabric). Women on Zanzibar often wear a large, black shawl called a *buibui*.

CUSTOMS AND COURTESIES
Greetings

The most common Swahili greeting is *Hujambo* (*Hamjambo* for more than one person), usually followed by a handshake. A more casual greeting is simply *Jambo*. A common response to *Hujambo* is *Sijambo* (I'm fine). *Hatujambo* means "We're fine." This exchange is followed by questions about one's home, family, work, or other activities. For example, one might ask *Habari za nyumbani?* (How are things at your home?). A common response is *Salama* (In peace, without problems). Each geographic region has a variety of non-Swahili greetings particular to the local ethnic groups, but Swahili is understood by the vast majority of Tanzanians. Men and women shake hands with each other, although a man may wait for a woman to extend her hand before offering his.

Mothers are commonly addressed by the name of their oldest son (or daughter until a son is born), rather than by their given name. Thus, the mother of Albert would be known as "Mama Albert."

Gestures

People use the right hand or both hands to pass and accept items. The use of the left hand alone, even in gesturing, is improper. The verbal *"tch-tch"* sound is considered an insult. In many cases, it is impolite to let the bottom of one's foot or shoe point at someone. Therefore, when sitting, one does not prop up the feet on chairs or tables but places them on the ground. It is impolite to photograph another person without permission. A person will rarely refuse but expects the courtesy of being asked.

Visiting

Among Muslims, visiting is an important social custom; friends and family visit often. All Tanzanians enjoy friendly social visits and enthusiastically welcome their visitors. Hosts do their best to make guests comfortable. Unannounced visits are common and warmly received. Most times of the day are acceptable for a visit except late in the evening (after 8:00 P.M. or so). A host also does not appreciate repeated visits at mealtime. Any guest arriving at mealtime, even if unannounced, will always be offered part of the meal. Not offering a meal would show a lack of hospitality and refusing the offer is impolite. If a visit is arranged, a person does everything possible to keep the appointment. Not showing up for a scheduled visit is rude. It is polite for hosts to serve tea (often with milk and sugar), coffee, or another beverage. *Maandazi* (small doughnuts) or *kitumbua* (a fried bread, plural is *vitumbua*) may also be set out. Refusing these refreshments is impolite.

A first-time visitor customarily brings a small gift to the home. This may include sweets or cookies but not flowers. Flowers are used to express condolences. Guests of the opposite sex are entertained with the outside door open. When guests depart, hosts customarily accompany them part of the way (a few hundred yards) to see them off properly.

Eating

Throughout the country, a bowl or basin of water is offered for washing hands before each meal. This is especially important because most meals are eaten with the hand. But even if diners use utensils, they wash the hands before eating. Because the left hand traditionally is used for personal hygiene, people use only the right hand when eating without utensils. They might use the left to handle difficult foods, such as meat with bones, but never to take food from a communal bowl. Eating from a communal dish is common, especially when it contains *ugali* (see Diet) or rice. Families along the Indian Ocean coast, as well as in villages and towns along the three lakes (Nyasa, Tanganyika, and Victoria), sit on woven mats on the floor to eat meals. Muslims tend to sit cross-legged on these mats, but others sit with one leg tucked and the other stretched out sideways away from the food. Among Muslims, as well as some rural non-Muslims, it is common for men and women to eat separately. When guests are invited, dinner is usually served first and socializing is reserved for afterward. Therefore, it is impolite for guests to leave a home immediately after a meal. During the Islamic month of *Ramadan*, Muslims do not eat or drink from sunrise to sunset; meals are served in the evening.

LIFESTYLE

Family

Tanzanian socialism is based on *ujamaa*, or "family-hood." The nation's extended families have been encouraged to act as economic as well as family units. Families traditionally are large, usually including either the father's brothers and their families or (less often) the mother's sisters and their families. Urban families usually are smaller and less cohesive than those residing in rural areas. Christian marriages tend to be monogamous. Males in Muslim and traditional families, however, may legally have up to four wives. Polygamy is more common in rural areas.

Dating and Marriage

Western-style dating habits are uncommon among the majority of the people. Traditionally, marriages have been arranged, often within the extended family. Today, while individual preference is permitted, cousin marriages are still encouraged—especially in rural areas. This practice is becoming less common in cities. The husband's family normally gives a dowry to the bride's family for one of two reasons. First, it is a way of showing respect for the bride's parents—of thanking them for raising the woman. Second, it helps compensate for the loss of a productive member of the bride's family. This is important especially in rural areas because extended families share work responsibilities.

Diet

Tanzanians eat grains, fruits, and vegetables. Meat is served less often, the most common being chicken, goat, and lamb. *Kitumbua* is a popular snack or energy food, as is sugarcane. A daily staple is *ugali*, a stiff porridge made from maize (white corn), millet, sorghum, or cassava. Cooked bananas are a starch staple in much of northern Tanzania (particularly around Lake Victoria and in the foothills of Mount Kilimanjaro) and in the southwest around Mbeya and Lake Nyasa. Bananas are prepared in a variety of ways, including roasted, fried, or made into a paste and mixed with meat and gravy. Sweet bananas are also consumed as a fruit. Other fruits are mangoes, guavas, pineapple, jackfruit, breadfruit, and oranges.

Rice is the staple of much of the coastal area and is often cooked with a variety of spices (including cloves, curry, cinnamon, cumin, and hot peppers), which are mixed directly into the water as the rice cooks. This is called *pilau*. Dishes that are prepared as a relish to go along with the main starch food (*ugali,* rice, or bananas) are commonly meat stews, green leafy vegetables (cabbage, Swiss chard, spinach), and beans or cowpeas. Devout Muslims in Tanzania do not eat pork or drink alcohol.

Recreation

Soccer, track-and-field, and boxing are popular. Tanzania is known for its world-class runners. Big-game hunting is permissible under certain restrictions. Tanzania actively fights elephant poaching and ivory smuggling. It has created game parks to protect endangered species. Water sports are popular along the coast. People enjoy socializing at coffeehouses or at home. In their leisure time, men play *bao*, a strategy game for two in which each tries to earn his opponent's pebbles or seeds by moving them in a certain fashion around a board (or the ground). There are many variations, but the game is over when one player is out of playing pieces.

Holidays

Civic holidays include New Year's Day, Zanzibar Revolution Day (12 January), Union Day (26 April), Labor Day (1 May), *Saba Saba* (Farmer's Day, 7 July), *Nane Nane* (International Trade Day, 8 August), and Independence Day (9 December). In addition to national holidays, the people honor Christian and Muslim religious holidays. Christians celebrate Easter (including Good Friday and Easter Monday) and Christmas. Islamic holidays are based on the lunar calendar and fall on different days from year to year. At the end of the holy month of *Ramadan*, a three-day feast is held to break the fast. The Feast of the Sacrifice, held 40 days later, honors Abraham for his willingness to sacrifice his son. Muslims also mark the birthday of the prophet Muhammad.

Commerce

General business hours are from 8:30 to 11:30 A.M. and 2:00 to 6:00 P.M., Monday through Friday. Most businesses close by noon on Saturday. Government offices do not re-open in the afternoon; they close at 11:30 A.M. each day. The government regulates certain business dress standards. Most office workers wear Western-style clothing.

SOCIETY

Government

Tanzania is a democratic republic containing 25 regions. The president is chief of state, and a prime minister is head of government. The National Assembly (*Bunge*) has 232 seats. While CCM still dominates politics, opposition parties do provide balance and pressure. The most important include the National Convention for Construction and Reform (NCCR-Mageuzi), the Union for Multiparty Democracy (UMD), and Zanzibar's Civil United Front (CUF), among others. The voting age is 18.

Zanzibar (population 700,000) has a separate Parliament and elected president (Salmin Amour)

Economy

Agriculture dominates Tanzania's economy, employing 85 percent of the population and accounting for 85 percent of all exports. Key exports include coffee, cotton, sisal, cashew nuts, meat, tobacco, tea, cloves, and coconuts from Zanzibar, and pyrethrum (a pesticide made from chrysanthemums). Tanzania is also a major producer of diamonds and other gems.

Economic liberalization since 1990 has encouraged private investment and the creation of new export products. Economic growth has risen and inflation fallen. But corruption, mismanagement, and regional problems have kept growth at less than 4 percent. New trade relations with South Africa, as well as continued democratic reforms, are expected to boost economic performance in the future. On Zanzibar, trade and tourism are expected to lift people from grinding poverty.

Real gross domestic product per capita is $620. Sixty percent of people live in poverty. To generate some cash income, a family will often run an informal shop (*duka*) that sells produce, soda, soap, and sundries. Or they may find odd jobs to supplement low-paying wage jobs. Tanzania's currency is the Tanzanian shilling (Sh).

Transportation and Communication

The transportation system is only partially developed. Most roads are not paved, and the system is not extensive in the rural interior. People often travel by foot or bicycle, ride on or carry loads with donkeys or oxen, and hitchhike. Buses, trains, and taxis are available in some cities, especially Dar es Salaam. Taxi fare is negotiated in advance. Trains and buses run between major cities. Between smaller towns, one can ride a small truck or van that has been converted into a passenger vehicle. Few people own cars. Following the British tradition, traffic moves on the left side of the road. The communications system also is not fully developed. Few telephones are available, and the country is served by only two daily newspapers.

Education

Tanzania's adult literacy rate is 64 percent. Primary school instruction is in Swahili, and English is the main language in secondary schools. About 70 percent of all school-aged children begin primary school, but less than 10 percent progress past the seventh grade. Boys are more likely than girls to get an education. Students pay fees and wear uniforms. Most secondary schools are boarding schools. The University of Dar es Salaam emphasizes community service rather than strictly academic pursuits. Technical training is available at other institutions, as well.

Health

In rural areas, malaria, sleeping sickness, and a wide variety of intestinal parasitic diseases are common. Quality medical care is really only available in large cities, with the exception of a few remote, well-run mission hospitals. Rural clinics are available, but they often lack trained personnel and sufficient medical supplies. Tanzania has only one doctor for every 24,000 inhabitants. With an infant mortality rate of 109 per 1,000, the need for expanded health care is great. Life expectancy averages 45 to 50 years.

FOR THE TRAVELER

A valid passport and visa are required of U.S. citizens to enter Tanzania. It can take one month to process a visa application. Travelers should have vaccinations for yellow fever and cholera, as well as other diseases, and should use malarial suppressants.

Water is not safe for drinking, for ice cubes, or for brushing teeth, unless it has been boiled. Eat only food that is hot and has been well cooked. Peel and wash all fruits and cook all vegetables before eating. Photography of certain government installations may be restricted. When one is taking pictures of people, they may first want to change clothing or pose. Taking pictures of objects rather than people is considered odd. Dress modestly. Learn some Swahili.

Tanzania's game reserves, mountains, lakes, and islands are all worthy attractions. For more information, contact the Tanzania Permanent Mission to the United Nations, 205 East 42d Street, 13th Floor, New York, NY 10017; phone (212) 972–9160. The Embassy of Tanzania is located at 2139 R Street NW, Washington, DC 20008; phone (202) 939–6125.

 Printed on recycled paper

CULTURGRAM ™ '97

Kingdom of
Thailand

Boundary representations not necessarily authoritative.

BACKGROUND

Land and Climate

Thailand is located in the heart of Southeast Asia and extends down the Malaysian peninsula. Some have compared its shape to the head and trunk of an elephant or the shape of an ax. Covering 198,455 square miles (514,000 square kilometers), Thailand is about the size of Arizona and Utah combined. The central region is dominated by fertile agricultural land and Bangkok. The northeast (covering one-third of the country) consists of the Khorat Plateau. Forested mountains and steep, fertile valleys form the northern quarter of the nation, an area once rich in timber (primarily teak). The southern peninsula is comprised of rain forests and rubber and coconut plantations. The climate is mostly tropical. Cooler temperatures prevail between November and February, but the rest of the year is fairly hot. Rains fall mostly from June to October.

History

Thailand's early history, which may have begun four thousand years ago, is linked with that of southern China. Studies show migration occurred both from Thailand to south China and later from China to Thailand. Between the ninth and thirteenth centuries, present-day Thailand was part of a vast Khmer empire that covered much of Southeast Asia. Upon overthrowing the Khmer, the Thai established a kingdom at Sukhothai in 1238. A Thai ruler, Ramathibodi, introduced Theravada Buddhism in the 14th century.

After a struggle against the Burmese in the 18th century, Rama I founded the Chakri Dynasty and established Bangkok as the capital in 1782. At that time, the Thai kingdom was known as Siam. The Thais successfully kept European colonialists from their soil. The wise rule of King Mongkut and the reforms of Rama V (Chulalongkorn) kept the kingdom independent. Military leaders forced the government to become a constitutional monarchy in 1932, and Siam changed its name to Thailand in 1939.

Japan occupied Thailand for a short time during World War II, and Thai leaders allied the country with Japan. After the war, however, Thailand allied with the United States and became an important base for U.S. activities in the region during the 1960s and 1970s. Since 1975, Thailand has been home to many Indochinese refugees. The present king has ruled since 1946. He is known as Rama IX, but his name is Bhumibol Adulyadej. Despite several military coups, terrorist violence, drug trafficking, crime, and problems with neighboring nations, Thailand's king has always been a symbol of national unity and stability.

Thailand's military has long been politically active. Its 1991 coup led to a governing crisis that eventually incited riots, a violent military response, and then royal intervention. In September 1992 elections, pro-democracy parties combined to win a narrow parliamentary majority, a victory against the military that strengthened civilian institutions. A July 1995 election brought the *Chart Thai* (Thai Nation) Party to power.

THE PEOPLE

Population

Thailand's population of 60.2 million is growing annually at 1.2 percent. Less than one-fourth of the population lives in cities. Bangkok is the largest city; its population varies between five and nine million depending on the time of year and the constant movement of migrant workers. About 75 percent of the population is comprised of Central Thai, Northeastern Thai, Northern Thai, and Southern Thai. The Chinese form the largest minority, composing about 14 percent of the people. However, intermarriage over many generations has made it difficult to distinguish between the Chinese and the Thais. There are also many Thais of Malay, Khmer, Vietnamese, and Lao ancestry. Ethnic Khmer, Vietnamese, and other refugees inhabit Thailand, mostly in border regions. About 500,000 mountain people form a number of distinct ethnic groups. Thailand's Human Development Index (0.827) ranks it 58th out of 174 countries. Adjusted for women, the index (0.798) ranks Thailand 33d out of 130 countries. The figures suggest Thailand has performed reasonably well in providing the average citizen with health, education, and income sufficient to empower him or her to choose life's direction.

Language

Central Thai is the official language and is used in schools. Other Thai dialects are spoken in various regions of the country. Lao is spoken in some northern areas, and Khmer is spoken along the Cambodian border. Thai is a tonal language, meaning that a given syllable can have different meanings depending on the inflection with which it is pronounced. Central Thai has five tones. Many people speak Chinese and Malay. Those with advanced education often speak English. Some minority groups, such as the Mon and Hmong, have their own languages.

Religion

Although Thailand guarantees freedom of religion, and many religions are represented in the country, 95 percent of the population is Theravada Buddhist. Muslims compose about 4 percent of the population. There is also a small number of Christians in Thailand.

Buddhism deeply affects the people's daily lives. Buddhist *wats* (temples) dominate Thai communities. Traditionally, all young men were expected to become Buddhist monks for at least three months of their lives, during which time they studied Buddhist principles. While the practice is not strictly enforced today, it is still important to the people, and large ordination ceremonies are often held for young boys entering their training. Ancestor veneration is practiced as part of Buddhist worship. Food is offered in memory of deceased relatives, and special ceremonies serve to remind the living to honor the dead. Buddhism in Thailand also incorporates rites and principles from other Eastern religions such as Hinduism, as well as animism, which espouses a special reverence for life based on a belief that all living things possess spirits.

General Attitudes

Thailand means "Land of the Free," and Thais are proud of the fact that their country has avoided foreign rule (except during Japan's occupation in World War II) throughout its long history. The King and Queen are the most respected and honored persons in Thailand. A Thai would be offended by any joke or ill reference to them. Even images of the King are treated with respect. For example, rather than lick a postage stamp with the King's picture on it, one wets it with a damp sponge. It is illegal to say or write anything offensive about royalty. Traditionally, success was measured by a person's religious and nationalistic attitudes. The trend is now toward wealth and education. Wealth is generally looked on as a reflection of virtue. Thais have much respect for those who unselfishly help others and lead virtuous lives.

The Thai expression, *Mai Pen Rai* (Never mind), characterizes their general feeling toward life, that it is to be enjoyed; problems and setbacks should not be taken too seriously. While Thais are by no means lazy or unproductive, they are generally happy with what they have and who they are. Another name for Thailand is "The Land of Smiles." Thais are a reserved people and usually consider criticism of others to be in poor taste. A sense of humor, laughter, and a pleasant, smiling attitude are highly regarded. On the other hand, showing a lack of reserve by speaking loudly or showing anger in public is offensive and may cause one to lose another's respect.

Thais are proud of their cultural heritage and are often offended by those who see "development" as a need to Westernize and change people's religious and cultural habits. What may seem poor to a Westerner may be a fine lifestyle to a Thai, especially in rural regions where life has not changed for many centuries.

Personal Appearance

While Western clothing is common in most areas, especially Bangkok, traditional clothing is also often worn. There are, of course, the highly stylized costumes of Thai dancers, but most clothing is simpler. Men and women frequently wear straw hats because of the heat. Simple blouses and *sarongs* (tube skirts) are common for women. Men might wear pants and a shirt in public but change into a long *sarong* or short wraparound at home. Men and women of Chinese descent wear calf-length loose pants and jackets. Intricate headdresses may accompany the traditional clothing of the mountain people. Sandals are popular, but shoes are worn in formal situations. Rural people may wear rubber thongs or go barefoot. Children are required to wear shoes to school.

CUSTOMS AND COURTESIES

Greetings

The traditional and most common greeting in Thailand is called the *wai*. How the gesture is performed depends entirely on the relationship between the people, and there are many variations. Generally, however, a person places the palms of the hands together, with fingers extended at chest level, and bows slightly; women curtsy. The younger person greets first, and the more senior person responds with a *wai* in a lower position. Bows and curtsies are more pronounced to show greater respect. In addition, the higher one's hands are placed, the more respect is shown. The fingertips only go above the level of the eyebrows to reverence Buddha or greet royalty. For other honored persons, the fingertips may reach to between the eyebrows, with the thumb tip touching the tip of the nose. It is an insult to not return a *wai*, unless there is great social or age distance between the two people, in which case the senior does not return the *wai*. For example, an adult does not exchange a *wai* with a small child. Buddhist monks never return a *wai*. The gesture can mean not only "Hello" but also "Thank you," "Good-bye," or "I am sorry."

Very close friends do not use the *wai,* but greet informally and address one another by nickname. Thais otherwise address each other by their first names, preceded by *Khun* (for example, *Khun Sariya*), and reserve surnames for formal occasions. In formal situations, visitors may address Thais by using *Mr., Mrs.,* or *Miss* with the first or last names.

Gestures

A person's head is considered sacred and one should neither touch another's head nor pass an object over it. Parents pat their children's heads, but this is the only exception. People try to keep the level of their heads below that of social superiors. The bottoms of the feet are the least sacred part of the body and should never be pointed in the direction of another person. Thais avoid stamping their feet, touching people with them, or using them to move or point at objects.

Body posture and physical gestures are extremely important in polite company and will speak volumes about one's character and regard for others. It is usually offensive to cross the legs while sitting in a chair, especially in the presence of an older person. Placing one's arm over the back of the chair in which another person is sitting is offensive. Men and women generally do not touch or show affection in public. However, good friends of the same sex sometimes hold hands. Among the youth, it is becoming more common for members of the opposite sex to hold hands. Women must never touch images of Buddha or a Buddhist monk or offer to shake hands. All religious monuments and shrines are sacred and should not be defiled or treated disrespectfully. One passes and receives items, especially gifts, with the right hand only, never the left. For heavy items, one uses two hands.

Visiting

Thais are very hospitable hosts and enjoy having visitors. The person of highest social rank or age is treated with the greatest respect. In all cases, how one sits, walks, or otherwise interacts with others depends on the status of each person present. It is customary to remove one's shoes when entering a Buddhist temple or private home. Because Thai tradition says a soul resides in the doorsill of a *wat,* visitors avoid stepping on the doorsill.

It is not necessary to take gifts when visiting, but it is not uncommon for guests on extended stays to present their hosts with a gift of appreciation. In the home, people commonly sit on the floor. They do not stretch out their feet in front of them. Women generally tuck their legs to the side and behind them and men sit cross-legged. Men might also sit with their legs tucked to the side to show special respect to the hosts. Guests may offer compliments on the home or children but should avoid admiring any specific object excessively because this may embarrass the host.

Eating

Thais use forks and spoons at the dining table. They hold the spoon in the right hand and the fork in the left, pushing food onto the spoon with the fork. Knives are usually not necessary because foods are served in bite-size pieces. Rural families may eat around a straw mat on the floor. In northern areas, people eat a steamed, sticky (glutinous) rice with their fingers. Chopsticks are used with noodle dishes and in Chinese homes. Guests usually receive a second helping of food and are encouraged to eat as much as they can. Diners choose small portions from various dishes at the center of the table to eat with rice. Bones and other such items are placed on the plate. Water, the standard mealtime drink, is drunk at the end of (not during) the meal. When finished, one places the utensils together on the plate. In restaurants, tips are not usually necessary, but some people give a small amount (5 percent) to the waiter or waitress for special service.

LIFESTYLE

Family

Thai families are close, and several generations may live in the same household. The oldest male is customarily the patriarch of the family. Members of the family (even adults) are usually expected to abide by the advice of their elders, although this is becoming less true with time and modernization. Still, Thais have great respect for their parents and the elderly. Families usually have two or three children. On a farm, all members of the household share the work. When the elderly live with their married children, they often tend the grandchildren. Polygamy was legal until 1935, and having many wives was a sign of wealth. Because traditions change slowly, many men openly keep mistresses in addition to their legal wife. However, Thai women are becoming less accepting of the practice, and the younger male generation is becoming increasingly willing to commit to one woman. A family's youngest daughter inherits the parents' home. In return, she and her husband care for the parents in their old age.

Dating and Marriage

In Thailand, girls have traditionally led a more sheltered life than boys, but this is no longer the case. Boys and girls generally have equal access to society. Although Western-style dating is popular in Bangkok, it is not as common in rural areas. According to tradition, if a boy wishes to marry a girl, he must first become well acquainted with the entire family and make himself agreeable to them. He then sends his parents to the girl's family to make his wishes known. If both families agree on the marriage, a wedding date is set. The groom traditionally pays a bride-price to the bride's parents as "compensation" for raising her. Some parents later return the items or cash to the couple as a wedding gift. Pink is the traditional color for bridal gowns. Grooms wear either a Western-style suit or pants and a high-necked jacket (*sua phrarachathan*). Rural newlyweds often live with the bride's parents until they have a child.

Diet

Rice (plain in southern and central regions, glutinous in the north) is the staple food of Thailand. It is usually served with spicy dishes that consist of meat, vegetables, fish, eggs, and fruits. Curries and pepper sauces are popular. Typical meats include beef, chicken, and pork. Thailand boasts a wide variety of tropical fruit year-round.

Recreation

The most popular sports in Thailand are soccer, table tennis, badminton, volleyball, and basketball. *Takro* (a traditional sport played by trying to keep a wicker ball in the air without using hands) and kite flying are favorite activities. The youth enjoy various martial arts. Movies and television provide leisure entertainment. Thai chess, played without a queen and under unique rules, is a popular urban spectator sport.

Holidays

Although the government uses the Western (Gregorian) calendar, Buddhist holidays are set by the lunar calendar and vary from year to year. Official holidays include New Year's Day; Chinese New Year, Chakri Day (6 April); Labor Day (1 May); Coronation Day (5 May); Royal Ploughing Ceremony (11 May); the Queen's Birthday (12 August); Chulalongkorn Day (23 October), honoring the "beloved monarch" (1868–1910) who abolished slavery and introduced many reforms; the King's Birthday (5 December); Constitution Day (10 December); and New Year's Eve.

Some important religious holidays include *Makha Bucha*, *Asalaha Bucha*, and *Visakha Bucha*, which mark important events in Buddhism's history. For *Songkhran*, the Thai New Year, people throw buckets of water on each other. *Loy Krathong* honors the water goddess for providing water throughout the year; people float small "boats" with candles, coins, or flowers on waterways.

Commerce

Most businesses are open Monday through Friday from 8:30 A.M. to 4:30 P.M., although some are open until 6:00 P.M. Retail shops are often open seven days a week, especially small, family-owned stores, and many stay open until 10:00 P.M. each day. When prices in small shops are not fixed, bargaining is expected but should be done in good taste because the people make very little profit. Thais buy fresh food in open markets.

SOCIETY

Government

In Thailand's constitutional monarchy, the King is head of state but has few executive responsibilities. The prime minister (Banharn Silpa-archa) heads the government. The National Assembly has two houses: a 270-member Senate, whose members are appointed by the King, and a 360-seat House of Representatives, whose members are directly elected. The voting age is 21. In villages, local chiefs are elected by the people. In addition to the Thai Nation Party, the Democratic Party, National Development Party, and New Aspiration Party all have significant voting blocs in the House.

Economy

Agriculture has traditionally been the backbone of the nation's economy, employing more than 70 percent of the labor force. But industry, which employs 11 percent, provides the bulk of Thailand's export earnings. This gives the country the reputation of being one of the most advanced nations in Southeast Asia.

Tin, textiles, fish products, rice, tapioca, and jewelry are among the most important exports. Thailand is the world's third largest producer of tin. The country's manufacturing base also includes electric appliances, furniture, integrated circuits, and plastics. Tourism is an important source of foreign-exchange currency and helps many local economies. Inflation is generally low. While official unemployment is low (4 percent), underemployment is a significant problem. The currency is the *baht* (B).

Thailand's real gross domestic product per capita ($5,950) has dramatically increased in the last decade. Urban poverty is decreasing, but poverty still affects one-third of rural people. Income distribution is highly unequal and economic prosperity is only slowly extending to rural areas. Still, more people than ever before can meet basic needs and have access to economic opportunities.

Transportation and Communication

Most large cities are connected by rail, highways, and air service. Local transportation is by bus, taxi, *samlor* (three-wheeled motorized taxi), and *silor* (mini-cab). In rural areas, pedicabs are most common. While most people still do not have cars, greater ownership has significantly increased urban traffic problems. Traffic moves on the left side of the road. Canals (*klongs*) are often used for transportation in rural and some urban areas. The Chao Phraya River serves as the most important waterway for Bangkok. Merchant and commuter traffic on this river is common. The government communications system is well developed, and the public telephone system is adequate for most needs.

Education

Education has been a priority of the government, and literacy and enrollment rates have increased dramatically over the last generation. The literacy rate is 93 percent. Universal, free, and compulsory education lasts for six years (seven in some areas). Nearly all primary-aged children are enrolled, although the figure drops to less than half for secondary education. Entrance to universities is by examination and there is stiff competition for a limited number of places. Sometimes boys, if they come from distant provinces, have greater opportunities than girls to study at universities. This is because boys can live in one of the many *wats* while girls must live in boarding schools and hostels, which can be expensive. Marriage is discouraged until one's education is complete.

Health

Health services have expanded greatly in the last decade, but they are still limited in remote rural areas. Tropical diseases are common outside the cities. The infant mortality rate is 36 per 1,000. Life expectancy ranges from 65 to 72 years. HIV/AIDS is one of the country's most serious problems, with some 100,000 children expected to be orphaned by the disease by the year 2000.

FOR THE TRAVELER

A visa and passport are necessary for U.S. travelers. No vaccinations are required; however, visitors to rural areas should take malarial suppressants and vaccinate against typhoid, cholera, and rabies. Drink bottled or boiled water. Eat only well-cooked meats; peel and wash all vegetables and fruits. Shorts are not appropriate attire in most public places. Thailand is a favorite tourist destination because of its unique architecture, rural villages, and ancient temples. For information, contact the Tourism Authority of Thailand, 5 World Trade Center, Suite 3443, New York, NY 10048; phone (212) 432–0433. The Royal Embassy of Thailand is located at 1024 Wisconsin Avenue NW, Room 101, Washington, DC 20007.

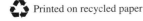

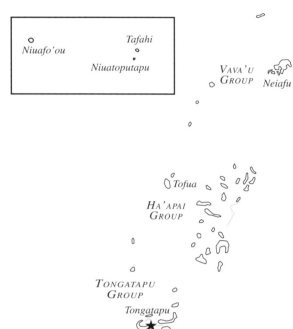

Kingdom of
Tonga

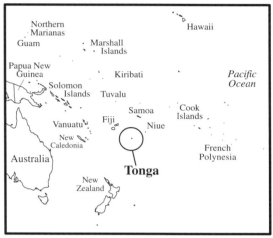

Boundary representations not necessarily authoritative.

BACKGROUND

Land and Climate

Tonga is composed of 170 islands, of which only 36 are inhabited. They stretch north to south across 500 miles (800 kilometers) of the Pacific Ocean. The total land area is less than 300 square miles (750 square kilometers). About half of the land is under cultivation and the soil is very fertile. Surrounding waters provide an abundance of fish and other seafood. The Tongan islands are composed of coral or volcanic formations. Tongatapu is mostly flat, with high cliffs in the southwest. Niuafo'ou, located about 210 miles (338 kilometers) northwest of the Vava'u group, is the world's only home to the *Malau* bird (a flightless bird), which lays large eggs in the sand that are incubated by heat from an active volcano. The volcano has a freshwater lake in the crater. 'Eua has several endemic plants and will eventually be home to a national park. Its rolling hills give way to high eastern cliffs, but the island is surrounded by many beaches. Other islands have similar features.

Tonga is divided into three island groups: Ha'apai, Tongatapu, and Vava'u. The largest individual islands are Tongatapu and 'Eua. The capital is Nuku'alofa. Although located in the tropics, Tonga experiences few extremes in heat, rain, or humidity. Nuku'alofa's average temperature is about 76°F (24°C); humidity averages 76 percent. Northern islands are somewhat warmer and more humid. Cyclones are possible from October to April, and the dry season is from June to November.

History

Written histories do not exist for Tonga before the 17th century, but experts believe the islands were settled by at least 500 B.C. According to tradition, the Tongan ruler was known as the Tui Tonga and was descended from the Creator, Tangaloa 'Eitumatupu'a. The heridatary monarchy reached its zenith in the 13th century, when it ruled not only over Tonga but also other Pacific islands (Samoa, Niue, Fiji, and others). The empire eventually declined, even as the population grew. Society became unstable and several Tui Tonga were assasinated. In 1470, a new office was created by the Tui Tonga called the *hau*, or Temporal Ruler. The Tui Tonga became Sacred Ruler, more distant from daily government. The first *hau* created the Tu'i Ha'atakalaua Dynasty. In the 17th century, another dynasty was formed by a descendant of the first *hau*. The monarchy was stable and generally presided over a prosperous people. The Tui Tonga tradition continued into the 19th century. Because the high chiefs lived on Tongatapu, the main island group, and the royal subjects lived on other islands, Tongatapu was known as the Land of Chiefs and the other islands were called the Land of Servants. Great honor was paid to the Tui Tonga and other chiefs.

The Dutch were the first Europeans to visit Tonga in 1616. Britain's Captain James Cook visited in 1773 and returned in 1777. He named Tonga "the Friendly Islands" for the way the inhabitants treated him. British missionaries from the Wesleyan Methodist Church arrived in 1797. Civil war erupted in the 1790s and continued through the 1820s. An

OCEANIA

important struggle between Taufa'ahau, the chief of Ha'apai, and the Tui Tonga was impacted by the spread of Christianity. A Wesleyan Mission was established in 1826. Taufa'ahau converted to Christianity in 1831, chose the name George (after the current English king), and was victorious in his struggle against the Tui Tonga. He founded the present royal dynasty in 1845, proclaiming himself King George Tupou I. The Wesleyans helped develop a written code of Tonga's laws. When the king fully united all Tongan islands in 1850, the Code of Laws was in effect for all subjects. Serfdom was abolished in 1862, and a constitution was promulgated in 1875.

Facing economic troubles, King George Tupou II asked for and received British aid. The two nations signed a treaty of friendship in 1900. In 1905, Britain made Tonga a protectorate, which was not dissolved until 1970. Tongans point out that Britain never colonized the island, and the Tongans remained essentially sovereign. They look to 1970 as a year in which they rejoined equality with other countries rather than as a date of independence. Queen Salote Tupou III ruled from 1918 to 1965. She was followed by her son, King Taufa'ahau Tupou IV, who currently reigns.

THE PEOPLE

Population

Tonga's population of about 105,600 is growing annually at 0.8 percent. About two-thirds of the people live on Tongatapu, and Nuku'alofa has some 35,000 inhabitants. Tongans of Polynesian descent make up the bulk of the population. Small minorities of other Pacific Islanders and a few hundred Europeans also reside in Tonga.

Language

Tongan and English are both official languages. Government documents are in both languages, but Tongan is the language of daily communication. English is used in business correspondence and is taught as a second language in school. Tongan was an oral language prior to the 20th century but a written form based on the Latin alphabet was established in 1897. The alphabet includes 16 letters plus a glottal stop (indicated by an apostrophe). Tongan spelling is phonemic; words are spelled the way they are pronounced. For instance, the traditional greeting *Malo e lelei* is pronounced "MAH-low eh leh-LEH-ee." All consonants are separated by a vowel, all vowels are prounounced, and all words end in a vowel.

Religion

Nearly all Tongans are Christians. The royal family, nobles, and about 30 percent of the population belong to the Free Wesleyan Church, which is the official state church. The king is the head of the church. The Church of Jesus Christ of Latter-day Saints (Mormon) is the second largest church, followed by the Roman Catholic Church, the Independence Church of Tonga, and the Church of Tonga. According to royal edict, rules of the Sabbath are quite strict and widely upheld in Tonga. Virtually everything is closed on Sunday, except for emergency facilities.

General Attitudes

Tongans are proud of their independent nation, their royal heritage, and their Polynesian culture. The "Tongan way" of life (*FakaTonga*) is easygoing and relaxed. Whatever does not get done today can be done tomorrow. This is not an attitude of laziness but an expression of a relatively worry-free approach to life. Tongans are generous, devoted to family and religion, gentle, and friendly. They value cleanliness, good manners, a good education, and respectful behavior, especially toward elders. Men and women who drink alcohol or smoke are not considered good role models.

The youth are becoming more interested in pursuing a Western lifestyle, and pressures to emigrate abroad are increasing. Young people more often associate their agricultural heritage with a hard lifestyle and low income; they see getting a good education and seeking urban or foreign employment as a way to rise above those roots. While they retain their devotion to core Tongan values, their pursuits cannot help but change Tongan society in the future.

Personal Appearance

Because modesty is valued, most females do not wear short skirts or low-necked dresses. Pants are inappropriate for women. By law, males older than age 16 must wear shirts in public places. Long hair is not appropriate for men. The Tongan word for clothes is *valas*. For many generations, men wore *tupenus* (calf-length pieces of material wrapped around the waist) with a *ta'ovala* (a piece of fine material, made from the leaves of the pandanus tree, that is wrapped around the waist and tied with a coconut-fiber rope). Open-necked shirts were also worn as a sign of respect. Today, Western clothing, including ties, suit jackets, and trousers, is common for everyday use. Still, *tupenus* and the *ta'ovala* are required attire (along with a tie) for formal occasions such as associating with royalty. Tongan women traditionally wore a *kiekie* (an ankle-length skirt), often accompanied with a *ta'ovala*. Today, blouses are worn with the *kiekie*, and women also commonly wear Western clothing.

CUSTOMS AND COURTESIES

Greetings

It is appropriate to greet people either with a handshake or a verbal greeting. Men often hold the handshake for several seconds during a brief conversation. *Malo e lelei* (Hello) is a common daytime greeting, in addition to several different phrases that can be used to say "Good morning." Two such phrases are *Malo e lelei ki he pongipongi* and *Malo e tau mo eni.* "Good evening" is expressed as *Malo e lelei ki he efiafi ni.* Visitors might be greeted with *Talitali fiefia* (Welcome). Nobility are greeted with different phrases.

Upon being introduced, one might say *Fefe hake?* (How do you do?). The polite response is *Sai pe, Malo* (Fine, thank you). When parting, one says *'Alu a,* to which the other replies *Nofa a* (both of which mean "Good-bye"). Tongans customarily call acquaintances by their given names. People meeting for the first time often use titles and family names, since doing so shows respect. If professional titles are not used, *Tangata'eiki* (Mr.), *Fine'eiki* (Mrs.), and *Ta'ahine* (Miss) are appropriate.

Gestures

The use of body gestures is important in communication. Raising the eyebrows means "Yes" or "I agree." It is not appropriate to call anyone other than children by using hand motions. A downward wave of the arm is a gesture meaning

"Come here." A forward and upward wave means "Go" or "Good-bye." Young men and boys often walk holding hands as an expression of friendship, but physical displays of affection between members of the opposite sex (or even kissing between parents and children) are considered inappropriate. When one sits in a chair, it is proper to cross one's legs at the knee. Eating or drinking while standing in public is inappropriate.

Visiting

Tongan society is closely knit and socializing is an integral part of daily life. Women seldom go anywhere without being accompanied by another woman. Tongans passing each other while walking always greet each other, even if not personally acquainted. And relatives (who are often neighbors) frequently visit each other, especially on Sunday afternoon.

Most visits during the week are spontaneous. Unexpected guests are usually welcomed in. However, if a family feels their house is not adequately furnished or cleaned, they may be reluctant to invite a visitor in. Visitors remove their shoes upon entering and are often directed to the best seats in the house. In a traditional home, men sit cross-legged on the floor and women sit with both legs tucked behind them to one side. Children are kept out of the way as much as possible. Hosts usually offer refreshments such as water, coconut, *otai* (a mixture of cut fruit), or soda. The family always tries to accommodate the guests' needs. If guests arrive unexpectedly at mealtime, the hosts will invite them to stay and eat. A complimentary speech from departing guests is a high honor to the family.

Tongans generally enjoy giving and receiving personal compliments. Guests often compliment the home or family but should avoid admiring any one object too specifically. This may cause the host to feel obligated to offer the item as a gift. Tongans welcome but do not expect gifts from guests. Gifts are not opened in front of the person giving the gift. Flowers are considered gifts on special occasions (weddings, funerals, etc.), but other items may be more appropriate when visiting the home socially. Hosts may give a gift to honored or new guests when they leave. It is a terrible insult to decline such offers, which may include fruit, tapa cloth, or handicrafts.

Eating

Families eat their meals together whenever possible. On outer islands, they sit on woven mats to eat, but urban households more often have dining tables and other Western furniture. Although Tongans traditionally ate with their hands, standard utensils are now common. A prayer is offered before eating. Conversation is kept to a minimum. When guests are present, they usually eat with a few selected members of the family. Children are sent away or eat in a different place. Guests are served first and the person who prepared the meal usually eats last.

Standing while eating and drinking is not appropriate, even though others may do it. In restaurants, Tongans do not tip and servers do not accept tips from foreigners.

LIFESTYLE

Family

Families are close-knit and care for each other in almost every situation. In addition to parents and siblings, one's family unit includes grandparents, uncles, aunts, and cousins. In many cases, all family members work together to plant, harvest, cook, and fish. When young married couples live with the woman's parents, the man takes responsibility to provide food for that family. Although families are getting smaller, they remain fairly large by Western standards, averaging three or four children.

In a traditional Tongan family, the father is the head of the family and the mother is his subordinate. However, brothers are subordinate to their sisters (when close in age). That means that the oldest daughter (rather than the oldest son, as in many societies) receives the best of the family's resources. A father's eldest sister (*mehekitanga*) is the leader (*fahu*) over that nuclear family in the highly organized extended-family system.

Homes in modern Tonga vary from the traditional coconut-leaf and timber *fale* in rural areas to the frame, tin, or cinder-block *fale* in wealthier areas. All families own their homes, but sometimes two families (often two generations of one family) will live in the same house. Technically, all land is leased by heirship allotment from the nobles and is owned by the king. In practice, though, the people "own" the land they live on.

Dating and Marriage

Boys and girls are kept separate from a fairly early age, so interaction is limited until they get older. Teenagers meet at supervised school, church, or village activities. The traditional practice of "dating" only inside the girl's home allows a boy to get acquainted with the girl, her parents, and her family. To date at other locations, a girl is often accompanied by her mother or another family member. Marriages are times of great celebration. Ceremonies follow the traditions of the people's religious affiliation. Festivities after the ceremony can include hymn singing, a large feast, and many speeches. Young couples generally have their own home but may choose to move in with the bride's parents.

Diet

Tongans traditionally eat two meals each day, which may consist of yams, taro leaves, sweet potatoes, cassava, fish, or pork. European-style meals (a light, early breakfast, a meal at noon, and one in the evening) are becoming popular.

A popular dish is cooked taro leaves with coconut cream and corned beef (*Lu pulu*). Pork and chicken are the primary meats, and fish (tuna, shark, grouper, and parrot fish) is a typical main dish. Roast pig is a favorite. Tongans enjoy abundant mangoes, guavas, citrus fruits (oranges, mandarins, lemons, limes, and grapefruits), papayas, watermelon, squash pumpkin, passion fruit, bananas, plantains, avocados, and coconuts. Local vegetables include tomatoes, carrots, onions, green peppers, and cabbage. Tongans produce most of their own food, but an increasing amount is being imported.

Recreation

Tongans are sports enthusiasts. Rugby is the national sport. Most villages compete in rugby, cricket, volleyball, basketball, and tennis. Girls play *netball*, a court (grass, wood, or blacktop) sport very similar to basketball. Movies and dances are also major forms of recreation in larger villages. When dances are restricted to traditional Polynesian music, boys and girls do not dance together. They may dance together to modern music, but girls often have chaperones. Younger boys play with marbles and slingshots. Picnics on the beach celebrate special occasions. People often drink kava root juice and converse late into the night. Men enjoy building boats, canoes, and houses; wood carving is a popular hobby. Women weave mats and baskets, make dolls, and string special flower leis.

Holidays

The official holidays in Tonga include New Year's Day, Easter (Friday–Monday), Anzac Day (25 April), the Crown Prince's Birthday (4 May), Emancipation Day (4 June), the Birthday of King Taufa'ahau Tupou IV (4 July), Constitution Day (4 November), King George Tupou I Day (4 December), Christmas Day, and Boxing Day (26 December). Boxing Day comes from the British tradition of giving small boxed gifts to servants and tradesmen. It is now a day for visiting friends and relatives. Anzac Day is a New Zealand and Australian holiday honoring the armed forces; Tongans celebrate it for the Tongan soldiers who fought in World War II. There are also various local celebrations and festivals throughout the year.

Commerce

Generally, business hours extend from 8:00 A.M. to 5:00 P.M., Monday through Friday, and until noon on Saturday. All businesses close on Sunday. Many women may weave baskets for much of the day to sell locally. Except for produce in the market, merchandise is sold at fixed prices. Purchased items are often wrapped in newspapers. Some supermarkets operate in Nuku'alofa, but most shopping occurs at open markets. People on outer islands without refrigeration must acquire and prepare perishable items daily.

SOCIETY

Government

Tonga is a hereditary, constitutional monarchy. Tongans hold their royalty in high esteem. King Taufa'ahau Tupou IV is head of state. A prime minister (currently Baron Vaea) is head of government. The king and his cabinet form the Privy Council, which is part of the executive branch with the prime minister and his cabinet. Cabinet ministers are appointed by the king and hold their posts until retirement. The Legislative Assembly (*Fale Alea*) includes the executive branch members, nine members of Tongan nobility (elected by the nobility), and nine directly elected representatives. Legislators are elected as independents; political parties are a relatively new concept. All literate, tax-paying males are allowed to vote, as are literate females older than 21. The last legislative elections were held in 1996.

Economy

Agriculture and fishing are the mainstays of the economy and provide nearly all of Tonga's export earnings. Important products include coconuts (coconut oil and copra), bananas, taro, vanilla beans, fruits, vegetables, and a variety of fish. New export opportunities, such as squash pumpkin to Japan, have provided a recent boost to agricultural expansion. A growing manufacturing industry accounts for about 10 percent of all economic activity. Agricultural activities employ 70 percent of the labor force. Tonga must import consumer items and machinery. It is somewhat dependent on Western aid. Tourism has grown to become an important source of income and jobs. Tongans are not wealthy, but they generally have enough to meet basic needs. The currency is the *pa'anga*.

Transportation and Communication

Many Tongans own and use private cars for local transportation. Public buses and taxis serve the entire island of Tongatapu but are limited on other islands. Ferries travel between the islands, and air service is available to the main island groups. Most Tongans listen to daily broadcasts of the one radio station or watch broadcasts of the one television station. Television reception from New Zealand and Australia is also possible. There are few telephones and international links are limited. Two weekly newspapers serve the population.

Education

The government provides free and compulsory education for children ages six to fourteen. One year of kindergarten at age five is optional. Tonga has a high level of school enrollment. About two-thirds of secondary school students attend church-sponsored schools. A trade school offers technical skills to post-secondary students. 'Atenisi University offers a college education, and the University of the South Pacific also has a campus in Tonga. The literacy rate is nearly 100 percent.

Health

Tonga enjoys a generally healthy environment and freedom from most tropical diseases. The government provides free health care to all citizens; private clinics also exist. While each island group has a hospital, the most modern one is in Nuku'alofa; it is the only one that can offer advanced care. Most doctors are trained abroad. Traditional healers play an important role in primary health care; they often prescribe traditional remedies for illness. The infant mortality rate is 20 per 1,000. Life expectancy averages 68 years.

FOR THE TRAVELER

U.S. travelers do not need a visa for stays of up to 30 days, although a valid passport and proof of onward passage are required. Travelers are issued a visitor's permit at the airport. Valid yellow fever and cholera vaccination certificates are required of all travelers (except infants) who have been in an infected area prior to arrival. Other vaccinations are not required. Water is potable in the capital and resort areas.

Tonga is a lesser-known tourist destination in the South Pacific, but its beauty, friendly people, and improving facilities are enticing to many travelers. For information, contact the Tonga Visitors Bureau, PO Box 37, Nuku'alofa, Tonga. Tonga does not maintain an embassy in Washington, D.C., but the Consulate General may have more information: 360 Post Street, Suite 604, San Francisco, CA 94108; phone (415) 781–0365.

 Printed on recycled paper

Republic of
Tunisia

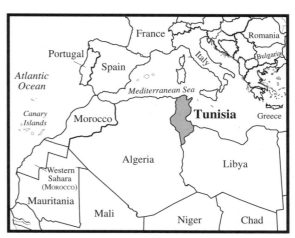

Boundary representations not necessarily authoritative.

BACKGROUND

Land and Climate

Tunisia covers 63,170 square miles (163,610 square kilometers) and is a bit larger than the state of Georgia. Hundreds of miles of sandy beaches line the northern and eastern Mediterranean coasts. Mountains along the Algerian border are balanced by oases in the southern desert. Orange orchards are found in the Cap Bon (northeastern peninsula) and olive farms in the Sahel (southern semidesert). The climate is mostly mild, with average temperatures ranging from 52°F (13°C) in winter to 80°F (26°C) in summer. Toward the desert, temperatures are much hotter, especially when the south wind (*sirocco* or *sh'hili*) blows. Sea breezes moderate the coastal climate. Winter nights can be cold throughout the country.

History

Throughout its history, Tunisia was a crossroads of many civilizations. Tunisia's indigenous inhabitants are known collectively as Berbers, but a more accurate indigenous term for them is Imazighen (Amazigh, singular). Phoenicians founded Carthage in 814 B.C. and fought the Romans in the Punic Wars. Carthage was captured and eventually destroyed by the Romans. Tunisia's ancient heritage is evident in well-preserved archaeological sites and excellent museums.

The two major influences shaping Tunisian society are Islam and the remnants of French colonialism. Islam came with invading Arabs in the seventh century. Indigenous groups gradually adopted the Arabic language and customs, and Tunisia became a center of Islamic culture. The Turkish Ottoman Empire ruled the area between 1574 and 1881. Economic difficulties and French colonial interests led to the Treaty of Bardo (1881), which made Tunisia a French protectorate. French culture soon became very influential and its influence continues to a lesser extent today. Because of its relation to France, Tunisia was a major World War II battleground.

Before the war, many Tunisians had pressed for independence, and the movement picked up again after 1945. Independence was finally secured relatively peacefully in 1956. Habib Bourguiba, who had led the movement since the 1930s, became Tunisia's first president in 1957. Bourguiba was re-elected every five years, always running unopposed, until he was named president for life in 1974. When he became too old to govern (in 1987), his prime minister, Zine El Abidine Ben Ali, legally removed him from power and took over as president. Bourguiba's 31 years in power left a strong imprint on Tunisia, his greatest achievements being in education, women's emancipation, and social modernization.

Ben Ali was reelected in 1989 and 1993. Other political parties have always been legal in Tunisia, but they have little power against the governing party. The Islamic Fundamentalist Movement (*Ennahdha*) is banned because political parties of a religious or linguistic nature are illegal. Islamic fundamentalism has caused social unrest in the past few years and is therefore subject to government controls.

THE PEOPLE

Population

Tunisia's population of 8.9 million is growing at 1.7 percent annually. About 37 percent of the population is younger than age 15. Most people (98 percent) are of Arab descent. Others, mostly of European descent, live mainly in and around Tunis or on the island of Djerba. More than half of all Tunisians live in urban areas. Greatly influenced by the French, who ruled the country for more than 75 years, some urban Tunisians consider Tunisia the most Westernized state in the Arab world. Still, most Tunisians identify more with their "Arabness" than their "Westernness." People in small towns and villages tend to be more conservative than those in cities.

The country's Human Development Index (0.763) ranks it 75th out of 174 countries. Adjusted for women, the index is only 0.641, reflecting gaps between men and women in income and education. Opportunities for personal advancement are expanding, as is the middle class.

Language

Although Arabic is the official language, French is spoken in business and official circles. Urban Tunisians easily switch from one language to the other in the same sentence. Many high school students or graduates speak some English, since it is considered imperative to national and individual success. *Derija* is the Arabic dialect spoken in Tunisia; it dominates in rural regions. *Derija* is a variation of the classical Arabic found in the *Qur'an* (Koran), but it is so different that a speaker of classical Arabic might not understand spoken *Derija*—although he himself would be understood. All Arabic nations speak a dialect, with North African dialects related and Middle Eastern dialects related.

Religion

Islam is the official religion, and 98 percent of the people are Muslim. The majority are Sunni Muslims of the Malikite tradition, as founded by Malik ibn Anas. He codified Islamic traditions and stressed the importance of community consensus (as opposed to Shiites, who emphasize the authority of Muhammad's descendants). Islam plays an important role in daily life, especially during family events such as births, circumcisions, weddings, and burials. Friday is Islam's holy day; government offices and many businesses close at 1:00 P.M. In addition to attending Friday prayer services at the mosque, Muslims pray five times daily. They accept the *Qur'an* (Koran) as scripture, believing it was revealed by *Allah* (God) to the prophet Muhammad. Abraham is honored as the father of Muslims. Muhammad is considered the last and greatest prophet, although many biblical prophets are accepted as important messengers. In villages without mosques, *zaouia* (small mausoleums built in memory of especially holy men) are the main centers for religious activity. One percent of the population is Christian and a smaller number is Jewish.

General Attitudes

Tunisians are a traditional, yet adaptable, friendly, and open people. They tend to act more formally with international visitors in order to give them the best impression of Tunisian culture. Tunisians are eager to share their culture with others. This might include taking foreigners to their homes for a meal or to museums, cafés, or archaeological sites. Tunisians enjoy learning about these guests' families, food, and politics. They value hospitality, warmth, and generosity and place importance on cultural arts.

While Tunisians often are relaxed and informal with each other, they also emphasize showing respect for one another, especially their elders. Conformity to a group (family or community) and concern for its well-being are usually more important than individual desires. Still, social status and possessions are valued, especially by men. Tunisians tend to use phrases such as *Inshallah* (God willing) and *Allah ghalib* (God is stronger) for expressing hopes or intentions. Difficult times are explained as *maktoub* (fate), an attitude that provides comfort and perseverance. A Tunisian's concept of time is loose; most people do not keep to a rigid schedule, and some things can take a long time to get done. "Three days" can easily mean three weeks.

Personal Appearance

In Tunis and other large cities, fashion is influenced by western Europe, particularly Italy and France. Most rural Tunisians, however, still wear traditional North African clothing. Older women, both in the city and countryside, might wear a white *safsari* (rectangular piece of cloth that completely covers the clothing) while in public. Once worn mainly out of modesty, the *safsari* today also protects clothing from dust and rain. Older Amazigh women might wear a *futah*, a dark red wraparound dress. Shorts and immodest attire are not worn in public, except in resort areas. However, young urban women might wear short skirts, while their rural counterparts are sure to at least cover their knees and shoulders. Rural women wear their hair up and covered; they let it down for celebrations and special occasions.

CUSTOMS AND COURTESIES

Greetings

Greetings in Tunisia are an important and expressive part of personal interaction. Friends and family members often greet each other by "kissing the air" while brushing cheeks. Among strangers, both men and women, a handshake is the most common form of greeting. Men may also shake hands when parting. Standard greetings include *Ass'lama* (Hello), *Bisslama* (Good-bye), *Sabah El-Kheer* (Good morning), and *Tass'bah Ala Kheer* (Good night). Asking about someone's health and family is expected before further conversation. People say *Assalama Allekuhm* (Peace to you) when joining a group or entering a crowded room. When entering a store or office, a person greets the owner or staff. Neglecting to greet someone upon meeting is a serious oversight. Personal warmth is characteristic of all greetings.

Gestures

Hand gestures are an integral part of communication between Tunisians in everyday discussions and price negotiations. For example, the thumb and all fingertips pulled together and pointing up, while being waved toward the body, can either mean "Good!" or "Wait!" depending on the context. One beckons by waving all fingers toward the body while the palm faces down. Using the index finger to point at objects or people is considered rude. Winking at someone in public is inappropriate.

Not all Tunisians subscribe to the tradition of avoiding the use of the left hand. Many urbanites use both hands freely. However, rural and some urban residents use only the right hand for shaking hands, passing objects, touching others, and eating. The left hand is reserved for bathroom hygiene. Like other Mediterranean peoples, Tunisians are spirited in conversational gestures and appreciate the same from visitors. Touching between members of the same sex is common to emphasize speech and communicate warmth. Friends of the same sex often walk hand in hand, but this does not suggest anything beyond friendship. Men and women, however, usually do not hold hands in public because public displays of affection are inappropriate.

Visiting

Family and friends visit each other frequently and unannounced—often in the late evening. Visits can last several hours, and guests usually are invited for a meal. It is especially important to visit neighbors and family on religious holidays.

Because hospitality is important, a host usually offers food and drink to guests. Such an offer is accepted, even if only for a taste. Invited guests might bring gifts of fruit or chocolate (never alcohol) to the host. Hosts commonly give first-time visitors a tour of the home, especially if a new room or new furniture has been added. On such an occasion, guests might congratulate the hosts with *mabrouk*, a congratulatory wish also used for weddings, graduations, or new employment.

Eating

Tunisians wash their hands before and after meals. Eating from separate plates with utensils is common only among the Westernized upper class. Otherwise, people sit on the floor around a low, round, wooden table (*mida*) at mealtime. They eat with the hand or use bread as a scoop, and customarily eat from a common plate or group of dishes. Tunisians do not like to eat alone. A host will often insist that guests have second or third helpings, and it is polite for guests to accept. When a person has eaten enough, he or she says *Hamdullah* (Thanks to God) to express the meal was good. Burping after a meal is considered rude. In restaurants, the tip usually is included in the bill.

LIFESTYLE

Family

The extended family is the most important social unit. Honor, reputation, and mutual support are important family values. Polygamy has been outlawed since Tunisia's independence in 1956, even though Islamic tradition allows a man to have up to four wives. Generally, men and women command equal respect in the home. By tradition, however, men dominate and a woman's role is clearly defined. Women are responsible for the household and children.

Although many women work outside the home in important positions, society is as male dominated as the home. Still, women comprise one-fourth of the labor force. Tunisia is the most progressive among Muslim countries in its laws concerning women's rights at work and in matters of divorce and inheritance. However, attitudes are changing more slowly than the law.

Dating and Marriage

Since Western dating practices generally are not accepted, weddings and social gatherings provide a chance for young people to meet. Marriage is not only a union between individuals but a link between two families. Rural marriages are often arranged by the parents—sometimes between cousins—but urban young people have increasing opportunities to meet

and get to know one another independently. Their parents still have a strong voice in who they marry, but the couples have the final say.

Traditional weddings, particularly in rural areas, are celebrated over several days, even weeks, through ritualized ceremonies and parties. The most important festivities occur in the last few days before the wedding. Men and women have separate parties. In one (*seqer*), the bride's body hair is "waxed" off with a sugar, water, and lemon paste. A henna party follows on the night before the wedding. Women invited to the bride's home apply patterns to her hands and feet using a paste made from henna leaves (the dried paste is removed after several hours, leaving patterns behind that last for several days). The bride also has her hair and makeup done. On her wedding day, a bride may wear one or two traditional dresses as well as a Western gown. After the ceremony, relatives and friends celebrate with dancing, music, and food.

Diet

Couscous is Tunisia's national dish; it is made of steamed and spiced semolina, and topped with vegetables and meats. Appreciated for its delicacy and lightness, *couscous* is prepared in many ways. *Breek*, another favorite dish, is made of a thin, fried dough stuffed with an egg, cooked vegetables, and tuna. *Tajine* is a crustless quiche of vegetables and meats. Tunisians frequently eat fish, lamb, and chicken. Tomatoes, potatoes, onions, olives, oil, and peppers are common to Tunisian cooking. A large variety of fruits are sold in the markets, including dates, oranges, apricots, watermelons, and nectarines. Cactus fruit (*hindi*), called the "sultan of all fruits," is widely available in the summer. *Tabuna* is a round bread baked in a cylindrical clay oven by the same name. Alcohol and pork are forbidden by Islam, but alcohol is available in large towns.

Recreation

Listening to music, watching movies (increasingly on VCRs) or television, going to the beach, playing soccer and beach volleyball (mostly men), and visiting friends and relatives are among the most popular leisure activities. Most people enjoy *shkubbah*, a traditional card game. Summer art festivals are organized throughout the country and attract large crowds. Coffeehouses are extremely popular among men, who go there to play cards, discuss sports and politics, conduct business, and drink coffee. Women usually do not go to coffeehouses unless in the company of male relatives.

Holidays

Although Tunisia's secular holidays follow the Western calendar, religious holidays follow the Muslim (lunar) calendar, so they fall on different days each year. The most important holiday period is *Ramadan*, a month of fasting and prayer. While Muslims do not eat, drink, or smoke from sunrise to sundown each day during *Ramadan*, they participate in lively evenings that involve special foods, carnivals, shopping, and festivals. Non-Muslims, while not expected to fast, should exercise good judgment about eating in public and taking part in the evening celebrations. *Aid El Seghir*, a two-day holiday, marks the end of *Ramadan*. People wear their best clothes to visit friends and relatives, and they trade presents of pastry. Other holidays include *Ras El Am El Hejri* (Islamic New Year),

El Mouled (prophet Muhammad's birthday), and *Aid El Kebir* (commemorating Abraham's willingness to sacrifice his son). For *Aid El Kebir*, each household sacrifices a lamb at dawn and feasts on grilled lamb throughout the day as relatives visit one another.

Secular holidays include New Year's Day (1 January), Independence Day (20 March), Martyr's Day (9 April), Labor Day (1 May), Republic Day (25 July), Women's Day (13 August), Evacuation Day (15 October, the day in 1963 when the last of the French troops returned to France), and the "Second Revolution," or the day that Ben Ali assumed power from Bourgiba (7 November).

Commerce

From September to June, business hours are Monday through Thursday, from 8:00 A.M. to 12:30 P.M. and 2:00 to 6:00 P.M. On Friday and Saturday, hours are from 8:00 A.M. to 1:00 P.M. Businesses are closed on Sunday. Many private companies, including banks, have slightly longer working hours during the week and are closed all day Saturday and Sunday. Tunisia has a shortened work schedule for July and August, when most businesses operate Monday through Saturday 7:00 A.M. to 1:00 P.M.

The weekly *souk* (market) is the focal point of local economic activity; people come to buy goods and produce, to trade, and to socialize. On the night of a *souk*, families often enjoy a meal of *couscous* topped with the freshest vegetables.

Tunisian businesspeople usually have tea or engage in small talk before discussing business, but this practice is disappearing among more Westernized Tunisians, especially as time pressures and business contacts with the West increase. Many details in business arrangements are not written down because the business environment does not always guarantee that such things as deadlines will be met.

SOCIETY

Government

Tunisia is a republic divided into 23 governorates. The central government is headed by a president who appoints a prime minister and a Council of Ministers. Members of the unicameral legislature, the 141-seat Chamber of Deputies (*Majlis al-Nuwaab*), are elected by the people. All citizens may vote at age 20. The ruling party is Ben Ali's Constitutional Democratic Rally Party (RCD, locally called *Destour* for "constitution"), although a number of independents and Islamists are represented in the legislature and smaller political parties do function.

Economy

Agriculture, light industry, and services all play key roles in Tunisia's economy. Agriculture is especially important in the interior and along the Sahel coast; olives and dates are exported. The textile industry (mostly for export) provides jobs for thousands of laborers, as does tourism, Tunisia's main source of hard currency. Remittances from Tunisian workers in France and income from oil and phosphates are also vital. Most exports go to Europe; most tourists come from Germany and France. The currency is the Tunisian *dinar* (TD).

Tunisia's economy is shifting toward a free market, and economic growth is about 4.5 percent. In 1995, export earnings rose an impressive 19.6 percent. The workforce is educated and productive. Real gross domestic product per capita is $5,160. Inflation is low, but unemployment (16 percent) remains a significant problem with serious social implications. The higher the unemployment rate, the more radical the fundamentalist movement can be.

Transportation and Communication

A good network of paved roads and highways links all cities and towns. Major railroads serve northern and coastal areas. Tunis, the capital, has an efficient light-rail system (*Métro Leger*). Buses are the most common form of public transportation. *Louages* (group taxis) run on set routes between cities and are faster than buses. Most families do not own cars. Motorcycles and bicycles are common. In rural areas, people may use donkey carts to transport goods and vegetables. There are airports in major cities. Phone service is good, but it may be slow in summer because the shorter work schedule strains the system. Most people do not have telephones in their homes, but they access them at post offices. The press is regulated by the government. There are four television stations. Postal delivery is efficient.

Education

Education has been an important element in Tunisia's development since independence. One-fourth of the government's budget is spent on education. This allows even the most remote regions to have free schooling. *École de Base* (Basic Education, grades 1–6) is compulsory and nearly all children are enrolled. Advancement depends on passing tests. About half of all students go on to the *Lycée* (grades 7–13). In tenth grade, students choose between two tracks: *Lettres* (humanities and social sciences) or *Sciences* (math and science). The rigorous Baccalaureate Exam is taken at the end of the 13th grade; successful students may go on to a university. A student's passing the test is a great source of pride for his or her parents. While classes are taught in French and Arabic, there is a trend to promote Arabic and the use of Arabic textbooks. Tunisia's literacy rate is 65 percent.

Health

The government provides free medical care to all citizens. There are also several private clinics in major cities. Rural health care may be limited to clinics for child immunizations, family planning, and other basic services. The infant mortality rate is 32 per 1,000. Life expectancy averages 71 to 75 years.

FOR THE TRAVELER

A valid passport is required for U.S. citizens to enter Tunisia, but no visa is required for visits of up to four months. There are no required vaccinations. Bottled water is recommended for drinking. Wash fruits and vegetables thoroughly before eating. Tunisia offers many well-run coastal resorts and sites of interest. For more information, contact the Embassy of Tunisia, 1515 Massachusetts Avenue NW, Washington, DC 20005; phone (202) 862–1850.

CULTURGRAM™ '97

Republic of
Turkey

Boundary representations not necessarily authoritative.

BACKGROUND

Land and Climate

Turkey is located at the juncture where Europe meets Asia, forming a bridge and a link to each continent. Covering 301,382 square miles (780,580 square kilometers), Turkey is about the size of Texas. The western portion is called Thrace, while the eastern portion is known as Anatolia or Asia Minor. Several countries, as well as the Aegean, Mediterranean, and Black Seas, border the country. Anatolia is a plateau that becomes more mountainous to the east. Mountains are also found along the Black Sea. Both the Euphrates and Tigris Rivers flow through Turkey. The coastal regions are generally low. Winters can be very cold in some portions of the country, although they are mild along the coasts. Summers are pleasant but can be hot in some areas.

History

Modern Turkey is the most recent in a series of important states and empires that have inhabited the Anatolian peninsula since the beginning of history. The oldest known site of human urban habitation is located in central Turkey at Chatalhuyuk (6500 B.C.). The great Hittite Empire (3000–2000 B.C.), which dominated much of the Middle East, was centered east of Ankara. Ancient Troy, the scene of much of Homer's *Iliad*, was located near the Dardanelles. Alexander the Great captured Anatolia in the fourth century B.C., and the Romans followed three centuries later, establishing important cities, such as Ephesus and Antioch, as major provincial capitals.

In A.D. 330, the Roman Emperor Constantine founded the city of Constantinople, which later became the center of the Byzantine Empire. This great state dominated eastern Europe for one thousand years. The Muslim Seljuk Turks entered Asia Minor in the 11th century and began the long process of Islamization and Turkization. In 1453, the successors of the Seljuks, the Ottoman Turks, captured Constantinople and went on to create a vast empire, stretching beyond the bounds of the Byzantine Empire into the Balkans, the Middle East, and North Africa. The Ottoman Empire survived until World War I when it allied itself with the Central Powers. With the defeat of the Central Powers, the empire was dismembered.

In 1923, out of the ruins of the Ottoman Empire, General Mustafa Kemal (known as Atatürk) fashioned the Republic of Turkey. Under Atatürk, the nation was reformed from an Islamic empire to a secular state with an Islamic majority. Although most of Turkey is in Asia, it has always had important European ties. In 1952, Turkey joined the North Atlantic Treaty Organization (NATO) and provided land for a U.S. military base.

Over the next three decades, the country went through various cycles of political turmoil. In the late 1970s, serious economic problems and political upheaval, which nurtured widespread domestic terrorism, so paralyzed the government that the military seized control in 1980. The military restored stability, called for elections in 1983, and withdrew from power after the elections. The military commander responsible for these actions, Kenan Evran, was elected president. His prime minister, Turgut Özal, became the dominant political figure in the 1980s.

In 1989, Özal was elected by Parliament to be president for a seven-year term. Parliamentary elections in 1991 brought Özal's rival to power as prime minister. Suleyman Demirel had been prime minister before and was twice (1971 and 1980) ousted in coups. When Özal suddenly died in 1993, Demirel was elected by Parliament as the new president. Mrs. Tansu Ciller was chosen to replace Demirel and became Turkey's first female prime minister. Ciller's government was immediately faced with economic challenges and the ongoing insurgency by Kurdish rebels. A cease-fire declared in 1993 did not hold and violence only worsened. In 1995, Turkish troops swept into Northern Iraq to wipe out rebel bases from which Kurds had staged terrorist attacks. Some Kurdish leaders offered to end the fighting in exchange for more cultural rights, but rebels connected with the Marxist Kurdish Workers Party (PKK) prefer to fight and have expressed a desire to establish an independent Kurdish state.

PKK terrorist attacks and government retaliations against Kurds, a rise in Islamic conservatism, and economic difficulties combined to give the Islamic leader Necmettin Erbakan's Welfare Party (RP) a slim victory in December 1995 parliamentary elections. When the RP was unable to form a government, Ciller joined with a former rival to create a center-right coalition. When infighting caused that government to fall a few months later, Erbakan was given an opportunity to form a viable coalition. In June 1996, Erbakan worked out an arrangement in which he is to alternate with Ciller as prime minister, with each serving for one year at a time.

THE PEOPLE

Population

Turkey has 63.4 million inhabitants, a population that is growing at 2 percent annually. Ankara, the capital, has more than 3.5 million people. Istanbul (ten million), once called Constantinople, was the center of the Byzantine Empire. It is still the industrial, commercial, and intellectual center of the country. About 80 percent of the people are Turkish, 17 percent are Kurdish, and 3 percent belong to a variety of smaller groups. Kurds live mostly in the southeast. As in most cultures, urbanization has increased over the years, and 64 percent of Turkey's population now lives in urban areas. Turkey's Human Development Index (0.792) ranks it 66th out of 174 nations. Adjusted for women, the index (0.744) ranks Turkey 45th out of 130 countries. These figures indicate Turkey has done reasonably well in providing most citizens with the potential to live well and participate in society.

Language

Turkish, the official language, is related to the Uralic-Altaic languages spoken across Asia (from Finland to Manchuria). Arabic script was used during the Ottoman Empire period, but a Latin-based alphabet has been used since 1928. Most of the Kurdish minority speaks Kurdish. However, Kurdish was banned for many years and some people forgot how to use it. Bans on its use in education and domestic broadcasting are still in effect, but Kurdish can be used in some publications and public speaking. Arabic is also spoken. English is an increasingly popular second or third language.

Religion

Although 98 percent of Turkey's population is Sunni Muslim, the government makes it clear that Turkey is a secular state with complete freedom of religion. Islam's status as the state religion was abolished in 1923. Still, Islam maintains an important influence on society. This became even more significant when the Welfare Party nearly took national power through elections in 1995. The party still controls some city governments and its influence is seen in an increased observance of Islamic dress and other behavioral codes.

Muslims believe in one God, *Allah*, and that his will was revealed to the prophet Muhammad through the angel Gabriel. These revelations were recorded in the *Qur'an* (Koran), the holy book of Islam. Muslims accept many Judeo-Christian prophets but proclaim that Muhammed was the last and greatest. Throughout life, they strive to live the five pillars of Islam: professing Allah's name and Muhammad's role as prophet; fasting during the holy month of *Ramazan*; giving aid to the poor; making a pilgrimmage to Makkah, Saudi Arabia; and praying daily at five specific times.

General Attitudes

Turkey is often described as a bridge between East and West. Due to centuries of interaction with Europe and Asia, Turks have incorporated features from both areas into their lifestyle and thinking. At the same time, they are patriotic and have developed a unique society. The people are proud of the achievements of their modern state as well as the accomplishments of their ancestors, who ruled great empires. Turks consider their society to be progressive, Europe-leaning, and strongly influential in the region. They often feel misunderstood by European and other Western nations because of the often publicized Kurdish rebellion. Turkey is known in the United States, Turks believe, mostly for its past and the terrorist violence; Turks emphasize another side of the country, one that is modern and ethnically diverse but tolerant and democratic.

Individually, Turks prize a good sense of humor; it is considered a sign of intelligence. Group orientation is valued over personal assertiveness or aggression, and honesty and cleverness are admirable qualities. People value a good education, secure employment, social status, and an honorable heritage.

Personal Appearance

Western-style clothing is most common. European fashions are especially popular among the youth. Some Muslim women may wear a turban (scarf) to cover their hair. Some traditional costumes are still worn in rural areas or for special occasions. The design of a costume's headdress and the type of material used signify a person's social status.

CUSTOMS AND COURTESIES

Greetings

When greeting friends or strangers, one shakes hands and says *Nasilsiniz* (How are you?) or *Merhaba* (Hello). A typical response to *Nasilsiniz* is *Iyiyim, teshekur ederim* (Fine, thank you). Greetings among friends are followed by polite inquiries about one's health, family, and work. Among close friends of the same (or sometimes the opposite) gender, Turks clasp hands and kiss on both cheeks when greeting. To show respect to an older person, their hands may be kissed and touched to the greeter's forehead. The youth often greet each other with *Selam* (Salute). Someone entering a room, office, or teahouse might say *Günaydin* (Good morning) or *Iyi günler* (Have a nice day). When parting, it is customary to wish for blessings from *Allah* (*Allahaısmarladık*) and respond agreeably (*Güle güle*).

Upon joining a small group, one greets each person in the group individually. When addressing others formally, one uses professional titles. Otherwise, the title *Hanım* is used for women and *Bey* for men among peers or with younger persons. These follow the given name: *Leyla Hanım* or *Ismail Bey*. With older people, one uses *Abla* for women (*Fatma Abla*) or *Aabey* for men (*Ahmet Aabey*). These terms mean "sister" and "brother." If there is a great age difference, one uses *Teyze* (aunt) and *Amca* (uncle) after the first name.

Urban people generally do not greet strangers when passing on the street; rural people are more likely to greet strangers.

Gestures

Turks generally use their hands a great deal during conversation, forming gestures that add meaning and emphasis.

Social courtesies are valued in Turkey. One does not put feet on a desk or table, point the sole of the foot toward another person, smoke without asking permission, or cross the legs while in the presence of an older or superior person. It is not proper for adults to eat or smoke on the street. Public displays of affection are not acceptable. To some more traditional people, it is an insult to pass an item with the left hand. "No" can be expressed by either shaking the head or lifting it up once quickly.

Visiting

Turks enjoy visiting one another in their homes, and hospitality is an integral part of the culture. Friends, relatives, and neighbors visit often. In large cities, people call ahead, but this is not practical in smaller villages, where unexpected visits occur more frequently. As hospitality is customary, guests are always invited in and offered refreshments. This usually involves something to drink (tea, coffee, soda) and sometimes to eat (crackers and cookies). It is impolite to decline these refreshments. Many Turks remove their shoes when entering a home and replace them with slippers. Guests are expected to do the same at homes where this custom is followed. Visitors are expected to bring a pleasant presence to the home; bad news or accounts of problems are saved for other occasions and locations. It is not polite to ask personal questions of hosts. First-time visitors to a home may bring a small gift, such as candy, fruit, or flowers. Turks work hard to make their guests feel comfortable. For example, even if the hosts do not think smoking is appropriate, they may allow visitors to smoke in their homes.

Eating

Breakfast is usually eaten around 7:00 A.M., or earlier in rural areas. Lunch is at midday and dinner is around 7:00 P.M. Dinner is the main meal and the family generally expects to sit down together for this meal.

Eating habits vary with the region and the food being eaten. Turks generally observe the continental style of eating, with the fork in the left hand and the knife remaining in the right. Some foods are eaten with the hand. To begin or end a meal, one might say *Afiyet Olsun* (May what you eat bring you well-being). One may compliment the cook on the meal by saying *Elinize saglik* (roughly, Bless your hand). Meals can be lavish, and Turks are quite proud of their rich cuisine. Types of restaurants range from those offering fast-food to international cuisine, but the most common is the Turkish kebab restaurant. Some restaurants include a service charge in the bill (about 10 percent), in which case a 5 percent tip is customary. If no service charge is included, a 15 percent tip should be given.

LIFESTYLE

Family

The primary social unit in Turkey is the family. In rural areas, traditional, patriarchal values prevail. An individual is loyal to and dependent upon the family. The Turkish household often consists of an extended family: a mother and father, their unmarried children, and, in some cases, married sons with their families. The married sons remain until they are financially independent. In urban areas, nuclear families are the standard and traditional authority structures are less pronounced. It is uncommon for a person to live alone, mostly for economic reasons. Polygamy, as permitted by Islamic law, was abolished in 1930. Women gained the right to vote in 1927 and the right to divorce in 1934 when civil marriage contracts were introduced. Urban women frequently work outside the home. Thirty-three percent of the labor force is female.

Dating and Marriage

Except perhaps at universities or in large urban areas, dating in the Western sense is not common. Young people associate more in groups. In the cities, this association is generally open and casual. In rural areas, chaperones are common. Rural families are heavily involved in deciding who a person will marry, but the choice is generally the couple's in urban areas. It is against the law for women to marry before age 15 and men before age 17. In the cities, many wait to marry until they have completed their education and sometimes military service. Hence, the average age for marriage is 22 for women and 25 for men. Most Turks expect to marry and have children.

Traditional wedding celebrations last three days and are still practiced by some in rural areas. Urban couples often follow more European traditions when marrying. Traditional festivities begin with the *Kına Gecesi* (henna evening), an event only for women. They decorate the hands and fingers of the bride with henna leaf dye and dance and sing. On the second day, both sets of parents serve lunch and dinner to their guests. On the third day, the bride is taken to the groom's home on a horse after folk dances are performed. This tradition is increasingly rare because of the time and expense involved.

Diet

Turkish cuisine is among the finest in the world. Lamb and rice are served with many meals. Seafood is more abundant along the coast. The famous *kahve* (Turkish coffee), a thick brew served in very small cups, is served with nearly every meal. Breakfast is usually light, consisting of tea, white cheese, bread, butter, marmalade or honey, and olives. The main meal of the day is eaten in the evening and may consist of several courses. Turkish cuisine is famous for many things, among them the *meze,* a tray or table of hors d'oeuvres, including stuffed grape leaves, salads, shrimp, and a variety of other items. There are also many unique Turkish soups. Shish kebabs (chunks of lamb on a skewer) are a favorite, as are vegetables prepared in olive oil. Rice *pilav* is common. Turkish desserts are famously sweet, including *baklava* (syrup-dipped pastry) and *muhallebi* (milk pudding). The most popular drink next to coffee is *raki*, a drink made of fermented grapes (not a wine).

Recreation

The most popular sport for both spectators and participants is soccer, which was introduced by the British in the 19th century. Volleyball, basketball, cycling, grease wrestling, traditional wrestling, swimming, and a variety of other sports are also enjoyed. Picnics are common family activities. August is the month for most vacations. During their leisure time, urban residents may watch television, eat out, visit others, or attend movies. Women often do volunteer work. Rural women visit one another in their homes or watch television. Men throughout the country gather at teahouses (like cafés) to socialize. When at home, they also watch television. Folk dancing and other cultural arts are popular.

Holidays

The ninth month of the Muslim lunar calendar is *Ramazan*, during which practicing Muslims fast from dawn to dusk. At the end of *Ramazan* is a three-day holiday called *Seker Bayrami* (sugar holiday), during which sweets are eaten to celebrate the end of the fast. A second Muslim holiday is *Kurban Bayrami* (sacrifice holiday), which marks the season of pilgrimage to Makkah. It also commemorates Abraham's willingness to sacrifice his son. An animal is usually sacrificed and the meat distributed to the poor. Other official holidays include New Year's Day, National Sovereignty Day (23 April, also Children's Day), Atatürk's Memorial Day and Youth Day (19 May), Victory Day (30 August), and Republic Day (29 October).

Commerce

Businesses are generally open from 9:00 A.M. to 5:00 P.M., Monday through Friday. Some are open for a half day on Saturday. Most people buy fresh produce at open-air markets but get other goods from supermarkets (in large cities) or neighborhood shops.

SOCIETY

Government

Turkey is a parliamentary democracy composed of 73 provinces. The president is head of state; the prime minister is head of government. The Grand National Assembly (Parliament) has 550 members. In addition to the Welfare Party, major parties include Ciller's True Path Party and the Motherland Party. The voting age is 21.

Economy

Agriculture is the traditional backbone of the economy, once providing the bulk of all exports. Today, it still employs half of the labor force and accounts for one-fifth of all exports. Chief agricultural products include cotton, tobacco, fruit, cereals, nuts, and opium for medicine. Manufacturing employs 15 percent of the labor force but accounts for nearly 60 percent of all exports. Its success is therefore vital to the economy. Mining and tourism are also important. Turkey enjoyed solid growth until about 1993, when mismanagement and other problems sent inflation above 100 percent and led to economic decline for 1994 and 1995. Industrial production slipped, and many factories laid off workers or cut output. The government implemented reform measures to address the problems. A high number of migrants, especially in Istanbul, has increased unemployment and strained urban infrastructure. Real gross domestic product per capita is $5,230, which has tripled since 1960. Income distribution is unequal: urban residents enjoy far higher incomes than rural people or migrants. The currency is the Turkish *lira* (£T).

Transportation and Communication

Around major urban areas, the roads are paved and in good condition. In rural areas, infrastructure is generally adequate but not always well maintained. Taxis, buses, streetcars, and *dolmus* (shared taxis) provide public transportation. The railroad is used for travel between cities, as are the airways. Turkey is connected with other countries by international air links. The overall communications system is fairly good, with several television and radio stations broadcasting throughout the country. The press is free and active. Telephone service is best in urban areas.

Education

Primary and secondary education is free and coeducational. Primary schooling lasts five years and secondary education lasts three. Additional years are possible to about age 17. Nearly all children complete the primary level, and about half go on to the secondary level. A foreign language is required. Exams determine university entrance. There are more than 25 universities in Turkey, the oldest of which was founded at Istanbul in 1453. Some 250 specialized colleges and institutions offer vocational and other training. Adult literacy averages 81 percent. It is higher among men and urban residents.

Health

The government provides basic health care, but it is not sufficient to meet the country's needs. Urban facilities are generally modern and adequate, but rural facilities are not as well equipped. Besides public health care, institutions such as the military, state-owned enterprises, etc., provide care to their personnel. Reform measures have been introduced to address the most serious problems, including a relatively high infant mortality rate (46 per 1,000) attributed to poor education about child care and the lack of family planning. The government seeks to reduce the figure to fewer than 30 by the year 2000 through improved child immunizations, prenatal care, education, and other programs. Life expectancy averages 72 years.

FOR THE TRAVELER

U.S. citizens need a valid passport and visa to enter Turkey. For tourist visits of less than three months, a visa can be obtained at the border. Bottled water is recommended. Fruits and vegetables should be cleaned and peeled before eating. Air pollution in the winter, particularly in Ankara, can be hazardous to those suffering from respiratory ailments. A number of interesting sites are worth visiting. For information regarding travel opportunities, contact the Turkish Tourist Office, 821 United Nations Plaza, New York, NY 10017. You may also wish to contact the Turkish Embassy's Tourist Office, 1717 Massachusetts Avenue NW, Suite 306, Washington, DC 20036; phone (202) 429–9844.

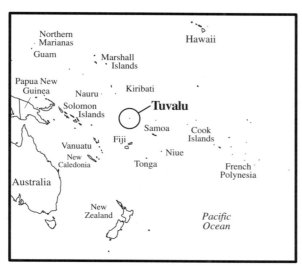

Boundary representations not necessarily authoritative.

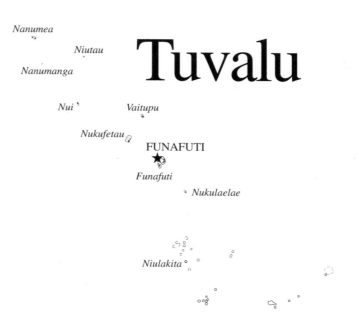

Tuvalu

BACKGROUND

Land and Climate

Tuvalu (too-VAH-loo) is a group of nine small atolls scattered 350 miles (565 kilometers) north to south in the south-central Pacific Ocean. Named for the eight inhabited atolls, *Tuvalu* means "eight standing together." Niulakita is a bird sanctuary and was not inhabited until recently. Tuvalu is one of the world's smallest countries, with a total land area of about 10 square miles (26 square kilometers). Six atolls enclose large lagoons; the land portion consists of sand-covered coral rock. Tuvalu also claims an exclusive economic zone (for fishing) of 200 nautical miles.

Tuvalu's tropical climate is pleasant, with high humidity moderated by easterly trade winds from March to November. The average annual temperature of 84°F (29°C) changes little during the year. Westerly gales and heavy rains come between November and March. Severe tropical storms have been rare, but cyclones and tidal waves can threaten this country whose highest point is less than 17 feet (5 meters) above sea level.

History

The original inhabitants were probably Polynesian and Southeast Asian travelers who came to the islands at various times from six hundred to two thousand years ago. Each Tuvalu island developed its own political and social system before European contact. Ceremonial and social visits took place between islands.

In 1568, Spanish explorer Alvaro de Mendana sited Nui (and in 1595, Niulakita), but the islands remained largely unknown by outsiders until a passing ship captain named one atoll Ellice Island in 1819. By 1825, the atolls were on European maps and by 1830 all had been visited and charted (and given various names by the explorers). In 1841, the entire group was named the Ellice Islands.

Whalers from New England were the most frequent foreign visitors. The London Missionary Society (LMS) of Samoa began founding churches and schools in the 1830s at about the same time the copra (dried coconut meat) trade spread throughout the Pacific. The islands were considered of low economic value and so remained mostly unexploited by outsiders.

By the 1860s, however, peaceful visits were replaced by the establishment of permanent trading posts, missions, and disastrous encounters with slave-trader ships. In 1863, Peruvian slavers raided the southern atolls of Funafuti and Nukulaelae, carrying away forever two-thirds of their population to work in Peruvian guano mines.

The Ellice Islands were claimed by the British in 1886, receiving protectorate status in 1892. The colonial administration left most local government in the hands of island councils. The LMS handled education until the 20th century, when the British established a boys' primary school under the direction of Donald Gilbert Kennedy. Kennedy left a legacy in administration, land tenure, cooperative and resettlement efforts, language, and technical skills.

In 1916, the Gilbert Islands (now Kiribati) and Ellice Islands were joined to form the Gilbert and Ellice Islands Colony (GEIC). World War II brought airstrips, U.S. soldiers, and money. During GEIC's independence movement in the 1960s, Ellice Islanders demanded separation from the Gilberts, being heavily outnumbered and culturally different. A referendum was held under United Nations auspices, and the Ellice Islands became a separate British colony in 1975. A subsequent vote changed the name to Tuvalu, and three years later Tuvalu became an independent nation within the Commonwealth.

OCEANIA

PEOPLE

Population

About ten thousand people inhabit Tuvalu, with one-third living on Funafuti, the capital island. Population growth is about 1.7 percent. All nine atolls are inhabited, with a single village on each outer island (islands other than Funafuti). The majority of Tuvaluans (96 percent) are ethnic Polynesians, while the remainder include mixed descendants of Polynesians and Europeans.

About 1,500 Tuvalu citizens are either studying, living, or employed overseas. More than seven hundred work in the phosphate mines on Nauru and Ocean Island. Nauru is set to close in the near future. The government is seeking alternate job opportunities to help keep the workers abroad. Short-term work is available in Tuvalu when projects are in development, but the economy is otherwise not large enough to accommodate all of Tuvalu's workers.

Language

English is Tuvalu's official language and is taught in all schools. However, most people speak Tuvaluan on a daily basis. It is related to several languages in the region (especially Samoan). Its written form uses the Latin alphabet. Each island has its own dialect. The differences are mostly in sound and vocabulary, and most Tuvaluans understand all the dialects. The Vaitupu dialect is most often used between islands.

The language spoken on Nui is related to Kiribati (Gilbertese). According to legend, I-Kiribati warriors once conquered the island and remained after their victory. They effected a radical change in the language, such that people say it is three-fourths Kiribati and one-fourth Tuvaluan.

Religion

Prior to the introduction of Christianity, Tuvaluans worshipped a number of island gods, placating them with offers of food and possessions. Powerful priests (*Vaka Atua*) acted as intermediaries between the people and the gods, and they presided over special ceremonies.

Today, 97 percent of Tuvaluans are members of the Christian Church of Tuvalu (*Ekalesia Tuvalu*), derived from the Congregationalist foundation of the LMS. Other faiths include the Roman Catholic Church, the Church of Jesus Christ of Latter-day Saints (Mormon), Seventh-day Adventist, and Baha'i.

The flow of community life, especially on outer islands, centers on religion. A typical day in a village begins with family prayer at 5:30 A.M. and ends with another at 7:00 P.M. Sunday church services are held at various times and are well attended. Virtually no work is performed on Sunday. The pastor is one of the most important men on the island. Villagers provide him with food and money, and build and maintain his home. They also take great pride in crafting beautiful churches for their meetings.

General Attitudes

Tuvaluan behavioral codes are concerned more with "how things seem" than with what actually occurs. Social offenses that do not become public knowledge are not treated, essentially, as offenses and little guilt is felt by those involved. This non-absolute social code suits the small population because society is based on kinship and devotion to the group.

Tuvaluans admire and expect of each other generosity, a willingness to help, sharing, caring for those who are alone, a sense of humor, and an ability to work hard. Tuvaluans are toughened by living in a close-to-nature existence. They easily adapt to the whims of nature, and they can fix just about anything. Tuvaluans are reserved but friendly and social. As the population aspires to a better education as a means of gaining access to paid employment, basic life skills are becoming less valued. On outer islands, there is a desire for such Western goods as flashlights, fishing gear, guitars, and radios.

Personal Appearance

Funafuti men and women with wage jobs wear light, casual Western-style clothing to work. At home, they wear a shirt or blouse with a *sulu*, a colorful medium-to-long cotton wraparound cloth. Some businessmen, clergy, and civil servants wear tailored *sulus* with pockets and a short-sleeved shirt. Outer islanders also wear a colorful *sulu*, but when they work they substitute a sturdier and less colorful *sulu* and T-shirt.

School children wear uniforms: shorts and shirts for boys, skirts and blouses for girls. Scanty dress is offensive; women do not wear pants or shorts (except some younger women on Funafuti). Many people wear flower garlands (*fou*) in their hair on festive occasions. Shoes are rare, but plastic flip-flops or sandals are worn for such activities as reef fishing or office work.

CUSTOMS AND COURTESIES

Greetings

Welcoming people is an important ritual in Tuvalu. When people first meet or when they arrive from another island or abroad, they shake hands and say, or are welcomed with, *Taalofa!* (Greetings!). Relatives use a *sogi* (sniffing) gesture, pressing their face to the other's cheek and sniffing deeply. They may use this when someone leaves or arrives at the island, or as an affectionate way to greet children. If meeting after a long absence, old friends may slap one another on the back as they exchange several phrases that show how close they are and how pleased they are to see each other.

Since most Tuvaluans see the same people often each day, *Taalofa!* is not a casual greeting. Instead, people say *E fano koe ki fea?* (Where are you going?) or *E aa koe na?* (What are you doing/How are you?). Greetings may continue with inquiries about one's family and friends.

Titles and last names are not often used when addressing others. Most all Tuvaluans know and use others' first names. Even the pastor is called by his first name. When speaking English, Tuvaluans adapt to the English custom of using titles when appropriate.

Very special occasions call for a feast (*fakaala*) in the *maneapa* (community hall; *ahiga* on northern islands), with food served on a tray woven from coconut fronds. The meal ends when the main chief is finished. It is followed by formal speeches, dances, and more speeches as hosts and recipients thank each other.

Gestures

It is improper to touch another person's head, the most sacred part of the body. In a *maneapa*, one keeps the head low, stooping to walk through a group. Pointing directly at someone or using one finger to beckon is rude. One beckons by waving all fingers with the palm facing down. Looking down while conversing shows respect to the other person.

Staring is impolite. Raising the eyebrows indicates agreement.

Visiting

Unannounced visiting is an important aspect of Tuvaluan society and guests are always welcome. Sunday is a popular day for such visits, but anytime will do (especially if it is raining hard and no one is working). One wouldn't normally visit early in the morning or when people usually prepare meals or work. Friends do drop by, but mostly relatives visit one another; daughters frequently visit their mothers.

The traditional house has no permanent walls, so visitors need not knock to announce their presence. It is customary to remove any footwear, enter, and sit down on the pandanus mat (*papa*). If the mat is not down, the visitor waits for it to be spread out. If walking past a sitting or lying person when entering, one says *Tulou* (Excuse me) to apologize for being above the level of the person's head. One also says *Tulou* when reaching for something above another person's head.

On the *papa*, one sits cross-legged (or women may extend one leg laterally and tuck the other under it). Except during formal *maneapa* speeches, one might also stretch the legs out straight. Hosts normally offer guests some fresh toddy (coconut tree blossom sap) or share green drinking coconuts or tea. If it happens to be mealtime, guests are invited to eat. If a friend or relative passes by the house during mealtime, someone in the house might call out *Vau o kai!* (Stop and eat with us!). The passerby will stop and chat briefly but does not normally stay to eat.

Eating

Tuvaluans eat three meals a day. Breakfast (*kaiga i taeao, inuti*) often includes a cup of warm, freshly cut toddy (*ssali kaleve*). Toddy is cut twice daily by older boys/young men who have responsibility for a few trees each. Toddy is a primary source of vitamin C, especially when fresh. It can also be made into a syrup for cooking or fermented as an alcoholic beverage.

Meals are prepared in an *umu* (cooking house), a separate structure that contains an open fire. Meals may be eaten at home or sometimes away, such as when food is taken by women to a returning fishing party. All meals begin with a blessing. Most food is eaten with the hand. The midday meal (*kaiga i ttuutonu*) is a major occasion on Sundays with families eating together, sitting cross-legged on the mat-covered floor. A water bowl is passed for washing before and after the meal. Neighbors share food, especially after a successful fishing trip or harvest.

LIFESTYLE

Family

Most Tuvaluans are in some way related to each other. Each person knows everyone's general kinship ties and uses the information as a behavioral guide. For example, boys are protective of but do not closely interact with sisters or female first cousins. Since one shares character and reputation with one's relatives, one is also bound to share material goods. To be stingy (*kaiu*) is to be despised, and one can ask for goods from relatives without shame.

Households are shared by the extended family. The elderly are cared for by their children and often help raise their grandchildren. Indeed, grandparents are considered the most qualified to raise children and teach them how to behave in culturally required ways. Mothers, however, are the main disciplinarians and fathers take action in cases of severe punishment.

All family decisions are finalized by the elders. Parents are responsible for providing for the family unit. Women cook, feed the livestock, make household items (mats, thatched roof panels, etc.), see to the needs of the family, and work in the *pulaka* (swamp taro) pits. Men fish, help in the *pulaka* pits, and are responsible for agriculture. Older men become more involved in community discussions, and elderly men make *kolokolo* (coconut fiber string) for use around the home.

The typical house (*fale*) is a rectangular structure made of timber posts from matured coconut stumps. A pandanus thatch roof covers the loose coral-stone floor (concrete in some homes). The floor is elevated above a coral-rock foundation and is made comfortable by rough coconut-frond mats under fine pandanus mats. The home is fitted with coconut-frond shutters that are lowered when it rains.

Dating and Marriage

Young people meet at community activities, but dating in the Western sense is not common. It is improper for members of the opposite sex to show affection in public, so young couples often meet secretly at night. Mothers are very protective of daughters. Virginity is highly prized in a bride. Some weddings are quietly arranged several years in advance by the families involved; otherwise, couples make their own choice.

Traditional competition between the bride's and groom's families to provide the best and most food at a wedding feast is discouraged on some islands, either by prior agreement between the families about their respective responsibilities or by a pastor sponsoring a group wedding of several couples and a combined feast afterwards. Celebrations can last for days. The newlyweds spend their first night at the groom's family home and their second at the bride's family home.

Diet

The Tuvalu diet is comprised of *pulaka*, breadfruit (*fuaga mei*), plantains or cooking bananas (*futi*), cooked or raw fish, crayfish, pork, chicken, and such local vegetables as spinach (*laulu*). Many dishes are prepared in coconut cream (*lolo*). Tropical fruits like papaya (*oolesi*) and bananas are eaten. Foods are normally steamed, boiled, or roasted in a ground oven. Tuvaluans quench their thirst with drinking coconuts (*pi*). Imported items have also made their way into the diet, including flour, sugar, rice, salt beef and corned beef, and tea. They are expensive and less nutritious but accorded higher respect than locally available food.

Recreation

Sports popular in Tuvalu include soccer, basketball, cricket, and volleyball. Young people also play a traditional sort of elongated volleyball (*te ano*). Movies are shown in *maneapas* with generators or electricity.

Tuvaluans love dancing. Special occasions nearly always include the traditional *faatele* or more modern *siva* dance. Young people enjoy the more casual *tuisi* (twist) dances, which are popular fund-raising events. The *faatele* is a line dance performed by men or women (most commonly young women) dressed in pandanus-leaf skirts and wearing greenery and flower garlands. Dancers tell stories through their body actions, and are accompanied by others who sing, clap, and beat wooden "drums" made from boxes or biscuit tins covered with mats. The *siva* is performed by young women who dance and sing as young men play the guitar and sing.

Holidays

Public holidays include New Year's Day; Easter; Queen Elizabeth's birthday (in June); National Children's Day (4 August), which features children's sports and crafts; Independence Day (1 October), marked by a parade on Funafuti airstrip and dancing; Hurricane Day (21 October), recalling Hurricane Bebe of 1972; Prince Charles's Birthday (14 November); and Christmas. On Funafuti, Bomb Day (23 April) commemorates the day in 1946 when a Japanese bomb fell through the church roof and destroyed the interior. A U.S. corporal had directed 680 villagers out of the building just moments before.

Commerce

Office hours are 7:30 A.M. to 4:15 P.M., Monday through Thursday, with an hour break for lunch, and 7:30 A.M. to 12:45 P.M. on Friday. All stores and offices close on Sunday. Each island has a *Fusi* (co-op) store that carries staples and sundry items. Funafuti's is the largest; outer island stores often run out of supplies. Prices are set by the government. Other small businesses sell clothes, handicrafts, and nonfood household items.

SOCIETY

Government

Tuvalu is a democracy whose head of state, Britain's Queen Elizabeth II, is represented by a local governor general (currently Tomu Malaefono Sione). The 12 members of the unicameral Parliament (*Palamene*) are elected. Each island has representation. All adults may vote at age 18. There are no political parties. Parliament's members choose a prime minister to lead the government. Kamuta Latasi was elected prime minister in 1993. Local government is managed through elected Island Councils (*Fonopule*). The next elections are in 1997.

Traditional chiefs (*Aliki*) still play a significant role in influencing island events. A long-held distinction between chiefly families and commoners is slowly changing, with chiefs now more often selected on the basis of social standing rather than birth. One's behavior, ability to participate in ceremonies and communal gatherings, and public support figure most prominently in establishing one's social status.

Economy

Lacking industry and minerals, and with exports limited to small amounts of copra and coins, Tuvalu's self-sufficiency at a Western level is impossible. Subsistence farming and fishing are the primary economic activities. The islands are too small and too remote to support a large tourist industry. Many women own small businesses that sell handicrafts. A major source of income is remittances sent to relatives from Tuva-luans working abroad. The country earns some licensing fees from offshore Asian fishing boats that harvest skipjack tuna. An international trust fund established in 1987 by Australia, New Zealand, and the United Kingdom (also supported by Japan and South Korea) gives the government annual revenues. Foreign assistance provides funds for development projects. Employment opportunities are limited chiefly to the civil service. The currency used is a combination of the Australian dollar ($A) paper money and Tuvalu dollar ($T) coins.

Transportation and Communication

Local transport needs are met primarily by bicycles, motorbikes, and walking. Only a small number of trucks, tractors, and emergency vehicles travel the mostly gravel roads. A minibus and a taxi do run between the government center at Vaiaku and the wharf on Funafuti. One passenger/cargo vessel based at Funafuti provides interisland transport, delivering supplies to and collecting copra from outer islands every one or two months. Flights from the Funafuti airport go to Kiribati and Fiji for connection with international carriers.

Radio Tuvalu, a public AM station, broadcasts 40 hours per week, including local programming in English and Tuvaluan and twice-daily world news from Radio Australia. The government news sheet (*Sikuleo o Tuvalu*) is published in Tuvaluan, while another paper, *Tuvalu Echoes*, is in English. Funafuti has extensive phone service, while the outer islands communicate via radiophones.

Education

Each island has a public primary school and Vaitupu has a secondary school. The bilingual curriculum places greater emphasis on English at the secondary level. Private kindergartens and primary schools are available. Primary school graduates may go to one of eight community training centers. A maritime school trains merchant seamen. The University of the South Pacific (based in Fiji) has an extension center on Funafuti. The literacy rate is 96 percent.

Health

Dispensaries staffed by first aid *dressers* are located on all outer islands, and Funafuti has a hospital. Care is provided free. The population is generally healthy, due to a reasonable climate, a good basic diet, and a strong tradition in medicinal skills and natural remedies. With population growth, greater contact with overseas lifestyles, and increasing consumption of imported foods (higher in sugar and starch), the rates of obesity, diabetes, tooth decay, and hypertension are rising. The infant mortality rate is 27 per 1,000; life expectancy is 61 to 64 years.

FOR THE TRAVELER

U.S. citizens need a passport and proof of onward travel to visit Tuvalu. Visas are issued upon arrival. Travelers pay a $T5 departure tax. Water is usually treated and safe for drinking. No film is sold locally. Be sensitive to local dress standards and do not abuse the many privileges granted to visitors. For trips to outer islands, it is customary to take small gifts (sticks of tobacco, matches, chewing gum, sporting gear, T-shirts, or cloth). Travel information can be obtained from the Tuvalu Embassy, PO Box 14449, Suva, Fiji; phone (649) 301355.

Printed on recycled paper

United Arab Emirates

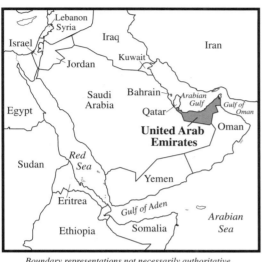

Boundary representations not necessarily authoritative.

BACKGROUND

Land and Climate

The seven shaikhdoms of the United Arab Emirates cluster along the south shore of the Arabian Gulf, covering 29,182 square miles (75,581 square kilometers). Abu Dhabi, the capital, is the largest emirate; Dubai is the business center. The other emirates are Sharjah, Ras-al-Khaimah, Ajman, Umm-al-Qaiwain, and Fujairah. Although distinct differences make each emirate unique, they are all conditioned by a harsh geographical combination of mountain, desert, and sea.

In the south and west, sand dunes and salt flats (*sabkha*) are interspersed with the occasional desert oasis. The largest oases are Al-Ain, one hundred miles east of Abu Dhabi, and Liwa in the southwest. Beyond Liwa is the Empty Quarter where endless sand dunes stretch into Saudi Arabia.

Summers are very hot, with temperatures rising to as high as 122°F (50°C). The coast is humid. Desert temperatures drop sharply at night. Winter (November–February) features pleasant temperatures (average 75°F in the day and 50–60°F at night) and a little rain.

History

Pockets of human habitation date back to 3000 B.C. in the emirates, including in Abu Dhabi, Al-Ain, and Sharjah. The area was known through the ages by a variety of names, depending on who was using it and for what purpose. At various times, the coast has been known as Pirate Coast or Trucial Coast. Under British colonial rule in the 19th century, the region was called the Trucial States. The British prized the Gulf as a principal route of communication between India and Britain. But to the Qawasim, the powerful local tribe, the British and their allies were conspicuous foreign intruders in Muslim waters. On several occasions, the British raided and ultimately destroyed the fleets of Ras-al-Khaimah. Britain's interest in the region was so strong that it came as a surprise when Great Britain announced in 1968 a pending withdrawal from its political and military commitments in the Gulf. At the initiative of Abu Dhabi and Dubai, the shaikhdoms decided to construct a federation. The United Arab Emirates (UAE) were officially declared a nation in December 1971.

The ruler of Abu Dhabi, Shaikh Zayid bin Sultan Al-Nahyan, became president of the federation and serves in that capacity today. Shaikh Zayid used the riches of his emirate to benefit all the federation's citizens. Since independence, the UAE has emerged as a major oil producer and a land with a high standard of living. In 1981, the UAE joined with other Arab Gulf countries in forming the Gulf Cooperation Council (GCC), which proved vital in the areas of economy and defense, including during the Gulf War.

In 1991, the elderly Shaikh Zayid was elected by the Supreme Council of Rulers to a fifth five-year term as president. It is expected he will continue to be reelected until he dies. In such an event, his son, Shaikh Khalifa, would replace him as ruler of Abu Dhabi but not necessarily as president of the UAE.

PEOPLE

Population

The United Arab Emirates is home to 2.37 million people, but nearly 80 percent of these are expatriates (*wafidiin*) from other countries who live and work in the UAE. Of the *wafidiin*,

45 percent are from the Indian subcontinent (mostly Indian), 17 percent are from Iran, 13 percent are from other Arab nations, and 5 percent are from Western nations. Expatriates have no political power or citizenship rights, but they are valued members of society.

The remaining 20 percent of the UAE's population consists of *muwatiniin* (locals). These native people of the emirates are either Arab descendants of great tribal confederations that have dominated the land since the 17th century, or long-time immigrants from both Persia and Arab Gulf countries. Many *muwatiniin* are actually a mix of these groups. Abu Dhabi has a population of more than 800,000. Dubai has 635,000 residents.

Muwatiniin and *wafidiin* men might socialize together or at least intermingle on a professional level, but women are less likely to be involved socially. A *muwatiniin* woman would almost never marry a *wafidiin* man, but local men often take foreign brides. This is done to avoid certain local traditions such as paying high bride-prices.

Language

Arabic is the country's official language and is used for daily communication. However, English is used widely in business and the public sector. Among expatriates, Persian, Urdu, Malayalaam, and Tagalog (among Filipinos) are most common. The country's many languages contribute to a pleasant cosmopolitan environment.

Religion

Islam is the official religion and *shariah* (Islamic law) is state law. This influences most aspects of life in the UAE. For example, the consumption of alcohol is prohibited for locals and Muslim expatriates. However, non-Muslims are exempt, except in Sharjah and on holy days. Non-Muslims are also free to practice their own religions, and main population centers are home to many thriving Christian churches. Emirati are tolerant of other religions and there are no clashes between the different groups.

All *muwatiniin* are Muslim and a good portion of the *wafidiin* are also. Most are Sunni Muslims of the Hanbali or Maliiki sects, but about 10 percent adhere to Shi'ah Islam. The Shi'ah and Sunni both celebrate Islam's major feasts and they coexist in harmony; however, they do have different traditions and different minor holy days. All Muslims accept Old Testament prophets as messengers from God but believe Muhammad to be the last and greatest prophet. Muslims show their devotion to Islam through such actions as praying five times daily, following dietary restrictions, acknowledging *Allah* as the only God and Muhammad as his prophet, giving to the poor, fasting during the month of *Ramadan*, and making at least one pilgrimage to Makkah, Saudi Arabia.

During *Ramadan*, Muslims refrain from eating, drinking, and smoking each day from dawn to dusk. They break the fast with an evening meal. Families gather to recite passages from the *Qur'an* (Koran), Islam's book of scripture. Special prayers, called *Al Tarawiah*, are also offered. The evening is then spent in the company of family and friends.

General Attitudes

The tribe is the basic unit of UAE society. Tribal values play a key role in social life. Emirati often identify themselves by their tribal origins and associate mainly with those who share their tribal affiliations. Tribal values are mostly derived from Islam and the family's heritage. They encompass one's political, social, and financial endeavors. A good education is considered extremely important, especially to women. Degrees of higher education are precious commodities; the more one has, the more respected one is. This has led to some abuses (mostly by men) such as buying degrees, but on average people are committed to learning. Success in business (for men) and family stability are the primary goals in life. The ability to lead, be charming, and yet be serious-minded are the most admired traits in men. *Wafidiin* usually desire to succeed in business and acquire wealth.

The Bedouin (called *Bedu* in the UAE), a once nomadic but now settled people, continue to lead a traditional agrarian lifestyle and do not necessarily share urban attitudes.

Personal Appearance

Despite the pace of Westernization in almost every aspect of life, Emirati still wear traditional clothes as a symbol of national identity. Modesty is required for both men and women. In public, a woman wears an *ab'a*, a black robe that covers her dress, and a *shailah*, a scarf that covers the head. In Abu Dhabi and other conservative emirates, women wear a *burqa* (veil) over their faces. At home, women wear modest dresses. Long skirts and blouses are also common.

Men wear a *dishdasha* or *kandurah*. Each is a white robe. A man's head is covered with a *kitra* (white scarf) tied by an *agal* (black headband). Due to the climate, both men and women wear sandals, which they remove before entering the home. During the short winter months, some people wear shoes. *Wafidiin* usually wear Western-style clothing and shoes. *Muwatiniin* in Dubai dress less conservatively than those in other emirates. Children wear both Western and traditional clothing; tradition becomes more important as children get older.

CUSTOMS AND COURTESIES

Greetings

Personal greetings take many forms depending on the relationship between the speakers. Men shake hands when greeting and, if already acquainted, add a kiss to both cheeks. Women greet by kissing each other on right and left cheeks several times. When not well acquainted, they may only shake hands. Men greet women only verbally unless the woman extends her hand to be shaken. A common verbal exchange is *Assalaam alikum* (May peace be upon you) and *Wa alikum assalaam* (And peace be upon you). Another common phrase, *Kaif halak?* (How are you?), is often replied to with *Bikhair al-hamdu lillah* (Good, thanks be to God).

Friends and relatives of the same sex address one another by first name. Acquaintances or persons of the opposite gender use professional titles (Dr., Engineer, Mr., Mrs.). Or adults may be addressed as the mother (*Um*) or father (*Abu*) of their eldest son (e.g., the mother of Mohammed might be called *Um Mohammed*). Members of the ruling family are addressed by the title *Shaikh* (for men) and *Shaikhah* (for women).

Gestures

People use the right hand for shaking hands, eating, and gesturing. Use of the left hand is extremely rude. One passes items with both hands. Pointing with the finger is impolite;

one uses the entire hand instead. It is improper for the foot or shoe to point at another person. Members of the opposite sex do not touch in public even if they are married. It is impolite to walk in front of a person who is praying. Emirati show respect for their elders by opening doors for them, giving up seats on public transportation, or seating them in the front in private vehicles.

Visiting

Visiting is one of the UAE's most important pastimes, and it is also a sign of social solidarity. Indeed, social commitments are an essential part of life, and Emirati are known for their hospitality. Married children visit their parents daily and often are accompanied by the grandchildren. People like to invite each other for meals and socializing in their homes. Declining an invitation is considered impolite. If a person cannot accept for certain, *In shallah* (God willing) is the common response.

Friends and relatives may visit one another without prior arrangement, although it is polite to avoid stopping by during mealtimes and between 1:00 and 4:00 P.M. If someone does arrive without an appointment, it is considered an offense or *aib* (shame) not to invite them in for refreshments.

Due to strict customs of segregation and seclusion, men and women usually socialize separately. Men receive their male guests in special rooms called *majlis*, and they do not introduce their wives. The women socialize elsewhere in the house. Older male children stay with the men, but all other children will be with or supervised by the women.

Guests are treated to coffee and the smell of incense as soon as they arrive. The coffee is served in small cups and it is common to take more than two cups. One shakes the cup to indicate one does not desire more. Otherwise, the server is free to refill an empty cup. Tea and soft drinks soon follow the coffee. First-time visitors are treated to *fualah*, a custom of serving sweets and fruits. These first-time guests usually present gifts of sweets, fruits, or flowers (sweets are most appreciated). Frequent visitors only bring gifts for special occasions. After *fualah* or after a meal, hosts serve coffee and guests are expected to leave thereafter. It is impolite to stay after coffee has been served.

Eating

People in the emirates usually eat three meals each day: breakfast between 7:00 and 8:00 A.M., lunch between 12:30 and 2:30 P.M., and dinner between 8:00 and 9:30 P.M. The family eats all together when possible. Although many families, especially more Westernized ones, have tables and chairs, families eating without guests usually prefer to sit in a circle on the floor. Diners sit cross-legged, using their long dresses or robes to cover their legs and feet. This shields the women from exposing their legs and keeps men from accidentally pointing the soles of their feet at another person. Family members eat from separate plates, using their right hands. Hands are washed before and after meals. Likewise, thanks to *Allah* is given before (*Bism Allah*, In the name of God) and after (*Al hamdu lillah,* Praise be to God) the meal. The meal is an occasion for conversation. Fathers especially like to ask their children about their well-being.

When guests are present, the family might use the table, but it is a greater honor to be seated on the floor. Women and children often do not eat with unrelated male guests. Food is served in abundance, so one is not expected to finish all the food on the plate. An empty plate will be refilled as a sign of hospitality. The most common dish served to guests is roasted sheep on a pile of rice or bread. To make a guest feel more welcome, he is often offered the sheep's internal organs.

LIFESTYLE

Family

The extended family is a prominent feature in UAE society, but nuclear families usually constitute a single household. Family ties are extremely important and can take priority over the nuclear family. For example, one is expected to share resources with extended family members. Women play a central role in the family. They enjoy respect and security but also have the freedom to own property and businesses, drive cars, and have other social access. It is not acceptable, however, for females to live alone. Children do not leave the home until they get married. Adult children expect to care for aging parents.

The government encourages people to have large families and offers *muwatiniin* economic incentives to have children. The average local family has five children. Homes are surrounded by walls to protect the family's privacy.

Dating and Marriage

As in other traditional societies, dating is socially unacceptable. Arranged marriages still exist, and marriages from within the extended family (preferrably between cousins) are most popular. In the current generation, young people have the option to accept or reject a proposed mate. Men marry around age 26 and women at about age 22. An engaged couple may not socialize before the wedding. Weddings are very elaborate celebrations lasting three days. The actual ceremony is performed on the third day. The other days are filled with various festivities and plenty of food and drink. The government helps finance weddings between locals and provides free housing to couples after they marry.

Cohabitation is prohibited. The penalty for extramarital activities is severe for men and women. Men may take up to four wives, but most younger men prefer to have only one.

Diet

Rice is a staple food in the UAE and is served essentially every day. The most common dish is *kabsa*, rice mixed with fish or meat (usually lamb). *Biryani* is rice with either meat or chicken cooked with certain Indian and Persian spices and saffron. *Majbous* is rice cooked in a sauce until it is yellow and then served with chicken, fish, or meat. The UAE is famous for its seafood, which is plentiful year-round. Fish and shrimp are most popular. Fruits and vegetables are eaten each day. Of approximately 23 kinds of bread, the most common is *raqaq*, a very thin bread served with a sauce.

Coffee and tea are served before and after meals; ginger, mint, and other herbal drinks are also popular. Muslims do not drink alcohol or eat pork or pork products.

Recreation

Men enjoy sports, soccer being the most popular. Falconry is enjoyed as a sport, although it was once also used to help supplement the diet. Camel racing is the primary spectator sport. Races take place around the country during winter months. Traditional *dhow* (sailboat) races are quite popular, although younger nationals like powerboating and jet skiing. Both local and expatriate men enjoy sportfishing.

Women do not play sports but enjoy family outings to the parks and beaches. Families like to camp in the desert. At home, watching movies is a common pastime.

Holidays

Secular holidays include New Year's Day (1 January), Shaikh Zayid's Ascendancy to the Throne (6 August), and National Days (2–3 December). Religious holidays are governed by the lunar calendar and fall on different days each year. The most important are *Eid-al-Fitr*, a three-day feast at the end of the month of *Ramadan* during which people buy new clothes, visit each other, and eat well; *Eid-al-Adha*, on the tenth day of the month of *Dhul al Hijjah* in which the *Hajj* (pilgrimage) to Makkah takes place; the birth of the prophet Muhammad; *al-Isra wal-mi'raj*, the occasion of Muhammad's ascendancy to the sky; and *Hijra*, the Islamic New Year.

Commerce

Government business hours extend from 7:30 A.M. to 1:30 P.M., Saturday through Wednesday, and to noon on Thursday. Private businesses determine their own working hours. Shops and open markets are open from 7:00 A.M. to 2:00 P.M. and again from 4:30 to 10:00 P.M., Saturday through Thursday. On Friday, the Muslim day of worship, business hours usually extend from 8:00 to 11:30 A.M. and then from 4:30 to 10:00 P.M. Public offices are closed on Friday.

SOCIETY

Government

The UAE is a loose federation of seven emirates. Within each emirate, the hereditary ruler is sovereign. Each emirate is named after its principal city. The Supreme Council of Rulers, composed of the seven emirate rulers, is the federation's highest authority. It elects the president, who serves as head of state. The head of government is the prime minister/vice president. Currently that post is held by Shaikh Maktum of Dubai. All emirates have members in the Council of Ministers, which initiates legislation for ratification by the Supreme Council. Both bodies are advised by a 40-member National Council. Each emirate also has its own local government. There are no political parties or elections.

Economy

The UAE's vast oil reserves and its strategic location at the mouth of the Arabian Gulf have attracted a number of international businesses that have based their Middle East operations in Dubai's Jabal Ali Free Zone. The country's ample financial resources, derived from producing an average of 2.5 million barrels of oil per day, have allowed the government to improve the quality of life in nearly every aspect. Houses, roads, hospitals, schools, telecommunications systems, and other facilities have been and are being constructed. Many foreign firms are part of this rapid development. The UAE is self-sufficient in the production of vegetables and dairy foods but must import most other items.

The UAE's Human Development Index (0.861) ranks it 45th out of 174 nations. Real gross domestic product per capita is $21,830. An ever-increasing number of people enjoy a high standard of living, access to economic prosperity, and opportunities for personal advancement. The unit of currency is the UAE *dirham* (Dh).

Transportation and Communication

The UAE has one of the best highways in the Middle East and the network is continually expanding. Travel between emirates is most convenient by car. Air travel is available between Abu Dhabi and Dubai. Public transportation in the form of buses and taxis is also available both between and within cities. In the desert, the camel is still used for transportation. Most homes have phones and access to television. Eight daily newspapers, three of them in English, are distributed throughout the emirates.

Education

Public education began in 1953 for males and in 1958 for females. Prior to this time (and the discovery of oil), formal education was available only in a few small Koranic schools.

Children begin school at age six; after kindergarten, boys and girls attend separate classes. The first six years of schooling are mandatory. After those primary years come optional elementary and secondary years. Advancement is based on exams. Nearly all students finish the primary years and about 70 percent finish the other levels. Young men often join the army and young women may work as clerks after leaving school. Among young people, the literacy rate is very high, but the adult level is 77 percent.

The government pays for all qualified citizens to attend the UAE University in Al-Ain; two-thirds of its students are women. Overseas scholarships are also available to those (mostly men) who wish to pursue higher degrees. Locally, citizens may also attend technical colleges. Women tend to go into teaching and medicine, while men pursue business and government careers.

Health

Free medical treatment is available to all citizens of the UAE, but a small charge is imposed for *wafidiin*. Each emirate has at least one major hospital and several clinics to serve the populace. These are modern and well equipped. Several private hospitals offer advanced, but expensive, treatment. The infant mortality rate is 20 per 1,000 (down from 59 just a few years ago). The life expectancy rate is 72 years.

FOR THE TRAVELER

For entry, U.S. citizens need a passport and visa. The UAE does not issue tourist visas through its embassy, but two-week transit visas are available through hotels or through sponsorship by a resident. Those who are sponsored by a UAE organization may obtain business visas. Visitors will enjoy fine food, friendly people, and sporting opportunities, including sand skiing (using a snow board or snow skis to navigate the country's many sand hills and dunes). For more information, contact the UAE Embassy, 3000 K Street NW, Suite 600, Washington, DC 20005.

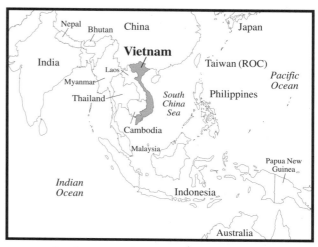

Boundary representations not necessarily authoritative.

Socialist Republic of
Vietnam

BACKGROUND

Land and Climate

Covering 127,243 square miles (329,560 square kilometers), Vietnam is just larger than New Mexico and stretches from north to south for nearly 1,000 miles (1,600 kilometers). Flat deltas in the north and south are separated by central highlands. Hills and mountains are found in the far north. Summer rainfall is heavy in the deltas and highlands. While the south experiences a mostly tropical climate, the north has four seasons (two are short); winter months are chilly, but temperatures do not reach freezing. In the south, May to September is hot and rainy, while October to March is warm, humid, and dry. Temperatures are often above 84°F (29°C). Approximately 22 percent of the land is arable; 40 percent is covered by tropical and highland forests.

History

Vietnam's history dates back four thousand years. Centuries of Chinese domination ended in the 1400s. A succession of Vietnamese dynasties followed until French colonial rule took over in the latter 1800s. The French divided Vietnam into three areas: the colony of Cochinchina (south) and the protectorates of Annam (central) and Tonkin (north).

French rule was interrupted by the Japanese occupation in World War II. Following Japan's defeat, the Allies divided Vietnam into two zones for the purpose of disarming the Japanese. In the south, the British completed the task and restored French rule. In the north, China also completed the task but ceded power to Vietnam's emperor, Bao Dai, who abdicated in favor of Ho Chi Minh. Even before 1945, the north had resisted colonial rule and Ho was very powerful. He declared Vietnam's independence and led his Viet Minh troops in an insurgency against the French and their southern allies. The war culminated in France's defeat in 1954 at Dien Bien Phu.

The 1954 Geneva Accord called for national elections in 1956. The southern regime led by President Ngo Dinh Diem refused to recognize the accord. Diem did not hold elections as required, and southern Communists rebelled. Northern Communists first aided and then joined the civil war with their southern comrades under North Vietnam's leadership. The United States supported South Vietnam, sending troops and supplies to fight the Viet Cong (southern and northern Communists). The war spread to Laos and Cambodia, and U.S. bombs caused widespread destruction throughout the region. Eventually, South Vietnam's government could no longer maintain popular support. With the government's demise imminent, U.S. troops withdrew and Saigon fell to the Viet Cong in April 1975. Saigon's name was officially changed to Ho Chi Minh City, but most Vietnamese still call it Saigon. All three Indochinese lands—Vietnam, Laos, and Cambodia—became Communist states. Thousands of families fled, and those who remained faced difficult years of poverty, isolation, and repression.

In 1976, Vietnam's north and south were officially reunited as the Socialist Republic of Vietnam. The United States refused to recognize the government and imposed an economic embargo that, until the 1990s, was observed by most other

Western nations. After the "American War" (as the Vietnam War is known in Vietnam), troops under Cambodia's Pol Pot regime repeatedly attacked provinces of southern Vietnam. In December 1978, Vietnam invaded Cambodia, deposing the genocidal Pol Pot regime and installing a government loyal to Hanoi. Not long after, China invaded from the north. Depleted and war torn, Vietnam withdrew from Cambodia in 1989.

Since then, Vietnam has concentrated on internal development. In 1986, *doi moi* (renovation) became the guiding economic policy. *Doi moi* is characterized by private enterprise, international trade, market prices for retail goods, openness to overseas Vietnamese, and tourism.

The 1989 peace treaty with Cambodia allowed Vietnam to seek renewed relations with the United States. Washington, D.C., opened an office in Hanoi in 1991 to coordinate the search for U.S. Americans missing in action and to pave the way to better relations. The U.S. trade embargo was lifted in 1994, allowing U.S. businesses to fully participate in Vietnam's economy and to trade with Vietnam. The Vietnamese greeted the end of the embargo as the final end of the American War. American investment began pouring into the country, joining many other countries that had no longer supported the U.S. embargo.

In 1995, both nations settled long-standing property claims, opened liaison offices in their respective capitals, stepped up efforts to search for the remains of U.S. service personnel still considered missing in action, and then established formal diplomatic relations with embassies in each capital.

THE PEOPLE

Population

Vietnam's population of 76 million is growing at 2 percent annually. More than 40 percent is younger than age 15. The majority of people live in rural regions, mainly in the Red and Mekong River Deltas and along the coastal plain. The largest cities are Saigon (five million) and Hanoi (three million). About 88 percent of the population is ethnic *Kinh* (Vietnamese). The Chinese (2 percent) form an important merchant class. The rest of the population consists of Khmer, Hao, and Cham peoples in addition to more than 50 highland minority groups, each with its own language and culture.

Over the years, many Vietnamese fled their country, often in difficult circumstances, in search of better conditions. There are large immigrant and refugee communities in the United States and elsewhere. Many refugees are being repatriated from other Asian nations; others would return voluntarily if the political system in Vietnam were to change.

Language

Vietnamese is the official language, although ethnic minorities still speak their own languages at home. Vietnamese is monosyllabic; each syllable is a word, but up to four syllables can be joined together to form a new word. For instance, *thanh* (fresh) joins with *nien* (years) as *thanh nien* (youth). Each word has six tones and therefore six possible meanings. The word's tone is indicated by a symbol usually located above the word's main vowel. English is the most popular foreign language to study. Older people may speak some French; middle-aged Vietnamese might speak Russian or another language from a former Communist country.

Religion

Vietnam's constitution has always guaranteed freedom of religion, but only now are people able and willing to take advantage of it. Buddhism is practiced by 55 percent of the population. Temples and pagodas are busy with people offering prayers for success and health to various gods and goddesses. About 12 percent of the population is Taoist and 7 percent is Roman Catholic. Christianity is becoming more popular in cities. Some ethnic minorities remain animists, practicing a reverence for all living things.

Regardless of one's religion, nearly everyone participates in ancestor veneration. The Vietnamese believe the deceased are accessible to help or hinder the living. Almost every Vietnamese family has an altar for ancestor worship. Family members place fruit and/or flowers on the altar on the first and middle days of the lunar month. Incense is also burned and prayers are offered to ancestors for support in overcoming misfortune and achieving good luck.

General Attitudes

Vietnamese respect those who respect others. Children must respect teachers and parents. Vietnamese value marital fidelity, generosity, gentleness, and hard work. The lazy, selfish, and disloyal are despised. Neighbors help each other and families support one another. Vietnamese hope for a future of wealth and security but worry that traditional family and cultural values will be lost in a modern economy.

The Vietnamese lived under Chinese domination for one thousand years, followed by almost one hundred years of French colonialism (1858–1954). Then came 30 years of civil war that included the war against the United States. This long struggle for independence has given the Vietnamese a deep sense of national pride. People focus on the future rather than the past. They are often baffled by the fixation many Americans still have with the American War, which they see as past history. In fact, rather than being anti-American, most people have an interest in all things American.

As Vietnam faces the future, people are both happy and unhappy. Urban areas are enjoying better basic services, a more open political and cultural atmosphere, and a booming economy. Unfortunately, the countryside—where three-fourths of the population lives—continues to be neglected. Peasants are still dominated by party officials, still lack access to cultural opportunities and basic services (health care and education), and still live in grinding poverty. The inequality between urban and rural encourages urban migration and strains urban infrastructure.

Personal Appearance

Everyday dress for both men and women generally consists of slacks worn with a casual cotton or knit blouse or sport shirt. For special occasions, women wear the graceful, traditional *ao dai*, a long dress with front and back panels worn over satin trousers. Men might wear shorts without pockets at the beach or shorts with pockets at the work site, but not otherwise in public.

CUSTOMS AND COURTESIES

Greetings

Vietnamese shake hands when greeting formally, but otherwise greet verbally, bowing the head slightly and standing at a distance of about three feet. A formal greeting between strangers is *xin chao*. In other situations, Vietnamese greet with a variety of phrases that nearly always are accompanied by a title. *Di dau day?* (Where are you going?) is the most common greeting among friends. *Co khoe khong?* (How are you doing?), *Lam gi day?* (What are you doing?), and *Chao* (Greetings) are also popular. The title used depends on the relationship of the two individuals. Titles are based on family, as if everyone were related. For instance, a person greeting a man about the same age as the person's father calls the man *bac* (uncle): *Bac di dau day?* If the man is of the person's brother's age, the title used is *anh* (brother). If a man greets an older woman of his mother's generation, he greets her as "aunt" (*co*) and refers to himself as "nephew" (*chau*).

Peers might call each other by their given names, and younger people are addressed by given name. Names in Vietnam are structured with the family name first, followed by a middle name and a given name (e.g., Nguyen Huu Minh). Professionals or officials are addressed by their appropriate title (e.g., *Bac si* for "doctor") or a combination of those titles.

Gestures

One does not touch another person's head, the body's most spiritual point. It is rude to summon a person with the index finger. Instead, one waves all four fingers with the palm down. Hand gestures otherwise are limited because verbal communication is preferred. Men and women do not show affection in public, but it is common for members of the same sex to hold hands while walking. Vietnamese use both hands to pass an object to another person. Crossing the index and middle fingers is impolite.

Visiting

Vietnamese friends and relatives visit each other as often as the distance between their homes permits. Evening and weekend visits are most common. Most visits occur without prior arrangements in rural areas, but urban families with phones are beginning to prefer a call in advance. Holidays are the best time to visit distant friends and relatives. Relatives also gather for the death anniversaries of their ancestors. Urban residents take rural hosts a gift of something from the city, such as candy for the children, tea, bread, and so on. Rural visitors take urban hosts something from their farm (sticky rice, a live chicken, fresh produce).

During a short visit, hosts serve tea and cigarettes and chat about local matters. Guests politely wait for the host to begin drinking first. The host may invite the visitor to stay for the upcoming meal; if the individual has a long way to travel home, he or she is expected to stay. The invitation is extended before meal preparation begins so as not to make the guests feel they need to leave.

Eating

The Vietnamese eat three times a day; they use chopsticks and rice bowls for most meals. They hold the rice bowl in the hand; it is considered lazy to eat from a rice bowl on the table. Spoons are used for soup. Dishes of food are placed in the center of the table. Diners choose small portions from these dishes throughout the meal and place the food in their individual rice bowls. One is careful not to take the last portion of any dish so as to leave it for someone else. This means food may be left on the serving dishes, but no one should leave rice or other food in his or her individual bowl. Meals usually are taken at a table, although people may sit on a mat for certain occasions (e.g., when guests are present and the table is not big enough). The host might serve guests but usually just invites them to help themselves. Female guests help female hosts with doing the dishes after the meal.

LIFESTYLE

Family

The rural family unit includes parents, their unmarried children, and married sons and their families all living in the same household. However, as married sons establish their own households, the youngest son inherits the parental home and cares for the elderly parents. Single-family homes are more common in urban areas. Extended families provide members with assistance and support as needed. Men and women share most responsibilities in the family, although men are considered the authority and women care for the children and household. Both are breadwinners and both (if farmers) work in the fields.

Dating and Marriage

Youth begin dating in their late teens. In urban areas, young people generally go as couples to coffeehouses or movies. In rural Vietnam, they tend to socialize in groups. Young people are free to choose their mates; they are encouraged to marry after the man is at least 25 and the woman 23. Some weeks or months before a wedding, the two families meet to get to know each other. Later, there will be a formal proposal ceremony when the boy asks permission of the bride's parents to marry her. At a traditional wedding, the two families sit on opposite sides of a table in front of an ancestral altar. After a formal ceremony, they share a feast.

Diet

White rice is eaten with every meal. A fermented fish sauce called *nuoc mam* is the main seasoning used for flavoring dishes or dipping food. The main meal includes rice, a salty dish (such as *thit kho*, pork cooked in fish broth), a vegetable dish (such as *rau luoc*, boiled vegetable), and soup. *Canh ca* (fish and vegetable soup) is the most popular. Abundant local fruits include watermelon, papaya, bananas, and citrus fruits.

Commerce

Most offices are open Monday through Saturday from 8:00 A.M. to 4:30 P.M., closing at noon for one hour. Shops often close for two hours at noon but stay open until about 7:00 P.M. Some larger government stores remain open until 8:00 P.M. People may shop daily for perishables. Open markets and traveling traders are common in rural areas. An initial business meeting may begin with informal conversation over tea or coffee and fruit or sweets. Promptness is important to the Vietnamese; the time stated is the time meant.

Recreation

Vietnamese men enjoy team sports such as volleyball and soccer. Badminton, table tennis, swimming, and tennis are popular in cities. Only young, unmarried women tend to engage in sports. Urban people of all ages like to get out early in the morning to jog, do *tai chi* or yoga, or exercise. Men play Chinese checkers in their leisure time. Rural people have less leisure time but spend it in the company of friends and relatives. Traditional music is played on a variety of stringed instruments, such as *dan tranh* (multiple-string) *dan bau* (single-string), and *dan vong co* (modified guitar). Rural people love traditional opera: *cai luong* in the south and *hat cheo* in the north.

Holidays

There are 11 major lunar holidays (*tet*) in Vietnam, but the most important one is the Lunar New Year (*Tet Nguyen Dan*) in late January or early February. On this day, everyone becomes a year older. For three days, the Vietnamese spend their time feasting and visiting. Beforehand, houses are cleaned, ancestral graves are refurbished, debts are settled, and strained relationships are mended. Of the other *tet* celebrations, *Tet thuong nguyen* and *Tet trung nguyen* are most significant. The former is on the first full moon of the new year. The latter is on the full moon of the seventh month. It is a day to pardon the sins of the dead by reading the *Vu lan* (Buddhist prayer book).

Public holidays include International New Year's Day (1 January), a day commemorating the 1975 defeat of South Vietnam (30 April), Labor Day (1 May), and National Day (2 September, the anniversary of Ho Chi Minh's death).

SOCIETY

Government

Vietnam is a socialist state, led by a president (Le Duc Anh), a prime minister (Vo Van Kiet), his deputies, and a Government Council. Also powerful is the Communist Party's chairman, Do Muoi. The Vietnamese Communist Party is the only legal political party. All citizens may vote at age 18. The National Assembly (*Quoc-Hoi*) has 395 seats. The last legislative elections were in 1992; the next are scheduled for 1997.

Economy

With the success of *doi moi*, state-owned firms have had to be profitable to remain in business (six thousand were shut down or merged between 1990 and 1995). With U.S., Japanese, and other Asian investment, new plants are opening, previously underdeveloped industries (manufacturing, textiles, mining, and oil) are experiencing growth, and entrepreneurs have turned Ho Chi Minh City into a bustling commercial center. Even Hanoi is becoming more cosmopolitan and business oriented. In 1995, the government worked to streamline management in public firms, set terms for foreign companies exploiting mineral resources, revised other business procedures, and strove to keep inflation at less than 15 percent. Growth was nearly 10 percent.

Many urban Vietnamese desire to be a trader or businessperson, so many small shops are opening throughout the country. Despite these advances, rural farmers remain locked in poverty. Many men migrate to cities to work temporarily between harvests or at night. Vietnam's great potential for economic progress faces challenges from a growing population, poor infrastructure (i.e., lack of adequate laws, transportation links, skilled managers, and efficient government institutions), very low salaries, corruption, and a rapidly growing gap between rich and poor. In addition, skilled Vietnamese do not want to work for the government, which desperately needs talented people to improve Vietnam's education, health, and bureaucracy. Agriculture remains the primary activity, employing two-thirds of the labor force. The country's Human Development Index (0.539) ranks it 120th out of 174 countries. Real gross domestic product per capita is $1,010. The currency is the *dong* (D).

Transportation and Communication

The Vietnamese highway system is extensive, although road quality is variable and rural roads often need repair. Many roads damaged by war are still in need of repair. A rail service runs from Hanoi to Saigon through the coastal lowlands. Few individuals own cars, but most urban families have at least one motorbike. Bicycles are also used for private transportation. Rickshaws (pedicabs) are commonly used as taxis in cities. Most people depend on local public transportation, which includes bus service to district towns. The communications system is not well developed but is being updated. The press is controlled by the government, but opportunities for freedom of expression are increasing.

Education

Primary education is free to all, beginning at age five. In some areas, school facilities do not adequately handle all children, so students attend on a half-day basis. The school week is Monday through Saturday. All children are encouraged to finish high school. The drop-out rate is increasing as young people leave to look for work. The literacy rate is about 92 percent. University education is free to qualified students, but there is stiff competition for limited space. Vietnam has begun allowing students who can afford tuition, but do not qualify for a government subsidy, to enter a university as paying students. Three private universities have recently opened.

Health

Vietnam's health-care system offers free or low-cost medical care to all people, but facilities are often inadequate, especially in rural areas. Every commune has a clinic, but it may lack modern medicine or other supplies. Traditional healing and natural medicines play an important role in health care. People grow herbs and use local raw materials to make medicine. Malnutrition affects a large proportion of rural children. Vietnam's infant mortality rate is 42 per 1,000; life expectancy ranges from 64 to 68 years.

FOR THE TRAVELER

U.S. citizens need a passport and visa to enter Vietnam. No vaccinations are required, but travelers may call the U.S. Centers for Disease Control International Travel Hotline for updates: (404) 332–4559. The travel industry is growing, but facility quality is not always high. Water should be treated or boiled, and fruits and vegetables should be peeled and washed. Eat well-cooked meat served hot. Avoid using pedicabs not associated with hotels or restaurants; agree on a fare before starting out. First-time visitors should probably travel in a group with a Vietnamese-speaking guide. Major credit cards are accepted at most tourist destinations. For information, contact the Embassy of Vietnam, 1233 20th Street NW, Suite 501, Washington, DC 20036; phone (202) 861–0737.

A *Culturgram* is a product of native commentary and original, expert analysis. Statistics are estimates and information is presented as a matter of opinion. While the editors strive for accuracy and detail, this document should not be considered strictly factual. It is a general introduction to culture, an initial step in building bridges of understanding between peoples. It may not apply to all peoples of the nation. You should therefore consult other sources for more information.

West Bank and Gaza

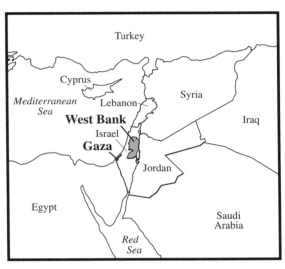

Boundary representations not necessarily authoritative.

BACKGROUND

Land and Climate

The West Bank is situated between the State of Israel and Jordan, while Gaza is further south, near the Sinai Peninsula. Covering 2,263 square miles (5,860 square kilometers), the West Bank is about the size of Delaware. It has a generally rugged terrain; vegetation is scarce in the east but there is some to the west. There are few natural resources. The West Bank borders the Dead Sea, which, at nearly 1,300 feet (390 meters) below sea level, has the lowest elevation on earth. In the highlands, the climate is cooler and moderate. Overall, the West Bank experiences a temperate climate. About 27 percent of the area is suitable for cultivation.

Gaza borders the Mediterranean Sea and is only about twice the size of Washington, D.C. It covers 147 square miles (380 square kilometers). The climate is also temperate, with mild winters and dry summers. As a coastal plain, much of Gaza is covered with sand dunes. Only 13 percent of the land is suitable for cultivation. Gaza has no natural resources but does have the capacity for a sea port.

History

The area known to Christians as the Holy Land was named *Palestine* by the Romans. The history of the West Bank and Gaza is naturally linked to the history of the entire area. Because of its central location between Asia and Africa, Palestine was conquered by many nations. Some three thousand years ago, a Hebrew kingdom was established by the descendants of the 12 tribes of Israel under King David. After the rule of David's son Solomon, the kingdom was split into two states—Israel and Judah. Both were destroyed by Assyria and Babylonia in the eighth and sixth centuries B.C.

After the Persian conquest of the Middle East, Jews dispersed by previous invasions returned to establish a state and build a temple. But the area later fell to the Greeks and then the Romans. In the 600s, Palestine was conquered by the Arabs, who subsequently settled the region. In the 1500s, the Ottoman Turks began to rule and remained in power until after World War I, when Palestine was declared a British mandate. The Balfour Declaration of 1917 pledged British support for the establishment of a national home for the Jews in Palestine, but it also insisted that nothing be done to prejudice the civil and religious rights of the existing non-Jewish communities in Palestine. These two goals conflicted and resulted in problems throughout the mandate.

The United Nations (UN) voted in 1947 to partition the area into two states—one Arab and one Jewish, with Jerusalem having a separate status (because of its significance to both). The Jewish State became the independent nation of Israel in 1948. Arab states who had opposed the UN partition immediately declared war. Israel withstood initial advances, but hostilities erupted again into open war in 1956, 1967, and 1973. During the 1967 war, Israel occupied the West Bank, Syria's Golan Heights, the Gaza Strip, and the Sinai Peninsula. East Jerusalem was also occupied and came under Israeli jurisdiction. As a result of the 1979 Camp David Accords, the Sinai was returned to Egypt and the final status of the West Bank and Gaza became subject to negotiation.

Peace negotiations during the 1980s broke down several times. Out of frustration for their situation, the Palestinian Arabs rebelled in 1987 and declared an independent Palestinian state. Their uprising is known as the *intifada*. It led to violent clashes between residents of the occupied territories and Israeli military forces but also resulted in peaceful demonstrations, civil disobedience, and other forms of resistance.

A peace conference between Israel, its Arab neighbors, and Palestinians convened in 1991. It marked the first time the Palestinians were able to hold direct talks with the Israeli government. The talks continued into 1993, with little progress due to continuing violence and political conflicts. Only when secret talks in Norway occurred did a breakthrough allow the two sides to sign, in 1993, an initial peace agreement. An actual framework for peace took several more months to construct, and the full agreement was signed in May 1994. The agreement ended 27 years of occupation and provided for eventual self-rule in Gaza and in the West Bank city of Jericho. Israeli troops withdrew from Gaza and Jericho in 1994 and were replaced by a Palestinian police force. Some Israeli soldiers remained to protect Jewish settlements. Yasir Arafat, chairman of the Palestine Liberation Organization (PLO), was sworn in as head of the Palestine National Authority. Israel released many political prisoners and many exiles returned to Gaza.

A wave of enthusiasm for self-rule, as well as diligent work by Palestinian officials to establish the new government, characterized the first weeks of the new arrangement. Even Israelis welcomed the peace and greatly reduced tensions that immediately followed the accord. Conditions soon soured, however, as the Islamic Resistance Movement *Hamas* rejected the agreement and vowed to fight both Israel and the Palestinian Authority. A rash of violent terrorist attacks took the lives of several Israeli citizens, restoring a climate of distrust. Right-wing Jewish groups pressured Israeli officials to slow talks on further self-rule and to crack down on the violence.

In September 1995, an accord was signed to grant self-rule to most of the West Bank. Israel withdrew from six cities and more than four hundred villages by the end of 1995. In January 1996, Palestinians held a historic free vote, in which Yasir Arafat was elected president. His government, the Palestinian Authority, now governs with an 88-member legislative council (Palestinian Council).

THE PEOPLE

Population

There are some 1.3 million people in the West Bank and nearly one million in Gaza. These figures do not include Palestinian Arabs who live in the State of Israel as Israeli citizens. The figures also do not include about 250,000 Jewish settlers who live in the West Bank and East Jerusalem through an Israeli housing program. Gaza is nearly 100 percent Palestinian. There are also many Palestinians living abroad, either as citizens of other countries (such as Jordan) or in refugee camps. All together, there are about 5.8 million Palestinians in the world. Several Bedouin groups also reside in the area; they retain some traditions but are no longer nomadic.

Language

The language of the Palestinian Arabs is Arabic. A high percentage also speaks English or French. English is required as a second language in schools, and French is a popular third language in many (especially private) schools. Because of the Israeli occupation, a large number of Palestinians have also learned Hebrew, although it is an optional language in public schools (except in East Jerusalem).

Religion

Of the Palestinian Arabs, between 92 and 97 percent are Muslims (mostly Sunni). Most of the rest are Christian—generally Greek Orthodox or Roman Catholic, although some are Protestant. Most Christians live in the West Bank. Most Muslims say they are religiously observant, while only about 22 percent are secular. Likewise, only about 18 percent of all Muslims characterize themselves as politically militant because of their religion. Muslims accept major biblical figures as prophets but do not accept Jesus Christ as the son of *Allah* (God). They believe Muhammad was the last and greatest prophet of *Allah* and that he received the *Qur'an* (Koran) by revelation. Devout Muslims pray five times daily while facing Makkah, Saudi Arabia; fast during the holy month of *Ramadan*; try to make at least one pilgrimage to Makkah; donate money to the poor; and follow certain dietary codes. They confess *Allah* to be God and Muhammad to be his prophet. Regardless of religion, being Palestinian unites the people as a group. Christians and Muslims respect each other's religions and honor the respective holidays. Schools are out on Friday and Sunday. Shops close according to the owner's religion.

General Attitudes

Palestinian Arabs value courage, hospitality, and generosity. They generally believe the establishment of the State of Israel in 1948 was illegal and assert they have the right to a sovereign state that provides them with basic human rights. Even self-rule does not go far enough to satisfy those who seek full independence. Since Israel can seal the borders at will and control movement between Gaza and the West Bank, Palestinians under self-rule still feel as if they are an occupied land. And since the Palestinian Authority is finding it difficult to bring order and structure to society, many people have become as critical of their leaders as they are of Israel. However, the average person is still pleased by the new freedoms that have come with autonomy. They realize the future will not be easy, as they must build an economy and a peaceful society, but they are hopeful that a better future will be possible. Indeed, for all their problems, most Palestinians are surprisingly optimistic about the future. They all share a dream for a Palestinian State.

Most Palestinians say they respect Judaism, and even Israel's right to exist as a state, but they oppose Zionism as a movement to establish the entire region as only a Jewish homeland. They point to the fact that they, too, have lived in the area for centuries. Palestinians are therefore sensitive to references to the Holy Land as "Israel" because they consider the Holy Land to be Palestine.

Personal Appearance

Western clothing is most common in urban areas and more common in the West Bank than Gaza. Elderly men, or those following traditional Muslim practices, wear long, white, loose-fitting robes and sometimes a turban. Women usually cover their heads with a scarf, although less-traditional women wear it loosely and a few choose to go without. During the *intifada*, urban women (more so in Gaza) began to wear tightly drawn scarves; long, loose-fitting dresses; and sometimes even a veil. This switch from Western dress was partly in response to greater religious devotion and partly in response to pressure from religious fundamentalists. With the end of the *intifada*, some urban women are again choosing to wear Western attire or at least loosen or remove their scarves. In small villages, the Muslim dress code remains standard practice.

CUSTOMS AND COURTESIES

Greetings

Al-Salaam 'Alaykum (Peace be upon you) is the usual greeting among Palestinian Arabs. Close friends of the same sex frequently exchange a kiss on the cheek. A pat on the back or shoulder is a sign of affection. Handshakes are also common. Important to the greeting are various expressions of goodwill and welcome. Friends call each other by their first names. The elderly and other respected individuals are called *Abu*, meaning "father of." For example, *Abu Ahmed* refers to the father of Ahmed (the oldest son), whose own personal name might be Ibrahim.

Gestures

It is impolite for the bottom of one's foot to point at another person; in addition, one never props the feet on a table or chair in the presence of others. Burping in public is inappropriate. It is important to show respect to all elderly individuals, no matter their social status or level of education. People, especially Muslims, pass and receive objects with the right hand or both hands.

Visiting

Except for close friends and relatives, a person will not visit another without an invitation. Relatives and friends may drop by at any time and often do. Visiting is an important part of Arab culture and is a social obligation. When one visits acquaintances, it is polite to ask about their family, health, and work. Men also enjoy visiting one another in coffeehouses to smoke waterpipes, drink coffee, and discuss daily concerns. Women more commonly socialize in the home. Entire families socialize at the beach.

Eating

Eating habits vary between families according to lifestyle. For example, in traditional homes people may eat food with the right hand, often taking their portions from a common plate. More Westernized families eat with utensils from separate plates. In some cases, men will eat separate from women, but families generally enjoy eating at least their main meal together. It is polite for guests to accept additional helpings.

LIFESTYLE

Family

Families are often large and play an important role in the life of the individual. The father is head of the family and the mother takes care of the housework and children. Although few women work outside the home, the number is increasing. Children are encouraged to cherish their heritage as Palestinians. Parents take great pride in their children and find personal success in their accomplishments. Because of this, they will do all they can to help their children succeed and will even support married children if necessary. In turn, children expect to care for their parents in their old age. It is not proper for a family member to die in anger or anguish, so every effort is made to keep the elderly happy. Most homes are equipped with the basic necessities of running water, refrigeration, and electricity. But luxury items are found only in the homes of wealthier families.

Dating and Marriage

Dating is not common. In traditional families, it is forbidden. Girls marry at about age 18 and boys at age 22 or older. Those who do date enjoy going to the beach, seeing movies, or having parties in private homes. At such parties, excessive behavior (drinking, immorality, etc.) is not tolerated. Individuals engaging in such behavior are not accepted by their peers. Cousin marriage is common among the Muslims. Marriages between Christians and Muslims occur but are fairly rare. A marriage is a time for great family celebration. Fall is the most popular time of year for a wedding. Separate parties are held for men and women during the day, and then the entire wedding party enjoys an evening of dancing and eating—often at beachside wedding clubs.

Diet

The main meal is eaten at midday or in the afternoon, rather than in the evening. Spicy food, such a *qedra* (a rice dish), is typical. *Falafel* (filled pocket bread) is popular. Other well-liked foods are stuffed grape leaves and spiced rice with nuts. Turkish coffee, tea, and fruit juice are common. Observant Muslims do not eat pork or drink alcohol.

Recreation

Soccer and basketball are the most popular sports among Palestinian Arabs. Playing cards, attending movies, and visiting friends are common activities. Camping is becoming a favorite way to spend leisure time. Gazan families enjoy having a barbecue on the beach. In fact, families often go the beach in the evening to play, drink sodas, and relax. Adults love to socialize at coffeehouses or cafés, and many people attend performances of the cultural arts when possible. Many new cafés are being built, especially in Gaza.

Holidays

Palestinian Arabs observe both Muslim and Christian holidays. Christmas celebrations in Bethlehem and Easter commemorations in East Jerusalem are known throughout the world. *Ramadan* is the month of fasting for Muslims, who go without food or drink during daylight hours. In the evenings, they eat a meal and visit friends or relatives. At the end of *Ramadan*, a three-day feast called *'Aid al Fitr* is held.

Muslims also celebrate *'Aid al Adha,* which comes after the pilgrimage to Makkah and celebrates the willingness of Abraham to sacrifice his son.

Commerce

Business hours vary according to personal choice, religion, and the current political climate. Under the *intifada,* leaders often called for strikes and other shop closures. These measures are seldom necessary today but are still possible. More likely, however, is that business is idled when Israel closes the borders: workers cannot get to jobs in Israel, supplies from outside the West Bank and Gaza cannot get into stores and small factories, and businesspeople cannot conduct trade. In the first 450 days of autonomy, about 200 days of potential commerce were lost to closed borders. Commerce is increasing, however, as private enterprises are opening.

SOCIETY

Government

The Palestinian Authority has responsibility for specific internal matters, including education, health, taxation, tourism, and social welfare. They also have some control over commerce and day-to-day order. Israel continues to maintain foreign borders and runs joint patrols with Palestinian police officers along key roads. Palestinians continue to need Israeli-issued identification cards and may not leave the country without permission. Jewish settlements in the area remain under Israeli jurisdiction. Since the West Bank and Gaza depend on Israel for so many things, the actual power of the Palestinian Authority is limited.

Economy

The economies of both the West Bank and Gaza are poor and struggling. Unemployment and inflation fluctuate according to political relations with Israel. On average, though, Gazans suffer from a 50 percent unemployment rate. People in the West Bank generally have higher incomes than those in Gaza. Gazans have a per capita gross national product of about $2,400 and residents of the West Bank average $2,800. Both regions are in need of substantial foreign investment. The skilled workforce is capable of building a solid economy if the necessary infrastructure can be established. Unfortunately, electricity, sewer, and water systems are all inadequate. Private enterprise is beginning to expand as wealthy exiles return to invest in promising ventures. Construction is proceeding at a rapid pace. A new port and airfield are planned for completion sometime in 1997. Beach resorts are planned.

Most current industries are small-scale and operated by families. They include cement, textiles, and souvenirs. Agricultural crops include fruits, olives, vegetables, beef, and dairy products. Both the new Israeli *shekel* (NIS) and the Jordanian *dinar* (JD) are acceptable legal tender.

Transportation and Communication

Buses are the primary mode of mass transit. Taxis and private cars are also common. Roads generally are in poor condition. Travel between Gaza and the West Bank must follow specified routes. A growing number of people have private cars, adding to traffic problems. About half of all families have televisions, but only about 10 percent have telephones in their homes. This inhibits communication and is an area of focus for future development. Newspapers are popular.

Education

Despite a general lack of facilities, Palestinian Arabs have a high literacy rate of about 80 percent. Unfortunately, this translates into about 89 percent for men and only 72 percent for women. Education is valued by society; even when schools were closed during periods of the *intifada,* parents organized classes and continued the educational process in their homes. Some private schools are supported by international Christian and Muslim organizations. Public schools lack space, materials, and teachers, so Palestinian authorities are seeking aid from donor nations. Nine percent of all Palestinians have had at least some college education.

Health

Health conditions are better in the West Bank than in Gaza. However, hospital and medical care are difficult to obtain in either region. Facilities that do exist are often inadequate. Health care is therefore another priority of the new Palestinian government. The United Nations sponsors some medical care programs. The infant mortality rate is much higher in these areas than in the State of Israel. In Gaza it is 31 per 1,000, while in the West Bank it is 30 per 1,000. Life expectancy ranges from 66 to 71 years, depending on gender and the territory.

FOR THE TRAVELER

U.S. travelers need a valid passport, but no visa, to enter Israel. A U.S. passport is also valid for entry to Gaza and the West Bank. Travel may be restricted by the Israeli government. Care should be exercised when traveling because of potential violence. For a recorded message on current travel advisories, call the U.S. Department of State at (202) 647–5225. Contact U.S. embassy authorities in Israel for further information. For more information on travel to the West Bank and Gaza, contact the Palestine Arab Delegation, PO Box 608, New York, NY 10163; phone (212) 758–7411; or the PLO Office to the United Nations, 115 East 65th Street, New York, NY 10021; phone (212) 288–8500.

CULTURGRAM '97

Republic of Zaire

Boundary representations not necessarily authoritative.

BACKGROUND

Land and Climate

With 905,563 square miles (2,345,410 square kilometers), Zaire's land area is about the size of the United States's land area east of the Mississippi River. It is situated in central Africa, almost entirely within the equatorial zone. The Mitumba Mountains are part of Africa's Great Rift system, running north to south along Zaire's eastern border and separating most of the country from Lake Tanganyika on the border. This range is also prominent in the extreme south. Other important mountain ranges include the Ruwenzori and Virunga, both located in the northeast. Most of the country lies within the vast lowlands of the Zaire (Congo) River Basin. The Zaire is the world's fifth largest river.

Much of Zaire (47 percent), especially in the west, is covered with tropical rain forest. To the north and south of the central rain forest are grasslands, and then north and south of those areas are savanna. Only 3 percent of the land is under cultivation. Temperatures in the eastern mountains and the southeast savanna are cool from May to September, and they occasionally drop below freezing.

The rain forests experience high humidity and warm temperatures throughout the year. Rainfall varies from 40 inches (101 centimeters) in the south to 80 inches (203 centimeters) in the central Zaire River Basin. The dry season is generally from April to October, although these months comprise the wet season above the equator, which runs through northern Zaire. The country has many natural resources, including copper, oil, diamonds, gold, silver, zinc, tin, uranium, bauxite, iron ore, and coal.

History

Long ago, Bantu peoples from western Africa moved into the Congo Basin. Several kingdoms existed in the centuries before Europeans arrived. The Kongo Kingdom controlled southwestern Zaire when the Portuguese arrived in the late 1400s. Little European intervention took place until the late 1800s, when Leopold II of Belgium formed an international trading company to exploit the Congo region. The so-called Congo Free State, recognized by the Conference of Berlin in 1884, became, in effect, a feudal estate. Leopold enslaved the people and plundered the land. His harsh treatment of the region inspired Joseph Conrad's novella, *Heart of Darkness*, Mark Twain's *King Leopold's Soliloquy*, and other publications. These eventually aroused an international outcry, and the Belgian Parliament was moved to seize the private royal domain from King Leopold in 1908. The area then became known as the Belgian Congo.

After World War II, and following the trend in much of Africa, the people negotiated with Belgium for their independence. This was granted in 1960, although the new leaders were not fully prepared to govern such a large country, which they named the Democratic Republic of the Congo.

Soon after the first elections, the province of Katanga seceded. Katanga's separation was followed by general upheaval, the prime minister's assassination, and unrest throughout the region. United Nations troops were called in to help keep peace in the area. After years of bloody fighting, the revolts subsided in 1965. Mobutu Sese Seko seized power that year with help from Western nations. In 1971, he began an "Africanization" campaign and renamed the country the Republic of Zaire, after the Portuguese name for the Congo River. Zairians were told to reject foreign models and draw upon their own heritage in shaping their nation's future. As part of this national campaign, cities and individuals were required to replace their Christian or other foreign names with African names, Western-style clothing was banned, and other changes were implemented.

Mobutu ruled a one-party dictatorship through the Popular Movement of the Revolution (MPR). He robbed the national treasury, living in luxury while ignoring the needs of his people. Under pressure in 1990, he lifted the ban on political parties and granted other freedoms that people thought might open the door for democracy. Mobutu allowed a national political conference to open in 1991 with the purpose of establishing a framework for a transitional government and free elections. Unfortunately, Mobutu refused to accept as binding many of the conference's decisions, including one to abandon the name *Zaire* for *Congo* and one to dissolve Mobutu's Parliament. He did agree initially to the appointment of his chief rival, Étienne Tshisekedi, as prime minister. But when Tshisekedi began challenging Mobutu's authority, the two became locked in a power struggle, and Mobutu attempted to replace Tshisekedi, who refused to leave office. Western governments demanded that Mobutu relinquish power, but he refused. In 1993, Mobutu had Tshisekedi ejected from his office building and the country had, for a few months, two governments and two constitutions.

Outside of Kinshasa, the capital, the power struggle resulted in the deterioration of services, schools, transportation networks, and other institutions. Rampaging underpaid soldiers, corruption, and a collapsed economy plunged the country into chaos. Most Westerners left. People in interior towns were cut off, their only means of long-distance travel is by boat on the Zaire River, and the passenger boats operated by the government stopped working.

Total collapse was averted in 1994 when a new constitution was adopted and Mobutu agreed to share power over the military. Parliament nominated Kengo wa Dondo as prime minister, and he was accepted by Mobutu. Kengo moved to reduce the size of the military, repair roads and other infrastructure, and reform state enterprises. By 1995, the economy and social structures remained in serious condition, particularly because of the strain of Rwandan refugees, but the government was able to begin addressing the country's many problems. Tribal violence raged in many areas in 1996, mostly as spillover from Rwanda and related conflicts. Mobutu has lost much of his power but continues to command a vast security force. Some regions function with near autonomy from Kinshasa. Even if elections scheduled for 1996 or 1997 are held, it will be difficult for any government to reunite Zaire.

THE PEOPLE

Population

The population of Zaire is approximately 44.1 million and is growing at 3.2 percent annually. About 45 percent of the population is younger than age 15. During the last decade, migration to cities has caused the urban population to grow from 25 to 40 percent. The rapid shift has hurt both rural and urban areas: cities cannot provide for their expanding populations and villages are losing their labor force.

There are more than two hundred distinct African ethnic groups in Zaire, with Bantu peoples accounting for the majority (80 percent). The three largest Bantu groups (Mongo, Luba, Kongo), together with the Mangbetu-Azande, make up 45 percent of the total population. Some minority groups include the Pygmy, Nilo-Saharan, and Afro-Asiatic peoples who mainly inhabit the northeastern part of the country. There are fewer than one million Europeans and Asians concentrated in urban areas. Kinshasa, the capital, has some four million inhabitants and Lubumbashi has more than 800,000.

The country's Human Development Index (0.384) ranks it 143d out of 174 countries. Real gross domestic product per capita is $523, a figure that is lower than before independence. Most people have no access to resources that would allow them to pursue personal goals.

Language

With more than two hundred different languages, Zaire has had to adopt a special language policy. French is the official language and is used in larger businesses, education, and government administration, but it is spoken by only about 10 percent of the population. Lingala is increasingly used as the national language of government (military and bureaucracy). Broadcasting, local business, daily communication, and primary school instruction occurs in one of the four national or regional languages, all of which are Bantu: Lingala (in the west and in Kinshasa), Kikongo (in the west and southwest), Tshiluba (in central and southern Zaire), and Swahili (in the east). Most people speak their own ethnic language as well as one or more of the official national languages. It is increasingly common for urban people to speak a mixture of local languages and French.

Religion

Eighty percent of the population is Christian. Fifty percent is Roman Catholic and 20 percent belongs to various Protestant organizations. Another 10 percent participates in the indigenous Christian sect known as Kimbanguism, a Protestant offshoot. It was established in the 20th century by Simon Kimbangu. Many Christians also mix traditional animist beliefs with Christianity. About 10 percent of the people are Muslim, residing mainly in the east but also in Kinshasa. The remaining 10 percent follow traditional beliefs.

General Attitudes

The majority of Zairians are members of one of the many Bantu ethnic groups. Most Bantu peoples share a common cultural heritage. Most distinctive, perhaps, is their general politeness and genuine concern for the welfare of others. This politeness sometimes manifests itself as a gentle disposition and shyness with strangers, which outsiders occasionally interpret as reticence. Although they may seem shy, Zairians reciprocate open and sincere friendliness.

One characteristic of Lingala-speaking Zairians seems to contradict their politeness. Their speech is often abrupt; they may make requests without a "Please" and accept help without a "Thank you." This is not impolite; it is simply a cultural habit. Lingala was specifically promoted by Belgian colonialists for use by official institutions (such as the police force) because of its directness. Even if a person does not say "Please" (*Bolimbisi* in Lingala or *Tafadhali* in Swahili) or "Thank you" (*Botondi* or *Aksanti*), he or she will show gratitude or politeness through actions.

In general, Zairians are careful not to offend. The desires of friends, family, and colleagues, as well as one's responsibility to maintain the status quo, are paramount forces controlling personal actions. Individualism is acceptable only if it does not conflict with a group's needs. Time is elastic in Zaire and does not have the importance it does in Western society; Lingala has only one word for both "yesterday" and "tomorrow." Which day a person is referring to is determined from the context. Because schedules are not as important as people, appointments may run 30 to 60 minutes late.

Personal Appearance

Western-style clothing is common in most urban areas. A locally styled, two-piece suit (*Abacost*) is also worn by some men. It was introduced by the Mobutu regime in the 1970s as part of the Africanization campaign. Until 1990, it was technically a crime to wear Western clothing. Zairian women wear a *pagne*, a long dress made of a five-yard length of fabric, more tailored than an Indian *saree*. Adults rarely wear shorts and immodest attire. Children do wear shorts.

CUSTOMS AND COURTESIES

Greetings

In urban areas, men and women generally shake hands, smile, and greet each other verbally. The urban elite use the French term *Bonjour* (Good day). But *Mbote* (Hello) is more common. It is followed by *Sango nini?* (What's new?) among Lingala speakers. Outside urban areas, men usually do not shake hands with women but will shake hands with men. Some rural women greet men by clapping their hands a few times and bowing slightly. In the eastern and southeastern parts of the country, the Swahili greeting *Jambo* (Hello) is common. Other greetings vary by ethnic group.

Gestures

Pointing directly at a person with the index finger is impolite. One beckons by waving all fingers. Objects are passed with the right hand or both hands.

Visiting

Visiting is important in Zaire and hospitality is traditional. Most visiting occurs in the home. Family and close friends often drop by unannounced, but strangers are expected to make arrangements in advance. When a person first visits a Zairian home, a gift is not appropriate. Visitors may give small gifts, such as food or an item for the house, after a relationship is established. First-time visitors are directed where to sit by the hosts and they generally remain seated. Good friends and extended family members have greater liberty to make themselves at home. Children are expected to greet each adult with a handshake and perhaps a kiss on the cheek. They usually are then dismissed while the adults socialize.

If a Zairian offers to share a meal, the guest is first expected to show reluctance to join the host's table. But the guest should ultimately accept the offer. Not doing so is impolite. Even if guests are unable to eat the meal, they should try some of the food as a gesture of goodwill. Zairians often judge guests' sincerity by the way they eat. Even if hosts do not offer a meal, they usually serve refreshments.

Eating

Meals usually are eaten with the fingers of the right hand only. When Zairians ues utensils, they observe the continental style of eating, with the fork in the left hand and the knife remaining in the right. Men and women eat from separate communal bowls. When sharing a bowl, people eat only from the space directly in front of them. Only the eldest can distribute meat with both hands to those eating the meal. Diners wash hands before and after each meal.

LIFESTYLE

Family

The family is the most important focus in a Zairian's life. Although family structure varies greatly between different ethnic groups, they all place emphasis on group goals and overall family welfare. Large extended families are the norm in Zaire. They usually live under the same roof or in a group of closely joined homes. In western Zaire, families are mostly matriarchal; the mother's brother, rather than her husband, is the male with the greatest authority in the family. In other areas of the country, patriarchal and polygamous (with multiple wives) families, as well as combinations of these, are common. Urban families, particularly among the more affluent, tend to be more patriarchal and include fewer relatives in the extended family.

Dating and Marriage

Casual dating only occurs among the wealthy in large urban areas. Otherwise, if two young people meet and desire to date, the boy and his family seek permission of the girl's family for him to see her. Subsequent dating usually leads to marriage. Traditionally, marriage is a family affair and is at least partly arranged by parents. Among matrilineal families, the preferred marriage partner is a cousin (one of the mother's brothers' children). However, that pattern is slowly changing, especially in urban areas.

Diet

Staple foods include cassava, rice, potatoes, bananas, yams, beans, corn, fish, peanuts, and various fruits and vegetables. Common fruits include mangoes, oranges, pawpaws, and coconuts. Sugarcane is grown in Zaire. People must purchase some perishable foods on a daily basis. Adequate supplies of food are becoming harder to find in some areas, and malnutrition and starvation are affecting from 4 to 10 percent of the nation's children.

Recreation

Soccer is the most popular sport. Rural Zairians enjoy gatherings that consist of dancing and drum music. Many urban people spend their leisure time socializing, dancing, or listening to Zairian jazz.

Holidays

Zairian holidays include New Year's Day; the Commemoration of the Martyrs of Independence (4 January); Easter; Labor Day (1 May); MPR Day (20 May), which honors the national political party; Independence Day (30 June); Parents' Day (1 August); the President's Birthday (14 October); Three "Z" Day (27 October), which marks the day in 1971 when Mobutu changed the name of the country, currency, and river from Congo to Zaire; Veterans' Day (17 November); the Anniversary of the Second Republic (24 November), which began in 1965; and Christmas.

Commerce

Most people live in small villages and farm small plots of land or catch fish. In the cities, business hours vary. Businesses may open anytime from 7:00 to 9:00 A.M. and close between 4:00 and 5:00 P.M. Government offices close by 4:00 P.M. In the current situation, both government and business offices may be closed for extended periods of time.

SOCIETY

Government

Zaire is a republic, but Mobutu has ruled more as a dictator than as a president for most of his tenure. However, with Mobutu's power decreasing, Kengo and Parliament are trying to strengthen democractic institutions. Parliament is equally divided between presidential supporters and opponents and is to be a transitional parliament until elections can be declared. The main political parties include the MPR and the Union for Democracy and Social Progress (Tshisekedi's party). Zaire has ten regions or provinces. The voting age is 18.

Economy

Vast mineral deposits and other resources make Zaire potentially one of the richest nations in Africa, but this potential remains largely untapped. Inflation has been so high (10,000 percent in 1993) that a new currency has had to be reintroduced three times in the past few years. The new *Zaire* (Z) was introduced in October 1993 and it immediately began losing value. The devaluation continued into 1995. Urban unemployment is at 80 percent, and many government workers have not been paid for months. An informal economy functions in most rural areas, as money and jobs do not exist.

The bulk of the labor force (75 percent) is involved in agriculture. Main products include cassava, corn, palm oil, bananas, rice, rubber, and timber. Coffee is the most important cash crop. Zaire is the world's largest producer of diamonds. It was a principal supplier of cobalt and a major exporter of copper. Mining and mineral processing were the most important industries, but productivity has slipped by 90 percent and many mines are now closed. The most important state-owned mining company, Gecamines in Lubumbashi (Shaba province), remains open but barely functioning. It was reorganized in 1995 in an attempt to save its future. South African and other foreign firms are seeking partnerships with Gecamines to tap Zaire's wealth.

Vast inland waterways give Zaire great potential for hydroelectric energy. It has one of the largest dams in Africa, the Inga Dam near the mouth of the Zaire River on the Atlantic Ocean. Power is transmitted more than 1,000 miles from the Inga to the southern copper-mining region—one of the world's longest direct-current hydroelectric transmission lines.

Transportation and Communication

While several thousand miles of roadways exist, few are paved and most are unimproved dirt roads. A number of paved roads are crumbling and difficult to travel. Many roads are impassable in the rainy season. Public transportation in cities is all but nonexistent. Private trucks provide transportation, along with taxis in larger cities. The communications system is barely adequate for domestic use. There are no pay phones. The press is generally free to operate, and many new publications have emerged since 1990.

Education

Like the economy, the education system has faltered. Facilities and staff are lacking, and enrollment levels are very low. Few viable institutions exist in interior rural areas. Literacy is much lower than the official estimate of 74 percent. A severe "brain drain" of the skilled and educated is undermining the country's ability to provide adequate education.

Health

There are few physicians in Zaire. Medical help is available in Kinshasa, but adequate health care is a serious problem in rural areas. Medical supplies are lacking throughout the country. International relief organizations or traditional healers are often the only sources of care. Zaire's infant mortality rate is 109 per 1,000. Life expectancy ranges from 52 to 56 years. Malaria, yellow fever, AIDS, and cholera are widespread. Disease epidemics are common. In 1995, an outbreak of the Ebola virus was discovered in Kikwit, a city of 500,000. Through widespread education and precautionary measures, health officials tried to keep the virus from spreading to Kinshasa and elsewhere. There is no cure for the disease, which causes one to bleed to death internally. Other epidemics also afflict people, including measles, malaria, hepatitis, tuberculosis, sleeping sickness, and AIDS.

FOR THE TRAVELER

A visa and valid passport are required of U.S. travelers entering Zaire. Fees vary according to the length of stay, and a person must prove return passage before a visa will be issued. Travel to Zaire at this time may not be wise. Crime and instability make travel in some areas hazardous. For recorded travel warnings from the U.S. State Department, call (202) 647–5225. Vaccinations for yellow fever and cholera are required. Malarial suppressants are recommended. Water must be boiled before use, even for brushing teeth. Eat only foods that are well cooked and hot. All fruits and vegetables should be washed and peeled or cooked before being eaten. Do not remove Zairian currency from the country. Be aware of restrictions on photography. For more information, contact the Embassy of Zaire, 1800 New Hampshire Avenue NW, Washington, DC 20009; phone (202) 234–7690.

CULTURGRAM '97™

Republic of
Zambia

Boundary representations not necessarily authoritative.

BACKGROUND

Land and Climate

Zambia is a landlocked country sharing borders with Zaire, Tanzania, Malawi, Mozambique, Zimbabwe, Botswana, Namibia, and Angola. It covers 290,583 square miles (752,610 square kilometers). The plateau on which the country lies rises from 3,000 to 5,000 feet (900–1,500 meters) above sea level. Except for the capital, the most populous cities congregate in a region known as the Copperbelt. The Copperbelt lies on Zambia's border where Zaire nearly bisects Zambia. The famous Victoria Falls are near Livingstone on the southern border. In the north stand the Muchinga Mountains. The country shares lakes with Zaire, Tanzania, and Zimbabwe. Three large rivers, the Zambezi, Luangwa, and Kafue, flow through the country. The cool, dry season is from April to August; the hot, dry season runs from August to October or November; the warm, rainy season is from November to April. The northwest gets the longest and heaviest rainfall. Average temperatures in the capital of Lusaka are 70°F (21°C) in January, 60°F (15°C) in July, and 75°F (24°C) in October.

History

Between 300 and 1500, Bantu peoples replaced Zambia's original inhabitants and introduced their languages, culture, and institutions, including that of chieftainship, to the area.

The 1800s brought Western missionaries and explorers, among them the Scottish missionary, David Livingstone. The British South Africa Company took control of Zambia in the 1890s, and Zambia became a British protectorate in 1924. The discovery of copper deposits led to the establishment of the Copperbelt and precipitated urbanization in that area.

In 1953, the area's European settlers formed the Central African Federation of Rhodesia and Nyasaland from Northern Rhodesia (now Zambia), Southern Rhodesia (now Zimbabwe), and Nyasaland (now Malawi). Northern Rhodesia gained independence when the federation was dissolved in 1963, and the country became known as Zambia in October 1964. Former African National Congress (ANC) official Kenneth Kaunda became president and head of the ruling United National Independence Party (UNIP). A one-party state was declared and all other political parties were banned in 1972. Kaunda united the country's many ethnic groups, built schools, and attempted to develop a health-care system. However, his socialist policies and autocratic style prevented the realization of his expressed goals.

In 1990, after severe food riots, Kaunda agreed to allow multiparty elections, which took place in October 1991 without violence or fraud. Kaunda lost the presidency to union leader Frederick Chiluba. Unlike other long-ruling African leaders, Kaunda peacefully accepted the election results and retired to a modest home in Lusaka.

Chiluba won the election with 84 percent of the vote, and people were enthusiastic for change. He inherited a poor country, however, and could not meet people's high expectations. While he allowed a free press and promised basic human rights, his government was soon accused of being corrupt and unable to provide the nation with strong leadership. In 1993, Chiluba temporarily declared a state of emergency due to the threat of a coup from his opponents. That threat passed, but a number of his cabinet ministers were forced to resign over allegations of corruption. Chiluba worked to privatize state industries, ended food shortages, and encouraged foreign investment, but transition to full democracy has been difficult.

In 1995, Kaunda came out of retirement to declare his candidacy for president in October 1996. Popular disillusionment with Chiluba, railway strikes, and economic woes are expected to create a volatile election atmosphere.

THE PEOPLE

Population

Zambia has a population of more than 9.4 million. The annual growth rate is about 2.7 percent. With half of its people living in cities, Zambia is one of the most urbanized countries in Africa. Half of the population is younger than age 15; less than 1 percent is older than age 65. Close to 99 percent of the population is African. Only 1 percent is European. The Africans are divided into 73 ethnic groups, including various Bantu peoples.

Zambia's Human Development Index (0.425) ranks it 136th out of 174 nations. Adjusted for women, the index (0.403) ranks Zambia 97th out of 130 countries. These figures indicate that Zambians have few opportunities to pursue personal goals, with women lagging behind men in terms of income and adult literacy.

Language

English is the official and administrative language spoken by literate people. It is more common in urban areas than in rural areas. Additionally, Zambians speak seven major languages: Ichibemba is used in the Copperbelt, Luapula, Northern, and Central provinces; Chinyanja in the Lusaka and Eastern provinces; Chitonga in the Southern province and Kabwe rural areas; Silozi in the Western province and Livingstone urban areas; and Kikaonde, Lunda, and Lovale in the North-Western province. Swahili is spoken to a limited extent in the Copperbelt and northern Zambia. There are as many languages as there are ethnic groups. Most Zambians speak their ethnic language in addition to one of the seven national languages.

Religion

It is difficult to determine how many people practice any one religion in Zambia. Many people adhere to a combination of two or more religions or belief systems. Estimates as to how many people practice Christianity vary between 50 and 90 percent, depending on the source of the estimate and whether it considers the combination of Christian principles with indigenous beliefs as practicing Christianity. Likewise, estimates as to how many people practice Islam, Hinduism, and other religions vary. Only a small number of people actually practice indigenous beliefs exclusive of the world religions.

General Attitudes

Zambians are warm and welcoming people, although they may be wary of suspicious-looking strangers. Most Zambians, especially those in the rural areas, are very patient and take life as it comes. In urban areas, where the pace of activities is faster, people are more time conscious. The elderly, chiefs, and persons of high status are shown great respect. People consider caring for the elderly a privilege rather than a burden. Homes for the aged are discouraged, as care is the responsibility of the family. Funerals of near and extended relatives and neighbors are considered extremely important and must be attended as a sign of solidarity and respect for the dead.

Personal Appearance

Western-style clothing is common throughout Zambia. Men wear trousers or shorts and a shirt in rural and urban areas. Some elderly rural men may wear a short wraparound skirt-like cloth with a shirt. Women wear wraparound skirts with blouses. They commonly wrap their hair in a cloth matching the skirt or blouse. Rural women often sew their own clothing.

CUSTOMS AND COURTESIES

Greetings

Greetings vary according to the region and situation. For example, in the Copperbelt region, a common phrase is *Mwapoleni* (Welcome); in and around Lusaka, *Mulibwanji* (How are you?) is common; and, in the south, the preferred term is *Mwabonwa* (Welcome). Adults respectfully address each other on formal occasions as "Mr.," "Mrs.," or "Miss" with their last names, rather than their given names. All local languages have equivalent forms of these terms. People in most areas generally greet by shaking hands, with the left hand supporting the right to show respect. Kneeling down before the elderly or social superiors is common. Greetings that incorporate clapping and the gentle art of thumb squeezing are also practiced, especially by ethnic groups in the Western, North-Western, and Luapula provinces. Making bodily contact while greeting a member of the opposite sex traditionally is not acceptable. In most ethnic groups, parents-in-law and their children's spouses also avoid physical contact.

Gestures

Zambians use handshaking widely as a gesture of thanks and friendship. Women commonly clap hands while conversing with others. Girls and women often kneel when addressing elders; men and boys curtsy slightly. Direct eye contact, embraces, and public displays of affection are avoided. Spitting in front of people is a sign of disrespect. Finger pointing is not acceptable.

Visiting

Official and business matters call for making appointments, especially in urban areas. In rural areas or traditional situations, however, people tend to be flexible about time, so allowance is made for delays. An important exception is a visit with the local chief, when scheduling is always taken seriously. Having a visitor in a home at any time is considered an honor to the family. In many Zambian cultures, an unannounced visitor at mealtime is expected to share the food with the hosts. It is considered inappropriate for the host to have to invite the guest to partake of the food. It is also discourteous for the visitor not to join the hosts in eating the meal. Among friends, gift giving is an accepted practice. One extends both hands when presenting and receiving a gift; kneeling when giving a gift is also customary in many parts of Zambia.

Eating

In many homes, families eat meals from communal dishes. Zambians normally eat with the fingers of the right hand. They wash hands before and after eating. Utensils are used in some homes, mainly with foods such as rice or potatoes but also with *nsima* (see Diet). Water is served with meals. In some areas, especially in villages, men eat in a place separate from women and children.

LIFESTYLE

Family

Extended families are important in Zambia, and they are often large. The family structure is somewhat different than in Western societies. For example, in the extended family, a father's brothers are also considered "fathers" in the family and a mother's sisters are also considered "mothers." Cousins are basically considered brothers and sisters. Other members of the same clan who are not actually blood relations may also be considered siblings. Some families are matriarchal, but most are patriarchal. In patriarchal families, the father is the head of the family. In matriarchal families, the mother's brother has the greatest authority.

Dating and Marriage

Traditional marriages take place soon after a girl matures and, in most cases, without dating. Modern marriages are preceded by some dating. In both approaches, elders are consulted and negotiations for the *lobola* (bride-price or dowry) take place. Church weddings are common, although some couples choose only to register at a district office. The influence of Christianity has decreased the traditional practice of polygamy. Marriages are expected to be fruitful and families are large. On average, a woman bears seven children, although not all live to maturity. Marital infidelity is common for men and is culturally acceptable.

Diet

Nsima, made from cornmeal, is the national food. It can also be made from cassava (common in the north) or millet (common near the Zambezi River). *Nsima* is prepared as a dough or thick porridge. It might be eaten with a relish made of fish or meat stew and vegetables. Breakfast consists of bread or *nsima* and tea. Rural Zambians often eat sweet potatoes and groundnuts (peanuts) as well. Fresh fruits and vegetables are fairly abundant during and following the rainy season. Financially secure families generally eat two hot meals, lunch and supper, plus breakfast. Other families must make do with one hot meal and breakfast. Consumption of beer is heavy. Although bottled beer is available, many rural inhabitants brew their own alcohol.

Recreation

Drinking and traditional dancing are the main forms of entertainment in rural areas. Urban life offers soccer, tennis, basketball, golf, discos, *ifisela* (drama), church activities, volunteer organizations, and social clubs.

Holidays

Holidays celebrated in Zambia include New Year's Day, Easter (Friday–Sunday), Labor Day (1 May), Youth Day (19 March), African Freedom Day (25 May), Heroes' and Unity Day (first Monday and Tuesday in July), Farmers' Day (first Monday in August), Independence Day (24 October), and Christmas.

Commerce

Business hours usually extend from 8:00 A.M. to 5:00 P.M., Monday through Friday. A one-hour lunch break is usually observed. Banks close for a half day on Thursday but are open from 8:00 to 11:00 A.M. on Saturday. Shops are open 8:00 A.M. to 6:00 P.M., Monday through Friday. They close on Saturday at 4:00 P.M. Rural life revolves around small-scale farming, the main source of income. With the exception of public-sector jobs, rural work schedules are not fixed. Most people are not wage earners.

SOCIETY

Government

The Republic of Zambia has nine provinces. The central government is headed by a president and his cabinet. The cabinet is drawn from the National Assembly. Members of the 150-seat National Assembly are elected by the general population to serve a five-year term. The voting age is 18. In October 1996, voters will cast ballots for both the president and the National Assembly. The main political parties include Chiluba's Movement for Multiparty Democracy (MMD) and Kaunda's UNIP.

Economy

Over the past decade, Zambia's economic performance has declined along with the world price of copper. This, combined with high oil prices, high inflation (up to 60 percent), and a growing foreign debt, caused severe economic problems for the country.

Rather than growing, the economy declined by 2 percent per year in the 1980s. Economic problems led to a lower standard of living for most people and are one reason why people demonstrated for change in 1990. The government introduced some fundamental changes in its economic policy in 1990 and some growth was recorded, but voters did not accept the reforms as sufficient. Chiluba's government emphasized free-market principles (such as the end of subsidized food prices) and private enterprise. Reforms encouraged growth of up to 4 percent (1994), but copper prices and transportation problems continued to hold the economy back. The copper industry also suffers from low output and outdated technology. Yet copper remains the most important industry and export. Diversification and additional progress is necessary to allow for greater economic growth.

Real gross domestic product per capita is estimated at $1,230, which is only slightly higher than it was in 1960. This reflects the fact that people are not able to earn a decent income. Indeed, many have no income but rely on subsistence agriculture. About 64 percent live in poverty (80 percent in rural areas). Still, the existence of an educated labor force indicates that the economic situation for many people could improve with long-term stability, government commitment, and effective social change.

Zambia relies on imports for most of its essential commodities. Zinc, cobalt, lead, and tobacco are exported. There is a fairly large manufacturing sector. The currency is the *kwacha* (K).

Transportation and Communication

A rail line connects Livingstone in the south with Mufulira in Copperbelt province. The Tazara (Tanzania-Zambia) Railway links Zambia to the Tanzanian port of Dar es Salaam. Buses are the main means of transportation in rural areas, although they are not often punctual. Some Zambians own cars, but they are found almost solely in urban areas. Taxis are available in the cities. Breakdowns are a major problem due to the lack of spare parts for vehicles. Following the British tradition, traffic moves on the left side of the road. A national air carrier, Zambia Airways, operates international and domestic flights. The telephone system is one of the best in sub-Saharan Africa. It, several radio stations, and a number of daily newspapers (two in English) serve all areas of the country down to the district level. Television is available in urban areas and larger towns.

Education

The average literacy rate in Zambia is 75 percent, but it is higher for males and lower for females. Although education is free, the requirement that students provide their own paper is a barrier to many prospective pupils. About 80 percent of Zambian children attend primary school. Because of financial constraints and insufficient facilities, only 20 percent are educated in secondary schools and only 2 percent in institutions of higher education. There are two universities, fourteen teacher-training colleges, and fourteen vocational and technical institutions.

Health

Zambia has 12 large hospitals and more than 60 smaller medical centers, but they are concentrated in urban areas. Health facilities are beginning to operate on a fee-paying basis for such services as medical reports and vaccinations. Medical treatment is free for those who cannot pay, but non-Zambians are required to pay for all medical services. Treatments used range from traditional to modern medicine.

Common childhood diseases such as measles, malnutrition, and diarrhea contribute to an infant mortality rate of 86 per 1,000. Malaria, pneumonia, bilharzia, and AIDS are major health problems among adults. Shallow latrines, open garbage pits, and polluted water create hygiene problems that allow for serious epidemics. Life expectancy averages 43 years.

FOR THE TRAVELER

A visa and valid passport are required for U.S. citizens to enter Zambia. Zambia is in the yellow fever endemic zone and a vaccination is strongly recommended. It will be required by any country visited after Zambia. Other vaccinations, such as for cholera, are also advised, as are malarial suppressants. Water is not potable, except in Lusaka. Do not swim in freshwater lakes or rivers. They can be contaminated with a parasitic worm that enters through the skin and causes schistosomiasis. Wash and peel fruits and vegetables before eating, and be sure food is well cooked. For current health guidelines, call the Centers for Disease Control and Prevention International Travel Hotline at (404) 332–4559.

Victoria Falls and national wildlife reserves are popular tourist attractions. Travel in these areas is safe, but the U.S. State Department warns travelers to beware of crime or potential election violence in other areas. Travel at night is considered unsafe in most regions. For travel information, contact the Zambian National Tourist Board, 237 East 52d Street, New York, NY 10022; phone (212) 758–1110. You may also wish to contact the Embassy of Zambia, 2419 Massachusetts Avenue NW, Washington, DC 20008; phone (202) 265–9717.

Printed on recycled paper

Republic of
Zimbabwe

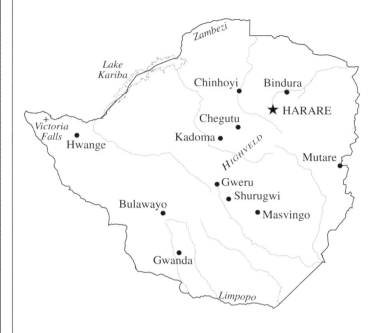

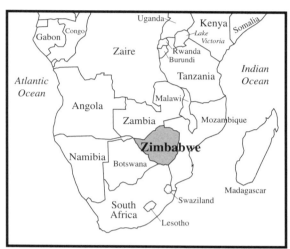

Boundary representations not necessarily authoritative.

BACKGROUND

Land and Climate

Zimbabwe is a landlocked country located on southern Africa's Great Plateau. Covering 150,803 square miles (390,580 square kilometers), it is slightly larger than Montana. The country is divided into three regions. The Highveld, where the major cities are located, is the central plateau with altitudes over 5,000 feet (1,500 meters). The highest mountain is Inyangani (8,502 feet or 2,592 meters). On both sides of the Highveld lies the Middleveld, which sends water from the Highveld into the Zambezi River (north) and the Limpopo River (south). Near each of these rivers, altitudes drop below 1,000 feet (300 meters); these areas are called the Lowveld. Despite its location in the tropics, Zimbabwe has a pleasant and mild climate because of its elevation. Days are sunny but not extremely hot; nights are clear and cool. The winter months of June and July are somewhat cooler, but still pleasant. Severe weather is rare.

History

Between the ninth and thirteenth centuries, the area of Zimbabwe was populated by a people that had established trading contacts with commercial centers on Africa's southeastern coast. In the 15th century, the Karanga people (ancestors of the Shona) established a major trading empire at Great Zimbabwe (near present-day Masvingo). Today, remains of the main city comprise the Great Zimbabwe National Monument. The empire lasted until the end of the 17th century, when it came under Portuguese domination. The Ndebele people entered the area in 1830 and conquered the Karanga.

In the 1890s, whites, hoping to discover new gold fields, began to trek north from South Africa. In 1897, the imperialist Cecil John Rhodes claimed the Matabeland (home of the Ndebele) and Mashonaland (home of the Shona) regions for England under the terms of a Royal Charter from Queen Victoria. Rhodes ran the British South Africa Company (BSAC), which colonized much of the region. In 1922, the white voters chose to become a British colony (rather than just a possession of the BSAC) as Southern Rhodesia. A federation including Southern Rhodesia, Nyasaland (now Malawi), and Northern Rhodesia (now Zambia) was created in 1953 but dissolved in 1963. Southern Rhodesia, however, was a British colony for two more years.

In 1965, the white-minority government led by Ian Smith issued a declaration of independence from Great Britain. His rule led to ethnic unrest, sanctions from United Nations members, and several years of civil war. In 1979, an agreement was reached that allowed power sharing with blacks and paved the way to elections in 1980. Zimbabwe's independence was then officially recognized by the nations of the world. Originally, the constitution called for a ceremonial president and a prime minister to form the executive branch of a multiparty parliamentary democracy. The elected prime minister was Robert G. Mugabe.

Mugabe was reelected in 1985 as he worked to increase his power and curb opposition. In 1987, his Zimbabwe African National Union (ZANU) political party merged with the country's other large party, Zimbabwe African People's Union (ZAPU), to form a strong ruling party called ZANU-PF. The constitution was amended to eliminate the office of prime minister and create a strong executive president. Mugabe was named to the new post.

In 1990, Mugabe was reelected with only token opposition. Dissatisfaction with ZANU-PF grew in the 1990s but was disorganized and divided. Mugabe's government cracked down on dissent, even as it heralded the democratic nature of upcoming elections. With little opportunity to mount an effective campaign, opposition leaders were unable to gain much of a legislative foothold in 1995 elections, in which ZANU-PF received all but three of 150 parliamentary seats. They also had no way to influence the revision of election rules regarding the 1996 presidential race; the rules provided for campaign funds only for the ruling party. Mugabe was to have faced two challengers, but they felt compelled for various reasons to withdraw prior to election day. Mugabe declared the voting would take place anyway, and he was reelected.

THE PEOPLE

Population

Some 11.1 million people inhabit Zimbabwe. The population is growing at 1.8 percent annually. All but 2 percent of the population is Black African. Individuals of European descent (mostly British) account for 1 percent, and those of mixed descent or Asian heritage make up the remaining 1 percent. A variety of ethnic groups comprise the Black African population. The largest of these are the Shona (71 percent) and Ndebele (16 percent). While urbanization has increased over the years, 70 percent of the people continue to live in rural settings.

Relations between the races were harmonious after blacks gained political power in 1980. Even though whites held most of the wealth and land, the majority blacks accepted their important role in Zimbabwe's future. And while whites lacked political power, they welcomed the peace that came with full democracy. Unfortunately, when economic hardships hit in the early 1990s, blacks began resenting white wealth and the government began seizing land from whites to give to landless blacks. By 1994, tolerance between the two groups was low and cooperation ended on many fronts.

Zimbabwe's Human Development Index (0.539) ranks it 121st out of 174 countries. The nation has yet to provide sufficient opportunities for people to enjoy a decent standard of living and determine their own futures.

Language

English is the official language of the republic and is spoken by most educated people. It does not predominate in rural areas, however, where people converse in the tongue of their native ethnic group. Shona and Ndebele are commonly spoken. People often speak more than one language and many mix parts of several languages in daily speech. Both Shona and Ndebele are written languages and are taught in school.

Religion

Zimbabwe has many established Christian churches and missions and a few minority religions (Judaism, Hinduism, and Islam). About one-fourth of the people are Christian. Half practice a mixture of Christian values and traditional beliefs. Traditional beliefs vary and often emphasize ancestor veneration and faith in spirits and magic. About 24 percent of the people continue to practice traditional beliefs.

General Attitudes

Zimbabwe has an interesting variety of customs. It is, in many ways, a very modern and developed country. In urban environments, one can expect to find the cosmopolitan habits that prevail in Western cities. In remote rural districts, customs are more traditional. Zimbabweans are generally friendly, cheerful, optimistic, and courteous. While open and enthusiastic among friends, they are more cautious and reserved with strangers. Humility is esteemed. Individually, Zimbabweans are sensitive to racism and discrimination because of the years of colonial subjugation.

Personal Appearance

Generally speaking, Zimbabweans wear Western-style clothing. Traditional African dress is reserved for performing or for special occasions, but fashions from other African countries are becoming more popular. Dressing neatly in clean clothes is important. People do not purposely dress in worn or tattered clothing. Men prefer a suit for conducting business. Young girls sometimes wear shorts, but women generally wear long or short cotton dresses in both modern and traditional styles. It is not uncommon for a woman to wear a scarf on her head.

CUSTOMS AND COURTESIES

Greetings

A handshake is commonly used in greeting. "Good morning, how are you?" is the usual greeting understood by all language groups. "Hello" is also popular. Common Shona greetings include *Manguanani* (Good morning), *Masikati* (Good day), and *Maneru* (Good evening). Greetings among friends may include lengthy inquiries about one's family. A person claps hands when asking how things are. Traditionally, to pass a stranger without any word of greeting is considered bad manners, but this is no longer true in cities. Zimbabweans do not commonly address others by title, except in urban areas where people often follow English customs.

Gestures

Traditionally, one gives and accepts items with both hands. This is still practiced, particularly in rural areas. A person may clap the hands as a gesture of gratitude or politeness. Women and girls, especially in rural areas, often curtsy as a gesture of politeness. Direct eye contact during conversation is considered rude, principally in rural areas, because it shows a lack of respect.

Visiting

People in rural villages live a slower-paced life than those in the cities. The concept of time is much more flexible in the village than in the city, where people expect invited guests to arrive on time. Unannounced visits are common, especially in villages. While visiting in rural areas, a person may sit or stand without waiting for an invitation. In Westernized urban areas, visitors wait for an invitation from the host before being seated. Small practical gifts for both urban and rural families are appreciated but not customarily expected. Zimbabweans are hospitable and try to make their guests comfortable. Hosts always offer refreshments, including soft drinks or tea and sometimes a snack. Inviting friends or relatives for afternoon tea is quite popular, and people also enjoy having guests for dinner. Refusing refreshments or offers of food is impolite. Patience and politeness are important in conversation.

Eating

While many people use Western utensils, those in rural areas also commonly eat with the fingers. Regardless of how people eat, they first wash their hands with water that is provided. Rural families may eat from a communal dish, depending on the food. In rural areas, parents eat together but children eat in a separate location. When guests are invited, the hostess usually serves each plate; it is polite to leave a little food behind to show one is not greedy. A person asks permission of the others to leave the table when he or she is finished eating.

People eat breakfast before going to or beginning daily work and eat the main meal after work. Lunch is usually light.

LIFESTYLE

Family

The father is usually the leader of the family, but the mother also exercises influence in the home. The father expects to make all final decisions and to support his family (including children, wives, and any mistresses). Polygamy is still common among some groups. The traditional, extended family unit is strongly evident in rural areas, with more than one generation living together. Urban families tend to be more nuclear. Still, family ties are strong and important. A child is an investment; parents take care of their children and expect to be taken care of in their old age. The concept of nursing homes is highly offensive. The elderly are considered a family treasure and there is always room for them. While urban families often have electricity and running water, some rural families continue to live a more traditional life in thatched-roof homes without such conveniences.

Dating and Marriage

In the past, marriages were most often arranged by families, and affection was never shown in public. However, Westernized social patterns are replacing these traditions. Public affection, while not widespread, is not unknown. Young people usually choose their marriage partner. When a couple is ready to marry, customary visits and gifts are exchanged between the groom's representative and the bride's family. The parents plan the wedding. A bridal token, known as a *roora* (or *lobola*), is paid to the bride's parents. Over time, this practice has become more difficult to afford because the bride's family demands more and more. Some segments of society are trying to abolish the tradition, which was once only a small

token or gesture. A church wedding ceremony for a Christian couple often is just one of many ceremonies that mark the marriage. It is not uncommon for men to engage in extra-marital affairs with the knowledge of their wives. This culturally accepted practice is considered necessary by men to prove virility.

Diet

Sadza, a stiff porridge made from maize (cornmeal), is the staple food of most Zimbabweans and is served at nearly every meal. Various local vegetables serve as a garnish, and meat is eaten when available. In the cities, people tend to eat a more Western diet, including meat and potatoes or rice instead of *sadza*. Locally grown fruits, such as mangoes, bananas, melons, guavas, and papayas *(pawpaws),* are enjoyed at various times of the year. Tea is popular with meals and in the office. Zimbabwe's rich agricultural land usually produces enough food to feed the nation adequately, although the recent drought caused widespread hunger and suffering.

Recreation

Soccer is the favorite sport, but tennis, boxing, rugby, cricket, polo, bowling, field hockey, squash, golf, and horse racing are enthusiastically pursued by various segments of the population. Naturally, income and location help determine one's recreational activities. Swimming in open-air pools is a favorite pastime, but swimming in rivers and lakes is dangerous due to bilharzia (a parasite that has been carried in African rivers for centuries and infects the liver). People also enjoy watching television and going to movies.

Holidays

The national holidays in Zimbabwe include New Year's Day, Easter (including Good Friday and Easter Monday), Independence Day (18 April), Worker's Day (1 May), Africa Day (25 May), Heroes' Days (11–12 August), and Christmas. Heroes' Days honor the dead. Local religious celebrations are also held throughout the country each year.

Commerce

In cities, businesses, government offices, and shops are open Monday through Friday from 8:00 or 8:30 A.M. to 5:00 or 5:30 P.M. Retail shops remain open until noon on Saturday. Small shops, where necessities and perishables are sold, are open longer each day and also on Sundays. Shops in rural areas keep flexible hours. Banks close at 2:00 P.M. most days and at noon on Wednesday. Because the majority of the people are engaged in agriculture, work schedules vary and can be long. Women form an important part of the agricultural labor force, often carrying small children on their backs as they work.

SOCIETY

Government

Zimbabwe is a nominal parliamentary democracy. Mugabe is chief of state and head of government. He has two vice presidents and a cabinet. Parliament has 150 members, 120 of whom are directly elected. Twenty members are appointed by the president and ten positions are reserved for traditional chiefs. The voting age is 18. The next elections are scheduled for 2000. The country is divided into eight provinces:

Manicaland, Mashonaland Central, Mashonaland East, Mashonaland West, Mavingo, Matabeleland North, Matabeleland South, and Midlands.

Economy

Before the 1965 declaration of independence, Southern Rhodesia was one of the most economically developed countries in sub-Saharan Africa. Between 1965 and 1980, civil war, economic sanctions, and other problems damaged the economy and slowed development. Zimbabwe is struggling to recover from its worst drought in this century, which has forced it to import food and caused a strain on economic growth. The country is trying to improve its economic situation, basing reforms on a market-oriented economy. The plan to acquire 20 million acres of land held by white farmers and give it to poor black farmers worries some who fear that if the land is given to unproven farmers, the country's food production will decrease. But Mugabe says it is time to allow more people access to fertile land.

Agriculture employs about three-fourths of the labor force. Agricultural products such as tobacco and cotton account for 40 percent of all export earnings. Corn, tea, and sugar are other important products. Manufactured items, including footwear, furniture, and equipment, are very important to the export economy. The mining industry engages in the exploitation of coal, copper, gold, tin, and other mineral resources. The country also promotes its potential as a tourist destination. Unemployment is 50 percent and inflation is 24 percent. Strikes over low wage increases threaten economic growth for 1996. The currency is the Zimbabwean dollar (Z$).

Real gross domestic product per capita is estimated at $1,970, which has fallen slightly in the last few years. Up to 60 percent of rural Zimbabweans live in absolute poverty.

Transportation and Communication

Private cars in the cities are relatively common but generally are not used in rural areas. Those who do have cars often use them to provide taxi service (illegally). Buses are the principal means of motorized transportation in rural areas. Bicycles are common, especially among schoolchildren. A railway connects key cities. Zimbabwe is dependent on ports in South Africa and Mozambique for its exports because it has no outlet to the sea. The telecommunications system is extensive but often poorly maintained and therefore not always reliable. Newspapers are readily available in the cities, but the press is restricted by the government. Televisions and radios are likewise common in cities but limited in rural areas to villages that have electricity. There are two government television stations.

Education

The adult literacy rate in Zimbabwe is about 83 percent, and education is a high priority for Zimbabweans. The government has been working to provide education for all and

has built many rural schools to help achieve that goal. While less than half of all school-aged children attended school in 1980, nearly all are enrolled today. Children attend seven years of primary school. Half of all children go on to secondary school, an excellent rate for Africa. Students attend four years of secondary school before entering vocational training or ending their studies; six years are required for those who intend to go to college. Church-sponsored missions own or operate many schools, and most private schools receive some government funding. Students pay fees if they can; government grants pay the balance. Several teacher-training colleges operate in addition to the University of Zimbabwe in Harare. Commercial and technical training are offered at the polytechnic schools in Harare and Bulawayo.

Health

Towns and cities usually have good plumbing and sanitation systems. Rural areas often lack these, although improvements during the 1980s were substantial. The malarial mosquito has been eradicated in some areas but is still active in others. Yellow fever and other diseases are also widespread. All basic health services are free to the poor. People often turn to traditional healers for help with certain types of illnesses. The quality and availability of medical facilities varies between cities and rural areas. Clinics may be available but are usually underequipped. The infant mortality rate is 73 per 1,000. Life expectancy ranges from 41 to 45 years.

FOR THE TRAVELER

A visa is not required for U.S. travelers to visit Zimbabwe, but a valid passport is mandatory. Officials will also ask for proof of sufficient funds, a travel itinerary, and proof of return passage to the United States. Without these, one may be required to leave on the next flight. Vaccinations are recommended for widespread diseases such as yellow fever. Malarial suppressants are strongly advised.

Zimbabwe has invested many resources into creating an attractive and affordable tourist destination. Wildlife parks, steam-engine trains, safaris, a pleasant climate, Victoria Falls, and much more make the country worth visiting. The government encourages travelers not to feed wild animals because animals often will have to be destroyed (they begin expecting food and may harm people). Hotel bills must be paid in foreign currency or by credit card; Zimbabwean dollars will not be accepted. Be aware of photography restrictions, especially regarding government property. Information on travel opportunities is available through the Zimbabwean Tourist Office, 1270 Avenue of the Americas, Suite 2315, New York, NY 10020; phone (212) 332–1090. You may also wish to contact the Embassy of Zimbabwe, 1608 New Hampshire Avenue NW, Washington, DC 20009; phone (202) 332–7100.

Culturegrams Africa, Asia, and Ocean
David M. Kennedy Center for In

23896
910 Dav

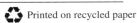

Printed on recycled paper

This book may be kept

FOURTEEN DAYS

A fine will be charged for each day the book is kept overtime.

GAYLORD 142			PRINTED IN U.S.A.